THINK LIKE AN ARCHITECT

How to Develop Critical, Creative and Collaborative Problem-solving Skills

RIBA Publishing

Randy Deutsch

Published by RIBA Publishing, 66 Portland Place, London, W1B 1AD

ISBN 9781 85946 931 6

British Library Cataloguing-in-Publication Data
A catalogue record for this book is available from the British Library.

Commissioning Editor: Elizabeth Webster
Assistant Editor: Clare Holloway
Production: Sarah-Louise Deazley
Designed and typeset by The First 47
Cover illustration by Bruce Bondy
Printed and bound by Pureprint Group

www.ribapublishing.com

Contents

Acknowledgements

A huge thank you to RIBA Publishing Director Helen Castle, who was there from the very beginning, identifying a need for this book. It has been wonderful to have the opportunity to work with her on yet another book project, this time at 66 Portland Place. And to Senior Commissioning Editor at RIBA Publishing Elizabeth Webster for her eternal patience, expert advice and support throughout the writing process, and also Clare Holloway. To Production and Design Assistant Sarah-Louise Deazley and Copyeditor Liz Jones for their steadfast and assured input and advice throughout. And to Alex Synge for the excellent graphic design and typesetting of the book. If the book you hold deserves praise it is due to them – any shortcomings are entirely my own. To illustrator Bruce Bondy of Bondy Studio, whose drawings add depth, dimension and richness to the book. He was the best collaborator an author could ask for and a champion of the book from day one. Thanks to Sharon, Michol and Simeon for their companionship and support while I wrote not one but two architecture books during a global pandemic. Lastly, to my former professors and mentors Vernon Shogren, Olivio Ferrari and Dan Wheeler, from whom I learned the importance of thinking in the midst of – not in spite of – life.

Dedication

This book is dedicated to encouraging you to become someone a human, machine or robot would want to collaborate with.

Preface

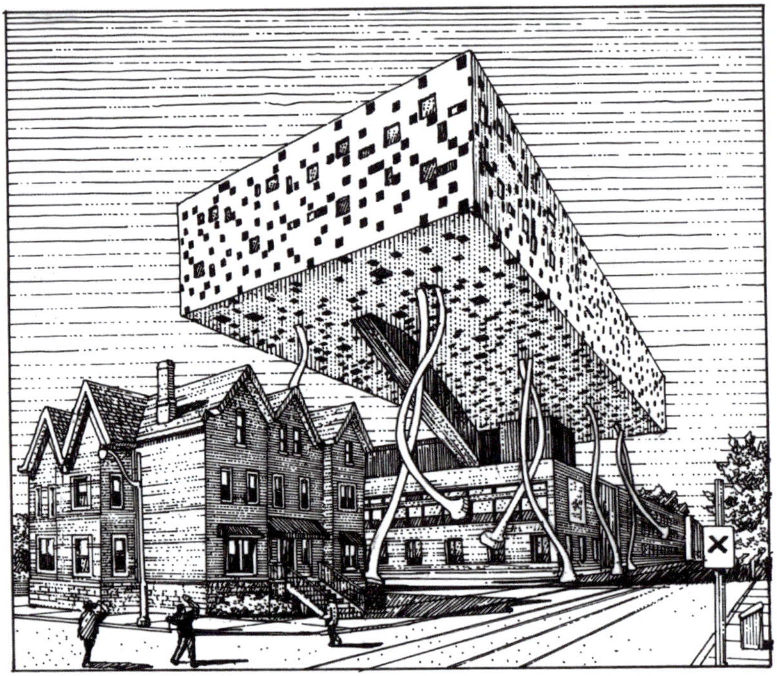

Fig 0.1: Architects think in pretty remarkable ways. Sharp Centre for Design by Will Alsop by way of Little Nemo in Slumberland by Winsor McCay

'But what is seeing without thinking?'
Johann Wolfgang von Goethe

There is something your tutor or professor, school administrator or employer want you to know that they can't tell you:

You may be talented as a designer and adept using the latest technology, but you have some room for improvement when it comes to the oldest technology: thinking.

One area that students, professors and practitioners typically struggle with is tacit knowledge. Knowledge that professionals gain over time but have difficulty explaining – knowledge that you either have or don't. Most students and emerging practitioners can grasp technical skills fairly readily. Soft skills, on the other hand – including mindsets, attitudes and thinking skills – are rarely covered in university courses or training in practice.

There is evidence that today's students and emerging practitioners struggle with thinking and communicating their ideas, and learning and acquiring soft skills, multiplied by the decrease in mentoring of the upcoming generation by firms' more senior members. Yet mastery of such tacit knowledge is arguably critical for both academic success and career longevity. This book addresses both this dearth and dichotomy.

School's absolutely the right place to emphasise the combination of critical thinking, creative thinking and interpersonal intelligence. A school's ability to blend or fold such vital content into other courses is a sign of both the course's – and the school's – relevance and ability to sustain itself into the future.

Think Like an Architect is about the ordinary work required by you to achieve extraordinary results. I wrote it to share insights, strategies and skills picked up over my career as a practising architect, employer, professor and administrator, backed by science and the research of others. Between these covers is a world of ideas that will make everything you do and say about what you do better. The only technology required is that found between your ears.

One tool we often overlook is the human mind, the most powerful tool we possess. The problem comes when we trust our instincts without questioning our assumptions or seeking evidence to back up our hunches. This book is here to help.

Why do we continue to design buildings that ought to last decades without the capacity to accommodate all users on day one? Or design using the latest computational design tools but forget to show the surrounding context in our design studio presentations?

Why are reason, science and evidence so ineffective against magical thinking? Why is it so difficult to influence people's deeply held beliefs? Are ethical beliefs more like facts or more like preferences? How can we focus on long-term thinking when so many who we design and build for are focused on short-term thinking?[1]

While architecture is both a science and an art, architects and future design professionals have to be above the fray and can't afford to engage in magical thinking. We have a duty to others – building users, neighbours, the public-at-large and not-yet-born future generations; the planet and its inhabitants. Even as the role of the architect faces an existential threat with the rise of technology, the way architects think ought to be preserved, practised and perpetuated.

Why think like an architect?

I am interested in the way architects think, the value that brings to the profession, and have done a lot of thinking about thinking – aka *metacognition* – lately, and this book is the result. It will encourage the development of your own metacognitive abilities to spur your cognitive growth and career trajectory.

Think Like an Architect is about the way architects think critically, creatively and collaboratively to address the increasingly complex problems facing us all. For some readers this will be a refresher. For others this will help connect the dots. For others still it will offer nuanced and myriad ways in which the architect adds value by the way they think.

Buildings, and the process of building, have become increasingly complex undertakings, and there are several societal and industry challenges that could be overcome – including wicked problems where the answer either does not exist or is not readily apparent – if the reader had access to the information this book provides. The world today is filled with intractable, complex, wicked problems without obvious solutions. The insights, mindsets and thinking tools presented in this book will go a long way to help the reader address intractable wicked problems such as climate change, the health and wellbeing of the larger population, and urban issues, while addressing the deterioration of our infrastructure. Addressing these complex problems requires navigating and getting results from diverse teams, which in turn requires us to think in terms of others.

Writing this book at a time of great upheaval, challenges to our wellbeing, and change ought to make acquiring the act of thinking critically, creatively and collaboratively all the more urgent. We're living in a world with rising use of AI and machine learning; machines that think. Technological disruption and change makes the need to think effectively all the more urgent. Our increasingly intelligent tools may be optimised based on criteria we establish, but all lack common sense – something that humans have in abundance.

To think like an architect prepares you for the world to come: the world of robots, automation, autonomous design, AI and machine learning, but also a world of mass migration, housing shortages, rising oceans and other impacts brought about by climate change. With the rise of AI and robots, process-driven tasks and jobs are going away. Creative and soft skills (i.e. empathy, collaboration) are more important than hard skills, since they are precisely the skills robots can't automate. In the era of AI students need to rely on their thinking ability.

Future skills vs capabilities

Continuously evolving economic, technological and social changes will inevitably impact the employment marketplace long after you leave school and begin your career.[2] Students attend architecture school for a variety of reasons: to learn how to design buildings; to learn how to practise architecture; to acquire marketable skills. But less frequently students pursue a degree to foster human capabilities that go beyond skill building.

This book has 'skills' in the subtitle, but it easily could have read *capabilities.* Why? If architecture school better equips students, job seekers, and future career professionals for the realities of the twenty-first-century economy, it does so not just by focusing exclusively on acquiring marketable skills, but on investing in human capabilities like critical, creative and collaborative thinking.[3] Many of the skills architects have today will in time become obsolete, whereas their capabilities – to place buildings in a larger context, to propose and develop alternative outcomes, and to apply creative thinking to achieve improved results – will endure, likely becoming even more important than any individual skillsets.

In my most recent book, *Superusers,* readers were encouraged to address the future with both confidence and aplomb. The book urged them to be open to acquiring new technology skills while honing their soft skills, demonstrating how so-called *superusers* have done so with substantial and meaningful career success.[4]

We often receive advice to 'futureproof yourself' by keeping your eyes open (on what?), becoming indispensable (how?) and staying abreast of the latest trends in technology (which?). Stay relevant and valued in school and in the workplace? OK. But *how?* Without offering specifics or addressing practical realities, this well-intended advice amounts to little more than platitudes at best, and at worst conflicting and confusing career advice.[5]

Three current capabilities happen to be among the most sought-after by professors, architecture school administrators and employers to thrive into the future: the ability to think critically, creatively and collaboratively[6] – and demand for these skills is only increasing.[7] In other words, to stay relevant and avoid career obsolescence, focus less on what you do (skills) and more on how you *think* (capabilities).[8]

What is it about the architect that no machine can replace? This is the question that *Think Like an Architect* seeks to answer. There are critical thinkers and creative problem solvers as well as collaborative thinkers, but few beside the architect bring this triple-threat combination of thinking abilities together in one person. This book is less a celebration of this fact than an assurance that these qualities continue. This book will help you recognise these thinking capabilities in yourself and show you how to build them into your own unique repertoire or toolbox. To assure your continued relevance, think critically, creatively and collaboratively – think like an architect.

Why read a book like this?

Many books focus on what to think. This one focuses on *how* to think, providing a foundation and establishing good thinking habits early on. The focus throughout is on the thought process – to help designers design better and present their ideas more effectively, and to think more rigorously, logically, thoroughly, creatively, intuitively, and in tandem with the thinking of others.

Think Like an Architect is the book I wish I had read when I was just starting out, represents what I want my students to be aware of before they are my students, and what I want emerging professionals to understand before joining the firm.

There are books on how to design buildings, detail buildings, draw buildings, understand buildings and become an architect. There are videos and books on how to write, speak, read, sketch, draw, travel, act, shop at a flea market (go on, google it) and dress like an architect. But no book that focuses on the ways an architect thinks.

A primary purpose of this book is to fill your thinking toolbox with easy-to-access tools. Thinking like an architect is a learnable behaviour with the tools to become a lifelong habit. This book is about you and what you bring to your classroom discussions, studio projects, research and job interviews, as well as the unexpected serendipitous situations that open doors for you in your career as you evolve from being a student to a contributing design professional. *Think* will challenge you to higher levels of critical and reflective thinking, increasing your tolerance for ambiguity and uncertainty, and enable you to gather, analyse and synthesise information.[9]

College students are falling behind. The book *Academically Adrift: Limited Learning on College Campuses* reported that critical thinking is no longer progressing during college compared with previous generations of students.[10] When young adults between the ages of nineteen and thirty (both current college students and recent graduates) were given a test designed to test their ability to detect fake news, only 24% were able to correctly answer eight out of nine questions; 44% could not correctly answer six out of nine questions.[11] There is a gap in learning – and this book seeks to fill this gap.

This book serves as a roadmap for what questions to ask along the way: of yourself, of your project, of your instructor and critics; how to make the most of your situation and education. Those who learn how to think critically, creatively and collaboratively earlier in their academic or professional career will become more effective, resilient and sought-after problem solvers no matter the application, field or interests.

Becoming an architect takes time. It's not like you start out in architecture school establishing a foundational vocabulary – line, plane, mass, volume, form, shape, space – then *yada yada,*[12] you're designing and building skyscrapers. No book can provide all of the *yada yada* – that can come only from education – including reading and experience. This book aims to fill in the missing links.

How to read this book

'Sometimes, first you think and then you do; and sometimes first you do and then you think.'
Olivio Ferrari[13]

Architects tend to work fluidly, iteratively – between the rational and intuitive – and aren't excited by the notion of working with action plans or checklists. Consider what is presented in this book more as insights to shape your mindset than presenting steps in a design method.

The book is divided into three parts:

PART I: Critical Thinking
PART II: Critical Creative Thinking
PART III: Critical Collaborative Thinking

Each part has three sections. Why critical thinking first? IF you think critically first, your creative thinking will be grounded in reality. This will improve your design and help you to be more effective. In truth, it doesn't matter where you start, as long as you pass through all three.

Why *critical* creative thinking? Because architects take their creativity critically. Too often creative thinking is thought of, incorrectly, as being right-brained (it's both right *and* left, or *whole-brained*) intuitive, fantasy-based, visual thinking. The way architects think creatively goes beyond these – and has to – because what they come up with has to work, be buildable, using available materials and labour; it has to protect the health, safety and welfare of those who use it and live in and around it; it has to come within budget and schedule; it has to address its context, it cannot use too much energy. In other words, architects – unlike artists – need to think critically even about their creative output.

There are critical thinkers and creative thinkers. Few bring the two together in one person as well as the architect. This book emphasises both critical and creative thinking so that one's solutions are both sound and unexpected. By the end of this book it is my hope that you will agree we all need to start thinking like an architect, because it will become increasingly necessary to do so in light of the rise of machines, sea levels, AI and the deluge of information.

Each chapter that follows concludes with a set of useful questions, reading suggestions and practical tips to try – ASK THIS, TRY THIS, READ THIS – aimed at students and emerging professionals who are interested in improving the quality and outcomes of their thinking. The practical tips are short and simple so they're easily digested. Here's an example from the Critical Collaborative Thinking section on *Thinking Like Others:*

TRY THIS

Make it your aim to know how others think, know what others do in the process, so you know who to go to when you're in need of information that you don't possess or have access to. As a generalist, specialise in people. Zoom out to better see connections and join the dots. Appreciate specialists but be the one who actively seeks to get them out of their silos to solve holistic problems with common sense solutions. Know just enough to be able to communicate the overall contours of the assignment, the problem you are trying to solve, and your ideas – then strive to get others including stakeholders involved in helping you solve it.

To address the most challenging of problems – problems that you have never faced before – and to be assured, indeed confident, that your ability to think, to gain insights, and to imagine, is commensurate to any problems you may face. And not just any problems – *open-ended* problems without easy solutions. *This* is what it means to think like an architect.

Introduction: Solving Wicked Problems

Fig 0.2: The rapidity of climate change has led to sea level rise

The past decade was the warmest ever recorded.[14] The rapidity of climate change that has led to sea-level rise, the scale of massive extinctions, acidification of our oceans, slow-decay pollutants, contamination of fresh water, and industrialisation, to name just a few, are realities we as inhabitants of this planet all must face.[15]

We live at a time with increasingly intractable unsolvable problems. Fortunately, as you are about to witness in this book, architects think in pretty remarkable ways.

Instead of feeling helpless, understanding and applying how architects think can empower you in the face of wicked problems. The kinds of problems architects face – dwindling natural resources, climate change and its repercussions, overpopulation – will keep them busy for the foreseeable future.

Learning how to think like an architect enables you to address and solve wicked, complex, intractable problems – aka non-obvious problems without a single, definitive solution – and apply what you learn to other future, not-yet-imagined problems.

Design technology and software are all just tools in your virtual toolbox. Three tools that are often missing from the designer's toolbox are critical thinking, creative thinking and collaborative thinking – tools that will give you an edge and act as differentiators throughout school and well into your career. They're the focus of this book.

Even more than these thinking tools, this book is about *you* – what you bring to these thinking tools. And thereafter, what you bring to class: to classroom discussions; to studio projects; to lectures; and, later still, to job interviews, and your first assignments at work.

Challenges the world is facing are due to pervasive and accelerating change including climate change, poverty, inequality and the need to house refugees will all require the architect's thinking capabilities: not only to think critically, creatively and collaboratively, but quickly, assuredly, and with care, quality and conviction.

In other words, they will require all of us to think like an architect.

Wicked problems can be found when people come together to improve a site, situation or condition. As you'll read in the book, architects are ideally suited to:

- address inevitable density in cities without resorting to high-rises
- house the homeless in high-rises so that they are people-friendly
- locate millions displaced by immigration, including refugees
- design for rising sea levels due to climate change
- convince others that climate change is real and worth paying to ameliorate.

In a later chapter we'll revisit the topic of wicked problems, but here let's just look at the fact that buildings account for one-third of global carbon emissions, energy consumption and waste.[16]

Seventy per cent of greenhouse gas emissions in the world come from the built environment – with buildings alone making up close to 40% of CO^2 emissions.[17] The last four years (at the time of writing) were the four hottest on record, and winter temperatures in the Arctic have risen by 3°C since 1990.[18] The latest analysis shows that if we act now, we can reduce carbon emissions within twelve years and hold the increase in the global average temperature to well below 2°C – and even, as asked by the latest science, to 1.5°C above pre-industrial levels.[19]

Roughly 11% of the global carbon footprint is related to what buildings are made out of.[20] Take concrete, third only to water and stone as the Earth's most used material and the second-largest producer of carbon dioxide (CO^2), with manufacturing of cement accounting for 8% of total CO^2 emissions.[21] This has architects and others turning to alternatives that are better for the environment.

Artificial intelligence and machine learning, cloud-based and quantum computing, additive manufacturing and nanofabrication, advanced automation and robotics – these disruptive technologies are already impacting every industry.[22]

The key components of critical thinking for design professionals include:

- asking questions to gather relevant information
- identifying biases and minimising their influence
- evaluating all available data relevant to the situation or problem
- asking for feedback and collaborating with those involved in the situations, including people with different backgrounds, perspectives and knowledge specialities
- generating a variety of possible solutions and determining the optimal implementation, given the desired consequences.[23]

Coinciding with your career, over the next forty years it is estimated that nearly 2.5 trillion square feet of new construction will be needed to support growth in the world's increasingly dense urban areas.[24]

Sea levels are rising, coral reefs are dying, and we are starting to see the life-threatening impact of climate change on health, through air pollution, heatwaves and risks to food security.[25]

Virtually every country is experiencing an increase in the number of older people – those aged sixty and over – in its population. An ageing population will have implications in terms of housing of the elderly.[26]

When it comes to atomic energy, more than thirty countries worldwide are operating 444 nuclear reactors for electricity generation, and sixty-six new nuclear plants are under construction. In 2014, thirteen countries relied on nuclear energy to supply at least one-quarter of their total electricity.[27]

Climate change is one of the major challenges of our time. From shifting weather patterns that threaten food production, to rising sea levels that increase the risk of catastrophic flooding, the impacts of climate change are global in scope and unprecedented in scale.[28]

In response to climate change, architects must design for rising sea levels, and the impact this will have on communities and entire regions where people live and work.

Today, more people than ever before live in a country other than the one in which they were born. The world is witnessing the highest levels of displacement on record. An unprecedented 59.5 million people around the world have been forced from home. Among them are nearly 20 million refugees, over half of whom are under the age of eighteen.[29]

In response to decolonisation and immigration, architects will not only be needed to design housing for the Earth's rising population, but also for refugees and displaced people around the globe.

Thinking about the thinking that will be required of us

There are books on how to design buildings, detail buildings, draw buildings and understand buildings. There are books devoted to detailing to keep water out and to building a thriving practice, but no book that focuses on thinking like an architect.

Frankly, we have bigger fish to fry. While most architects come to discover that a bathroom redo for a discriminating client can be as challenging to design as a high-rise – and client relations, customer service and being a trusted adviser will always be important – the world won't wait or be put on hold. You, future architect, were meant for bigger things.

Why architects? Because of your passions and the way you were trained and educated – and are therefore comfortable with ambiguity and uncertainty – you can take on and tackle difficult-to-define, seemingly unsolvable problems. It's what we *do.*

In fact, by definition *an architect is someone who is asked to do impossible things they know nothing about.*

And they don't let that stop them. They leverage critical thinking to ask pertinent questions, and separate facts from fiction. They leverage creativity to propose previously unconsidered solutions and have the wherewithal to evaluate until they arrive at one that is effective and amenable to all involved – including those not represented at the table (or even yet on the planet). They leverage their vast network to assure that the decision is informed and backed by experience and sound judgement, and can indeed be acted on and implemented. They, in other words, think like an architect so as not to be overwhelmed by the near-constant bombardment of seemingly impossible problems that demand to be solved.

A rejection of rational thinking

The world today has become a far less rational place. The fact that you have an architectural education doesn't guarantee that you will think rationally or critically once out of school.

An acceptance of critical thinking and, conversely, the rejection of the subjective, emotional and irrational thinking as acceptable criteria for decision-making, only comes with deliberate, conscious choice and some significant effort.[30] In other words, it requires us to rethink the way we think.

Architects are rightfully encouraged to use simpler, non-technical terms and are justifiably chastised for speaking in a way that is understandable to fellow professionals but hard to follow by nearly everybody else. And yet, urged to simplify, they risk over-simplification, and the diminishment of critical thought – so they strike a balance by leveraging multiple thinking types at once.

Instead of the exclusive use of rationality to get their message across, architects utilise other thinking types, including creative thinking to help others understand and accept their ideas.

Architects, as we'll see, are masters at thinking like others and, in doing so, shape both the content of their message and the terms in which it is delivered, so as to be better understood and ultimately reach consensus on the decision at hand.

Instead of dumbing down their message, they leverage a form of thinking – collaborative thinking – that helps projects proceed towards an amicable conclusion.

Thinking rationally and critically alone isn't enough today to assure that we'll be understood, that our messages get across and persuade others to act. We also need emotion, creativity and the ability to think like others – attributes that architects possess, having acquired them during years of architectural education and practice. The unique combination of thinking types used by the architect is the subject of this book.

Mind the gap

The shift from theory to practice is as difficult and unpredictable for the soon-to-be-graduating architecture student as the shift from analysis to synthesis,[31] and represents an inherent conflict where architects find themselves caught between the opposing identities of a service profession where you are expected to meet a client's needs, and a design profession where you are expected to create culturally significant works of architecture.[32]

There's a gap between the theoretical knowledge you learn in school and the practical knowledge you acquire in practice. The *mind the gap* message broadcast at London's underground stations ought to be broadcast to every architecture student who plans on embarking on a career in architecture, because what students are taught in school, and what they need to know to succeed throughout their careers – as many come to discover – can be two entirely different things, and a leap that can be as difficult and unpredictable as the leap from analysis to synthesis.[33] It's the difference in architectural education between knowledge-based development (theoretical) versus skill development (practical).[34]

Architecture school is designed to provide a foundation, establishing good habits to build on. The problem is that design education was never intended to address such a litany of intractable, seemingly unsolvable problems, all occurring at the same time. There are so many problems requiring our attention it is hard to know where to focus. In response to the situation we find ourselves in today where outcomes are unknown, 'today's curricula needs to focus on developing adaptive and agile systemic and integrative thinkers rather than focusing on disciplinary adherence and skill building'.[35]

What the world needs now

What if architects, due to AI and automation, were to go away tomorrow. How would we describe them? What they did? How they were different from others who purported to perform and deliver similar services? What about them would we want to preserve? What would we want to discard? What about the architect is timeless and ought to continue in perpetuity into the future?

In this book I make the argument that it is the way architects think that distinguishes them and is of the utmost importance to preserve and emulate – no matter your field or calling, or who or *what* in the end will do the designing. Especially now, in this time of wicked, seemingly unsolvable problems. The book argues that the unique way the architect thinks ought to continue. That the world needs this way of thinking now more than ever.

Writing this book at a time of great technological, economic and demographic upheaval, with challenges to our wellbeing, and near-constant change, ought to make acquiring the act of thinking critically and creatively all the more urgent. The focus here isn't on the design or even the designer, but on the thought process – to help designers think better as a means to designing better solutions.

What's past is prologue

In the section that follows, the prologue paints a picture of what it will look like once you have internalised the lessons in the book. While fictional, this critique represents what goes through the mind of an architect when evaluating someone's work. It also represents a simplified account of what goes through the mind of an architect when designing. Simplified, because questions concerning cost-effectiveness, time constraints, availability of materials and labour and more would normally need to be taken into account. It is clear, whether designing or evaluating, architects have to think of *everything.* Granted, they don't have to *know* everything – for example, they don't need to be experts in crowd control or on the impact of monsoons on public plazas – they just need to know enough to be able to ask questions. They need curiosity. They need imagination. They need a network they can turn to for feedback and for timely responses to their enquiries. And most of all, they need to know how to think.

Prologue: How to Think Like an Architect in Under Three Minutes

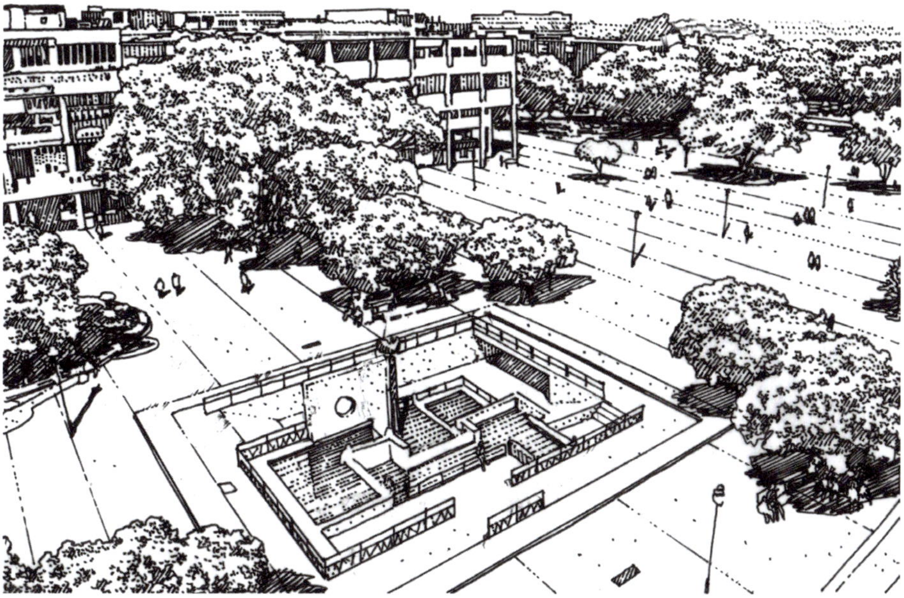

Fig 0.3: Retail designs were proposed for the commercial sector of Chandigarh, India

At the last minute a tutor volunteers to critique the four-week assignments of ten second-year students in the Strategies of Architectural Design course.

Reviewers are given eight minutes to critique the interventions of each student. Their retail designs in Sector 17, the commercial sector of Chandigarh, India, include the student's urban analysis, context plan, site section and physical model.

The student presents. Then in the remaining time the reviewer asks questions, providing feedback. When the eight minutes are up, the reviewer moves on and repeats with the next student, until all students have been addressed. Each reviewer has ten students to review. In a row. While standing: a bit like playing chess with ten players blindfolded – the grandmaster playing ten boards simultaneously.

As explained to each reviewer, students have been introduced to the history of the Chandigarh urban plan and have completed some basic urban analysis at the city scale. Their projects comprise an architectural intervention including a covered pavilion for outdoor retail vendors, and seating for 300 people (adults and children) in the existing plaza. Students were asked to pay particular attention to the environmental conditions of heat, sunlight and monsoon rains. Their projects – their *imagined constructed reality* – should respond to the need for shading and protection from the rain, and demonstrate an ability to think about public urban space planning for multiple users and age groups.

The first student presents for five minutes, leaving three minutes – 180 seconds – for the reviewer's feedback.

When it is the reviewer's turn to respond, she starts with what is positive about this student's solution to the assigned problem, followed by a critique, concluding with something positive. A *compliment sandwich:* praise, critique, followed by praise. Lessens the sting, improves the aftertaste. The praise – earned or not – is good manners. It is in the critique (the creamy filling) that learning – if learning is to be had – takes place.

Quickly, the reviewer, using a rubric to organise her succinct feedback, considers *what is actual?* She needs to size up the situation and understand what is existing vs what is the student's intervention (the separation is not always clear). What is the situation this student is entering into and potentially changing with their intervention? The reviewer assesses the site conditions from the site analysis – prevailing winter and summer winds, the best and least desirable views, flows of people to and from the site – and considers how successfully the student's intervention addresses them. Did the student consider how the sun's path could influence the orientation of the pavilion to maximise wanted daylight while shading unwanted sun's rays? Did the student orient the pavilion based on this existing information – or was its orientation based on other forces?

The reviewer asks herself *what is necessary?* She imagines a client – assigns them a persona – to assess their specific needs, answering *what is the general functionality required of this design?* As for necessities, the prompt listed the project's minimum requirements: the covered pavilion for outdoor retail vendors, seating for 300 people in the existing plaza, and engagement with a pre-existing fountain. What are the intervention's space requirements, and how successfully has this student met them?

Without regulations available – zoning ordinances, building codes, environmental regulations – the reviewer supposes the project's health, safety and welfare requirements. Does the seating for 300 accommodate people in wheelchairs? Does the retail pavilion take both children and the elderly into consideration? Did the student coordinate their plans, sections, elevation and model so that the information in each was consistent and clear? If not, the reviewer looks for clues as to which is the latest version of the design. Is there evidence that the student had another pair of eyes – a studio-mate, a friend – look at the presentation before printing?

The reviewer recognises the inspiration for the green roof from an Instagram post that went viral, and wonders if the student looked at books, periodicals or websites devoted to landscape design for additional information. Is there enough depth for the pavilion's green roof? Can people access and maintain it? Will the openings to the pavilion accommodate people's flow and movement? Will the vendors' tables block physical and visual access to the existing retail? That also needs to thrive and can't suffer at the expense of the student's intervention. Did the student study lines of sight and the visual impact of the intervention to enhance user experience? Does the student's scheme capitalise on prevailing winds, air flow and local air quality? The prompt talked about monsoons and need for shade: how well does this student's solution address these? Did the student consider water management – keeping water out, directing it away from the pavilion and potentially reusing it for the surrounding landscape? Did the student consider how people will approach the pavilion from all directions, how they will experience, circulate within and exit the pavilion as a matter of routine or in an emergency?

With ninety seconds left, the reviewer then considers, *what is desirable?* Beyond actualities and necessities, what would this imaginary client *want?* While only a four-week assignment, did the student consider integrating technologies to complement the efficiencies of the design? Did the student use integrated thinking in the design of their intervention? The pylons holding up the pavilion roof are large enough that they could double as storage or support lighting. Had the student considered this? The reviewer looks to see if there is nearby transit infrastructure – bus stops, bicycle stands, side roads or alleys – to consider the direction that people would approach the intervention from. She considers whether this student's retail intervention solves the client's problems, is strong conceptually and creates a sense of place; whether the design is innovative, with clear organisation, circulation to accommodate large crowds, form and appropriate use of materials, while still fitting into its surroundings; whether it communicates its function to those who might use it; whether it uplifts or would oppress the moods of people who use it.

Closing in on the eight-minute time allotment, the reviewer asks herself *what is possible?* Did the student develop alternative conceptual designs to explore possibilities? The reviewer considers other possibilities and tries to understand why the student went with this one. What hasn't the student considered? *Why this and not something else?* Retail on covered buses that could take retail goods and food to the people, so they didn't have to travel to the commercial sector in the heat? Or proposing doing nothing at all – would *that* have been an improvement? What could the student have done to make something more of this opportunity to design in this situation? What would be non-obvious? What would differentiate this project from others? What would make people who use the intervention happy and look forward to going to it? Proud of it as an addition to their community?

The reviewer glances at the site survey, the aerial photo, to assess the surrounding architectural form – however traditional or contemporary. She looks at the site section to consider the building elevations in the distance, to assess how the intervention's scale relates to or contrasts with the surrounding buildings, and relates to the sector's buildings, pedestrians and shoppers. But none are included in the presentation.

The reviewer observes if the student is taking notes or for signs that the student is listening to the feedback or just relieved the interminable tribunal is nearing its conclusion. Does the student ask questions in response to what the reviewer says? Does the student attempt to defend their design – or themselves? Does the student present their design solution as a sacrificial offering then await the attack? Or do they persevere with an open mind and the intention of learning from what they present, and the response their work triggered?

The reviewer's three minutes – the eight-minute time allotted to this student – are up, and they move on to the next student.

Fig 1.0: Critical thinking as a go-to tool in your toolbox

PART I: CRITICAL THINKING

Architects think critically. Architects recognise that there are consequences for their architectural actions. For them it cannot be out of sight out of mind. Architecture has serious consequences – people may get hurt – and so, architects are responsible for the health, safety and welfare of inhabitants and passersby alike. They can't be flippant or sloppy in their work. If they are to build, architects can't just design for themselves. They need to think not only in terms of the owner – who pays for the work, and with whom the architect is contracted – but the building's users, neighbours and the public-at-large who will have to live with the resulting building. The architect uses real materials that obey physics, physical constraints and laws – but architects also have to consider future generations, giving heed to their voiceless concerns.

SECTION 1: CRITICAL THINKING

1: What Were They Thinking?

Fig 1.1: View of Hunters Point Library across New York City's East River

Architects need to think of everything.

The new Hunters Point Library in Long Island City is the third completed building in New York City by the New York-based, internationally recognised prize-winning architectural firm Steven Holl Architects.

And unlike the first two, this third innovative work made the headlines for all the wrong reasons.

There is certainly much to like: landings and terraces, natural light, stunning views of Manhattan across the East River.

But to take in those views, and despite disability rights laws, the library relies heavily on stairs – to get to some of those landings and terraces – making it difficult for people who cannot climb them to access all of the library's levels.[36]

There were reportedly other barriers at the library, including a potential hazard on the children's stairs, and the fact that the five-storey building has only one lift, one that does not stop at certain levels.

So, a class-action lawsuit was filed, calling out the architectural firm over the library's alleged Americans with Disabilities Act (ADA) violations.[37]

You would be right to ask: *how did no one catch these oversights?*

Architects – at least those who want to see their buildings built – don't design in isolation. In the library's case, among others, there's the client and approval agencies with their lengthy planning process.

Focusing on the architect – this book is after all about how architects think – while one might question the architect's QA/QC or code analysis check process, we will question their thinking.

Suggestions that architects should be required to go through sensitivity training, or spend time with kids so they understand how kids behave – while well-meaning – miss the point.

This isn't about codes, mores or public sentiment changing from the time the building was first designed until it was constructed and opened. Things change – and people, including architects, adapt.

This isn't about the building needing to adapt or the staff needing to adapt but the architect needing to adapt so that this doesn't happen again.

Thankfully, because architects don't design in isolation, they don't need to know everything.

When necessary, we turn to experts for answers. But: architects need to think of everything – with an emphasis on the word 'think'.

People will assume everything in a building is deliberate – the architect might as well make it so.

And so, architects need to learn how to think more critically: so they can adapt in real time – ideally during the design process when potential problems are still digital – before there is a need for sticking plasters, roping-off or retrofits.

Fig 1.2: Hunters Point Library, on the banks of New York City's East River, was never intended to be an island

For starters, it's not always clear what is meant when we say 'critical thinking'.

If almost 90% of faculty consider critical thinking to be important to instruction, why can only 19% of them adequately articulate what critical thinking is?[38]

More than half of companies say that new employees aren't sufficiently trained to think critically.[39]

Critical thinking is like jazz or obscenity: you may not be able to say what it is, but you know it when you see it.

Professors, university administrators and employers all want you to have it – even if they can't explain exactly what it is.

They know when students have it and – as importantly – when they don't.

TRY THIS

Critical thinking is a lot of things, especially the ability to: look at facts in order to come to sensible conclusions to help make decisions; analyse the way you think then present proof for your ideas, rather than presenting your personal opinions as sufficient evidence; see both sides of an issue, be open to new evidence that challenges your ideas, reason equitably, expect claims to be backed by evidence, deduce conclusions from available facts, and identify and solve problems.[40]

ASK THIS

Why open a section on thinking critically with an example where the architect apparently wasn't? To emphasise the fact that buildings are complicated? That there is too much to think about? To point out that to think critically it helps to have some industry knowledge? Or some common sense?

ASK THIS

As some of the alleged accessibility problems are rooted in the design itself,[41] here we must ask: *is there a way the architect could have thought to make the outcome better for all involved – the architect, the owner, the library's current and future patrons, community members and the city beyond?*

2: Architecture Can't Be Reduced to a Formula

Fig 2.1: Hunters Point Library interior

Architects are expected to think both deliberately and intuitively.

Architecture and design critic Alexandra Lange visited the Hunters Point Library before it opened, and to her credit asked at that time whether all of the levels were accessible. It's a good question – but one that could be answered, with room for interpretation (accessible to whom?) in the affirmative.

Soon, though, she realised that she could have asked another, more specific, question. Evaluating her thinking process, questioning her question. Not to have gotten a scoop on what would become a headline-making story, but to identify the question behind the question. That question would have been: *if you are unable to climb stairs, can you still access every level?*[42]

Had the architect asked precisely *this* question during the design process, perhaps they would have avoided many of the building's preventable shortcomings, not to mention the lawsuit and unwanted publicity.

As an architect, would you have been able to come up with the second question?

It's a subtle difference – between the word *accessible* and the ability to climb stairs – but the specificity of the follow-up question is an exemplar of critical thinking.

Today there is an imbalance in our thinking – where less rational thinking is winning out.

Glancing at the headlines, nobody would mistake our time period for an Age of Enlightenment.

'There are enormous challenges for the built environment ahead,' explains Alexandra Lange. 'Sea level rise. Wildfires. Decaying infrastructure. Insufficient housing. But access should not be difficult. The design imperative to make public spaces that are open, usable, and even fun for the widest possible audience isn't new, or novel, or much affected by technology. It is a design problem that's solvable and, at this moment of crisis, the need for public space for people of all abilities only gains imperative.'[43]

This section attempts to address this imbalance and provide some tools for thinking more critically about your designs, thoughts and ideas, helping you along the way to *think like an architect.*

There are specific kinds of critical thinking characteristic of different subjects, helping you to, say, think like Sherlock Holmes or like a futurist. This is what is meant when we say we want to think like an architect.

Here's a quick way to remember what's involved in the critical thinking process. In this book, critical thinking is defined much like the design process, where you:

Conceptualise: consider, visualise and conceive
Analyse: take apart, inspect, observe, scrutinise and study
Synthesise: incorporate, bring together, converge, unify and integrate
Evaluate: assess, check and decide

While shortcuts like CASE can be helpful in the short run, like design, critical thinking isn't a simple formula or linear process – first this, then this – otherwise everybody would already be doing it. The architect gathers and analyses information and is expected to synthesise all of the information obtained from numerous disciplines.

Unlike the steps implied in this example, when an architect thinks critically it pretty much happens concurrently, in ever-tightening loops of analysis and synthesis: the designer appears to work within these two modes simultaneously.[44]

But we're getting ahead of ourselves.

Because it is deliberate, and because it is a process, critical thinking prevents us from jumping to conclusions like CASE.

Instead, critical thinking takes you through step by step, opening up the way you look at things, expanding your point of view, your sources, which findings you accept, helping you to put aside personal biases. With some practice, over time, you will be able to do this all at once.

This is not to imply that architecture is completely rational and doesn't involve emotions. It does.

As architecture is both an art and a science, it requires the imagination born of the unconscious as well as conscious rational thinking: both ineffable and applied thinking.

Thinking and feeling are related responses to information. There's a relationship between thought and feeling, reason and emotion, explaining why creativity can't be ignored when thinking critically.

The knowing-thinking gap

Since a domain's received wisdom evolves over time, being an architect is less about how much you know and more about how you think.

In fact, when intelligence and critical thinking are pitted against each other, critical thinkers fare better.[45]

Critical thinking isn't domain-specific – it's a transferable skill – so should you decide to leave architecture for another major or career or take on another career on top of or alongside architecture, the time you put in here won't be wasted.

Does it help to have domain knowledge to think critically? Sure. That can only come with experience – something admittedly in short supply while still in school. But it will come.

For example, you know how to ask questions – like the ones Lange asked about accessibility and people who are unable to climb stairs – and can improve at asking increasingly relevant questions when it counts. Doing so takes some focus and attention – things like experience that may be in short supply at the start, but that we'll work on in the pages to come.

This critical ability has particular relevance for you and the education of architects. In the course of their studies, and into their role in the profession and industry, architecture students need to be able to raise relevant questions, formulate arguments, compare positions and consider consequences for their architectural actions – again, all things we'll discuss in the pages that follow.[46]

Though sometimes confused with intelligence, unlike IQ – which is mostly genetic – critical thinking can be learned and built on,[47] as this book will show you.

TRY THIS

The thing is, you soon come to realise that enough credit isn't given to common sense and a lifetime observing the world around you. In other words, you know and can do more than you think. Take a moment and give yourself some credit.

TRY THIS

Learn to question and evaluate the information you have been given or happened upon, including the very problems you have been given to solve, your assumptions and preconceived ideas.

ASK THIS

When given or finding information, question your assumptions and evaluate your beliefs by asking: Why do I think this is the case? Why do I believe this? Am I attached to this idea emotionally? Is there another way I could be looking at this?

3:
What's Critical About Critical Thinking

Fig 3.1: Architects are nothing if not critical

Architects serve as role models for how to think.

An architecture student is asked to draw a section of an existing house. Never having drawn a section before, the student repurposes a section they find online. It turns out that the section the student copied is inaccurate: the student didn't use critical thinking.

Architects are nothing if not critical. So, you'd think critical thinking would come easily to them.

And yet critical thinking apparently doesn't come easily to *anyone.*

Thinking isn't the only thing modified by the critical modifier. Among others, there are critical theory, critical practice, critical regionalism, critical architecture and critical modernism.

For example, use of the word critical in *critical regionalism* contrasts with reference to the vernacular. Critical regionalism is a heightened, i.e. *critical,* study of vernacular architecture.

To be critical means to make a critique of something in the mainstream. So, for an architect to practise critically means to be critical of the mainstream ways one might practise architecture; to go beyond the status quo in which architects normally work, beyond the economic realities, construction constraints and commercial interests of a client.[48]

To be fair, architecture is a bigger topic than the design of buildings. Architecture includes design, history, theory, technology and building performance, and urban, social and professional studies.[49]

Critical practices often focus more on theory and history than on building, construction or building performance – which are seen more as the *status quo.* A critical practice therefore might be one that focuses on activist architecture, on computational urbanism, or on serving the underprivileged, displaced or disadvantaged.[50]

What does this have to do with critical thinking? Similar to the use of the word *critical* above, to think critically – to be a critical thinker – means to think purposefully, deliberately.

Be critical, but be nice

Sometimes the word critical is equated with being negative. But being critical isn't an invitation to be a troll or do a hatchet job. To be critical implies being respectful, whereas critical thinking is an act of kindness (or at least being *cruel to be kind*).

By communicating your design intentions, you are helping others to understand your thought process and in turn, when critiquing your peers, they are helping you understand theirs. So be nice.

Every time you think critically and communicate your findings, you are serving as an example, modelling behaviour.

So, it should be clear that the way we are using the word critical here is not intended to imply a strictly negative approach to thinking. Critical can also mean vital, useful, even indispensable.

But here *critical* implies the way we evaluate our thoughts and the thoughts and ideas of others: consciously, creatively and collaboratively.[51]

So how about the word *crit* – derived from and related to critical, criticism and critique – dating from the nineteenth-century Beaux-Arts school of architectural education?[52] The two most common types of crit are those that occur informally in studio[53] – *desk crits* where tutors move from student to student reviewing progress and offering feedback – and those that serve as studio project milestones – *design jury* or *design review* where students present their design projects to a panel of tutors and external critics – usually involving pin-ups and more formal verbal and graphic presentations.[54]

Crits – where students are expected to communicate their design intent and be prepared to discuss their work[55] in an effort to continuously improve – are the heart of the development of design thinking, distinguishing architecture and design education from just about every other subject taught at university level.

4: 12 Challenges of Thinking Critically

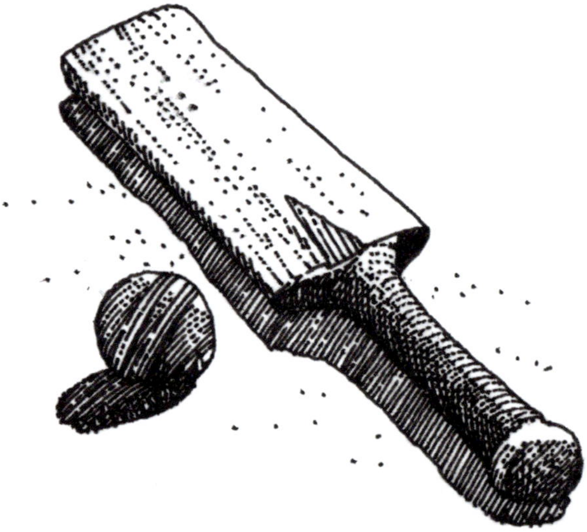

Fig 4.1: A cricket bat and a ball cost £1.10. The bat costs £1 more than the ball. How much does the ball cost?

If architects were *only* deliberate thinkers, they'd be unemployed and their buildings would be uninspiring.

A cricket bat and a ball cost £1.10. The bat costs £1 more than the ball. How much does the ball cost? If you answered ten pence, you are an intuitive thinker – you instinctively or impulsively relied on intuition to arrive at your answer. A deliberate thinker – more rational in their thinking – would have spent time thinking about it. When they did, they'd see that the ball costs five pence. Then, if the bat costs £1 more, it comes out to £1.05, which, combined, gives you £1.10. That is how automatic, habitual, intuitive thinking can lead to mistakes. Arriving at solutions habitually and intuitively will mean we are frequently wrong. Most professors will say that their students need more deliberate thinking – that their ineffable ideas and designs were brought into existence by instinctive or intuitive thinking, relying heavily on emotions and feelings rather than rationally addressing the problem that needed solving. Yet if architects were *only* deliberate thinkers, they'd arguably be unemployed, and their buildings would be uninspiring. As long as architecture is both an art and a science, architects will continue to need both intuitive and deliberate thinking.

Critical thinking is exhausting. Students soon learn that quiet reflection is a lot of work. Because thinking is fatiguing, it is hard to continue doing it except in short bursts (try thinking on a low-carb diet). The brain uses 20% of the body's energy intake,[56] the most energy of any organ in the body.

Critical thinking is hard. If it was easy, everybody would be doing it. There are other things in our environment vying for our attention. Some are shiny and a lot more fun to do than thinking. It's hard to change, to take on new habits – especially the thinking kind. Thinking deliberately may be difficult – but the consequences of *not* thinking more than make up for any hardships.

Critical thinking is deliberate. You have an intractable problem without an obvious solution – the kind that would really benefit from your concentrated thinking – and you realise that you deliberately need to make time/place/space to think about it. So, it doesn't happen. People didn't evolve to think deliberately but to navigate plains and forests, identifying predators. Our brains have numerous hardwired heuristics, rules-of-thumb that often gets us to the right answer. To think deliberately we have to go against our own brain wiring.

Critical thinking involves others. Thinking often needs to be done in real time, on our feet, with others present: *reflection-in-action.* In these situations, thinking becomes a kind of performance – which can cause anxiety. Critical thinking is the most interdisciplinary design skill, and for that you need others.[57]

Critical thinking is unfamiliar. Yes, you may have taken a course in critical thinking, but learning how to think critically as a result of real-life problems – that's something else altogether. And what that something else is – is *unfamiliar.* It may be possible to learn critical thinking while you are doing everything else you are asked to do without resorting to using, say, *Star Trek* to learn critical thinking, despite the fact that critical thinking is unfamiliar and *Star Trek* is familiar and makes you feel comfortable.[58]

Critical thinking is the exception. There is not a lot of evidence that others are doing it – just turn on the news or go online and read the comments: anti-intellectualism and *un*critical thinking are rampant. If world leaders aren't thinking, the argument goes, then why should we?

Critical thinking is > Ctrl+C Ctrl+V. Architecture students tend to misuse the internet to seek ideas, images and information that reinforces already-held positions – as opposed to seeking other points of view and ideas that challenge their preconceived ideas. Critical thinking requires us to pause, consider, apply any one of several thinking tools, and repeat – which is hard to do in a fast and-only-getting-faster world that values Instagram.

Critical thinking is too rational. It took me a long while as a teen to come to realise two facts: that thinking isn't brooding, and that thinking doesn't always have to be rational. There's the belief that doing *any* thinking (as opposed to feeling or intuiting) will lead to a too-rational (i.e. boring, repetitious, inhuman) design. Can critical thinking be abused or taken too far? Sure, by not taking emotions into consideration, ignoring people and their all-too-human needs, resulting in an overly rational, imbalanced solution.

Critical thinking has too many rules. Architects are gregarious, independent thinkers, and they don't like to follow rules, menu items or checklists.

Critical thinking is a process. Not a thing but a process, and people are usually rewarded for results (i.e. things) – not reasons. Similar to action, the world rewards not just words but outcomes. So, in addition to deliberately concentrating and thinking, you have to commit to *making something* out of your decision. True, students are often rewarded for both their results and the thinking that led to them (ask any Year 6 student doing maths homework who is expected to show their work), but in the real world (IRL, i.e. once you graduate) the work that led to your results is seldom scrutinised outside of court or unless something goes awry. Being judged on results not reasons works against the person who needs to do some deliberate thinking. The thinking that led to your results will only be scrutinised when asked, thank you. The sign ought to read: *Justify only upon request.*

Critical thinking requires action. You are rewarded for action – not thinking. In the US, with its Puritan work ethic, you are rewarded for performing. The British have a similar work ethic and are even more action-oriented.[59] So, in addition to concentrating and thinking, you have to commit to acting on the decision: to action, to actually *doing* something. People have a preference/inclination/bias for action – not thinking. Once out of school you will only be rewarded for action. We live in a world where learning is increasingly actionable and project-based. If you are to conduct research, it will probably be *applied* research. If you are studying one of the fine arts, it is increasingly likely to be an *applied* art – like architecture. We are predisposed towards applying what we learn – and not studying or learning for its own sake. (Yes, people once did that. Hard to believe, right?)

Less art for art's sake, more art for-profit. Likewise, our thinking is expected to be applied to real-world problems – not just abstractions. R&D today requires more development and less research. Which is a good thing, but nonetheless a challenge.

Critical thinking takes focus. Lastly, the London architect John Pawson says he thinks more clearly when put in a situation where he is unable to do anything else apart from think.[60] He's not alone: minds wander, and it is hard for anyone to concentrate for long periods of time. The ability to focus without distraction and to work in long uninterrupted stretches is a skill worth cultivating, a tool worth adding to your kit. Focused attention improves outcomes:[61] like a muscle that you build when you work out, focus improves as we use it and weakens or even atrophies when we don't. So, to differentiate yourself, focus. Frankly, because all architects need to stand apart, given the competition – people and technology – the ability to focus is a non-negotiable skillset and mindset. We need to focus to accomplish important things; to be assured that we won't wait until the last minute to address hard work that needs to be completed; to work smart – not long, providing us with some semblance of balance in our lives. According to a University of California Irvine study, after a distraction such as looking at email or social media it takes an average of 23 minutes and 15 seconds to get back to the task.[62] Recognise that designing buildings where people will live and work – and public safety is at stake – is important and deserves concentrated, undistracted, focused effort. We need to stop multitasking, move beyond good intentions and show up – bums on seats, eyes on the road.

You can address your distractions – social media, email – during your breaks. As noted previously, architecture is an art *and* a science. We need both focused awareness and down time where our minds are allowed to drift. It is often thought that attention needs be in the service of problem solving, but often our best ideas come when we allow the mind to drift. (Who hasn't had a great idea when showering?) For designers, focused attention does not have greater value than daydreaming, where we allow the mind to wander. What you're aiming for is a combination of abilities to have extreme concentration at times, and allowing time for reflection, the wide-open mental wandering kind at others. Accept that all things of lasting and deep value require time, some nurturing and only come to us after a little effort. That said, your goal should be to learn how to work smarter – not longer, or harder.

READ THIS

Indistractable: How to Control Your Attention and Choose Your Life
by Nir Eyal
Deep Work: Rules for Focused Success in a Distracted World
by Cal Newport
Digital Minimalism: Choosing a Focused Life in a Noisy World
by Cal Newport

5: Unlimited Benefits of Thinking Critically

Fig 5.1: With the architect here are those not usually present at the table where decisions are made

The benefits of thinking critically like an architect are unlimited.

Having the ability to think critically will help you pass the *sleep test.* When you do your own thinking and problem solving, you can rest assured that everything has been considered and thought through – you will sleep well at night knowing you left nothing to chance.

Thinking critically ensures that you will not be a victim of others' manipulation or bullying – since critical thinking provides you with the ability to see through spurious arguments, unsupported reasoning and persistent bullying. As an architect, critical thinking reminds you that you – and you alone – represent those not present at the table where decisions are made – including current and future building users, neighbours, the public at large, and even future generations (not yet born), who will have to live with these decisions. All of these – and more – are seen as benefits of thinking critically.

As with the challenges, here are twelve benefits:

Critical thinking encourages curiosity. The more you enquire into something, the more you learn about it, the more you want to know – it becomes addictive. Critical thinking and curiosity have a symbiotic relationship: each spurs the other on.

Critical thinking encourages creativity. Critical thinking requires curiosity, and curiosity leads to more innovative ideas.

Critical thinking increases problem-solving ability. Because it forces us to focus and consider both sides of an argument, critical thinking improves our ability to amicably and constructively address situations, solve problems and resolve issues in a way that will be acceptable to all involved.

Critical thinking is a transferable skill. Are architecture students in pursuit of skills they are told are useless as soon as they reach the job market? Why bother? Time spent invested in developing critical thinking pays off.

Critical thinking is hard. That's right – but not too hard. And that is a good thing. Your ultimate goal is to take on work where most of your time is in a state of flow.[63] Ideally, the work you do is neither too hard nor too easy, but just challenging enough to keep your mind occupied. Critical thinking requires just the right level of focus, concentration and effort to keep you engaged for long periods of time.

Critical thinking is deliberate. And a good thing it is. No one becomes an architect because they want to sleepwalk through life. Better to pursue a career that requires you to think purposefully than habitually and automatically.

Critical thinking requires you to engage with others. Studies show that we find more fulfilment when working with and among others. Engaging with others in the thinking process also keeps our thinking honest. Critical thinking is considered the most interdisciplinary design skill.[64]

Critical thinking is the exception. In today's marketplace, you need to stand out and differentiate yourself. There is no better way to do that than to think critically. Do so and you will probably be the exception – and before long you will be recognised, sought after and rewarded for it.

Critical thinking is not domain- or discipline-specific. Time invested in developing this capability pays off. Critical thinking is not domain- or discipline-specific. The ways architects think – critically, creatively and collaboratively – is transferable to multiple fields and roles including start-ups and entrepreneurs, and they're necessary to your everyday tasks in architecture.

Critical thinking is sought after by employers. Considered a current and future capability, employers look for and reward those who possess critical thinking capabilities.

Critical thinking is associated with wellness and longevity. Critical thinkers experience fewer bad things in life than people who simply have a high degree of intelligence, and critical thinking has been associated with wellness and longevity.[65] Having the ability to think critically empowers people, lowering their anxiety.

Critical thinking strengthens self-reliance. Developing critical thinking skills enables you to think more independently, relying less on others and other sources to do your thinking for you.

Critical thinking has its challenges, but it should be clear by now that the benefits win.

6:
Deliberate Thinking

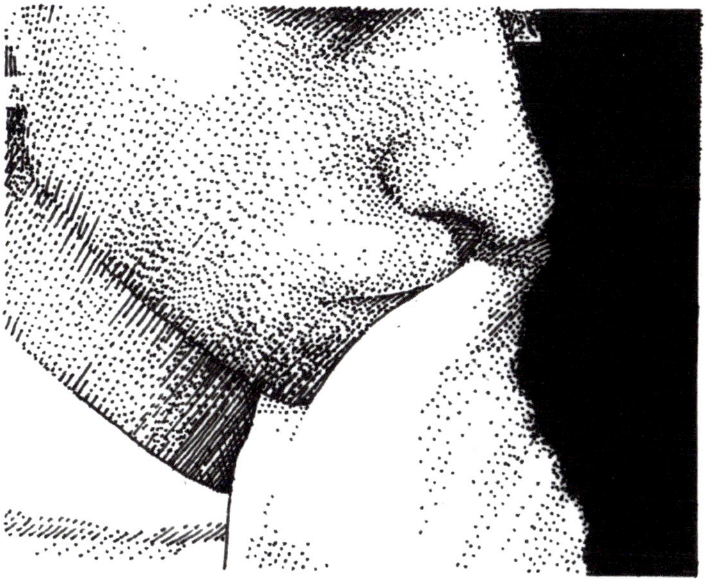

Fig 6.1: The good news about critical thinking being deliberate is that you are not expected to do it all the time – most of the time, habitual thinking works just fine

Architects think deliberately about how inhabitants experience their buildings.

Do you imagine the experiential qualities of spaces as you create architecture? Do you think of spaces you design in these terms? Do you sense the quality of the light streaming in through the windows at various times of the day and year? Do you feel the cooling breezes which are a result of the manipulation of the section and openings? Do you feel the heat baking the occupants of unshaded south-facing windows in the summer? Do you hear the deafening roar of air through the ventilation ducts from HVAC systems desperately attempting to reach the setpoint of the thermostat?[66] When you design, do you imagine how the senses are impacted by the decisions you make?

Professor Terri Meyer Boake posed these questions to architecture students, then offered a reply of her own:

'I would venture to say that the majority of students, as well as designers, never think in these terms.'

Imagine designing a building without imagining how the spaces in that building would feel to its inhabitants. According to Boake, it is unlikely that students and designers in the design process give this much thought, and she concludes her enquiry by posing a question to educators of these students and designers:

'How can we enlighten students to think critically in these terms?'[67]

This is what deliberate designing looks like. There's a level of curiosity, specificity and detail when thinking and designing deliberately.

It is intentional, rigorous and holistic, whereas most of the time the type of thinking we do is selective, automatic, uncritical and habitual.

Critical thinking isn't haphazard – you have to will it, make time for it, and expend some energy and effort to make it happen.

The fact that it is deliberate – where you consciously set time aside to focus on a problem – is what differentiates critical thinking from other types of thinking.

Yet, just because it is deliberate doesn't mean that it is entirely rational. It just means that the thinking that takes place is purposeful – on purpose – and not haphazard or random. For that reason, deliberate thinking often includes other thinking types – specifically intuitive and analytical thinking: both are important to make assured decisions that stick.

People assume that what architects do – including the buildings they design – is deliberate: they might as well make it so.

The opposite of critical thinking isn't critical mindlessness, it's uncritical thinking: automatic, non-deliberate thinking: the kind of thinking we do most of the time, when driving home, while brushing our teeth or taking the stairs.

But deliberation is slow. Usually we don't have time to stop and think critically. What then?

Coming to conclusions too quickly can be counterproductive, resulting in shortsighted or superficial results that aren't thoroughly vetted, in the long run costing you more time and effort than you might have saved. The opposite is also true: if you deliberate too slowly, you might miss out by missing deadlines.[68]

Reflection-in-action

To counter the counterproductivity of working too fast and the missed opportunities of working too deliberately, architects and other designers partake in a particular kind of thinking: reflection-in-action, or thinking on your feet: where they don't stop what they're doing to navel-gaze; where they learn how to think in real time, on the fly. Reflection-in-action is a coveted and sought-after ability, up there for effectiveness with sketching in front of people.

The good news about critical thinking being deliberate is that you are not expected to do it all the time: most of the time habitual thinking works just fine. Most activities don't require deliberate thinking. Habit and routine work are just fine to complete day-to-day tasks and challenges.[69] If you had to think about every movement you make in walking down a flight of stairs you would probably trip! Most of the time, automatic or habitual thinking serves us well. It is only when we have to create that gap in time and turn our attention to the problem at hand that we think deliberately and critically.

The opposite of superficial, surface thinking, deliberate thinking requires you to probe deeper. Examples of automatic or habitual thinking include memorising facts that can then be regurgitated come exam time, and repeating information you may have read or overheard somewhere without analysing or comprehending it.

So, while we don't have enough clues yet to know how an architect thinks, we have an inkling as to what it means to *not* think like an architect:

Base decisions on assumptions that go untested; ignore feedback; go with hunches and habitual thinking without resorting to reason; let preconceived ideas drive design decisions; copy/paste ideas from other sources as your design direction; and, go with what feels right to the exclusion of evaluation.

When designing, there is a lot of pressure to come up with a brilliant idea. When given an assignment, the tendency is to do an online search where you zero in on what appeals most to you, and *that* becomes the impetus or inspiration for your design. The next time this happens, don't just mindlessly see an image online and copy/paste: ask questions of it. What sorts of questions?

TRY THIS

Create a time and place for deliberate thinking, a ritual for deliberate thinking, or a trigger such as making a cup of coffee or tea; have a favourite place to sit and think; minimise distractions and make it easy for yourself to concentrate. Concentration – like any habit – takes repetition: rinse and repeat.

TRY THIS

Approach your next design assignment by using deliberate thinking, setting aside any preconceived ideas, keeping track of the questions that arise while you design and the decisions you make. Seriously consider feedback, whether from classmates or your tutor. Your goal in this exercise is to surpass habitual thinking to think thoughtfully, contextually, rigorously, exactingly, self-critically and equitably.

ASK THIS

Ask questions of a project's context: What is this project's location? Region? Weather conditions? Ask questions of its origin: Who made this? And why? Why is this the way it is? Ask existential questions: Why this and not something else? What are the forces that drove or determined this into existence? What were the constraints that led to this as a solution to a problem? What was the nature of the problem that this is the solution to?

7:
A Tool in Your Toolbox

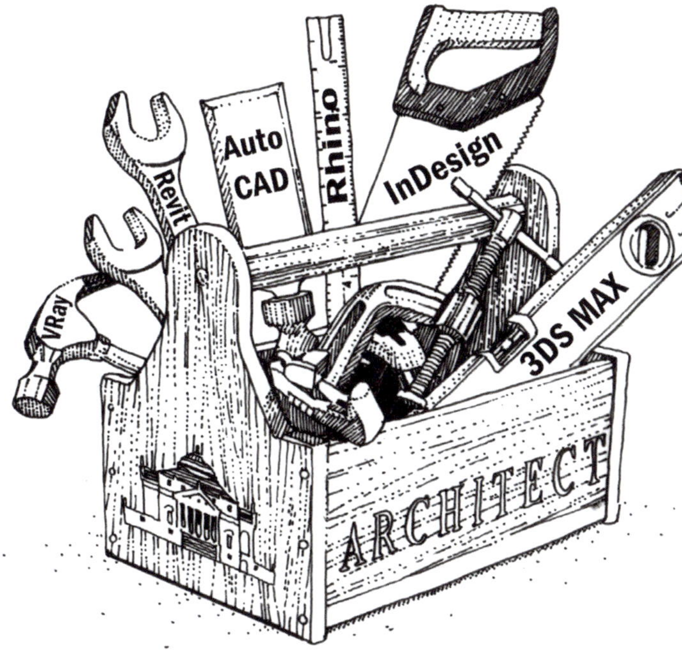

Fig 7.1: Critical thinking is a go-to tool in the architect's arsenal

Critical thinking is a go-to tool.

It is important to think of critical thinking not just as a scholastic subject or academic achievement, but as a tool in your toolbox.

It is a tool like any other tool that you want to have at the ready, and tool belt and toolbox analogies work particularly well for the architect – even if they're associated more with construction than design.

Critical thinking belongs there alongside the architect's scale, mechanical pencil, Moleskine notebook and metal swing-arm LED desk lamp; with CAD, Revit and Rhino; with your scalpel, tracing paper and Prismacolor pencils, laptop and Monte Blanc pen with sepia ink.

Pritzker Prize-winning architect Alejandro Aravena has gone so far as to suggest that 'rather than architecture being presented as a profession, it should be seen as a set of tools to understand society. You may end up designing buildings with your training, or you may use your degree as a way to understand reality, and given the global challenges we are dealing with, that is also desirable.'[70]

As you work your way towards being able to think on your feet – reflection-in-action – you can reach for that tool in your tool belt.

You want to avoid thinking of critical thinking, though, as a tool in your tool shed. It's not something you learn and then store or park – where it might be out of sight and out of mind.

As critical thinking is one of your go-to tools, you'll want it close at hand as you design.

TRY THIS

If it is too hard to think of critical thinking as a tool in your toolbox, break it down into its constituent parts – reason, intuition and reflection – and ask yourself: which will serve me best here, in this situation? A thinking process can begin with any of them.[71]

ASK THIS

Use critical thinking to evaluate the other tools in the toolbox. Before using, for example, Rhino or Revit, ask: Is this the right tool to accomplish what I need to do? How do I know? Does this tool work well (from an interoperability standpoint) with other tools in my workflow? Is this worth doing? If working in a team, will others need access to the file, and do they have this software? How will the deliverable be presented? Is it value-added? Will this tool help to explain my project? How so?

8:
Argument in Architecture

Fig 8.1: The interior rotunda of Frank Lloyd Wright's Solomon R. Guggenheim Museum in New York City. If natural light harms photographs and paintings, then why is there direct natural light where the art is hung?

Architects argue effectively by appealing to reason, the emotions and ethics.

Frank Lloyd Wright's Solomon R. Guggenheim Museum on Fifth Avenue in New York City turned sixty in 2019.

A beloved building; nonetheless, the architecture competes with the art for your attention.

There's the difficulty of installing and displaying art – especially wall-hung pictures – along a continuous ramp.

And while it is a known fact that daylight can irrevocably harm artworks, natural light bathes the central rotunda of the museum via its nearly 20-metre-diameter oculus skylight.

If natural light harms photographs and paintings, then why is there direct natural light where the art is hung?

Why indeed. Because Wright was adamant there should be abundant light in the museum's rotunda.

And what argument did he use?

He alluded to the museum director's comment in 1955 that pictures – photographs and paintings – are among things that could be found in nature, and that nature benefited from the effects of natural light.[72]

So ... here we have Wright arguing for natural light in the Guggenheim even though light is known to permanently harm artwork.

A spurious argument at best, but Wright could be persuasive – and, Wright being Wright, got his way.

Of course, an architect's work isn't done once they come up with a design for a building.

If, while presenting multiple schemes, there is one in particular that solves most of the problems within the project constraints, they have to argue on its behalf.

As you might imagine, there are more or less effective ways to do that.

We can't all have the gall and persuasive powers of Wright. So, in addition to presenting the facts and evidence discovered in the design process, for when it matters most it would behove architects to learn to argue effectively.

Cut to Aristotle

Aristotle famously put forward three appeals to argument: logical (logos), ethical (ethos) and emotional (pathos), where the best arguments are a balance of all three.

For example, when architects cite evidence (such as facts, data and statistics) to support their actions – presenting evidence-based decisions – they are able to convince others of the design direction by means of reason or logic.

Architects will appeal to the emotions, not as a substitute for logic or ethics, but responsibly – because they know for example that the visual appeal of buildings can persuade on an emotional level.

When architects serve as a trusted adviser to an owner – while taking the needs of others into consideration, including users, neighbours, the public-at-large and even future generations – arguments made on behalf of their designs are considered balanced, fair, equitable and ethical.

When an architect argues in support of a design direction, they offer reasons with an aim of persuading others that their design is right, or another is wrong.

Argument in architecture needs to use facts, data and evidence to support positions on issues like regenerative or whole systems design, sustainability and resilience.

Make it compelling

It is essential to learn to defend your ideas, and to argue on behalf of your architectural decisions.[73] To do so requires persistence, persuasiveness and no small amount of eloquence. Minoring in rhetoric while majoring in architecture in college was one of the best decisions I ever made – not because I write books, but because for thirty years I designed buildings and, if they were to be built, I had to argue persuasively on their behalf.

Your argument needs to be rational and logical, but also well spoken and compelling.

'Eloquence is what's needed to resist the so-called inevitable futures and influence. People let bullies get away with it because they don't know any better – and retreat because it's overwhelming,' explains futurist David Zach. 'Most design schools ignore teaching how to defend ideas. At one school of architecture a professor told me (and the crowd) that "we teach design, not sales". If you can't explain and defend your ideas in compelling and logical ways – you're probably not really a designer.'[74]

ASK THIS

A homeowner wants to add a bedroom and bath to their house and turn their one-car garage to fit two cars, requiring the widening of the driveway. A contractor tells a client that they can handle this, but that working with an architect will slow down the construction process. Is this true? It is true that architects want to do things right, and where required by law will follow local rules, seeking a permit for construction. Following the rules, designing and detailing accordingly as opposed to just doing it will probably slow things down. Breaking the law will speed things up. So yes, the contractor's statement is correct: working with an architect will slow down the construction process. The contractor is itching to get moving on the project, and by not breaking the law the architect will probably need to slow down that process. But getting caught doing work without a permit *will* also slow things down, not to mention cost even more. And doing work that doesn't require a permit may not get you what you are looking to do.[75]

9:
Can Buildings Argue?

Fig 9.1: Philip Johnson's Palladian curtain wall at One International Place

Buildings can't argue, but their architects can and must.

The best thing one could say about Philip Johnson's Palladian curtain wall at One International Place in Boston was that it was mischievous[76] and even silly. In fact, that is what *The New York Times*'s architecture critic called it,[77] explaining that the architect intended for the tower to look like a nineteenth-century crystal palace stretched out into a skyscraper.

But we may never know the real reason Johnson repeated the historical Palladian windows *ad nauseum* over the high-rise facade. The public outcry partly against the project's design eventually led to a lawsuit to block the project, causing only one of two proposed towers with Johnson's Palladian window wall-papered curtain wall to be built.[78]

Today, with the world on fire, arguments about style and (bad) taste may seem at best quaint and at worst beside the point. In the previous pages I argued that architects, if they are to see them built, must argue on behalf of their buildings. But how about buildings? Are buildings – made of masonry, concrete, steel and glass – really mute, or is architecture able to argue on its own behalf? And if so, how?

After all, architect Peter Zumthor believes that the building itself is an architect's best argument – irrespective of what their argument may be.[79] Rhetoric, or the art of persuasion, influence and argument, has a primary goal – to achieve consensus. To get others on board to agree with you. So, even if buildings could argue, before your building can argue on your behalf, you have to argue on its behalf.

Making arguments in architecture

What we're really talking about when we ask if buildings can argue, is *discursive* architecture, where a building whose main purpose is not functional has been intentionally embedded with discourse and is used to stimulate discussion.[80]

Architecture, if it can be said to make arguments, does so either directly – using signage boards – or indirectly and abstractly. One example, the Eiffel Tower, was constructed in part to demonstrate France's industrial boldness to the world.

It's not like you can hand out pamphlets in front of your built projects explaining what your building means. Once a project is built – leaving aside architectural guidebooks and architectural websites – the building has to do the talking. At some point, your designs belong to the world and have to stand on their own.

Architects can try to speak on their behalf. But if they mean something, if they have an argument to make, buildings will just have to make it on their own. Architecture either creates our world – the built as opposed to the natural environment – and says something about our place in the world,[81] or serves as a backdrop for people's lives in the world.

Architecture can have an impact on how people feel, and the best architecture can make us feel profoundly.

To the extent that a building urges you on, it can be said to be making an argument in terms of directionality and movement. But buildings can also be said to *move* you in a different way, emotionally, impacting your mood.

Similarly, buildings make arguments when they play with your emotions, change your attitude or encourage you inside, manipulating you to look around or make a purchase. Or they serve an economic end – to make the building developer money or improve the economic conditions or prospects of the community – as in the case of Frank Gehry's Guggenheim Museum Bilbao, and the so-called 'Bilbao effect'.

For some, a building is an argument – where the building is a means to an end.[82] Yet even in those cases, a building has to fulfil a function, dictates and obligations that go beyond any discourse. As long as those are also met, buildings should be free to speak. The question is, given the various demands on people's attention, will people look up and listen?

ASK THIS

If we can embed our projects with discourse, come crit time why not let our presentation boards – the combination of our drawings, renders and words – speak for themselves? Where the student who is about to present their design at a review starts their presentation with: *Any questions?* Can buildings make their own case? Do they need their architects to make their cases for them?

ASK THIS

When an architect designs a building that addresses the climate crisis, *they* may be able to declare a call for carbon reduction, but can the building? A building can be designed with the climate in mind, i.e. to save energy. But can a building argue in favour of saving energy[83] or can only the architect do so?

ASK THIS

Think of a building you have designed. Looking at it from the perspective of the public, what is your building trying to say? How well does it say it? What means does your building use (style? scale? materiality?) to communicate its message? Put this message in the form of an argument: What is the building arguing for?

10:
Test and Evaluate

Fig 10.1: An architect's work is iterative, more like a spiral (directional, leading towards their goal) – like the spiral in Frank Lloyd Wright's Solomon R. Guggenheim Museum – than circular, cyclical or wheel-like. Less spinning of their wheels than spiralling towards a solution

Architects don't wait to evaluate – it happens throughout the design process.

Often associated with learning objectives, Bloom's taxonomy (knowledge, comprehension, application, analysis, synthesis, evaluation) is also a useful guide to determine what level of thinking is required for a given task.

A lot of mid-term and final exams, for example, test for rote memorisation – the lowest tier of learning in this model.

Testing and evaluating – making informed judgements – for example, are significantly higher-level orders of thinking: above remembering, knowing and memorising; above understanding, comprehending and being able to put something into your own words; even above applying what you know.

In fact, next to creating, evaluating is the second highest order of thinking ability in Bloom's taxonomy.

Despite what we've been told, while evaluation requires a higher-order level of thinking, testing and evaluation is not a set phase at or near the end of the design process.

When architects design, however microscopically small each design move may appear, each line we make is put to the test.

That's because architects design iteratively.

Architects think something, place a mark on paper or a line on their monitor, then test the mark or line in their imagination, or using a simulation tool to evaluate it against all the known constraints: building codes, sun orientation, energy use, aesthetic appeal, cost, schedule implications, adjacent uses, common sense and more.

Architects, in other words, test as they go. Testing and evaluating is something that occurs every step along the way.

Many experts on creativity advise that brainstorming and judgement are two separate acts or phases.

They are – but they're only separated by fractions of a second.

Despite what you might have read or been told about the right brain vs left brain, evaluating as you go doesn't stifle creativity – it *improves* it.

Architects are constantly bouncing ideas back and forth between their left and right brains: passing back and forth across the brain's tennis net, the corpus callosum, weaving together so-called right- and left-brain thinking.

It's wrong to think – like so many design processes indicate – that evaluation is a one-time phase or stage.

And like evaluation, when in the design process does critical thinking occur?

Hopefully it does, at every step along the way.

In Albert Camus's last complete work of fiction, *The Fall,* narrator Jean-Baptiste Clamence says: 'Don't wait for the Last Judgment. It takes place every day.'

Likewise, for architects in the design process there is no last judgement. Don't wait to evaluate – it takes place every day!

Trust but verify

The best architects start by programming the spaces needed by the client and see how these can best fit the space of the site and its surroundings.

Architects trust themselves and the design process to assure that everything will work out.

They trust but verify. For architects, facts matter.

To verify, they test the soundness of claims made and evidence used to support the claims.

Architects assess the inferences and logical assumptions they make, asking themselves: is this True, Probably True, Requires More Information, Probably False, or False?

Critical and creative thinking are not linear processes or steps. There's a simultaneity of critical and creative thought while the architect designs.[84]

Architects don't wait for the building to be built before testing it on its inhabitants – that would be cruel and unusual. They test as they go.[85]

For the sake of clarity, when architects design, one stage they go through is test-fit, which tests how something works – for example, how the programme works in the space that has been allocated, confirming that the client's needs and requirements can be accommodated within a space.[86] It's a form of reality-check.

TRY THIS

One time I worked on the design of a new manufacturer's headquarters. We designed the facility based on their space requirements, but by the time the building was complete, they had already outgrown the facility. For this reason, when doing a test-fit, architects factor in growth projections.

TRY THIS

Draft a test-fit drawing – a simple plan used to confirm that the stated programme requirements can be accommodated within the given or allotted spaces. Now try this using an app or digital tool. What did you learn?

TRY THIS

Next time you read something online, evaluate the source of your information. Use more than one source. Get in the habit of judging the quality of what you read online. The ability to evaluate the quality of sources is becoming more important – and most of us aren't getting better at it.[87] Since what they design must address the health, safety and wellness of its inhabitants and the public, architects especially need to get better at this.

ASK THIS

Architects go from radical thinkers to grounded thinkers seemingly in the same thought. How about this? How about this? Let's test it. What does it mean to test our ideas?

ASK THIS

Design something. Does it exceed the square footage, the budget, does it defy gravity? How do you know? When in the design process do you ask and find out?

ASK THIS

Can the place or space you are designing accommodate the client's plans for growth?[88]

11: Analogous Thinking

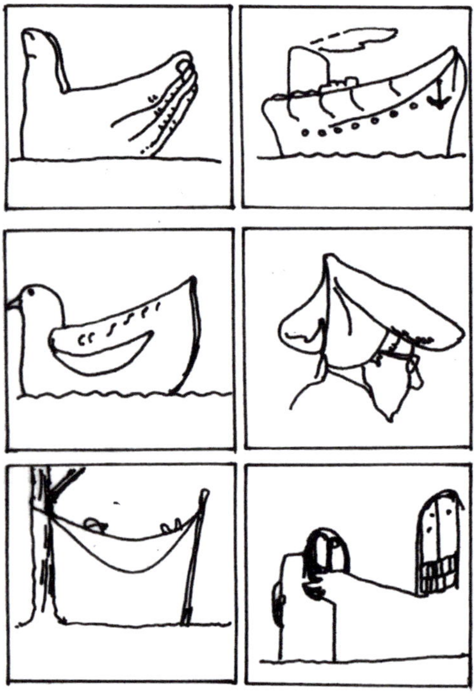

Fig 11.1: Metaphors of Le Corbusier's Ronchamp based on drawings by Hillel Schocken in a seminar on architectural semiotics at the Architectural Association,[89] and a guy on a hammock

Architects use metaphor to provide order and meaning to the built environment.

If architecture could be said to be discursive, one way would be through metaphor.

Metaphor is where one substitutes one thing to stand in for another so it can be understood.

It makes sense to use metaphors and analogies to help explain domain-specific or otherwise difficult-to-explain ideas or forms to someone not trained to see like an architect.

We use them to help others understand what they don't know, and to explain unfamiliar things to people in terms or images they can readily understand.

At its best metaphor helps make the not-understandable understandable – especially to non-specialists (non-architects) by speaking of one thing in terms of another. At its worst, it serves as a substitute or even a crutch for critical thinking.

Metaphor is important to help you understand – to understand something that you don't know in terms of something that you do.

For example, when making critical points, architect Eric Owen Moss provides analogies, explaining the way – by combining two analogies – he would like architectural thinking to be.[90]

The use of analogies and metaphors is also important to help explain something you know, for example your design, and to explain or communicate it to someone who is not as familiar with it.

Because metaphor can be thought of as a shortcut to meaning, too often we use metaphor – and metaphoric thinking – as a form of verbal shorthand for thinking in lieu of presenting facts or communicating the truth about something.[91]

This is especially true when we resort to similes in architecture. As Figure 11.2 shows, when the multistorey headquarters of a basket maker is in the shape of a basket – or a music school resembles a grand piano – the idea is too literal. Similes are too literal – where the architect hasn't enabled abstract thinking – to serve the more poetic purpose of metaphor. Here the comparison between things (e.g. building = basket) is too direct, where a building becomes the constructed version of a thing itself, and not something that implies something else.

When stretched beyond credibility metaphors can misinform or mislead.[92] Israeli psychologist Amos Tversky considered metaphors to be cover-ups and false storytelling,[93] especially when compared with more rigorous scientific thinking.

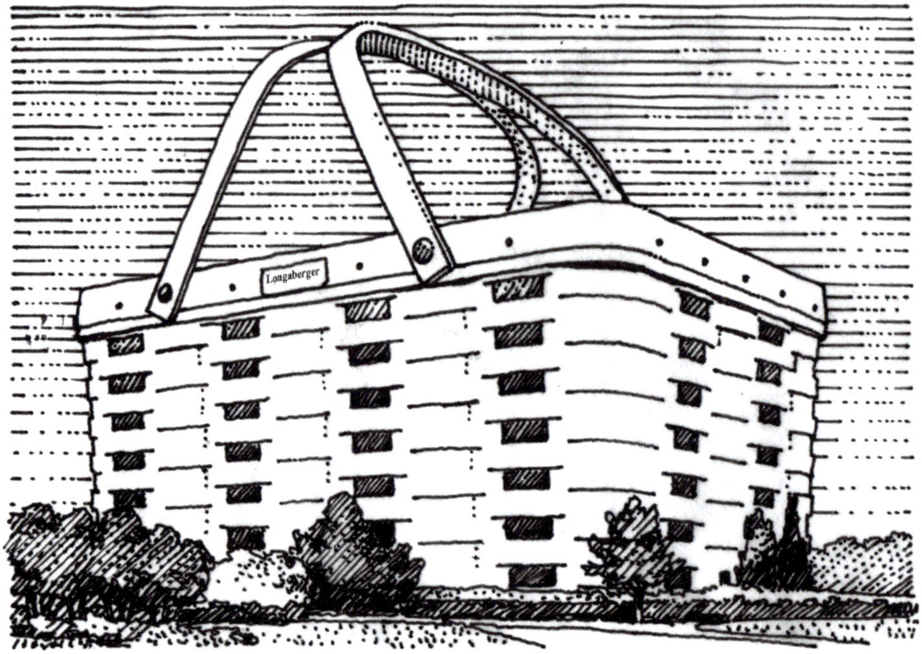

Fig 11.2 Longaberger's old headquarters building in Newark, Ohio, USA

Far from serving as a fallacy, metaphors are critically important in expressing the element of poetry in architecture. For metaphor, at its best, can explore and express the poetry of architecture.

From the earliest ages, architects used metaphor to provide order and meaning to the built environment.[94] Yet metaphor as a stand-in for critical thinking is lazy thinking.

Nothing is a substitute for critical thinking.

ASK THIS

Why does analogical thinking appear in the critical thinking and not, say, the creative thinking section of this book? Because metaphor can be misused as a stand-in or substitute for thinking clearly and communicating directly.

READ THIS

Metaphor: An Exploration of the Metaphorical Dimensions and Potential of Architecture by Simon Unwin. Consider this volume as an addendum to Unwin's foundational book, *Analysing Architecture.*

12: Describe Explain (Rationalise) Justify

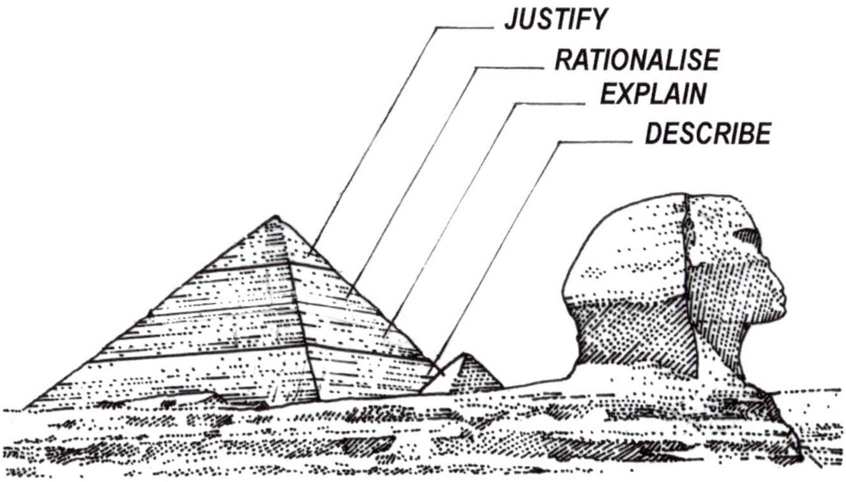

Fig 12.1: Justifications for our architectural acts are built on a solid foundation of reasons, explanations and descriptions

Architects only need to justify their decisions when challenged, but a good critical thinker prepares for this inevitability.

Here are two bits of wisdom that pertain to most presentations architects give, from formal crits to design competitions.

The first: Your project is only as good as your weakest image.

A weak image undermines the argument you are making on behalf of your project.

And the second: Know what you are being asked – the so-called *question behind the question.*

The emphasis can be subtle but important. Take the question: *Why did you do that?*

Where's the emphasis? Look at the context of the question. What came immediately prior?

Why did you do that?
Why **did** you **do** that?
Why did **you** do that?
Why did you do **that**?

It is important to know what you are being asked to do.

To help you build a thinking repertoire, here are terms to become familiar with so you know what is being asked of you:

Describing
Are you being asked to describe your project? Then literally report what you see: plans, elevations, sections, whatnot.

Explaining
Are you being asked to explain your project? Then you are being asked to share how you arrived at your solution. The emphasis is on *how* – not on you. *Occam's razor* is often used to find the simplest explanation that fits all facts.

Rationalising and Self-Justifying
Are you being asked to rationalise your project? That's a trick question – because you will never, ever be asked to rationalise why you did what you did. If you respond to a request for an explanation in terms of yourself, you are self-justifying: you're providing a rationalisation. This is sometimes referred to as post-rationalisation, where you are rationalising after the fact as opposed to providing reasons and evidence before you act. Rationalisations are important – they're the stories architects tell themselves for why they do what they do. Just be selective whom else you tell, and consider what you hope to gain by doing so.

Justifying

Are you being asked to justify your solution? This is rare. You can provide a description or explanation unprompted, but almost no one offers a justification for *why* they did what they did – their solution – without being prompted or asked to do so. A reviewer might ask something like *Tell us how this is a viable solution for the problem you were asked to solve?* In such a case it would be inappropriate to respond by describing the project – they clearly see what you presented; how you arrived at this outcome. They are in essence asking *Why this and not something else?* Your response is a justification.

When justifying your solution, you can appeal to certain authorities: climate, context, economy, aesthetics, codes, etc.

We learned in a previous chapter that architects argue effectively when they appeal to reason, the emotions and ethics.

But a justification would be an appeal to values held by others: especially the paying client – whomever commissioned the project or created the project description – and the *non-paying* client or larger society that will support and use it.

The building might have been oriented a certain way to save energy – to make use of the sun. But the people on the street are unlikely to know this. They will wonder why the building turns its back on its neighbours.

A crit is where reviewers ask of your project a series of questions.

- It is where your project is vetted, scrutinised, questioned, poked and prodded.
- And sometimes it is subjected to public merriment and ridicule – the veritable spanking machine.
- It puts your idea through the ringer to see if it is strong enough to withstand the test of gravity, typology, energy, climate, sustainability, context, regional fit and materials.
- And it finds whether *you* are strong enough to withstand a test of resilience.

In a crit the burden of proof is on you.

So, *have a reason* for doing what you are doing, a reason why you did what you did.

Don't just put a function somewhere because you have the space in your building – make it deliberate, purposeful.

Just like Bloom's taxonomy, introduced earlier, which offered levels of thinking and learning objectives, these steps represent levels of questioning, parts that make up an argument for your solution.

Some responses are more persuasive than others. You want to use the more effective ways to argue your points.

Because they are more effective ways to argue for your idea, you want to use reasoning, logic, evidence, justification, explanation, demonstration – and avoid less-effective self-justificatory behaviour.

Employers and tutors don't just want to take your word for it – that you think critically, creatively and collaboratively – they want to see *evidence* of it in your writing, in your work, in your speaking and in your projects. In other words, in your *behaviour.*

The time may come when clients require architects to justify design decisions by using evidence and hold them accountable by using data: proactive architects will be prepared for such a future.

TRY THIS

Responses to reviewers' enquiries are almost always examples of the socialisation of your idea. Think of a review or crit as your idea's coming-out party, where your solution goes from private and personal to public.

TRY THIS

Tell a story about what your building will do. Walk the client down the path. Create a narrative. The decisions will appear to be sequential, inevitable. Stories have momentum and their own inherent logic. *I did this then this* is not a story: it is a self-justification. *This led to this which led to this* is a story.

ASK THIS

When you are asked a question during a crit, how do you know what is being asked?

ASK THIS

Who benefits from your decision? And who will be left out?

ASK THIS

Imagine your design is built. Looking back – as though in a rearview mirror: how is the building used? Received? Put yourself in the shoes of a future inhabitant or passerby. What impact does the building have on others? Was this what was intended?

ASK THIS

Ask yourself, *What am I being asked?* To justify yourself? Or your decision? To defend your project? To defend yourself?

SECTION 2: FACTS, FALLACIES AND PHOTOSHOP

13: Fact or Fiction?

Fig 13.1: Ole Scheeren in front of CCTV

Architects are like investigative reporters who scrupulously explore details to verify facts.

Architect Ole Scheeren likes to tell the story of how, when his team was working on the CCTV tower in Beijing, China, many in the office had never worked on a project of that size (their previous largest project was a Prada store), and they felt it was important to understand the scale they were working at. To understand the project's size in terms of human scale, he had his team cut out 10,000 cardboard people and add them to the physical model. In doing so, he had his employees go from imagination to reality, fiction to fact. Architects deal with real people, places and things. Despite the considerable virtual and digital tools available to him, with simple cardboard Scheeren had everything he needed at hand to get his point across.

Meanwhile, we all know the benefits of trees in cities. Urban trees help to save energy, lead to better air and water quality, reduce stormwater run-off, store carbon and increase property values. And a large, healthy tree removes approximately seventy times more air pollution per year than a small, newly planted tree.[95]

In fact, there's even an easy-to-remember acronym on the four primary ways that urban trees affect air quality:

Temperature reduction and other microclimatic effects
Removal of air pollutants
Emission of volatile organic compounds and tree maintenance emissions
Energy effects on buildings[96]

But, fact or fiction, what about the claim that greenery may also make cities safer, especially in low-income, blighted areas?

A growing body of research suggests buildings surrounded by lots of foliage saw 56% fewer violent crimes. Let's briefly explore that claim.

By comparing aerial photos and police crime reports, researchers calculated that buildings still surrounded by lots of foliage saw 48% fewer property crimes, on average, and 56% fewer violent crimes than buildings with low levels of vegetation. In one city, tree loss was associated with an uptick in property crimes, assaults and violent crimes

To be clear, the analysis doesn't *prove* the trees caused the phenomenon. But a small but growing body of research supports the idea that trees can have a calming effect on crime.

If you shared this claim, you might be asked what, exactly, makes foliage a possible deterrent to delinquency? Researchers have a few ideas:

Some say trees might signal that the area is well cared-for, similar to the 'broken windows theory' which suggests that disorder invites crime.[97]

Some say green spaces make an area inviting and can lead to more informal surveillance, or 'eyes on the street'.[98]

Other theories point to the well-documented calming effect of vegetation, or the idea that greenery promotes trust within a community.[99]

Let's look at another fact – this one an example of critical thinking in green architecture:

Fact or fiction? Cutting down trees to make buildings does not sound environmentally sensitive.

That, of course, is not a fact but an opinion – in part because mass timber wood could be harvested from sustainably managed forests,[100] but as importantly, the sentence should have clued you in on what rendered the sentence someone's opinion: the phrase 'does not sound'.

Fact or opinion? Wood is more dangerous to build with because it is more flammable.

There's the question: more dangerous for whom? But generally, it's an unsupported fact, i.e. someone's opinion, because the evidence doesn't bear it out.

It is a fact that while wood is combustible, structural members of treated engineered wood in a fire form an insulating layer of char before the strength of the member is significantly impaired, making it not more dangerous to build with.

How about the oft-heard claim that wood is stronger than steel?

Pound for pound, wood *is* stronger than steel.[101] But the source of the quote shows that the claim is made not by a researcher or scientist, but by a manufacturer, i.e. someone with a conflict of interest who might benefit from your believing the claim.

Facts are admittedly hard to prove, but prove we must. In one test, wood was slightly better than steel in relation to fatigue and stress of a simulated earthquake,[102] but one test does not a fact make.

On the other hand, science demonstrates that untreated wood is rarely as strong as metals used in construction,[103] and while we're on the topic, it is true that wood can be *transformed into* a material that is stronger than steel.[104]

That a structure supports a building, except of course when it doesn't,[105] or that a roof is intended to protect the structure from the elements are both examples of facts.

Let's now explore the claim that architecture – through elements like space, light, geometry and materials – can impact our mood.

Taken at face value, it is not an evil claim with malicious intent. No one is deliberately trying to dupe you by getting you to believe the claim – however increasingly cited – that architecture can impact people's wellbeing and moods.

Numerous studies document *healthy building* impacts such as reduced illness and absenteeism among workers, higher worker productivity, higher test scores among students, and greater workplace satisfaction.

Natural light, for example, can help hospital patients to recover and school pupils perform better.[106]

But still, despite articles stating that *numerous studies show* ... what is the *science* behind such a claim? What, in other words, are the facts?

We know that people in modern societies spend 90% of their time indoors.[107] We also know that buildings can impact a person's health.[108] IRL the information we find is not black and white – it still requires us to make informed judgements, for example by finding and citing a tutor whose research is legit.[109]

TRY THIS

Follow this line of thinking concerning indoor air quality (IAQ). One of the responses to the energy crisis of the 1970s was to seal up our buildings in order to reduce heating and cooling loads. But an unintended consequence of doing this was stagnant air. We know that indoor air is on average two to five times more toxic than outside air.[110] This led to the rise of sick building syndrome,[111] so we allowed our buildings to breathe more. But an unintended consequence of this was raising heating and cooling loads. Passive House (Passivhaus) does not recommend that we seal our buildings (they are better insulated and much more airtight than regular builds). Will airtight buildings lead to another rise of 'sick' buildings? One can always open a window, but opening a window wreaks havoc on the mechanical consultant's mechanical system. People can unintendedly leave windows open. And so on ... This is the kind of back-and-forth thinking that architects do when making difficult decisions.

TRY THIS

Some problems are inconclusive: open vs closed office plans? Which lead to increased productivity and wellbeing? Happiness? Gensler recently redesigned its Chicago offices as open. Research this topic and see if you can find conclusive evidence one way or the other. Note: Some generative design tools are being used to design office layouts but lack common sense as criteria for selection.

ASK THIS

What is a fact? Is a fact something that is based on objective reality and, using evidence, can be proven to be true?

ASK THIS

Next time you have a design assignment, and are considering shopping for a design online, consider the source. Where did you get your ideas? Ching? Google? Instagram? Your imagination? Many find projects that they like online and *Ctrl+C Ctrl+V* the project, using it to serve as inspiration for their design. Did you read up on the project to understand why it is the way it is, why certain decisions were made? What its location is and the influence the region had on its design? For example, Alvar Alto's work doesn't make sense out of context, because Alto was all about context. So, copying his building details verbatim doesn't make sense in another context.

Fig 13.2: Notre-Dame du Haut, or the chapel in Ronchamp by Charles-Édouard Jeanneret, or Le Corbusier?

ASK THIS

Because it departed from his architectural principles and machine aesthetic, Ronchamp is unlike anything in Le Corbusier's oeuvre. Therefore, Le Corbusier must not have designed Ronchamp, seen here in Figure 13.2 but instead – and this is a fact – the architect Charles-Édouard Jeanneret designed the site-specific chapel at Ronchamp. Yet, that Le Corbusier designed Notre-Dame du Haut, the chapel in Ronchamp, France, is an irrefutable fact. So how do we explain the discrepancy? By realising that Charles-Édouard Jeanneret *was* Le Corbusier's name at birth before he changed it and so they are one and the same.

Having fun? Let's do another one.

ASK THIS

For 50 quid: fact or fiction? The Olympic stadium designed by Jan Wils for the 1928 Games earned the architect an Olympic gold *in architecture?* Fact. How do we know? During the first four decades of the modern Olympic Games, 151 medals were awarded for the arts ... including architecture.[112] We find a reliable, trusted source – then another and another – until we're assured the claim is corroborated and no longer refutable. That's how.

ASK THIS

Fact or fiction? The designer of the Vietnam Memorial in Washington DC, Maya Lin, is the niece of the first female architect in modern China, Lin Huiyin? Find more than one reliable resource that either backs up or refutes this claim. Start here.[113]

However trivial, these architecture facts that seem untrue *are* true – and are indeed facts – because they can be proven with evidence. And not just because the internet says so.

There is corroborating evidence from reliable sources in the form of written biographies and history books, historical designations that provide proof beyond a reasonable doubt.

Regardless of source, discriminating architects-to-be should get in the habit of being more like investigative reporters who scrupulously explore details, verify facts and probe original sources for themselves.

Separating facts from intuition, rationalisations and specious heresy requires us to demand quality information from quality sources.

Architects have the responsibility to try and separate information that's relevant and useful from less helpful distractions.

Just like your parents told you to *consider the source* when someone said something that upset you, *consider the source* is excellent advice when seeking data, information, knowledge and wisdom.

Too often we conflate information with opinion. In fact, only 9% of fifteen-year-olds can tell the difference between fact and opinion.[114]

14:
Facts Matter

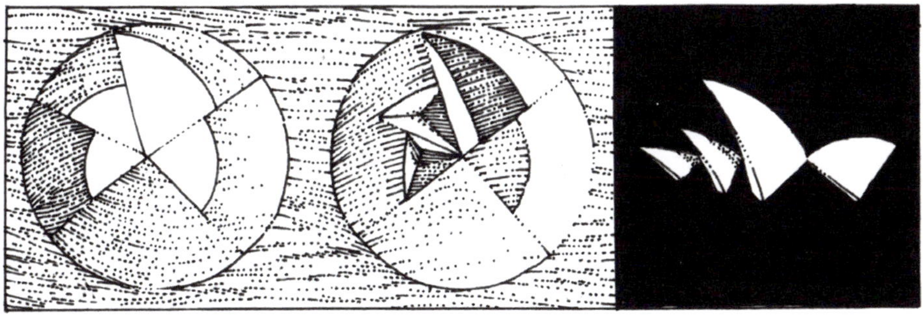

Fig 14.1: Jørn Utzon claimed that the final design of the Sydney Opera House's shells was inspired by peeling an orange. True or not, the solution can be demonstrated in this way

Architects trust, but verify.

True or false? A cow's weight can vary by up to 75 pounds in a day.[115] Ducks and bees can see ultraviolet light?[116] [117] The last country to outlaw slavery did so in 1981?[118] The advantage for STEM (science, technology, engineering and mathematics) graduates fades steadily after their first jobs, and by the age of forty the earnings for graduates in social sciences or history have caught up.[119]

As you might have guessed, these are indeed facts – and are all true.[120]

But all, except perhaps the last two, are also trivial. Nice to know perhaps to impress your studio mates – but not really must-know information.

Now, let's try a few more.

True or false: Penn Station is today the busiest transit hub in the Western Hemisphere, through which more than 600,000 commuters pass each day?[121] The twenty warmest years on record have all come in the past twenty-two years?[122] The number of airline passengers worldwide has more than doubled since 2003?[123] Across the world, only 9% of all the plastic ever made has been recycled?

Just like the first group, these also are all true.[124] But you might find these to be more applicable to your area of study or career – especially if you are designing, say, for transit in NYC or an air terminal in another city.

Facts matter to architects because architects are educated, trained and responsible for the health, safety and welfare of the public.

Seventy per cent: the percentage of energy use in UK buildings devoted to heating. Nineteen per cent is devoted to cooling, 7% is devoted to hot water, and 4% is devoted to lighting.[125] [126]

Architects are drawn to and many collect facts – relevant facts – such as the ones above, well in advance of needing them, that help support arguments they make on behalf of their designs.

In a world surrounded by *alternative facts,* architects don't take facts, statistics, metrics and data at face value – they verify that the source is a reliable one.[127]

When considering whether or not to reference a fact, architects recognise the need for common sense, to think for oneself – independently, while considering other sides.

And they make sure that the fact is relevant for their intended use. Because while facts matter, as important is your ability to evaluate them.

TRY THIS

While writing this chapter, a meeting I was to attend across the country, to address the impact of climate change on the future of architectural education, was cancelled. The host said the cancellation was due to budget cuts: they were being sensitive of spending at this time. Another reason they could have given for cancelling the trip that wasn't mentioned: meeting virtually vs in person can help save costs while reducing the carbon footprint, given the purpose of the meeting – a relevant reason for not travelling. Think of a problem that you have or announcement you have to make and come up with multiple reasons why. While all may be true, one may have more of an impact when you consider the situation, timing and audience of your message.

ASK THIS

You're designing a tower in a residential neighbourhood. The neighbours are against having your tower built due to increased traffic it will cause – but realise this argument didn't stop previous towers from being approved for construction. The neighbours hire an architect who determines that your tower will cast a shadow on a nearby playground for two hours a day, and a psychologist who attests that children's growth and mental development can be stunted when they are unable to play in sunlight. You are not an expert on child development, so cannot speak to whether their claim is true. What questions could you ask that would potentially undermine the expert's claim?

15:
Evidence-Based Ideas

Fig 15.1: The burden of proof is on you – the architect. The more credible your evidence, the better

It is down to the architect to present evidence in support of their design decisions.

When it comes to building design, what is meant by evidence?

Evidence refers to information that rationally supports a design decision in the form of a hypothesis or point of view.

Evidence-based design then is simply when you base your design decisions on evidence.

Evidence doesn't have to originate in science, an industry-endorsed website, or from an authoritative resource such as a reference book.

Unlike forensics, design ideas can come from many sources – including oneself.

Architects use evidence all the time. Evidence can come from you – your intuition, your experience – and doesn't have to come from a rigorous investigation of credible sources.[128]

Show me the evidence

Some architects prefer to have data drive the design.

Some architects prefer to come up with a design, then provide evidence later.

The thing to avoid is post-rationalising design decisions – where excuses are offered to back your ideas in lieu of evidence. Most clients don't want reasons but results.

While some firms invest in research, collecting data via sensors and other means, most projects don't warrant or allow for lengthy, involved analysis and testing to support decisions. As with justification, you usually only have to provide evidence when asked.

The thing is, when asked, the burden of proof is on you. You don't want to support your design decisions with opinions and heresy when you can back them up with facts.

That said, you need to consider your audience, as it has been demonstrated that even facts don't always change people's minds.[129]

Even when evidence for your ideas isn't requested or required, having it can only improve your design decisions – both for yourself and others.[130]

ASK THIS

Is the requirement to provide evidence for one's ideas too limiting and rigorous an expectation for an art form such as architecture? In architecture – which is a science and an art – what is considered evidence?

16:
Information Gathering

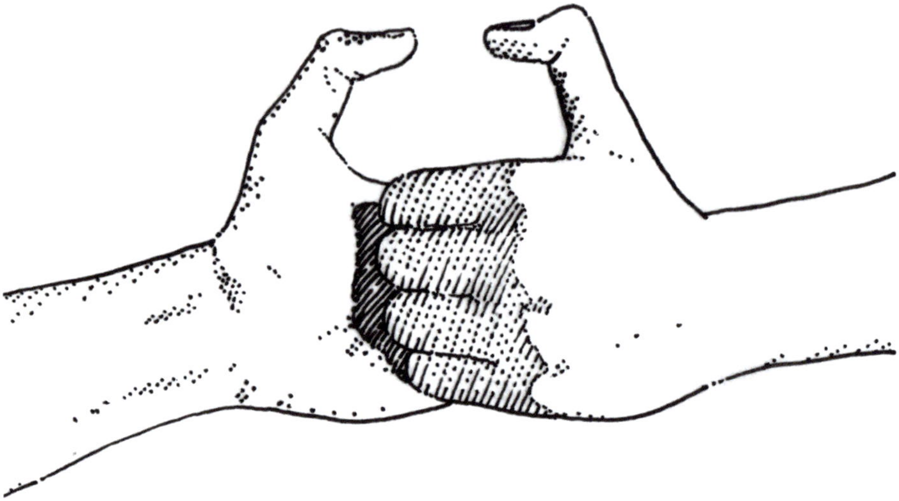

Fig 16.1: The opposable mind, like the opposable thumb, demonstrates the brain's ability to hold two conflicting ideas in constructive tension

Architects move from not knowing towards knowing by gathering information.

When faced with a problem, engineers seek a solution. Architects add an element between the problem and solution that makes all the difference: an idea, sometimes referred to as a big idea. Then they iterate – or refine – the idea. In a sense, the design process becomes a kind of *refinery* for ideas. The architect gathers information and is expected to synthesise all of the information obtained from numerous sources.

Students need to graduate with one more tool in their virtual toolbox: an ability to gather information, then integrate it seamlessly into their projects,[131] recognise misinformation when confronted with it, and differentiate reliable from superficial sources.[132]

When your tutor or employer says they want you to think critically, what they primarily want is for you to develop into an architect who can tell truth from lies and fact from fiction.

Simply put, when you work on a project you are going from a state of not knowing to knowing. When gathering information, don't settle for the first answer you find. See things from multiple perspectives – including points of view that are at odds with your own.

Like the fact that people have opposable thumbs – a characteristic of primates that allows digits or fingers to grasp and handle objects – the idea of the *opposable mind* is that we can hold two contradictory ideas in our mind (for example, your idea and that of your tutor) and still be able to function. The brain's ability to hold two conflicting ideas in constructive tension is an important skillset, enabling decision makers (such as architects) to synthesise new and better ideas.[133]

What information?

Architects work with information found from reliable sources including online sources and other types – such as yourself – in the form of intuition, experience and prior knowledge, but not preconceived ideas or preconceptions from their past.

A few useful tips for analysing online sources:

- Scrutinise the domain name
- Read the 'About' section
- Look for a lack of quotes
- Is the person quoted a reputable source?
- Don't share or spread false content

'The most essential gift for a good writer is a built-in, shockproof, (bull) shit detector,' said Ernest Hemingway.[134] With perhaps the exception of the colourful language, the same is true for a good architect.

Architects defend their design ideas – sometimes referred to as their design intent – with instinct and intuition. They are increasingly backing up their design ideas with public and private data, because data is becoming a universal language understood and, when reliable, trusted by all.

TRY THIS

Architects consider opposing arguments or views that contradict their own even if they make them feel uncomfortable. This is what is meant by *cognitive dissonance* – the discomfort one feels when simultaneously holding two thoughts that are in conflict.[135] F. Scott Fitzgerald called this the test of a first-rate intelligence, 'the ability to hold two opposed ideas in the mind at the same time, and still retain the ability to function'.[136]

ASK THIS

Architects scrutinise. They are amiable sceptics who don't take things at face value. They want to understand what makes things work. So, when given a problem to solve, ask: What do you know? What do you know to be true? How do you know? What is the source?

ASK THIS

Name three things that the leveraging of data can accomplish in architecture and design. Why is it necessary for architects to back up their design ideas with data? What makes data a particularly effective means for explaining, defending or justifying one's design decisions?

READ THIS

Professor Melissa Zimdars offers many more in-depth tips for analysing news sources in *False, Misleading, Clickbait-y, and/or Satirical 'News' Sources.*[137]

READ THIS

Seeing and Making in Architecture: Design Exercises by Taiji Miyasaka

17:
Seeking Clarity

Fig 17.1: Two students pin up for a review. One student's work is presented in a clear and straightforward way. The other?

An architect is someone who makes sense of the 10,000 things that go into the making of a building.

A student pins up their boards for a review. Their design work is presented in a clear and straightforward way.

A second student is unprepared, their presentation unfocused, with no coordination between the plans, elevations and sections; they are missing information that would help reviewers understand the project more quickly and assuredly.

The focused and disciplined presenter has something a lot of people lack: coupled with empathy (considering the reviewer's time and energy) and a deep understanding of the assignment (what was asked of the student), not just in general terms but also specifics, is the ability to think clearly and communicate what they come up with in a clear way.

If your building is hard to navigate, if its circulation leads people into a rabbit warren or on a wild goose chase, so they never arrive at their destination – your goal as the architect must have been to obfuscate. Why else was the building designed this way?

I tell my students that 10,000 decisions go into the making of a building. That's quite a mess.

When you start a project, think of the mess of data or information gathered about the project as a tangle of yarn.

Each line or strand (in the mess) represents something that needs to be accommodated.

Each is either an adjacent, related or competing force.

Each represents criteria that need to be prioritised.

Fig 17.2: Knitters with hopelessly tangled yarn – *detanglers*

How to wrangle this mess

Thinking like an architect is a bit like being a data wrangler, where data + wrangler = detangler.

As Figure 17.2 illustrates, knitters with hopelessly tangled yarn are *detanglers.*[138]

Architects are too. For that is what you are, a data detangler.

Making disparate pieces of data manageable, understandable and meaningful.

Your goal is not to keep the mess from getting out of control – but to make sense of the mess.

You are also a bit like a lion tamer when you are taming a mess.

In detangling the mess, you are seeking clarity, always looking to clarify and to simplify.

The same goes for architects who need to review what they come up with – what they design – with a critical eye, and remove the offending parts, the parts that do not add to the whole, the parts that obfuscate and don't make clear.

Architects don't solve anything by throwing more stuff at a problem to see what sticks. By removing things – by playing a veritable game of pick-up sticks with their design – architects arrive at clarity.

TRY THIS

There's a tendency at the start of your career to put every idea you ever had into your project. I have walked through architects' first projects that look like Museums of Every Idea the Newly Minted Architect Ever Came Up With in their Sketchbook. It is OK to be eager – designing your first building and seeing it built is an extraordinary experience. But take a breath. As you mature as a designer, you realise that there will be more than one opportunity – this won't be your only chance – and you become more selective in what you put in and what you leave out.

TRY THIS

Another way to seek clarity is to follow the classic advice for writers: *kill your darlings.* Writers are advised to find their favourite line and delete it. The thinking is that a favourite line or paragraph made it into the final draft because the author particularly liked it or is otherwise (irrationally) attached to it, and is therefore blind to the fact that the (offending) words don't add to but take away from the completed piece: an example of how *all writing needs to be self-editing.*

ASK THIS

Looking at the mess under a magnifying glass, you will see that some strands are more important than others. But in what way? To whom? Each strand in the tangle cries out for attention: honour me! In this way you can start to build a wish list for your building.

ASK THIS

Clarity starts with you. First and foremost, your intention has to be clear. Do you intend to *mean* – to connect, to make clear – or to obfuscate? People assume that what the architect did was intentional, whether it was or not. You might as well make what you do intentional.

ASK THIS

How do you communicate with yourself? It will be a *tell* (like in poker) for how you communicate with others. Are your sketches clear? Are your annotations or journal entries clearly articulated? Even if not meant for public consumption – they are for your own eyes alone – what kind of conversations are you having with yourself? What is the quality of these chats? Are you being clear to you? If yes, you are more likely being clear with others. To be clear with others you first need to be clear with yourself.

ASK THIS

You are about to present to the jury. Are you about to make their lives hard – or easy? How hard have you made finding answers to questions they may have about your design? How clear is the information you are about to present? Are the plans oriented the same way? People like to work with (and support, and hire) those who make their lives easier – not unnecessarily harder. That's not to say your project needs to spell everything out and be obvious. The best art and architecture is rich enough to work on several planes. Aim to be like Shakespeare – where you address the plebeians – the base, the masses – using straightforward information simply expressed, but also more advanced or educated patrons. Be like Rudyard Kipling in his poem 'If': 'If you can talk with crowds and keep your virtue, Or walk with Kings – nor lose the common touch'. Ideally, your work communicates clearly enough to address and speak to all audiences.

READ THIS

How to Make Sense of Any Mess: Information Architecture for Everybody by Abby Covert

18: Fallacies and Myths

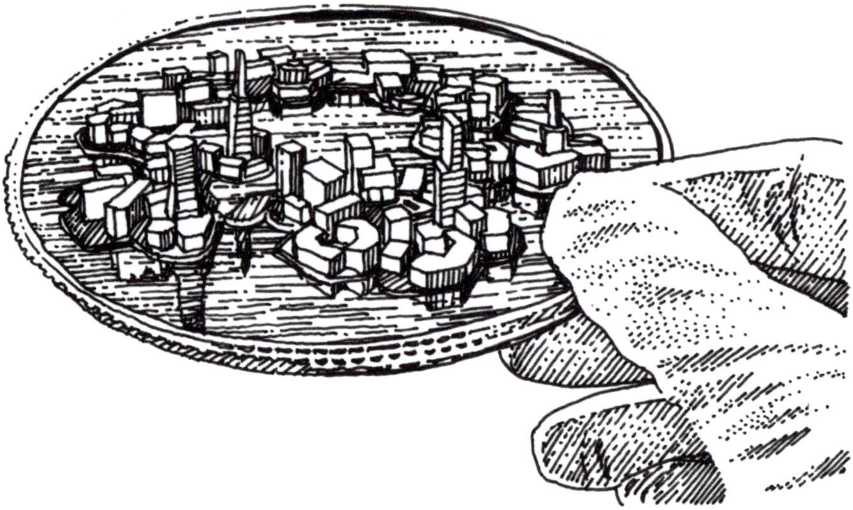

Fig 18.1: Floating city in a petri dish. Are floating cities a good plan for the future – or magical thinking?

Architects familiarise themselves with fallacies in thinking so they can catch themselves and others who resort to them.

Recently, in response to the climate crisis, architects, students and other visionary types have been floating the idea of floating cities. Are floating cities a good plan for the future – or magical thinking? Practical or unrealistic? Supporters say that it would be magical thinking to *not* consider floating cities.[139] What do you think? Why? Floating cities may in the past have been seen as whimsical or fanciful – but are they worth another look?

More people are moving to cities. There will be a need to house more people in cities as seas and populations rise, and people are displaced. Perhaps building offshore habitats comprising many of the same services and places afforded by the world's best cities will address these needs? Time is short and we need to strategically look at realistic and effective solutions.

Fallacies are statements that are logically false, but which often appear to be true.

You want your design to be approved and also liked, so you use what you can to gain approval. Your brain resorts to using half-truths or altogether untruths – using fallacies to support your argument – whatever it takes.

Aristotle listed thirteen fallacies; today, over 100 have been identified.[140]

Many fallacies rely on appeals: to tradition, to fear, to pity, to novelty, to authority.

Architecture tutors are susceptible to myths based on erroneous information about the brain. For example, it is widely assumed that students learn best when they're taught according to their preferred learning style. Most architecture students, for example, prefer to learn visually. But this idea is false. Research[141] suggests that there is not only no evidence to support the idea that people learn best when taught in their preferred learning style, but that doing so may actually hinder learning.[142]

Debunking myths

It's easy to buy into the hype, especially concerning a new product or technology. Take for example smart cities such as now cancelled Google spin-off and Alphabet company Sidewalk Labs in Toronto, Canada. It is a smart city that uses sensors, data and ever-present cameras in an increasingly complex network to increase their efficiency, safety and sustainability, while raising questions about privacy and bias due to prevalent use of algorithms for automated decision making. Architects can't afford to take hype at face value, instead needing to question and when necessary debunk myths put forward as 'the next thing'.[143]

TRY THIS

According to *The Debunking Handbook,* an effective debunking requires three things. To avoid sharing and exposing the misinformation, the rebuttal or disproval should focus on essential facts rather than the myth. Precede any mention of a myth with the word *alleged* or a warning to notify readers that the information you're about to mention is not true. Lastly, when refuting the myth include an alternative explanation – especially one that accounts for significant qualities in the initial misinformation.[144]

TRY THIS

Familiarise yourself with fallacies in thinking so you can catch yourself when resorting to them – and catch others when they use them on you, so you're not swayed.

ASK THIS

What technology would be needed to help create floating cities? What would the project's merits be? What are the challenges? Where should the first floating city be built? Where is the greatest need? How would it be paid for? Hint: All three of these last questions can be answered with the one fact that in most countries offshore waters can be inexpensively leased.[145] Does it make sense to place the greatest populations in the path of increasingly lethal storms rather than on dry land? Does it make sense to focus on solutions in response to climate change rather than putting our attention, creativity and resources into stopping climate change?[146]

ASK THIS

A fallacy in architectural design may include the belief that traditional architecture is nostalgic, sentimental, Disneyesque dishonest pastiche, while modern architecture, in contrast, is honest and authentic. What does it mean for architecture to be honest?[147]

READ THIS

Professor and former architecture school dean Douglas Kelbaugh writes of seven design fallacies that can be found in professional practice and in studio culture at most schools of architecture, in *Seven Fallacies in Architectural Culture.*[148] A few of the seven self-imposed and externally driven fallacies consist of The Forgotten Middle – where architects serve only the rich and poor; The Solo Artist – where architecture is practised primarily as personal expression; and Mandatory Invention – on the difference between originality and creativity.

READ THIS

Why People Believe Weird Things: Pseudoscience, Superstition, and Other Confusions of Our Time by Michael Shermer

READ THIS

The Debunking Handbook by J. Cook and S. Lewandowsky

READ THIS

Robin Evans's *Translations from Drawing to Building* represents a debunking of the common architectural myths associated with notions of drawing buildings and building drawings.[149]

19:
Assumptions and Beliefs

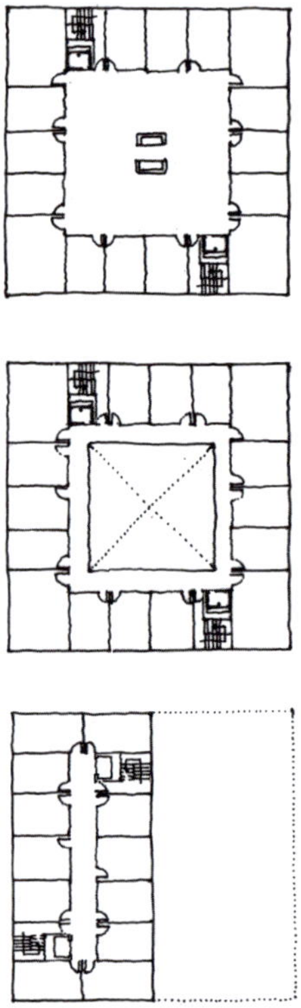

Fig 19.1: Alternative hotel plans

Architects let what they are already familiar with inform what is new and unfamiliar.

You're given a 40m x 40m site and asked to design a high-rise hotel with sixty guest rooms. You decide to build out the site by making the first floor the size of the site: that's good urban design. After laying out the ground floor public spaces you start laying out the typical guest room floor. At first you do so using the entire site. Rooms need light, so you put them along the perimeter. But there's all this space in the middle! You have 85% more space on each floor than you need so you add a few sofas and make the core a lounge. The sofas look kind of lost. Do people hang out outside their private guest rooms with other hotel guests? You never have – but maybe other people do? Make it circulation? Wait, make it an atrium. OR – instead of trying to solve a problem that you created – make the guest floor footprint smaller than 40m x 40m!

At first, the typical guest room floor was given the same footprint as the ground floor, 40m x 40m, because it was assumed that you needed to build out the site on the upper floors rather than ask how big the floor plate needed to be based on the rooms + circulation: which turns out, without an atrium, to be *much* smaller than the first floor building footprint. Less area on the upper floors means there ought to be more money to spend on the ground floor public spaces shared by all.

This is one example of how the assumptions we make can shape our thinking process when we design.

And how often the problems we solve are those we created in the first place.

Why does this happen? You wouldn't deliberately give an answer in a maths or science class that was 85% off.

This happens when designers are not aware of the alternatives or options available to them (e.g. redesign), or because they lack curiosity (e.g. What do other hotel guest room floors look like?), because they lack rigour and critical thinking, or because they feel like they don't have agency (believing *it is what it is.*)

Don't blame yourself for making faulty assumptions: assumptions are necessary. Like hypotheses in science that you prove or disprove, they're different from facts and you need to recognise when you are making one.

To think critically requires you to recognise your own point of view, and the assumptions that frame how you look at and interpret the problem you are trying to solve.[150]

Recognise the difference between a belief and argument. Beliefs are preconceived ideas and can keep you from innovative, creative thinking – especially when the beliefs are wrong, are not held by others, or are unnecessary. Beliefs can hold you back, keeping you from seeing what is there, envisioning what is possible and attaining insight.

Get to know your beliefs; become familiar with what you believe and why. You are not a blank slate. You bring with you life experiences. Don't discount them – they are your strength. Instead of seeing yourself as a blank slate, with no beliefs or prejudices except those that must be scrubbed clean before your true education can begin, recognise that there is value in the experiences you have had prior to entering architecture school or the profession.[151]

For one, you are or will be designing for non-architects. Since you are currently or recently were one yourself, you will never be able to relate to your project's users more than you do right now. This point of view is your superpower – don't discount it.

Don't throw the baby out with the bathwater, but instead let what you are familiar with inform the new and unfamiliar.[152] Simply by having lived in the world, begin with the premise that you actually know more about architecture than you know about almost anything else.

Our core values inform our worldview and how we think by influencing the way we interpret information. We have a tendency to cling to our beliefs even in the face of evidence that contradicts them. We feel comfortable sticking with our beliefs in the face of challenges to them – as when you have a desk crit, and you receive feedback that may contradict an idea or thought that you value or hold dear.

Your beliefs don't represent objective reality. They're made up of partial truths, selected facts and subjective experiences. Your beliefs blind you to opportunities to improve your design, and from exploring valid possibilities. Because beliefs are subjective and personal, we associate with them, and come to feel that we are inseparable from them. In order to change our beliefs, we need to change ourselves, and that requires work.[153]

There's a saying: *Unless the pain of not changing is greater than the pain of changing, I'm not going to change.* In other words, change only happens when the pain of staying the same is greater than the pain of change. That's why change is so hard – and why banking on changing ourselves is not always a good bet.

TRY THIS

Like assumptions, beliefs can deceive. It's hard, but try to understand what beliefs you hold. Beginning in the early 1950s, radio pioneer Edward R. Murrow asked people from all walks of life to write brief essays about their most fundamental and closely held beliefs that became a popular five-minute radio programme. Write a *This I believe ...* statement for yourself, listing what it is you believe, and asking what are your most closely held beliefs.

TRY THIS

In lieu of holding on to beliefs that might work against you and all you want to achieve, consider *pragmatism.* Beliefs are limiting and self-limiting. When making an important decision about yourself or your career, instead of asking what you believe, pragmatism asks: What would work for you? What would be nurturing? What would be growth promoting? Do that instead. Instead of trying to change your beliefs, get to know yourself better: what motivates you, what your likes and dislikes are. When challenged, reframe what you do in terms of pragmatism.

ASK THIS

Does doing what you are about to do work for me? Will it help me or my project move forward? If yes, irrespective of everything else, do it. Go with the suggested change. Don't ask: Do I like it or not? Or, does it fit my worldview/philosophy or not? Instead ask: Does it work?

ASK THIS

Are memories a type of belief? As they are private, your memories may be personal and not shared by others, so question them. Are there shared memories? Part of the collective unconscious? How do you know? Referencing projects you've seen and places you've been to, memory can play tricks on us so can be unreliable: what we remember may not be what happened. How important is historical accuracy in the memory you are referencing, leveraging or using to inspire or inform your idea?

READ THIS

Liminal Thinking: Create the Change You Want by Changing the Way You Think by Dave Gray

20:
Biases

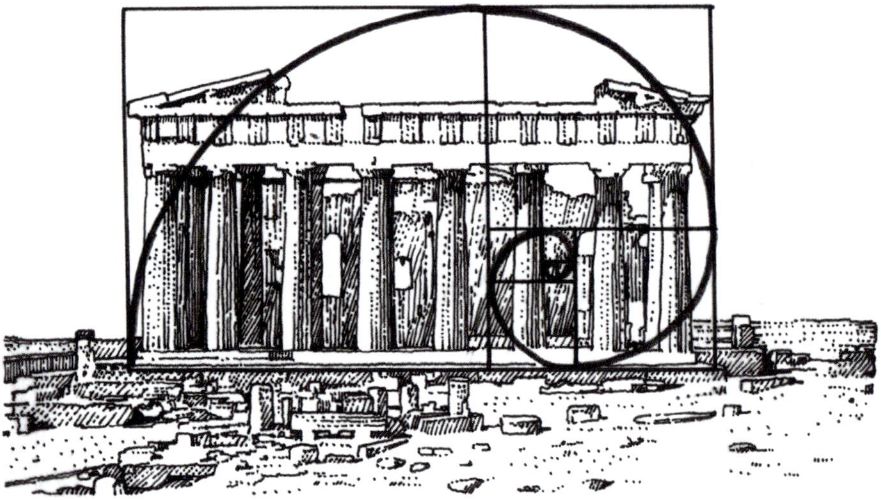

Fig 20.1: Was the Parthenon designed using the golden ratio – the hidden maths that allegedly explains beauty?

Architects turn their biases from compulsions to preferences and choices.

Was the Parthenon designed using the golden ratio – the hidden maths that allegedly explains beauty? Or is this an urban legend with little or no science to support it?[154]

Before we answer that, what's a bias? If a reader in the UK said they wouldn't read this book because it was written by an American, that would be a bias. Their bias? Well that depends, but some might say that, with rare exceptions, American authors or US architects have nothing to offer a UK architect.

So why look beyond our own biases? Doing so provides us with diverse points of view and perspectives, enabling us to become more well-rounded designers, not to mention better humans.[155]

When architect Robert Adam describes the three fallacies of classical architecture, he is only really defending a preferred style. It's his word – as an authority – against yours (a comparable novice) that classical architecture is relevant, doable, buildable and desirable.[156] But that's his bias – it proves nothing.

I once had an architect colleague who only would work on modern buildings – which she defined as contemporary buildings with flat roofs. The problem was that at that time our firm did primarily traditional architecture. She didn't last long. What she needed to do was turn her bias for modern architecture to a preference (that, or go and work for a firm that only did modern architecture).

Like assumptions, biases are important and even necessary. They're one of the ways architects distinguish themselves – and enable prospective or potential clients to tell them apart. But architects need to turn their biases into preferences, or at least a higher-order bias that is less a compulsion – where you adamantly *must* do something – and more of a choice.

The problem with approaching your assignment with biases is much like doing so with preconceptions. It allows for less innovation and fewer fresh ideas. Instead of reframing a problem, someone who approaches a problem with strong biases doesn't make room for new ideas. They are less likely to listen or seek out ideas from others. In doing so, they demotivate others around them because they appear to already have their solution. That solution may please and, importantly, convince them, but will it do so for others? Or address others' needs? Working from one's biases doesn't leave room for empathy – or empathising with others and their needs.

Biases of course aren't limited to humans. Attempting to solve problems with technology doesn't preclude the possibility that there will be biases inherent in the data or baked into the algorithms we use to generate building designs. This is a good thing to be cognisant of as we move forward.

Oh, and the golden ratio? It makes for a cool graphic but is total made-up nonsense.[157]

TRY THIS

One way to overcome biases is to ask questions. In this book, question asking may seem like the panacea for whatever ails you. That's because it is! Challenge your assumptions and biases – and those of others – by asking penetrating questions.

TRY THIS

When asked to design a home or chair, beginning design students tend to reference houses or chairs that are favourites of theirs or that they are familiar with, and end up replicating them in their own designs instead of letting go of familiar examples. That is why their tutors will try to get them to let go of preconceived ideas, biases and assumptions, and address the unfamiliar. Every time I assign beginning students to design their dream home, most design a suburban split-level home similar to the one they grew up in – because that is all they know. Your tutor's job is to help you to see beyond the familiar. They help students to let go of preconceived ideas and biases by keeping them off-balance.[158]

ASK THIS

This is something architects also need to consider: if using a generative design tool, what assumptions and/or biases were baked into the algorithms? Also consider what data was used to come up with optimised design solutions. How do you know? Always ask: *Optimised for whom?* Biased data and algorithms can lead to biased conclusions.[159]

21: Facts, Fake News and Photoshop

Fig 21.1: One architect has taken the extreme step to ban renderings from their design process

Instead of over-promising and not delivering, architects under-promise and over-perform.

Due in part to our rendering tools' ability to stretch the truth or render designs in terms of all-out lies; in part because the rendering fixes an idea of the design when in the process it is still very fluid; and in part because they discourage a collaborative approach to design, at least one architect has taken the extreme step to ban renderings altogether from their design process until the final design stage,[160] opting instead to present models, sketches and collages which can accommodate changes, unintended inaccuracies and mistakes. Perhaps in time we will see more of this among other firms?

Firms are increasingly designing in Photoshop, setting client expectations, misleading themselves and others on what they can deliver.

They don't do this deviously, but due to expediency. It's just easier and faster. If the project doesn't get the green light, nothing is lost.

The problem comes when the firm is given the go-ahead to move forward and the design must become a viable building. Some firms discover that what was presented in their renderings over-promised and cannot be replicated in drafting or modelling programs. In such cases they have to back-pedal with their client, or hope the revised design – including its parameters such as height restrictions and unit count – will be overlooked.

Today there's arguably an over-reliance on technology. Designing using the computer can be constraining, yet designing in Photoshop can have the opposite affect – where it's too easy to lie to ourselves and, worse, to others.

As technology improves, so does the seeming completeness or realism of a design, however early in the design process or under-cooked it may actually be. Research shows that the more complete drawings appear, the more clients and others with a vested interest in a project assume the design to be final or complete. Such a misreading of the design – and the architect's intention – can lead to a reduction in interest in engaging and collaborating, since it assumes that most of the important decisions have been made. In most cases, nothing could be further from the truth.

And the firm that banned renderings from their design process? Ironically, to capture the spirit of their design process, they now use Photoshop in the making of their collages.

22: Magical Thinking in Architecture

Fig 22.1: Magical thinking can be found not just in architecture, but in many life events, when there may not be a clear or obvious explanation for why something occurred

Architects are critical thinkers and avoid attributing outcomes to magical thinking.

A fellow designer explained to me how to get the client to pay for a lake in my project. *Put two lakes in it,* he explained. *The client will inevitably remove one and you'll have your lake.*

If only it were that easy! Tutors and school administrators complain that there is too much magical thinking in architecture. Like the *Seinfeld* episode where someone explains something that happened, skipping over the unmentionable part by saying 'yada yada', too often designers blur over, cover up or don't adequately explain, let alone justify, the inexplicable magic – the *yada yada* – that takes place in the design process.[161]

I did this, then this, and *voila* – any questions?

The concept of magical thinking was made popular with the publication of Joan Didion's *The Year of Magical Thinking* in 2005, an account of the year following the death of her husband.

Magical thinking can be found not just in architecture, but in many life events, when there may not be a clear or obvious explanation for why something occurred. For example, when a child miraculously recovers from a dire illness, we sometimes attribute their otherwise unexplainable recovery to various interpretations. Among the possible occurrences that could have contributed to the recovery of this child we might mention blind luck, the emergency medical personnel who attended to them, their family's insurance coverage, those who so generously contributed to the online campaign, the selfless people who assisted them, the fact that they live in a country at a particular time in history when life-saving technology and medicines are available, among several others. The possibilities are seemingly endless. Too often, we forgo critical thinking and go to the convenient explanation, irrespective of its validity.

Magical thinking can occur when strong emotions are involved, which are more likely to result in distorted and inaccurate perceptions.[162]

Architecture too encourages magical thinking. It is after all a combination of art and science, and art can excuse a lot of bad behaviour – and, also unfortunately, thinking.

Architects – for example, when they offer hoped-based outcomes in lieu of planning – sometimes fall back on old habits and offer magical thinking when the time and hard work of actually thinking is what is called for.

SECTION 3: DECISION MAKING

23: Good Decision Making

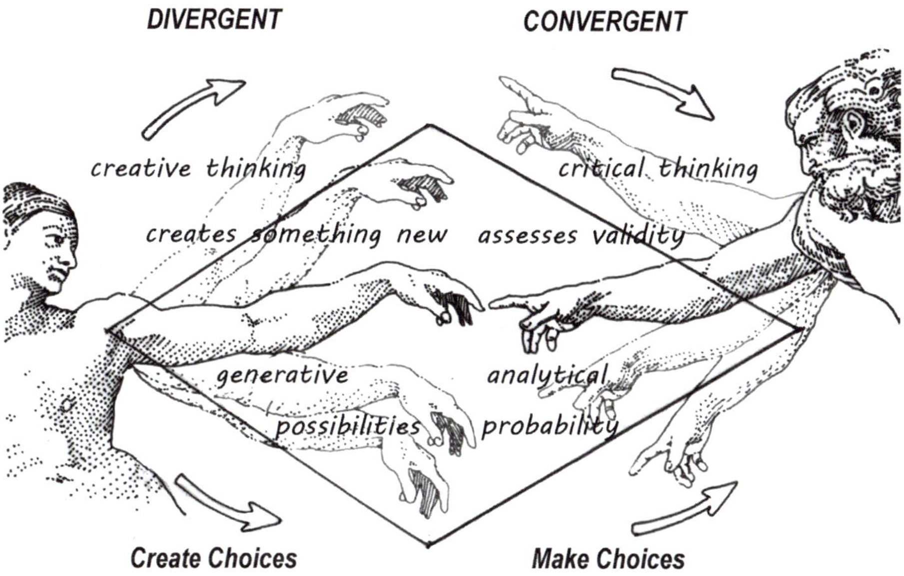

Fig 23.1: Think of the divergence/convergence phases as a tool for making effective decisions

Architects have to make or facilitate a series of decisions based on trade-offs.

If a typical person makes approximately 35,000 choices per day[163] and 2,000 decisions every waking hour,[164] and if 10,000 decisions go into the design of a typical building, why is it that architects can't design them in five hours?

Because, unlike the automatic and habitual decisions that comprise most of our choices, the decisions that go into the making of a building must be critically weighed by the architect.

Critical thinking is tied to decision making in that thinking critically results in our deciding what to do or trust. And decision making is tied to design in that design is informed by the decisions we make.

What, then, makes for a good decision?

You are making an assured decision when you are able to identify and comprehensively understand the situation you are designing for and determine which alternative solutions most effectively address the situation.

Facilitating decision making

Architects aren't always the decision maker, and less so now than in the past. More often, their role is to help someone else make a decision. In this case they act more as decision identifiers – identifying what decisions need to be made – and decision facilitators than decision makers, and can reframe their role accordingly. Frequently, architects will come up with alternatives and variations and will present them to help the owner decide, or as often help your boss or team leader decide, by identifying and weighing options and the pros/cons for each. The architect's task – their most difficult task – is always selecting or helping someone else to select.

The reality is that architects don't design in a vacuum. Their designs are realised by using other people's resources, including land and money; by following others' laws and ordinances; by working within constraints ranging from availability of materials and labour to the bank's willingness to extend a loan. Due to these realities – taking all of these factors into consideration and more – architects often have to make compromises, where they are choosing between two less-than-ideal options or recommending the better option for someone else to decide on.

But critically thinking architects have to base their decisions and conclusions on something. As we've seen, they tend to base their design decisions on facts, experiences and assumptions. We need to approach problems with some assumptions, as they help us to progress and move forward. But the problem with approaching an assignment with baked-in assumptions is that we need to question our assumptions to ensure that they accurately represent reality and aren't preconceived ideas that will keep us from innovating and trying something new.

Architects can also base their decisions and outcomes on observations and beliefs. The problem with approaching your assignment or solving your problem with beliefs is that a belief can be misguided, stifle a good idea or otherwise limit your thinking.

As we've seen, the decisions architects make are significant and deliberate, not minor, insignificant, unconscious, automatic or habitual – like what we decide to eat for breakfast or what show to watch. Because they aren't working alone, architects have to formulate their decisions then try to convince others to go with them – or do all they can to help others to make them.

Because the decisions architects identify, make and facilitate take concentration, real thought and have consequences for others – significant consequences, often having a direct impact on the health, welfare and safety of the building's inhabitants, neighbours, the public-at-large and even future generations not yet born – they can't take them lightly or make them out of habit.

It is important to remember that architects, being human, make better decisions on a good night's rest and less assured decisions when stressed, overworked, or hungry – so have a healthy mindset, and take frequent breaks, or better yet make important decisions when your mind and body are fresh to avoid decision fatigue. In a well-known example, a prisoner is more likely to have parole approved by a judge in the morning than when their case is heard in the afternoon.[165] Following are the usual culprits that get in the way of making good decisions:

Multitasking and distractions

Ever catch yourself saying you don't have enough time to accomplish a certain task? We waste a lot of time – not by procrastinating or avoiding what we need to do, but by overtaxing our cognitive system. Most people lose 28% or 2.1 hours a day of productive time to constant interruptions and the time it takes to recover and return to the task where we left off.[166]

There is a real need to remove unnecessary distractions when making important decisions. Clifford Nass, a researcher at Stanford University, suggests that rather than making frequent switches, you should try to dedicate twenty minutes to a single task, then switch to the next. He calls this the twenty-minute rule.[167]

Anger and other strong emotions

Architects need to be able to control their emotions, remaining calm and level-headed, not letting emotions get the better of them when making decisions. While their best work is often infused with emotion – it is not their emotions per se, but with the recognition that what they are designing is for other people. Thus decisions need to be made with others' feelings in mind

– not the emotions, whether anger or righteous indignation, they may be feeling at that particular moment.

Too much information

We are increasingly buried in data, and need to be able to manage the flow of information that bombards us day in, day out. Designers famously don't know when to stop 'researching', where researching itself becomes a form of procrastination (writers do this too!). When it comes to making assured decisions, having too much information and too many options to choose from can be paralysing and immobilising.[168]

Biases

As discussed in a previous chapter, our biases can affect the way we make decisions, so we need to be on the lookout for them. Architects tend to be optimistic by nature, as would anyone be who expects their designs to be built. Optimism is fine – both a job requirement and a liability; it's when it becomes expected that overconfidence can cloud our clear thinking and negatively impact our decisions.

We need to develop an understanding of how biases can distort our reasoning. *Confirmation bias,* the tendency people have to embrace information that supports their beliefs and reject information that contradicts them, for example leads us to ignore evidence that contradicts our preconceived notions,[169] whereas another bias, *groupthink,* causes us to go along with the crowd, and *loss aversion* makes us too cautious, and so on.

If they are to inspire, and help transform lives of those who live in and among the results, architectural decisions require an element of intuition. Many architects' decisions are based on intuition, even when purportedly arrived at using lists of pros and cons, appearing to be informed and not made flippantly. Architects especially have to watch for biases when relying on their instincts or intuition to make decisions by testing their intuition and occasionally going against their gut instincts.[170]

It may be surprising to discover that your big decisions are often less calculated than your small ones,[171] but we often find that we have to make or facilitate big decisions in less-than-ideal circumstances that can keep us from considering things thoroughly.

With so many ways to decide, it is hard for architects to decide which is the best way to decide!

When designing architects' decisions often unfold in stages, a divergence phase (where information is sought and alternatives developed) might be followed by a convergence phase (where options are pared down and recommendations or a selection made.) One can think of the divergence/ convergence phases as a tool for effectively making decisions.

In the past few years, we have been advised by Malcolm Gladwell to make decisions in a *blink,* by Michael Mauboussin to *think twice,* and by Nobel Prize recipient Daniel Kahneman to think *fast and slow.*[172] Thinking fast – automatic judgements that stem from associations stored in memory – and slow thinking – what we have been calling deliberate thinking – are both necessary: the first for immediate, instinctive decisions where we need to react quickly (like stepping out of the way of a moving car). But in architecture, the more deliberate kind of thinking – slow thinking – is called for to make sound decisions that stick.

Making more informed decisions

In a project's earliest phases, a great deal of time is spent evaluating your design, ensuring it follows regulations including building codes and zoning ordinances, and delivering information required by your client. In school, and in your first job out of school, it's important to learn what takes place in these project phases, and to be able to experience them for yourself. But once you've experienced them, why wouldn't you want to use a computational- or generative-design tool to help determine this information, one that would free you up to spend more time doing what you are there to do – namely design? Why, in other words, wouldn't you want to leverage technology that can help you evaluate thousands of designs fast and provide the information you need to make an informed decision?

Crowdsource decisions

The averages of multiple guesses are usually more accurate than the best guess by an individual. Why then not harness the collective intelligence – intuition, judgement and wisdom – of the crowd as a baseline to arrive at decisions that matter? When making decisions on their studio projects, architecture students have been known to poll their friends – though they often do so until they hear what they want to hear (see *confirmation bias,* above.)

TRY THIS

No matter the decision process used, a gut check on important decisions would be prudent. Of the criteria used in making a decision, common sense is too often not among them.

TRY THIS

Architects can make more informed decisions using simulations and AI. You can work in a software environment that you are accustomed to – CAD, BIM, etc. – or in a standalone program. Either way, leveraging these tools, you will be able to make or help others make decisions faster and more assuredly.[173]

TRY THIS

There are simple decisions that still manage to confound us. Take, as one example, the thinking that goes into deciding where to cut a section through a building. Unless you are asked or required to do so, it is unnecessary to cut a building section through a lift shaft or through structural columns. Think about it: a section is a kind of detail – where you are showing how the building comes together – and all detailing is joints, where two materials/components/systems come together. So, instead of cutting mindlessly through materials or columns, cut through a wall. And not just any wall. Cut through a wall with windows or doors. If it is a multistorey building where one floor is the same as the next, don't mindlessly repeat them: use cut lines. And don't show a cut line through the entire plan – where it may conflict with or obscure other information – but abbreviate it just at the walls. Only show something once. This is good advice as redundancy creates mistakes but is also an unwise use of time.

ASK THIS

How did you decide to study architecture or become an architect? Did somebody influence you? What were the circumstances? Was it a drawn-out and calculated decision?

ASK THIS

What does it mean when it is said that architects don't make any decisions – they make recommendations? What is an example of decision identification? In what way(s) can architects serve to facilitate decision making?

READ THIS

The Wisdom of Crowds by James Surowiecki. In the book Surowiecki explores the idea that large groups of people are smarter than a few, no matter how smart or how much better at problem solving they may be. He gives examples where large groups of people foster innovation, guess the number of jellybeans in a jar, arrive at good decisions, and predict the future better than individual experts.

24:
The Four Questions

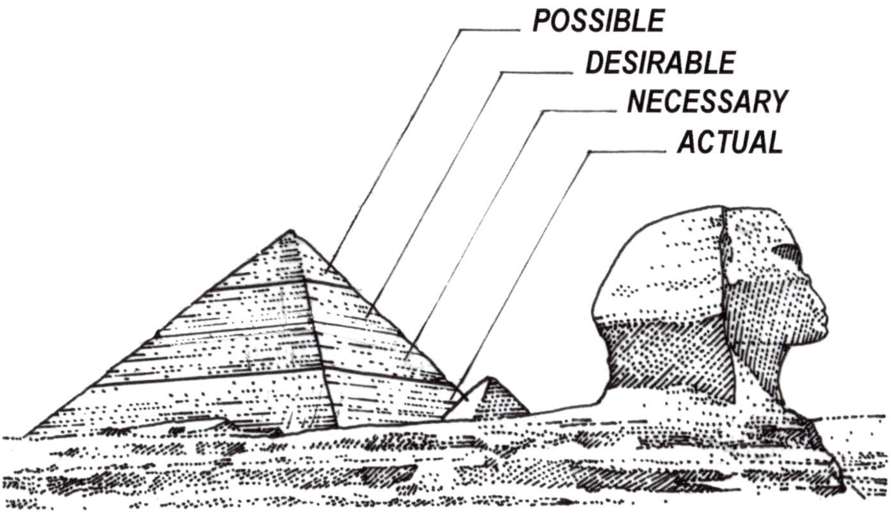

Fig 24.1: Architects try to make sense of their projects by asking four questions

At the start of every project architects ask what is actual, necessary, desirable in order to discover what is possible.

Bombarded with a lot of information at the start of every project, architects try to make sense of it all. One way they do this is by organising data and other inputs into categories. Whether explicitly or implicitly, architects try to make sense of their projects by organising the responses to four questions:

What is actual?
What is necessary?
What is desirable?
What is possible?

How do you know the answers to each of these questions? You ask questions in the form of information gathering and research.

For the question *What is actual?* you enquire into what is meant by *site* and *context.* To the Scandinavian architectural firm Snøhetta, asking questions of site and context is considered *prepping* and *zooming out,* providing a factual basis for, and having a significant impact on, the quality of their resulting creative ideas.[174] Architects – unless they are paper architects – have a particular place in mind that they are designing for. Is it limited to the property lines within which your building will be placed? Most likely, it will extend beyond in terms of the flows that come to your site (people, traffic, deliveries, sunshine) and those that flow out (rain run-off, light pollution, views).

Associated with reality capture and analysis, the question *What is actual?* asks, just as it sounds, what exists – in both the site and situation – that you will be designing for and/or building in? What is the literal context of your immediate site? Are you building in a historic district? Are you building in a flood plain? A residential neighbourhood? A rural or dense urban site?

To ask *What is actual?* is not only a place-specific question. What is the larger context – the historical, political, environmental and social context – of your project? These are all part of the question *What is actual?* What often happens in school is that the larger contexts are ignored when you don't start with this question. You will know when it – and not your project – becomes the focus of discussion at your crit.

Most projects are different because they have a unique site, circumstance, climate, culture. Your responses to the question *What is actual?* represents constraints that you can then seize upon and turn into opportunities.[175] Design involves a reflective conversation with the situation.[176]

It is natural to want to jump in and start designing as soon as you're given an assignment. But most architects find that the design process can only begin in earnest only after the given parameters, constraints and inputs – site information, client information, building type/typology – for a project are gathered and assessed.[177] For example, Australian architect and emeritus professor Alec Tzannes placed particular importance on needing extensive analysis and a full understanding of all parameters associated with the project prior to beginning to think creatively about a design solution.[178]

To understand what is actual, architects sometimes go virtual to both capture and simulate reality out of convenience, to save time, but also to look at circumstances more holistically and comprehensively. Technology enables architects to look at a multitude of constraints, inputs and options they otherwise might not have the time or capacity for.

The world needs architects – the Earth, our continent and country needs architects – to address national issues. Your region needs architects to represent what distinguishes one locale from another, to make sure that buildings belong to a specific place and time. Your county or borough needs architects, your city needs architects, and especially your suburbs. Architects create works that are inseparable from their environments and the way we think about them, at the same time expressing and infusing local or regional character so that their buildings appear to belong to the place where they reside. Architects may be comfortable with change but recognise that they first have to make change palatable for and acceptable to others.

For the architect in practice the question *What is actual?* includes what type of project you are proposing: residential, commercial, institutional, mixed-use, etc., and the allowable occupant load based on use; legal constraints such as building setbacks and height restrictions; the direction of prevailing winds and both desirable and undesirable views and adjacencies; site topography and whether any parts cannot be built on; the make-up of the soil below ground and what the implications might be for foundations, etc.

If the question *What is actual?* is realistic/phenomenological, then the next question architects ask to make sense of the mess of information *What is necessary?* is practical/pragmatic.

The question *What is necessary?* – where the architect tries to nail down every discoverable detail – is straightforward. What is the bare minimum that if delivered in response to the design problem or assignment would be acceptable? What is needed to minimally fulfil the obligations of the client's brief?

What is necessary? is an especially important question today as architects are increasingly seen as a luxury, and architecture is perceived as something unaffordable by the masses, even as basic shelter and housing remains a dire necessity for many. Human beings the world over have built homes with nothing more than their own two hands. Until recently, the world existed without architects. But architects – for all they do – are seen by some as an indulgence that most cannot live without. As purveyors and perpetuators of good design, architects are truly needed: good design is not a luxury, but a necessity.

Architects are essentialists who tap into what is necessary, what is core. And they provide something more by searching for what is essential – not by embellishing the frivolous and unnecessary. It was an architect after all who coined the phrase *less is more.*

Architects use what they have available to them and strive to do more with less. Architects try to make the most with what they have and are given – even if it is not expected or asked for. If they did not, the built world would be confined to making shelters. Like Helmut Jahn, we strive for an architecture from which nothing can be taken away. Architects thrive on less, and becoming one represents a case where less is truly more. Architects recognise that in tough times better architecture can be the result. That constraints may in fact lead to *better* architecture. This is important because the opposite could occur – were architects to believe that fewer resources result in lesser buildings, less pride of place – with all of us being the worse for it.

Where the questions *What is actual?* and *What is necessary?* are questions of what is realistic and practical, the next question *What is desirable?* represents an enquiry into the emotional and aspirational.

Ever since the Bible declared that *Man shall not live by bread alone,* people have aspired to live beyond necessities. At the start of every project, architects ask themselves: *Given what is actual and necessary, what is on everyone's wish list?* Architects strive to fulfil these often more emotional than rational aspirations.

After all, Vitruvius's three design principles that guide the architect's creation of space are commodity, firmness and delight (*firmitas, utilitas* and *venustas*) – or, alternatively, structural integrity, usefulness and beauty – all of which can be found in the majority of buildings throughout time.[179]

Vitruvius could have stopped short of three principles: *You had me at commodity and firmness.* The added element of delight is what makes architecture something more than mere building. Architects strive to make architecture that delivers commodity, firmness and delight, where the actual and necessary address commodity and firmness, and desirable and possible satisfy delight.

Constraint and uncertainty are the two existential conditions for design to take place. What is actual and necessary addresses constraints, while what is desirable and possible addresses uncertainties.

Designers are comfortable with ambiguity and uncertainty, a required part of the design process, where there are no known, right and wrong answers.

While others can ask, the architect working with their team answers *What is possible?*

Just as architects can envision what isn't there – veritably seeing through walls – they can also imagine possible futures, scenarios based on the consequences of their architectural acts, their imagination, and also on what they have come to understand about the world. They can project what has not been built into situations and ask: *What will the potential impacts be?* For this, the question What is possible? has a spiritual or transcendent component: the *quest* in the word question. They may never be able to anticipate all possible futures – but if thoughtful, persistent, and patient they may anticipate many of them.

Answering *What is possible?* is the architect's ultimate purpose, one that cannot be replaced by machines. The architect's job is to give the client not what they want, but what they never dreamed they wanted; when they get it, they recognise it as something they wanted all along.[180]

With the advent of climate change and the expense of ground-up construction, it is projected that we will see an increase in the adaptive reuse of buildings. Architects will increasingly be asked *how else can this existing building be used?* There will be more and more of this, as reuse of existing buildings and infrastructure is more environmentally friendly: the most sustainable building is an existing one. And a greater percentage of the projects an architect will work on during their career will be existing buildings – whether renovating, restoring/preserving, reusing, rehabilitating or reimagining.

While the questions *What is actual?* and *What is necessary?* are questions requiring critical thinking, the questions *What is desirable?* and *What is possible?* – because other people need to be involved to help determine what is desirable and possible (desirable and possible *for whom?*) – represent creative and collaborative thinking: the subjects of the next two sections.

TRY THIS

In practice, when presenting alternative designs to the client, the first scheme is usually what they asked for. By giving them what they asked for you assure that they've been heard. Next, give them two other schemes that represent ways to solve or resolve their problem: Here is what you asked for and ... here is this ... and *this.* Underpromise and overperform. In my experience, once a client sees what is possible – the third scheme – most will abandon their original idea. Just make sure you can live with any scheme you present.

TRY THIS

Expand the meaning of *What is actual?* beyond the site by expanding your awareness of the physical, social and emotional environment.

ASK THIS

How can buildings designed for a specific site address issues on a national or global scale? How can architects ensure that the buildings they design appear to belong to the sites where they reside? Since buildings represent change (from what was there before), how can architects make change palatable and acceptable for others?

ASK THIS

Name a situation in which engaging an architect is a necessity. If working with an architect is not a necessity, give three reasons why someone would nonetheless want to engage an architect. In what ways is engaging an architect a luxury and an indulgence that most cannot live without?

ASK THIS

What are the attributes necessary to an architect's identity? Why are architects interested in finding the simplest and most essential way to do something? By designing to what is essential, can a project be somehow more, not less, than it would otherwise be? How so?

ASK THIS

In what way is less *more?* How does Mies's dictum *less is more* support our desire to design and build sustainably? What is the real benefit in following it? Does it take creativity to do more with less? Does it take an ethical stance, or conscience, to do more with less? Why do architects thrive on less? Do others? What role do constraints play in enabling an architect to work creatively?

25:
Good Judgement

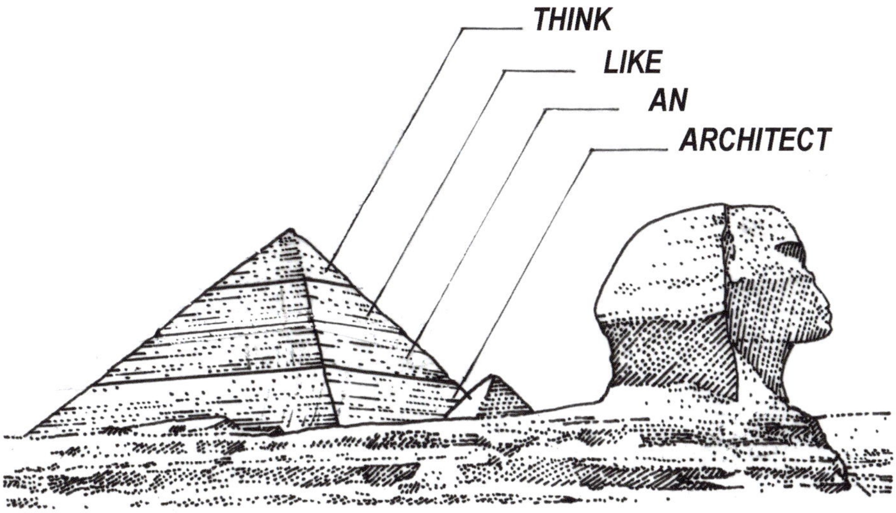

Fig 25.1: Developing good judgement in all things is a worthwhile use of a future architect's time and resources

Architects improve their design judgement by building their experience, knowledge and intuition.

We don't talk too often about judgement anymore – having all but replaced it with decision making – but we ought to.

Practical and applied knowledge have taken the place of what are seen as more effete or highbrow subjects – including correct usage of grammar.

Would you sooner say, *The worst cricket player around here is I?* Probably not. You'd sooner say, *The worst cricket player around here is me,* right? And yet, the first is an example of proper grammar, while the second is an example of good judgement.[181]

Developing good judgement in all things is a worthwhile pursuit and a good use of a future architect's time and resources.

Architects are still valued and even sought after for their professional judgement, so it is probably worth spending a moment refamiliarising yourself with this concept.

An architect's professional judgement is based on three things: experience, knowledge and intuition.

You could even write it out this way:

Professional judgement = knowledge + experience + intuition

The problem when first starting out with your architectural education or practice, of course, is that you are lacking in all three.

Knowledge comes from experience and exposure to information.

The problem with experience is that, through no fault of your own, you usually are operating at a deficit in experience at the start of your academic or professional career.

And intuition of course is not magic, but direct access to internalised experience and knowledge.

Architects who work in a dashboard on their monitor, with immediate feedback on their design moves in the form of data visualisations, pie charts and bar graphs, not only find that their intuition is informed by the data, but it is improved as well.

Two people can experience the same thing and have two different experiences in part because of where they are developmentally and the filters they have in place – what information they let in and what they block. That is why two students can have completely different reactions to a design studio course. Similarly, despite each drawing's shared precedent in a precedent study, it happens that no two will turn out alike.

It is not often discussed this way, but one of the outcomes of design studio is to help you, the designer – through near-constant feedback during crits – develop your judgement.[182] Design judgement is a critically important capability for anyone charged with synthesising disparate views, inputs and objectives from a diverse array of stakeholders.[183]

TRY THIS

You've heard it before, and I'll repeat it here: it would behove you to read more, to experience more, and internalise what you read, do and learn along the way. All experiences, good and bad. Billionaire entrepreneur Warren Buffett spends five to six hours a day reading. Reading enables you to access and internalise the experiences of others. As a reader, you are of course at an advantage in that you can learn from others' experiences. When you read, you are in essence living life twice.

26:
How to Prioritise

Fig 26.1: To prioritise means to identify what is pertinent and relevant

Architects have an unspoken social contract to make life better.

I often see students check all the boxes for what is asked or required of them, except one: prioritising.

By that I don't mean identifying which is urgent, which is important and so on in terms of time, but what is pertinent and what is relevant?

Just as physicians swear to uphold the Hippocratic Oath and its critical dictum *first, do no harm,* so design professionals follow what Will Alsop referred to as an architect's social contract to make life better.[184]

What criteria do you use to prioritise your design work?

As has hopefully been made clear, architects' work depends on rational criteria found in critical thinking.[185] They reference these objective criteria when deciding what information is important to others. But it is not until the architect gives the outcome a gut check – engaging their instincts, intuition and emotions – that they know what the hierarchy ought to be.

TRY THIS

Too often we are prisoners of our ordering systems, the non-printing light-blue guidelines that organise our design layouts – all good – but have you circled back and asked: What is the first or most important thing I want them to know about my project? Have I emphasised that using light/dark, size, position or colour? Why bury your best work in your portfolio because of your decision to present your work chronologically – to accurately tell your story as a designer over time, where your best work is likely to be presented last – rather than in reverse chronological order or, alternatively, grabbing the one or two images that say the most about you and your design ability and placing them up front where the table of contents normally goes: *no one* will miss the table of contents.

TRY THIS

Using the terms from the previous chapter, at the lowest level, base your decisions on constraints or what is *actual.* At mid-level, necessity and desirability; at the highest level, prioritisation of your ideas, answering the question *What is possible?* After the other questions have been answered, this is where your core competency is as an architect, and where your value and strength reside.

ASK THIS

Is there a hierarchy? Have you prioritised one image over another? Is one image more important? What is the second most important? And so on. In journalism, there is a saying: *don't bury the lede,* i.e. the story, the main point that you are trying to communicate. We do this in our presentations and portfolios mainly as a result of not asking ourselves what is important, then prioritising.

ASK THIS

Too often students throw whatever they have drawn or modelled up on the wall and, like spaghetti, hope it sticks. Instead, determine the relevance of what you are about to present. Of each drawing. Ask yourself: Is there any redundant information here? Do two drawings essentially say the same thing? Does one of them say it more clearly, coherently or strongly? Your presentation is only as strong as the weakest image. Which images can you remove – and, in doing so, make your presentation not weaker but stronger? Remember the dictum *kill your darlings.* Identify your favourite, most clever image, take a deep breath, remove it, and then ask yourself if your presentation is stronger for it. Figure out what information is most relevant to the decisions you need to make. Have the discipline to reject even exceptional ideas if they are not relevant for the problem at hand – you can always save them for a future project.

ASK THIS

One way to prioritise from the start is to start with the end in mind. Ask: Will this information end up in the final project or presentation? How do you know? As you develop your ability to anticipate consequences of your architectural acts, you enlist this muscle to envision or visualise what your final presentation will look like. Use decision-making devices by creating hierarchies, setting priorities and selecting filters. Ask: Is the information nice-to-know or must-know? Present the must-know.

27:
Consequences of Decisions

Fig 27.1: Architects know that their architectural acts have downstream consequences and take responsibility for them

Architects understand that their actions have consequences and work to imagine and anticipate what they are.

One thing that distinguishes design in architecture school from designing in practice is that, perhaps beyond an impact on your grade and character, there are no consequences for your decisions. But to learn to make decisions that stick, from the time they begin their architecture studies students need to consider the consequences of their actions.

Architects know that their architectural acts have downstream consequences and take responsibility for them. To consider the possible impacts – both positive and negative – of architectural acts that take place in school, we need to project out far beyond our projects into the outer world and enlist our imagination. Architects justify their decisions in part based on the consequences of their architectural acts.

To anticipate the consequences of their architectural decisions, architects need to think clearly. They need to be able to project from their decision out into the future, and ask: what consequences will this have on people who I do not know; on inhabitants and the building users; on neighbours; on the public at large; into the future – on people not yet born?

We of course cannot know entirely, but we can imagine, and on that base our best professional judgements.

Consequences and foresight

The ability to anticipate the future impact of a course of architectural action or decision making is foresight. Project consequences of your architectural acts and decisions into the future, adjust and respond accordingly.

Architects look to the beyond. Beyond the immediate problem. Beyond the immediate issue at hand. Beyond the immediate surroundings – to look at the impacts of what they're creating on the world beyond. Architects often ask themselves what the consequences are for any course of action. Architects are said to be thoughtful and ethical in that they are concerned with the consequences of their actions.

TRY THIS

Think about future consequences of your decisions. If you do this – what will the outcome be? Don't stop with the first thing that pops into your head. Stick with this question and take it further. What else? What are you blind to? What haven't you considered? Who else will be impacted by your decision? What other consequences will there be? Reference similar projects you've seen and places you've been to.

ASK THIS

Based on one of your design projects, consider questions to ask before you make decisions. How might your project impact the site where it is located? Consider all of the possibilities, throughout the seasons, during day and night, weekdays and weekends. What impacts might there be beyond the site, on its immediate surroundings? Neighbourhood? Community? City or region? What are they? For whom? How might your responses to these questions – a form of feedback loop – potentially impact the design of your project?

ASK THIS

What are potential consequences of deciding to slope a roof steeply? In terms of adjacent neighbours? In terms of the region you are building in? In terms of cost, labour and material availability? In what ways do architects look beyond the immediate problem they are asked to solve or project they are asked to design? What can potentially occur if the consequences of an architect's decisions aren't considered?

28: Self-Editing

Fig 28.1: Many of the best architects learn to edit as they go, and find that self-editing becomes not an impediment to their creativity but instead plays a crucial role throughout the design process

Architects self-edit by focusing not only on the content but on the negative or white space.

A few years back, at another university, I served as a reviewer of presentations on the importance of working with integrated teams. There is a built-in efficiency in working in an integrated manner and I was looking forward to seeing what the students came up with. Three students on the first team took turns speaking. The first student presented, then the next, each student repeating information already delivered by the previous student. Despite their words and excellent PowerPoint slide deck, it was apparent that the students hadn't learned a thing because their delivery wasn't integrated. They didn't look at their topic and ask themselves: Does the delivery support or detract from (or even completely contradict) the topic?

If you were to only take away one thing from this book, it should be for you to become your own best editor. Practice at self-editing leads to automatic self-correction. If you can self-correct as you go, you'll save time, energy, resources – and those of others. Having received feedback from a desk crit or from a test score, your response ought to be to find the relevant take-aways and self-correct. Self-edit your drawings to prepare for desk crits, and be ready with questions. Reference your tutor's suggestions from your last desk crit or pin-up, asking yourself: *how did I respond, and why?*

We're often taught in school that editing is a separate phase from ideating, best left for the end of the design process. But many of the best architects learn to edit as they go, and find that self-editing becomes not an impediment to their creativity but instead plays a crucial role throughout the design process.

One way architects self-edit is to focus not on the content – the words and images – but on the negative or white space on the page, sheet or presentation board. Increasing the amount of white space communicates confidence to the viewer – that the person presenting is able to zoom out and use the whole space available to them, not just focusing on the images or messages. They recognise that the negative space is part of the message as well.

This also goes for the *white space when speaking:* using pauses and silences to your advantage.

Focusing on the negative space – on the silence as much as the noise – is similar to Nobel Prize-winning playwright Harold Pinter's use of silence as poignant and meaningful content – the pregnant pauses in his scripts being referred to, fondly, as 'Pinter pauses'.

Architects avoid the tendency to fill every white space with something. They try not to repeat the rookie mistake of putting everything they know into their design or presentation. Be selective – life is long, and there will be other opportunities.

A rule I tell my students: only draw what you know. Or, to put it negatively, don't draw what you don't know. Drawing what you don't understand will come back to bite you. With 10,000 decisions that go into every building design, you aren't expected to know everything. Ask questions if you don't know something.

Self-editing requires self-awareness and some self-reflection but not self-criticism: when you self-edit you are looking critically at your work, not you. Self-editing isn't about beating yourself up but turning your critical eye on your own thinking, ideas, project, decisions in order to achieve a more purposeful and assured outcome. So self-edit ruthlessly – just be easy on yourself.

There is no better way to communicate to your tutor that you understood than to show them a sketch where you tried it and either incorporated the suggestion, rejected it, or came up with an alternative way to go. Your tutor wants to know they were heard. They are not talking just to hear themselves talk, nor sending you on a wild goose chase for sport, but to improve your prospects. If your tutor makes a suggestion they do so because they think it might improve your design. Don't reject it outright, even silently. Don't forget what they suggested. Immediately after your desk crit write a summary including suggested next steps: this is good preparation for practice.

TRY THIS

When self-editing, look dispassionately at what you produced – as though you were seeing your work for the first time through another person's eyes. Walk away from your work – take a break – then, when you return, look at your work objectively. Professional writers have been known to put their writing in a drawer for forty-eight hours, then take it out and review it with a fresh pair of eyes. Move on to another task while you wait. Or give this a try on the off-chance you complete your work with time to spare.

TRY THIS

You are expected to review and edit your own work but, unless specifically told otherwise, there is nothing wrong with engaging another point of view. Ask a classmate, studio mate, roommate or friend to look at your presentation layout and help identify opportunities to make your message clearer. As a rule of thumb, don't share your first draft until you have had a chance to review it yourself. You will only learn and benefit from another's input if you first have had a go with it yourself. Critical thinking involves not only the awareness of others' thinking but the constant monitoring of your own. I have seen students present two identical plans as well as plans side by side that were at two different scales or showing a concrete slab 600 mm thick when it should be 100 mm thick: apparent to me – the tutor, critic or reviewer – but apparently not to the student. There is a need for information to be socialised: this is where having another pair of eyes can help.

ASK THIS

Before showing your work to your tutor or reviewers, have you:

- Coordinated?
- Revisited previous comments and suggestions?
- Shown your work to a classmate or friend for their input – another pair of eyes to catch things you might have missed?

ASK THIS

You've designed an eight-storey building and are asked to present all eight floor plans. If you have eight floor plans displayed side by side, do you need eight north arrows? Maybe one is enough? If three of the floor plans are identical, do you need to print all three, or label one *Floors 3–5?* We are bombarded with information from the time we awaken until the time we go to bed. Architects try not to contribute to information overload by looking to simplify wherever possible; removing redundancies that can complicate their message; and, generally reducing the amount of information in their communications, including when presenting.

ASK THIS

What is it your tutor wants you to know? If your tutor makes a design suggestion, try it. Then, the next time you meet let them know that you tried it or looked at it. You don't have to use their idea – but as a courtesy, and because they have your best interest in mind so it would benefit you to do so, consider their suggested idea or change to your project. Most students don't do this, and their tutor wonders if they were even heard – or, if heard, were understood. Some students self-report that they are not in studio (or school) to learn – but to embellish their portfolio, improve their job prospects or simply to graduate.

29:
Think Like César Pelli

Fig 29.1: César Pelli's ability to contend with a vast array of facts and figures in his head is an ability that most architects can develop

Architects strive to manage an increasing set of variables and alternatives in their head.

César Pelli was an Argentine architect who designed some of the world's tallest buildings and other major urban landmarks. He also happens to be a graduate of the architecture programme where I teach. Two of his most notable buildings are the Petronas Towers in Kuala Lumpur and the World Financial Center in New York City. He passed away in 2019.

Why should architects strive to think like César Pelli? For two reasons: his ability to contend with a vast array of facts and figures in his head, and his refusal to support the *systematic generation of useless alternatives.*

Pelli's ability to contend with a vast array of facts and figures in his head is an ability that – if they make it a goal – most architects are able to develop ten to fifteen years into their careers. Pelli warned of the computer's *systematic generation of useless alternatives,* and architects subsequently being buried in alternatives from which they were then responsible for choosing an optimised option.[186] [187]

One difference between emerging professionals and students, and more senior design professionals is the ability (or not) to manage an increasingly larger set of variables in their head. César Pelli was able to keep many pieces of information in his mind, balancing and weighing each one against the other, editing out pointless or impractical alternatives, preventing his team from going in a dead-end direction.

Theoretically, we treat the design activities of ideation and judgement separately, but in reality – especially over time, as one matures as a design professional – they happen virtually simultaneously.

César Pelli's thought process isn't something he was born with, but an ability he developed over a long career. Your goal is for this to become second nature. Strive to think like César Pelli.

TRY THIS

Find something you would like to make part of your thought process or design repertoire. To commit it to memory, write it down. Instead of highlighting a passage in a book, research has shown that informally quizzing yourself on the content is a more reliable way to learn. Create a checklist of the information you want to learn, then turn this into a mental checklist. You will learn over time how to consider all factors, criteria and consequences for each path in your head – simultaneously – and be able to edit out unpromising paths *before* you spend time and energy heading down them. Eventually you won't need to rely on doing a Google search; by building your thinking muscles you will be able to rely on yourself, by going through this thinking process in your head, owning it and making it part of your experience.

TRY THIS

The information in this book is not meant to stay in this book, but be put into practice and action. Whether as actionable information, applied knowledge, or news you can use, the goal is for you to read it, *grok* it (understand it intuitively), then forget it. Why forget it? The most important knowledge for design professionals to understand is tacit knowledge – things you know but can't necessarily explain, like how to tie your shoes. In order to learn, we have to internalise information, and one of the best ways to learn something is to know when to let go of it, trust the process and access the information when you need it: the same process you go through when studying for an exam that isn't open book or open note. Here, forgetting something doesn't mean it is erased clean from your memory, but rather it is internalised so it can be accessed later, becoming part of your behaviour – your ultimate goal.

READ THIS

Moonwalking with Einstein by Joshua Foer

30:
Aim to Be an Amiable Sceptic

Fig 30.1: Architects as *amiable* sceptics will also be needed to provide a healthy dose of common sense

Architects strive to be independent thinkers while engaging others in decision making.

Thinking for yourself is not the same as venting, speaking your mind just to hear yourself talk, or saying whatever is on your mind: *you being you.* It's about not being beholden to anyone, avoiding groupthink and standing up for what you believe, however unpopular, in the name of factfulness, honesty and what you see as truth. A year after the first *Star Wars* film came out, on a television talk show American astronomer and author Carl Sagan critiqued the popular movie saying that it got science wrong – and, worse, accused it of white supremacy and chauvinism.[188] *That* is independent thinking!

In previous chapters we've suggested that engaging with others in the design process could be helpful. That advice doesn't preclude us from also recommending that you learn to think for yourself. One doesn't cancel out or contradict the other – they're complementary.

Architects are nothing if not independent. They're also independent thinkers. They have a reputation for not accepting advice from others ... something that an author who writes books doling out advice to architects – and their publisher – ought to keep in mind.

The recommendation to think for youself is less about disengaging from or otherwise disregarding the input and feelings of others, and more about thinking independently and striving for self-reliance.

When starting out in architecture school, students find themselves in a time of social, intellectual and creative self-discovery. It can be an exciting time, but also one that can be filled with self-doubt and uncertainty. How can you think for yourself at a time when you are just starting to learn about your area of specialisation? You come to discover that the first years of your architectural education are actually more about establishing self-initiated enquiry than learning discipline-specific tasks.[189] Learning to become an architect is ideally a process where tutors trigger the growth of self-reliant, self-driven thinking by students.[190]

Thinking for yourself is less about external sources – such as Google, Instagram, your network – than learning to rely on your inner resources: your ability to question; your imagination and ability to come up with original thoughts and ideas and to project those into the future; and, your lifetime of experiences, memories and impressions.

If you look at design studio like a competition – where at the start of every assignment students jockey to come up with the Next Big Idea, as opposed to an opportunity to learn from both successes and errors, to grow as a designer, to gradually come into your own, building self-confidence – you might short-circuit the learning process by shopping for a design on Instagram, ArchDaily or Google images. I say this because I sense the pressure students feel under. As a professor in the United States, in studio I recognise many of the student projects from online sources: where students feel they are under such pressure to come up with a strong idea that they don't even bother shopping for design inspiration in the library – as many of my peers did in a previous generation – but take the more expedient route of fishing for a design online. These students curtail or delay their development as designers in that they, in many cases, don't even consider themselves as a source of original ideas.

Sagan's example is who you want to strive not to *be* – work to become your own person – but to *be like:* thinking about everyday familiar things in ways that no one else has. *That* is independent thinking.

With the rise of technologies such as artificial intelligence it will be all the more important for architects to rely on their own critical thinking, especially when the temptation will be to rely on algorithms and generative design tools for answers and design outcomes. In such circumstances, architects will need to think for themselves, independently, not taking the machine's word as the final arbiter. Architects as amiable sceptics will also be needed to provide a healthy dose of common sense – something missing from current design technology offerings.

To be self-directed and to think independently, accept the fact that you are not a passive receptacle to be filled with information. You have agency – with the ability to act on the world. Take responsibility for your education and who you will become. The sooner you come to this realisation and acceptance of it, the steeper your career trajectory.

TRY THIS

The next time you are given a design assignment, before automatically going online in search of inspiration, pour a cup of hot chocolate, coffee or tea, find a comfortable seat somewhere, open a Moleskine, sketchbook or roll of tracing paper, and empty your mind of any preconceived ideas you may have for the project. Some designers believe that among these initial ideas is The Big Idea, whereas others see these for what they are – preconceived notions that are largely obvious and unoriginal. Think of this exercise as emptying yourself of stale thoughts and ideas; by committing them to paper, you free your imagination up for new, more original thoughts. If you can stay seated sketching every idea that pops into your head for twenty to thirty minutes, you may find that an unexpected idea occurs to you – something you would never have thought of if you went with the first thought that popped into your head. Sometimes an original idea will occur later, after this emptying exercise, while on a walk or in the shower, when you aren't thinking about your assignment and the pressure is decidedly off, even for a moment – voila, the idea appears. In either case you end up with two gifts: one, an idea for your assignment; but, as importantly, you will find that you have relied on yourself – that you are a reliable resource you can count on for ideas, that you can and will turn to again and again throughout your career. This is a thought that doesn't occur to most of your peers, whose go-to habit is to see what's online.

TRY THIS

This is the time in your life when to get to know yourself, your preferences. Sure, seek help and feedback, but in the end, you decide: *that* is how you grow and evolve as a designer. Live (and hopefully not die) by your decisions. Then afterwards, take a breath or a sip of tea and ask yourself: *Based on how it turned out, based on feedback received, how would I do it differently next time?* That is how you evolve as a designer.

Fig 31.0: Creative thinking as a go-to tool in your toolbox

PART II: CRITICAL CREATIVE THINKING

Architects think creatively. Architects think of ways to explain their ideas in terms that non-architects can understand – in a layperson's terms. They do this to assure project progress, moving the ball forward, improving upon what came before. To do this, they work iteratively – not in circles spinning their wheels, but in a spiral working towards a solution. Ultimately, they use their head and heart to address people's reason but also to appeal to their emotions, their needs and wants.

SECTION 4: CRITICAL CREATIVE THINKING

31:
Critical Creative Thinking

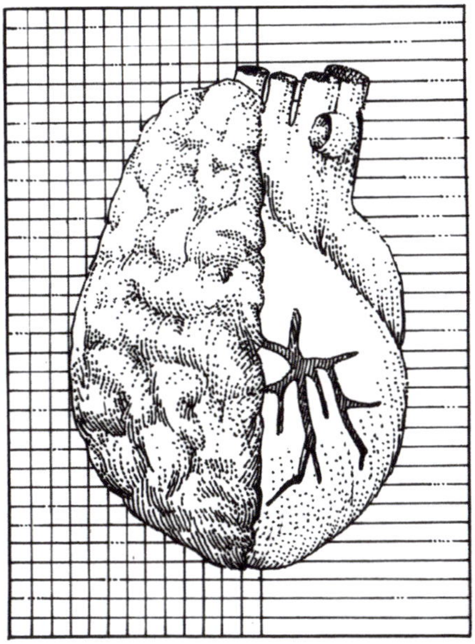

Fig 31.1: As an art and a science, architecture involves both rationality and emotions

Architects rely on critical creative thinking to draw on both sides of the brain.

Say you were asked to translate a two-dimensional abstract painting into a three-dimensional object with a series of spaces – a pretty typical translation/abstraction project found in many beginning design programs. How would you go about doing it?

Most students would look at this assignment and produce a 3D extrusion of the painting.

But not you – that would be too literal or obvious an interpretation of the assignment.

What is a non-obvious way of interpreting the assignment?

The intent of this project is not for you to produce a 3D extrusion of the painting.

Instead, recognise that you are being asked to decide for yourself which are the most important attributes of the painting, and you might translate these ideas into 3D form.

This assignment, you conclude, requires you to interpret the painting as you see fit, distilling the painting down to the core issues, then using the 3D abstraction to communicate these ideas.

Using this example, how does one consider design assignments in terms of critical thinking?

As you can see, applying creative thinking *critically* results in a very different outcome from producing a 3D extrusion of the painting![191]

Architects and other creative types are often advised that reasoning and judgement can mess with creative output, so should be sequestered for a later time, ideally after they're done ideating.

Yet in this time of rapidly developing design and delivery technologies – including parametric, computational, generative design tools and robotic fabrication – it is critical that we consider creative thinking as fundamentally a critical thinking process, not something separate from it.[192]

That's why this section is called not 'creative thinking' but *critical* creative thinking – because we don't abandon the critical thinking we learned in the previous section. And because, as we'll see, critical thinking isn't a separate phase that comes at the end of the design process, but is something that we access and engage with throughout.

Fig 31.2: Think outside the building

Architecture, as an art and a science, involves both rationality and emotions. We need both, and solutions need to address both. While we have come to associate creative thinking with idea generation and critical thinking with analysis, in practice the two – analysing and synthesising, critical thinking and creative thinking – occur at the same time.[193]

Neuroscience bears this out. Architects aren't more right-brained than left-brained – or more left-brained than right-brained. The cerebrum is divided into left and right hemispheres. The two sides are connected by the nerve fibres of the corpus callosum. Returning to our question, they need both, with the corpus callosum – the bridge between the left and right sides of the brain – connecting the two hemispheres. As astronomer, cosmologist, astrophysicist and author Carl Sagan wrote, 'to solve complex problems in changing circumstances requires the activity of both cerebral hemispheres: the path to the future lies through the corpus callosum'.[194]

If we were to watch our brain under an MRI, we might think that when we are being creative the right brain lights up, and when we are, say, solving a maths assignment the left side lights up – but the reality is that both light up in each instance. The reality is we need both.[195] Creative thinking draws on both sides of the brain – involving multiple brain regions – and that's why the brains of architects and other creative types are so unusually well connected.[196] In fact, the connection between critical and creative thinking is especially strong from the time when one first starts out in architecture school.[197]

As pointed out in the previous section, critical and creative thinking increasingly take place simultaneously, or nearly so, as one advances in one's career. While creativity is seen as the most important skill in the world,[198] for architects critical thinking is never far behind.

If your goal is to design paper architecture – unrealistic, unbuildable, theoretical – then perhaps start with creative thinking. Innovation is sometimes referred to as *useful* creativity. So is innovative architecture – fact-based, grounded in reality and by gravity – even as it aspires to transform the lives of those who inhabit it. Critical creative thinking depends on working within constraints while seizing opportunities.[199]

Critical thinking and creative thinking are sometimes expressed as divergent and convergent thinking, where with divergent thinking architects seek to understand, expressed by doing research – asking *what more can this be?,* and *how can I expand this?* – whereas convergent thinking zeroes in on a solution, narrows the field, and evaluates options.

Creative thinking involves learning to generate and apply new ideas in specific situations, seeing existing situations in a new light, identifying alternative reasons, and seeing or making new connections that generate a positive outcome. Architects engage in creative thinking to differentiate themselves and their designs, to continually improve, to be both more efficient and more effective, to make something of their time, and to advance novel ideas in the name of progress.

If creative thinking is the process of generating new ideas and possibilities, *critical* creative thinking sees creativity as a thought process as well as a design process.[200] Critical thinking requires one to think for oneself, questioning usually accepted ways of understanding things and avoiding uncritically accepting the ways others commonly see things. The difference between critical and creative thinking is the difference between IBM's 'Think' and Apple's 'Think different'. To think creatively means to *think differently.*

TRY THIS

With your next assignment, think independently, for yourself. Think not in terms of another's ideas – whether from the internet, sneaking a peek at a classmate's or studio mate's ideas, nor based on what you think your professor wants – but ideas from you and you alone. Be alone with your writing/drawing/modelling instrument of choice and the paper/monitor. Pour a cup and wait. *Thinking means concentrating on one thing for long enough to develop an idea about it.*[201] This is how, over time, you build confidence and a reputation for being a creative thinker.

TRY THIS

First perceive critical aspects of a painting; analyse these aspects to understand their meaning and impact in the painting; choose which aspects are most important; and lastly, decide how to best communicate them in three dimensions.

ASK THIS

This[202] illustrates how you can think critically about each design assignment you are given by asking: What are we being asked to do here, both literally – superficially, on the surface – and also more deeply?

ASK THIS

Isn't there the fear of rejecting a good idea before it had the chance to be thoroughly vetted? At first, when you are starting out, perhaps. But as you develop your ability to think like an architect, your flow of ideas is free of evaluation and judgement – until it isn't. The two phases – critical thinking and creative thinking – remain separate: over time, architects just become better self-editors and judges of ideas that are relevant, pertinent to the task at hand.

ASK THIS

What does that even mean – to *think outside of the box?* It means to be able to see what others don't (yet) see – but once you do, and show them, they will. Ask: What is really being asked here? What are others not seeing? What is another way of interpreting what is being asked here? What is this most like or similar to – and how would it be solved in that context?

ASK THIS

If you could only choose one, given the choice between critical thinking and creative thinking – criticising and creating – which would you choose? Fortunately you don't have to choose – you can have both. Design studio ensures that you are exposed to, and if you work at it, develop, each virtually at the same time as the feedback loop is almost instantaneous.

32: Why Critical Creative Thinking?

Fig 32.1: BIG's CopenHill waste-to-energy plant doubles as an urban ski slope for those in and around Copenhagen

Architects don't let everyday problems distract them from addressing major, wicked problems with non-obvious solutions.

Located in an industrial area near the city centre, Bjarke Ingels Group's CopenHill waste-to-energy plant first opened in Copenhagen in 2019. What's different about this new plant is not only that it aimed to become a model in the field of waste management and energy production, but that it also doubles as an urban ski slope for those in and around Copenhagen.

The design of a building is not exclusively a creative act. Architects not only have to be creative in terms of novelty, but have to solve major – intractable, complex, unsolvable, wicked – problems as well as minor problems: where to locate the mechanical room or breakfast nook, the sill height of windows, or what the roof slope ought to be – or what other uses the roof could have.

A big part of creative thinking is to challenge assumptions – our own and others' preconceived ideas – by asking questions such as: Why is it this way? And, does it need to be this way?

So, why *critical* creative thinking? Is it because creativity without the critical component emphasises art over science? Architecture doesn't have the luxury of being able to ignore the elements, living conditions, building codes, budgets, gravity – nor the opportunity to serve the larger community.

Or is it because these two ways of thinking are complementary and equally important,[203] because man cannot live by reasoning alone? Hopefully by now you're on board with the idea that creative thinking is not separate from critical thinking. They're in sync – *simpatico* – and are compatible. As Carl Sagan wrote, 'mere critical thinking without creative and intuitive insights, without the search for new patterns is sterile and doomed'.[204]

It is because creative thinking is table stakes for being invited to play the game of architecture. To succeed at the game, you have to apply what you learned in the previous section to creative thinking.

The heart of the architecture curriculum is the design studio and what students learn there is less about how to design buildings than about learning a thinking process – a way to address design problems so you are more likely to arrive at an optimal outcome.[205]

This thinking process requires students to think about their thinking – referred to as *metacognition* – where the student actively thinks about their design process *in situ* in the midst of designing. Anyone who wishes to solve meaningful problems with original discoveries or wants to learn to think differently and gain an edge over their routine way of problem solving would do well to reflect on their design process. Supportive tutors encourage the development of metacognitive abilities in their students, recognising it as a critical part of critical creative thinking and growth as a designer.[206]

Australian architect and emeritus professor Alec Tzannes believes that teaching people to think is missing from architectural education. From his experience he thinks that being aware of one's own design methods leading up to conceptual realisation of an idea 'lubricates and facilitates the process and creates the basis of creativity'.[207]

TRY THIS

Donald Schön wrote about a range of professionals who self-monitor, calling them *reflective practitioners,* and saw design as a reflective activity in which the designer has a reflective conversation – a form of metacognitive thought – with the situation.[208] There is no faster way to develop as a designer than to be the sort of designer who reflects on their decisions as they are made. Make a habit of thinking about your thinking as you design.

33: Challenges of Creative Thinking

Fig 33.1: When the Shenzhen Library opened in China, umbrellas also opened

Architects use their comfort with ambiguity and uncertainty to their and others' advantage.

When the Shenzhen Library opened in China, due to glare and heat from the sun patrons were forced to shelter under umbrellas. For the superstitious, opening an umbrella indoors brings bad luck. For others, it is an inconvenience. For still others, using umbrellas indoors is just part of the culture. But was it a failure of empathy on the part of the designers with the student patrons? Was it a failure of imagination? Or a failure of asking questions: How will the space be used? Is glare a concern or an issue? Or ... do people in Shenzhen just use umbrellas indoors?

A student's first studio represents a new way of thinking and working. This in itself can be challenging – especially for those who relied on memorisation to succeed and counted on there being a right and a wrong answer to get ahead – neither of which count for much in studio. While most students expect to learn how to design buildings of different types and scales in studio, architecture students will tell you that what they learned in design studio is to make form, translate concepts or foster human interactions.[209]

The benefits of creative thinking in studio are many: learning the iterative process; first-hand immersion in design thinking; camaraderie among studio mates; the perseverance of repeatedly trying; working with faculty to arrive at solutions you never thought possible. Perhaps most beneficial of all, creative thinking is a renewable resource: it never runs out – though it helps to make it part of your routine and use your creative muscles often. But there are also challenges.

As we saw in the previous section, the challenges of critical thinking – that it is exhausting, hard, deliberate and involves others, that it is unfamiliar, too rational, has too many rules, requires action, takes focus – are different in number and kind from the challenges of creative thinking. But creative thinking has challenges, nonetheless.

Here I will focus on one such challenge: design – and creative thinking – is largely subjective and open-ended. The open-endedness of architectural problems and assignments – exacerbated by the ambiguity and uncertainty inherent to the design process – can create anxiety in some students. Students respond to this uncertainty differently. Some architecture students lower their anxiety by opting to seek out and emulate (or in some instances all but copy) an existing design online so they can compete and move forward in studio. In this way, they are largely abdicating creative thinking; they are not thinking but imitating. Others learn to live with some anxiety until – working with their tutors, talking with their studio mates – their designs materialise, and answers fall into place.

Unlike other subjects students might study, there are no right or wrong answers in architectural design – there is no one way – only better or worse solutions. This open-endedness is a complaint of many who study architecture; its subjectivity one of the most-cited reasons for why students drop out. Ironically, even if you are comfortable with uncertainty you will come to learn that your clients and the public in general are more comfortable with certainty and need to communicate in their terms – thus the further importance of *critical* creative thinking.

It's hard to come up with a novel, original design. Then add to that the requirements of the brief and all of the additional burdens our designs aspire to accommodate: a tall order, and asking a great deal of anyone who is working on becoming an architect. What a student may consider novel their tutor may have seen a thousand times, and instead of being encouraged to abandon their borrowed design some students will persevere only to be dismissed months later during a mid-term or final review by a reviewer who has also seen that particular scheme a thousand times before. Today, with social media and the breadcrumbs of the internet, it's almost impossible to obscure one's sources of inspiration.

There is a palpable tension between conserving resources and using what is available. This may come as a surprise to some, but even with the shortage of natural materials and resources, one contrarian lesson I've learned from a career in architecture is to use what you're given – the whole site, the whole programme, the whole schedule, the whole budget. The good architect isn't the one who heroically uses half the budget and schedule, but the one who uses up what they are given for the best of all concerned: paying client and non-paying client (i.e. the public). Unless you have a good reason not to use up all available resources – i.e. conserving resources, materials, labour or energy – you are expected to best serve your clients by making the most of resources, including budget and time, that have been made available to you.

A further challenge of creative thinking is learning to work creatively with others, either on team projects or on shared parts of individual projects, such as building a model of the site or completing a site analysis – which will be addressed in the next section.

ASK THIS

Another challenge is for creative thinking to accommodate innovative form and all of the other needs made explicit by the client's brief, while also doing the right thing for those who are impacted by your design. In other words, ask of your design these questions: Does your design have a negative impact on the environment or lead to the decarbonisation of the built environment? Does your design contribute to urban sprawl or increase urban density and access to public transportation while reducing the necessity for additional infrastructure and cars? Does your project contribute to the health and wellbeing of its users, inhabitants and future generations? Does your design – irrespective of what you were asked to design – address the need to house billions, many of whom cannot afford market-rate housing – in the years to come? Design may be subjective, but we must get beyond saying we did something because we like it. It is assumed that you like what you did – why would you design something you dislike? – and it should not be offered as a reason for why you did what you did. That you like it is a self-justifying rationalisation, never a justification for doing something. Your reasons for doing what you did can and should be expressed, a belief that is in contrast to the subjectively based *I did it because I like it* approach to design which some beginning design students – and not a few seasoned practising architects – assume to be sufficient.[210] It is OK to be passionate about your ideas, but for others to appreciate your passion you have to think not only creatively but critically. Critical thinking teaches you to anticipate reasonable objections to your ideas.

34:
Comfort with Ambiguity and Uncertainty

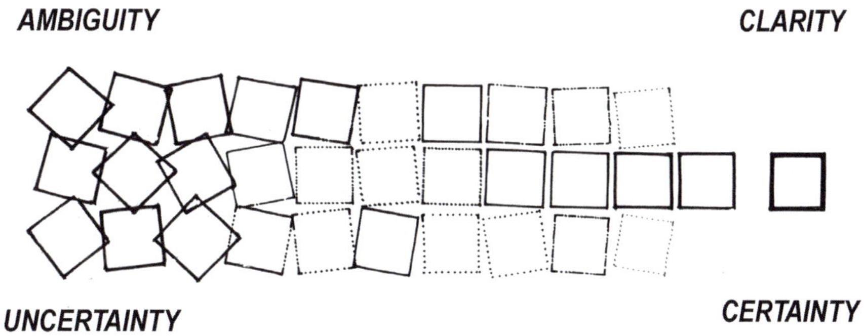

Fig 34.1: Architects are comfortable with ambiguity and uncertainty while others look for clarity and certainty

Architects are asked to do impossible things they know nothing about.

If the first section – critical thinking – was about understanding, this section – creative thinking – is about discovery and the importance of building confidence. The fact that you are comfortable with ambiguity ought to be a point of pride, because it is a distinguishing characteristic of the architect. Soon after enrolling in architecture school you come to learn among roommates and those you grew up with that not everybody is comfortable with uncertainty – but you are, and it is one of your standout superpowers.

Hold that thought

Many architecture students have a tendency to go with their first idea. But studies show that to make decisions that stick, we're better off delaying choices for as long as practically possible. According to Frank Partnoy in *Wait: The Art and Science of Delay,* prepared professionals understand how long they have available to make a decision, and then, given that timeframe, they wait as long as they possibly can. People are hardwired to react quickly, yet are often better off resisting the urge to go with their first idea.

The length of time you can hold an idea in your head while vetting it – putting it to the test of scepticism and scrutiny, not to mention questioning by others and sometimes even public ridicule – is a direct indicator of an idea's strength. And also your comfort with ambiguity. If you killed an idea as soon as someone verbally shot holes at it, you would never know whether it was a worthwhile idea or not.

Architects need to keep everyone's needs, wants, aspirations and wishes – their ideas and ideals – in mind throughout the design process, like trying to keep so many balls in the air at one time. As discussed, architects primarily deal with wicked problems, which are ambiguous and don't have an obvious solution. On the one hand, the longer you keep a question open – the more likely that you'll arrive at an amicable, insightful or creative solution. Few, though, have this luxury. While Le Corbusier wrote that 'creation is a patient search', with today's reduced timelines, schedule crunches and fast-track projects, creation needs to be more like an *impatient* search. Architects rely on data, but creative thinking challenges them to welcome what is still undefined.

As we saw in the previous chapter on challenges, it is easier for some students to handle the ambiguity inherent to architecture design studio than others, and there are theories as to why that's the case.[211] Some students complain that assignments aren't explained clearly or with enough specificity – when the point of the assignment is to be open-ended, so students can interpret what is expected of them. Some students harbour conspiracy theories and try to second-guess the tutor, trying to figure out what they are looking for[212] or sweet-talk them into sharing the right solution – when the point of the assignment is that there is no right answer. Nonetheless, students who until that point in their academic career have been focused primarily on STEM subjects try to understand open-ended design assignments in right or wrong terms that are more familiar to them:

'How can everyone come up with different solutions to a problem and everyone be correct?'[213] For some, ambiguous assignments in architectural education come as a shock.[214]

What students really want is certainty, direction and an end to the open-endedness. After being given an ambiguous assignment by their tutor, ostensibly to help develop their imagination and creative thinking, some will request that they just point-blank tell them what to do. Ideally in writing. And make that triplicate. These students miss the clarity of studying for quizzes – at least then they knew what was expected, correct and incorrect. What students don't realise is that over time, especially as they progress with their designs, their self-provided decision-making criteria are often replaced with reality-based less-open interpretations and criteria: what works in this situation; how it relates with the context; what will keep it from falling down; what is most relevant and warranted to do here, etc.

Here's a recent email I received from a student who had been given no instructions, just general guidelines for an assignment:

Dear Prof. Deutsch,
The assignment sheets are well written, but the example photos/models are never very accurate of the assignment and this leads to a lot of confusion.
Signed,
Just tell me what to do

What I want to tell them:

Taking photos of previous assignments/students' work is not a substitute for thinking.

Little by little, these students come to realise that they don't need everything pinned down and perfect from the get-go. That having some parts of their design indeterminate will not kill them, and that what does not kill them makes them stronger.[215] That living with some anxiety is necessary and OK as long as it doesn't get out of hand. That they should learn to trust themselves and build confidence in the amount of anxiety they can handle. And in doing so, they will learn how to remain in an ambiguous state, to live with this uncertainty, for as long as possible. Students look back on their initial experiences in design studio, and what they remember most is being shocked by the lack of instruction or direction on assignments, the uncertainty about their tutor's intent or expectations. Students persevered despite this uncertainty – and some because of it – while it proved too ambiguous for others. What's important for the architect is to remain agile, not fragile.

TRY THIS

As the semester progresses, watch to see if your professor gradually introduces more or less ambiguity into the project assignments.[216]

35:
Design Thinking in Architecture

Fig 35.1: Two architects examine an untangled thread of yarn

Architects consider design thinking less a process than a mindset, one that may lead to intangible results.

There's a joke where one fish asks another fish, 'How's the water?' The other fish replies, 'What is water?'

Just as humans cannot see the air that surrounds them, because water is all they know, it's easy for fish to forget it's there.

Architects are like fish in that they are trained in design thinking through the iterative design studio experience (Tim Brown, the CEO of IDEO, went so far as to say that 'architectural education is the best systems design education in the world'[217]) – they're arguably[218] the original design thinkers and are surrounded by it – but you wouldn't know it from architects themselves.

Because architects more often focus on objects (buildings) over processes, and don't like to follow linear methodologies (they're too inhibiting) – and perhaps also because they don't engage as much as they ought to in public discourse outside of their architecture circles – architects are not associated with design thinking: but they ought to be.

Architecture students learn first-hand the back-and-forth, divergent/convergent iterative process via desk crits in studio, converging towards a solution; an experience that can't be replicated nor replaced by a diagram or article in a business journal.

Architects engage in design thinking when they gain a deep understanding of the environment and the user's context – when they ask, what is actual and necessary? – requiring field work in the user's environment, but also empathy in terms of the extent to which they try to understand the user and their situation.[219] Architects also commonly participate in design thinking when they ideate, visualise, prototype and evaluate solutions to address the user's explicit and implicit needs, through their iterative process. For it to be design thinking, the emphasis is on people.

Design thinking in business, product development and marketing – three areas that have taken design thinking and run with it – hasn't helped the architect much where their goal is a new product or service, not a place that people will use and that will serve as the backdrop of their lives. Where design thinking really helps the architect is where they scale up and creatively address problems beyond the individual building.[220]

The important thing for architects isn't that they are swimming in design thinking and don't realise it. It's that their doing so gives them an edge in addressing complex issues and wicked problems – messy problems without obvious solutions – due to their ability to not just problem solve but identify problems worth solving, then apply critical creative thinking to turn issues such as addressing homelessness into opportunities.[221]

There is a duality at the heart of what makes an architect an architect, and design thinking is nothing if not a duality. The architect exists as a balancing act between two extremes: practicality and dreaming; necessity and luxury; actual and virtual; science and art. Yet architecture isn't an either/or proposition, but the careful balancing of extremes. It is for this reason that architects can continue designing buildings but also social systems, businesses and solutions to intractable problems like climate change, ageing and the need to house the homeless, using the same critical creative thinking to address not only private architecture but our age's most hard-to-solve urgent public problems like pending ecological catastrophe.[222]

Design thinking requires you to step back and see problems in a wider context, one that requires you to empathise with people and their circumstances over yours. Historically, an architect would design a building and say, 'I designed the building to your brief and design intent as you requested.' Today, a design thinker might reply, 'Do we even need a building?'[223]

Take the case of a school district that engaged an architect to design an addition to their school building that was in need of additional classroom space.[224] Architectural projects often begin with a defined problem that embodies its solution – namely, a building. By contrast, defining the problem based on insights gained through empathising with the client and users, design thinking stresses discovering the right problem to solve over finding a predetermined solution.

Leveraging design thinking, instead of proposing alternative building designs, the architect might conclude that what is needed is not an addition to the school but a tweaking of the teaching schedule to make better use of the current school classrooms. Here, design thinking is less a process, methodology or set of steps to follow than a mindset; one that may result in an intangible outcome.

36:
Designerly Ways of Thinking

Fig 36.1: Three architects examining a tangle of information

Architects think in a way that is worth studying, preserving and applying to problems large and small.

So, hopefully by now we've established that architects think differently from others. They have more ways to think at their disposal, and when they think they do so as both a process and a mindset. But there is an additional way architects think that can have an impact on the resulting design.

For architects, design can be a wrestling match between abstract ideas/form/appearance – line, plane, mass, volume, form, point, shape, time, scale, space – and more practical ideas/reality/necessity – climate, materials, site forces, constructability[225] – between the ideal and the real, resulting in either a healthy tension or outright conflict.

This concept of thinking comes from Nigel Cross's influential 1982 essay, 'Designerly ways of knowing: design discipline versus design science,[226] which tried to distinguish between scientific ways of knowing and the ways that designers gain knowledge, asserting that design has a legitimate body of knowledge.

Similarly, a designerly way of *thinking* asserts that the way architects think is worth studying, preserving and applying to problems large and small. This book is a case in point.

A designerly way of thinking keeps both the ideal and real in balance throughout the design process until a agreeable solution is arrived at.

Additionally, a designerly way of thinking:

- implies that an open mindset is required to see possibilities others might miss, overlook or not consider
- means to think in terms of bringing something new into the world, even if what you propose is a modification to or adaptation of something that already exists
- keeps those in mind who will be impacted by the design, especially those who are under-represented or don't have a seat at the table
- keeps all voices, forces, constraints and impacts in mind as deep into the design process as possible
- exhibits confidence that the design is both a powerful force that can bring about positive change while also being synthesised into a cohesive whole
- requires a big idea that informs the project throughout the entire design cycle, guiding the design and providing a hierarchy for decisions
- looks for opportunities to delegate the mindless, laborious, repetitive (i.e. for some, boring) parts of the design process to free oneself to focus on one's core competency: namely, to design. That said, most designers benefit from doing everything at least once themselves, so they at least know what it is they are abdicating when they automate
- asks the architect to continually reconcile the ideal and real into a satisfying work
- requires metacognition – thinking about thinking – to help one see the big picture, provide support and keep the whole design process on target.[227]

Architects tend to see everything as a design opportunity. While non-designers might make disparaging comments – that *architects are always designing* or *architects don't know when to stop designing* – don't let that stop you. So much of our world is under-designed that it demands the attention of architects.

Think of design as a lens through which you see the world – that is a designerly way of thinking.

37:
Design Process

Fig 37.1: In 1946 Le Corbusier met Albert Einstein at Princeton University after travelling to New York City to present his project for the UN Headquarters at the United Nations

The architect's design process moves a project forward from concept to a piece of architecture.

If we were to believe Le Corbusier, he committed the design assignment to memory, deliberately forgot about it for several months, then one day *voila* – Ronchamp.[228]

Few architects today – and I suspect even at that time – have the luxury of waiting days, let alone months, to deliver.

But Corbu's hurry-and-wait design process turned out not to be true. Architects have a tendency to romanticise or exaggerate their design process. In Le Corbusier's view, instead of doing the hard work of making drawings and study models, he *incubated* for months at a time, after which the project – Ronchamp in this case – appeared whole cloth[229] in a moment of inspiration.[230]

What actually happened is that Le Corbusier designed Ronchamp by sketching. His version of how his projects materialised made for a better story – but for the pesky fact that it was untrue.

If there is one thing to understand about the design process it is that there is one: that there is a means to develop your big idea into a viable project remains a surprise to some architecture students when first starting out.

A second thing to understand about the design process it is that there is more than one.

The critical creative thinking you bring to the design process is important, because the thought process that goes into making architecture has an impact on the resulting architecture.[231] While we may discuss them separately, in reality the two cannot be separated.

Think Like an Architect doesn't try to present a reductionist understanding of the architectural design process but addresses the tangle in all its messy glory.

Each architect has a different design process, yet as long as the outcome is deemed a success – however that is defined – they are all permissible.[232] Ever malleable to one's needs, the design process cannot be reduced to a formula.

Typically, architects place the emphasis on product, not process: on projects that *look like* architecture. But they do themselves – and their stakeholders – a disservice, as the design process is equal parts process and results. In an environment that is more results oriented, you may find that that a focus on process is associated with a decrease in efficiency. Some feel that a focus on process is less practical and more academic, while industry and business are more interested in results. Results are as important to those who aspire to think like an architect, but equally so is an understanding of one's process. An inefficient process, for example, even with satisfactory results, could still be improved on. To think like an architect means to treat the design process like a design assignment – designing more effective work procedures rather than designing objects like furniture or buildings.

The design process is about how you get from a concept to a piece of architecture – the big idea of the previous chapter. No PowerPoint lecture can teach it; to learn the design process, one must *do* it.

There wouldn't be a need for a design process if architectural design was straightforward and easy. As mentioned, buildings are becoming increasingly complex and architects have to reconcile often-conflicting demands including social, economic, political and technical. These inputs that every architect contends (wrestles) with can be likened to a tangle – one that the architect must unravel to arrive at a synthetic solution: whether a building, urban plan, or anything else they might have the opportunity to design. Only the tangle can't be amicably and satisfactorily unravelled in a systematic, rational way. This, then, is the architect's design process.

While you should be encouraged to explore and implement your own unique way of solving problems, most design processes have several steps in common, going by various names: you start with a design problem, collect information about the project, then allow the information to digest. Next, the designer comes up with schemes based on this absorbed data, resulting in a solution or design direction. But these are the barest of bones, as each architect has their own version of the design process. Alvar Aalto, for example, started with childlike, instinctive sketches from which his big idea took shape. That's how Aalto said he brought the many mutually opposed issues vying for attention and resolution into a harmonious whole.

Fig 37.2: Some architects do their best thinking in the shower

TRY THIS

Especially as some architects still see what they do primarily as art – where they ideate first then when required justify – standardising the design process will help to create needed efficiencies and improve productivity. In the near future, with the continued rise of technology, the design process may become more routinised, where architects will be pressured to look for opportunities to automate parts of the design process – so why not identify these opportunities now before being forced to do so?

TRY THIS

Most students stick with their initial idea. That they do this is a basic misunderstanding of the iterative design process. Some students come up with an idea for a project and spend the rest of the semester protecting it. This is a misunderstanding of the collaborative design process – in this case between the tutor and student. 'Some architects can probably find the right solution on the first try. I am not one of them,' admits architect Paul Michael Davis. 'Neither is Frank Gehry, for whom I worked at the beginning of my career. Neither, it seems, is OMA, Jeanne Gang, Morphosis, or a host of others in the canon of remarkable contemporary architects. Rather, these designers seem content to go back to the drawing board as many times as it takes to get the design right. And it usually takes a lot of tries.'[233] If it doesn't work for them, why should it for you?

Fig 37.3: Some architects do their best thinking while cycling

TRY THIS

No architecture lecture course can teach the design process. To learn the design process, one must do it. While each architect has their own version of the design process, one commonality is that when first starting out they think like an architect, then they make, and only with some practice and experience does thinking and making become concurrent.[234]

ASK THIS

What's the neuroscience behind arriving at the big idea? There are two theories. One hypothesises that after a period of down time the brain has enough energy to deliver a solution. The other suggests that the down time – whether during sleep, meditation, taking a shower or bath, or going for a bike ride or walk – enables the designer to let go of mental obstacles while helping the mind to consider the assignment from a different point of view.

38: Make It Break It Fix It

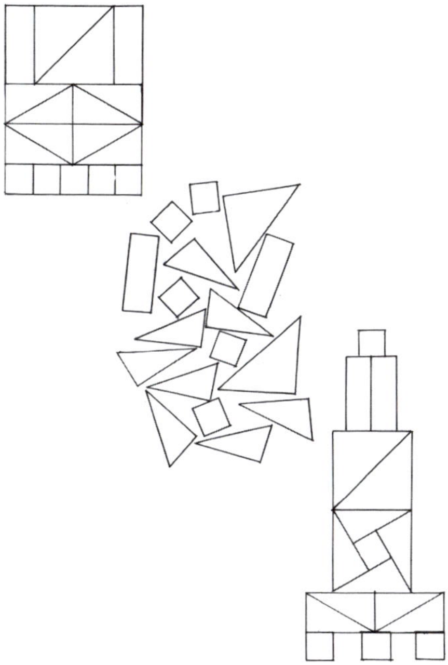

Fig 38.1: Architects are comfortable taking their initial ideas and breaking them down, then building them back up into something else to move the project forward

Architects have the confidence to take their project apart if it means improving it as they put it back together.

If you are not going to go with your initial idea – and we have seen good reasons so far not to – then how do you come up with a second (and third, and fourth) idea? Not by poking at it. Not by making tweaks. You break it.

One method that works for designers is to take their initial idea and break it down, then build it back up into something else. In this way a project transforms, ideally improves, and the process moves forward – spirals forward – towards a successful resolution. This is how projects progress.

At first, breaking your idea apart is a bit like taking a bungee jump: you take a deep breath, close your eyes and hope for the best. As with everything, it becomes easier over time.

Why break your idea apart? Breaking a problem apart allows you to reassess it, and then find a way to put it back together again that improves it: make it break it fix it.

To make it break it fix it – or if you prefer, design, critique, revise[235] – you first have to stop and assess your progress. The critique can be done on your own, but it can also occur right after a desk crit, or in practice it can come from a client or team leader. In the case of a crit, if you are honest with yourself, your tutor provided you with some good insights and ideas to improve your project: ignore them at your peril. Better to consider those that resonate with you, that you think might indeed improve your design, then break it and fix it!

Keep making it, breaking it and fixing it until you arrive a place where you are satisfied with the results.

TRY THIS

To make it break it fix it is how the project improves and how you improve. Architects are OK with breaking things. After you do it once or twice, you realise that the world doesn't end, that life goes on. To make it break it fix it is a form of iterative design – you keep doing it until your project becomes acceptably refined, or until time (or, in practice the design phase budget) runs out. Think of your initial design as a first draft – it was never meant to see the light of day. Like the first pancake that gets thrown out to make way for an almost-OK second pancake, and a considerably improved third pancake, it is OK to make mistakes – in fact, mistakes are encouraged at the initial stages of the design process – just try to do them fast!

39:
Recognising Patterns

Fig 39.1: One of the most creative and transformative acts an architect can experience is the ability to recognise patterns

Architects alternate between focused attention and a relaxed state in order to recognise patterns.

One of the most creative and transformative acts an architect can experience is the ability to recognise patterns: to see something others can't; to relate then combine two seemingly unrelated things; to connect things that previously seemed dissociated; to see commonalities where previously none existed; and to explain one thing in terms of another so it is understood by all.

Some architects are superstitious, preferring not to describe or explain their creative thinking process.[236]

By alternating between a focused then a fuzzy state – first rational then irrational – one can better recognise patterns that before may not have been apparent. To achieve an optimal state requires a balance of linear and creative thinking – switching between focused attention and a relaxed state. Like the incubation stage in the creative process, getting into the right frame of mind in order to be able to recognise patterns requires making time in your day for just chilling, even doing nothing. Eventually you may be able to do this on command anywhere – but while still in school it is probably best practised away from stimulating places like the studio and distractions like your phone while lying in bed or lounging on a couch.[237]

Pattern recognition requires both critical and creative thinking. Some patterns can deceive – where we see things that are just not there due to wishful thinking, or when we will them into existence. Also, to see patterns requires a background in a topic – such as architecture – to know what to look for when you are seeking patterns. In other words, in order to connect the dots, it helps to be familiar with the dots you are connecting.

To put two and two together, it helps to be an associative thinker. To make associations between things, let go of the literal and rational and welcome the fuzzy logic of the dream state.

TRY THIS

To recognise patterns, it helps to be in a loose, before- or after-sleep fuzzy state of creative thinking. When thinking creatively, architect Eric Owen Moss explained that he almost always worked in the middle of the night after having been asleep. The important thing, explains Moss, is the change of environment – from studio or the office[238] – where one can disassociate by thinking in a dream-like state.

TRY THIS

How to disconnect in a time when connecting is hard to avoid? Here are four suggestions: make a long phone-free walk a part of your daily routine; get out of your comfort zone by taking a different path to studio or work; make more time for recreational activities;[239] alternate between doing focused work and activities that are less intellectually demanding.[240]

ASK THIS

How are architects able to recognise patterns that are otherwise undetectable to others? How do architects make these patterns discernible or understandable? Is it the architect's job to make sense of the random and the complex?

40:
Intuitive Thinking

Fig 40.1: The biggest argument architects have against critical thinking is that it doesn't give enough credit to intuition

Architects develop their hunches and intuition at the same time as their rational thinking.

Once, when still in high school, I said to a friend 'I don't think I have ever *thought!*'
'What do you mean?' he asked.

I meant that I couldn't think of a time when, given something to think about – say, a problem – I'd focused on that one thing and responded to it.

I didn't know it at the time, but I had indeed been thinking: I was an *intuitive* thinker. Thinking for me wasn't a conscious effort. Thoughts just came to me.

I didn't have the vocabulary then, but what I was trying to say was that I hadn't thought *deliberately.* That I'd never (like Rodin's statue, *The Thinker*) ever put my chin on my fist, leaned forward and, well ... *thought.*

Instead, I just came up with ideas intuitively that I would turn into cartoons, paintings, plays, songs for the piano and, yes, buildings. They would pop into my head and I would just go with whatever stuck.

Probably the biggest argument architects have against critical thinking – especially as it applies to creative thinking – is that it doesn't give enough credit to intuition.

This book emphasises critical thinking – in this section with critical creative thinking – not because the rational is better than intuition (it's *not*) but because intuition takes experience and judgement – two things beginning students lack. For what is intuition but internalised experience and knowledge?[241]

As Daniel Kahneman made popular as an idea, intuition is fast or quick thinking; a gut reaction or sense that something is right. As a designer, you don't want to wait until you have years of experience and have gained professional judgement before you develop your intuition. You want to develop your hunches and intuition at the same time as your rational thinking ability. Just as rational thinking alone would lead to predictable, dry, uninspired work – buildings, not architecture – so too rational thinking without emotion, eloquence or finesse would lead to logic, not poetry.

We've seen how it's too easy to romanticise how a project like Le Corbusier's Ronchamp came into being – via the architect waiting months for the moment of insight – instead of the much more *prosaic but true* series of sketches and rational decisions. Ronchamp wasn't just intuited into being.

We tend to see intuition as being the opposite of thought, but intuition is a normal and important component of thought[242] and has its roots in tacit learning. You can begin your design process with either rational or intuitive thinking – the important thing is that your design eventually passes through each type of thinking, often through the iterative process multiple times. Once background information is gathered, some architects start their design process with intuition which is then verified by analysis,[243] while others start their design process with data, information and rational thought, then subject it to the subconscious – where creativity starts with analysis which is then verified by intuition.

Architect Lindsay Clare deliberately avoids intuitive thoughts until he has fully understood the problem on a practical level. In this process, he first lays the groundwork, then does the necessary research, and answers what is the actual and necessary *before* addressing the desirable and possible. For Clare, the problem needs to be understood before he is free to act on what he has learned, supporting the process of an immersion into the problem prior to concept realisation.[244]

Thom Mayne talks about the need for spontaneity in the design process; distinguishing between intuitive logic and conventional logic; that architects are always working on the design problem in both a conscious and subconscious state; and that ideas come to him incrementally, not all of a sudden in a eureka moment. Thom Mayne prefers a randomness or 'asymmetric thinking', not to do anything to formalise or systematise the design process.[245] This echoes the architect's preference for not using logical formulas or checklists when designing. Daniel Libeskind, who is suspicious of using a generic model for creative thinking, admits that he tries not to burden the creative process with any parameters or discipline.[246]

Architect Peter Wilson himself is suspicious of using design methods or checklists when designing.[247] While beginning architecture students just want to be told what to do – if only to alleviate the anxiety of uncertainty – by the time they are working architects they prefer to figure things out for themselves.

Architect Glenn Murcutt has likened designing to dreaming, where every line he draws is seen or visualised in his mind's eye beforehand.[248] Alvar Aalto attributed much of his success as an architect to the confidence he allowed himself to have in his intuitive ability.[249] Meanwhile architect Peter Zumthor's design process comes closest to an ideal balance, based on what he describes as an ongoing interplay of intuitive and rational thought, intuition and analysis, feeling and reason.[250]

TRY THIS

Architect Peter Tonkin uses doodling to clarify his thinking and translate his subconscious thoughts into architectural form. You are more likely to gain insight when relaxed. In a relaxed state, use a drawing instrument to make marks on paper and see where it takes you. For Tonkin, doodling in this way is the process of letting the subconscious mind come through without consciously thinking of the logistics.[251] For intuitive doodling to be most effective, it helps to do some preparation and critical thinking first.

41: Thinking Through Making

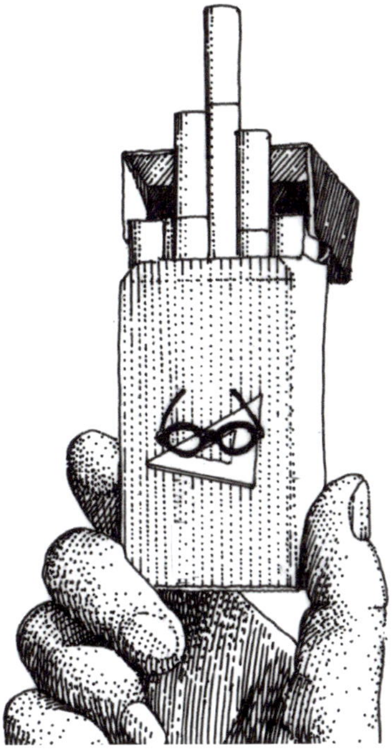

Fig 41.1: Architect Bruce Graham attributed the story of the Sears Tower's origins to a bundle of cigarettes

Architects think through making, where the two are not separate acts but seen as correlated.

The Sears Tower in Chicago (today known as the Willis Tower) consists of nine interlocked tubes. Architect Bruce Graham, a smoker, attributed the Sears Tower's origins to the time he had lunch with structural engineer Fazlur Khan. According to Graham, to prove the tower could be tall, slender and attractive, he grabbed a handful of cigarettes, cupped some in his hands, and slid a few past the others, demonstrating to Khan what came to be called the *bundled tube* concept the tower is famous for.

Thinking gets a bad rap. Associated with inaction, in recent years thinking has taken a back seat to doing and making. Doing, making and *applied learning* today are seen as more necessary. So much so that Pritzker Prize-winning architect Alejandro Aravena calls his think tank Elemental a *do tank*.[252] Even architect Steven Holl believes that drawing is a form of thought.[253]

Doing and making point to a return to the things themselves, where the goal isn't to think more – it's to do, to make, to create, and to have actionable, applied research that has an impact. Even the pronunciation of the word 'think' has 'thing' in it: think·er */THiNGkər/*, where to think is not abstract but part of the making process.

Some architects do not see thinking as *part* of the design process – where a solution comes about by separate acts of thinking, then doing – but instead by thinking *through* doing, where the two are seen as correlated. Similarly, one develops a critical eye not through intellectual exercises but through the act of drawing. According to Douglas Kelbaugh, 'Design is a serendipitous conversation between the sketching hand and the critical eye.'[254]

A designer is someone who thinks through making: *thinking through making* is the way one learns in architecture school, where learning through making is haptic learning. The studio is a learning-by-doing environment, and the crit is the setting in which students acquire design skills and knowledge, under the guidance of the teacher. In architecture school – whose goal is to educate *thoughtful makers*[255] – you make the things you draw, whereas in practice others make (i.e. build) the things you draw.

To make or to think?

Which comes first: thinking or making? To make first then analyse? Or to determine what you want to make and then think? In other words, is it better to think about what you intend to make? Or to make something then to think about it? Professor Matthew Brehm has argued that making – drawings, or physical or virtual study models – should be the first step, where the expectation that students first develop their thinking before they are able to act can lead to a type of paralysis.[256] Others contend that it is better to think and strategise before one puts pen to paper to design.[257] As my one-time professor, Olivio Ferrari, put it: 'Sometimes, first you think and then you do; and sometimes first you do and then you think.'[258]

Architects have always thought in action, through drawing and sketching, where drawing is a way of thinking; solving problems through design. Thought is seen as too abstract for some architects, including Carlo Scarpa, who needed to see something drawn, or better yet draw it himself, in order to trust the results.[259]

We saw in the previous chapter how architect Peter Tonkin uses doodling to clarify his thinking and translate his subconscious thoughts into architectural form. Tonkin acknowledges that the architectural goals for projects come about through what he refers to as *thinking through doodling*[260] and he is often pleasantly surprised to find at the end of a project that the building matches the doodles.

As an alternative to drawing, diagramming is a way of visual thinking that mediates between words and images/things.[261] Either way, drawing and diagramming are tools in the architect's toolbox.

Making and doing are a form of craft. And craft is at the core of architecture, writes Catharine Rossi. 'Craft contains the critical thinking that could unpack the current state of architecture,' says Rossi. '... [It] already contains within itself critical thinking that could not only help unpack its current situation, but that of architecture too. Thinking about craft today ultimately offers ways of meaningfully thinking through how we make, and unmake, a world that is entirely manmade.'[262]

Thinking through our fingers

The critic R.P. Blackmur, who taught biographer Robert Caro when a student at Princeton, admonished him to 'stop thinking with your fingers'.[263] We have long had hand–eye coordination, but today – especially with the internet's impact on our thinking – our fingers are increasingly becoming an extension of our brain.[264] In fact, recent research indicates that we think as much with our hands as our head. *Embodied cognition* is the name given to the recognition that our hands play an increasingly significant role in how we think.[265] Architects have long known that they think with their hands as much as their brains – but psychologists are only now coming to this realisation.[266]

ASK THIS

Do you have a propensity for understanding things? Do you have a predilection for making? Do you prefer to think things through completely – where you have an outline or plan in place – before acting? Or do you have a preference for action?

42:
The Ineffable in Architecture

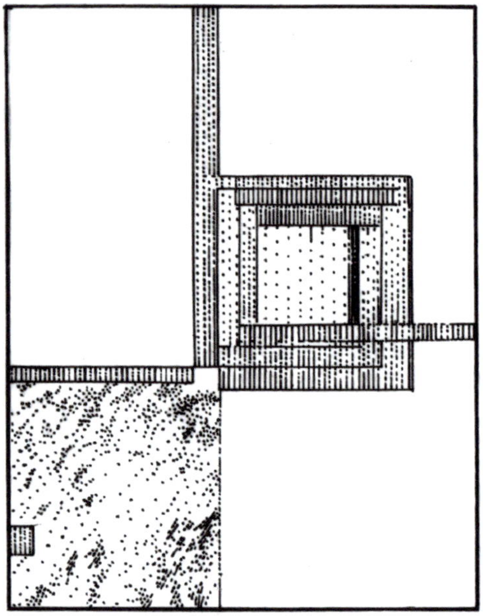

Fig 42.1: A bronze and matt gold detail set in a stone wall panel by Carlo Scarpa

Architects see design as a reconciliation of the ideal with the real and are influenced by both abstract and practical ideas.

Is architecture art? That was the question discussed online on 10 January 2020 on Twitter, in response to AIA National's tweet: 'Like architect Renzo Piano once said, "architecture is art".'

The response to this tweet by the Twitterati was fierce.

All three Vitruvian characteristics – structural integrity, usefulness and beauty – can be found in most buildings. We have beauty or delight because man cannot live by commodity and firmness alone.

That said, when there are larger problems to contend with – climate change, affordable housing – the question of whether architecture is art seems almost beside the point.

There is a long history of distinguishing between mere building and architecture – look no further than Nikolaus Pevsner's 'A bicycle shed is a building; Lincoln Cathedral is a piece of architecture' – and this score won't be settled here.

What this chapter asks is whether there is a place for the ineffable – something so great or otherworldly that it cannot be described in words – in architecture?

An engineer is given a problem and solves it. Two steps:
1. Given problem; 2. Provides solution.

An architect adds a third step:
1. Given problem; 2. Has idea; 3. Provides solution.

In that second step – the idea, or what we've been calling the *big idea* – are a whole lot of potential complications, time expenditure and heartbreak.

Why? Because as we've seen, ideas – imagined, created – can conflict with the reality presented by the problem that requires solving. Design, as a reconciliation of the ideal with the real, is influenced by both abstract and practical ideas.[267]

Where do ideas come from? Experience, the imagination, books, research; often, the architecture student – feeling they are under a great deal of pressure to come up with a solution – panics and feels anxiety. To alleviate their anxiety, they look through the most expedient and familiar websites and social media for images to inspire, borrow or steal. Students are not alone in feeling this anxiety: Pritzker Prize-winning architect Glenn Murcutt admitted to feeling a lack of confidence and nervousness when approaching a design problem, even to the point where he admitted that the anxiety of design made him ill.[268]

If there is a time and place for mystery – for obscurity even – architecture school isn't it. Or is it? Are students rewarded for designing mysterious, inexplicable, *ineffable* buildings? Perhaps – and this may be a good thing as the ineffable, what makes design *good,* is the one thing that robots cannot replicate or replace,[269] and is what humans do best.[270]

Just as design is a reconciliation of the ideal with the real, so too must architecture balance between the ineffable and the rational.[271] As Louis Kahn so eloquently put it, 'A great building must begin with the unmeasurable, must go through measurable means when it is being designed and in the end must be unmeasurable.' If students are overburdened by too much reality, and not enough of the ineffable – where the focus is on function at the expense of wonder – they and their design will suffer. The ideal might be to balance and integrate the ideal and the real, the abstract and the practical, the ineffable and the rational – the *constant interplay of feeling and reason*[272] – where students explore creative solutions based on real situations.[273]

While some professors may welcome a diminution of the ineffable in student architecture, a preponderance of function doesn't relieve the architect of the necessity of wonder.

SECTION 5: CURIOSITY

43: Curiosity

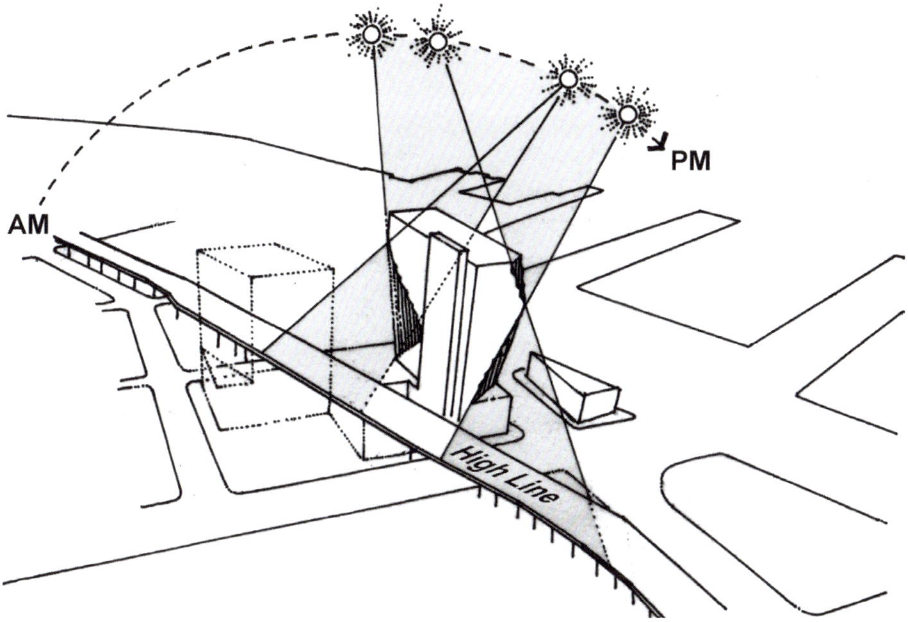

Fig 43.1: The Solar Carve office building by Chicago architect Jeanne Gang near the High Line in New York manoeuvres to let the sun through

Architects are naturally curious, and make an effort to continue to be so throughout their careers.

There is ample evidence of a deep and abiding curiosity throughout the architectural projects of Chicago architect Jeanne Gang.[274] Pick any of her projects – the Solar Carve office building near the High Line in New York and how it manoeuvres to let the sun through; the Rescue Company 2 fire station in Brooklyn that is designed around a giant void enabling the company to practise rescue scenarios; the Writers Theater in Glencoe, Illinois that energises and engages the larger community – each serves as an exploration of her persistent inquisitiveness and myriad interests.

Both architecture schools and firms are always interested in students and recent graduates who ask relevant questions, come up with new ideas, and are eager to evolve in their roles. The mindset they are looking for in their candidates is *curiosity* – the second most-mentioned attribute or quality after critical thinking that schools and firms are looking for in new candidates and hires.

To be curious means you are interested in something, *eagerly* interested in learning more about something. To be curious means there is a light on inside; that you are inquisitive and have a concern about something that drives you to look or delve into it further. Curiosity implies a motivation – to search, to find out, to know; to sleuth, to investigate, to find answers. It may seem that most people have a healthy curiosity, but as former professor and author Edgar Schein has suggested, curiosity and question asking – which are integrally related – are missing from most conversations.[275]

What does being more or less curious mean in terms of creative thinking? The highly curious person will seek out what makes experiences unique – for example, seeking out additional information when travelling to another country or visiting a well-known work of architecture – as opposed to seeing them exclusively through others' eyes. Then, when you return, find ways to integrate what you picked up along the way to make new knowledge that you can access and apply.[276]

Sometimes architects use the curiosity of a building's users or inhabitants in the design of their architecture. Alvaro Siza is such an architect, whose framed openings and layered boundaries create curiosity, drawing people in and through his spaces to explore what may exist beyond.[277]

When you leave school, you may want to consider adding curiosity to the criteria you use to choose where to work. In a recent survey of 23,000 people, 83% of company executives said that they encourage question asking and reward curiosity in their organisation, but in the same survey only 52% of employees agreed.[278] The implication being that a more curious organisation will be a more innovative place to work – but make sure that prospective employers and employees are on the same page in their assessment of the extent to which the company encourages curiosity.

Perhaps while discussing curiosity it is a good time to revisit the topic of self-motivation. Much of what architects need to know to become an architect is learned in practice, and much of what they think is learned by practising. This book exists to serve as a resource to help you develop these skills on your own. There are critical thinkers and creative thinkers, but few bring this unique combination of thinking abilities together in one person as well as the architect.

This book is less a celebration of this fact than an assurance that this quality continues and will help you recognise the thinking capabilities and show you how to build them into your own unique repertoire or toolbox. But it can only do so if you find a way to remain curious – today, and throughout your career. It is up to you to find and maintain a sincere interest in things – some of which you can integrate into your design, others for their own sake.

TRY THIS

The importance of staying curious for your career cannot be overstated. But also, it is critical for your development as an architect. All of us are born curious, but few are able to maintain the spark to enquire, explore and learn as we mature into adulthood. Some of us when young are discouraged from asking so many questions, while others find that question asking could be perceived not as an expression of curiosity, but ignorance. To be a critical creative thinker, and think like an architect, you need to nurture and build on this desire to understand. To be curious means to be inquisitive, not to be afraid of asking questions – to be the perpetual child asking *why* – and not be satisfied or satiated until you find an answer. For the curious, the more they learn, the hungrier they will be for information and knowledge. I am someone who learned early that I am motivated by learning. Curiosity is the opposite of being satisfied with the first idea that pops into our head. Can the first idea turn out to be the best idea? Sure – but, as we've discussed, it's unlikely – so continue the search until you discover something new. This is how we continue to innovate and bring something new into the world.

TRY THIS

How do you know if you have above-average curiosity? One way is to try an assessment: Do you bore easily? Do you not care how something works as long as it works? Are you intrigued by the unknown? Do you prefer repetitive tasks and word searches to riddles? Are you willing to try something once to see what it is like? Do you like trying new routes to class or work and approaches to things? Do you tend to ask few or many questions? Do you enjoy meeting strangers? Do you generally hang out with the same people? Do you like to do things your own way?

ASK THIS

Are you a multipotentialite, polymath or autodidact? Like many architects, a multipotentialite is a generalist with a multitude of interests and creative pursuits. Multipotentialites have no *one true calling* the way specialists do. We have many paths and we pursue all of them, either sequentially or simultaneously (or both). Similarly, architects consider themselves polymaths – in that they have wide-ranging interests – and also self-taught or self-educated autodidacts.

READ THIS

Curious: The Desire to Know and Why Your Future Depends On It by Ian Leslie

44: Possessing a Growth Mindset

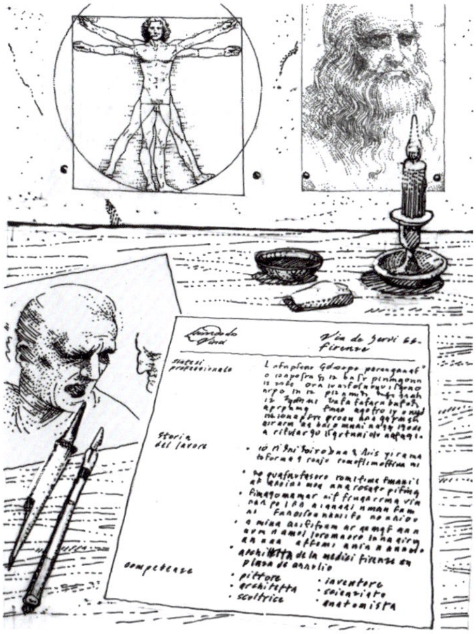

Fig 44.1: The world's first CV downplayed an impressive list of accomplishments in preference for playing up the way one thinks

Being open to feedback, change and growth is critical to one's development as an architect.

Who created the first CV?

I'll give you a hint. It was a jobseeker who was trying to impress a prospective employer, only this CV didn't list their achievements – it explained how this person *thinks.*

Give up? The first CV goes back almost 450 years, the employer was the Duke of Milan, and the CV writer – the CV inventor – was none other than Leonardo da Vinci.[279 280]

By downplaying his impressive list of accomplishments and playing up the way he thought, Leonardo was unwittingly expressing that he was in possession of a growth mindset – something that employers today look for in their job candidates.

With a fixed mindset, individuals see their abilities as unchangeable gifts that they had at birth: this is who I am, take it or leave it. Whereas with a growth mindset, students and emerging professionals see their abilities as developable and their intelligence as evolvable through hard work and feedback. They are open to – not threatened by – challenges because they see them as unlimited opportunities for growth and transformation.[281] In her research, Stanford professor and psychologist Carol Dweck discovered that students who believe that they can improve with effort, i.e. those with a growth mindset, exceeded and surpassed those with a fixed mindset.[282] Dweck coined the phrase *growth mindset* after decades of research on how children and teens become successful. Dweck's book[283] explains that accomplishment goes beyond abilities to students' attitudes. Those with growth mindsets see themselves as works-in-progress, while those with fixed mindsets see their abilities as static, so they avoid challenge and failure.[284]

With all there is to learn, no matter how innately talented one is, it is hard to imagine being an architect without having a growth mindset. Being open to change and growth is that important to development as an architect. As shown in Figure 44.2, a growth mindset is required for a 'Make It Break It Fix It' approach to design.

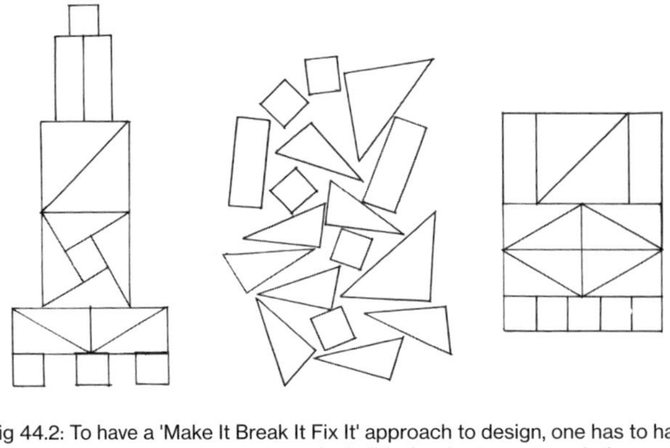

Fig 44.2: To have a 'Make It Break It Fix It' approach to design, one has to have confidence that failing fast – even when it requires one to start over and rebuild – is a better approach than making minor, incremental adjustments

Intellectual humility

To have a growth mindset, it is incumbent on you to make mistakes. Make them fast, if you must, make them as pain-free as possible, but make them. This is part of the *fail fast, fail often* ethos.

To do so requires intellectual and creative humility – where you invite criticism. You don't need to be a masochist – like pulling off a plaster it will hurt, but like muscle building over time you become stronger where the scars are.

So, don't be unnecessarily hard on yourself. Accept that this is where you are now developmentally. Each student is different, but you will grow and expand over time – it is happening even if you don't immediately see results. To have intellectual humility means to consider the possibility that others know something you could benefit from learning. See everyone as your teacher, including your classmates: you never know who you can learn from. How to overcome a lack of humility? Curiosity. Curiosity is the antidote to arrogance.[285]

Architect Paul Michael Davis sees the critique of one's work in a positive light: '... no design proposal escapes without criticism. Indeed, a strong academic critique can be one of the most energizing, inspiring moments of an architect's education. In that instant of receiving and internalizing criticism, the designer grows. They see how their work falls short through the eyes of someone else – someone more trained and experienced in the subject they chose to study – and they see other possible solutions to the problem in that understanding.'[286]

Growth mindset and perseverance

A growth mindset is especially important for the work of architects, since their projects can take years to complete and this requires perseverance, where perseverance and resilience are associated with a growth mindset.[287]

At the start of a project architects spend hours acquiring knowledge about the situation, enquiring with as many people as possible to gain a clear picture, before setting out to act on the knowledge gained via design. In these situations, architects often find they face circumstances they don't know anything about.

A few chapters back you might recall that we defined architects as people who are asked to do impossible things they know nothing about.

This *not knowing* about something or how to do something doesn't cause all architects anxiety. On the contrary, most architects thrive when given such assignments, especially where expectations are high, because each assignment is an opportunity to learn and architects are motivated by learning.

Architecture is an immersive experience. You can't look on from the sidelines, with one foot in and one foot out. There is an expectation of being *all in* – you're in it for the long haul, investing in yourself over a long period of time.

TRY THIS

Make a shift in your design process from linear to non-linear thinking. This will require you to be open to new ideas, having the courage to make mistakes, and learning from them. Be a sponge. Be open-minded. Be receptive to new ideas – having a growth mindset requires a level of receptiveness. Architect Harwell Hamilton Harris anecdotally acknowledged this quality of receptiveness in architecture students at the beginning of their studies, but observed that their enthusiasm peaked in the second and third years then declined until graduation was in sight,[288] implying that one has to work at being receptive and open-minded.

ASK THIS

While I am writing a book that suggests you should learn to think like an architect, I am teaching design studio to final-year students who do not yet think this way. On their presentation boards, one project used five different styles of trees (I pointed out four, but another student found a fifth). One project didn't show any context. How could these liabilities or oversights be overcome? *Intellectual humility.* Listen to your tutor. Remember when they said 'fit' as a design criteria? Remember 'show context'? Tutors know that they need to repeat themselves multiple times to get their point across. You know how you don't like to read the instructions that come with your IKEA furniture? This is architecture school: read the instructions that come with the assignment. Read the assignment. Listen to your tutor. Take notes when your tutor speaks. Request clarification when you need it. Use it as a checklist. Intellectual humility requires that you question yourself. Is it possible you are wrong? Are you ignoring or forgetting something? Are you blind to an obvious idea? Develop your willingness to rethink your conclusions based on new information or feedback.

READ THIS

Humble Inquiry: The Gentle Art of Asking Instead of Telling by Edgar Schein

45: Beginner's Mind

Fig 45.1: Emergency responders, firefighters, fellow drivers and pedestrians try to come up with a way to dislodge the truck stuck under a viaduct

Architects deliberately put themselves into a state of creative ignorance so they can approach problems with an open mind.

A truck driver who tried to pass under a low bridge failed, and the truck found itself stuck, causing traffic to back up, resulting in emergency responders, firefighters, fellow drivers and pedestrians trying to come up with a way to dislodge the truck. Should they dismantle parts of the truck or remove parts of the bridge? Each suggested a solution from their respective point of view.

A child walking by looked at the truck, at the bridge, then looked at the road and said, matter-of-factly, 'Why not just let the air out of the tires?'

This story represents the challenges we face where the best solution is often the one most difficult to arrive at because of the self-imposed constraints – our respective point of views – we work within.

It also illustrates the importance of seeing a problem with fresh eyes. And the great news is that being able to do so is not a one-time thing – the ability to see anew is a renewable resource – a mindset we can take on again and again.

Some architects will deliberately put themselves into a state of creative ignorance – or *deliberate ignorance* – in order to address complex problem solving. Architect Will Alsop was one such architect, who avoided extensive building-type research – preferring to work in a state of ignorant bliss – prior to commencing creative thinking and the search of fresh possibilities.[289]

Preparing them for the unknown

The concept of beginner's mind was popularised in Shunryu Suzuki's classic book, *Zen Mind, Beginner's Mind,* where he noted two conditions for beginner's mind to arise: having no thought of achievement, and having no thought of self. In other words, to have new, innovative ideas it would behove the architect to not concern themselves with a successful outcome, nor with concern about themselves.

For example, when asked to design a home or chair, beginning architecture students tend to reference houses or chairs that are favourites of theirs or that they are familiar with. When they do this they end up replicating vs re-seeing the familiar example through fresh eyes. Their tutors – design studio teachers, studio masters, professors or instructors – when they see this occurring, try to get them to address the unfamiliar. Some tutors will attempt to address this condition – which can lead to preconceived, conventional or habitual ideas – by trying to keep students off-balance, or knocking them (proverbially) off-track. Doing so challenges preconceived notions and has longer-term benefits. In a quote attributed to Oliver Wendell Holmes Sr, 'One's mind, once stretched by a new idea, never regains its original dimensions.' One such suggestion or new idea is when tutors try to get object-oriented beginning students to see architecture not as buildings but spaces, or instead of adding-on have them carve out of form, and in doing so provide them with a whole new way of thinking.[290]

When architect Daniel Libeskind won the Berlin Jewish Museum competition, he felt that having no experience didn't put him at a disadvantage but on the contrary gave him an advantage, in that if you have too much experience, or any experience for that matter, you already know where you're going design-wise. Libeskind believed that without experience he was free to think differently, and able to convince others that there are other ways of doing and building things. He explains how in order to have fresh ideas he has to get rid of his expertise.[291]

Libeskind discusses beginner's mind in terms of the architect being a perpetual amateur, pointing out that the word *amateur* comes from a French word meaning *lover of,* where an amateur is a lover of something. He notes that Thomas Jefferson was an amateur architect, as was Alberti, especially since the profession of the architect is a relatively new invention.[292]

When they first start out in architecture most architects think they are at a deficit, and in some ways perhaps they are. But they are also at a distinct advantage in that they have beginner's mind, a state that they will try to re-create voluntarily throughout their career, over and over again.

The architect is charged with transforming what has come before into something that speaks to its time. For the armchair architect we have precedent studies – the acquisition of precedent, the internalisation of past architecture[293] – or legitimate ideas that have come before and are worth becoming familiar with, visiting while travelling, and thinking about.

TRY THIS

As you go through the architecture curriculum you are gaining, growing, expanding, becoming deeper, more thoughtful. Some of the onus is on your tutors to ensure that you are learning, but why not go through college as a autodidact – self-taught? If you learn from school, great, but ultimately you are responsible for your own education. This mindset enables you to go where your interests are, get to know yourself, and discover what special life experiences and insights you bring to the class. Even having no experience can be seen as an advantage, in that you are experiencing beginner's mind not as a paradigm or concept to follow, but for real.

ASK THIS

Here we are talking not just about a subjective creative act, or creativity per se. A big part of critical creative thinking is challenging assumptions and the aforementioned preconceived ideas. Tutors do this by asking questions: *Why is it this way? Why does it need to be this way?*

46:
Observation, Mindfulness and Alertness

Fig 46.1: An architect sketching Villa Savoye on an iPad

Architects make a special effort every day to be observant, mindful and alert.

For the young Le Corbusier, known then as Charles-Édouard Jeanneret, the sketchbook emerged during his extensive travels as his primary tool for observing, recording and learning, where drawing became for him an essential medium for architectural training. In the first decade of the twentieth century, Jeanneret made hundreds of drawings. With each trip he gained a broader view of the world. As his interests expanded, so did his ability to document what he saw. Many architects travel, especially – in the tradition of what was known as the Grand Tour – following school. But what distinguished Jeanneret's travels from those of his classmates and fellow graduates was his awareness of *being able to begin again,* something that is apparent on nearly every page of his notebooks.

The phase during construction for architects in the US used to be called 'construction administration'. More recently, for legal and liability reasons – *administration* could be interpreted as *inspection* – it was changed to 'construction observation', taking the implied agency away from the architect. *Don't mind me – I'm just observing.* Many contracts read that, during construction, the architect will perform periodic observations.

Your goal as an architect is to provide *continuous* observation (living in a perpetual state of wonder is also recommended), and to always be in a mindful state. Doing so will lead to active listening, identifying problems worth solving, and an increase in insights and creative solutions.

Observation may be a weasel word when it comes to contracts, but it is a reminder of one of the architect's prime strengths and capabilities: the power to observe. To take in one's environment. To zoom in and zoom out – observing at all scales – to get a more complete picture. Make it your goal, as Henry James advised writers, to 'try to be one of the people on whom nothing is lost!'[294]

With the rise of new technologies, we forget that the old ways of looking and seeing evolved over millennia, for example, served us just fine. Children do this naturally, and we all need to get back in touch with how, when walking down the street, or in a park or nature, we would take in the world around us – without overthinking, judging, analysing what we saw or drowning it out with music. While learning new ways of seeing is encouraged, it is also important to not leave behind our more accustomed ways of seeing and taking in what is around us.[295]

The place where architects begin has to be in observing the world. When first starting out in our academic and professional careers, it's easy to miss so much of what is right in front of us because our attention is elsewhere – we are not actively looking at, listening to and taking in what surrounds us. It is incumbent on each of us to see with our own eyes, to record what we see, with a goal to understand and join the dots in the natural and built environment, between people and how they engage with each other and the world.[296]

Now admittedly, observation isn't as sexy as winning recognition from professional organisations and your peers. Observing seems passive – something you just do naturally – but in reality it is active (just as you can passively hear or actively listen), and it takes deliberate effort, concentration and attentiveness. What it takes more than anything is your presence.

If we're being honest, we know we can be counted in attendance in a class without necessarily being present. Your body might have showed up, but your mindful attention could well still be back in bed, lost in some reverie or going over a conversation you had the night before. What you aren't in these situations is *there*.

This is what is meant when, as one professor stated, 'you know you're starting to think like an architect when you are concerned about, when needing to mail a letter, the stamp, the envelope, and the stamp's relationship with the envelope'.[297] Yes, aesthetics are involved: the type of envelope, quality of the paper, whether to handwrite or type the address, what font you will use, what stamp you will use and what it may communicate to the recipient, where you will place the stamp, even whether you will actually post a letter or send an email or text. But as importantly, you find you are concerned about things that architects concern themselves with: questions about the relationship of the part to the whole; the process you use (the postmaster offers to use a franking machine, but you have your eye on that commemorative architecture stamp). All of this speaks to how an architect thinks.

Fig 46.2: Notre-Dame du Haut in Ronchamp, France by Le Corbusier

There are only so many ways that the outside world enters our inside world. How does information come to us? Putting telepathy (ESP, clairvoyance, sixth sense) aside for the moment, through experience (including right now experiencing this book), reflecting on that experience, reasoning, communicating with others, and through observation. One of the most important ways information comes to us is this last one, *through observation* – our ability to perceive and understand the world around us: seeing and documenting details, capturing reality and mapping our world.

We do this by paying attention, by observing. You need to fill yourself up with knowledge and information, not to have preconceived ideas about things but so the mind can take two unrelated things and put them together, and in doing so bring something new into the world; so you can go beyond the utilitarian or obvious solution and approach something from a new perspective; so you can create something that meets all the criteria and also provides something more. It's not a formula, it's a mindset, a capacity you create within yourself, by bringing your entire life experience to the fore. Architecture isn't for the meek or faint of heart: it requires you to have the courage to see.

When you meditate, you concentrate on your breathing. When your mind wanders, you make note of this – you don't judge yourself or berate yourself – you just acknowledge that your mind has wandered and return to the breathing. Our mind wanders again – we recognise this – and bring it back to our breathing ad infinitum. We are able to do this because we create a gap – between our automatic thoughts and our mindful attention. Our ability to do this is like building a muscle, only it's in our consciousness. Similarly, we don't just plough into a project by rote or by habit; we create a gap in time to consider what we are doing. A gap to think about the problem or assignment. This gap requires us to let go of assumptions, preconceived ideas, and what we want to believe. This doesn't come easy to everyone. Like most effective habits that are worth considering, it takes practice.

TRY THIS

Many students and emerging professionals feel a lot of pressure to achieve early wins, to find success fast, to build their brand. This leads to feeling anxiety and fear about one's prospects and how one stacks up, compares or fits in. The problem is that this mindset is outside-in – wanting and expecting recognition to come from outside. By doing this – and we may not even be aware that we do this – we are putting the power in others, not ourselves. You are the one thing you can control in the beginning stages of your career. While acknowledgement from others will inevitably become part of the equation for how you define success, in your early years when first starting out, it is more important to become a gifted observer and develop your ability to replicate, represent what you see, and imagine.

TRY THIS

Try meditation or yoga to increase awareness. Most people go through their day on autopilot – and there are certainly things we don't need to give 100% of our attention to. But through the increased awareness that yoga and meditation bring, and focusing on otherwise natural processes that come automatically to us (like breathing), we can learn to be in the moment and see opportunities that may not have come into our consciousness before.[298] Learning how to see what is – learning from observation – will teach you to see, really see, not to see what you think you are seeing.

TRY THIS

Create a gap. Among so many other benefits, meditation teaches you the importance of the gap that exists between the trigger and your response. In that gap is a space – calm like the eye of a hurricane – where you have a choice: to react automatically, or deliberately. Rather than doing something because it's the most expedient – it's what your studio mate is doing, it's what you think your professor wants you to do, it's what you've always done in similar situations, or accepting what you've read or been told – take a deep breath and spend some time thinking. One of the most powerful secrets of the universe is in this gap – and being able to recognise its existence. The gap between stimulus and response[299] allows us to act less automatically or habitually – like animals – and more like the enlightened human beings we are and strive to become, and recognise that we are doing so.

ASK THIS

Can you remember a time when you just observed – for example, looking out of the car window on a family holiday? Do you recall what you saw? How do you feel about what you saw today? William Cronon, in the introduction to his book *Nature's Metropolis,* describes the first time he saw Chicago from the backseat window of his family's car while on vacation as a child. His observations led to a brilliant career – and a brilliant book.

READ THIS

Drawing on the Right Side of the Brain by Betty Edwards

READ THIS

Read books to gain different perspectives on how to see a building. Like the proverbial blind men describing an elephant, treat these as ways to help you see anew:
Translations from Drawing to Building and Other Essays
by Robin Evans
A Critic Writes by Reyner Banham
Mathematics of the Ideal Villa and Other Essays by Colin Rowe
Modernity and the Classical Tradition by Alan Colquhoun
Experiencing Architecture by Steen Eiler Rasmussen

47:
Question Asking

Fig 47.1: Creative thinking is most readily achieved by simply asking questions, and *critical* creative thinking by asking good questions

Architects care about the quality and character of their questions to ensure their relevance and applicability.

In an interview for a new project, the client asked our architecture firm how many design schemes they should expect to get.

One said the pennywise manager.
Three said the pleaser principal.
As many as you want said the design-happy designer (that would be me).

The emerging professional – who until then had been silent, taking notes – wisely asked: *How many do you want?*

Silence. Stunned, that was it! This last response – in the form of a question – showed critical creative thinking (and maturity beyond her years).

The emerging professional's response – in the form of a question – is surprising and situational, taking into consideration the context. Her question recognises that we didn't have enough information to respond with an actual answer. Plus, it's just good marketing and customer service: it responds to a question with a question – to further clarify and to engage with the client. It was risky for her to have said – *asked* – this in front of her bosses, but why else had she been invited to the interview, if not to provide value?

Researchers asked ten-year-olds and college students to come up with a plan to protect bald eagles from elimination. Both groups came up with ideas of equal quality. Besides having better spelling skills, the primary difference between the fifth graders and the college students was that the latter had developed the capacity to ask questions.[300]

Creativity and question asking

Creative thinking is most readily achieved by simply asking questions, and *critical* creative thinking by asking good questions – relevant, thoughtful and incisive questions – coupled with cultivating the ability to make sound decisions that lead to strong ideas.[301] The difference between architecture and building, or good and bad architecture, is related to the kinds of questions that are asked: the quality or *character* of questions.[302] One of the most critical skills for an architect to develop is the facility to ask relevant and perceptive questions.[303]

According to architect Peter Zumthor, what should be taught in architecture school is the asking of questions, because design is itself a form of questioning. The acts of creating or making things are themselves questioning.

What questions?

Design is not just about asking questions. It's about asking the *right* questions. Relevant questions. Meaningful and insightful questions.[304] And not asking other types of questions, for example these that Edgar Schein identifies in *Humble Inquiry:* leading questions, statements as questions, shaming questions and rhetorical questions.[305] Asking pertinent questions –

and not accepting and (worse) using just any information that you come across online – is of course part of critical thinking, but also of creative thinking.

TRY THIS

Here are the three most important words you will ever use (besides *I love you*). At our architecture school career fair most of the interview or job offers go to graduate students. I tell my undergrad students when they are told by a prospective employer 'Sorry, we only hire graduate students' or 'We only hire those with graduate degrees' to reply with these three magical words: Help me understand ... *Help me understand* what a graduate student can do that I can't do? This three-word query frequently catches employers off-guard, and in many cases impresses them enough to invite the candidate for an interview, and sometimes even to hire them. When I served as associate director of my architecture school's graduate programme, one of my duties was to read letters of recommendation written on behalf of applicants. One letter was written by an applicant's employer, who wrote 'I will never forget [the applicant's] reply when I told him we don't hire undergraduates. His reply – *Help me understand* – was equal parts mature beyond his years and disarming. I hired him on the spot.'

TRY THIS

Among Edgar Schein's suggestions for cultivating a habit of honest questioning, expanding your powers of observation, and exercising your natural ability for creative thinking in his book *Humble Inquiry:* travel to unfamiliar lands and cultures, develop your observation skills by taking courses in art or mindfulness, attend theatre productions, and write in a journal.[306]

TRY THIS

Anticipate the questions students may be asked at a design review (mid-term or final). Work backwards from these questions to the beginning. Design to the questions.

TRY THIS

Say you're given an assignment to report on the architect Le Corbusier. There are many ways you might go about researching it: biographies, periodicals, architecture books. You soon discover that one book is no more an authority on the subject than another. Instead, you try a *rabbit holes* strategy. Come up with a bunch of questions about Le Corbusier you want answered, and then simply do whatever you must to pursue them. Here are a few possible questions: *How did Le Corbusier's architecture draw on earlier styles? How did Le Corbusier's ideas about architecture evolve? Furniture? Urban design? What were the origins of Le Corbusier's work in Paris?* 'Here is the thing: simply pursue the list of questions,' suggests economist Tyler Cowen. 'It may well induce you to find books, or it may lead you down Googled rabbit holes. Or it may lead you to ... Follow the questions, not the books per se. Don't focus on which books to read, focus on which questions to ask. Then the books, and other sources, will follow almost automatically.'[307]

ASK THIS

What do you like or dislike about your design? What design issues have/have not been addressed at this point? What areas of this design do you feel are/are not resolved at this point? What is the base concept/parti of this design?[308]

ASK THIS

Consider asking questions that are important for journalists to ask: *Why do you think of that? How did you learn that? Am I understanding this? What else should I know?*[309] At your next desk crit, pin-up or review, ask yourself: What was I asked to do – literally asked to do? So why am I presenting something else?

ASK THIS

You just sat through a lecture. Instead of passively taking down notes to review in the days before the exam, in the hours – not days – after the lecture, ask yourself: What do I think about what was said? How would I agree or disagree with this? Are there any other similar answers I can think of with alternative routes?[310] Such an approach improves retention better than underlining, highlighting and cramming before an exam.

ASK THIS

For Thom Mayne of Morphosis, creative problem solving starts with posing questions: What does architecture contribute to the solution?[311] As important as it is for salespeople to recognise they've made the sale, and to stop selling, it's just as important for the architect to know when to stop questioning. Ask yourself: Have I achieved my goal (e.g. to change another person's mind, or to figure out what architecture contributes to the solution)? Then stop.

READ THIS

The Book of Beautiful Questions: The Powerful Questions That Will Help You Decide, Create, Connect, and Lead by Warren Berger
Questions Are the Answer: A Breakthrough Approach to Your Most Vexing Problems at Work and in Life by Hal B. Gregersen
A More Beautiful Question: The Power of Inquiry to Spark Breakthrough Ideas by Warren Berger
Leading with Questions: How Leaders Find the Right Solutions By Knowing What To Ask by Michael J. Marquardt
QBQ! The Question Behind the Question: Practicing Personal Accountability in Work and in Life by John G. Miller

READ THIS

Humble Inquiry: The Gentle Art of Asking and Not Telling by Edgar Schein. Yes, I'm recommending this book again! *Humble Inquiry* means asking questions to which you do not already know the answer and building a relationship based on an interest in the other person. Ask instead of tell.

48:
Asking *What If ...?*

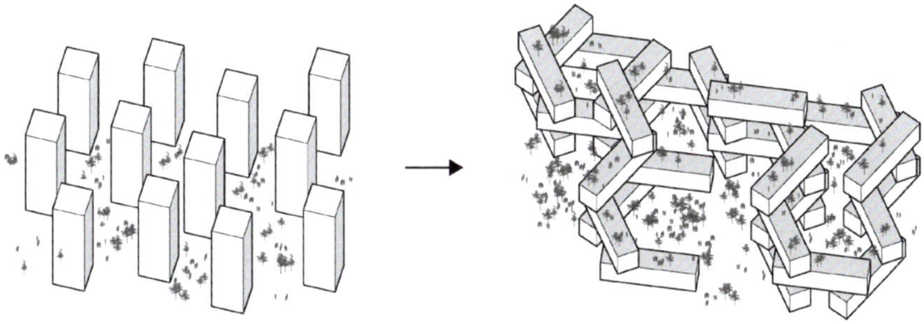

Fig 48.1: With the design of Interlace, Ole Scheeren asked how models with the density of a skyscraper could improve people's lives

Architects ask *What if ...?* to lead to new directions in research and future development.

Is it possible for a project to have 112% green space? In other words, can a project have *more* nature than had it not been built?

Ole Scheeren is an architect who applies critical thinking to the design process beyond the conventional extents of the making of architecture. In doing so, the firm asks how architects can rethink things for which there are no existing models.

The Interlace, a 1,040-unit residential complex in Singapore, one of the last projects Scheeren designed while at OMA, and named the World Building of the Year at the World Architecture Festival in 2015, redefines what a skyscraper can be.

Housing is an example of a project type that has become standardised and formulaic, and Interlace is an example of how – using the same components, requirements and density – something new is possible. Its organisational structure is a hexagonal grid, in which horizontal twelve-storey building blocks are stacked up to create abundant, open, interconnected and permeable outdoor courtyards.

Interlace is an example of a building that moves beyond a focus on the object to one that shapes spaces for people. Completed in 2013, atop its hexagonal plan of horizontal buildings are rooftop gardens, and below are open plazas and pool decks that encourage human interaction.

As Scheeren said in his TED Talk in 2015, if all the green space that was left on the ground was counted, subtracting the footprint of the buildings, and the green of all the terraces was added back – essentially serving as each building's thirteenth floor – this would result in 112% green space. In other words, *more* nature than had the building not been built.[312]

What if ...?

Want a simple, one-sentence shortcut to thinking like an architect? Ask questions like this:

Next time you ask yourself *Should I fix my old car or invest in a new one?* instead ask *Can I get a job within bicycling distance of my residence?* or *Can I relocate near public transport?*[313]

In other words, substitute the either/or proposition – the trigger and response – with asking: *What if ...?*

Your tutor asks you to design a community centre with a swimming pool. Thinking divergently, ask:

What if the pool doubled as a filtration plant? Or, in off-hours, doubled as a homeless shelter? What if the building created more power than it used? What if by swimming, people generated the additional power? What if the building educated the community on resilience? Or included a pool where local pets could swim?

The question *What if...?* was the central question asked of students in a graduate seminar on Building Envelope Design taught by architect and Associate Professor Scott Murray in the School of Architecture at the University of Illinois at Urbana-Champaign. In this seminar, students were asked to think creatively about the future, and to envision new types of building envelopes or new types of performance for which the technology does not yet exist, but which may point to new directions in research and future development. The students' quick sketch proposals involved asking a question that begins with the provocative phrase: *What if...?*

What if the facade could act like human skin? What if glass was made of electromagnetism? What if windows could light up the interior? What if a facade could become a room? What if the walls of a building could grow?

What if the facade could act like human skin? asks Amal Tariq

What if glass could change its colour based on users' stress level? What if building envelopes could store rainwater? What if building envelopes could breathe? asks Arpana Pillai

What if a building envelope could be made of textile waste? What if a building envelope could repel pests? asks Marilia Sa Ribeiro

What if facades were Non-Newtonian Liquids? asks Marlom Vargas

What if a building could moult? What if a building is a rubik? What if we can live in balloons? asks Teng Long

What if buildings grew like plants? What if 'wind panels' could be used on the building envelope? What if the building skin behaved like that of an armadillo? asks Sharanya Reddy

What if building skin is made of generative bio-roots? What if building envelopes could mutate? asks Ravideep Singh

What if the building skin could be made of upcycled plastic waste? What if the building skin was stretchable? What of the building skin could use wind loads to generate power? asks Raksha Magal

What if old tires could be pressed into bricks? asks Rachel Sloan

What if it would be possible that buildings transform CO^2 to O^2? asks Daniela Beerens

What if the envelope is designed to be folded open or closed? asks Shuquin Xu

What if the facade was electromagnetic? What if the building skin was edible? asks Prathiksha Chandra Mohan

What if glass could perform photosynthesis process? asks Ramya Pattanur Vasudevan

TRY THIS

Give your assignment – what you are asked to do – a twist by making something more of it.

SECTION 6:
PROBLEM SOLVING

49:
Problem Solvers, Definers and Identifiers

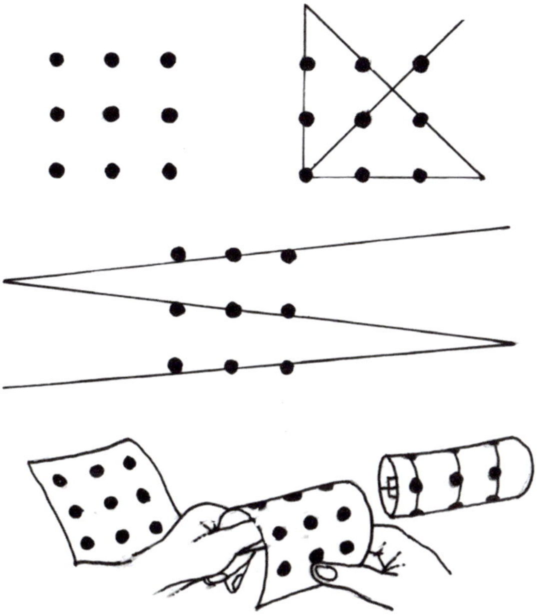

Fig 49.1: Presented with dots in a three-by-three grid, the Nine Dot Problem asks you to connect all nine dots – without lifting your pencil from the paper – using the fewest possible number of straight lines. Here are solutions for connecting the dots using four or three lines, and even one line – all by creatively interpreting the rules. Can you connect them using two lines? Email your solution to the author at info@randydeutsch.com

Architects are not only creative problem solvers but problem definers and identifiers.

Design requires and develops decision making and problem solving, both of which are important to everyday life.

Architects are primarily creative problem solvers and *More than just designers of buildings, architects are creative problem solvers* are clichés and a myth. Every professional is a problem solver. What is different is *how* architects solve problems – they do so iteratively.

What is also different is that architects don't just problem solve but also problem define and problem identify. They find what problems are worth solving.

All architects face and address problems that need to be solved. And a big part of being able to think like an architect requires one to be able to solve difficult design problems throughout the planning, design and construction process. Problem-solving stages include: define the problem; generate solutions; evaluate solutions; select a solution; and, make a plan.

Yet architects are also problem identifiers. Architects recognise that identifying the right problem to solve can be 80% of the solution. Often, the problem they have been assigned is not the one – or the most important or urgent one – that truly requires addressing. Architects work efficiently and effectively to make sure that everyone is focused on the most pressing, pertinent problem. In doing so, architects identify problems worth solving.

The problems architects address go well beyond the boundaries of a building. Today, they frequently include wicked problems – those intractable, hard-to-solve problems without an obvious solution. While solving building design problems architects may also be tackling important issues such as rising sea levels, affordable housing for displaced immigrants, and preparation for natural and manmade disasters.

Architects realise that even when the problems they address appear to be solved, there is often still more work to do. Sometimes the solution solves one problem but creates others. For example, architects may create more problems in terms of the environmental impact of a newly designed building. Sometimes the architect discovers that the solution solved the problem – but not in the way that they intended – and they need to learn from this experience. Are their solutions so comprehensive that they solve the entire problem – or only parts?

Instead of thinking of what they offer as solutions – which implies a level of completeness and finality that no one can be assured of – architects see what they contribute as a positive response to a problem. In this way, architecture is about change: where architects are problem responders and architecture a catalyst for change.[314]

This is all another way that architects express their intellectual humility and acknowledge their limitations.

There's no point in pretending problems are simpler than they are. Critical creative thinking and problem-solving necessitate a willingness to acknowledge both the problem's and outcome's inherent ambiguity, uncertainty and complexity. Doing so will lead to the discovery of fresh ideas and outcomes.[315]

TRY THIS

Reframe the problem, issue or question. Zoom out – place the problem into a larger context. Look at it from a different angle.

READ THIS

Problem Seeking: An Architectural Programming Primer by William Peña

50:
Iterative Process

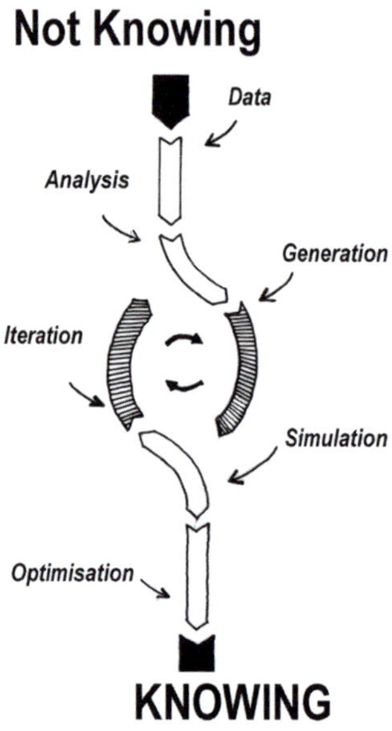

Fig 50.1: Everything the architect does takes them from a state of not knowing to knowing

Architects see the creative process not linearly or as a circle, but gradually moving forward as an iterative spiral.

Sitting in the sun, notebook in hand, looking at leaves and thinking of what inspired a recent design and led to a breakthrough, architect Nicholas Grimshaw explains that he is a collector of things – in his mind, where he stores impressions. He first composes in his mind before drawing on paper, then he closes his notebook and lets the idea simmer, and uses this time to think about the idea, then has another go at it.

Like a lot of architects, Nicholas Grimshaw sees the creative process as going around in circles, with the centre gradually moving forward: an iterative spiral. While doing searches out in different directions, it may feel as if you are going in circles, but you are progressing and the primary path is gradually moving forward.[316]

Beginning architecture students arrive with a predisposition for a linear thought process: they have an idea: then this happens, then this, and done. It is their first experience with the way one learns in studio and its culture of experimentation, and the non-linear, iterative process of design. The iterative process can trip up some students at first – with the understanding that your first idea isn't necessarily the best, and even once you think you've found a solution you continue to receive feedback and continue to evolve the design. It's the realisation and acceptance that architecture is not only a thing, but a process – an iterative process – that requires some creative destruction in order to be fully realised. As my academic colleague Associate Professor Emeritus Paul Armstrong has written, 'The iterative process of drawing or modeling, critiquing, and redrawing or remodeling is the fundamental pedagogical tool of architectural design education.'[317]

The iterative design process is more like a stair – a spiral stair – than a conveyor belt, and more like a spiral than a circle: you aren't just going around and around in circles, you are proceeding towards a resolution. In this way, the design process is cyclical, not linear: not cyclical as in a circle – spinning wheels – but more like a spiral, where you are receiving feedback in the form of analysis, working towards something. Architects think laterally – not linearly – and design is a process and outcome, cause and effect – where effect can become a new cause – requiring divergent and convergent thinking.[318]

Architect and professor Jonathan Ochshorn, when he designed and built a home extension explained his design process in terms of cause and effect. For example, at the start of the process, he points out that the site survey shows possible extension locations based on zoning, then describes the Cause: Decision to design and build an extension. Then, after looking at what he calls Options and Analysis (the extension can be placed on one of four sides of our site; west requires purchasing a neighbour's property (not possible); north garden is not big enough, etc.) leading to the Effect: Decision to design an extension on the east side of the house. Ochshorn does this – identifying cause, options and analysis, effect – for all the decisions that need to be made: Need more space; Decision to design extension on east side of house; Decision to design a floating slab foundation for the main block; and so on.[319]

51: Unravelling the Tangle

Fig 51.1: Situations that each architect confronts in the early stages of a project can be compared to a complex tangle that cannot be unravelled in a linear, methodological or systematic way

To remain open to experimentation and discovery architects try not to be attached to a specific outcome.

When Finnish architect Alvar Aalto faced an architectural obstacle that he found difficult to surmount he would attribute the burden to the fact that design presents the architect with contradictory information – social, human, economic and technical inputs that impact both individuals and larger groups of people – which is often in conflict. He likened this situation, a situation that each architect confronts in the early stages of a project, to a complex tangle that cannot be unravelled in any linear, methodological or systematic way.

So, he tried a different approach – one that Aalto compared to abstract art – where he took in all of the contradictory information and started to draw. Not in a technical or linear way, but by instinct, making drawings that he equated to childlike compositions. And as long as he continued to work in this instinctive, abstract way, a big idea gradually took shape, where the previous complex, conflicting and contradictory information now resulted in a harmonious resolution.[320]

How does this work? I experienced this many times in my career as an architect. On the one hand, the client has a commission for a new laboratory building and hands you a 1,500-page building programme containing a data entry point for every room, piece of equipment, and their ideal and less-than-ideal adjacencies. Add to this the need to deal with inputs and constraints including building codes, budgets, schedules, material and labour availability; the whole shebang. On the other hand, you are alone in a field, or what is now a car park, imagining what will go there and *yada yada* you arrive at a new building design with everything resolved. I have no explanation for how this works – it just does: as long as you trust the process.

Suggestions like *break the problem down into smaller parts* seem almost irrelevant. If I were to hand you a tangle of yarn and asked you to unravel it, *break the tangle down into individual strands of yarn* would be accurate, even obvious, but unhelpful. *How* exactly is this accomplished?

First – and this is required of every architect entrusted with a large, complex building design – trust that there is a solution. In other words, have confidence the 500-, 1,000- or 1,500-page building programme emphatically *will* result in a building more or less all will be happy with. Even with all the critical thinking in the world you cannot accomplish this near-superhuman feat unless you believe – i.e. envision – that you can do it. First believe, then synthesise.

Then do what Alvar Aalto did. Don't force a solution into a preconceived idea, but work with the information at hand – all of it – in an instinctive, slightly loose and abstract way. Gordon MacKenzie, author of *Orbiting the Giant Hairball,* said it best when he wrote, 'What is the biggest obstacle to creativity? Attachment to outcome. As soon as you become attached to a specific outcome, you feel compelled to control and manipulate what you're doing and, in the process, you shut yourself off to other possibilities. Creativity is not just about succeeding. It's about experimenting and discovering.'[321]

The perfectionism sometimes needed from architects – say, to detail a roof so it won't leak or design a stair to meet regulations and so people won't trip – won't help you here. Design is experimental – requiring more fuzzy logic than logic – until it isn't, then back and forth between fuzzy and pragmatic, unfocused and focused, dreaming and practical, until the tangle is untangled, and a building is born.

ASK THIS

WWLCD? (What would Le Corbusier do?) Louis Kahn? What would (fill in your favourite architect) do? A method suggested by Neil Durbach for a starting point in your thinking is to anticipate how various other people might solve the problem. This allows him to quickly produce and get out of the way more conventional solutions, resulting in his being able to work toward a more precise response to the problem. There are no shortcuts; it takes work to come up with ideas.[322] He considers this approach more of an editing process than a collaging process, less about adding things, than about taking away or editing out.

READ THIS

How to Make Sense of Any Mess: Information Architecture for Everybody by Abby Covert

52:
Synthesis and Meaning

Fig 52.1: Alejandro Aravena's Villa Verde, Chile. Half-houses can be completed later by their inhabitants when the time comes to add rooms and expand

Architects are synthesisers of social, functional, economic, environmental, technical and aesthetic factors.

Chilean architect Alejandro Aravena designs half-houses – one of his big ideas – making housing affordable by designing homes where half of the house is unfinished. His *half of a good house* projects, such as Villa Verde in Chile, can be completed later by their inhabitants when the time comes to add rooms and expand. One half is enclosed, while the other half remains incomplete, to be finished by homeowners. In this way Aravena solves a wicked problem – making housing affordable to more people – through design.

Man cannot live on analysis alone, as the architect's ultimate goal isn't to take things apart but to bring new things into being that look and feel as though they have always been there.

In their design process architects both analyse and synthesise, where to synthesise means to select, decide, make a choice, bring things to a conclusion, make sense of the mess, and work towards a solution.

Synthesis provides meaning in that, unlike analysis – which is associated with investigating, probing, and taking things apart – synthesis is about combining, merging and bringing together, creating at least the semblance of something complete, connected and whole.

We have seen that design involves both analysis and synthesis – back and forth, or in the case of Cesar Pelli, both at the same time[323] – where the two are required, however unpredictably,[324] back and forth in ever smaller cycles for creative thinking.

As we've discussed, the ability to simultaneously analyse and synthesise is a superpower that architects need years to develop. Roger Martin explained in *The Opposable Mind* that most people don't want a trade-off or either/or proposition, they want a synthesis.[325] And architects who build the capacity to live with the tension that comes with working towards a synthesis – to hold two contradictory ideas in their head at the same time and build from there, without caving or settling for a lesser solution, will benefit in the long run.

Making meaning is important, especially in a universe that doesn't automatically provide one. For, as Simon Unwin has said, along with language and mathematics – which correspondingly deal with words and numbers – architecture, which organises space into place, is one of the basic means we have to make sense of the world.[326]

Instead of accepting the world as random, with disconnected objects and people, architects look for ways to relate things together to create if not a cohesive whole, the semblance of one. Similarly, architects work with meaning in their projects by relating parts to the whole. They know that it is important for people to have meaning in their lives, that the g*enus loci* of a place ought to come through and be represented in architectural interventions, so it doesn't look like the project just landed on their site from outer space, but instead *belongs* there.

While creative thinking ultimately leads to a synthesis, it is a creative and some even say mysterious or alchemical process in which a mess – or, as we've been calling it, a *tangle* – is critically applied to a problem to produce an effective or optimal outcome for all concerned.[327]

For the architect, it is not enough to keep the building user in mind. Architects keep all in mind – paying client and non-paying client, the building user and the public at large. While they may make use of analysis and analytical tools, architects are entrusted to bring everything – and everyone – together in the end. It's in this way that they are considered synthesisers, where the resulting whole is always greater than the constituent parts. Architects transform analysis into synthesis, and in doing so, transform chaos into order, and hopelessness into something meaningful.

Architect Peter Wilson describes the act of synthesis in almost mystical terms. Working with the facts and as much information as he can find at the project start, Wilson commits all of it to memory until he intuitively understands it. Then he forgets it. And as if by chance, something catches his attention and by association he is able to give order and structure to what had been until then a bunch of parts. Doing the groundwork – of asking then answering what we have called *What is actual?* – is critical, as is an awareness that you are looking for something that will tie everything together.[328]

Don't take the ability to synthesise for granted – it is a rare and sought-after skillset. The ability to look at a mess and see how the disparate parts interconnect is a gift.

53:
Perseverance

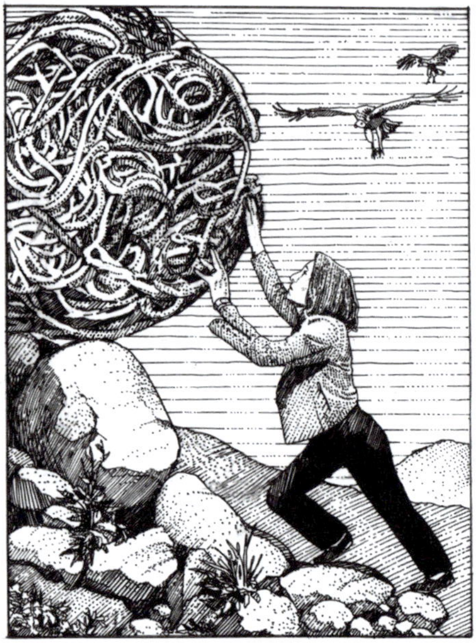

Fig 53.1: To persevere – like Sisyphus – architects must wake up each day to roll their tangle up the hill again

Architects require patience, resilience, perspective and above all perseverance for architecture to happen.

Imagine designing a building every day for three years. If in three years you designed 1,000 buildings, what would you have learned?

This is exactly what architect Will Alsop disciplined himself to do early in his career, to take himself well beyond what he knew and was capable of at that time.

This theoretical exercise helped him to evolve and grow as a creative designer, especially when he compared it with the two dozen or so buildings he would have designed in that same period of time had he not challenged himself with this exercise.[329]

Architects of course don't achieve what they set out to accomplish every time they design. Sometimes this occurs through no fault of their own – due to budget limitations or a fickle market – and other times due to a lack of curiosity or imagination. Like Sisyphus, they wake up the next day to roll their boulder up the hill again.

Buildings can be constructed seemingly overnight. Architecture, on the other hand, takes patience, resilience, perspective and above all perseverance on the part of the architect.

Our world today is designed for short attention spans and instant gratification, which makes it harder for people to do the hard work that doesn't have an immediate pay-off. Architecture – where buildings can take years to design and construct – requires the opposite of instant gratification. It requires *deep work,* or long, uninterrupted stretches of work that push you to your limits.

Once you have committed to architecture, everything you do – no matter how menial, inconsequential or tertiary – will matter to you and be enjoyable because you are working towards your longer-term goals.

It takes a determined and tenacious search for the architect to discover a design solution. And to achieve excellence in one's work requires not only talent and persistence in one's pursuit, but even an obsessive interest in the outcome.[330] While architects can make a good living practising architecture, most architects who persevere find that they do what they do for its own sake.[331] You find that you forego the flashier and more obvious perks for longer-term pay-offs of intrinsic rewards.

Albert Einstein once said, 'It's not that I'm so smart; it's just that I stay with problems longer.' Do what you do because you like it. If you do, you will persevere.

Trust the process

There will be times when you don't feel like the project is advancing, or that you are making progress. Don't despair. Sometimes we cannot see the progress we are making – it comes about gradually or is occurring under the surface. You may find during times when it seems like things are not advancing you have the most profound thinking. It is especially when things seem stagnant that it is most important to be persistent, to persevere – however uncomfortable it might feel. You have to trust that it is part of the process and you will be rewarded.[332] Get comfortable being uncomfortable. Learn how to *stay.*

That said, be easy on and patient with yourself. We are all works in progress. One outcome of the fact that most architects don't peak until their fifties is that there's time to learn how to do this. It becomes easier when you commit, when you are in it for the long haul.

Daniel Libeskind's Jewish Museum in Berlin took over a decade to come from design competition to plan to fruition, and his plan for the Ground Zero reconstruction took similarly long. Libeskind attributes his ability to maintain his patience and motivation to remaining positive, developing a thick skin and not falling into the trap of becoming cynical. You can't just go through the motions but have to have patience and believe in what you are doing.[333] Play the long game. China is producing students with some of the strongest critical thinking skills in the world, with studies showing Chinese students outperforming their global peers in reading, maths and science. But a new study by researchers at Stanford University found that Chinese students lose their advantage in critical thinking in college. That is, they excel at critical thinking until college, showing no improvement while their American and Russian counterparts did show improvement. The cause is attributed to exhaustion coupled with a lack of incentive to improve once in college.[334]

This speaks to the importance of gestation, incubation, scheduling down time, and giving the problem time to solve itself; time for the brain to do its magic; the importance of sticking with and not abandoning a problem before it has a chance to resolve itself.

TRY THIS

People who persevere do so because they aren't attached to the results. They don't get burned out by their efforts because they are not attached to the outcome. I used to wake up every day and say *I am grateful that I have a job where I get to design* – and I was happy nearly every day of my twenty-five-year career designing buildings. Others would say *I will be happy if my project gets built.* Many of them got burned out and left the field. The difference was that the first was ultimately in my control, while the second put their happiness in the hands of others or even chance. A lot of factors go into whether a project gets built or not, often beyond any one person's control.

TRY THIS

Architecture is not a sprint but a marathon. Recognise that down time is important to ensure focus, to recover, to restore energy, to build up the willpower that is depleted from the moment you awaken.

TRY THIS

Push for the third third! As we've seen, the best idea is often not the first idea. One incentive for not giving in or giving up too quickly – for example in the first third of the process, and for sticking with it when creative problem solving, is that the best ideas often come later in the process, in what Tim Hurson calls the *third third*.[335] By persevering, there's a benefit in that you achieve a deeper level understanding and insight, but also a challenge, in that it takes time and effort to persevere.

READ THIS

Working by Robert Caro. It is hard not to be impressed and inspired by the biographer's phenomenal patience, stamina and perseverance, and you learn about what went into the writing of his Pulitzer Prize-winning biographies. Better yet, listen to Caro read it.

54:
Impact of Technology

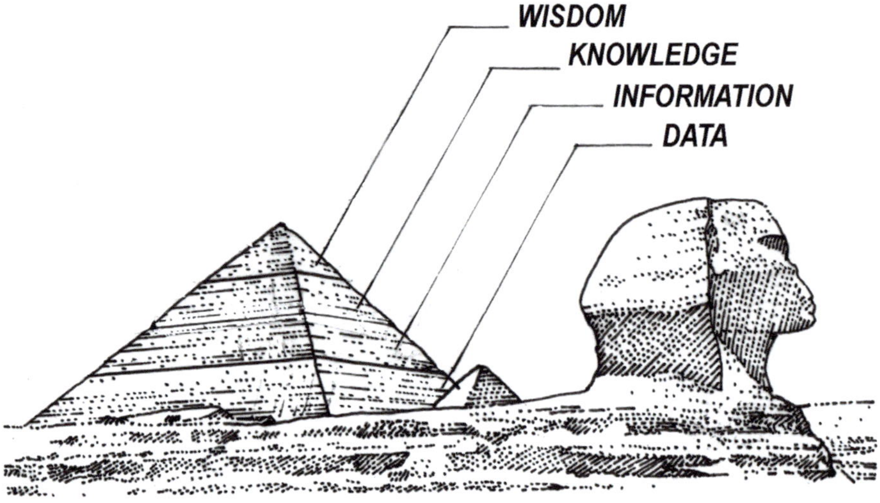

Fig 54.1: DIKW pyramid

Architects think critically and creatively without technology, and should be able to do so even more assuredly and quickly with it.

At the start of the semester, I ask my students to measure a house. I have them form teams of two and do this using a tape measure. Then I have them do it again – this time using a laser distance meter, with an app that measures spaces using the phone camera, or with an app that measures and then draws the spaces for you. I do this to show them that there are many ways to measure a room; why they should use one method over another; the importance of being aware of different options; to always be growing and progressing; and to always ask: *Is there a better way to do this?*

What is the one fundamental skill architects need in the twenty-first century? What is the one skill you'll need as an architect? Should we learn to code? Not necessarily.

First, I tell architects, learn to *think.*

Yes, some familiarity with coding could be helpful. But more important than learning any specific tool is to learn to think more generally.[336]

Architect, professor and writer Witold Rybczynski recalls a time when analogue tools such as hand drafting and model building allowed the architect sufficient time to think. 'The fierce productivity of the computer carries a price – more time at the keyboard, less time thinking.'[337]

Much has been written on how first the computer and now the internet have changed the way we think, and on whether anyone benefits from this change. And thinking *has* changed.

Thinking has changed due to working with computers, but also due to the almost constant distraction of shiny new toys like video games and VR headsets that arguably make it even more difficult to truly think.[338] The bottom line is that we ought to be able to think critically and creatively without technology, and even more assuredly and quickly with it.

When the computer is used as a substitute for thinking

Architectural historian and critic Mario Carpo has said that digital technologies 'are no longer the tools for making: they are primarily tools for thinking'.[339] This is an important distinction, especially as architecture has leveraged technology for other uses such as form-making, communication, construction and building performance. There is a fear that, by letting the computer do the thinking for us, it makes us lazy – *just google it.* In architecture, we have seen how the rise of CAD, BIM and various modelling tools have atrophied the ability to hand-draw. Where due to our modelling tools there are fewer people today who can visualise in their mind. One can only wonder what other abilities we currently possess will atrophy with the introduction of even newer tools. Even the way we use language has changed *because internet.*[340]

Soon AI and generative AI tools will help architects expand their human cognitive capabilities, and machine learning will augment the architect–client relationship by providing additional insight. But they will be no substitute for what the architect can contribute, offer and provide to the design process. We have a tendency to blame technology for all of our shortcomings – including our inability to think creatively. So instead of abdicating what architects do to machines, a better use of our time and energy would be for architects to focus on what they do best – while enabling our technology to do what it does best.

This will be the case because a lot of our decisions will be based on data, with companies rewarding employees who leverage data – and think regarding data[341] – when working in BIM and other tools. But outcomes are only as good as the data we put into our models, so making sure the data we use is compatible will be important. But more important will be our ability to think – and to ask questions of the data: starting with what it will be used for, and why.

In the midst of recent advances in data analytics, artificial intelligence and other technologies, it is important for architects to not just turn everything over to machines but to rely on their own reasoning[342] and especially their creative thinking ability. The human brain is just too powerful and valuable to carry out routine acts. Instead it should be used for creative thinking.

TRY THIS

Architects will need to do something to differentiate themselves from those who purport to provide similar services in less time, at lower cost. They also will need to differentiate themselves from each other. Add to this the very real possibility that they will need to differentiate themselves from computers, machines, robots and algorithms. As this book argues, architects differentiate themselves by learning how to think critically, creatively and (in the next section) collaboratively when problem solving. As we increasingly rely on machines to carry out basic tasks, *thinking* will give architects the advantage.[343] In the section on critical collaborative thinking, we'll discuss how the most reliable outcomes can be achieved when computers and humans work collaboratively, assigning tasks based on each other's strengths.

TRY THIS

Tools for thought. Architects have tools for drawing and modelling that help them design and document. Why can't they have tools that augment human intelligence and help them think? What tools, you ask? They're called books. But unfortunately, like hand sketching, they too have fallen out of favour.

ASK THIS

New autonomous design tools are emerging that aim to automate much of the design and documentation processes, enabling architects to speedily and effortlessly configure working and living spaces in the early design stages to increase efficiency and productivity, saving time and money. Are the tasks that the autonomous design tools replace so repetitive and tedious that they ought to be given over to algorithms to complete? If these new tools are able to lay out efficient floor plans, should architects be relegated to designing building enclosures? For places where people live, do the tools prioritise decision making in terms of affordability?[344]

ASK THIS

Moving ahead, the important question will be: Will architects be able to integrate and balance the combined advantages of human and artificial intelligence?

READ THIS

The Death of Drawing: Architecture in the Age of Simulation by David Ross Scheer

55: Detangling Wicked Problems

Fig 55.1: Ole Shereen's Interlace

Architects should apply their unique way of thinking not only to buildings but to challenges facing society such as poverty, inequality and segregation.

You're interviewing for a job and your prospective employer asks you: 'How many piano tuners are there in Chicago?'[345] They are not being cruel – they want to know how you think in action.

While the topic of wicked problems is covered in this book's introduction, it is such an important topic for those who hope to think like an architect that it is worth revisiting.

More than a half century ago, Nobel laureate physicist Enrico Fermi would dare his University of Chicago students to estimate absurd quantities without looking anything up. Perhaps the best-known 'Fermi question' was to estimate the number of piano tuners in Chicago.[346]

As for the interview question, no one expects you, architect or otherwise, to know any statistics about piano tuners. Googling the answer isn't the point (and besides, there is no answer to be found).[347]

The interviewer just wants to know how you think. And how *you* think – if not yet, then by the end of this book – is like an architect.

Fig 55.2: Wicked problems are easier to detangle when we involve others

Definition of a wicked problem

About twenty or thirty years after Fermi came up with his questions, two professors – Horst Rittel and Melvin Webber – divided all important problems into two categories: Tame or Wicked. The main difference is that tame problems can be solved while wicked problems have no obvious solution.[348] They identified essential characteristics of wicked problems: every wicked problem is unique; they have no agreed-on definition; they have no single, correct solution; no solution is right or wrong, but only bad, good, better, best; there is no rule for knowing when to stop working on them; and, they can never be truly 'solved'.[349] They're also problems that are created and exacerbated by people.

TRY THIS

Apply your education and training to the challenges of society: global issues such as crime, sanitation, housing shortage, traffic, waste, migration and pollution. Extract lessons from your most recent projects that go beyond them. By offering viable, actionable suggestions – or better yet, solutions – aim to go beyond conscience-clearing good intentions and go for real world results. For example, by 2030 it is thought that five billion people, many in extreme poverty, will live in cities, and currently there isn't adequate housing. Architects can respond by coming up with affordable housing models, such as a portable housing shelter.

ASK THIS

Would it be over-reaching if we were to ask architecture to help us solve real-world issues? Can thinking like an architect help the world contend with and ultimately find solutions to tangible issues that affect everyone, such as inequality, migration and climate change? As Olivia Butcher has asked, 'is it arrogant to even ask: can architects succeed where others have struggled or even failed?'[350] Pritzker Prize-winning architect Alejandro Aravena believes we should encourage architecture students to apply what they learn in school to challenges facing society.[351] A contrarian take would be that architects over-reach when they claim physical buildings can address and solve social problems. But what about architects themselves? Can the thinking tools employed by designers of buildings be applied to solve the most intractable, wicked problems felt in the world today?[352]

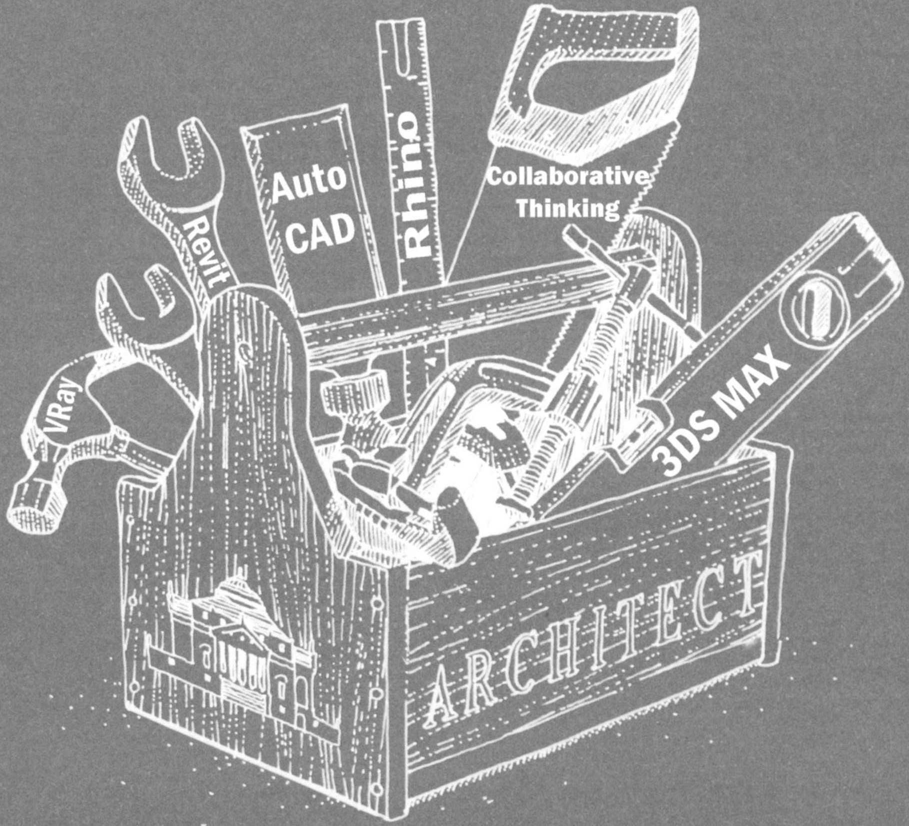

Fig 56.0: Collaborative thinking as a go-to tool in your toolbox

PART III: CRITICAL COLLABORATIVE THINKING

Architects work collaboratively. Buildings are too complex for any one architect to know everything. Thinking collaboratively, they know which experts to go to for answers. Architects have *intellectual humility* and know they are not, nor can ever be, experts at everything. In fact, architects know that their real superpower is their curiosity; the fact that they know a little about a lot of things. It is because of this that they know who to have in the room, on Skype or on the phone, to chime in when the time comes with their expertise. Architects are expert coordinators. They think of others, and ask: who needs this information, and how does it jive with what we have heard so far? Able to see the big picture, the architect is best placed to orchestrate the whole.

SECTION 7: CRITICAL COLLABORATIVE THINKING

56: Critical Collaborative Thinking

Fig 56.1: The game of exquisite corpse leads to the creation of a disjointed building in lieu of a unified synthesis. The same thing happens when we cooperate but do not collaborate

To achieve the architects' social contract to make life better it helps to work with others.

Why work with others? Why not just do everything yourself? When projects are large and complex, no one architect can know everything that goes into designing and realising the building. It serves as an ideal case for collaborative thinking and decision making, requiring people to make decisions together. Are decisions made together better? Are they more likely to stick? Often, yes – but, as with most things, it depends on the circumstances. Project size is one circumstance that necessitates a collaborative effort.

In addition to when problems become more complex and buildings become larger, other reasons to think collaboratively include when it helps to have a diversity of opinions, insights or inputs – for example to avoid cultural blindness, and gender or age bias; to see problems from different angles and point of view, as you strive to understand the context in which you will be building. Especially today, buildings are too complex to do alone. They require large teams made up of lots of players from many trades and backgrounds. Architects reach out into their network to identify who can best address the problems at hand.

As architecture requires the involvement of many people, it's likely that as you enter practice you will be collaborating with a wide range of professionals, and that the need for you to be able to collaborate effectively will become more important over time. The architect working on collaborative teams has implications for education. Recently, more than 80% of architects rated collaboration with stakeholders as important/critical, yet fewer than half that many, only 31.5% of interns and recently licensed architects, indicated that they had performed collaboratively prior to completion of their education programme.[353] With 10,000 decisions going into every building design, you can't be expected to know everything – especially with buildings becoming more complex. That's one reason why we turn to others.

I have a rule in studio: only draw what you know. Don't draw what you don't know. It will come back to bite you. It is clear that this last student didn't follow this rule. Ask questions if you don't know something – or, better yet, have a classmate look at what you are planning on presenting well before the pin-up. While most tutors want students to do their own work, in its most fundamental form, this is what collaboration can do for you: provide you with another pair of eyes.

Can collaborative thinking be abused? Sure. For example, when a student goes from tutor to tutor, student to student, asking each for their input, not stopping to evaluate their feedback – not stopping at all – just asking until they hear what they want to hear: a case where collaborating is really just looking for praise or consensus, and design becomes a numbers game. People are social animals, and architects have what Will Alsop referred to as an architect's social contract to make life better.[354]

Why is collaboration important? You'll soon be entering a quickly transforming, global design practice environment, one where emerging technologies are enabling – and a world increasingly in environmental, economic, and societal crisis that requires collaboration.[355]

Not everyone who says they collaborate, collaborates. Look at just about every architecture firm's website; most say they are collaborative. They can mean a lot of different things by this: think of it as a continuum with, on the far left end, corruption, conflict and conspiracy, and on the far right cooperation, collaboration and chaos, with a gradation of competition, conversation, communication, community and coordination between.

The important thing is for you to think of collaborating – the ability to work well with others, and engage in teamwork and consensus decision making – as just another tool in your toolbox. Collaborate when you need alignment; when the solution isn't straightforward and obvious; when it isn't a distraction from getting the job done.

That's not to say that collaboration doesn't have its challenges. For starters, collaboration is hard and takes time – to build relationships, to clear up misunderstandings, to listen and to get things done; it can be experienced as challenging when you are first starting out. On large teams especially, beware of 'social loafing' – the tendency to abdicate responsibility when there are others who can do the heavy lifting. It's easy to underperform on large teams, especially when roles are blurred or ill-defined and it is unclear what role you are supposed to perform.

Among the top obstacles to successful collaboration, for many collaboration means compromise, resulting in watered-down design – a product of groupthink, a race towards the lowest common denominator – and they have difficulty connecting the development of collaboration abilities with desired design outcomes, let alone design excellence and the contribution of one's design ideas in relation to the overall project.[356] The fear in collaborating is that we and our work will be mediocre. For a designer whose singular voice is their expression through their work, collaboration is equated with joint authorship – to some the antithesis of creative expression, muddying the message of the work, dispersing and diluting the voice and design intent of the creator. This thinking is of course mistaken, as leaders need to make clear. One only needs to compare a Beatles' tune with any of the band members' solo efforts to recognise that teams make better decisions – and importantly, achieve better results – than individuals.[357] Collaboration can be time-consuming and resource-intensive.

In addition to challenges, there are benefits to collaborating. Collaboration helps build consensus – by getting everyone on board – and envisions the problem from multiple points of view, and at its best it engages a diversity of problem solvers. By *not* collaborating, architects become marginalised, and not knowing how to effectively collaborate could lead to your irrelevance.

There's one way in which being a relative newcomer to the field can be seen as an advantage: with little or no past experience you also don't have a lot of the mental baggage that can hold teams back, and one of the barriers to collaboration remains organisational silos.

There's an alchemy to working with others. Where – as with the Beatles' lead songwriters – two are better than one. Where 'the alchemy of collaboration does not merge the two authors into a single voice but rather proliferates them to create the chorus of a multitude'.[358] To collaborate you have to be more focused on the outcome than on who gets credit for what. In the best collaborations it's hard to tell who did what: that is why the songwriting credit is shared for most Beatles' compositions, reading Lennon–McCartney.

TRY THIS

At some point when you are presenting your work in your portfolio, the prospective employer wants to hear you use *we* more than *I*.

TRY THIS

The image of the individual architect working independently is largely a myth. That said, architects tend to be independent types – to a fault. During the global economic downturn of 2008, 30% of architects in the US lost their jobs. Adding insult to injury, most architects didn't help each other during this trying time: instead, it was mostly every person for themselves. Therefore, be the architecture student or emerging professional who looks out for others.

TRY THIS

Become acquainted with the disciplines related to the architect: landscape architects; structural engineers; mechanical, electrical and plumbing (MEP) engineers; civil engineers; conveyancing solicitors; estate agents – the list goes on. Introduce yourself to people in these related professions, tell them where you are in your academic or professional career, and request an informational interview over coffee or lunch. Most will be more than willing to help out a fledgling architect at the beginning of their career.

READ THIS

Idea Work by the Scandinavian architecture firm Snøhetta about activities concerned with generating, selecting, realising, nurturing, sharing, materialising, pitching and communicating ideas in organisations. The book features ten patterns or qualities identified as being present in extraordinary idea work.[359]

57: Communicating with Non-Architects

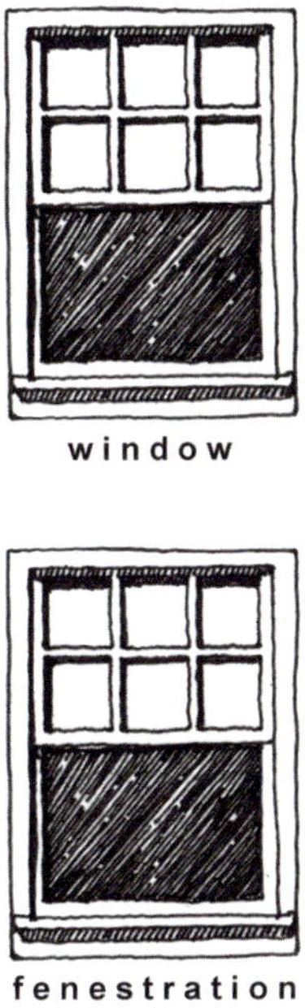

Fig 57.1: Calling a window a window requires architects to consider their audience

Life experiences prior to becoming an architect should be used and considered a strength.

Architecture students and architects too split their lives into two phases: before architecture school and after, where the experience prior is discounted or altogether ignored. There is value in the experience of students prior to entering architecture school. Architects design for non-architects, so since architecture students are still non-architects themselves, they will never be able to relate to a project's users more than they do now.

In other words, you are not a blank slate. You bring with you your life experiences, and these should be considered a strength, as opposed to seeing yourself as a tabula rasa with no beliefs or prejudices except those that must be wiped clean before real learning can begin.

Communication is a social act. Learning to communicate with non-architects goes beyond saying 'window' when you think *fenestration.* To communicate with others requires a sincere interest in others. Communicating well requires empathising with those you are trying to reach: actively listening and speaking in terms of their interests and concerns.

And even when we do communicate, how can we be sure what we said has been heard? True communication has four steps. You haven't communicated until you've spoken, they've heard and said what you said back to you in their own words, and you've heard them. Anything short of that is just talking to – or worse, at – each other. It isn't communicating if they aren't listening, if they or you are multitasking, if they aren't figuratively or literally looking into your eyes when you talk.

How do you talk to your client when your client is your tutor? To get buy-in from your tutor, go over what you spoke about last time. It is your idea – not theirs – but you still need to sell them on it. Here's how: *I looked at the suggestion you made. I didn't like it* (it didn't achieve x, y and z).

Be prepared. Anticipate questions and reasonable objections. You don't have to be a know-it-all. (I *knew* you were going to say that!) Just behave *as if.* As if they will respond a certain way (based on past behaviour and what you know about them). Don't worry about pleasing them – your tutor is your biggest champion. They will write recommendation letters on your behalf. They will nominate you for awards. They will stand up for your design.[360]

TRY THIS

When presenting your idea, represent both sides. People will be more convinced of your idea if you mention that you thought of the negative consequences or thought of alternative approaches.

TRY THIS

Practise adaptability. Practise resilience. Learn how to take feedback. It's not personal. It's business. Even in school! Stay on topic. It's not you against them. Work with them. You are defending your design – not yourself. Communicate to others how they have arrived at their solution. Criticism isn't a personal attack. They are looking out for your best interests. Act as though this were true. There's a place for poetry. For the ineffable. Avoid tangents. Stay focused. Be completely present. As Pritzker Prize-winning architect Alejandro Aravena advises, 'architects need to understand people and places and be able to read between the lines. Communication is only 90 per cent verbal – we need to be face to face to fully communicate. We have access to sophisticated technology but it's completely mismatched to the primitive emotions humans have been dealing with for millennia; fear, desire, love and envy.'[361]

58:
Diverse Points of View

Fig 58.1: People think differently from one another, and architects benefit when they collaborate by filling in blind spots and overcoming weaknesses

Architects design with others in mind.

The architect draws a building facade – an image turning the object over (in their mind, or on their work surface) to see what it would look like from another angle or on a different side of the building. This requires spatial intelligence – something architects possess. Architects will turn their drawings upside down to see from another perspective or another point of view (POV), to shake up their complacency, to not be so attached to one POV, because they know that their POV is only half of the equation. Architecture students in particular develop a critical consciousness for design when they extend their POV even larger by considering historical, economic, social, cultural or political contexts for their designs.[362]

Architects design with others in mind, and this mindset extends to *the way* they design. The importance of inviting different voices to work on diverse teams – and not being on teams made up of people just like yourself, where each brings something of value to the team and the project stems from the need to consider other sides and diversity in every dimension: race, gender, nationality, company size, industry and role. People think differently from one another, and we benefit when we collaborate with them by filling in our blind spots and overcoming weaknesses.

So where to start? While the architecture profession itself is famously undiversified, those who make up most architecture school student bodies are often quite diverse, as students come from different parts of the world and some from non-architectural backgrounds.

TRY THIS

While nobody likes to have their design criticised, in the spirit of science, ask for feedback. You want to know if your idea is any good, and the sooner the better.

TRY THIS

To start a collaboration, look for mutual interests. Consider meeting to discuss a book or film you all enjoy, or start a reading group to learn more about a topic you mutually care about. Pay attention to how you benefit from a diverse set of sources of information, insight and inspiration relative to each other's backgrounds.

ASK THIS

Are there students on your course previously from different subjects? What insights do they bring? Can you suggest an interdisciplinary exchange, where students or tutors from other courses critique your work, and vice versa? Come to appreciate why studio culture – working together in studio, keeping your headphones off so you can engage with and share ideas, spontaneously explaining your project to others when they ask, receiving impromptu feedback – is so valuable for your academic, professional and personal growth. Consider how you might benefit from reaching out and getting to know and understand each other.

59: Solving Wicked Problems With Collaboration

Fig 59.1: Wicked problems are found whenever people try to make the world better

Because they are comfortable with ambiguity and uncertainty, architects are ideally suited to solving wicked problems with others.

As discussed in the introduction and the last section, wicked problems (problems that have no single, definitive solution) and tame problems (which, well, do) are two types of problems that architects address. If the problem is tame then the architect can DIY and consider it done. If the problem is wicked – if the building is unique or complex, or the issues associated with it difficult to solve, for example due to climate change or lack of affordable housing – then the architect will need to bring others in to help solve it via a transdisciplinary team.

Even interior design projects face intractable, hard-to-solve problems. Open office plans are intended to encourage spontaneous collaboration, but most evidence suggests they accomplish the exact opposite: they are noisy, distracting and lead to lower productivity. Now, with the pandemic, they may increase the possible spread of the virus.

In other words, wicked problems are found whenever people engage with the world and try to make it better, for example by asking: How to address inevitable density in cities without resorting to high-rises? How to design high-rises so that they are people-friendly? How to address millions displaced by immigration and crises? How to design for rising sea levels due to climate change? How to convince others that climate change is real and worth paying to ameliorate?

How, in other words, to approach deep and complex problems not simplistically, but in deep and complex ways? And applying rational thought and technology or working harder and longer won't solve them: only working smarter. And one way for the architect to work smarter is by engaging with others, which brings to the design process new viewpoints, skills, insights – increasing the odds that the problem will be solved. What will solve wicked problems in the future is arming a critical mass of people with the ability to think like an architect.

There has been talk of bringing back the Renaissance idea of the architect as the master builder. But with buildings becoming more complex, the possibility that any single individual can tackle wicked problems has passed. Other options include master builder teams,[363] allowing machines themselves to be master builders, and collaborating with technology. At one time the best chess *player* in the world was a couple of teenagers and a laptop – people working side by side with machines. It's best to prepare for a world where technology is complementing rather than substituting people.

TRY THIS

Start by identifying tame and wicked problems. In architectural education, your tutors could help by, instead of offering increasingly complex projects throughout the course, offering a continuum of projects from tame to wicked. Architects like Ole Scheeren purposely choose larger wicked problems to tackle rather than only addressing and solving the client's assignment or needs. This is because architects try to progress with each project, to improve on what came before, but also to address those not represented at the table: the public at large, the users, the neighbours and future generations. It's not that architects need to take tame projects and make them wicked, or that architects need to turn every project into a wicked problem. It's that architects, because of their social contract to make the world better, look for opportunities to make something more than the narrow assignment they have been given. Because they are comfortable with ambiguity and uncertainty – a transferable skill – architects are ideally suited to address and attempt to solve wicked problems with others.

60:
Intuition and Collaboration

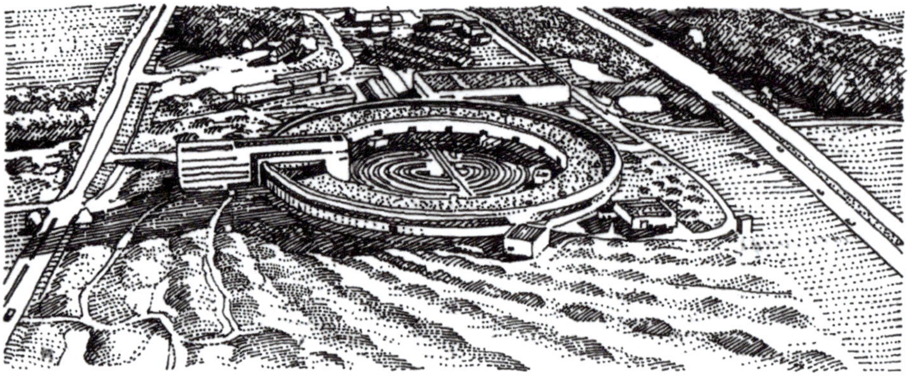

Fig 60.1: Snøhetta MAX IV Laboratory in Lund, Sweden

Architects rely on their intuition to make design decisions; it turns out, so do the best teams.

It could have been a wall. The MAX IV Laboratory in Lund, Sweden was built near a highway which created unwanted ground vibrations that had a negative impact on lab experiments. Snøhetta were hired, and instead of a wall they came up with several solutions, settling on a landscape in the form of a wave field. Maya Lin had created a sculptural wave field in North America, but the one Snøhetta proposed was different. Using computational design tools, their wave field was designed to model the effects of the vibrations. But that's not all: their wave field absorbs vibrations while creating public space, a constructed meadowland that also captures stormwater. And best of all, to build this landscape Snøhetta uploaded the 3D model directly into the GPS system that then guided bulldozers to carve out the shapes.

Architects rely a great deal on their intuition to make design decisions. But what role, if any, does intuition have on teams?

First, it is important to recognise that intuition is private, so its role in collaborative efforts is put into question. It doesn't help if, when working on a collaborative team, your gut tells you to go in a certain design direction. You need to articulate your intuitive feeling in terms others can understand and be persuaded by.

What about collaborative teams? Could a team be said to possess intuition? Some teams who have worked for many years together – teams who have shared experiences and access to information – might answer in the affirmative. You only have to look as far as the name of Snøhetta's most recent monograph, *Collective Intuition.*

An architect who works everything out in their head, who considers drawing a waste of time and resources – as opposed to communicating their thoughts in words and sketches – would have to consider a more social means of working when working on a team. Working in one's head precludes a collaborative process, rendering it opaque.

When collaborating, architectural thoughts can be personal, but not isolating. To think like an architect on a team means, as in the case of Snøhetta, to think collectively; where creativity isn't the province of the few but the purview of the many, and where working collaboratively isn't a sometimes thing but daily habit.[364] Where intuition has a place, not in the privileged but in the collective.

SECTION 8: THINKING WITH OTHERS

61:
Thinking Like Others

Fig 61.1: It is unlikely that everyone is thinking what you're thinking

Architects think like others to be more observant while avoiding the pitfalls of drawing faulty conclusions.

As important as it is to think like an architect, it is equally important for the architect to think like others: to speak in terms they can understand; to understand how your idea applies to them; to empathise with their situation and circumstances. To think like others means to be more observant while avoiding the pitfalls of drawing faulty conclusions.

To put yourself in others' shoes, you have to feel empathy, and consider how people will experience and use the spaces you design or propose.

How can you know for certain what people want? You can ask or interview them. Some say that focus groups and user interviews don't work for innovation. Ford Motor Company founder Henry Ford famously said, 'If I had asked people what they wanted, they would have said faster horses.' That said, there is always something to be gained by listening.

For the same reasons you want to think like an architect, you want to think like others. To prepare for an exam it helps to think like the tutor, right? What advantages would this give you?

This is one reason why taking non-architectural courses is so important: in addition to what you learn and are exposed to, these courses help you think like others outside the industry. This also applies to joining organisations outside your field. Thinking like others helps you to develop what is referred to as an outward orientation or mindset[365] that will serve you well in both your career and your personal life.

Architects can lead collaborative teams by thinking like other team members, anticipating their concerns and questions before they arise. Architects see through others' eyes; they empathise with and understand what is important to others. In trying to predict the consequences of any course of action, the architect needs to anticipate the responses of each of the integrated team members. To do this, an architect must know enough about each discipline to negotiate and synthesise competing demands. Architects don't need to be plumbing or electrical contractors, but they ought to be aware of what these entities do and the services they provide.

TRY THIS

You have the ability to think like others. Ask yourself: What will my tutor think? What will the structural engineer think? The MEP consultant? How would someone who does maintenance feel about my creating an all-glass facade? Anticipate what others will think, including their objections. You could ask them – but if you have imagination and empathy you can imagine their responses – and adjust your message accordingly.

TRY THIS

To think like others, get your hands on every *Think Like a _________* book. There are hundreds: some general – *Think Like an Artist, Think Like a Fish* – while others are more specific – *Think like a Graphic Artist, Think Like a Bass.* There are books that will teach you how to think like a game designer or to how to think like a venture capitalist or a horse. I read these types of books early in my career (OK, not the ones about fish or horses) because I wanted to understand how others thought so I might understand how I thought. So I could communicate better with others – speak in terms they understood – and to see if maybe there was some insight I might glean that could help me become a better architect.

TRY THIS

To better understand why some people think differently from you, deliberately read an essay, interview or book by someone with ideas or viewpoints diametrically opposed to your own. As futurist David Zach suggests, think into other boxes without abandoning your own (which you probably invested a lot of time and money in to build).

62:
Collective Intelligence

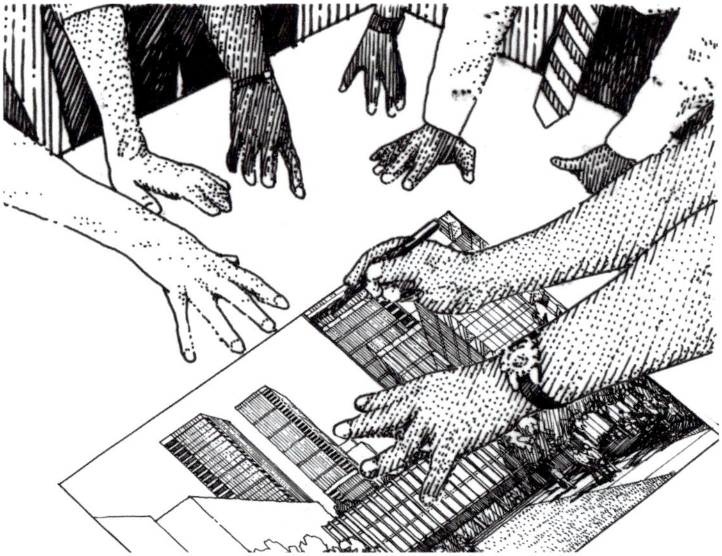

Fig 62.1: No single individual can fully grasp all that goes into a building project

Project teams possess a collective intelligence above and beyond the intelligence of the individual architect.

It has been suggested that an ant colony possesses memories that its individual members don't have, where memory itself is considered the result of collective action.[366] Buildings are becoming increasingly complex with more people involved, more demanding construction systems, budgets and schedules, and stricter performance goals. We have reached a point where no single individual can fully grasp all that goes into a building project. Window walls, roofing and other building parts have become areas of specialisation requiring the input of consultants. Buildings of any but the smallest size or scope today require the collective intelligence of the many.

This kind of collective thinking is what a firm like Snøhetta – a firm where thinking, intelligence, and knowledge are social – does especially well; not on selective projects, but daily, in everything they do.[367] One wonders whether an organisation such as Snøhetta, which works as a collective, could – like the ants – be said to possess memories that its individual firm members don't have? Or project teams whose collective intelligence can be thought of as being above and beyond the intelligence of each individual team member.

Architect Daniel Libeskind describes his creative process in similar terms – where he starts by immersing himself into the project site, picking up or internalising on an intuitive level the history of the place and what he refers to as *invisible wavelengths.* The resulting concept for Libeskind isn't something that can at first be put into words, but emerges from his immersion and can only be realised in form.[368] But how can such a personal and intuitive approach involve other people? At what point does Libeskind bring other people into the process? He brings others into the design process once the nascent design – not yet a building – starts to take shape. Other architects have the core team present before so much as starting the design process.

We live, work and go to school in a culture that celebrates individual talent over that of collaborative teams. Few architects have been the focus of laudatory media coverage over the past decade more than Jeanne Gang of Studio Gang Architects – yet she is the first person who will point out the team effort required on complex projects. For Chicago's Vista Tower, Gang and her firm have what she refers to as a symbiotic relationship with bKL Architecture, working together throughout to make the building design a reality. While these firms are mentioned the most frequently in the media, literally hundreds of teams – including thirty consultants – from various industries have been involved in the project: a true collective.

TRY THIS

Make your next project a group project instead of a solo assignment. If you carefully pair yourself with another student so that you symbiotically learn from each other, you'll end up learning not only about design, but how individuals work together, while developing necessary interpersonal skills.

TRY THIS

A rookie mistake is to have a DIY mindset. You work on a team begrudgingly, you give lip-service to input from others, and you go to others when you need something – but you don't add to the gestalt or overall work or project. Instead, think of collaboration as supplementing your weaknesses. You are expected to have weaknesses, as you are still only starting out. Why not make use of the input of those around you? Think of collaboration – whether collaborating with people or machines – as bigger thinking. This bigger mind has the potential to solve increasingly complex design assignments. Work on developing a collaboration mindset. It's different from you working among others; on truly collaborative teams, the dynamic changes; the roles and titles blur.

TRY THIS

You are responsible for your own creative output. Your tutor on the other hand is trying to manage the creative output of others – you and your classmates – which is even more difficult. Your tutor has had to master the transition from maker to manager, with a goal of managing consistent, systematised output from an unpredictable design process. No one knows for certain what will result from a design studio assignment: not you, not your tutor. The secret? Leading by influence, not by direct control. Some have likened managing architects to herding cats or even tigers.[369]

ASK THIS

The single most important issue confronting architecture, engineering and construction (AEC) leadership is, as MIT research fellow and author Michael Schrage asked, how to pose problems and opportunities in forms that will elicit and inspire a collaborative response. Consider reframing questions so that they lead to responses that engage the intelligence of the collective.

63:
Impact of Culture

Fig 63.1: Given the complex issues architects will face in the years ahead, you want to attend a school, take classes and work in firms that encourage collaboration when appropriate

Architects strive to build, learn and work in cultures that support collaborative problem solving.

Architecture is of course part of a culture and a particular time and place, and the individuals who participate in its design and making contribute to its culture. Used slightly differently, the culture of a place – a school, an architecture firm – is sometimes referred to as the way we do things around here, and it can have an outsize impact on whether and how well people collaborate.

If you attend a school or work at a firm that places greater importance on competition, and on individual rather than team performance, it can be an uphill battle to get the support and encouragement you need to develop cooperatively at a team member, and to find opportunities to work together while building your interpersonal skills. Given the complex issues architects will face in the years ahead, you want to attend a school, take classes and work in firms that encourage collaboration when appropriate.

Asking relevant questions, from an attitude of respect and curiosity, requires critical collaborative thinking, and is the basis for building trusting relationships. Trust facilitates better task-related communication, thereby ensuring collaboration not only to complete the assignment but also to make sure all constituents and stakeholders are represented. Question asking is especially important for complex problems like those that architects face, that cannot be solved by solitary designers.

TRY THIS

There is a stigma attached to students and emerging professionals who ask questions. Does asking a question imply that they are ignorant and don't know? Some say they're fed up with mansplainers (or we may be afraid we unwittingly act like one ourselves), but being ask assertive as opposed to tell assertive can put pressure on us to become one.[370] Instead of giving orders, see if you can find a way to get people to do what needs to be done by putting your request in the form of a question. An impatient, task-oriented culture discourages us from building community. As Edgar Schein explains in *Humble Inquiry,* if you 'don't care about communicating or building a relationship with the other person, then telling is fine. But if part of the goal of the conversation is to improve communication and build a relationship, then telling is more risky than asking.'[371]

ASK THIS

Look at how you were raised. Were you rewarded for individual contributions or when you helped others out? Does your school culture now make it safe to speak up? If you work or are educated in a culture that doesn't encourage question asking or collaboration, what are other ways you can gain this experience (for example by joining organisations)? A culture that rewards the DIYers is a culture that is more about just get it done rather than honest enquiry and research.

64:
Being a Master Generalist

Fig 64.1: To become effective collaborators, architects should strive to become master generalists, polymaths and T-shaped people

Architects, by definition, are multidisciplinary generalists.

Architects are multidisciplinary generalists[372] who, since the time of Vitruvius and then Alberti, have been encouraged to familiarise themselves with various branches of knowledge. It makes sense, given that architecture is both an art and science, while being not entirely one or the other. Martha Thorne has said that architecture is not just art, or just science, but – as it draws on psychology, sociology, economics, politics and more – is more than either of these.[373] As generalists, architects thrive in environments where wicked problems prevail.

And given the complexity of buildings and the number and kinds of people involved in any building project, it is important for architects to be familiar with a lot of things. David Gilmore, president and CEO of DesignIntelligence, calls on architects to become *master generalists* and polymaths[374] who, by definition, know a whole lot about a whole lot. But as important as knowledge is, it is equally important that architects feel comfortable engaging with others who may hold specialised knowledge and insights that can move the project forward. This combination of deep smarts and wide social wingspan is sometimes referred to as being a T-shaped individual.

To relate well with others, it is important to think like them and to empathise with them. But there is no substitute for actually switching roles with them on project teams. Snøhetta use a concept they call *transpositioning*[375] – where firm members are invited to break from their professional role and actually switch perspectives with others on the team. Earlier in my career, when designing transportation stations, the public transportation client would have their employees one month serve as project managers, then as conductors, or as safety engineers. The thinking goes that by exposing ourselves to others' roles for a short period of time we release ourselves from disciplinary conventions, which can – as Snøhetta have learned – foster a greater sense of what is possible, freeing teammates from conventional domain-specific thinking, and yes, build empathy for others you may work with in the process. Snøhetta liken doing this to how some orchestras encourage their musicians to rehearse on each other's instruments to better appreciate the challenges and possibilities of other musical parts, and better communicate across cultures and disciplines. On returning to your own instrument, what you learned can elevate the collective quality of the performance.

TRY THIS

Make it your aim to know how others think, and know what others do in the process, so you know who to go to when you need information you don't possess or have access to. As a generalist, specialise in people. Zoom out to better see connections and join the dots. Appreciate specialists, but be the one who actively seeks to get them out of their silos to solve holistic, common sense solutions. Know just enough to be able to communicate the overall contours of the assignment, your ideas and the problem you are trying to solve – then strive to get others involved in helping you solve it.

TRY THIS

Increase your use of metaphor, so you can explain new things in terms others can relate to. Make it your goal to be relatable, to use language others can relate to, and that doesn't exclude others. Have something you are known for (you're more likely to work on important projects), but also develop diverse interests and consider what it is beyond specific skillsets that you bring to projects and teams.

READ THIS

Range: Why Generalists Triumph in a Specialized World
by David Epstein

65: Agility

Fig 65.1: With the blurring of roles and responsibilities, you want to aim to be agile enough to adapt to different demands and situations

Architects design for resilience and are themselves resilient, remaining agile not fragile throughout their careers.

As 10,000 decisions go into the design and making of a building, architects have to think of many things.

What's important for the architect is to remain agile, not getting caught up or stuck on any one question, issue or point; maintaining an open mind when others are speaking; zooming in and out to look at decisions at different scales; and remaining flexible in their thinking.

With the blurring of roles and responsibilities, working remotely and together earlier, and increasing complexity and speed of projects, you want to aim to be agile enough to adapt to different demands and situations. Some problems or assignments will be similar to ones that you have encountered before – and then it's more expedient for you to do it yourself. Doing it yourself makes sense when the schedule or budget won't support a team effort, or when the simplicity or lack of complexity of the assignment calls for a more direct route to a solution. In addition to everything else, architecture is a business, and problems often have to be solved quickly. There isn't the luxury of dwelling on them endlessly – sometimes the more expedient decision is made for the sake of time. DIY is when your boss unforgivingly promises something to a client by the end of the day and you are the go-to person to get it done. It doesn't make sense collaborating in these situations. Remaining agile throughout your career will help you to pivot between working collaboratively and independently, depending on the circumstances, and be seen as someone who is flexible and easy to work with.

Few right out of school are given DIY assignments, because emerging professionals tend to work on a team from the start. While it may seem that technical ability – building technology and digital or design technology – is more important at the start of your career, in part because you are given fewer opportunities to engage with clients and consultants, people skills are still important when you first graduate, and increasingly so as you continue in your career.

Architects can famously maintain two simultaneous lines of thought: their own and their client's; their client's and that of the public-at-large; the paying client and the non-paying client; the 99% and the 1%; the circumstantial and the ideal; science and art; reason and intuition; evidence and the ineffable; HSW and aesthetics; practical and dreamer. Doing this takes agility.

TRY THIS

While you don't always need to be the expert, the question of memorisation – how important is it, can't you just google it? – comes up when collaborating. Some memorisation is useful and important. You will be of more use to others in real time if you keep some information in your head. You want to work around others in studio – to be in the room where things are happening. You may be more comfortable wandering off doing things in your own place and time. But you can miss important messages and information. More importantly, when you are off on your own you don't learn from other students – or only from those you hang out with. Some architects find that they do the most learning when eavesdropping on nearby conversations. (Some people speak loudly – what can you do?)

ASK THIS

In response to the increasing wicked problems where outcomes are unknown, instead of focusing exclusively on disciplinary fidelity and skill building, today's schools really ought to focus on developing resilient, adaptive and agile multidisciplinary thinkers. Short of this goal, what can you be doing in your academic and professional career to remain as agile as possible, adaptive to a variety of roles and situations?

ASK THIS

If the best results tend to be achieved when computers and humans work collaboratively – allocating tasks to each other's strengths, rather than working in competition – what can you be doing today to increase your responsiveness to working with technology? Can you take a course or watch tutorials to help you learn to code? Can you take software home and open the bonnet, so to speak, finding ways to customise the tools you and others use to be more accessible and user-friendly? What other things could you try to build a bridge between you and the tools that will help you get ahead in your academic and/or professional career?

SECTION 9: PERSUASION

66: Rationalisation and Persuasion

Fig 66.1: People will be swayed by information that is made rational, i.e. translated into something relevant, understandable and usable

As with building facades, architects rationalise their subjective ideas by translating them into something relevant, understandable and usable.

As we saw in the first section on critical thinking, like many people, architects like to rationalise.

But architects also take part in another form of rationalisation – when they rationalise building facades, which they usually do computationally.

Often associated with facade design, rationalisation is used where complex geometries made up of unique components need to be translated into understandable and buildable form. This type of rationalisation is how an architect like Frank Gehry has been able to build his complex ideas. Complex shapes that are becoming easier to design still raise the question of how they can be built feasibly and affordably.[376] Gehry first works with physical models, then creates a computer model by scanning the physical model. It doesn't make sense for him to do more conventional elevations of his buildings, as contractors won't build from them – they'll build from the model. However, municipalities require elevations to issue a building permit, so his firm provides them.

What this has to do with persuasion is that people will be swayed by information that is made rational – i.e. translated into something relevant, understandable and usable. Just as metaphor is one way to take something new and make it understandable to others, rationalising intuitive or subjective information is a way to verify it logically. Unlike post-rationalisation, where the architect comes up with reasons after the fact, rationalisation is a way to size up and measure what you are being told.

An architect like Steven Holl starts his design process with watercolor sketches that result further along in built form that is subjected to all of the regulations, constraints and forces of other built works. In the process his abstract intuitive ideas are rationalised so they can be realised.

TRY THIS

While playing Devil's advocate is not always an effective way to advance your ideas, to persuade others it helps to represent both sides. People will be more convinced of your idea if you mention that you thought of the negative consequences or thought of alternative approaches. This communicates that you are not so irrationally obsessed with an idea that you have failed to see it in context, from another's perspective.

67:
The Role of Emotion

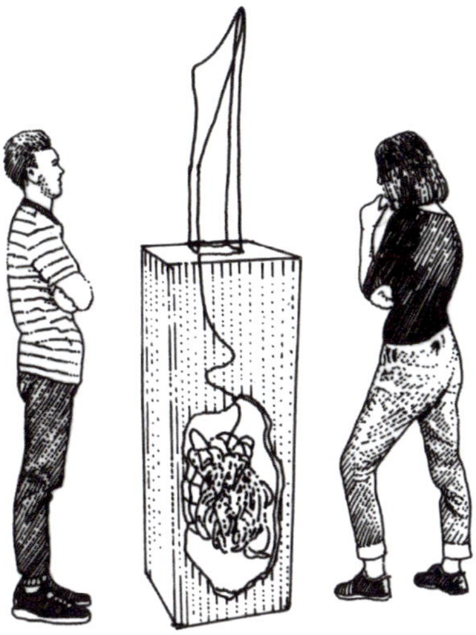

Fig 67.1: Arguing using not only reason but passion and emotion can make all the difference to a project others will stand behind and defend

Architects learn when and how to use emotion when presenting their design ideas.

During his Ground Zero interview, Libeskind allowed himself to express emotion – thus making a strong connection with the design jury, while differentiating himself from teams that took a different approach or established a different tone in their interview presentation. From the emphasis that Daniel Libeskind placed on emotion in architecture, one could be led to believe it was Libeskind's expression of emotion during his presentation that led to his being selected to oversee the rebuilding of the World Trade Center.

Using facts and figures – appealing to the rational and logical, while critically important to arrive at a decision and move a project forward, is seldom enough.

For this reason, it is important to appeal to the emotions to take decision makers to the final step.

Arguing using not only reason but passion and emotion can make all the difference between a project that is understood but doesn't build excitement, and a project that builds consensus others will stand behind and defend.

Architects have to learn when and how to use emotion when presenting their design ideas. Emotion communicates that you care – that you have conviction in what you are presenting – and relates to the rhetorical tool of pathos, the quality that stirs up emotions in the listener.

Buildings, likewise, make emotional connections, perhaps none so prevalent as what is known as the 'wow effect'. Architects provide the wow effect, that sense of awe when we are standing before something manmade, masterful and inexplicably beautiful or grand. This is the gift architects give to the world: creating places that inspire, where people live out and realise their dreams and destinies. Architects aim to wow.

This bit of wisdom is here in the collaboration section because while it is always a good idea to keep your emotions in check, you don't need to manage emotions as much when by yourself. Emotions primarily have to do with the presence of, and potential impact on, others.

TRY THIS

Learn how to manage emotions – not to be overcome by feelings when having a bad day. Easier said than done, but always try to keep the long game in mind and have faith that things will come through for you in time, just perhaps not exactly when you'd hoped. Keep your eyes on the prize and you will prevail over short-term setbacks.

68:
Beware the Cookie

Fig 68.1: Beware of the product sales representative who tries to win you over to their product via your stomach, not your head

Architects think independently and can't be manipulated or swayed by extrinsic enticements.

A product manufacturer's sales representative makes the following claim: Wood is stronger than steel!

Pound for pound, they say, wood is stronger than steel. Is it? How can you know?

Once out of school and working in a firm you will be invited to attend lunches arranged by your firm and hosted by product manufacturers.

These events can be hit or miss in terms of learning opportunities. The best cover general content about a topic for the first two-thirds of the time and only in the final third is the product itself specifically mentioned as an example.

One thing to be on the lookout for is that the product sales representative will try to win you over to their product via your stomach, not your head.

They want your firm to specify their product – and that explains the free lunch.

Economics in nine words: *There is no such thing as a free lunch.*

Don't be swayed by the cookie! Look under the product's bonnet, take a sample for a spin. But don't be pressured into using someone's product, nor buy into the hype. A professional is someone who is not swayed by either self-interest or commercial interests. Architects think independently. It is essential that architects are not manipulated or swayed by enticements and remain neutral – that they seek out and hear from both sides of an argument.

Architects must make an effort to see beyond the free lunch and the cookie to create their own continuing education, for as one architect has said, 'once the Part III certificate is filed away all too many of us rest on our laurels, skimming an online journal or listening to a product rep murder building physics in pursuit of product sales'.[377]

ASK THIS

You want to scrutinise what others are saying. If they are speaking for an hour, is the first forty minutes general information about the category and industry knowledge, with the final twenty minutes about their product, plus Q&A? Is it a marketing person or an engineer who is presenting? An engineer will often be able to respond to questions more thoroughly – based on experience in the field.

Epilogue

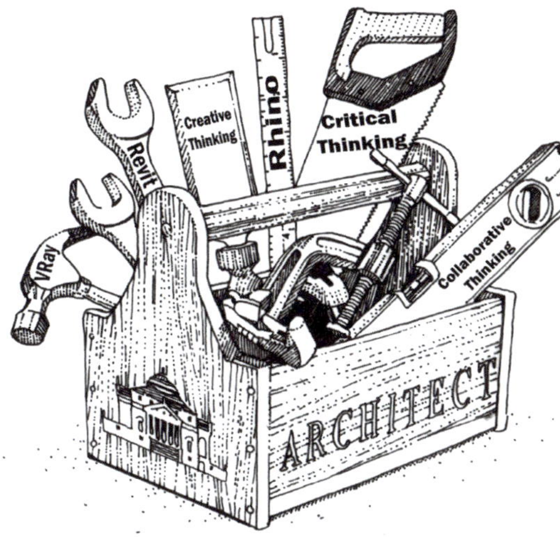

Fig 69.1: Use critical, creative and collaborative thinking to help you get what you want

A conclusion is simply the place where you got tired of thinking.

– Fortune cookie, New Year's Eve 2019

How do we decide to end? When is a building complete?

Was the Hunters Point Library *complete?* Who decided it was so?

The purpose of this book isn't to ensure that there will be more thinking, just better thinking. If we need to think, I cannot think of a much better way to do so than the way an architect thinks.

The thinking that goes into the design and delivery of buildings all but assures their longevity and impact, and the positive impression they will have on their communities.

A friend decided to work on her Michigan beach house renovation without an architect, explaining that it wasn't rocket science, that she could handle it. I recently asked her how that's going; what, if anything, is missing? Someone who sees the big picture, she said. How everything pieces together. Someone who understands the minute details and the larger overall view; who thinks beyond the immediate situation and keeps others in mind.

Your goal isn't to think. Your goal is to get your building design liked, approved or esteemed. Or to get someone to throw money – and lots of it – or prizes at it. Or to make places where people can afford to live well. Or thrive in their schools or workplaces. To feel at home wherever they are.

Your goal isn't thinking. Thinking, though, is how you get there (that, and some hard work). It's what will help you arrive at your longed-for, long-sought-after goals. To arrive at your goals, you'll have to do some thinking, and there is no better way than to think like an architect.

The goal isn't thinking for the sake of thinking. Or to turn you into a logician or philosopher. The goal is to use thinking to help you get what you want.

Your goal is to be whomever and whatever is needed in the situation you find yourself in.

Sometimes what is needed is someone to take tracing paper out and start sketching while others are talking, describing what needs to happen, or what their preferences are.

Sometimes what is needed is someone who listens, taking in what is said, then reframing it in clear, actionable terms, eliciting a response along the lines of *yes, that's what we meant.*

Sometimes what is needed is someone to walk a client away from doing something potentially catastrophic for the neighbourhood/context/situation/environment.

It's not about what software you use – it's about your personal operating system (OS): your brain hardware and mind software.

No matter what technology or wicked problem comes your way, you will have the wherewithal and intestinal fortitude to respond using the new tools you've acquired.

There is no better OS than one that encourages and enables you to think like an architect.

Aim to be an augmented architect. In this book we've discussed what it means to be able to think critically, creatively and collaboratively.

Time spent improving these mindsets and skillsets will pay dividends throughout your career.

As you make your way through school then practice, return to these often; make them the air you breathe, and the water you swim in.

Wear them like an exoskeleton as you go about your life.

TRY THIS

Australian architect and emeritus professor Alec Tzannes uses three pencils. They are all in black casings but they have black, red and blue lead. When he draws freehand to scale, black initiates ideas, blue discusses ideas and red audits. So, use black for creative thinking and initiating ideas, use red for critical thinking and evaluating ideas, and use blue for collaboration, to discuss ideas – who else to work with to communicate your thought process with the office and beyond.

ASK THIS

Size up the situation you are entering. What is needed? A helping hand, resource, catalyst for change, provocateur, voice of reason, or clearing-house? Can you provide what is needed here?

READ THIS

Read this book over again. This time return to chapters that resonated most with you. Identify what you want to work on next, and how you will go about doing so. Consider this book a career companion you can return to again and again, until you are no longer emerging but a full-fledged design professional.

APPENDIX

68 Ways To Think Like An Architect

Critical Thinking

1. Architects need to think of everything.
2. Architects are expected to think both deliberately and intuitively.
3. Architects serve as role models for how to think.
4. If architects were *only* deliberate thinkers, they'd be unemployed, and their buildings would be uninspiring.
5. The benefits of thinking critically like an architect are unlimited.
6. Architects think deliberately about how inhabitants experience their buildings.
7. Critical thinking is a go-to tool.
8. Architects argue effectively by appealing to reason, the emotions and ethics.
9. Buildings can't argue, but their architects can and must.
10. Architects don't wait to evaluate – it happens throughout the design process.
11. Architects use metaphor to provide order and meaning to the built environment.
12. Architects only need to justify their decisions when challenged, but a good critical thinker prepares for this inevitability.

Facts, Fallacies and Photoshop

13. Architects are like investigative reporters who scrupulously explore details to verify facts.
14. Architects trust, but verify.
15. It is down to the architect to present evidence in support of their design decisions.
16. Architects move from not knowing towards knowing by gathering information.
17. An architect is someone who makes sense of the 10,000 things that go into the making of a building.
18. Architects familiarise themselves with fallacies in thinking so they can catch themselves and others who resort to them.
19. Architects let what they are already familiar with inform what is new and unfamiliar.
20. Architects turn their biases from compulsions to preferences and choices.
21. Instead of over-promising and not delivering, architects under-promise and over-perform.
22. Architects are critical thinkers and avoid attributing outcomes to magical thinking.

Decision Making

23. Architects have to make or facilitate a series of decisions based on trade-offs.
24. At the start of every project architects ask what is actual, necessary, desirable in order to discover what is possible.
25. Architects improve their design judgement by building their experience, knowledge and intuition.
26. Architects have an unspoken social contract to make life better.
27. Architects understand that their actions have consequences and work to imagine and anticipate what they are.
28. Architects self-edit by focusing not only on the content but on the negative or white space.
29. Architects strive to manage an increasing set of variables and alternatives in their head.
30. Architects strive to be independent thinkers while engaging others in decision making.

Critical Creative Thinking

31. Architects rely on critical creative thinking to draw on both sides of the brain.
32. Architects don't let everyday problems distract them from addressing major, wicked problems with non-obvious solutions.
33. Architects use their comfort with ambiguity and uncertainty to their and others' advantage.
34. Architects are asked to do impossible things they know nothing about.
35. Architects consider design thinking less a process than a mindset, one that may lead to intangible results.
36. Architects think in a way that is worth studying, preserving and applying to problems large and small.
37. The architect's design process moves a project forward from concept to a piece of architecture.
38. Architects have the confidence to take their project apart if it means improving it as they put it back together.
39. Architects alternate between focused attention and a relaxed state in order to recognise patterns.
40. Architects develop their hunches and intuition at the same time as their rational thinking.
41. Architects think through making, where the two are not separate acts but seen as correlated.
42. Architects see design as a reconciliation of the ideal with real and are influenced by both abstract and practical ideas.

Curiosity

43. Architects are naturally curious and make an effort to continue to be so throughout their careers.
44. Being open to feedback, change and growth is critical to one's development as an architect.
45. Architects deliberately put themselves into a state of creative ignorance so they can approach problems with an open mind.
46. Architects make a special effort every day to be observant, mindful and alert.
47. Architects care about the quality and character of their questions to ensure their relevance and applicability.
48. Architects ask *What if ...?* to lead to new directions in research and future development.

Problem Solving

49. Architects are not only creative problem solvers but problem definers and identifiers.
50. Architects see the creative process not linearly or as a circle, but gradually moving forward as an iterative spiral.
51. To remain open to experimentation and discovery architects try not to be attached to a specific outcome.
52. Architects are synthesisers of social, functional, economic, environmental, technical and aesthetic factors.
53. Architects require patience, resilience, perspective and above all perseverance for architecture to happen.
54. Architects think critically and creatively without technology and should be able to do so even more assuredly and quickly with it.
55. Architects should apply their unique way of thinking not only to buildings but to challenges facing society such as poverty, inequality and segregation.

Critical Collaborative Thinking

56. To achieve the architects' social contract to make life better it helps to work with others.
57. Life experiences prior to becoming an architect should be used and considered a strength.
58. Architects design with others in mind.
59. Because they are comfortable with ambiguity and uncertainty architects are ideally suited to solving wicked problems with others.
60. Architects rely on their intuition to make design decisions; it turns out, so do the best teams.

Thinking With Others

61. Architects think like others to be more observant while avoiding the pitfalls of drawing faulty conclusions.
62. Project teams possess a collective intelligence above and beyond the intelligence of the individual architect.
63. Architects strive to build, learn and work in cultures that support collaborative problem solving.
64. Architects, by definition, are multidisciplinary generalists.
65. Architects design for resilience and are themselves resilient, remaining agile not fragile throughout their careers.

Persuasion

66. As with building facades, architects rationalise their subjective ideas by translating them into something relevant, understandable and usable.
67. Architects learn when and how to use emotion when presenting their design ideas.
68. Architects think independently and can't be manipulated or swayed by extrinsic enticements.

Notes

1 J. Brockman, ed., *The Last Unknowns: Deep, Elegant, Profound Unanswered Questions About the Universe, the Mind, the Future of Civilization, and the Meaning of Life* (William Morrow, 2019).

2 K. Willyerd, B. Mistick, *Stretch: How to Future-Proof Yourself for Tomorrow's Workplace* (Wiley, 2016).

3 J. Kaji, R. Moses, B. Hurley, R. Bhat (2019), *Skills Change, But Capabilities Endure,* https://www2.deloitte.com/content/dam/insights/us/articles/6332_From-skills-to-capabilities/6332_Skills-change-capabiliites-endure.pdf (accessed 16 April 2020).

4 R. Deutsch, Superusers: *Design Technology Specialists and the Future of Practice* (Routledge, 2019).

5 M. Trinetti, 'How to Future-Proof Yourself: Skills, behaviors & mindsets to adopt today for uncertain tomorrow', mission.org, 27 February 2018, https://medium.com/the-mission/how-to-future-proof-yourself-2dab379f953d (accessed 16 April 2020).

6 A. Gray, 'The 10 Skills You Need to Thrive in the Fourth Industrial Revolution', World Economic Forum, 19 January 2016, https://www.weforum.org/agenda/2016/01/the-10-skills-you-need-to-thrive-in-the-fourth-industrial-revolution/ (accessed 16 April 2020).

7 National Association of Colleges and Employers (NACE) staff, 'The Four Career Competencies Employers Value Most', 29 March 2019, https://www.naceweb.org/career-readiness/competencies/the-four-career-competencies-employers-value-most/ (accessed 16 April 2020).

8 M. Bonchek, 'How to Stop Worrying About Becoming Obsolete at Work', *Harvard Business Review,* 11 January 2016, p 3.

9 A. Gribbin, *Design and Critical Thinking: Applying Perry's Theory of Intellectual Development to Foundational Design Instruction* (19th Proceedings on Beginning Design Student, 2003), p 204.

10 R. Arum, J. Roksa, *Academically Adrift: Limited Learning on College Campuses* (University of Chicago Press, 2011).

11 T. Williams, 'Study: Nearly Half of Millennials Get an "F" In Critical Thinking', *GoodCall,* 10 May 2017, https://www.goodcall.com/news/critical-thinking-011043/ (accessed 16 April 2020).

12 'The Yada Yada' is the 153rd episode, or the 19th episode of the eighth season, of the American NBC sitcom *Seinfeld.* It aired on 24 April 1997.

13 H. Lasala, A. Hines, *On the Verge: Designing First Design* (Tenth National Conference on the Beginning Design Student, 1993), p 313.

14 B. Dennis, A. Freedman, J. Muyskens, '2019 Capped Off the World's Hottest Decade in Recorded History', *Washington Post,* 15 January 2020, https://www.washingtonpost.com/climate-environment/2020/01/15/2010s-hottest-decade-world/?arc404=true (accessed 16 April 2020).

15 A. Tsing, 'Critical Care, Earth Stalked by Man', *Cambridge Journal of Anthropology,* vol. 34, no. 1, Spring 2016, p 2.

16 D. Benjamin, ed., *Embodied Energy and Design: Making Architecture Between Metrics and Narratives* (Lars Müller, 2017)

17 UN Climate Action Summit, 2019, https://www.un.org/en/climatechange/un-climate-summit-2019.shtml cited in D. Hoskins, A. Cohen, *Gensler's Latest Data on Climate Impact and Our Pledge to the Future,* https://www.gensler.com/research-insight/blog/impact-by-design-2019-genslers-latest-data-on-climate-impact (accessed 16 April 2020).

18 Ibid.

19 Ibid.

20 M. Green in S. Wallis, 'The Trees and the Forest of New Towers', *The New York Times,* 20 November 2019.

21 L. Rogers, 'Climate Change: The Massive CO² Emitter You May Not Know About', BBC News, 17 December 2018, https://www.bbc.com/news/science-environment-46455844 (accessed 16 April 2020).

22 M. Brown, '4 Cornerstone Skills Engineers Need for the Future of Work', engineering.com, 16 April 2018, https://www.engineering.com/JobArticles/ArticleID/16807/4-Cornerstone-Skills-Engineers-Need-for-the-Future-of-Work.aspx (accessed 16 April 2020).

23 Ibid.

24 Green in Wallis, 2019.

25 UN Climate Action Summit, 2019.

26 United Nations, Global Issues Overview, https://www.un.org/en/sections/issues-depth/global-issues-overview/ (accessed 16 April 2020).

27 Ibid.

28 Ibid.

29 Ibid.

30 D. Niose, 'Anti-Intellectualism: A Rejection of Critical Thinking', *Values of the Wise,* 13 December 2018, https://www.valuesofthewise.com/critical-thinking-2/ (accessed 16 April 2020).

31 T. McGinty, *Skillful Beginnings* (11th Proceedings National Conference on the Beginning Design Student, 1994).

32 C. Mead, 'Critical Thinking in Architectural Design' in *Architectural Design Portable Handbook* (McGraw-Hill Education, 2015), p 10.

33 McGinty, 1994.

34 A.J. Colmenares, *The Beginning Architectural Studio as an Object of Knowledge* (14th Proceedings on Beginning Design Education, 1997), p 29.

35 *Begin With Why: Ethics and Values In Beginning Design* (National Conference on the Beginning Design Student, 2017), p 33.

36 L. Stone, 'Steven Holl Hunters Point Library Is Being Sued Over ADA Violations', *The Architect's Newspaper,* 26 November, 2019, https://archpaper.com/2019/11/hunters-point-library-is-being-sued-over-ada-violations/ (accessed 16 April 2020).

37 Ibid.

38 R. Seevers, 'An Interview with Linda Elder: About Critical Thinking and Gifted Education', criticalthinking.org, January 2003, https://www.criticalthinking.org/resources/articles/an-interview-linda-elder.shtml (accessed 16 April 2020).

39 J. Berr, 'Employers: New College Grads Aren't Ready For Workplace', CBS News, 17 May 2016, https://www.cbsnews.com/news/employers-new-college-grads-arent-ready-for-workplace/ (accessed 21 January, 2020).

40 D.T. Willingham, *Critical Thinking: Why Is It So Hard to Teach?* (American Educator, 2007).

41 S. Otterman, 'New Library Is a $41.5 Million Masterpiece. But About Those Stairs', *The New York Times,* 5 November 2019, https://www.nytimes.com/2019/11/05/nyregion/long-island-city-library.html (accessed 16 April 2020).

42 A. Lange, 'New York City's Two Biggest Design Stories of 2019 Are Also Design Failures', *Curbed*

New York, 20 December 2019, https://ny.curbed.com/2019/12/20/21020969/hudson-yards-hunters-point-library-design (accessed 16 April 2020).
43 Ibid.
44 J. Postell, *Teaching Beginning Students: Introducing a Paradigm* (Proceedings 5th National Conference on the Beginning Design Student, 1988), p 26.
45 H. Butler, 'Why Do Smart People Do Foolish Things?', *Scientific American,* 3 October 2017, https://www.scientificamerican.com/article/why-do-smart-people-do-foolish-things/ (accessed 16 April 2020).
46 R. Handa, *Teaching Design Judgment* (11th National Conference on the Beginning Design Student, 1994), p 66.
47 Butler, 2017.
48 S. Wigglesworth in J. Rendell, J. Hill, M. Dorrian, M. Fraser, *Critical Architecture* (Routledge, 2007), p 310.
49 J. Rendell, *Critical Architecture: Introduction* (Conference Proceedings, The Bartlett School of Architecture, University College London, 2005).
50 M. Jarzembek, 'Critical or Post-Critical?', *Architectural Theory Review,* April 2002, p 149.
51 L.M. Murawski, 'Critical Thinking in the Classroom ... and Beyond', *Journal of Learning in Higher Education,* Spring 2014, p 25.
52 J.P. Healy, 'The Components of the "Crit" in Art and Design Education', *Semantic Scholar,* 2016, https://www.semanticscholar.org/paper/The-Components-of-the-%22Crit%22-in-Art-and-Design-Healy/95d5b96185536cc8373a272dde54e2acf59f2bd2 (accessed 16 April 2020).
53 P. Crowther, 'Assessing Architectural Design Processes of Diverse Learners', 29 February 2012, https://www.uts.edu.au/sites/default/files/Crowther.pdf (accessed 16 April 2020).
54 R. Sara, R. Parnell (July 2016), 'Fear and Learning in the Architectural Crit', http://field-journal.org/wp-content/uploads/2016/07/Field-51-Sara-Parnell.pdf (accessed 16 April 2020).
55 Healy, 2016.
56 N. Swaminathan, 'Why Does the Brain Need So Much Power?', *Scientific American,* 29 April 2008, https://www.scientificamerican.com/article/why-does-the-brain-need-s/ (accessed 16 April 2020).
57 B. Tippey, *Critical Thinking is Not Discipline Specific* (24th National Conference on the Beginning Design Student, 2008), https://smartech.gatech.edu/handle/1853/29122 (accessed 16 April 2020).
58 'Using "Star Trek" to teach critical thinking', *The New York Times,* Tech Talk podcast, 16 June 2010, https://bits.blogs.nytimes.com/2010/06/16/tech-talk-podcast-star-trek-and-critical-thinking/?searchResultPosition=32 (accessed 16 April 2020).
59 R. Wiseman, 'Self Help: Forget Positive Thinking, Try Positive Action', *Guardian,* 30 June, 2012, https://www.theguardian.com/science/2012/jun/30/self-help-positive-thinking (accessed 16 April 2020).
60 J. Pawson in an interview with M. Crick, *Exploring Excellence: How Architects Think,* 1998, https://www.architects.nsw.gov.au/download/BHTS/CrickMelanie_Exploring%20Excellence-%20How%20architects%20think_BHTS_1998_Report.pdf (accessed 16 April 2020).
61 D. Goleman, *Focus: The Hidden Driver of Excellence* (Harper, 2015).
62 K. Wong, 'How Long It Takes To Get Back On Track After a Distraction', *Life Hacker,* 29 July 2015, https://lifehacker.com/how-long-it-takes-to-get-back-on-track-after-a-distract-1720708353 (accessed 16 April 2020).
63 M. Csikszentmihalyi, *Flow: The Psychology of Optimal Experience* (HarperCollins, 1990).
64 B. Tippey, *Critical Thinking is Not Discipline Specific* (24th National Conference on the Beginning Design Student, 2008), https://smartech.gatech.edu/handle/1853/29122 (accessed 16 April 2020).
65 Butler, 2017.
66 T.M. Boake, *Oasis* (14th Proceedings on Beginning Design Education, 1997), p 113.
67 Ibid.
68 J. Sostrin, 'How to Act Quickly Without Sacrificing Critical Thinking', *Harvard Business Review,* 27 April 2017, https://hbr.org/2017/04/how-to-act-quickly-without-sacrificing-critical-thinking (accessed 16 April 2020).
69 T.L. Freeman, *Critical Thinking, Communications, and Teamwork* (Proceedings of the American Society for Engineering Education Annual Conference & Exposition, 2001), p 6.314.1.
70 F. Strachan, 'Architecture can help solve poverty, inequality, segregation', UNSW Sydney, 27 July 2017, https://newsroom.unsw.edu.au/news/art-architecture-design/architecture-can-help-solve-poverty-inequality-segregation (accessed 17 April 2020).
71 E. Danze, *Intuition* (19th Proceedings on Beginning Design Student, 2003), p 125.
72 M. Kimmelman, 'With the Guggenheim, Frank Lloyd Wright Built a Soaring and Intimate Sanctuary for Art', *The New York Times,* 18 October 2019, https://www.nytimes.com/2019/10/18/arts/design/guggenheim-frank-lloyd-wright-photos-60.html (accessed 17 April 2020).
73 S. Maser, see preface to the exhibition catalogue on Baste Design, *Grundlagen der Gestal tung,* Professor A.W. Oppermann Unl v. Gesamthochschul e Wueppertal, 1982.
74 D. Zach, 18 December 2019, email to the author.
75 M. Leeper, 'Do Architects Slow Things Down?', *Li Herald,* 6 December 2019, http://liherald.com/stories/do-architects-slow-things-down,120744 (accessed 17 April 2020).
76 C. Bjone, *Philip Johnson and His Mischief: Appropriation in Art and Architecture* (The Images Publishing Group, 2014).
77 P. Goldberger, 'Architecture View; Tale Of Two Towers On Boston Boylston Street', *The New York Times,* 24 January 1988, https://www.nytimes.com/1988/01/24/arts/architecture-view-tale-of-two-towers-on-boston-boylston-street.html (accessed 18 April 2020).
78 Ibid.
79 C. Turner, 'Peter Zumthor: Zinc Mine Museum', Norway, *Icon,* 28 July 2014, https://www.iconeye.com/architecture/news/item/10837-peter-zumthor-zinc-mine-museum-norway (accessed 18 April 2020).
80 B. Tharp, S. Tharp, 'What is Discursive Design?', *Core 77,* 9 December 2015, https://www.core77.com/posts/41991/What-is-Discursive-Design (accessed 18 April 2020).
81 W. Jones in C. Hume, 'Architecture As Argument For Creating Better World', *The Star,* 23 January 2009, https://www.thestar.com/life/homes/2009/01/23/architecture_as_argument_for_creating_better_world.html (accessed 18 April 2020).
82 Ibid.
83 A. Schopf, C. Squire, 'Moving Towards Design that Supports Climate Action', *IAI KnowledgeNet,* 26

August 2019, https://bit.ly/2YUrjjf (accessed 18 April 2020).
84 Antoine Predock in 'What is Good Design? Interview with Andrew Pressman', *Architectural Design Portable Handbook* (McGraw-Hill Education, 2001), p 10.
85 D. Jovanovic, 'Test Like An Architect', *DEV,* 30 November 2018, https://dev.to/damnjan/test-like-an-architect-25bo (accessed 18 April 2020).
86 E. Estep, 'Interior Architecture: Should You Do a Test Fit?', 5 November 2015, https://asg-architects.com/interior-architecture-should-you-do-a-test-fit/ (accessed 18 April 2020).
87 'Thinking About Thinking with Tyler Cowen [The Knowledge Project Ep. #39]', 2019, https://fs.blog/tyler-cowen/ (accessed 18 April 2020).
88 Ibid.
89 C. Jencks, *The New Paradigm in Architecture: The Language of Post-modernism* (Yale University Press, 2002), p 32.
90 E.O. Moss in M. Crick, 1998.
91 F. Downing, *Remembrance and Making of Places,* (12th Proceedings National Conference on the Beginning Design Student, 1995), p 53.
92 S. Unwin, *Metaphor: An Exploration of the Metaphorical Dimensions and Potential of Architecture* (Routledge, 2019).
93 Tweeted by Edward Tufte (30 January 2017), in Michael Lewis, *The Undoing Project: A Friendship That Changed Our Minds* (W.W. Norton, 2016).
94 Unwin, 2019.
95 D.J. Nowak, 'The Effect of Urban Trees on Air Quality', 2002, https://www.nrs.fs.fed.us/units/urban/local-resources/downloads/Tree_Air_Qual.pdf (accessed 28 April 2020).
96 D.J. Nowak, *Trees Pollute? A "TREE" Explains It All,* in: Proc. 7th Natl. Urban For. Conf., 1995, C. Kollin, M. Barratt, eds., *American Forests* (Washington, DC, 1995), pp 28–30.
97 O. Newman, *Defensible Space* (Macmillan, 1972).
98 J. Jacobs, *The Death and Life of Great American Cities* (Vintage, 1961).
99 J.F. Mogensen, 'The Surprising Science of Fighting Crime With ... Trees', *Mother Jones,* May/June 2019, https://www.motherjones.com/environment/2019/04/trees-crime-cincinnati-philadelphia-ida-b-wells-chicago/ (accessed 19 April 2020).
100 S. Wallis, *'The Trees and the Forest of New Towers', The New York Times,* 20 November 2019.
101 Appalachian Wood Manufacturers, http://www.appalachianwood.org/utilization.htm (accessed 19 April 2020).
102 W. Johnson, 'Strength of Steel Vs. Wood', *Hunker,* 2019, https://www.hunker.com/13401408/strength-of-steel-vs-wood (accessed 19 April 2020).
103 S. Perkins, 'Stronger Than Steel, Able to Stop a Speeding Bullet – It's Super Wood!', *Scientific America,* 7 February 2018, https://www.scientificamerican.com/article/stronger-than-steel-able-to-stop-a-speeding-bullet-mdash-it-rsquo-s-super-wood/ (accessed 19 April 2020).
104 M. Zastrow, 'Crushed Wood Is Stronger Than Steel', *Nature,* 7 February 2018, https://www.nature.com/articles/d41586-018-01600-6 (accessed 19 April 2020).
105 J. Fishman,,'The 50 Worst Architecture Fails', *Complex,* 21 December 2011, https://www.complex.com/style/2011/12/the-50-worst-architecture-fails/ (accessed 19 April 2020).
106 L. Edwards, P. Torcellini, *A Literature Review of the Effects of Natural Light on Building Occupants,* July 2002, https://www.nrel.gov/docs/fy02osti/30769.pdf (accessed 19 April 2020).
107 'The Inside Story: A Guide to Indoor Air Quality', EPA, https://www.epa.gov/indoor-air-quality-iaq/inside-story-guide-indoor-air-quality (accessed 19 April 2020).
108 B.C. Howard, '5 Surprising Ways Buildings Can Improve Our Health', 14 February 2017, *National Geographic,* https://www.nationalgeographic.com/environment/urban-expeditions/green-buildings/surprising-ways-green-buildings-improve-health-sustainability/ (accessed 19 April 2020).
109 https://www.hsph.harvard.edu/joseph-allen/ (accessed 19 April 2020).
110 Howard, 2017.
111 'Sick Building Syndrome', EPA, February 1991, https://www.epa.gov/sites/production/files/2014-08/documents/sick_building_factsheet.pdf (accessed 19 April 2020).
112 K. Kohlstedt, 'Olympic Architects: Forgotten Gold Medals Awarded for the Arts', *99% Invisible,* 9 May 2016, https://99percentinvisible.org/article/olympic-architects-forgotten-gold-medals-awarded-arts/ (accessed 19 April 2020).
113 https://www.geni.com/people/Lin-Huiyin-林徽因/6000000014110754421 (accessed 19 April 2020).
114 J. Anderson, 'Only 9% of 15-Year-Olds Can Tell The Difference Between Fact And Opinion', *Quartz,* 3 December 2019, https://qz.com/1759474/only-9-percent-of-15-year-olds-can-distinguish-between-fact-and-opinion/ (accessed 19 April 2020).
115 S. Lohr, 'Robotic Milkers and an Automated Greenhouse: Inside a High-Tech Small Farm', *The New York Times,* 13 January 2019, https://www.nytimes.com/2019/01/13/technology/farm-technology-milkers-robots.html (accessed 19 April 2020).
116 M. Wollan, 'How to Wear Camouflage', *The New York Times,* 16 January 2019, https://www.nytimes.com/2019/01/16/magazine/how-to-wear-camouflage.html (accessed 19 April 2020).
117 C. Claiborne Ray, 'How Bees Find Your Flowerpots', *The New York Times,* 1 April 2019, https://www.nytimes.com/2019/04/01/science/bees-flowers-pollen-honey.html (accessed 19 April 2020).
118 P. Scott, '4,000 Miles, Seven Countries: An African Adventure on Two Wheels', *The New York Times,* 28 January 2019, https://www.nytimes.com/2019/01/28/travel/africa-cycling-trip-adventure.html (accessed 19 April 2020).
119 D. Deming, 'In the Salary Race, Engineers Sprint, but English Majors Endure', *The New York Times,* 20 September 2019, https://www.nytimes.com/2019/09/20/business/liberal-arts-stem-salaries.html (accessed 19 April 2020).
120 A. Symonds, et al., '79 of Our Favorite Facts of 2019', *The New York Times,* 31 December 2019, https://www.nytimes.com/2019/12/31/reader-center/2019-best-facts.html?smtyp=cur&smid=tw-nytimes (accessed 19 April 2020).
121 M. Kimmelman, 'When the Old Penn Station Was Demolished, New York Lost Its Faith', *The New York Times,* 24 April 2019, https://www.nytimes.com/2019/04/24/nyregion/old-penn-station-pictures-new-york.html (accessed 19 April 2020).

122 'Pictures from Youth Climate Strikes Around the World', *The New York Times,* 15 March 2019, https://www.nytimes.com/2019/03/15/climate/climate-school-strikes.html (accessed 19 April 2020).
123 A. Newman, 'If Seeing the World Ruins It, Should We Stay Home?', *The New York Times,* 3 June 2019, https://www.nytimes.com/2019/06/03/travel/traveling-climate-change.html (accessed 19 April 2020).
124 A. Symonds, et al., 2019.
125 'Climate change', *UKGBC,* https://www.ukgbc.org/climate-change/ (accessed 19 April 2020).
126 N.P. Walsh, 'The Facts about Architecture and Climate Change', ArchDaily, 3 January 2020, https://www.archdaily.com/931240/the-facts-about-architecture-and-climate-change/ (accessed 19 April 2020).
127 D. Cuff, 'In the Face of Propaganda, Data-Driven Design Makes It Clear That Facts Matter', *Pool Magazine,* 14 October 2017, http://www.pool-la.com/cuff-act-like-an-architect (accessed 19 April 2020).
128 R. Brandt, G.H. Chong, W.M. Martin, *Design Informed: Driving Innovation with Evidence-Based Design* (Wiley, 2010), p 2.
129 E. Kolbert, 'Why Facts Don't Change Our Minds', *New Yorker,* 19 February 2017, https://www.newyorker.com/magazine/2017/02/27/why-facts-dont-change-our-minds (accessed 19 April 2020).
130 Brandt, et al., 2010, p 4.
131 A. M. Harris, *A Beginning Professor's Path Toward Effective Teaching: My Search for Balance* (08 Proceedings Beginning Design Education, 1990).
132 W. Davis, *Fake Or Real? How To Self-Check The News And Get The Facts, NPR,* 5 December 2016, https://www.npr.org/sections/alltechconsidered/2016/12/05/503581220/fake-or-real-how-to-self-check-the-news-and-get-the-facts (accessed 19 April 2020).
133 R. Martin, *The Opposable Mind: How Successful Leaders Win Through Integrative Thinking* (Harvard Business Press, 2007).
134 'The most essential gift for a good writer', ScienceBlogs, 22 July 2008, https://scienceblogs.com/thescian/2008/07/22/the-essential-writers-gift (accessed 19 April 2020).
135 J. Beck, 'This Article Won't Change Your Mind: The Facts On Why Facts Alone Can't Fight False Beliefs', *The Atlantic,* 13 March 2017), https://www.theatlantic.com/science/archive/2017/03/this-article-wont-change-your-mind/519093/ (accessed 19 April 2020).
136 F. Scott Fitzgerald, 'The Crack Up', *Esquire,* 1936, https://www.esquire.com/lifestyle/a4310/the-crack-up/ (accessed 19 April 2020).
137 https://docs.google.com/document/d/10eA5-mCZLSS4MQY5QGb5ewC3VAL6pLkT53V_81ZyitM/edit (accessed 19 April 2020).
138 C. Melago, 'Knitters With Hopelessly Knotted Yarn Call "Detanglers" for Help', *The Wall Street Journal,* 21 December 2015, https://www.wsj.com/articles/knitters-with-hopelessly-knotted-yarn-call-detanglers-for-help-1450751172 (accessed 20 April 2020).
139 A. Revkin, '"Floating Cities Could Ease The World's Housing Crunch", The UN Says', *National Geographic,* 5 April 2019, https://www.nationalgeographic.com/environment/2019/04/floating-cities-could-ease-global-housing-crunch-says-un/ (accessed 20 April 2020).
140 For a full alphabetic list of fallacies, see http://changingminds.org/disciplines/argument/fallacies/fallacies_alpha.htm (accessed 20 April 2020).
141 B. Supiano, 'Students Learn Best in Their Preferred Learning Style, and Other Neuromyths', *Chronicle of Higher Education,* 17 October 2019, https://www.chronicle.com/article/Students-Learn-Best-in/247360 (accessed 20 April 2020).
142 O. Khazan, 'The Myth of "Learning Styles"', *The Atlantic,* 11 April 2018, https://www.theatlantic.com/science/archive/2018/04/the-myth-of-learning-styles/557687/?cid=nwsltrtn&source=ams&sourceId=3364403 (accessed 20 April 2020).
143 S. Saxe, 'I'm an Engineer and I'm Not Buying Into Smart Cities', *The New York Times,* 16 July 2019, https://www.nytimes.com/2019/07/16/opinion/smart-cities.html (accessed 20 April 2020).
144 J. Cook, S. Lewandowsky, *The Debunking Handbook* (University of Queensland, 2011).
145 Revkin, 2019.
146 L. Alter, 'Floating cities: a good plan for the future or magical thinking?', *TreeHugger,* 9 April 2019, https://www.treehugger.com/urban-design/floating-cities-good-plan-future-or-magical-thinking.html (accessed 20 April 2020).
147 D. Otieno, 'The fallacy of honest architecture', 28 January 2010, http://blog.marcantonioarchitects.com/the-fallacy-of-honest-architecture/ (accessed 20 April 2020).
148 D. Kelbaugh, *Seven Fallacies in Architectural Culture* (2004).
149 'Lost in Translations (from Drawing to Building)', *afterstate,* 6 July 2017, https://afterstate.co/2017/07/06/lost-in-translations-from-drawing-to-building/ (accessed 20 April 2020).
150 C. Mead, 'Critical Thinking in Architectural Design' in *Architectural Design Portable Handbook* (McGraw-Hill Education, 2001), p 10.
151 R. Thallon, J. Young, *Pattern Language: Teaching Beginning Students* (Proceedings 5th National Conference on the Beginning Design Student, 1988), p. 203.
152 S. Piedmont-Palladino, *Absolute Beginners: Teaching Architecture to Pre-Architects* (Tenth National Conference on the Beginning Design Student, 1993), p 223.
153 D. Gray, 'Liminal Thinking: Six Principles', http://liminalthinking.com/six-principles/ (accessed 20 April 2020).
154 J. Brownlee, 'The Golden Ratio: Design's Biggest Myth', *Fast Company,* 13 April 2015, https://www.fastcompany.com/3044877/the-golden-ratio-designs-biggest-myth (accessed 20 April 2020).
155 W. Lau, 'Addressing Our Own Bias to Design Better', *Architect,* 27 November 2019, https://www.architectmagazine.com/practice/addressing-our-own-bias-to-design-better_o (accessed 20 April 2020).
156 R. Adam, 'Classical Architecture: Three Fallacies', *Architects' Journal,* 7 May 2010, https://www.architectsjournal.co.uk/home/classical-architecture-three-fallacies/5217216.article (accessed 20 April 2020).
157 Brownlee, 2015
158 F. Fantaumi, *Conspiring with the World* (16th Proceedings on Beginning Design Student, 1999), p 6.

159 D.A. Bray, R. Wang, 'Three People-Centered Design Principles for Deep Learning', *MIT Sloan Management Review,* 9 September 2019, https://sloanreview.mit.edu/article/three-people-centered-design-principles-for-deep-learning/ (accessed 20 April 2020).
160 A. Frearson, 'We Banned Renders From the Design Processs Says Tatiana Bilbao', *Dezeen,* 4 December 2019, https://www.dezeen.com/2019/12/04/tatiana-bilbao-banned-renderings-architecture-interview/ (accessed 20 April 2020).
161 'The Yada Yada' is the 153rd episode, or the 19th episode of the eighth season of the American NBC sitcom *Seinfeld.* It aired on 24 April 1997.
162 B. Duffy, *Why We're Wrong About Nearly Everything* (Basic Books, 2019).
163 Dr. J. Hoomans, 20 March 2015, https://go.roberts.edu/leadingedge/the-great-choices-of-strategic-leaders
164 E. Krockow, 'How Many Decisions Do We Make Each Day?', *Psychology Today,* 27 September 2018, https://www.psychologytoday.com/us/blog/stretching-theory/201809/how-many-decisions-do-we-make-each-day (accessed 21 April 2020).
165 S. Danziger, J. Levav, L. Avnaim-Pesso, 'Extraneous Factors In Judicial Decisions', 26 April 2011, https://doi.org/10.1073/pnas.1018033108 (accessed 21 April 2020).
166 N. Smith, 'Data Overload and the Myth of Multitasking', 20 April 2015, https://www.geckoboard.com/blog/data-overload-and-the-myth-of-multitasking/#.Wrbt2ZPwaV4
167 I. Flatow, C. Nass, 'The Myth Of Multitasking', NPR, 10 May 2013, https://www.npr.org/2013/05/10/182861382/the-myth-of-multitasking (accessed 21 April 2020).
168 B. Schwartz, 'More Isn't Always Better', *Harvard Business Review,* June 2006, https://hbr.org/2006/06/more-isnt-always-better (accessed 21 April 2020).
169 E. Kolbert, 'Why Facts Don't Change Our Minds', *New Yorker,* 19 February 2017, https://www.newyorker.com/magazine/2017/02/27/why-facts-dont-change-our-minds (accessed 21 April 2020).
170 J.B. Soll, K.L. Milkman, J.W. Payne, 'Outsmart Your Own Biases', *Harvard Business Review,* May 2015, https://hbr.org/2015/05/outsmart-your-own-biases (accessed 21 April 2020).
171 J. Rothman, 'The Art of Decision-Making', *New Yorker,* 14 January 2019, https://www.newyorker.com/magazine/2019/01/21/the-art-of-decision-making (accessed 21 April 2020).
172 J. Heskett, *Is There Still a Role for Judgment in Decision-Making?,* HBR, August 7, 2013.
173 J.T. Franco, 'Can a Machine Perform the Work of an Architect?', ArchDaily, 6 December 2019, https://www.archdaily.com/929300/can-a-machine-perform-the-work-of-an-architect-a-chat-with-jesper-wallgren-founder-at-finch-3d (accessed 21 April 2020).
174 A. Carlsen, S. Clegg, R. Gjersvik, *Idea Work: Lessons of the Extraordinary in Everyday Creativity* (Cappelen Damm, 2013), pp 332–340.
175 D. Leatherbarrow, *Making: Invention and Involvement* (Proceedings 26th National Conference on the Beginning Design Student, 2010), p 15.
176 John Dewey in D. Schön, *The Reflective Practitioner: How Professionals Think in Action,* (Basic Books, 1983).
177 E. Reinholdt, *30X40 Design Workshop,* https://www.youtube.com/user/30by40 (accessed 21 April 2020).
178 A. Tzannes in M. Crick, 1998.
179 J. Zukowski, *A Chronology of Architecture: A Cultural Timeline from Stone Circles to Skyscrapers* (Thames & Hudson, 2020).
180 Denys Lasdun in S. Brier, P. Guddemi, L.H. Kauffman, R. Glanville, *How to Live the Cybernetics of Unknowing,* (1965), p 185.
181 W. Strunk, E.B. White, *The Elements of Style* (1920).
182 G. Herman, *Not Only Design but Also Knowledge* (14th Proceedings on Beginning Design Education, 1997), p 50.
183 R. Handa, *Teaching Design Judgement* (11th National Conference on the Beginning Design Student, 1994), p 66.
184 W. Alsop in M. Crick, 1998.
185 P. Zumthor, *Thinking Architecture* (Lars Muller Publishers, 1998), p 20.
186 R. Deutsch, *Convergence: The Redesign of Design,* (Wiley, 2017), p 52.
187 P. Bernstein, *Architecture | Design | Data: Practice Competency in the Era of Computation* (Birkhauser Architecture, 2018), p 59.
188 G. Simpson, 'Carl Sagan SLAMS 'racist, chauvinistic, unscientific' *Star Wars* in classic interview', *Express,* 3 April 2017, https://www.express.co.uk/entertainment/films/787202/Star-Wars-racist-Carl-Sagan-The-Tonight-Show-Johnny-Carson (accessed 22 April 2020).
189 S. Temple, *Developing A Beginner's Mind* (Proceedings 21st National Conference on the Beginning Design Student, 2005), p 6.
190 A.M. Harris, *A Beginning Professor's Path Toward Effective Teaching: My Search for Balance,* (08 Proceedings Beginning Design Education, 1990).
191 B. Tippey, *Critical Thinking Is Not Discipline Specific* (24th National Conference on the Beginning Design Student, 2008), https://smartech.gatech.edu/handle/1853/29122 (accessed 23 April 2020).
192 M. Ozkar, *Rethinking Basic Design in Architectural Education: Foundations Past and Future* (Routledge, 2017), pp 141–2.
193 W. Bryant, 'At the Intersection of Creativity and Critical Thinking', *Getting Smart,* 7 November 2017, https://www.gettingsmart.com/2017/11/at-the-intersection-of-creativity-and-critical-thinking/ (accessed 23 April 2020).
194 C. Sagan, *Dragons of Eden: Speculations on the Evolution of Human Intelligence* (Random House, 1977).
195 C. Bergland, 'Einstein's Genius Linked to Well-Connected Brain Hemispheres', *Psychology Today,* 5 October 2013, https://www.psychologytoday.com/us/blog/the-athletes-way/201310/einsteins-genius-linked-well-connected-brain-hemispheres (accessed 23 April 2020).
196 Ibid.
197 M. Victoria Liptak, *Creative Criticality and Critical Creativity: Cross-wiring Bloom's Taxonomy* (25th NCBDS, 2009), http://ncbds.la-ab.com/25_Proceedings.pdf (accessed 23 April 2020).
198 P. Petrone, 'Why Creativity is the Most Important Skill in the World', 1 January 2019, https://learning.linkedin.com/blog/top-skills/why-creativity-is-the-most-important-skill-in-the-world (accessed 23 April 2020).

199 D. Leatherbarrow, *Making: Invention and Involvement* (Proceedings 26th National Conference on the Beginning Design Student, 2010), p 15.
200 Ozkar, 2017, p 142.
201 W. Deresiewicz, 'Solitude and Leadership', *The American Scholar,* 1 March 2010, https://theamericanscholar.org/solitude-and-leadership/#.Xf6isi2ZOgQ (accessed 23 April 2020).
202 Tippey, 2008.
203 D.J. Treffinger, 'Preparing Creative and Critical Thinkers', *Educational Leadership,* Summer 2008, http://www.ascd.org/publications/educational-leadership/summer08/vol65/num09/Preparing-Creative-and-Critical-Thinkers.aspx (accessed 23 April 2020).
204 C. Sagan, *Dragons of Eden: Speculations on the Evolution of Human Intelligence* (Random House, 1977).
205 S. Hoque, *An Ethnographic Study of Design Studio Practices* (Proceedings 25th National Conference on the Beginning Design Student, 2009).
206 R. Hargrove, 'Fostering Creativity and Creative Thinking in Studio', *Art Design & Communication in Higher Education,* vol. 10, no. 1, 2011.
207 A. Tzannes in M. Crick, 1998.
208 Hargrove, 2011.
209 S. Hoque, *An Ethnographic Study of Design Studio Practices* (Proceedings 25th National Conference on the Beginning Design Student, 2009).
210 R. Thallon, J. Young, *Pattern Language: Teaching Beginning Students* (Proceedings 5th National Conference on the Beginning Design Student, 1988), p 203.
211 A. Gribbin, *Design and Critical Thinking: Applying Perry's Theory of Intellectual Development to Foundational Design Instruction* (19th Proceedings on Beginning Design Student, 2003), p 201.
212 S. Piedmont-Palladino, *Absolute Beginners: Teaching Architecture to Pre-Architects* (Tenth National Conference on the Beginning Design Student, 1993), p 223.
213 Gribbin, 2003, p 203.
214 Ozkar, 2017, p 2.
215 German philosopher Friedrich Nietzsche: 'That which does not kill us, makes us stronger.'
216 Gribbin, 2003, p 204.
217 'Design is Our Answer – An Interview with Leading Design Thinker Tim Brown', *Architectural Design,* July–August 2015, p 37.
218 E. Lee, 'The Architecture of Design Thinking', *Practice of Architecture,* 29 March 2019, https://practiceofarchitecture.com/2019/03/29/the-architecture-of-design-thinking/ (accessed 23 April 2020).
219 C. Chanzaras, 'Architecture as System Design & Innovation Design Discipline, Relating Systems Thinking and Design', 2017, https://systemic-design.net/wp-content/uploads/2018/01/Chantzaras.pdf (accessed 23 April 2020).
220 R. Weddle, 'Thinking Outside the Design Box', SBJ, 15 July 2019, https://sbj.net/stories/opinion-thinking-outside-the-design-box,64667 (accessed 23 April 2020).
221 Ibid.
222 A. Rawsthorn, 'Can Design Solve Social Problems?', *Fast Company,* 1 November 2008, https://www.fastcompany.com/1042492/can-design-solve-social-problems (accessed 23 April 2020).
223 T. de Monchaux, 'A New Idea in Architecture? No New Buildings', *Metropolis,* 30 December 2019, https://www.metropolismag.com/architecture/new-idea-architecture-no-new-buildings/ (accessed 23 April 2020).
224 E. Lee in R. Deutsch, *Data Driven Design and Construction* (Wiley, 2015).
225 J. Ochshorn, 'Architect Designs and Builds Home Addition: Process Explained in Terms of Cause, Effect', 2004–5, http://www.ochshorndesign.com/cornell/writings/cause-effect/index.html (accessed 23 April 2020).
226 N. Cross, 'Designerly ways of knowing: design discipline versus design science', *Design Studies,* vol. 3, no. 4, October 1982, pp 221–7.
227 R. Hargrove, 'Fostering Creativity and Creative Thinking in Studio', *Art, Design & Communication in Higher Education,* vol. 10, no. 1, 2011.
228 Hargrove, 2011.
229 M.T. Brehm, *Think>Make and Make/Think: Beginning Steps in Architectural Design* (Proceedings 26th National Conference on the Beginning Design Student, 2010), p 171.
230 E.G. Bormann, *Theory and Research in the Communicative Arts* (Holt, Rinehart and Winston, 1965), p 131.
231 Hoque, 2009.
232 M. Lamster, 'The Virtues and Perils of Design Thinking', *Architect,* 8 July 2010, https://www.architectmagazine.com/design/the-virtues-and-perils-of-design-thinking_o (accessed 24 April 2020).
233 P.M. Davis, *Critical Skills for Solving Design Problems* (Images Publishing Group, 2020), p 5.
234 Brehm, 2010.
235 Davis, 2020.
236 E.O. Moss in M. Crick, 1998.
237 D. Beres, 'Being Busy is Killing our Ability to Think Creatively', *Big Think,* 3 July 2017, https://bigthink.com/21st-century-spirituality/creativity-and-distraction (accessed 24 April 2020).
238 E.O. Moss in M. Crick, 1998.
239 Beres, 2017.
240 C. Newport, *Deep Work: Rules for Focused Success in a Distracted World* (Grand Central Publishing, 2016).
241 E. Connell, *Teaching Intuition,* (14th Proceedings on Beginning Design Education, 1997), p 23.
242 G. Klein, *The Power of Intuition: How to Use Your Gut Feelings to Make Better Decisions* (Random House, 2007).
243 J.N. Baldeweg in M. Crick, 1998.
244 L. Clare in M. Crick, 1998.
245 T. Mayne in M. Crick, 1998.
246 D. Libeskind in M. Crick, 1998.
247 P. Wilson in M. Crick, 1998.
248 G. Murcutt in M. Crick, 1998.
249 *Alvar Aalto: Points of Contact* (Aalto Museum, Exhibition Catalogue, 1994), pp 14–17.
250 Zumthor, 1998.
251 P. Tonkin in M. Crick, 1998.
252 F. Strachan, 'Architecture Can Help Solve Poverty, Inequality, Segregation', UNSW Sydney, 27 July 2017, https://newsroom.unsw.edu.au/news/art-architecture-design/architecture-can-help-solve-poverty-inequality-segregation (accessed 24 April 2020).
253 V. Belogolovsky, 'Steven Holl: I am Interested in Architecture that "Speaks to the Soul"', ArchDaily, 21 September 2019, https://www.archdaily.com/925219/steven-holl-i-am-interested-in-architecture-that-speaks-to-the-soul (accessed 24 April 2020).

254 D. Kelbaugh in R. Kasprisin, *Play in Creative Problem-Solving for Planners and Architects* (Routledge, 2016).
255 K. Puljak, *Why Do You Always Make Us Think? Maintaining a Journal in the Beginning Design Studio* (18th Proceedings on Beginning Design Student, 2002), p 51.
256 Brehm, 2010.
257 J. Tate, *The Architecture Concept Book* (Thames & Hudson, 2018).
258 O. Ferrari in A. Anderson, *Design Process: A Teaching Pedagogy* (Tenth National Conference on the Beginning Design Student, 1993), p 317.
259 C. Scarpa, G. Zambonini, 'Process and Theme in the Work of Carlo Scarpa', *The Yale Architectural Journal* (The MIT Press, 1983), pp 23–4.
260 P. Tonkin in M. Crick, 1998.
261 M.T. Foster, *Diagramming: A Graphic Tool to Develop Conceptual Thinking and Organizational Skills* (08 Proceedings Beginning Design Education, 1990).
262 C. Rossi, 'Craft Contains the Critical Thinking That Could Unpack the Current State of Architecture', *The Architectural Review,* 7 February 2017, https://www.architectural-review.com/essays/craft-contains-the-critical-thinking-that-could-unpack-the-current-state-of-architecture/10016445.article (accessed 24 April 2020).
263 J. Szalai, '"Working", Robert A. Caro Gives Us a Brief Look at the Process of Writing His Epic Books', *The New York Times,* 9 April 2019, https://www.nytimes.com/2019/04/09/books/review-working-robert-caro.html (accessed 24 April 2020).
264 J.J. O'Donnell, 'How Is the Internet Changing the Way You Think? My Fingers Have Become Part of My Brain', *Edge,* 2010, https://www.edge.org/response-detail/11113 (accessed 24 April 2020).
265 R. Judkins, 'Think With Your Hands', *Psychology Today,* 26 August 2014, https://www.psychologytoday.com/us/blog/connect-creativity/201408/think-your-hands (accessed 24 April 2020).
266 Ibid.
267 J. Ochshorn, 'Architect Designs and Builds Home Addition, *Process Explained in Terms of Cause, Effect*', 2004–5, http://www.ochshorndesign.com/cornell/writings/cause-effect/index.html (accessed 24 April 2020).
268 G. Murcutt in M. Crick, 1998.
269 'At the Intersection of Technology and Professional Practice', *DesignIntelligence,* 15 May 2018, https://www.di.net/articles/intersection-technology-professional-practice/ (accessed 24 April 2020).
270 S.S. Szenasy, P. Bernstein, 'What Technology Can and Can't Do', *Metropolis,* 9 February 2016, https://www.metropolismag.com/sponsored/susan-szenasy-phil-bernstein-computing-technology-can-cant-do/ (accessed 24 April 2020).
271 R. Otani, 'How Far Can Automation Go?', 9 May 2018, https://www.thorntontomasetti.com/how_far_can_automation_go/ (accessed 24 April 2020).
272 Zumthor, 1998.
273 S. Hoque, *An Ethnographic Study of Design Studio Practices* (Proceedings 25th National Conference on the Beginning Design Student, 2009).
274 P. Sisson, 'How Jeanne Gang's Firm Designed a Better Police Station', *Curbed,* 2 October 2015, https://www.curbed.com/2015/10/2/9915166/jeanne-gang-architect-police-station-chicago (accessed 24 April 2020).
275 L. MacLellan, 'The Life-Changing Art of Asking Instead of Telling', *Quartz at Work,* 22 November 2018, https://qz.com/work/1472600/the-life-changing-art-of-asking-instead-of-telling/?hootPostID=f04fadb897850e856b5753fd3c5f6c16 (accessed 24 April 2020).
276 D. Beswick, 'A Lecture Presentation at the Centre for Applied Educational Research', University of Melbourne, 2000, http://www.beswick.info/psychres/curiosityintro.htm (accessed 24 April 2020).
277 'Curiosity: Beyond the Killing of Cats', *EBD Journal,* n.d., http://ebdjournal.com/blog/general-design/curiosity#fn:1 (accessed 24 April 2020).
278 E. Blanchard, 'The Curiosity Gap', December 2018, https://www.td.org/magazines/td-magazine/the-curiosity-gap (accessed 24 April 2020).
279 M. James, 'Critical Thinking, Problem Solving, Creativity are Skills Needed for the Future of Work in the 21st Century', 13 October 2017, https://www.masstlc.org/critical-thinking-problem-solving-creativity-are-skills-needed-for-the-future-of-work-in-the-21st-century/ (accessed 25 April 2020).
280 R. Gonzalez, 'Leonardo da Vinci's Hand-Written Resume Will Make You Feel Inadequate', *Gizmodo,* 7 February 2015, https://io9.gizmodo.com/leonardo-da-vincis-hand-written-resume-will-make-you-fe-1684441362 (accessed 25 April 2020).
281 G. Lindt, *Taking Time to Develop Metacognition for Deeper Design Learning,* (University of Cincinnati, 2018), p 4.
282 P. Mehrotra, 'Growth and Creativity Mindsets', 30 November 2017, http://blog.mindantix.com/2017/11/growth-and-creativity-mindsets/ (accessed 25 April 2020).
283 C. Dweck, *Mindset: The New Psychology of Success* (Random House, 2006).
284 Ibid.
285 Temple, 2015, p 9.
286 P.M. Davis, *Critical Skills for Solving Design Problems* (Images Publishing Group, 2020), p 5.
287 Mehrotra, 2017.
288 H.H. Harris in C. Rowe, *As I was Saying: Recollections and Miscellaneous Essays,* (MIT Press, 1996), p 51.
289 W. Alsop in M. Crick, 1998.
290 G. Goldschmidt, H. Hochman, I. Dafni, 'The Design Studio "Crit": Teacher–Student Communication', *Artificial Intelligence for Engineering Design, Analysis and Manufacturing,* 2 August 2009, pp 285–302.
291 'Daniel Libeskind on Working Unconventionally', *Harvard Business Review,* July–August, 2018, https://hbr.org/ideacast/2018/07/architect-daniel-libeskind-on-working-unconventionally.html (accessed 25 April 2009).
292 Ibid.
293 E. Jenkins, *The Acquisition of Precedent* (Tenth National Conference on the Beginning Design Student, 1993), p 187.
294 Henry James, 'The Art of Fiction', *Longman's Magazine,* no. 4, September 1884, https://public.wsu.edu/~campbelld/amlit/artfiction.html (accessed 29 April 2020).
295 J.A. Scelsa, 'Observing Time: Employing Positivist Observation As a Bridge to Abstraction in Early Design Education', 2018, https://journals.uc.edu/index.php/ncbds/article/view/763 (accessed 25 April 2020).
296 K. Alter, *Reel to Reel* (14th Proceedings on Beginning Design Education, 1997), p 63.

297 J.S. Hartnett, *Flat to Round and Back Again: Representations* (Proceedings 5th National Conference on the Beginning Design Student, 1988), p 135.
298 Krokow, 2018.
299 'Between stimulus and response there is space. In that space is our power to choose our response. In our response lies our growth and our freedom,' has been attributed to Viktor E. Frankl. Researchers have been unable to find this passage in the works of Viktor E. Frankl. https://quoteinvestigator.com/2018/02/18/response/ (accessed 25 April 2020).
300 D. Bartels, 'Critical Thinking Is Best Taught Outside the Classroom', *Scientific American,* 27 February 2013, https://www.scientificamerican.com/article/critical-thinking-best-taught-outside-classroom/ (accessed 25 April 2020).
301 Temple, 2015, p9.
302 R. Thallon, J. Young, *Pattern Language as a Tool for Teaching Beginning Students* (Proceedings 5th National Conference on the Beginning Design Student, 1988), p 203.
303 E. Danze, *Intuition* (19th Proceedings on Beginning Design Student, 2003), p 121.
304 Ibid.
305 MacLellan, 2018.
306 Ibid.
307 Based on a suggestion by Tyler Cowen, 'Reading and Rabbit Holes', *Marginal Revolution,* 10 August 2019, https://marginalrevolution.com/marginalrevolution/2019/08/reading-and-rabbit-holes.html (accessed 25 April 2020).
308 J. Numbers, *Interim Studio Critiques: Intentions and Outcomes* (08 Proceedings Beginning Design Education, 1990), p 126.
309 MacLellan, 2018.
310 L. Chesser, '50 Questions To Help Students Think About What They Think', *TeachThought,* 10 December 2017, https://www.teachthought.com/critical-thinking/metacognition-50-questions-help-students-think-think/ (accessed 25 April 2020).
311 T. Mayne in M. Crick, 1998.
312 O. Scheeren, 'Why Great Architecture Should Tell a Story', TED Global, London, September 2015, https://www.ted.com/talks/ole_scheeren_why_great_architecture_should_tell_a_story?language=en, (4:34) (accessed 25 April 2020).
313 K. Sawyer, *Zig Zag: The Surprising Path to Greater Creativity* (Jossey-Bass, 2013).
314 A. Salituri,, 'Design is Not Problem Solving', *Medium,* 22 December 2017, https://medium.com/@salituri/design-is-not-problem-solving-bace64318d56 (accessed 25 April 2020).
315 R. Kasprisin, *Play in Creative Problem-Solving for Planners and Architects* (Routledge, 2016).
316 N. Grimshaw in M. Crick, 1998.
317 P.J. Armstrong, *Figure/Field Permutation: The Cubist Syntax* (Proceedings 5th National Conference on the Beginning Design Student, 1988), p 188.
318 J. Ochshorn, 'Architect Designs and Builds Home Addition, Process Explained in Terms of Cause, Effect', 2004–5, http://www.ochshorndesign.com/cornell/writings/cause-effect/index.html (accessed 25 April 2020).
319 Ibid.
320 S.J. Kirk, K.F. Spreckelmeyer, *Creative Design Decisions* (Van Nostrand Reinhold, 1988) p 8.
321 G. MacKenzie, *Orbiting the Giant Hairball: A Corporate Fool's Guide to Surviving with Grace* (Viking, 1998).
322 N. Durbach in M. Crick, 1998.
323 J. Postell, *Teaching Beginning Students: Introducing a Paradigm* (Proceedings 5th National Conference on the Beginning Design Student, 1988), p 26.
324 T. McGinty, *Skillful Beginnings* (11th Proceedings National Conference on the Beginning Design Student, 1994).
325 R. Martin, The Opposable Mind (Harvard Business Review Press, 2007).
326 S. Unwin, *University of Dundee Keynote: Making Sense of Architecture* (Proceedings 26th National Conference on the Beginning Design Student, 2010), p 14.
327 L. Houghton, D. Tuffley, *Towards a Methodology of Wicked Problem Exploration through Concept Shifting and Tension Point Analysis,* 2013.
328 P. Wilson in M. Crick, 1998.
329 W. Alsop in M. Crick, 1998.
330 P. Graham, 'The Bus Ticket Theory of Genius', November 2019, http://paulgraham.com/genius.html (accessed 26 April 2020).
331 S. Sinha, *Autotelic Architect: Changing World, Changing Practice* (Routledge, 2016).
332 A.M. Harris, *A Beginning Professor's Path Toward Effective Teaching: My Search for Balance* (08 Proceedings Beginning Design Education, 1990).
333 S.G. Carmichael, 'Architect Daniel Libeskind on Working Unconventionally', *Harvard Business Review,* July–August 2018, https://hbr.org/ideacast/2018/07/architect-daniel-libeskind-on-working-unconventionally.html (accessed 26 April 2020).
334 J.C. Hernandez, 'Study Finds Chinese Students Excel in Critical Thinking. Until College', *The New York Times,* 30 July 2016, https://www.nytimes.com/2016/07/31/world/asia/china-college-education-quality.html?searchResultPosition=38 (accessed 26 April 2020).
335 T. Hurson, *Think Better: An Innovator's Guide to Productive Thinking* (McGraw-Hill Education, 2010).
336 Y. Brikman, 'Don't Learn To Code Learn To Think', 19 May 2014, https://www.ybrikman.com/writing/2014/05/19/dont-learn-to-code-learn-to-think/ (accessed 26 April 2020).
337 W. Rybczynski, 'Think Before You Build: Have Computers Made Architects Less Disciplined?', *Slate,* 30 March 2011, https://slate.com/culture/2011/03/have-computers-made-architects-less-disciplined.html (accessed 26 April 2020).
338 S. Greengard, 'Are We Losing Our Ability to Think Critically?', *Communications of the ACM,* July 2009, https://cacm.acm.org/magazines/2009/7/32082-are-we-losing-our-ability-to-think-critically/fulltext (accessed 26 April 2020).
339 M. Carpo, 'The Alternative Science of Computation,' *e-flux architecture,* June 2017, http://www.e-flux.com/architecture/artificial-labor/142274/the-alternative-science-of-computation/ (accessed 26 April 2020).
340 J. Szalai, 'Why Has Language Changed So Much So Fast Because Internet', *The New York Times,* 22 July 2019, https://www.nytimes.com/2019/07/22/books/review-because-internet-understanding-new-rules-language-gretchen-mcculloch.html (accessed 26 April 2020).
341 A. Quito, 'WeWork Is Retraining a Generation of Architects to Think in Terms of Data', *Metropolis,*

25 February 2019, https://www.metropolismag.com/architecture/workplace-architecture/wework-workplace-design-data-analytics/ (accessed 26 April 2020).
342 M. Özkar, 2017, pp 141–2.
343 J. Aoun, 'In An Age of Machines, Critical Thinking Gives People the Edge', *CXO Magazine,* 1 November 2017, https://medium.com/cxo-magazine/in-an-age-of-machines-critical-thinking-gives-people-the-edge-e2b80d0ff439 (accessed 26 April 2020).
344 Franco, 2019.
345 See Chapter 2 in D.J. Epstein, *Range: Why Generalists Triumph in a Specialised World* (Riverhead Books, 2019). I first came across this question fifteen years prior in W. Poundstone, *How Would You Move Mount Fuji?* (Little, Brown and Company, 2003).
346 Poundstone, 2003, p 163.
347 Ibid., p 8.
348 From Chapter 1 of an unpublished book, 'Explorations in Wicked Problems: What They Are and Why They Are Important' in J. Bentley, *Wicked Problems: An Idea Whose Time Has Come,* 11 November 2018, http://tamingwickedproblems.com/wicked-problems-an-idea-whose-time-has-come/ (accessed 26 April 2020).
349 Bentley, 2018.
350 O. Butcher, 'Can Architecture Help Us Solve Real World Issues?' 17 November 2017, http://warwickglobalist.com/2017/11/13/can-architecture-help-us-to-solve-real-world-issues/ (accessed 26 April 2020).
351 F. Strachan, 'Architecture Can Help Solve Poverty, Inequality, Segregation', UNSW Sydney, 27 July 2017, https://newsroom.unsw.edu.au/news/art-architecture-design/architecture-can-help-solve-poverty-inequality-segregation (accessed 26 April 2020).
352 R. Weddle, 'Thinking Outside the Design Box', *SBJ,* 15 July 2019, https://sbj.net/stories/opinion-thinking-outside-the-design-box,64667 (accessed 26 April 2020).
353 *NCARB Practice Analysis of Architecture* (2012), p 48.
354 M. Crick, 1998.
355 C. Brause, 'Collaborative Beginnings: Developing Collaboration Skills in an Interdisciplinary Design Seminar', 8 October 2018, https://journals.uc.edu/index.php/ncbds/article/view/774 (accessed 27 April 2020).
356 C. Brause, *The Designer's Field Guide To Collaboration* (Routledge, 2017), p vii.
357 R. Deutsch, 'How We Can Make Collaboration Work', *DesignIntelligence,* 4 February 2014.
358 'The Theory & Event Interview: Sovereignty, Multitudes, Absolute Democracy: A Discussion between Michael Hardt and Thomas L Dumm about Hardt's and Negri's Empire', in P.A. Passavant, J. Dean (eds), *Empire's New Clothes: Reading Hardt and Negri* (Routledge, 2004), p 163.
359 A. Carlsen, S. Clegg, R. Gjersvik, 'Idea Work: Lessons of the Extraordinary in Everyday Creativity', introduction in *Why Talk About Idea Work, and What Does It Matter?* (J W Cappelens Forlag AS, 2013).
360 C. Weber, 'How to Talk to Clients', *Architecture,* 12 February 2013, https://www.architectmagazine.com/practice/how-to-talk-to-clients_o (accessed 27 April 2020).
361 A. Aravena in F. Strachan, 'Architecture Can Help Solve Poverty, Inequality, Segregation', UNSW Sydney, 27 July 2017, https://newsroom.unsw.edu.au/news/art-architecture-design/architecture-can-help-solve-poverty-inequality-segregation (accessed 27 April 2020).
362 S. Hoque, *An Ethnographic Study of Design Studio Practices* (Proceedings 25th National Conference on the Beginning Design Student, 2009).
363 R. Deutsch, 'How We Can Make Collaboration Work', *DesignIntelligence,* 4 February 2014.
364 A. Carlsen, S. Clegg, R. Gjersvik, *Idea Work: Lessons of the Extraordinary in Everyday Creativity.* (Cappelen Damm, 2012), pp 332–40.
365 The Arbinger Institute, *The Outward Mindset: Seeing Beyond Ourselves* (Berrett-Koehler, 2019).
366 D.M. Gordon, 'An Ant Colony Has Memories That Its Individual Members Don't Have', *Aeon,* 11 December 2018, https://aeon.co/ideas/an-ant-colony-has-memories-that-its-individual-members-dont-have (accessed 27 April 2020).
367 Carlsen, Clegg, Gjersvik, 2012, pp 332-40.
368 'Architect Daniel Libeskind on Working Unconventionally', *Harvard Business Review,* July–August 2018, https://hbr.org/ideacast/2018/07/architect-daniel-libeskind-on-working-unconventionally.html (accessed 27 April 2020).
369 T. Henry, *Herding Tigers: Be the Leader That Creative People Need* (Portfolio, 2018).
370 MacLellan, 2018.
371 E. Schein, *Humble Inquiry* (Berrett-Koehler, 2013).
372 R. Handa, *Teaching Design Judgment* (11th National Conference on the Beginning Design Student, 1994), p 66.
373 V. Shah, 'The Role of Architecture in Humanity's Story', 8 June 2012, http://thoughteconomics.blogspot.com/2012/06/role-of-architecture-in-humanitys-story.html (accessed 22 January 2020).
374 Keynote address, University of Arizona CAPLA Futures Council, 17 February 2020.
375 https://snohetta.com/process/transpositioning (accessed 27 April 2020).
376 V. Henriksson, M. Hult, *Rationalizing Freeform Architecture: Surface Discretization and Multi-objective Optimization,* master's thesis (2015).
377 E. Jolliffe, 'Architectural Education is a Problem of Degrees', *Building Design,* 15 October 2019, https://www.bdonline.co.uk/comment/architectural-education-is-a-problem-of-degrees/5102123.article (accessed 27 April 2020).

Index

Page numbers in **bold** indicate figures.

Image Credits

Figure 37.1
F.L.C. / ADAGP, Paris / Artists Rights Society (ARS), New York 2020

Figure 48.1
The Interlace by OMA / Ole Scheeren

All other images by Bruce Bondy

modeste, mais il aura plus tard l'occasion de présenter ses projets à l'empereur Léopold I en 1688. Par ailleurs, il travaille pendant les années 1690, avec Jablonski et l'appui politique de Sophie Charlotte, à l'établissement d'une société des sciences à Berlin. Il en sera nommé le premier président en 1700. Par la suite, il travaille également sur des projets semblables à Vienne et à St. Petersburg[1]. Sa vision de la collaboration scientifique pour le bien commun et la gloire de Dieu trouvera son expression la plus émouvante dans le très beau *Mémoire pour des personnes éclairées et de bonne intention* de 1692[2].

Toutes ces activités de mathématiques, de physique, d'ingénierie, de théologie, d'historiographie, de politique, de diplomatie et de politique académique occupent Leibniz de manière continue pendant sa carrière à Hanovre. Mais elles ne l'empêchent pas de travailler sur sa pensée philosophique qui prend de plus en plus forme pendant la première moitié des années 1680. Si l'on devait identifier une *annus mirabilis* dans la biographie de Leibniz, ce serait l'année 1686, où il rédige quatre textes fondamentaux en physique, métaphysique, théologie et logique, respectivement: la *Brevis demonstatio erroris memorabilis Cartesii*, le *Discours de métaphysique*, l'*Examen religionis Christianae* (également connu sous le nom de *Systema theologicum*) et les *Generales Inquisitiones de Analysi Notionum et Veritatum*. C'est par ailleurs la période à laquelle, par la suite, Leibniz fera lui-même remonter sa première ébauche de philosophie complète. Cela dit, c'est une date à manier avec beaucoup de prudence : on note que Leibniz ne publie qu'un seul de ces quatre textes (la *Brevis demonstratio*). Le plus connu d'entre eux, le *Discours de métaphysique*, sera immédiatement soumis à des révisions importantes à l'occasion de la correspondance avec Arnauld. De façon générale, la pensée philosophique de Leibniz continuera à évoluer de manière importante[3]. Cela dit, ces quatre textes, dont les thèses s'appuient mutuellement sur des questions centrales et qui forment un ensemble relativement cohérent, donnent à première vue l'impression d'un esprit qui arrive à une première destination. Cela ne veut toutefois pas dire qu'il y reste. En témoigne le récit qu'il propose de son propre développement quelques années plus tard: « après avoir établi ces choses, je croyais entrer dans le bon port; mais

1. Voir Leibniz, *Le Droit de la raison*, 241-52.

2. *Mémoire pour des personnes éclairées et de bonne intention*, A IV, 4, 612-621 et dans Leibniz, *Le Droit de la raison*, p. 234-240.

3. Voir M. Fichant, « L'invention métaphysique ».

lorsque je me suis mis à méditer sur l'union de l'âme avec le corps, je fus comme rejeté en pleine mer »[1].

Cette dernière citation provient du *Système nouveau de la nature et de la communication des substances*, publié dans le *Journal des savants* en 1695. Ce texte représente en effet une nouvelle étape dans le développement philosophique de Leibniz : c'est le moment où il soumet à l'évaluation du monde intellectuel son « système ». Présenté notamment comme une alternative au cartésianisme, le *Système nouveau* provoque des critiques à la fois vives et perspicaces, entre autres de la part de René-Joseph de Tournemine dans les *Mémoires de Trévoux*, et de Pierre Bayle, dans l'article « Rorarius » de son *Dictionnaire historique et critique* (1697). Ces critiques inciteront Leibniz à approfondir des aspects clés de sa métaphysique, notamment sur la question de l'union de l'âme et du corps. À la même période, il rédige d'importants travaux scientifiques qui sont en partie reliés à ces considérations métaphysiques. On notera, en particulier, la *Dynamica de potentia* de 1689 et le *Specimen dynamicum* de 1695. Ces aspects métaphysiques et physiques sont d'ailleurs discutés avec de nombreux correspondants et, comme souvent, les lettres sont un complément nécessaire à la compréhension des positions leibniziennes. Soulignons notamment les correspondances avec Fardella, De Volder, Papin et Bernoulli, dans lesquels Leibniz discute de sa conception renouvelée de la substance et de son concept de force primitive qui sera à l'origine de la controverse sur les forces vives qui se déroulera jusqu'au milieu du XVIIIe siècle.

Vers 1704, Leibniz rédige les *Nouveaux essais sur l'entendement humain*, une réponse aux *Essais sur l'entendement humain* de John Locke qu'il lit dans la traduction française de Pierre Coste publiée en 1700 (laquelle est tirée de la 4e édition du texte). Son commentaire suivi sera achevé, mais jamais publié du vivant de Leibniz en raison de la mort de Locke en 1704. Le texte ne sera édité qu'en 1765 et constitue l'une des sources les plus importantes pour comprendre les thèses de Leibniz dans le domaine épistémologique. Vers la même époque, Leibniz commence également la rédaction d'un autre livre, lequel sera d'ailleurs le seul ouvrage philosophique d'envergure paru de son vivant : il s'agit des *Essais de théodicée*, publiés en 1710. L'occasion initiale en fut donnée par la deuxième édition du *Dictionnaire historique et critique* (1702) de Pierre Bayle. La discussion avec le scepticisme fidéiste affiché par Bayle dans son *Dictionnaire* est en effet centrale dans l'ouvrage. Toutefois, en proposant sa « théodicée », Leibniz réalise en même temps un projet de

1. GP IV, 483.

théologie naturelle en forme d'apologie de Dieu conçue bien des années auparavant[1]. L'ouvrage connaît un immense succès. À partir de 1710, il travaille avec le jésuite Bartholomeus des Bosses à une traduction latine. À la suite de cette publication, Leibniz s'efforcera également de résumer ses positions métaphysiques dans certains opuscules, le plus célèbre étant celui connu aujourd'hui sous le titre *La Monadologie*, rédigé en 1714 et qui est arrimé au contenu des *Essais de théodicée* (chaque article renvoie en effet aux sections correspondantes dans ce dernier ouvrage). La même année, il rédige un autre opuscule important, les *Principes de la nature et de la grâce fondés en raison*.

En 1714, Georg Ludwig, accède au trône d'Angleterre sous le nom de George Ier. La Cours de Hanovre déménage à Londres. Leibniz n'est jamais convié à la rejoindre et reçoit même l'ordre de rester en Allemagne, seul. Il faut aussi dire que ses rapports avec le monde intellectuel anglais se détériorent de plus en plus en raison de sa dispute avec les newtoniens, en particulier à propos de l'invention du calcul différentiel et intégral. Toutefois, il ne se décourage pas, et jusqu'à sa mort, compose des textes qui comptent parmi les plus connus, y compris la correspondance avec le newtonien Samuel Clarke en 1715-1716 contenant des discussions célèbres sur la nature de l'espace et l'attraction; les *Observations sur le projet de paix perpétuelle* de 1715, commentaire quelque peu sarcastique du projet de paix idéaliste de l'Abbé Castel de St. Pierre[2], et le magnifique *Discours sur la théologie naturelle des chinois* de 1715 où Leibniz revient sur son intérêt pour la Chine qui remonte à plus vingt ans et à son édition d'un recueil de « nouvelles de Chine » issues des missions jésuites, les *Novissima Sinica* de 1697[3].

Souffrant de la goutte et de l'arthrose qui l'empêchent d'écrire, Leibniz meurt à Hanovre le 14 novembre 1716[4].

On l'a déjà indiqué, Leibniz a non seulement entretenu des correspondances avec un nombre considérable de savants, théologiens et figures

1. Voir P. Rateau, *La Question du mal chez Leibniz*.

2. Pour ce texte et la correspondance associée, voir Leibniz et Saint Pierre, *Correspondance Leibniz – Castel de Saint Pierre*.

3. Voir Leibniz, *Discours sur la théologie naturelle des Chinois*.

4. Il n'existe pas de biographie de Leibniz en français. La première partie du *Leibniz. Initiation à son système* d'Y. Belaval contient un portrait assez détaillé mais le livre est, aujourd'hui, un peu daté. Pour ceux qui s'intéressent davantage à la vie de Leibniz, la biographie intellectuelle récente en anglais de M.-R. Antognazza est devenue la référence. Notons aussi le travail brillant d'E. J. Aiton. En allemand, il existe l'ancienne biographie de G. E. Guhrauer, la très précise chronique de K. Müller er G. Krönert, et le livre de E. C. Hirke, *Der berühmte Herr Leibniz : Eine Biographie*, un travail rigoureux et destiné au grand public.

politiques, mais a aussi conservé à peu près tous les textes de ces échanges. Il en est d'ailleurs de même des autres manuscrits qui composent le *Leibniz-Archiv* se trouvant à la Landesbibliothek de la Basse-Saxe à Hanovre : brouillons, plans, esquisses, notes de lectures, fragments, etc., qui représentent près de 50 000 pièces. L'état des archives de Leibniz est d'une certaine manière à l'image de sa pensée philosophique et scientifique, à savoir abondante et variée ; les pièces permettent par ailleurs de comprendre la manière dont Leibniz travaillait. Une thèse ou un argument est presque toujours l'objet de multiples tentatives, certaines plus complètes que d'autres. Il n'est donc pas rare que, pour un sujet ou un problème donné, nous soyons en possession de nombreux fragments ou textes plus achevés, la plupart du temps assez cohérents sur le plan conceptuel, mais parfois aussi plus difficilement conciliables. Prenons l'exemple des travaux en physique : de l'*Hypothesis physica nova* de 1671 au *Specimen dynamicum* de 1695 ou à l'*Essai de dynamique* de 1701, les positions de Leibniz changent, malgré la pérennité de plusieurs thèmes et arguments. On constate la même chose dans le domaine métaphysique : le *Discours de métaphysique* de 1686, le *Système nouveau de la nature* de 1695 et la *Monadologie* de 1714, bien que semblables sur plusieurs points, présentent des particularités qu'on doit prendre en considération. C'est que Leibniz semblait rarement satisfait du résultat final d'un opuscule ou essai et souhaitait presque toujours le retravailler. L'abondance des manuscrits permet ainsi de constater l'évolution des thèmes et des approches : sur près de soixante années de production scientifique et philosophique, Leibniz s'est intéressé à des objets qui nécessitent, pour en comprendre la portée, de déterminer leur contexte. Notons d'ailleurs que de cet ensemble, très peu a été publié par Leibniz lui-même. En philosophie, seuls quelques opuscules et l'*Essai de théodicée* de 1710 sont parus de son vivant. Des contributions qu'on juge aujourd'hui comme étant essentielles à la compréhension de la pensée leibnizienne, comme le *Discours de métaphysique* ou les *Nouveaux Essais sur l'entendement humain*, sont restées pendant longtemps inédits.

Il n'est donc pas difficile de comprendre que l'édition des œuvres de Leibniz a rencontré de nombreux obstacles. Celle-ci a certes souffert de conditions politiques défavorables, en particulier au XXe, mais il est aussi vrai que la nature du corpus pose à toute édition un problème qu'on ne rencontre pas dans la publication des œuvres complètes d'autres figures de l'histoire de la philosophie et des sciences. C'est l'une des raisons pour laquelle l'édition complète est non seulement toujours en cours de publication, mais il semble aussi que nous aurons à attendre encore quelques décennies avant qu'elle ne soit achevée. Avant le XXe siècle, il existe bien entendu des éditions importantes qui ont fait connaître de nombreux textes leibniziens. Au XVIIIe siècle, époque durant laquelle seul un nombre restreint de contributions sont connues, deux éditions ont quand même permis une diffusion élargie : les *Œuvres philosophiques latines et françaises* éditées par Raspe[1], lesquelles ont notamment rendu disponible les *Nouveaux Essais*, et l'édition des *Opera omnia* en 1768 (voir Dutens) qui contiennent des œuvres déjà publiées, mais souvent plus difficiles d'accès. Mais il faudra attendre le XIXe siècle pour que d'autres éditions fassent connaître des pièces centrales du corpus leibnizien. Le *Discours de métaphysique* sera notamment publié par Grotefend en 1846[2]. Notons toutefois surtout l'une des grandes éditions de textes leibniziens de l'époque, soit celle de Gerhardt. Ce dernier a en réalité édité deux séries, l'une mathématique et scientifique (GM), l'autre philosophique (GP). Ces publications sont toujours en usage pour les textes de la maturité, faute d'une édition plus complète. Finalement, au XXe siècle, certains chercheurs ont fait paraître d'autres inédits : on pense pour l'essentiel à l'édition de Couturat (C), contenant d'importants textes de logique et de métaphysique, et à celle de Grua (Grua), comportant des textes théologiques et de philosophie pratique.

Toutes ces éditions, on le comprend, sont partielles et ne rendent accessibles qu'une partie des manuscrits. L'édition qui vise à les remplacer est celle des *Sämtliche Schriften und Briefe* entamée au début du XXe siècle et toujours en cours (A, séries I à VIII)[3]. Comme on le soulignait, cette édition a connu des retards importants étant donné des situations politiques difficiles, surtout sous le régime national-socialiste et lors de la division de l'Allemagne. La complexité de la tâche nécessite l'investissement d'une pluralité d'institutions, dont le projet est chapeauté par les Académies des sciences de Göttingen et de Berlin-Brandenburg. Bien que le travail soit en partie centralisé à Hanovre où se trouve le Leibniz Archiv, plusieurs centres de recherche se répartissent le travail et mobilisent de nombreux chercheurs. L'édition est ainsi distinguée en séries selon les objets dont s'occupent ces différents centres. Le centre de recherche de Hanovre s'occupe de trois séries : la première série de la correspondance générale, politique et historique, la troisième série de la correspondance mathématique et scientifique et la septième série des écrits mathématiques.

1. Leibniz, *Œuvres philosophiques latines et françaises*.

2. *Briefwechsel zwischen Leibniz, Arnauld und dem Landgrafen Ersnt von Hessen-Rheinfels*.

3. Les plus récents tomes sont disponibles en ligne à l'adresse suivante : www.leibniz-edition.de.

Le centre de recherche de Münster édite l'œuvre philosophique, c'est-à-dire la correspondance dans la deuxième série et les écrits dans la sixième. Le centre de Postdam travaille pour sa part à l'édition des œuvres politiques regroupées dans la quatrième série. Le centre de Berlin a entamé il y a quelques années l'édition des écrits en sciences naturelles, en médecine et techniques dans la huitième série. Finalement, la cinquième série des écrits historiques et linguistiques est toujours en attente d'une structure institutionnelle d'édition. Certaines séries sont plus avancées que d'autres, dont celle de la correspondance générale qui a publié les lettres jusqu'au milieu des années 1700, mais d'autres tardent, le cas des écrits historiques et linguistiques étant le plus manifeste. De la correspondance et des écrits philosophiques manquent encore les textes de la période de maturité, mais ils seront édités dans les prochaines décennies.

Notre connaissance de la pensée de Leibniz est bien entendu liée à l'état d'avancement de l'édition complète des écrits et de la correspondance. Il est certes possible de consulter les manuscrits aux archives de Hanovre, mais la recherche est en bonne partie redevable de cette édition qui fait connaître, lors de la parution de chaque tome, un nombre toujours impressionnant d'inédits. Les grandes interprétations de la philosophie leibnizienne, sur lesquelles nous reviendrons, ont aussi été redevables de travaux d'édition. Le présent volume est bien entendu également en bonne partie fondée sur le fait que nous ayons aujourd'hui une meilleure connaissance de Leibniz grâce à la parution récente de plusieurs tomes de l'édition de l'Académie.

La publication de notre volume est toutefois aussi motivée par une autre raison. S'il existe, surtout en anglais, des ouvrages visant à introduire à la pensée de Leibniz, sous la forme de ce qu'on a coutume de nommer des *companions*, la production en langue française ne comprend finalement aucun ouvrage de cette nature. Plusieurs auteurs majeurs de la philosophie moderne ont fait l'objet de ce type de publication – Descartes, Spinoza ou Kant–, mais Leibniz a été à cet égard négligé. Ceci est d'autant plus surprenant que la recherche francophone sur la pensée de Leibniz a toujours été très dynamique. Pendant longtemps, seul le livre d'Yvon Belaval[1] pouvait prétendre introduire à la lecture et la compréhension du leibnizianisme. Même si cette contribution a pu être très utile, elle est maintenant datée et comporte des erreurs qui sont en partie dues à la connaissance du corpus que pouvait posséder Belaval à l'époque. Le présent volume vise à combler cette lacune. Il pourra servir aux enseignants, aux étudiants, mais aussi aux chercheurs qui souhaitent mieux

1. *Leibniz. Initiation à sa philosophie*.

connaître la pensée de Leibniz, puisque jamais la volonté d'introduire n'a nui à la rigueur scientifique et interprétative.

Ce recueil a été conçu de manière thématique afin de proposer des parcours dans l'œuvre et d'attirer l'attention sur les résonnances qui peuvent se produire d'un domaine à l'autre, notamment entre pensée philosophique et pensée scientifique. Chaque thème a été confié à un spécialiste qui s'efforce d'en livrer un état des lieux au regard du commentaire actuel, mais sans s'interdire pour autant de proposer ses vues propres sur le sujet. Partant des notions métaphysiques, substance (C. Leduc), théodicée (P. Rateau), esprit (J.-P. Anfray) et harmonie préétablie (J. McDonough), le volume évolue vers des domaines plus spécifiques. Au premier rang, les aspects scientifiques de l'œuvre : mathématiques (D. Rabouin), physique (F. Duchesneau) ou connaissance du vivant (R. Andrault), tous trois présentés dans la perspective de leur rapport à la philosophie. Viennent ensuite la morale et la politique (L. Basso), ainsi que la théologie (C. Rössler-Le Van). Une troisième section prend pour thème les questions de théorie de la connaissance, qu'elles suivent le fil de la logique et du langage (M. Favaretti Camposampiero), des considérations encyclopédiques (M. Lærke) ou des considérations de méthode (M. Picon). Enfin, une dernière section expose quelques éléments de la réception de la pensée leibnizienne au XVIIIe siècle, que ce soit en France et en Angleterre (A-L. Rey) ou au sein des Lumières allemandes (J.-F. Goubet), puis dans la première moitié du XIXe siècle en France, notamment à travers l'influence considérable qu'aura eu le philosophe de Hanovre sur le développement des différentes figures du « spiritualisme » français (J. Dunham).

Nous n'avons pas poussé l'étude de la réception au-delà de la seconde moitié du XIXe siècle pour des raisons qu'il pourra être utile d'expliciter pour finir cette introduction. Comme nous l'avons déjà rappelé, cette période coïncide en effet avec une efflorescence des publications de textes inédits de Leibniz qui n'a pas d'équivalent dans les périodes antérieures et dont le meilleur exemple est sans doute l'édition de Gerhardt, qui s'étala de 1849 à 1863 pour les œuvres mathématiques et de 1875 à 1890 pour les œuvres philosophiques[1]. Cette édition, qui sert encore souvent de référence aujourd'hui, mit à disposition des lecteurs non seulement un grand

1. On peut également mentionner le travail de Foucher de Careil éditeur des *Lettres et opuscules inédits de Leibniz*, en 1854, des *Nouvelles lettres et opuscules inédits de Leibniz* en 1857, mais également des *Œuvres de Leibniz publiées pour la première fois à partie des manuscrits originaux*, Paris, Firmin Didot, 1859-1887, en 7 vol. En Allemagne, de nombreuses éditions ont vu le jour durant cette même période : celles de G. E. Guhrauer (*Deutsche Schriften*, Bd. 1-2, Berlin, 1838-40), de J. E. Erdmann (*Opera philosophica quae exstant omnia*, 1839-40) ou de G. H. Pertz (*Leibnizens gesammelte Werke*, 1843-1847).

nombre de textes inconnus, mais surtout un noyau de réflexions issues de la logique et des mathématiques qui marqua les lectures à partir de cette époque. Le changement de point de vue et les discussions qu'elle suscita fut si grand qu'on parla alors d'une véritable «Renaissance Leibniz». Qu'on en juge: le début du siècle voit paraître coup sur coup *A Critical Exposition of the Philosophy of Leibniz* de Bertrand Russell (1900), *La Logique de Leibniz d'après des documents inédits* de Louis Couturat (1901) et le *Leibniz' System in seinen wissenschaftlichen Grundlagen* (1902) d'Ernst Cassirer. Tous ces ouvrages, qui ont marqué durablement le commentaire – qu'on s'en inspire ou qu'on s'en démarque – étaient accompagnés de la publication de textes et de traductions qui contribuèrent grandement à changer l'image qu'on se faisait alors de la pensée de Leibniz[1]. Ils plaidaient tous pour une centralité du logico-mathématique, un point de vue qui était très largement ignoré jusque-là dans le commentaire, et dont la forme la plus extrême fut la lecture «panlogique» qui se dégagea alors du philosophe de Hanovre.

Mais ce ne fut pas là le seul effet des éditions de la seconde moitié du XIXe siècle. Car elles ouvraient également la voie vers un continent jusque-là mal perçu par nombre d'interprètes: celui des milliers de pages de manuscrits inédits dans lesquels se dessinaient peu à peu les méandres d'une pensée complexe et en constante évolution. «Qui ne me connaît que par mes écrits publiés», disait Leibniz en une formule restée célèbre, «ne me connaît pas»[2]. Aussi le début du XXe siècle fut-il également celui de l'attention portée à l'évolution de la pensée de Leibniz et, en particulier, d'une réfutation philologique des lectures «panlogiques» à laquelle reste notamment attaché le nom de Willy Kabitz, un des premiers artisans de l'édition intégrale des textes de Leibniz[3]. Kabitz montra, en effet, que les préoccupations métaphysiques étaient au cœur de la pensée de Leibniz dès son départ et indépendamment des déterminations logico-mathématiques

1. Au premier rang le recueil de L. Couturat, *Opuscules et fragments inédits de Leibniz*, 1903. À la même époque Ernst Cassirer fait paraître avec une traduction d'Arthur Buchenau les deux premiers volumes de son édition des textes philosophiques fondamentaux: *Philosophiche Werke*, 1904-1906 (le premier volume s'ouvrant sur les textes de logique et de mathématiques).

2. Lettre à Placcius du 21 février 1696; A II, 3, 139

3. Lors de sa première session en 1901, la toute jeune Association Internationale des Académies commissionna les Académies française et allemande pour l'élaboration d'une édition des œuvres complètes. Pourtant, ce projet initial ne survécut pas à la première guerre mondiale et l'édition fut depuis lors prise en charge par l'Allemagne seule (le premier volume sortit en 1923).

qui s'y greffèrent progressivement[1]. Quelques années plus tard, Ivan Jagodinski éditait un ensemble de textes métaphysiques de la période parisienne qui formait une première manière de système et qu'il désigna sous le titre *De summa rerum*[2]. À la même époque Jean Baruzi insistait sur les déterminations religieuses, voire mystiques, qui préoccupèrent continûment Leibniz tout au long de sa vie[3].

On voit que retracer cette réception, dont nous ne venons de donner qu'un petit aperçu, revient d'une part à s'engager dans une tâche titanesque, d'autre part à se trouver pris dans un champ de bataille où il est difficile de progresser sans avoir à faire tel ou tel choix. Dès les années 1920, la profusion des études sur Leibniz était déjà si grande et si diversifiée que Dietrich Mahnke pouvait en faire le sujet même de sa thèse, soutenue en 1922 sous la direction de Edmund Husserl[4]. Qui voudrait avoir une vue des lectures alors proposées pourra d'ailleurs encore se reporter avec profit à cet impressionnant panorama. Mais on prêtera surtout attention à la difficulté qui se dégageait alors clairement et dont, en quelque sorte, nous ne sommes pas sortis. Entre ceux qui voyaient dans la logique et les mathématiques le cœur du système et ceux qui le situaient plutôt dans les questions métaphysiques, voire religieuses, liées à la liberté, à l'individuation et au mal, les images de Leibniz qui se dégageaient alors semblaient à la fois totalement irréconciliables et, dans le même temps, aussi plausibles l'une que l'autre. C'est pourquoi Mahnke appelait dès son titre à ce que soit enfin produit une synthèse de ces vues. Il en proposa d'ailleurs une esquisse à partir d'un perspectivisme revisité et nourri par sa propre inspiration phénoménologique. D'autres propositions ont été faites depuis. On pense notamment, en langue française, à celles de Yvon Belaval cherchant dans le « formalisme » de Leibniz opposé à l'« intuitionnisme » cartésien une clef d'interprétation[5]. En 1968, Michel Serres proposa un vaste tableau où tous les développements mathématiques pouvaient figurer comme autant de « modèles » d'un système métaphysique[6]. Plus près de nous, Gilles Deleuze proposa de suivre le fil d'un Leibniz baroque, dont la figure du pli et même, plus exactement, du repliement à l'infini, permettrait de parcourir l'œuvre et la pensée du philosophe[7]. Mais toutes ces lectures, et bien d'autres encore, laissent le problème soulevé par Kabitz intact :

1. W. Kabitz, *Die Philosophie des jungen Leibniz*.
2. Leibniz, *Elementa philosophiae arcanae de summa rerum*.
3. Voir *Leibniz et l'organisation religieuse de la terre*.
4. D. Mahnke, *Leibnizens Synthese*.
5. Y. Belaval, *Leibniz critique de Descartes*.
6. M. Serres, *Le Système de Leibniz*.
7. G. Deleuze, *Le Pli*.

faut-il voir la pensée de Leibniz comme un tout solidaire, comme un « système », dont le commentateur doit chercher la clef ? Ne faut-il pas prêter une attention particulière aux inflexions, parfois profondes, que l'auteur donna à sa pensée ? À vouloir à tout prix reconstituer un « système », ne manque-t-on des césures importantes dans l'invention métaphysique [1] ? Comment ignorer, par exemple, l'écart qui joint et sépare tout à la fois une définition de la substance de type « logique », à partir de la notion complète, et une définition de type « dynamique » à partir du concept central de force ? Ces questions sont encore les nôtres et ce recueil n'a pas vocation à les trancher. S'il peut aider le lecteur à les repérer comme telles et à y dessiner sa propre ligne de réponse, il aura déjà accompli une de ses missions [2].

Mogens LÆRKE (CNRS, IHRIM, ENS de Lyon)
Christian LEDUC (Université de Montréal)
David RABOUIN (CNRS, SPHERE, Université Paris Diderot)

1. M. Fichant, « L'invention métaphysique ».

2. Les éditeurs tiennent à remercier Adrien Saucier pour son aide dans la préparation du manuscrit. La présente publication a par ailleurs été rendue possible grâce au soutien du Conseil de Recherches en Sciences Humaines du Canada.

PREMIÈRE PARTIE

LA MÉTAPHYSIQUE

SUBSTANCE INDIVIDUELLE, MONADE ET MACHINE DE LA NATURE

La métaphysique de la substance se déploie chez Leibniz d'une diversité de manières selon les contextes théoriques dans lesquels elle est explicitée. La substance est d'ailleurs désignée différemment d'après ceux-ci : elle est entre autres substance individuelle, forme substantielle, entéléchie, monade ou machine de la nature. On remarque que cette pluralité terminologique est aussi conceptuelle, puisque la métaphysique leibnizienne se modifie en partie selon les époques et que celles-ci ne caractérisent donc pas exactement de la même manière le substantiel; son évolution se constate principalement des œuvres des années 1680 jusqu'à la période de la maturité [1]. On pourrait même affirmer que cette variété est présente à un même moment de la pensée leibnizienne, en ce que la diversité des dispositifs répond à des problèmes qui sont distincts les uns des autres [2]. Par exemple, la machine de la nature est une expression qui réfère aux unités substantielles dans le contexte d'une réflexion sur le vivant et la structure des corps organiques et ne se retrouve pas dans des textes à visée, par exemple, physique ou théologique. Il en est de même de la substance individuelle et de la doctrine de la notion complète, exposées surtout dans le *Discours de métaphysique* de 1686 et dans les lettres à Arnauld, lesquelles correspondent aux exigences d'une théorie logique de l'inhérence conceptuelle qui lui est contemporaine. Ces acceptions de la substance ne sont pas nécessairement contradictoires les unes par rapport aux autres, mais il importe de bien saisir pour chacune les conditions et les problèmes dans lesquels elles font leur apparition. Le présent chapitre vise

1. *Cf.* M. Fichant, « L'invention métaphysique » ; D. Garber, *Leibniz : Body, Substance, Monad.*

2. Catherine Wilson a tenté une analyse semblable du *Discours de métaphysique : Leibniz's Metaphysics*, p. 88-110.

à répertorier et à analyser les principales significations du substantiel chez Leibniz selon ces contextes théoriques, mais aussi à expliquer les problèmes particuliers auxquels le concept de substance vise à répondre.

LE FONDEMENT DE L'ACTION

Parmi les différentes manières d'introduire une conception renouvelée de la substance, l'une des plus fréquentes chez Leibniz repose sur son lien au problème de l'action. D'après lui, il est nécessaire de repenser le concept de substance pour comprendre l'origine causale du changement et du mouvement dans la nature. L'exigence d'un fondement de l'action se trouve dans plusieurs textes, mais est notamment connue par le *Discours de métaphysique*. Le contexte d'énonciation est manifeste : à cette époque, l'occasionnalisme d'inspiration cartésienne, surtout défendu par Malebranche, gagne de plus en plus en importance comme hypothèse métaphysique rendant compte de l'origine du changement dans les choses. D'après Malebranche, seul Dieu est cause véritable, c'est-à-dire agit selon sa propre force, et produit ainsi les changements de pensées dans l'âme et de mouvements dans le corps[1]. C'est en outre grâce à cette causalité divine que les deux ordres, spirituel et corporel, se correspondent, sans qu'il n'existe entre eux d'influence mutuelle[2]. L'âme et le corps sont ainsi les causes occasionnelles d'une véritable activité divine. Sans nier l'action originaire et créatrice de Dieu et son concours sur les substances de la nature, Leibniz entend néanmoins montrer que les créatures possèdent également un pouvoir causal qui leur est propre. En leur conférant une capacité d'action, on évitera notamment d'envisager l'action de Dieu sur le monde à la manière d'un miracle perpétuel, tel un *Deus ex machina*[3]. D'où la nécessité de donner une nouvelle définition qui saura rendre compte de l'action des êtres finis :

> Il est assez difficile de distinguer les actions de Dieu de celles des créatures, aussi bien que les actions et passions de ces mêmes créatures. Car il y en a qui croient que Dieu fait tout, d'autres s'imaginent, qu'il ne fait que conserver la force qu'il a donnée aux créatures : la suite fera voir combien l'un ou l'autre se peut dire. Or puisque les actions et passions appartiennent

1. *Traité de la nature et de la grâce*, OC V, 66.
2. *Ibid.*, 67-68.
3. *Système nouveau*, GP IV, 483.

proprement aux substances individuelles (*actiones sunt suppositorum*), il serait nécessaire d'expliquer ce que c'est qu'une telle substance[1].

Contre la position de Malebranche, mais aussi celle de Spinoza qu'on pourrait dans ce cas précis lui associer[2], la définition leibnizienne de la substance servirait entre autres à montrer que les créatures sont de véritables sujets d'actions; celles-ci ne sauraient être de simples occasions sans efficience causale ou des modes d'une substance divine unique. Dans le *Discours de métaphysique*, Leibniz propose dès lors de reprendre la définition d'Aristote, mais pour la renouveler et lui donner une orientation originale; il en sera question par la suite. Pour l'instant, insistons sur l'importance de conférer un pouvoir d'action à la substance, thèse que Leibniz conservera quasi intacte jusqu'à la période de maturité. Cette caractéristique sera par contre précisée : la substance individuelle est subséquemment qualifiée d'entéléchie, ce qui marque à nouveau un lien manifeste avec la métaphysique d'inspiration aristotélicienne. Le terme est absent du *Discours de métaphysique* et des lettres envoyées à Arnauld, mais fait son apparition dans les années 1690[3]. Il demeure également dans des textes du corpus métaphysique de la maturité et vise toujours à caractériser l'action propre des substances, désormais désignées sous le nom de monade :

> On pourrait donner le nom d'Entéléchies à toutes les substances simples, ou Monades créées, car elles ont en elles une certaine perfection (ἔχουσι τὸ ἐντελές), il y a une suffisance (αὐτάρκεια) qui les rend sources de leurs actions internes et pour ainsi dire des Automates incorporels[4].

Le pouvoir d'action est à ce point essentiel que Leibniz maintient l'idée que sans une telle capacité, il serait impossible de conférer une réalité à la substance[5]. Un être sans pouvoir actif, telle la *res extensa* de Descartes, n'est pas substance, car aucune activité ne lui permet d'exister et de s'individualiser en tant que telle. Une entité passive sans capacité ou force

1. *Discours de métaphysique*, § 8, A VI, 4, 1539-1540.

2. Leibniz traitera de la doctrine de Spinoza à plusieurs endroits afin de soutenir que la conception spinoziste de la nature divine enlève toute action aux créatures : *De ipsa natura*, GP IV, p. 515; *Réponses aux réflexions contenues dans la seconde édition du Dictionnaire critique de M. Bayle, article Rorarius, sur le système de l'Harmonie préétablie* : GP IV, 568; *Considérations sur la doctrine d'un esprit universel unique*, GP IV, 530.

3. *Cf.* Leibniz, *Discours de métaphysique, Correspondance avec Arnauld*, éd. par C. Leduc, « Introduction », p. 21-22.

4. *Monadologie*, § 18, GP VI, 609-610.

5. *De Ipsa natura*, GP IV, 509. Rappelons que les *Principes de la nature et de la grâce* s'ouvrent sur une telle assertion : « La substance est un être capable d'action », GP VI, 598.

de réalisation n'est pas une réalité métaphysique, mais une simple abstraction idéelle ou géométrique. L'argument est présenté de cette manière dans le *Système nouveau de la nature et de la communication des substances* de 1695 : la seule masse étendue des choses ne rend pas compte de la réalité métaphysique des choses, car rien ne la détermine actuellement; d'où la nécessité de recourir à des forces ou entéléchies primitives qui seront le fondement réel des substances dans la matière[1].

Leibniz voudra préciser ultérieurement ce pouvoir actif de la substance sur le plan métaphysique. Corrélativement à l'introduction du terme de monade, sur lequel nous aurons l'occasion de revenir, apparaît le qualificatif d'appétition servant à désigner la capacité d'action de la substance à passer d'une perception à une autre. Un passage célèbre de la *Monadologie* l'explicite :

> L'action du principe interne qui fait le changement ou le passage d'une perception à une autre, peut-être appelé appétition; il est vrai que l'appétit ne saurait parvenir entièrement à toute la perception, où il tend, mais il en obtient toujours quelques choses, et parvient à des perceptions nouvelles[2].

En opposition, toujours, à une hypothèse qui ferait intervenir Dieu comme seul agent causal dans le monde, Leibniz confère à toute monade une propriété fondamentale d'appétition. Par causalité interne, chaque substance est ainsi capable d'accomplir les changements actifs et passifs qui la caractérisent, causalité qualifiée dès lors de spontanéité[3].

Le retour à un vocabulaire d'influence aristotélicienne, qui conduit également à la réhabilitation des formes substantielles comme principe d'action dans les choses[4], se justifie chez Leibniz pour une raison supplémentaire : ses travaux en physique à partir de la fin des années 1670 l'ont convaincu que la propriété la plus fondamentale de la nature n'était pas l'étendue ou le mouvement, comme l'ont pensé Descartes, Hobbes ou Malebranche[5], mais bien la force active. Mieux, que les changements de figure et de mouvement de la matière reposent fondamentalement sur la détermination des forces primitives des corps. Leibniz forgera même une nouvelle désignation disciplinaire dans les années 1690, la dynamique, qui

1. *Système nouveau*, GP IV, 479.

2. *Monadologie*, § 15, GP VI, 609.

3. *Système nouveau*, GP IV, 484; *Essais de théodicée*, § 288, GP VI, 288.

4. *Discours*, § 10, A VI, 4, 1542-1543.

5. Leibniz a auparavant lui-même penché pour une position de type hobbesien, selon laquelle le mouvement est la propriété essentielle des corps : *Hypothesis physica nova*, A VI, 2, 223-224.

a pour objet l'explication des forces primitives et dérivatives corporelles[1]. L'importance de plus en plus accrue de la notion d'action dans le champ métaphysique n'est donc pas sans relation avec les réflexions leibniziennes en physique. La démonstration selon laquelle Dieu conserve la même quantité de force active dans la nature (mv^2), et non de force motrice comme le pensaient les cartésiens (mv), permet non seulement d'établir une physique plus solide, mais aussi de l'articuler adéquatement à la métaphysique. D'où, somme toute, l'importance de la thèse selon laquelle la substance est nécessairement pourvue d'action ou de force primitive.

La doctrine de la notion complète

Le *Discours de métaphysique* pose les deux points tout juste signalés : les substances individuelles et formes substantielles sont, d'une part, les principes d'action dans les choses et fondent, d'autre part, la notion de force qui permettra de réinvestir la philosophie naturelle[2]. La filiation aristotélicienne est encore une fois manifeste, même si les moyens métaphysiques et scientifiques sont propres à l'approche leibnizienne. Souvenons-nous que Leibniz entreprend ses réflexions à partir de la définition péripatéticienne de la substance, mais qu'il entend cependant compléter par des outils conceptuels nouveaux. Qu'est-ce à dire plus exactement ? La définition aristotélicienne de l'οὐσία est rappelée par Leibniz :

> Il est bien vrai, que lorsque plusieurs prédicats s'attribuent à un même sujet, et que ce sujet ne s'attribue plus à aucun autre, on l'appelle substance individuelle. Mais cela n'est pas assez, et une telle explication n'est que nominale. Il faut donc considérer ce que c'est que d'être attribué véritablement à un certain sujet[3].

Aristote affirme effectivement que la substance est ce qui n'est jamais dans un sujet ou attribuée à un sujet[4] ; contrairement aux genres, espèces et accidents, la substance occupe toujours la position du sujet dans une proposition. On peut attribuer à Socrate un ensemble de prédicats ou propriétés, énonçant ses états et actions, mais Socrate ne saurait être le prédicat d'une autre substance. Il s'agit de marquer l'individualité de la substance comme être premier agissant à titre de sujet d'un ensemble d'accidents et

1. *Cf.* Leibniz, *La réforme de la dynamique*, éd. M. Fichant ; F. Duchesneau, *La dynamique de Leibniz*.

2. *Discours*, § 17, A VI, 4, 1556-1558.

3. *Discours*, § 8, A VI, 4, 1540.

4. *Des catégories*, 3a7-9.

d'affections[1]. Leibniz considère que cette notion permet certes de distinguer la substance des autres catégories, faisant alors l'objet d'une définition nominale, mais que celle-ci ne nous indique pas en quoi consiste l'essence de la substance dans une définition réelle. Pour ce faire, il faut déterminer les différentes manières dont on peut rapporter un prédicat à un sujet au sein d'une structure propositionnelle. Le *Discours de métaphysique* ne donne que les grandes lignes d'une logique renouvelée qui sert à préciser le concept de substance, sachant que Leibniz a cependant consacré de nombreux textes à ces problèmes logiques, dont le plus complet est certainement les *Generales inquisitiones de analysi notionum et veritatum*[2].

Leibniz part du principe selon lequel toute proposition vraie exprime un rapport d'inhérence entre le sujet et le prédicat, plus précisément que le prédicat doit être contenu dans le sujet pour que la proposition puisse être tenue comme étant vraie. Il existe pour l'essentiel deux manières de rendre compte de l'inhérence conceptuelle ou *inesse :* 1) La première concerne les propositions identiques exprimant des vérités éternelles, par exemple les propositions de la logique et des mathématiques. Validées à partir du principe de non-contradiction, de telles vérités peuvent être dites exprimer un rapport actuel d'inhérence entre le prédicat et le sujet. Cette caractérisation a deux conséquences modales principales : d'une part, les vérités identiques sont nécessaires et expriment les essences telles que conçues dans l'entendement divin[3]. Elles énoncent des notions abstraites référant aux propriétés essentielles des choses. D'autre part, de telles vérités peuvent faire l'objet d'une analyse ou démonstration finie. C'est la raison pour laquelle elles sont aussi appelées des vérités immédiates[4]. Par exemple, le théorème de Pythagore énonce que, dans un triangle rectangle, le carré de l'hypoténuse est égal à la somme des carrés des deux autres côtés ($a^2 + b^2 = c^2$). Pour Leibniz, cette vérité serait nécessaire en ce qu'elle exprime une propriété essentielle à tout triangle rectangle ; mais il noterait aussi qu'elle fait l'objet d'une analyse finie, à partir d'un nombre limité de propositions premières que sont les axiomes et postulats de la géométrie euclidienne. Or, il appert que ce type d'inhérence conceptuelle ne peut rendre compte de la réalité des substances, puisqu'il porte sur les essences

1. *Métaphysique Δ*, 1017b23-25.

2. Il existe en traduction française un recueil de textes de Leibniz consacrés aux questions logiques et métaphysiques, comprenant entre autres les *Generales inquisitiones* (voir R).

3. *De natura veritatis*, A VI, 4, 1515.

4. Lettre à Arnauld de juin 1686 (brouillon), A II, 2, 56.

abstraites, et non sur les existences. Il faut alors chercher un autre type de prédication qui énonce la réalité individuelle de la substance.

2) Leibniz distingue par conséquent un deuxième type de relations propositionnelles qui s'expriment dans des vérités existentielles. Comme le nom l'indique, elles énoncent des rapports d'inhérence qui renvoient à des existences ou êtres réels. On comprend bien entendu que la substance y trouvera le fondement de sa réalité comme être individuel et concret. Elles s'opposent aux propositions identiques suivant les deux caractéristiques précédentes. D'abord, elles énoncent des vérités contingentes résultant non pas de l'entendement, mais bien de la volonté divine qui suit le principe du meilleur[1]. Autrement dit, leur contraire est logiquement possible, bien qu'il s'oppose aux décrets de la sagesse divine. À l'évidence, les propositions existentielles expriment tout de même des vérités, que Leibniz nomme nécessaires *ex hypothesi*, et énoncent aussi un rapport d'inhérence prédicative; mais contrairement aux vérités nécessaires absolues, cette inhérence est déterminée par le choix du meilleur. En d'autres termes, l'ensemble des événements qui expriment la réalité d'un être substantiel s'explicitent également dans une relation d'*inesse*. Toutefois, ce lien est virtuel, c'est-à-dire dont l'analyse nécessiterait de prendre en considération la suite infinie des prédicats d'un sujet individuel[2]. Par opposition aux vérités nécessaires immédiatement démontrées, Leibniz maintient que les vérités existentielles sont médiates et comprennent en puissance une suite infinie de qualités[3]. La notion complète d'une substance comprendra tous les prédicats qui la singularisent et la distinguent des autres substances dans son existence réelle. Les exemples d'Alexandre le Grand, de Jules César et d'Adam sont restés célèbres: la totalité des actions de César s'expriment sous forme de prédicats que Leibniz considère comme étant virtuellement inclus dans la notion du sujet César. Parmi ces actions, on sait qu'il franchit le Rubicon et devint ensuite dictateur et maître de la République[4]. Sur le plan logique, chacune de ces actions correspond à un prédicat participant de la notion complète d'une substance individuelle.

1. *Discours*, § 13, A VI, 4, 1547.
2. *De natura veritatis*, A VI, 4, 1516.
3. Lettre à Arnauld de juin 1686 (brouillon), A II, 2, 56.
4. *Discours*, § 13, A VI, 4, 1547-1548.

LE PRINCIPE DES INDISCERNABLES

À partir de cette théorisation, Leibniz en tire un principe d'individuation des substances : à chaque substance individuelle correspond une notion complète qui contient l'ensemble des événements qui la singularisent. C'est la raison pour laquelle Leibniz affirme que toutes les actions et passions passées, présentes et futures sont contenues dans la notion d'une substance individuelle[1]. Tout ce qu'on pourra énoncer à propos d'une substance devra se trouver dans cette notion, telle la qualité d'être roi qu'on attribue à Alexandre le Grand[2] ou même la descendance entière d'Adam[3].

Bien qu'il existe des différences importantes entre la théorie de la notion complète du *Discours de métaphysique* et les conceptualisations subséquentes, en particulier dans le *Système nouveau* et la *Monadologie*, l'idée d'une individuation par l'ensemble des actions et passions de la substance est un acquis que Leibniz conservera. Elle se retrouve d'une certaine manière dans la formulation du célèbre principe de l'identité des indiscernables. En effet, le principe stipule que deux êtres qui partageraient exactement les mêmes propriétés seraient indiscernables, à la manière des êtres abstraits de la géométrie. Au contraire, deux êtres substantiels constituent des réalités distinctes sur la base de séries différenciées de propriétés. La quatrième lettre à Clarke indique qu'une telle individuation des substances se répercute même sur les qualités sensibles des choses, à l'instar des feuilles du jardin de Herrenhausen :

> Il n'y a point deux individus indiscernables. Un gentilhomme d'esprit de mes amis en parlant avec moi en présence de Madame l'Électrice dans le jardin de Herrenhausen crut qu'il trouverait bien deux feuilles entièrement semblables, Madame l'Électrice l'en défia, et il courut longtemps en vain pour en chercher. Deux gouttes d'eau, ou de lait, regardées par le microscope, se trouveront discernables[4].

La différenciation des choses réelles se base ainsi sur l'ensemble des affections ou qualités qui les singularisent et en font des substances distinctes dans l'ordre métaphysique. Aucune substance ne partage exactement la même série de propriétés avec une autre substance, sinon il s'agirait du même être. En somme, bien que la définition aristotélicienne de la substance puisse être recevable, il fallait pour Leibniz la compléter

1. Lettre pour Arnauld de juin 1686 (brouillon), A II, 2, 52.
2. *Discours*, § 8, A VI, 4, 1540.
3. Lettre au Landgrave pour Arnauld du 12 avril 1686, A II, 2, 18.
4. Quatrième lettre à Clarke, GP VII, 372.

d'une théorie de la prédication et de la notion complète qui ouvre au final la voie au principe des indiscernables. Grâce à une doctrine de l'inhérence conceptuelle, il est alors possible d'expliquer en quoi consiste la substance individuelle, mais surtout d'établir une nouvelle thèse métaphysique quant à l'individuation des êtres réels.

Le principe leibnizien d'individuation a évidemment de nombreuses conséquences qu'on ne peut ici analyser en détail[1]. Retenons toutefois un élément sur lequel Leibniz est abondamment revenu : étant donné que la distinction d'une substance repose sur sa notion complète qui comprend tous les prédicats qui l'individualisent, il s'ensuit que seules les qualités qui sont inhérentes à cette notion contribuent à son discernement. De sorte que les dénominations extrinsèques ou numériques (*solo numero*), tels l'espace et le temps, doivent être exclues comme critères d'individuation. Il en est notamment question dans la correspondance avec Arnauld : Arnauld trouve problématique de recourir à la notion complète d'un individu, par exemple celle d'Adam, pour en déterminer l'existence, alors qu'un critère de type cartésien, grâce au *cogito*, semblerait suffire[2]. La position de Leibniz serait aux prises, d'après Arnauld, avec l'hypothèse d'une pluralité de notions possibles ou vagues d'Adam, telles que conçues dans l'entendement divin[3]. Or, selon Leibniz, tout critère qui serait strictement extrinsèque, notamment l'acte de penser *hic et nunc*, ne fonde pas le principe des indiscernables, justement parce qu'il y aurait un risque de devoir admettre deux individus exactement semblables sur le plan qualitatif, mais situés différemment. Par ailleurs, la notion de chaque individu est complète, ce qui interdit la possibilité d'une pluralité de notions vagues. De cette manière, seules les dénominations intrinsèques, qui font par conséquent partie de l'essence de la notion complète d'une substance, déterminent l'individuation. Leibniz conclut la discussion avec Arnauld par une généralisation du principe de Thomas d'Aquin :

> [...] je suis si éloigné de la pluralité d'un même individu, que je suis même très persuadé de ce que saint Thomas avait déjà enseigné à l'égard des intelligences, et que je tiens être général, savoir qu'il n'est pas possible qu'il y ait deux individus entièrement semblables ou différents *solo numero*[4].

1. *Cf.* C. Leduc, *Substance, individu et connaissance chez Leibniz*.

2. Lettre d'Arnauld à Leibniz du 13 mai 1686, A II, 2, 37.

3. À cette objection s'ajoute l'argument d'Arnauld selon lequel la doctrine de la notion complète semblerait conduire à un nécessitarisme absolu ou fatal, conséquence que Leibniz voudra aussi réfuter : Lettre à Arnauld du 12 avril 1686, A II, 2, 16-17.

4. Lettre à Arnauld, du 14 juillet 1686, A II, 2, 77-78. Leibniz mentionne déjà cette idée dans le *Discours* : § 9, A VI, 4, 1541.

L'UNITÉ SUBSTANTIELLE

Des travaux récents ont fait comprendre qu'une lecture systématique et parfois téléologique du développement de la métaphysique leibnizienne ne convient pas quand des comparaisons précises s'élaborent à partir des différentes pièces et périodes du corpus. Il est vrai que la théorie de la notion complète sera en partie reprise dans la formulation plus tardive du principe des indiscernables[1], mais force est d'admettre que ces différents cadres conceptuels ne sont pas entièrement homogènes, d'où l'importance d'opérer des analyses contextuellement adéquates. L'introduction du terme entéléchie pour désigner le principe actif des formes substantielles, évoqué précédemment, constitue un premier exemple patent. À l'égard de l'évolution générale de la métaphysique de la substance, on remarque un autre changement d'importance : si le concept de substance individuelle et la doctrine de la notion complète sont au cœur du dispositif argumentaire du *Discours de métaphysique*, de la correspondance avec Arnauld et de plusieurs textes qui leur sont contemporains, on remarque que ce dispositif tend à disparaître à partir des années 1690. À tel point que des œuvres phares comme le *Système nouveau*, les *Essais de théodicée* ou la *Monadologie*, ainsi que des correspondances majeures comme celles avec Bayle, De Volder ou Clarke n'en font plus mention. On pourrait prétexter que Leibniz propose avec ces contributions des perspectives différentes menant au final au même système métaphysique[2], mais une telle interprétation serait difficile à défendre, tant les positions semblent irréconciliables.

L'un des moments décisifs expliquant le délaissement de la théorie de la notion complète est certainement l'introduction du concept de monade qui fait son apparition dans les années 1690. Sa première mention publique se trouve dans le *De ipsa natura* de 1698 visant à désigner l'âme dans les êtres vivants et la forme substantielle dans les autres êtres[3]. Plus précisément, Leibniz affirme que la monade, accompagnée de matière, constitue une unité réelle et qu'en son absence le corps ne serait qu'un être par agrégation sans véritable statut substantiel. L'idée est en fait une reprise du *Système nouveau*, texte dans lequel n'apparaît cependant pas

1. *Sur le principe des indiscernables*, C, 10.

2. B. Russell, *The Philosophy of Leibniz*, p. 1 ; Y. Belaval, *Leibniz. Initiation à sa philosophie*, p. 158.

3. *De ipsa natura*, GP IV, 511. On s'entend maintenant pour dire que la première occurrence du terme de monade se trouve dans la correspondance avec Fardella : Lettre à Fardella du 3/13 septembre 1696, A II, 3, 192-193.

encore le terme de monade. Leibniz y rappelle l'importance de fonder l'action dans les êtres substantiels, mais ajoute l'exigence d'unité substantielle :

> [...] je m'aperçus qu'il est impossible de trouver les principes d'une véritable Unité dans la matière seule ou dans ce qui n'est que passif, puisque tout n'y est que collection ou amas de parties jusqu'à l'infini. Or la multitude ne pouvant avoir sa réalité que des unités véritables qui viennent d'ailleurs et sont tout autre chose que les points mathématiques qui ne sont que des extrémités de l'étendue et des modifications dont il est constant, que le continuum ne saurait être composé. Donc pour trouver ces unités réelles, je fus contraint de recourir à un point réel et animé pour ainsi dire, ou à un Atome de substance qui doit envelopper quelque chose de formel et d'action, pour faire un Être complet [1].

Dans des contributions récentes, Michel Fichant a montré que l'argumentation du *Système nouveau* apparaît en réalité dès la correspondance avec Arnauld et qu'il s'agirait du premier point de rupture par rapport à la métaphysique de la substance individuelle [2]. En réponse aux interrogations de ce dernier, Leibniz introduit l'unité comme marque du substantiel, idée jusqu'alors inédite dans le contexte de la correspondance [3]. La substance possède une unité *per se*, à la différence de l'agrégat matériel qui se comprend sous une unité *per accidens*. Autrement dit, la substance est non seulement pourvue d'action, mais elle doit désormais constituer une unité qui structure la matière et sans laquelle il ne saurait exister d'individus réels. Les substances sont des unités métaphysiques qui diffèrent par ailleurs des unités mathématiques, dont la nature est abstraite et incomplète. Dans le *Système nouveau*, Leibniz indique aussi qu'elles se distinguent des atomes matériels en ce qu'elles contiennent une réalité formelle et spirituelle, caractéristique déjà acquise depuis le *Discours de métaphysique*. En effet, l'étendue matérielle et ses modalités de figure et de mouvement ne sauraient constituer l'essence des corps, lesquels exigent un principe spirituel actif qu'est l'âme ou la forme substantielle [4].

Dans les œuvres de la maturité, Leibniz conserve cette caractérisation et les conséquences qu'il en tire dans le *Système nouveau*. Il en discute d'ailleurs abondamment avec l'Électrice Sophie de Hanovre qui

1. *Système nouveau*, GP IV, 478.
2. M. Fichant, « L'invention métaphysique », p. 81-95.
3. Lettre à Arnauld du 28 novembre/8 décembre 1686, A II, 2, 121.
4. *Discours*, § 12, A VI, 4, 1545.

s'interroge sur le concept de substance[1]. À la même époque apparaît toutefois un nouvel argument qu'on peut dire être constitutif de la métaphysique monadologique. Il s'agit de prouver l'existence des unités substantielles ou monades à partir de la composition des corps et de la matière. Le raisonnement sera énoncé à plusieurs endroits, mais la version la plus connue est très certainement celle qu'on trouve en ouverture de la *Monadologie* :

> La Monade, dont nous parlerons ici, n'est autre chose, qu'une substance simple qui entre dans les composés; simple, c'est-à-dire, sans parties. Et il faut qu'il y ait des substances simples, puisqu'il y a des composés : car le composé n'est autre qu'un amas ou *aggregatum* des simples[2].

À l'unité substantielle déjà acquise se joint alors la simplicité des monades qui rend compte du composé ou agrégat. La déduction est manifestement analytique : puisqu'il existe des corps composés, il doit y avoir à leur fondement des entités simples qui permettent de les rendre intelligibles. Le paragraphe suivant en tire une caractéristique auparavant attribuée à l'âme ou forme substantielle : puisque les monades ou substances simples sont les éléments premiers du composé, elles ne peuvent en conserver la divisibilité; de sorte que les monades doivent être sans parties et inétendues. C'est pourquoi Leibniz les considère comme étant « les véritables Atomes de la Nature et en un mot les Éléments des choses »[3]. La monade joue une fonction similaire à l'atome matériel défendu depuis Démocrite, mais en évitant une pétition de principe, puisqu'elle est simple et indivisible, de façon à rendre compte du composé. Au contraire, l'atome matériel et soi-disant insécable est une notion incomplète, étant donné que la matière est par définition décomposable, ce qui doit également être le cas de ses corpuscules[4]. Toute matière sera en somme constituée de monades qui la structurent et en représentent le fondement simple.

1. L'ensemble des lettres a été publié par O. Klopp, *Correspondenz von Leibniz mit der Prinzessin Sophie*, mais les extraits pertinents relatifs à l'unité des substances ont été regroupés par Fichant : « L'invention métaphysique », p. 333-362.
2. *Monadologie*, § 1 et 2, GP VI, 607.
3. *Monadologie*, § 3, GP VI, 607.
4. Cinquième lettre à Clarke de mi-août 1716, GP VII, 393-394.

La perception expressive

La suite de la *Monadologie* en tire une série de caractéristiques qui sont essentielles à la compréhension de l'ontologie leibnizienne. Résumons-en deux qui jouent un rôle crucial : d'une part, les monades ne sauraient être générées ou annihilées naturellement et doivent nécessairement commencer ou finir par création[1]. Leur génération ne pouvant tenir leur origine de l'ordre des choses a dès lors été l'œuvre de Dieu qui transcende et crée les substances finies[2]. Il ne faudrait donc pas considérer que les monades se forment par génération naturelle, mais plutôt qu'elles existent tant et aussi longtemps que Dieu les maintient dans l'existence. C'est pourquoi Leibniz leur confère une indestructibilité naturelle qui se répercute sur l'organisation du vivant, thème sur lequel nous aurons l'occasion de revenir[3]. D'autre part, et cette deuxième idée est intimement liée à la première, les monades ne peuvent interagir causalement les unes sur les autres :

> Il n'y a pas moyen aussi d'expliquer, comment une Monade puisse être altérée, ou changée dans son intérieur par quelque autre créature; puisqu'on n'y saurait rien transposer, ni concevoir en elle aucun mouvement interne, qui puisse être excité, dirigé, augmenté ou diminué là-dedans; comme cela se peut dans les composés, où il y a des changements entre les parties. Les monades n'ont point de fenêtres, par lesquelles quelque chose y puisse entrer ou sortir[4].

On sait désormais que la monade se fait attribuer une propriété d'action ou de changement que Leibniz nomme appétition. Cette capacité est en réalité un pouvoir interne de passer d'un état à un autre. Or, on comprend ici que ces changements internes sont au final les seuls qui puissent être possibles sur le plan métaphysique, puisque les monades ne sauraient s'altérer ou se modifier par causalité externe; elles sont fermées et n'ont pas de fenêtres par lesquelles leurs états pourraient changer de l'extérieur. Cela rejoint le principe des indiscernables qui stipulait que seules les dénominations intrinsèques, et non extrinsèques, rendent compte de l'individualité de la substance; il appert que c'est aussi de l'intérieur qu'elle se développe[5]. Pour se représenter l'idée que seule la causalité interne est effective dans l'ordre naturel, Leibniz emprunte souvent une analogie avec

1. *Monadologie,* § 6, GP VI, 607.
2. *Essais de théodicée*, § 396-397, GP VI, 351-353.
3. Lettre à Arnauld du 30 avril 1687, A II, 2, 188-189; *Système nouveau*, GP IV, 480-481.
4. *Monadologie,* § 7, GP VI, 607.
5. *Monadologie,* § 8-11, GP VI, 608.

la nature de l'âme pour la généraliser à toute substance simple : à la manière des idées de l'âme qui y demeurent et ne peuvent être transférées à une autre âme, les affections ne sauraient sortir de la monade et entrer dans une deuxième pour l'affecter[1].

Il reste toutefois à mieux caractériser l'état d'une substance simple ou monade. Plus précisément, en quoi consiste cette affection de la substance simple? Puisqu'il s'agit d'une réalité spirituelle et inétendue, Leibniz considère que l'état de la substance simple est une perception. Le terme peut porter à confusion compte tenu de sa signification épistémologique. D'où la nécessité de faire la distinction entre la perception, laquelle représente l'affection ontologique propre à toutes les monades, qu'elles soient conscientes ou non, et l'aperception d'une monade pourvue de cognition, tels l'âme animale ou l'esprit humain[2]. Dans les *Nouveaux Essais sur l'entendement humain*, Leibniz détaille longuement cette distinction que nous ne marquons qu'au passage: si plusieurs perceptions sont accompagnées de conscience et peuvent être considérées comme étant des aperceptions, une grande quantité, même chez l'être pourvu de réflexion cognitive, reste inaperçue, bien que ces perceptions constituent quand même des états internes et propres à la substance. Par exemple, nous apercevons le mouvement de la mer, mais nous percevons seulement, sans en prendre conscience, le mouvement de chaque vague qui compose ce bruit d'ensemble[3]. Ces états insensibles ou inconscients de la substance sont appelés des petites perceptions qui diffèrent par conséquent des aperceptions cognitives. Mais ces deux types représentent tout de même des états de la monade qu'elle cause de manière interne et spontanée.

Plusieurs raisons poussent Leibniz à exploiter ce concept de perception, notamment pour rendre compte de l'harmonie des choses. Rappelons que les substances n'entrent pas en relation causale les unes par rapport aux autres. Mais est-ce à dire qu'elles ne sont liées d'aucune manière et que la suite perceptive de l'une est entièrement hétérogène à la celles des autres ? Ceci irait à l'encontre d'une autre idée leibnizienne phare selon laquelle Dieu conçoit et crée non seulement chaque substance, mais aussi son inscription dans un monde selon une structure nomologique générale[4]. Dans ces circonstances, comment alors rendre compte de l'ordre des substances dans le monde, sans que n'opèrent d'influences causales? C'est ici qu'intervient un autre concept central de la

1. Lettre à Bernoulli du 17 décembre 1698, GM III, 560.
2. *Principes de la nature*, § 4, GP VI, 600.
3. *Nouveaux Essais*, « Préface », A VI, 6, 54.
4. *Essais de théodicée*, § 7, GP VI, 106.

métaphysique leibnizienne qu'on doit coupler à celui de perception. Chaque substance possède un ensemble de perceptions qui l'individualise, mais cet ensemble est ordonné suivant son rapport aux autres substances selon des relations dites expressives. Leibniz emploie ainsi la notion d'expression qui est un rapport réglé et constant entre les choses pour rendre compte des relations entre les perceptions des substances[1]. Dans la *Monadologie*, l'image, récurrente chez Leibniz, des points de vue sur une même ville illustre cet emploi de la doctrine de l'expression :

> Or, cette liaison ou cet accommodement de toutes les choses créées à chacune et de chacun à toutes les autres, fait que chaque substance simple a des rapports qui expriment toutes les autres, et qu'elle est par conséquent un miroir vivant perpétuel de l'univers. Et, comme une même ville regardée de différents côtés paraît toute autre, et est comme multipliée perspectivement; il arrive de même, que par la multitude infinie des substances simples, il y a comme autant de différents univers, qui ne sont pourtant que les perspectives d'un seul selon les différents points de vue de chaque Monade[2].

La théorie leibnizienne de l'expression est un acquis des années 1670, énoncée pour la première fois dans le *Quid sit Idea :* indépendamment des rapports causaux entre les choses, il est possible d'après Leibniz de dégager des rapports d'expression qui consistent en relations de correspondance entre l'exprimant et l'exprimé. L'un des exemples les plus souvent cités est celui qui existe entre l'équation algébrique et la figure qu'elle représente. À l'évidence, ces deux choses partagent une structure analogique expressive, sans qu'il n'existe de rapport de causalité entre les deux, ni même de ressemblance de nature[3]. Or, Leibniz emploiera ces caractéristiques de l'expression pour rendre compte des rapports entre substances : la perspective de la monade sur le monde, c'est-à-dire la série de ses perceptions, se structure précisément selon un ordre d'expression qui la met en relation avec les autres monades. Toutes les monades expriment un point de vue qui non seulement les singularise, mais aussi les lie aux autres substances de l'univers de manière non causale. Au lieu de concevoir l'harmonie générale des choses par des lois causales, à la manière de la physique, la métaphysique doit par conséquent s'appuyer sur les relations perceptives et expressives.

1. Leibniz définit l'expression comme rapport constant et réglé notamment dans la correspondance avec Arnauld : lettre à Arnauld du 9 octobre 1687, A II, 2, 240.

2. *Monadologie*, § 56-57, GP VI, 616.

3. *Quid sit Idea*, A VI, 4, 1370.

Les conséquences de la théorie leibnizienne de la perception expressive sont nombreuses, dont l'idée énoncée dans l'extrait précédent selon laquelle la monade est un miroir vivant de l'univers. Insistons pour le moment sur un autre aspect qu'on retrouve déjà dans le *Discours de métaphysique*[1] *:* même s'il n'existe pas d'influence causale entre les substances simples, il est quand même possible de parler d'une influence idéale selon l'ordre des perceptions respectives prédéterminé par Dieu. Effectivement, lors de la création, Dieu a prévu non seulement la suite des perceptions d'une monade, mais l'arrangement général des perspectives qui constitue l'harmonie universelle. Celle-ci se répercute sur la nature des perceptions elles-mêmes : une perception exprimant une action propre de la monade sera représentée de manière distincte par celle-ci, alors que les autres monades se représentent ce même état de manière passive et confuse. Les *Principes de la nature et de la grâce* reprennent cette idée en l'inscrivant dans le contexte de la doctrine de l'harmonie universelle :

> Car tout est réglé dans les choses une fois pour toutes avec autant d'ordre et de correspondance qu'il est possible, la suprême sagesse et bonté ne pouvant agir qu'avec une parfaite harmonie : le présent est gros de l'avenir, le futur se pourrait lire dans le passé, l'éloignée est exprimé dans le prochain. On pourrait connaître la beauté de l'univers dans chaque âme, si l'on pouvait déplier tous ses replis, qui ne se développent sensiblement qu'avec le temps. Mais comme chaque perception distincte de l'âme comprend une infinité de perceptions confuses, qui enveloppent tout l'univers, l'âme même ne connaît les choses dont elle a perception, qu'autant qu'elle en a des perceptions distinctes et relevées; et elle a de la perfection, à mesure de ses perceptions distinctes[2].

L'extrait comprend de nombreuses idées qui nous permettent de synthétiser les éléments de la métaphysique leibnizienne de la substance à l'époque de la maturité : 1) bien que chaque monade soit prédéterminée individuellement selon l'ordre de ses perceptions, elle existe toujours dans un monde ou univers selon une parfaite harmonie voulue par Dieu. C'est pourquoi les perceptions situées à des lieux et temps distincts sont tout de même reliées, d'où les formulations leibniziennes selon lesquelles « le présent est gros de l'avenir » ou « l'éloigné exprime le prochain ». 2) Chaque monade est une représentation ou perception particulière du monde en tant qu'elle exprime celui-ci sous un certain point de vue. Tous les états ou événements sont ainsi compris dans chaque substance, mais

1. *Discours*, § 15, A VI, 4, 1553-1554.
2. *Principes de la nature*, § 13, GP VI, 604.

d'une manière que Leibniz nomme virtuelle[1]. C'est la raison pour laquelle on pourrait connaître l'ordre du monde dans une seule monade en dépliant son développement qui correspond à l'harmonie générale des choses. Toutefois, la monade, même réflexive, est incapable de connaître l'infinité qu'elle contient virtuellement, seul Dieu saisissant parfaitement l'infini de manière actuelle et absolue[2]. 3) Le principe des indiscernables avait pour conséquence que deux suites de perceptions parfaitement exactes ne permettraient pas de distinguer des êtres réels. Si la beauté de l'univers se connaît dans chaque monade, car tous les événements du monde y sont contenus, comment alors respecter cette exigence d'individuation? C'est ici qu'intervient la distinction entre deux types de perception : d'une part, la perception distincte qui représente l'action ou véritable point de vue de la monade, d'autre part, la perception confuse des autres monades qui représentent ce même point de vue de façon passive. Si l'on reprend l'illustration par les points de vue sur une même ville, on peut ainsi dire que la perspective distincte et actuelle d'une monade A est concomitamment perçue de manière confuse par les monades B, C et D, que la perspective distincte et actuelle de B est perçue de manière confuse par les monades A, C et D, etc. Il existe donc bien une correspondance expressive entre les points de vue suivant la distinction et la confusion des perceptions. Notons un point sur lequel nous reviendrons : la distinction perceptive se rapporte principalement au corps propre de la monade[3] et pour lequel elle est entéléchie; tandis que l'action des autres corps sera perçue de façon confuse et passive par cette même monade. 4) Finalement, l'extrait soulève la thèse selon laquelle le niveau de distinction des perceptions représente la perfection d'une substance. Évidemment, cet aspect mène à des implications morales multiples dont font état plusieurs textes leibniziens[4], mais retenons surtout l'idée que l'ordre expressif des substances est aussi un ordre de perfection à proportion du degré de distinction perceptive. L'harmonie universelle repose sur un choix divin fondé sur le principe du meilleur et qui se répercute bien évidemment sur les perceptions des substances qui participent proportiellement à la perfection des choses selon leur distinction. Il est même possible d'établir une hiérarchie des substances ou chaîne des êtres selon la nature des perceptions : par exemple, la réflexion des esprits humains qui fait connaître les vérités nécessaires et abstraites a plus de distinction que la cognition animale qui

1. *Nouveaux Essais*, « Préface », A VI, 6, 52.
2. *Essais de théodicée*, § 403, GP VI, 356-357.
3. *Monadologie*, § 62, GP VI, 617.
4. Il en est notamment question dans les *Essais de théodicée* : § 357, GP VI, 327.

en demeure à une consécution empirique, de sorte que la première contient davantage de perfection que la deuxième[1].

L'ANALOGIE DU MOI

Les monades sont en somme des unités substantielles pourvues de perception et d'appétition, la première propriété explicitant principalement l'expression qu'elles ont du monde, la deuxième leur capacité d'action ou de force. L'argument principal utilisé dans des œuvres comme la *Monadologie* ou les *Principes de la nature et de la grâce* a été mentionné précédemment et procède analytiquement : les monades ou substances simples sont nécessaires à l'existence du composé parce que « sans les simples il n'y aurait point de composés »[2]. On sait également que ce raisonnement est différent de celui utilisé par Leibniz dans le *Discours de métaphysique* et la correspondance avec Arnauld, lequel reposait plutôt sur l'individuation que confère une notion complète. À ces deux argumentaires s'ajoute pourtant une troisième manière de prouver l'existence de la substance et qui permet de comparer l'approche de Leibniz à la tradition cartésienne. Rappelons que dans sa première lettre adressée à Leibniz, Arnauld objectait que l'individuation par la notion complète posait problème et qu'il serait préférable de recourir au *cogito* cartésien pour déterminer l'existence et la nature du moi[3]. En réponse à cette critique, Leibniz soutient que la notion du moi peut à juste titre être considérée comme référant à une substance individuelle, mais que cette notion « est infiniment plus étendue et plus difficile à comprendre qu'une notion spécifique comme celle de la sphère, qui n'est qu'incomplète [...] »[4]. Autrement dit, la notion du moi est certes celle d'une substance individuelle, mais sa connaissance ne saurait être aussi certaine que ne le croyait Descartes[5]. Il était alors nécessaire de jumeler au moi la doctrine de la notion complète longuement explicitée par Leibniz.

Il manque toutefois au *Discours de métaphysique* et à la correspondance avec Arnauld un argument qui fera son apparition avec la caractérisation de la substance comme unité à partir du *Système nouveau*. Effectivement, Leibniz affirme à cette occasion que l'unité véritable de la

1. *Monadologie*, § 28-30, GP VI, 611-612.
2. *Principes de la nature*, § 1, GP VI, 598.
3. Lettre de Arnauld à Leibniz du 13 mai 1686, A II, 2, 35.
4. Lettre à Arnauld du 14 juillet 1686, A II, 2, 75.
5. *Principia philosophiae*, AT VIII, 8-9.

substance « répond à ce qu'on appelle moi en nous »[1]. Tel que mentionné, le dispositif reposant sur la notion complète est absent à partir des textes métaphysiques des 1690 puisqu'il fait désormais place à une conception de la substance à partir de l'unité. Or, Leibniz reconnaît maintenant que cette unité se perçoit en nous. L'esprit humain, en réfléchissant à sa propre réalité comme moi, perçoit sa nature comme être substantiel. L'ego possède ainsi une unité *per se* et se comprend alors comme substance simple. Mais il y a plus : le *cogito* est certes pour Leibniz une vérité première, à laquelle il faut cependant ajouter une deuxième :

> Car je n'ai pas seulement conscience de mon moi pensant, mais aussi de mes pensées, et il n'est pas plus vrai ni plus certain que je pense, qu'il n'est vrai et certain que je pense telle ou telle chose. Aussi est-on en droit de rapporter toutes les vérités de fait premières à ces deux-ci : Je pense, et des choses diverses sont pensées par moi[2].

Le constat factuel de notre pensée nous donne accès à une structure que Leibniz attribuera plus tard à la perception[3], c'est-à-dire un rapport d'unité dans la multiplicité. Je me pense comme unité substantielle, mais je perçois aussi dans cette unité fondamentale une diversité de pensées. En d'autres termes, la représentation du moi est celle d'une substance simple capable de percevoir une multiplicité. Or, cette structure devient pour Leibniz la base d'un critère de reconnaissance du substantiel dans la nature : comme le moi permet de rapporter une multiplicité à une unité, Leibniz soutient que toute substance simple ou monade devra reproduire cette disposition ontologique. Il en fait part à la reine Sophie Charlotte :

> Cette pensée de moi, qui m'aperçois des objets sensibles, et de ma propre action qui en résulte, ajoute quelque chose aux objets des sens. Penser à quelque couleur et considérer qu'on y pense, ce sont deux pensées très différentes, autant que la couleur même diffère de moi qui y pense. Et comme je conçois que d'autres Êtres peuvent aussi avoir le droit de dire moi, ou qu'on pourrait le dire pour eux, c'est par là que je conçois ce qu'on appelle la substance en général [...][4].

1. *Système nouveau*, GP IV, 482.

2. *Animadversiones in partem generalem principiorum cartesianorum*, GP IV, 357, trad. *in* P. Schrecker, p. 39. Cette interprétation du *cogito* est beaucoup plus ancienne et est mentionnée lors du séjour parisien : lettre à Foucher de 1675, A II, 1, p. 388. C'est néanmoins une nouvelle fonction argumentative que Leibniz confère au *cogito* à partir du *Système nouveau*.

3. *Monadologie*, § 16, GP VI, 609.

4. *Lettre touchant ce qui est indépendant des Sens et de la Matière* à Sophie Charlotte, GP VI, 502.

Le troisième argument leibnizien principal pour prouver l'existence des substances repose ainsi sur une analogie avec le moi et une reconnaissance des êtres qui en partagent la même structure. Les autres monades posséderont par conséquent une capacité perceptive rendant possible une diversité dans une unité fondamentale. Ce que nous expérimentons en nous-mêmes fournit les moyens d'identification du substantiel dans les choses [1]. Évidemment, si un être n'est pourvu que d'une unité *per accidens*, et non *per se*, à la manière d'un agrégat phénoménal, il faudrait dès lors l'exclure du domaine de la réalité substantielle; sans véritable unité, reconnue en l'occurrence par le *cogito*, il ne saurait exister de fondement substantiel aux choses.

LA MACHINE DE LA NATURE

L'image générale qui ressort de cette conceptualisation monadologique a donné lieu à de nombreuses interprétations, en particulier dans la littérature récente. Plusieurs commentateurs ont soutenu que Leibniz adoptait une ontologie idéaliste, à la manière de Berkeley, suivant laquelle seules les monades spirituelles et inétendues existent réellement, reléguant les corps au statut de simples apparences phénoménales [2]. D'après cette lecture, le corps ne serait pas une substance, mais se réduirait, sur le plan métaphysique, à n'être qu'un agrégat de substances [3]. D'autres interprètes ont plutôt voulu insister sur des passages dans lesquels Leibniz maintient que la monade est un principe d'actualisation et d'organisation de la matière [4]; sans conférer à la matière un statut substantiel, certains textes suggèrent en effet qu'elle possède une réalité comme composante des substances composées [5]. En d'autres mots, une monade serait toujours constituée d'une certaine quantité de matière. Il est vrai que la diversité des affirmations leibniziennes relatives à la nature des corps peut laisser perplexe. Déjà à l'époque du *Discours de métaphysique*, Leibniz semblait hésiter à attribuer au corps une réalité substantielle [6]. D'ailleurs, il serait

1. Lettre à Lady Masham de mai 1704, GP III, 340.
2. *Cf.* R. M. Adams, *Leibniz*, p. 262-307.
3. C'est ce que Leibniz aurait notamment affirmé à Fardella dans une discussion mise par écrit : *De serie rerum, corporibus et substantiis, et de praedeterminatione*, A VI, 4, 1668.
4. L'extrait précédemment cité du *De Ipsa natura*, GP IV, p. 511, énonce cette idée, mais on la retrouve ailleurs dans une formulation rapprochée, par exemple dans les *Essais de théodicée* : § 195, GP VI, 232.
5. *Cf.* P. Phemister, *Leibniz and the Natural World*, p. 161-186.
6. *Discours*, § 10, A VI, 4, 1542.

possible de soutenir que l'ontologie leibnizienne évolue à cet égard, puisque la diversité des contextes théoriques permet très certainement des lectures tant idéalistes que réalistes du statut métaphysique des corps[1].

Parallèlement à ces discussions, force est de constater que le concept de substance, qu'il soit substance individuelle, entéléchie ou monade, est presque toujours élaboré chez Leibniz dans sa relation au corps[2]. La réhabilitation des formes substantielles ou l'idée plus tardive que la substance est une entéléchie démontrent d'emblée qu'il s'agit de penser le substantiel en rapport avec la matière. Les réflexions autour de l'harmonie préétablie montrent également que l'âme doit être pensée dans sa relation au corps[3]. La métaphysique monadologique précisera toutefois la fonction que joue la substance dans l'ordre corporel. En fait, la substance n'est pas seulement un principe d'unité et d'action, mais aussi un principe de vie. On sait que Leibniz s'est grandement intéressé aux sciences du vivant et que cet intérêt a marqué sa métaphysique[4]. Dans plusieurs textes d'importance, il est question de problèmes relatifs à la nature du vivant, qu'il s'agisse de la génération, de la transformation ou de la finalité des corps organiques. Dans la période de la maturité, Leibniz ira jusqu'à dire que « la nature est pleine de vie »[5] et que « chaque portion de matière peut être conçue, comme un jardin plein de plantes, et comme un étang plein de poissons »[6]. La structuration que permet l'unité substantielle de la monade est dans les faits le fondement métaphysique de l'organisation du vivant.

Pour mieux saisir la manière dont la métaphysique de la substance chez Leibniz peut à l'évidence être considérée comme étant une ontologie du vivant, il faut expliquer un concept employé pour la première fois dans le *Système nouveau*. L'organisation du corps vivant est appelée une machine de la nature[7]. Deux éléments mentionnés précédemment nous aideront à comprendre ce concept : d'une part, on a déjà indiqué que la substance simple ou monade possède une indestructibilité naturelle et que seul Dieu pourrait l'annihiler. Or, ce caractère indestructible ne concerne pas seulement la monade avec ses perceptions et appétitions, mais aussi le corps organique auquel elle est liée. Sachant qu'elle perçoit son corps de

1. *Cf.* D. Garber, *Leibniz : Body, Substance, Monad*, p. 303-388.

2. Je remercie Raphaële Andrault pour ses commentaires concernant les analyses qui suivent.

3. *Discours*, § 33, A VI, 4, 1582-1583 ; *Système nouveau*, GP IV, 485-486.

4. *Cf.* F. Duchesneau, *Leibniz, le vivant et l'organisme* ; J. E. H. Smith, *Divine Machine* ; R. Andrault, *La Vie selon la raison*.

5. *Principes de la nature*, § 1, GP VI, 598.

6. *Monadologie*, § 67, GP VI, 618.

7. *Système nouveau*, GP IV, 481-482.

manière distincte et agit sur lui comme entéléchie[1], la structure du corps organique en est de même préservée. Autrement dit, la machine de nature, à la différence de la machine artificielle conçue par l'être humain, est indestructible étant donné l'entéléchie primitive qui en exprime l'arrangement[2]. D'autre part, souvenons-nous que le substantiel se reconnaît à une disposition d'unité dans la multiplicité perçue notamment par la réflexion dans le moi. Pour Leibniz, cette organisation se répercute également dans le rapport de la substance au corps organique, en ce que la machine de la nature est formée d'une infinité de machines de la nature trouvant son unité dans une âme vivante. Sans que l'âme n'agisse véritablement sur le corps organique, puisque la doctrine de l'harmonie préétablie l'interdit, un rapport d'expression fonde leur unité respective. Pour ce faire, Leibniz fait une distinction entre la monade dominante qu'est l'âme animale et les monades dominées qui rentrent dans la constitution des machines de la nature. Un extrait d'une lettre à De Volder résume les éléments constitutifs d'un animal ou substance corporelle :

> Je distingue donc 1) l'Entéléchie primitive ou Âme, 2) la Matière, à savoir la matière première, ou puissance passive primitive, 3) la Monade complète avec ces deux choses, 4) la Masse ou matière seconde, ou Machine organique, à laquelle concourent d'innombrables Monades subordonnées, 5) l'Animal ou substance corporelle, que la Monade dominante sur la Machine fait Un[3].

Ce passage assez complexe a été abondamment mobilisé dans la littérature secondaire pour tenter de déterminer le statut du corps chez Leibniz. Mais ce qui nous intéresse concerne le rapport de domination entre l'âme comme entéléchie primitive et le corps ou machine organique constitué d'un nombre infini de monades subordonnées. Une machine de la nature s'accompagne ainsi d'une âme, ou un esprit dans le cas humain, et constitue une entité organisatrice tant dans le tout de la substance corporelle que dans ses parties ou organes *ad infinitum*. C'est précisément cette structure qui est indestructible et qui perdure, bien que les parties de matière changent continuellement dans l'animal. C'est la raison pour laquelle Leibniz affirme à plusieurs endroits que ni l'âme ni la machine de la nature ne sont détruites, c'est-à-dire qu'il n'y a pas véritablement de mort dans la nature, mais plutôt des changements de domination monadique dans la matière : « ce que nous appelons Générations sont des

1. *Monadologie*, § 62, GP VI, 617.
2. *Ibid.*, § 64, GP VI, 618.
3. Lettre à De Volder du 20 juin 1703, GP II, 252, trad. fr. A.-L. Rey, *Leibniz-De Volder. Correspondance*, p. 229.

développements et des accroissements; comme ce que nous appelons Morts, sont des enveloppements et des diminutions »[1]. Et bien entendu, ces changements d'accroissement ou de diminution de domination de l'animal tiennent leur fondement métaphysique de la perfection des perceptions distinctes et confuses de l'âme qui agit à titre d'unité et d'entéléchie primitive du corps organique.

Le concept de machine de la nature repose manifestement sur des acquis importants de la métaphysique de la monade; sans perception et entéléchie appétitive, l'âme ou monade dominante ne pourrait pas exprimer cette fonction structurante qui confère au corps organique une indestructibilité non seulement d'ensemble, mais aussi dans ses parties qui en font autant de machines de la nature dans une division infinie. On constate alors que la machine de la nature n'a pu apparaître comme notion fondamentale de l'ontologie leibnizienne qu'à la condition de considérer la substance comme unité simple. Le *Discours de métaphysique* comporte certes des considérations sur le vivant qui seront récupérées par la suite, mais force est d'admettre qu'elles ne sont pas articulées autour des notions de monade et de machine de la nature, lesquelles feront leur apparition dans les années 1690. La métaphysique leibnizienne de la substance s'est ainsi modifiée au fur et à mesure de son évolution, de manière à résoudre de nouveaux problèmes. Ces modifications pourraient même être considérées comme étant des discontinuités conceptuelles et théoriques, puisqu'il semble difficile de déterminer laquelle représenterait la version la plus achevée ou de les assembler sous un même système. Peut-être serait-il nécessaire, pour cet aspect comme pour d'autres, de renoncer à trouver un point d'achèvement de la métaphysique leibnizienne et d'en rester à une interprétation selon les contextes afin de mieux en apprécier l'appareil conceptuel.

Christian LEDUC
(Université de Montréal)

1. *Monadologie*, § 73, GP VI, 619.

LE MAL ET LA JUSTICE DIVINE

Leibniz aborde le problème du mal en le liant explicitement au thème de la justice[1]. La question première n'est pas, pour lui, « qu'est-ce que le mal ? » ou « pourquoi le mal existe ? » ni, celle, traditionnelle depuis Augustin, « d'où vient le mal ? » (*Unde malum ?)*, mais plutôt « à qui le mal est-il imputable ? ». L'enjeu est d'abord juridique et moral, avant d'être métaphysique et théologique. C'est seulement dans un second temps que l'enquête doit conduire à s'interroger sur l'essence du mal et sur son origine ultime. Pourquoi Leibniz privilégie-t-il cette approche ? Il est vrai que le modèle juridique est prégnant chez celui qui, juriste de formation, prétend, dans la préface aux *Essais de théodicée* (1710)[2], plaider la « cause de Dieu »[3], à l'instar de l'avocat qui défend un accusé dans un tribunal. Les règles de la controverse philosophique qu'il expose et applique lui-même dans le *Discours de la conformité de la foi avec la raison*[4] (par lequel s'ouvrent les *Essais*) sont d'ailleurs clairement – quoique non exclusivement – inspirées du débat judiciaire.

Leibniz pense le mal du point de vue du droit pour une raison cependant plus fondamentale : parce qu'il considère l'*injustice* – ce qui contredit une loi – comme le mal véritable, qu'il s'agisse de l'injustice commise (le péché) ou de l'injustice subie (la douleur en tant qu'elle est imméritée, c'est-à-dire ne suit pas d'un juste châtiment). Pour lui, l'existence du mal

1. Voir par exemple *De la toute-puissance et de l'omniscience de Dieu* [...], A VI, 1, § 1-3, 537 ; Y. Belaval, *La Profession de foi du Philosophe*, p. 29 (A VI, 3, 116). Dans *De la liberté, du destin, de la grâce de Dieu*, la démonstration de la proposition « Dieu n'est pas la cause du mal ou du péché » suit directement de la démonstration de la proposition « Dieu est suprêmement juste », A VI, 4, 1596-1597.

2. La *Théodicée* (y compris *La Cause de Dieu*) est citée ici dans l'éd. de J. Brunschwig, Garnier-Flammarion [dorénavant GF], suivie de la référence à l'éd. Gerhardt [GP VI].

3. GF, 39 (GP VI, 38).

4. Voir notamment § 58 et § 72-79.

– imperfection, faute, douleur – n'est pas *en soi* un « scandale », même sous un Dieu bon. Elle ne devient problématique et « choquante » qu'à partir du moment où la douleur échoit à qui ne la mérite pas, quand elle frappe l'homme de bien, ou lorsque le crime perpétré n'est suivi d'aucune sanction et profite à celui qui le commet. Les souffrances, les malheurs, les fléaux en tout genre (catastrophes et calamités d'origine naturelle ou humaine), y compris le fait qu'il y ait des méchants dans le monde ne poseraient pas réellement problème si ces souffrances, ces malheurs, ces fléaux n'arrivaient qu'aux seuls méchants ! Le « mal » serait facile à justifier en ce cas, dans la mesure où il apparaîtrait comme la punition de leurs fautes. Or l'expérience témoigne d'un ordre des choses parfois – d'aucuns pensent *souvent* – inversé, où l'innocent est persécuté et l'homme bon souffre, quand le méchant est libre d'agir en toute impunité et semble même récompensé par le bonheur qu'il retire de ses crimes. Voilà ce qui rend le mal véritablement *mauvais* – pour ainsi dire – et constitue le problème qu'il appartient à la raison de résoudre. Comment une telle contradiction entre le fait et le droit, entre l'être et le devoir-être est-elle possible supposé un Dieu que l'on dit bon, sage et tout-puissant[1] ?

Le mal met en cause la justice de Dieu, entendue selon ses deux acceptions, c'est-à-dire au sens du *droit* et au sens de la *perfection*. D'une part, la justice est la loi suivant laquelle Dieu gouverne l'univers et plus particulièrement l'ensemble des esprits – hommes, génies, anges – qui forment une communauté ou « République » dont il est le monarque. Sous son règne, chacun devrait être rétribué selon son mérite, aucune bonne action n'être laissée sans récompense ni aucun péché laissé sans punition. D'autre part, la justice s'identifie en Dieu à la sainteté qui n'est autre que le plus haut degré de bonté[2]. En vertu de cette bonté – qui l'éloigne infiniment de toute espèce de mal et d'imperfection –, il ne saurait vouloir ni faire que le bien. Or le désordre apparent des choses, notamment la prospérité des méchants et le malheur des bons, contredit la justice divine prise en son premier sens (comme *droit*) et semble renverser l'idée même d'une providence à l'œuvre dans le monde[3]. Le concours de Dieu au mal paraît, quant à lui, incompatible avec sa justice considérée dans sa seconde acception (comme *perfection*). Dieu prend part en effet aux péchés que réalisent ses créatures, par sa volonté et par sa puissance, puisqu'aucune

1. Voir par exemple *De la toute-puissance et de l'omniscience de Dieu* [...], A VI, 1, § 2, 537 : « Comment, malgré la misère présente des justes et le bonheur des méchants, peut-il tout de même exister une providence divine ? ».

2. Cf. *Théodicée*, § 151 ; *La Cause de Dieu*, § 50.

3. Voir par exemple *Théodicée*, § 4.

chose ne peut se produire dans le monde sans qu'il ne la veuille, ne la fasse arriver[1], ou tout du moins ne la permette. Ce concours physique et moral soulève ici le problème de la prédestination, de la liberté de l'homme et de la légitimité de sa punition. Que lui est-il imputable si Dieu, cause première et continuelle de toutes choses, sait à l'avance tout ce qu'il fera, n'empêche pas son péché de s'accomplir et même y contribue directement par sa puissance?

Étant donné la manière dont le problème du mal est posé, sa résolution passe nécessairement par une doctrine de la justice divine, c'est-à-dire, au sens propre, par une *théodicée* – terme dont Leibniz est l'inventeur[2]. Cette doctrine doit prouver l'innocence et la sainteté de Dieu, exposer les règles qui président à son action et les raisons pour lesquelles il n'a pu créer que le meilleur des mondes possibles. Or il n'est pas sûr que lecteurs et commentateurs aient vu ici l'originalité de l'entreprise leibnizienne, des arguments et des thèses qu'il avançait. Ce chapitre a pour but de remettre en cause deux interprétations habituelles de sa théodicée.

Selon la première, la plupart des arguments utilisés par Leibniz pour «justifier» Dieu et rendre raison de l'existence du mal dans le monde, n'auraient rien de nouveau, puisqu'on les trouverait déjà chez Platon, les stoïciens, les néoplatoniciens et Augustin[3]. Ainsi la définition du mal comme privation, sa réduction au statut de condition d'un bien plus grand – à l'instar de la dissonance en musique ou de l'ombre qui, dans le beau tableau, fait ressortir l'éclat de la lumière et la vivacité des couleurs –, la théorie de la permission divine du péché ne seraient que le réemploi d'un legs tiré de l'Antiquité et de la scolastique. Il est incontestable que Leibniz connaît bien cette tradition théologique et philosophique, à laquelle il se réfère explicitement[4]. Nous verrons cependant qu'il n'est aucun argument, concept ou distinction, apparemment repris de cet héritage, qui ne soit réinterprété et auquel il ne soit donné un sens nouveau.

Selon la seconde interprétation, la conception leibnizienne du mal et sa justification de Dieu auraient été établies et pratiquement fixées une fois pour toutes dès la *Profession de foi du Philosophe*, texte écrit dans les années 1672-1673 et souvent considéré comme une «première» théodicée ou une «théodicée de jeunesse»[5]. Dans les écrits ultérieurs, le philosophe

1. Puisque chaque créature tire son être de la puissance de Dieu et ne continue d'exister que grâce à cette puissance (sa conservation étant une création continuée).

2. Ce néologisme est formé à partir de deux mots grecs : *théos* (Dieu) et *dikê* (justice).

3. Voir G. Grua, *Jurisprudence universelle et théodicée selon Leibniz*, p. 370.

4. Cf. *Théodicée*, «Préface», GF, 43-44 (GP VI, 43).

5. Voir Y. Belaval, *La Profession de foi du Philosophe*, «Présentation», p. 25-26; G. Grua, «Avertissement», p. VII.

se serait contenté, sur cette question, de reprendre à peu près les mêmes thèses, la doctrine restant au fond inchangée, malgré quelques variations dans les exposés successifs. Or l'étude minutieuse des textes disponibles (des premières esquisses aux *Essais de Théodicée*) témoigne au contraire d'une importante évolution. Elle permet de repérer des changements significatifs, notamment dans la conception de Dieu et de ses rapports à l'action des créatures (son concours moral et physique), dans la définition de la nature du mal et de son origine, enfin dans les raisons alléguées en faveur de sa permission. Ce sont les principales étapes de cette réflexion nourrie et constante sur le mal et la justice divine que les pages suivantes s'attachent à retracer.

LA CRITIQUE DE LA TRADITION ET LE NÉCESSITARISME DES PREMIERS ÉCRITS

L'intérêt de Leibniz pour les questions relatives au mal, à la justice divine, à la liberté humaine et à la prédestination, fut précoce. Le philosophe le fait remonter à ses premières lectures, lorsque, adolescent, il passait son temps dans la bibliothèque de son père et, avide de connaissances, « y voltigeai[t] de livre en livre »[1]. À en croire une lettre à Jablonski (du 23 janvier 1700), il aurait eu, dès l'époque de ses études à Leipzig (1661-1663), l'intention d'écrire une «théodicée» pour y «défendre la bonté, la sagesse et la justice de Dieu, aussi bien que sa suprême puissance et son irrésistible influence »[2]. Ce dessein ne l'a jamais quitté et il est facile d'en retrouver les traces dans ses écrits, sous des formes différentes, tout au long de sa carrière philosophique. Ainsi l'ambitieux programme des *Démonstrations catholiques*, projet à la fois philosophique, théologique et religieux, initié dans les années 1668-1669 sous le patronage du baron de Boinebourg, annonce dans sa troisième partie des chapitres consacrés à la liberté des esprits (chap. XVI), au droit de Dieu et aux obligations qui existent entre lui et les créatures (chap. XVII), à la cause du péché (chap. XXI). L'objet du chapitre XVIII est résumé en ces termes : « Dieu n'est en rien la cause du mal de coulpe, mais seulement la cause par accident du mal de peine »[3].

Il faut pourtant attendre les années 1670-1671 pour trouver le premier essai leibnizien connu de résolution du problème du mal. Il s'agit d'un opuscule inachevé, écrit en allemand, intitulé par les éditeurs *De la toute*

1. *Théodicée*, « Préface », GF, p. 43 (GP VI, 43).
2. Leibniz à Jablonski, 23 janvier 1700, GP VI, 3.
3. A VI, 1, 496.

puissance et de l'omniscience de Dieu et de la liberté de l'homme[1]. Ce texte est un témoignage important de l'état de la réflexion du philosophe à l'époque. Son intérêt réside notamment dans les critiques adressées à la tradition et dans un traitement du sujet sensiblement différent de celui qui prévaudra dans les textes ultérieurs – et notamment dans la *Théodicée*.

Leibniz soutient que les objections contre la justice et la providence divines reposent sur deux principaux sophismes. Il réfute facilement le premier, connu depuis l'Antiquité sous le nom de « l'argument paresseux »[2], qui prétend que la vérité du futur – et en contexte chrétien la prescience de Dieu – est incompatible avec la liberté de l'homme. Le second affirme que Dieu est le véritable auteur du péché, dans la mesure où il ne se contente pas de le permettre, mais crée toutes les circonstances qui y conduisent et porte même l'homme à l'accomplir, alors qu'il pourrait l'empêcher. Le jeune philosophe répond d'abord en recourant à un argument d'ordre juridique et moral :

> La mauvaise volonté, d'où qu'elle vienne, requiert la punition. Sinon, aucun crime ne devrait être puni, car on trouve toujours une cause de la volonté hors de ceux qui veulent, et pourtant c'est la volonté qui fait de nous des hommes et des personnes, des pécheurs, des bienheureux ou des damnés[3].

Deux raisons sont ici invoquées. D'une part, la justice exige que tout péché soit puni, toute action bonne récompensée. D'autre part, en droit, l'imputation doit revenir à la cause la plus proche, en l'occurrence à la volonté de l'homme, et non aux causes déterminantes plus éloignées, ni *a fortiori* à Dieu, raison dernière des choses. Sans quoi le pécheur ne serait pas responsable du mal qu'il commet ni, par conséquent, punissable. Il trouverait toujours une excuse à son acte ; ce qui ruinerait toute justice.

Si l'argument vaut du point de vue juridique et moral et suffit à fonder l'imputation humaine, il laisse cependant entier le problème de la participation de Dieu au péché. À cet égard, la position défendue dans l'opuscule peut surprendre, comparée aux écrits postérieurs. Sans doute encore marqué par l'influence de Luther, mais aussi peut-être par sa lecture de

1. *Von der Allmacht und Allwissenheit Gottes und der Freiheit des Menschen*, A VI, 1, 537-546. Une traduction de ce texte, par les soins de Claire Rösler, se trouve dans la revue *Philosophie*, n°68, Éditions de Minuit, Paris, 2000, p. 66-88.

2. Parce qu'il conduit au fatalisme. *Cf.* Cicéron, *Du Destin*, XII, 28-29.

3. § 13, A VI, 1, 542. Le même argument est cité au § 264 de la *Théodicée*.

Hobbes[1], Leibniz ne cherche pas à nier ni à restreindre le concours divin. Il soutient que Dieu ne permet pas seulement le péché, mais *veut* son existence[2], considérant qu'il est meilleur qu'il existe. Dieu est l'auteur du péché, puisqu'il est l'origine de toute la chaîne des causes. On objectera alors que, s'il concourt moralement au péché par sa volonté, en revanche, il n'y concourt pas physiquement par sa puissance, parce que, comme l'ont montré Augustin et Thomas d'Aquin, le mal n'est *rien* en lui-même. Ces auteurs ont enseigné que Dieu est cause de tout ce qu'il y a de réel et de positif dans les créatures, mais pas de leurs défauts et de leurs manques, qui ne sont que des privations ou négations.

Cet argument, bien connu, est sévèrement critiqué par Leibniz qui le juge théoriquement indéfendable et dangereux sur le plan pratique. Il revient en effet à diviser ce qui est en soi indivisible dans une chose ou un acte : d'un côté, l'être (qui vient de Dieu), de l'autre, ses limites et ses défauts (qui seraient du seul fait de la créature). Une telle distinction est inadmissible, car il est impossible de dissocier dans le pécheur la créature (bonne) du vice qui la corrompt et qui fait précisément sa nature pécheresse, tout comme il est impossible de détacher dans le péché l'acte « pur » de son caractère peccamineux, afin d'assigner à chacun des causes différentes. L'imperfection et le péché de la créature, au même titre que sa perfection et ses bonnes actions, sont donc imputables à Dieu. Tenter de décharger ce dernier de la responsabilité du péché en alléguant qu'il ne produit que la réalité *physique* de l'acte, et non sa qualification *morale* (le fait qu'il est contraire à la justice) est aussi absurde que de prétendre qu'un mauvais violoniste est seulement cause des mouvements de son archet, sans l'être de la dissonance qui en résulte[3] ! Argument qui, s'il était recevable, vaudrait tout aussi bien dans le cas de l'homme et permettrait d'excuser tous ses crimes.

Cette division illégitime introduite dans le concours physique de Dieu conduit logiquement à définir le mal comme un non-être. À partir du moment où il est distingué de l'acte lui-même (seul réel « physiquement »), le mal n'est *rien* à proprement parler et n'a donc besoin d'aucune cause. Par suite, rien ni personne n'y concourt (puisque tout concours va à l'être), et ni l'homme ni Dieu n'en sont responsables. Et Leibniz d'ironiser : « Voilà les beaux avocats de la justice divine, qui vont rendre impunissables en même

1. Sur ce point, voir notre ouvrage *La question du mal chez Leibniz. Fondements et élaboration de la Théodicée*, sect. 1.3.4.

2. Voir § 16, A VI, 1, 544.

3. Voir § 18, 544.

temps tous les pécheurs. Et je m'étonne que le profond Descartes se soit aussi fourvoyé ici »[1].

Notre philosophe n'est jamais revenu sur cette critique. Il n'a jamais souscrit, en dépit de la reprise de certaines formules apparemment conformes à la tradition, à la conception du mal comme pur néant, et il a toujours rejeté l'idée d'un concours physique de Dieu partiel[2]. Quant au concours moral, il réaffirme dans sa lettre à Magnus Wedderkopf (mai 1671) que la distinction, en Dieu, entre une volonté positive absolue et une volonté seulement permissive (du péché) est sans fondement[3]. Il y défend également un nécessitarisme – qui n'était pas explicite dans *De la toute puissance et de l'omniscience de Dieu* – qui concilie la liberté avec la nécessité causale, sans remettre en cause la légitimité des peines et des récompenses. Rien n'étant sans cause, ni aucun effet sans une cause suffisante, tout est nécessaire. Dieu lui-même est nécessité par la considération du meilleur :

> Car la plus grande liberté est d'être porté au meilleur par la droite raison [...]. Il suit de là que, tout ce qui est arrivé, arrive, ou arrivera, est le meilleur et par conséquent nécessaire, mais [...] selon une nécessité qui n'enlève rien à la liberté, parce qu'elle n'enlève rien à la volonté ni à l'usage de la raison[4].

Ce nécessitarisme présente cependant deux caractéristiques qui le distinguent, par exemple, de celui de Hobbes. D'une part, la liberté est définie comme volonté du *meilleur*, car une volonté arbitraire, indépendante de la bonté intrinsèque des choses est contradictoire. D'autre part, l'harmonie universelle, suivant laquelle Dieu choisit et crée le monde, est elle-même incréée et ne dépend donc pas de sa volonté.

La *Profession de foi du Philosophe*, dialogue imaginaire entre un philosophe et un théologien, composé pendant le séjour parisien, témoigne encore de ce nécessitarisme, mais innove en introduisant une distinction importante entre la *raison* et l'*auteur* (du péché). L'application du principe de raison conduit à faire de Dieu la cause ultime du péché comme de toutes choses. Cela n'implique pas, pour autant, que Dieu le *veuille*. Il en est bien la *raison*[5], en tant qu'il est le premier maillon de la série des choses qui constituent le monde. Mais il n'en est pas l'*auteur*, c'est-à-dire la raison par

1. § 18, 545. Voir Descartes, *Méditation quatrième*, AT IX, 43.
2. Voir notamment *L'auteur du péché*, A VI, 3, 150-51.
3. Voir A II, 1, 187.
4. *Ibid.*, 186-187.
5. Puisque « tous les réquisits du péché viennent de Dieu », éd. Y. Belaval, p. 41 (A VI, 3, 120).

sa volonté, laquelle ne se porte qu'au bien. D'où cette explication paradoxale du mal : le mal est parce que Dieu est, et non parce que Dieu le veut. Dieu en est innocent, parce que l'origine du mal ne se trouve pas dans sa volonté, mais dans son entendement (qui contient toutes les essences)[1]. Il y concourt physiquement, mais en aucune façon moralement.

Cette manière de justifier Dieu n'est pas sans poser problème, dans la mesure où elle conduit à rendre le mal nécessaire. Le péché, comme n'importe quel événement ou acte se produisant dans le monde, est nécessaire car s'il manquait, un autre monde que le nôtre existerait à sa place[2] et, par suite, une cause première différente, c'est-à-dire un autre Dieu serait requis (ce qui est impossible). Le rapport de Dieu à la série des choses créées est en effet un rapport de dépendance réciproque : chaque terme de cette série (y compris le premier) est lié à tous les autres, de sorte qu'aucun ne peut être modifié sans que cela n'affecte tous les autres. Si Dieu est posé, *cet* univers qui contient le péché existe, à l'exclusion de tout autre, sinon Dieu n'en serait pas la raison suffisante et entière. Réciproquement, si cet univers qui contient le péché était changé, ou le moindre de ses événements supprimé, Dieu lui-même serait changé ou supprimé. Il en est ici exactement comme dans une proposition hypothétique : Dieu est au monde comme l'inférent d'une proposition hypothétique est à l'inféré : *si A (Dieu) existe, B (le monde) existe;* et, par contraposition, comme la condition au conditionné : *si B (le monde) n'est pas, A (Dieu) n'est pas*[3].

Un tel nécessitarisme a pour conséquence d'effacer le rôle de la volonté. Notre monde n'existe pas parce que Dieu le veut, mais parce qu'il est. Dieu apparaît comme une cause physique plutôt que comme une cause morale, comme la raison d'être du monde (son premier moteur) plutôt que comme son auteur. Comment le distinguer alors de la Nature, de la pure nécessité ou du Destin aveugle ? La différence s'estompe, et le doute peut s'insinuer quant à l'existence d'un être intelligent gouvernant l'univers, auquel nous devrions rendre grâce pour les biens qui arrivent. La volonté divine n'intervient pas, en effet, comme l'instance positive de choix entre divers possibles, instance faisant passer (avec l'aide de la puissance créatrice) du possible au réel. C'est bien plutôt l'harmonie universelle qui remplit ce rôle, en tant qu'elle est « déterminatrice [*determinatrix*] de l'existence des choses »[4]. Définie comme plaisir pris à l'existence de

1. Voir éd. Y. Belaval, p. 43-45 (A VI, 3, 121-122).

2. La possibilité d'autres mondes n'est pas exclue en soi, quoique ces mondes soient *par accident* impossibles, en raison de leur incompatibilité avec l'existence de Dieu.

3. *Cf.* éd. Y. Belaval, p. 47 (A VI, 3, 123-124).

4. *Ibid.*, p. 79 (A VI, 3, 137).

quelque chose[1], la volonté apparaît comme un consentement passif, un acquiescement à ce qui est et qui suit nécessairement de l'existence divine, au lieu d'être cet effort qui fait venir le monde à l'être. Comme si, loin d'inspirer l'acte créateur, elle venait après lui, pour en quelque sorte l'approuver et s'en réjouir.

Qu'en est-il alors des maux qui sont commis dans le monde ? Bien qu'il en soit la raison ultime, Dieu ne les veut pas, c'est-à-dire qu'il ne peut s'en réjouir, pris à part et considérés en soi. Il les *permet* seulement, en tant qu'ils entrent dans l'harmonie universelle. La notion de permission, explicitement rejetée dans *De la toute-puissance et de l'omniscience de Dieu*, réapparaît ici, mais dotée d'un sens nouveau. Le péché est admis dans la mesure où il est lié à la meilleure série de choses. Le permettre n'est ni le vouloir directement, ni indirectement, absolument ou même relativement. Ce n'est pas non plus ne pas le vouloir. La permission est une forme de suspension ou de « neutralisation » de la volonté. Elle n'est pas de l'ordre du vouloir, mais du savoir[2]. Elle ne consiste ni à se réjouir de l'existence du mal ni à en souffrir (sinon Dieu serait imparfait), mais à savoir qu'il est inséparable de l'harmonie universelle, où il est compensé par de plus grands biens.

Il est clair que cette conception de la permission diffère de celle qui sera exposée dans la *Théodicée*, où elle sera réintégrée au sein d'une doctrine de la volonté, fondée sur la distinction entre volonté *antécédente* et volonté *conséquente*. Il faut également souligner la portée exacte de l'apparente « réhabilitation » de la distinction scolastique entre nécessité absolue et nécessité hypothétique, opérée dans la *Profession de foi du Philosophe*. Cette reprise, loin de manifester une inflexion ou une atténuation du nécessitarisme leibnizien, n'est qu'une façon d'exprimer dans le langage ordinaire de l'École – sévèrement critiqué dans les écrits de jeunesse – une thèse établie sans son aide. La distinction des deux nécessités n'est donc pas entièrement assumée par le philosophe, qui la tient pour « superflue » et même « sophistique »[3]. Elle recouvre simplement l'opposition entre l'existence par soi et l'existence par une cause extrinsèque. Ce qui tire sa raison d'être de soi-même (Dieu) est *absolument* nécessaire, alors que ce qui tire sa raison d'être de quelque chose d'extérieur est nécessaire *ex hypothesi*, c'est-à-dire à condition que sa cause soit posée. C'est pourquoi tout ce qui

1. Cf. *ibid*., p. 55 (A VI, 3, 127).
2. *Ibid*.
3. *Ibid*. (A VI, 3, 126).

suit de l'Être absolument nécessaire n'est pas, par là même, absolument nécessaire[1].

L'emploi de cette distinction a seulement pour but d'expliquer en quel sens les péchés peuvent être dits nécessaires : ils le sont par accident ou *hypothétiquement* (et non absolument parlant). Cependant elle n'a qu'une portée très relative, puisqu'elle est appliquée dans le cadre d'une théologie qui, en faisant de la série des choses existantes (le monde) une suite de l'existence divine, considère que cette *seule* série est possible *par hypothèse*, c'est-à-dire en fait possible. Telle est la conséquence de la solidarité de chaque membre de la série avec tous les autres, le premier terme compris (suivant le modèle de l'implication logique). Pour qu'il y ait un autre monde il aurait fallu un autre Dieu – hypothèse absolument impossible, puisque Dieu ne peut être autre qu'il n'est. La possibilité en soi d'autres créatures et événements apparaît alors purement fictive, puisque l'existence de ces créatures et événements est en réalité incompatible avec l'existence de Dieu. Et la différence entre l'impossible par accident et l'impossible absolument s'efface ou, tout du moins, devient artificielle.

Pour établir solidement la contingence du monde, Leibniz sera amené à réviser certaines de ses thèses. Dieu ne devra plus être envisagé comme le premier terme de la série qui constitue l'univers, mais placé en dehors d'elle et considéré comme indépendant d'elle. Il sera alors possible de soutenir non seulement que d'autres mondes sont concevables, mais encore que Dieu pouvait créer n'importe lequel d'entre eux, sans cesser pour autant d'être ce qu'il est. Ce changement théorique suppose une conception nouvelle du possible (qui ne saurait se réduire à une pure fiction) et une redéfinition du rôle de la volonté divine, pour en faire une véritable instance positive de choix.

LA RÉVISION THÉOLOGIQUE ET LA NOUVELLE MÉTAPHYSIQUE DU CONCOURS

Dans la seconde moitié des années 1670, d'importants changements conceptuels conduisent à une révision de la conception de Dieu (1), à une nouvelle explication du concours physique et de l'origine du mal (2), enfin à une réinterprétation de la permission divine du péché (3).

1. éd. Y. Belaval, p. 57-59 (A VI, 3, 127-128).

1) Afin sans doute de souligner sa différence avec Spinoza, Leibniz prend soin de distinguer, dans les textes postérieurs à la *Profession de foi du Philosophe*, Dieu de la Nature, du Destin et de la nécessité, en insistant sur sa nature d'être spirituel, personnel, doué d'entendement et de volonté[1]. Il n'est plus désormais conçu comme le premier terme de la série des choses existantes, mais comme la cause de leur existence – cause extérieure et indépendante –, si bien que le monde aurait pu être autre sans que l'essence divine en soit affectée. D'autres univers sont donc non seulement possibles en soi, mais encore *réalisables* par Dieu sans contradiction. Cette nouvelle théologie est étroitement liée à la redéfinition de deux concepts majeurs : celui de *possible* et celui de *volonté*.

Un possible n'est pas une simple fiction, ni une chimère que nous nous forgeons, en pensant à quelque chose qui n'existe pas ou qui aurait pu exister. Il satisfait formellement au principe de contradiction et, métaphysiquement, renvoie à quelque chose de réel qui est indépendant de notre pensée actuelle[2]. Tous les possibles existent en effet dans l'entendement divin, où ils sont « réalisés »[3], c'est-à-dire sont des « choses » (*res*) à proprement parler, quand bien même ils ne seraient jamais amenés à l'existence. À partir des années 1677-1678[4], Leibniz les dote même d'une « propension à l'existence », ou encore d'une disposition à exister, exactement proportionnelle à leur degré de perfection, de sorte que plus ils sont parfaits ou possèdent de quantité d'essence, plus cette tendance est « puissante ». Ainsi un possible ne se définit plus seulement par la propriété logique de non-contradiction, et par la propriété métaphysique d'être en puissance (par opposition à l'être en acte), mais encore par une propriété pour ainsi dire « dynamique » : la tendance, l'effort (*conatus*)[5] vers l'existence.

Dans l'entendement divin, les possibles se combinent pour former des mondes, tous différents les uns des autres et incompatibles entre eux. Le meilleur est celui qui l'emporte sur les autres en raison de la plus grande quantité de perfection ou d'essence qu'il permet de réaliser. En dépit de son excellence, ce monde ne saurait pourtant par lui-même venir à l'existence – sinon il serait avant que d'être –, mais requiert pour cela l'intervention d'une force extérieure créatrice. C'est pourquoi un Dieu est nécessaire,

1. Voir par exemple A VI, 3, 474-75.

2. *Cf.* Leibniz à Foucher, 1675, A II, 1, 387-388.

3. Cf. *De l'origine radicale des choses*, Schrecker, 181 (GP VII, 305).

4. Voir A VI, 4, 1363. Leibniz parle de « *pretension* [...] à l'existence » dans le *Dialogue entre Théophile et Polidore* [1679 ?], A VI, 4, 2232.

5. L'usage du terme apparaît dans les années 1683-1685 (*cf.* A VI, 4, 557).

lequel embrasse et compare tous les possibles, choisit le meilleur et le fait exister par sa toute-puissance.

Le rapport entre entendement et volonté est, par suite, entièrement réévalué. Il suppose que le possible qui prétend à l'existence dans l'entendement de Dieu devienne une inclination dans sa volonté (pour laquelle il apparaît comme une fin à poursuivre). Leibniz s'écarte ainsi du modèle intellectualiste traditionnel, où la volonté est simplement subordonnée à l'entendement. La volonté se présente comme la traduction immédiate de la représentation mentale en effort, plutôt que comme ce qui viendrait après le jugement de l'entendement pour s'y soumettre et l'approuver. Entendement et volonté apparaissent comme les deux expressions d'un même et unique effort (*conatus*), qui n'est autre en Dieu que sa toute-puissance. Celle-ci ne doit pas être conçue comme une puissance absolue, aveugle et sans règles, mais comme la capacité à réaliser ce que l'entendement représente de plus parfait, qui est en même temps ce que la volonté recherche de meilleur.

Le même conflit, observé dans l'entendement divin entre les possibles en raison de leur incompatibilité, se retrouve dans la volonté entre les inclinations particulières (appelées, dans la *Théodicée*, « volontés antécédentes »), qui visent à obtenir chaque bien et à éviter tout mal. Comme celles-ci ne peuvent être toutes satisfaites[1] (à l'instar des possibles qui ne peuvent être tous réalisés), certaines (par exemple, que tous les hommes soient sauvés) n'aboutissent pas. De même alors que de la combinaison de tous les possibles naît le plan du meilleur monde possible, de la composition de toutes les volontés antécédentes, résulte la volonté dite « conséquente » ou « finale », par laquelle le plus de bien et de perfection est voulu, pour le minimum de mal.

2) Leibniz s'oppose aussi bien aux partisans d'un concours physique partiel[2] ou indirect[3] de Dieu au mal, qu'aux défenseurs d'un concours entier à la « matière » du péché, qui en laisserait au pécheur la seule responsabilité morale[4]. L'idée d'un concours partiel implique de diviser l'acte en deux, en attribuant une partie à l'homme et l'autre à Dieu. Or, quand bien

1. Ne serait-ce parce que certains biens ne peuvent être obtenus qu'à la condition que le mal soit permis.

2. Comme Occam, Erasme, Molina, ou encore Suarez.

3. Durand de Saint-Pourçain rejette l'idée d'un concours immédiat de Dieu à l'action des créatures (*In Sententias theologicas*, lib. II, dist. 37, q. 1). Parmi les défenseurs d'un concours général et médiat, Leibniz cite aussi Pierre Auriol, Pélage, Louis de Dole, François Bernier (*Théodicée*, § 27), et Nicolaus Taurellus (*ibid.*, § 381).

4. Suivant Thomas d'Aquin, *Somme théologique*, Ia, IIae Pars, 79, 2.

même cette répartition pourrait être établie avec exactitude, comment considérer la contribution « propre » à l'homme, sinon à son tour comme un acte, auquel, par conséquent, Dieu devrait encore concourir? La division se poursuivant ainsi à l'infini, la part réservée à l'homme diminuant à chaque fois, on serait bien obligé d'admettre, en fin de compte, que Dieu fait l'acte entièrement[1].

Dans l'hypothèse d'un concours intégral au péché, considéré dans sa réalité matérielle, on prétend cette fois séparer le *physique* du *moral*, en distinguant l'acte, entièrement produit par Dieu, de sa qualification morale. Le péché, dans ce qu'il a de réel et de positif (la force, par exemple, dont use un homme pour en frapper un autre), procède en dernière instance de Dieu, cause ultime de toutes choses, mais, en ce qu'il est condamnable (le meurtre est défendu), il vient du meurtrier, sa cause morale. Comme l'avait montré Leibniz dans *De la toute-puissance et de l'omniscience de Dieu* par l'exemple du mauvais musicien, et comme il le rappelle encore dans *L'Auteur du péché*[2], une telle séparation ne peut être admise. Elle suppose qu'un acte soit, ontologiquement, indifférent, neutre moralement : qu'il soit bon ou mauvais, sa nature demeure identique. Or, estime Leibniz, une action bonne et une action mauvaise ne diffèrent pas seulement parce que l'une est conforme à la vertu et l'autre y est contraire, c'est-à-dire par un rapport purement externe (le rapport à la loi), mais encore dans leur réalité physique même : la première contient davantage de perfection que la seconde.

À travers cette critique, c'est encore la conception augustinienne du mal comme non-être qui est visée. Délier le mal de tout fondement ontologique, en le rangeant entièrement du côté du moral ou du formel, conduit à le ramener à une pure négation, à un néant. Et si le mal n'est rien, il n'a ni auteur ni responsable. L'argument prouve trop, puisqu'il disculpe Dieu aussi bien que l'homme et anéantit toute justice[3].

Il faut par conséquent reconnaître que le mal est bien *quelque chose*, parce qu'il est inséparable de l'être qu'il limite et corrompt. Le péché est l'acte mauvais, pris comme un tout indivisible. C'est pourquoi il peut être dit une « créature » produite par Dieu[4] – lequel n'y concourt pas seulement mais le crée intégralement. Comment affirmer cette réalité du mal (qui,

1. Cf. *Conversatio cum Domino Episcopo Stenonio de Libertate*, 27 novembre 1677, A VI, 4, 1382.

2. Écrit vers 1673. Leibniz prend cette fois l'exemple d'un peintre auteur de deux tableaux de grandeur différente (A VI, 3, 151).

3. A VI, 3, 151.

4. « Le péché est une créature, toute créature est créée continuellement par Dieu, donc aussi le péché » (*Conversatio cum Domino Episcopo Stenonio de Libertate*, A VI, 4, 1382).

répétons-le, n'existe pas *à part* mais se confond avec l'être de la chose dite « mauvaise »), sans remettre en cause et la justice divine et la culpabilité humaine? Leibniz résout la difficulté en introduisant, dans la première moitié des années 1680[1], la notion d'« imperfection originale » de la créature. Parce qu'elles sont intrinsèquement et originellement limitées, les créatures bornent l'être, la puissance, la perfection qu'elles reçoivent de Dieu. Cette limitation métaphysique, antérieure au péché originel les rend faillibles, « peccables », sans les mettre pour autant dans la nécessité de pécher.

La thèse – qui fait consister l'origine du mal dans l'imperfection des créatures – peut ne pas sembler nouvelle. Leibniz s'écarte pourtant de la tradition, dans la mesure où cette imperfection ne signifie pas seulement, chez lui, le manque d'être, la négation propre à tout ce qui n'est pas l'Être tout parfait (Dieu) : elle est encore une répugnance à plus d'être, un frein à l'obtention de plus de réalité et de perfection. À ce titre, elle constitue une sorte d'effort négatif et contraire, exerçant une résistance qui est rapprochée, à partir des années 1685-1686[2], de l'inertie ou « tardiveté » observée dans les corps physiques. Cette imperfection originale permet de comprendre comment Dieu peut être la source de tout ce qu'il y a de réel, de positif, de parfait dans le péché, sans l'être de la limitation et du défaut que celui-ci renferme – puisqu'ils sont imputables à la créature.

3) Concernant le concours moral de Dieu au mal, la doctrine leibnizienne de la permission ne semble pas tout à fait fixée avant la reprise de la distinction scolastique entre volonté *antécédente* et volonté *conséquente*, à l'époque de la rédaction de la *Théodicée* ou peu auparavant[3]. Deux modèles explicatifs apparaissent successivement dans les textes, puis sont abandonnés. Le premier est celui défendu dans la *Profession de foi du Philosophe*, qui réduit la permission à un savoir et à une forme de suspension de la volonté. Le deuxième, au contraire, la ramène à une volonté positive, mais conditionnée, que Leibniz qualifie encore de volonté accidentelle (*per accidens*)[4], au risque de rendre Dieu complice sinon auteur du péché. C'est à partir des années 1680-1684 que se dessine

1. *Cf.* A VI, 4, 2577 (« Defectus originalis »); A VI, 4-A, 557 (« imperfectio rerum originalis »).

2. Voir A VI, 4, 1521.

3. Voir Grua 468, 474. La distinction était jusque-là utilisée dans le contexte de la discussion sur le salut (Grua 445, 449).

4. « Dieu ne veut pas les péchés, si ce n'est sous la condition de la peine qui les corrige, et par accident seulement, comme réquisits pour que la série soit entièrement parfaite » (*Conversatio cum Domino Episcopo Stenonio de Libertate*, A VI, 4, 1378).

la doctrine « définitive » – en tout cas celle qui s'imposera jusque dans la *Théodicée*. Elle consiste à penser la permission comme le résultat d'un processus complexe, interne à la volonté, où se mêlent des inclinations diverses qu'il est impossible de réaliser toutes en même temps.

Dieu veut chaque bien en particulier, ne veut pas le mal et veut même l'écarter, *pour autant que* l'harmonie universelle le permet. Cette condition introduit une restriction qui rend possible la permission. Celle-ci manifeste un infléchissement de la volonté divine, dès lors que cette volonté s'élève au point de vue de l'ensemble des choses, au lieu de s'en tenir à la considération du particulier. Il n'y a pourtant nulle contradiction ni velléité en Dieu, mais passage d'une volonté positive d'empêcher le péché (pris à part) à une volonté en quelque sorte *négative* de ne pas l'empêcher (le péché étant envisagé cette fois dans ses suites, avec le reste des choses). Autrement dit, « *permettre*, c'est pouvoir empêcher et ne pas empêcher, sciemment »[1].

La permission est l'effet dans la partie d'un choix qui porte sur tout l'univers. Elle ne peut s'expliquer ni se justifier que dans ce contexte universel, où toutes les choses sont liées. La prise en compte de cette liaison conduit à une approche inédite du problème du mal. Demander pourquoi Dieu n'a pas empêché tel ou tel crime de se commettre, par exemple, n'a pas donné à Adam cette grâce qui lui aurait permis de résister à la tentation et d'éviter la chute, revient à demander pourquoi il n'a pas choisi un autre monde que le nôtre – et corrélativement pourquoi il a créé *celui-ci*. Car Dieu, en raison de son infinie sagesse, ne saurait avoir de volontés détachées, indépendantes les unes des autres, c'est-à-dire particulières. Il ne règle pas les choses par parties et « à bâtons rompus »[2]. La permission du péché est donc contenue dans un décret général et unique[3], qui ne porte pas seulement sur Adam, mais sur l'ensemble du monde dont il est solidaire.

La justification de Dieu, sur le plan moral, repose en définitive sur deux principaux arguments. 1) N'étant pas l'auteur des essences, Dieu ne décide rien du contenu des mondes possibles. Il ne décide donc pas si Adam péchera ou non. Il voit seulement si la série de choses qui contient le péché d'Adam est préférable aux autres séries possibles qu'il trouve dans son entendement[4]. 2) Son choix de faire exister cette série (la nôtre, où Adam

1. A VI, 4, 941 (opuscule daté entre août 1688 et janvier 1689).

2. Leibniz à Coste, 19 décembre 1707, GP III, 400.

3. *Cf.* Leibniz au Landgraf Ernst von Hessen-Rheinfels, 12 avril 1686, A II, 2, 18; *Conversation sur la liberté et le destin*, Grua, 482.

4. Voir *Échantillon de découvertes sur les secrets admirables de la nature*, A VI, 4, 1619.

pèche) n'implique pas qu'il veuille *absolument* et *positivement* tout ce qu'elle comprend. Dieu veut le meilleur univers possible, le bien qu'il contient, mais permet seulement le mal qui s'y rencontre.

La réinterprétation des notions de possible et de volonté, l'identification de l'origine du mal dans l'essence même des créatures, la doctrine de la permission – corollaire de la thèse du décret universel unique –, permettent la mise en place progressive d'un dispositif conceptuel nouveau, dans lequel la justification de Dieu passe par l'explication de la création de *ce* monde. S'appuyant sur ces changements théoriques, les *Essais de Théodicée* offrent un exposé métaphysique et théologique complet, qui va bien au-delà de la réponse circonstanciée aux difficultés soulevées par Bayle touchant l'existence du mal et la bonté de Dieu.

LE PROBLÈME DU MAL DANS LA *THÉODICÉE*

Comment Leibniz, dans la *Théodicée*, résout-il les difficultés concernant le concours de Dieu au mal? La solution proposée se déploie dans le cadre d'une exposition des perfections divines et d'une explication générale du choix fait de notre monde parmi une infinité d'autres également possibles[1]. Dieu est doué d'un entendement infini, qui comprend tous les mondes possibles, d'une volonté absolument bonne qui ne peut manquer de choisir le meilleur, et d'une toute-puissance qui l'amène à l'existence (§ 7-8). Le mal contribue à la perfection du tout, au point que son absence aurait entraîné la création d'un univers, au total, moins parfait que le nôtre.

Leibniz recourt à la distinction entre la volonté *antécédente* et la volonté *conséquente* (§ 22 à § 25) pour expliquer le concours moral. Dieu veut *antécédemment* chaque bien particulier, rejette chaque mal pris en soi, mais il veut *conséquemment* le meilleur, qui implique d'écarter certains biens et de permettre certains maux. Pourquoi le meilleur n'équivaut-il pas simplement à la somme de tous les biens particuliers? Trois raisons peuvent être évoquées. 1) Tous les biens ne peuvent être réalisés en même temps car ils ne sont pas tous compatibles. 2) Certains biens sont liés à des maux (qui en sont les suites inévitables) ou ne peuvent être obtenus que si l'on admet certains maux (qui en sont la condition). 3) Les lois de l'harmonie demandent qu'il y ait de la différence, de la variété et de l'inégalité parmi les créatures. Ainsi « il se trouve que s'il n'y avait que vertu,

1. Pour un examen détaillé de cette question, voir notre livre *Leibniz et le meilleur des mondes possibles*.

s'il n'y avait que créatures raisonnables, il y aurait moins de bien. Midas se trouva moins riche, quand il n'eut que de l'or »[1]. L'homogénéité et l'uniformité sont contraires aux règles de la perfection et de la beauté.

La volonté conséquente ou finale de Dieu résulte de la prise en compte de ces trois contraintes, qui font que certaines volontés antécédentes n'obtiennent pas leur effet, mais que la meilleure combinaison de biens l'emporte. Ainsi le mal arrive « par concomitance »[2], par accident, comme une conséquence ou la condition de possibilité du bien. Il n'est jamais voulu antécédemment, pour lui-même et en lui-même. Cependant, son rapport à la volonté divine conséquente n'est pas le même selon qu'il est *moral*, *physique* ou *métaphysique*[3] :

1) Dieu ne saurait jamais vouloir, antécédemment ni conséquemment, absolument ou même relativement parlant, le mal moral (le péché). Celui-ci ne peut être permis qu'en raison d'un devoir indispensable, au nom d'une nécessité morale, non comme un moyen positif, mais « à titre du *sine qua non* ou de nécessité hypothétique qui le lie avec le meilleur »[4]. La permission consiste à ne pas empêcher le mal d'être commis. Et cela pour une raison à la fois morale et métaphysique. Dieu *pouvait* empêcher le péché (possibilité logique), mais il ne le *devait* pas (impossibilité morale), car en l'écartant, il aurait lui-même failli[5], il aurait agi contre la sagesse et la bonté. Pour l'éviter, il aurait dû renoncer au meilleur des mondes possibles – dont le péché est indissociable – et en amener à l'existence un autre, par définition moins parfait. La permission est *moralement* nécessaire parce que le péché est *hypothétiquement* nécessaire (inséparable du plus parfait univers). Elle suit d'une obligation essentielle, interne au divin, et exprime la prévalence d'un devoir sur toute autre considération. L'existence du mal, loin d'être ce qui accuse Dieu, devient paradoxalement ce qui le justifie, en manifestant sa bonté :

> La sagesse ne fait que montrer à Dieu le meilleur exercice de sa bonté qui soit possible; après cela, le mal qui passe est une suite indispensable du meilleur. J'ajouterai quelque chose de plus fort : permettre le mal comme Dieu le permet, c'est la plus grande bonté[6].

1. *Théodicée*, § 124, GF, 180-181 (GP VI, 179).
2. L'expression est employée à plusieurs reprises (*ibid.*, § 119, § 153, § 209).
3. Selon la distinction entre les trois sortes de maux (*ibid.*, § 21).
4. *Ibid.*, § 25, GF, 119 (GP VI, 117).
5. Il en est ici comme du soldat en faction qui ne peut abandonner un poste stratégique pour séparer deux de ses amis prêts à s'entretuer (cf. *ibid.*, § 24).
6. *Théodicée*, § 121, GF, 177 (GP VI, 175).

C'est, en effet, en permettant le mal que se réalise le meilleur univers possible. La perspective se renverse alors : le mal serait que le mal soit absent du monde, car cette absence signifierait l'imperfection du monde et de son auteur. Le plus grand mal n'est donc pas le péché que commet la créature, mais la faute que commettrait Dieu en l'écartant[1].

2) Dieu ne veut pas « d'une manière absolue » le mal physique (la douleur), qu'il tend à exclure, comme tous les autres maux, par sa volonté antécédente. Cependant il peut et doit parfois le vouloir, et pas seulement le permettre, conséquemment, d'une manière certes *relative* : en considération du péché, « comme une peine due à la coulpe », et en considération d'un bien à rechercher ou d'un mal à éviter, « comme un moyen propre à une fin, c'est-à-dire pour empêcher de plus grands maux ou pour obtenir de plus grands biens »[2]. Dans le premier cas, ce n'est pas le mal en tant que mal qui est voulu, mais le châtiment infligé au pécheur, conformément à la loi de justice selon laquelle tout crime exige une punition. Dans le second cas, le mal est voulu, mais en tant seulement qu'il sert le bien : comme un adjuvant et non une simple condition négative, un moyen par lequel s'acquiert une plus grande perfection (selon l'image du grain qui doit se corrompre pour germer[3]), ou par lequel est évité un plus grand mal.

Les maux physiques peuvent être ainsi assimilés à des « biens subsidiaires »[4]. Ils sont appelés « biens » relativement parlant, à cause du bien qu'ils rendent possible, et, pour cette raison, deviennent des objets légitimes de la volonté conséquente.

3) Le mal *métaphysique* – expression par laquelle Leibniz désigne toute imperfection, y compris les « désordres » naturels[5] – peut également être considéré comme un bien « subsidiaire ». Il est la limitation inhérente à tout ce qui est fini et ne tire pas son être de soi-même. Dieu le veut nécessairement, dès lors qu'il décide de créer quelque chose, puisque créer est forcément créer de l'imparfait, du limité – l'absolument parfait, Dieu, étant incréé. Le mal métaphysique est la condition *sine qua non* de la création, mais aussi le moyen par lequel s'obtient le plus de variété possible dans l'univers. Comme principe de différence, il est en effet ce par quoi les créatures sont diversement limitées. La multitude des espèces de créatures,

1. Cf. *ibid.*, § 129 et § 130.
2. *Ibid.*, § 23, GF, 118 (GP VI, 116). Voir aussi *La Cause de Dieu*, § 39.
3. Cf. *De l'origine radicale des choses*, Schrecker, 189 (GP VII, 307).
4. *Cf.* Grua, 474 ; GP III, 32 ; *La Cause de Dieu*, § 35.
5. Sur la notion de mal métaphysique et sur son ambiguïté, voir P. Rateau, *La question du mal chez Leibniz*, sect. 8.1.3.

spirituelles, animales, végétales, l'existence d'êtres inanimés, et les différents degrés de perfection à l'intérieur de chaque espèce font la beauté et l'excellence du monde. L'uniformité, l'homogénéité, l'identité, même dans le parfait, seraient un défaut. La sagesse exige la variété[1]. De plus, l'imperfection des créatures leur ouvre la possibilité d'un perpétuel progrès, elle est la condition de leur élévation et de leur mérite[2].

C'est également sous le nom de maux métaphysiques que Leibniz range les « désordres » naturels (cataclysmes, tremblements de terre, éruptions volcaniques, déluges, inondations). Comme le montre l'histoire de la Terre, ces bouleversements se révèlent utiles et bénéfiques à long terme, par les transformations qu'ils permettent à la surface du globe – notamment la formation des métaux et des sédiments. Ils rendent ainsi possibles l'industrie et l'agriculture humaines, de sorte que « nous leur devons nos richesses et nos commodités » et qu'il faut reconnaître que « ces désordres sont allés dans l'ordre »[3].

La réduction des maux physiques et métaphysiques à des biens « subsidiaires », susceptibles à ce titre d'être *voulus* conséquemment, non comme des fins (car cela serait contraire aux volontés antécédentes), mais comme des moyens relativement à des fins bonnes, restreint en définitive la permission au seul mal moral. Le péché n'est jamais un bien, même moindre ou relatif. Que Dieu le fasse servir à ses desseins, qu'il soit racheté ou contrebalancé, ne change en rien sa nature mauvaise. Il est un mal qu'il faut se résoudre à admettre, dès lors qu'est voulu le monde le plus parfait. Cela en fait une condition *sine qua non* (du meilleur) et non, à proprement parler, un moyen. Alors que le moyen est un instrument positif, qui *par lui-même* sert une fin bonne, la condition *sine qua non* est une donnée négative, qui renvoie moins à ce qu'elle permet qu'à ce qu'elle empêcherait si elle était supprimée, une circonstance par conséquent inévitable, dont Dieu tire cependant parti.

Sur ce point, une tension apparaît dans la théodicée leibnizienne entre deux conceptions du mal. Dans certains cas, le mal est ramené à un degré inférieur du bien, sinon réduit à une simple apparence, que la vue complète de l'harmonie universelle ferait se dissiper. Dans d'autres au contraire, sa « réalité » est soulignée, dans la mesure où il joue un rôle effectif dans l'obtention de biens impossibles à atteindre sans lui.

1. « Si chaque substance prise à part était parfaite, elles seraient toutes semblables ; ce qui n'est point convenable ni possible. Si c'étaient des dieux, il n'aurait pas été possible de les produire » (*Théodicée*, § 200, GF, 236-237 ; GP VI, 235).

2. Cf. *De l'origine radicale des choses*, Schrecker, 191 (GP VII, 308) ; *Théodicée*, § 120.

3. *Théodicée*, § 245, GF, 264 (GP VI, 263).

Selon la première approche, le mal est seulement l'effet d'une connaissance partielle et imparfaite des choses, qui est propre à la créature bornée que nous sommes. Ce que nous prenons pour des défauts et des désordres entrent, en fait, dans l'ordre général. Nous sommes pareils à celui qui, le nez rivé sur un tableau, se plaint de ne voir qu'un mélange confus de couleurs et de formes, au lieu de se mettre à la bonne distance pour l'apprécier comme il faut. Suivant la seconde approche, le mal n'est pas illusoire. Il est un défaut qui affecte l'être créé dans sa nature et dans son action. Quelle serait l'utilité d'une doctrine du concours et de la permission, quel sens aurait le dogme théologique de la Rédemption, si péchés et douleurs n'étaient qu'apparents? s'il suffisait d'adopter le bon point de vue pour qu'ils s'évanouissent? Tout le ressort de l'harmonie et toute l'intensité du plaisir que procure sa contemplation reposent sur la compensation d'un mal *réel*. La comparaison qui convient ici est musicale. Le compositeur talentueux est celui qui sait placer où il faut les dissonances, de façon à mettre l'auditeur mal à l'aise, dans l'attente inquiète de leur résolution. Le plaisir esthétique se produit au moment où cette résolution arrive et que « tout rentre dans l'ordre »[1]. Or, si dans le cas du beau tableau, l'adoption du point de vue adéquat permet de corriger la perception initiale – qui se révèle fausse –, en revanche, l'audition intégrale de la musique ne modifie en rien la nature de la dissonance. Celle-ci reste en elle-même un défaut irréductible, même si sa présence contribue à la beauté de l'ensemble. Elle demeure toujours un son désagréable, quel que soit le point de vue adopté (total ou partiel).

Ces deux approches, difficilement conciliables, relèvent de deux exigences différentes. La première est celle du philosophe mathématicien qui considère qu'il en est du mal comme des prétendues irrégularités en mathématiques. Il n'est pas de ligne si irrégulière qu'il ne soit possible à un géomètre d'en donner l'équation, ni de suite de nombres si désordonnée qu'un arithméticien ne puisse en donner la règle de construction[2]. La seconde est celle du théologien et du juriste qui, tout en voyant que le péché et la douleur s'inscrivent dans l'économie générale du salut, les considèrent selon les lois de la justice, respectivement comme une violation effective de l'ordre et comme un châtiment mérité du pécheur (sinon comme un moyen de perfectionner l'homme).

La nécessité d'assigner au mal un fondement ontologique – sans pour autant en faire une substance – montre que la tendance réductrice, visant en quelque sorte à le « déréaliser », quoique présente, ne prévaut pas dans la

1. *De l'origine radicale des choses*, Schrecker, 187 (GP VII, 306).

2. Voir *Théodicée*, § 242; *Discours de métaphysique*, § 6, A VI, 4, 1537-1538.

pensée leibnizienne. Parce que le mal n'exprime pas simplement notre rapport subjectif aux choses, ou la relation de ces choses à une loi morale, mais s'inscrit dans l'être, il est besoin de prouver que Dieu en y concourant n'en est ni l'auteur ni le complice. Leibniz défend l'idée d'un concours physique de Dieu à la fois intégral, continuel, immédiat et spécial. Tout ce qu'il y a de réel, de positif, de parfait dans les créatures et dans leurs actions émane constamment et directement de Dieu. Son concours est exactement proportionné à la nature et aux caractéristiques particulières de la créature et de l'acte considérés. Il est approprié à son objet « tel qu'il est, et selon l'état où il est », si bien que « la conservation d'un homme debout est différente de la conservation d'un homme assis »[1]. Il faut donc penser que l'homme de bien et le méchant ne requièrent pas la même quantité de puissance divine pour se maintenir dans l'être, parce que leur différence morale renvoie à une différence ontologique. Que l'un soit meilleur que l'autre signifie, sur le plan moral, que l'un est digne de louange et de récompense, l'autre de blâme et de réprobation, sur le plan métaphysique, que le premier participe à plus d'être et de réalité que le second.

Par son influence physique, Dieu ne produit que « ce qu'il y a de bon dans le mal »[2], c'est-à-dire la part de réalité positive contenue en lui. Mais ce que l'on pourrait appeler *le mal du mal*, ce qu'il y a de « mauvais » dans le mal, provient des créatures et résulte, originairement, de leur imperfection naturelle. Il est alors possible de distinguer, dans le même acte, ce qui revient à Dieu (être, perfection, force) et ce qui revient à la créature (limitation, imperfection, résistance), tout en considérant cet acte comme proprement indivisible dans l'instant même où il est accompli. Par suite, le péché devient imputable à la créature *dans sa réalité physique* même. Le pécheur est coupable, non seulement parce qu'il enfreint les règles de la justice (niveau moral), mais encore dans la mesure où il restreint l'être, borne la perfection et résiste à la grâce reçue de Dieu (niveau physique).

Le mal est une privation d'être. Il ne peut être abstrait sans contradiction du sujet qu'il affecte (la substance et ses actions). L'en distinguer serait aussi absurde que de considérer une limite séparément de ce dont elle est la limite. Il est un défaut de perfection, ce qui altère et diminue l'être sans l'abolir. Par conséquent, il ne requiert pas de cause efficiente, mais seulement, selon l'expression scolastique, une cause *déficiente*[3]. Là encore, la thèse peut sembler classique. Elle ne l'est pas, dans la mesure où Leibniz associe la privation aux notions de capacité et de réceptivité

1. *Théodicée*, § 27, GF, 120 (GP VI, 118-119).
2. *La Cause de Dieu*, § 68, GF, 438 (GP VI, 449).
3. Cf. *Théodicée*, § 20, GF, 116 (GP VI, 115).

propres à la créature. La nature d'une chose définit à la fois une aptitude à réaliser une certaine quantité de perfection et une résistance à davantage de perfection. Elle est positivement la détermination d'une réalité particulière et négativement le *non plus ultra* qui empêche un développement supérieur (la créature ne peut excéder les bornes de son essence). Cette opposition est pareille à l'inertie observée dans les corps par Kepler et Descartes[1]. La créature résiste à la perfection reçue comme la matière au mouvement communiqué. La privation n'est pas simplement un manque, une absence d'être, mais une répugnance à l'être, à plus d'être. C'est pourquoi le mal est irréductible au néant. Si le mal n'était rien, il ne ferait pas obstacle à la perfection et n'empêcherait pas le plein déploiement de l'être.

À l'instar de l'inertie, la résistance due à l'imperfection de la créature ne dérive pas d'une puissance active. Elle n'est ni la négation de la force (sinon rien ne s'opposerait au concours physique de Dieu), ni l'effet d'une force réelle antagoniste (l'hypothèse manichéenne étant exclue). Elle procède de la puissance passive et constitue une sorte d'*anti-conatus*, un frein plutôt qu'un effort contraire positif. Cette résistance explique nos fautes et notre malice. L'erreur résulte d'un défaut de réflexion et d'attention. Elle vient de ce que l'esprit s'en tient au témoignage des sens, par paresse, au lieu d'aller plus loin dans l'examen des choses[2]. La malice procède d'une volonté affaiblie, qui, au lieu de tendre au souverain bien (Dieu), s'arrête par facilité à des biens subalternes ou seulement apparents. C'est ainsi qu'elle s'attache « par inertie aux créatures »[3] et se borne aux plaisirs des sens. Tout comme l'erreur n'est pas de voir la tour ronde, mais d'en rester à cette perception pour former son jugement, la malice n'est pas de jouir des biens sensibles, mais de s'y limiter, sans s'aviser des biens supérieurs, seuls capables de donner la véritable félicité. Le mal consiste dans l'arrêt, dans « cette privation d'une tendance ultérieure »[4], qui caractérise aussi bien ce que l'on pourrait appeler l'*inertie de l'entendement* que l'*inertie de la volonté*.

1. Cf. *Théodicée*, § 30. Le rapprochement opéré entre métaphysique et physique ne relève pas de la simple analogie, puisque Leibniz considère l'inertie naturelle des corps « comme une parfaite image et même comme un *échantillon* de la limitation originale des créatures » (nous soulignons).

2. Voir l'exemple de la tour carrée vue de loin ronde évoqué au § 32 de la *Théodicée*.

3. *La Cause de Dieu*, § 73, GF, 439 (GP VI, 450).

4. *Théodicée*, § 33, GF, 123 (GP VI, 122).

CONCLUSION

Si le projet leibnizien de théodicée est ancien, sa forme, les arguments et les thèses avancés évoluent au cours de la vie du philosophe. Les premiers textes témoignent d'un nécessitarisme que l'auteur sera conduit à réviser, sans abandonner pour autant sa critique de la conception augustinienne du mal et des théories du concours divin existantes – en dépit de la reprise de certaines formules et distinctions apparemment conformes à la tradition. De la *Profession de foi du Philosophe* à la *Théodicée*, Leibniz affirme constamment que Dieu n'est l'auteur du péché ni par sa volonté, ni par sa puissance. Dans les deux textes, la justification passe par une explication paradoxale : la mal est parce que Dieu est. Mais la raison invoquée n'est pas la même. En 1673, la mal est, parce que Dieu est le premier terme de la série des choses, qui ne pouvaient être autrement sans qu'il en soit changé. En 1710, le mal est, parce qu'il est compris dans le meilleur des mondes possibles, que Dieu conçoit dans son entendement infini[1] et qu'il ne peut manquer d'amener à l'existence. Les autres mondes possibles ne sont plus de simples fictions – irréalisables car incompatibles avec Dieu –, puisque leur réalité est fondée et la possibilité de leur création effective assurée. La nécessité de choisir le meilleur n'est plus absolue mais seulement *morale*[2].

Dieu est la source de toute réalité et de toute perfection. Le mal, sous ses trois espèces (métaphysique, moral et physique), ne renvoie pas à une entité positive, mais à une privation et à une résistance. Il n'a pas d'efficace propre, mais peut engendrer des actions par accident, comme l'eau en gelant est capable de briser le canon d'un mousquet dans lequel elle est enfermée[3]. Le mal procède ultimement de l'imperfection originale des créatures. Cette limitation rend le péché possible, mais ne le rend pas absolument nécessaire[4]. Pour qu'il devienne actuel, il faut qu'intervienne

1. Ce qui autorise à faire de l'entendement divin le « principe du mal » (*Théodicée*, § 149, GF, 200 ; GP VI, 198).

2. *Cf.* Robert M. Adams, *Leibniz. Determinist, Theist, Idealist*, en part. chap. I et II. Leibniz ne serait pas parvenu à prouver la contingence du choix divin. Ses principes conduiraient, au contraire, à conclure qu'il est absolument (et pas seulement moralement) nécessaire que Dieu fasse le meilleur. Pour une critique de cette interprétation, voir P. Rateau, *Leibniz et le meilleur des mondes possibles*, « Introduction », p. 32-36.

3. Cf. *Théodicée*, § 153.

4. « Ainsi le fondement du mal est nécessaire, mais sa production est contingente ; en d'autres termes, il est nécessaire que les maux soient possibles, mais il est contingent que les maux soient actuels [...] », *La Cause de Dieu*, § 69, GF, 438 ; GP VI, 449.

la liberté. L'homme est ainsi le seul responsable du mal qu'il commet. Car il lui appartient de suivre les mouvements qui lui viennent de Dieu ou, au contraire, d'y résister, en s'opposant à l'effet bénéfique de son concours, en abusant de la force qu'il reçoit de lui, en la détournant de sa fin bonne.

Paul RATEAU
(Université Panthéon-Sorbonne)

PHILOSOPHIE DE L'ESPRIT

La philosophie de l'esprit de Leibniz peut être caractérisée tout à la fois comme traditionnelle, radicale et novatrice. Elle est traditionnelle lorsque l'on en énumère les principales thèses : l'esprit ou l'âme est une substance ; cette substance est immatérielle et immortelle ; elle est distincte du corps ; elle contient des idées et principes innés. Aucune de ces thèses n'est originale au XVIIe siècle : les premières sont communes aux scolastiques et aux cartésiens et les idées innées sont défendues par la tradition platonicienne, augustinienne et plusieurs cartésiens. Cependant la métaphysique de Leibniz leur confère un tour radical, notamment avec la théorie des monades développée dans les années 1700. Les réalités fondamentales, les monades, sont en effet de nature spirituelle, comme le souligne ce passage d'une lettre à Burcher De Volder : « En fait, en considérant la question avec exactitude, il faut dire qu'il n'y a rien d'autres dans les choses que des substances simples et en elles, de la perception et de l'appétit »[1].

Ce passage, très souvent cité par les commentateurs, paraît aller dans le sens d'une forme d'idéalisme, même si le statut ontologique des corps donne lieu à des interprétations divergentes[2]. Mais les propriétés des monades sont indiscutablement mentales : la perception, c'est-à-dire la représentation par la monade d'un état du monde, et l'appétition, ou la tendance à passer d'une perception à une autre, dont le désir et la volonté humaine fournissent le modèle[3]. Par un complet renversement du matérialisme, l'existence et la nature des corps dépend ainsi de la réalité de ces substances immatérielles analogues aux esprits : « la matière ne saurait

1. *Lettre à De Volder*, 30 juin 1704, GP II, 270 (notre traduction).

2. Voir G. Hartz, *Leibniz's Final System. Monads, Matter and Animals* et D. Garber, *Leibniz : Body, Substance, Monad*, en part. chap. VIII.

3. *Monadologie*, § 14-15, GP VI, 607-608.

subsister sans substances immatérielles, c'est-à-dire, sans les unités »[1]. Et puisque ces briques fondamentales de la réalité sont caractérisées par des propriétés mentales, la théorie des monades implique ainsi une forme de panpsychisme.

Enfin, le caractère novateur et original de la philosophie de l'esprit de Leibniz se manifeste dans la critique du paradigme cartésien qui fait de la conscience une propriété fondamentale de toute pensée, en sorte que tout état mental est essentiellement conscient. Pour Leibniz au contraire, la conscience, théorisée avec la notion d'aperception, n'est ni essentielle à la pensée en tant que telle, ni irréductible à d'autres propriétés[2]. La notion fondamentale est celle de représentation ou encore d'expression, dans la terminologie leibnizienne. Pour caractériser les substances ou monades, Leibniz recourt à la métaphore du miroir en les qualifiant de miroirs de l'univers et les esprits de miroirs de Dieu[3]. Sa philosophie de l'esprit donne corps à cette métaphore en définissant les perceptions en termes de représentation. En substituant la représentation à la conscience, la théorie de Leibniz ouvre ainsi de nouvelles perspectives originales. Sur le plan théorique ou conceptuel, elle permet de penser la conscience comme un type particulier de représentation. Sur le plan de l'analyse des phénomènes psychiques, elle ouvre la voie à un élargissement du champ des perceptions au-delà de la sphère des perceptions conscientes, à des représentations inconscientes ou « petites perceptions ».

Même si sa dernière métaphysique tend vers l'idéalisme, la distinction de l'âme et du corps et la critique de la conception matérialiste de l'esprit n'en occupe pas moins une place centrale dans la réflexion leibnizienne. La première partie de ce chapitre est consacrée à l'analyse du célèbre « argument du moulin » qui établit la fausseté du matérialisme à partir de la nature de la perception. On y présente le concept d'expression par lequel Leibniz définit la perception. Dans la seconde, on se penchera sur la manière dont la distinction entre perception et aperception se rattache à une division tripartite des genres de monades – entéléchies, âmes et esprits. Cette confrontation permet en effet d'éclairer les notions d'aperception, de réflexion et de mémoire et, par suite, la tentative leibnizienne d'une explication réductionniste de la conscience. Enfin, nous nous intéresserons dans

1. *Nouveaux Essais*, IV, III, § 6, A VI, 6, 379.

2. Voir en particulier A. Simmons, « Changing the Cartesian Mind : Leibniz on Sensation, Representation and Consciousness », p. 31-75 ; *id.*, « Leibnizian Consciousness Reconsidered », p. 196-215.

3. *Discours de métaphysique*, § IX, A VI, 4, 1542 ; *Monadologie*, § 56 et 83, GP VI, 616 et 621.

la dernière partie aux arguments établissant l'existence des petites perceptions, ainsi que leur nature et leur rôle dans l'explication des idées innées et des sensations[1].

PERCEPTION ET IMMATÉRIALITÉ DE L'ÂME : L'ARGUMENT DU MOULIN

Leibniz s'oppose au matérialisme en rejetant l'idée que des entités matérielles, exclusivement caractérisées en termes mécaniques de grandeur, figure et mouvement, soient capables de penser, percevoir ou sentir. À l'appui de cette affirmation, il recourt dans un certain nombre de textes postérieurs à 1702 à une expérience de pensée dont la *Monadologie* contient l'énoncé le plus célèbre :

> On est obligé d'ailleurs de confesser que la *perception* et ce qui en dépend est *inexplicable par des raisons mécaniques*, c'est-à-dire par les figures et par les mouvements. Et feignant qu'il y ait une Machine dont la structure fasse penser, sentir, avoir perception, on pourra la concevoir agrandie en conservant les mêmes proportions, en sorte qu'on y puisse entrer, comme dans un moulin. Et cela posé, on ne trouvera en la visitant au-dedans que des pièces qui se poussent les unes les autres, et jamais de quoi expliquer une perception. Ainsi c'est dans la substance simple, et non dans le composé ou dans la machine qu'il la faut chercher[2].

L'argument repose sur l'expérience de pensée d'une hypothétique machine pensante, d'une grandeur suffisante pour que l'on puisse y pénétrer et observer son mécanisme intérieur, tel un moulin. Cette expérience de pensée fonctionne comme une réfutation de l'hypothèse matérialiste dans la mesure où une telle machine ne permet précisément pas d'expliquer la pensée[3]. On conçoit le rôle heuristique de cette fiction

1. D'autres aspects importants de la philosophie de l'esprit ne peuvent être abordés dans ce chapitre, faute d'espace : la question de l'appétition et du corollaire des petites perceptions que sont des appétits insensibles, qui se manifestent à travers l'expérience de l'inquiétude ; le problème de la causalité mentale et de son rapport aux causes finales et aux explications téléologiques (esquissé dans notre conclusion); le statut des esprits comme personnes et la question de leur immortalité et de leur identité morale (Leibniz défend une conception intéressante dans laquelle la mémoire joue un rôle important, sans être pour autant constitutive de l'identité personnelle); enfin la question de l'union de l'âme et du corps, dont la solution dépend de la théorie de l'harmonie préétablie, est abordée dans le quatrième chapitre de cet ouvrage.

2. *Monadologie*, § 17, GP VI, 609.

3. La littérature consacrée à la discussion de cet argument est désormais abondante. Voir notamment P. Lodge et M. Bobro, « Stepping Back Inside Leibniz's Mill », p. 553-572;

d'agrandissement : selon le matérialisme, le cerveau produit la pensée. Or le cerveau est une machine subtile composée de corps fluides dont il est difficile de figurer en imagination le mécanisme produisant la pensée. En proposant pour modèle une machine composée de corps rigides et en agrandissant considérablement son échelle, cette expérience de pensée doit permettre de rendre compte en principe de ce mécanisme. Or selon Leibniz, « on ne trouvera rien en la visitant au-dedans [...] jamais de quoi expliquer une perception ».

Il ne s'agit pas de conclure à l'impossibilité que la matière pense à partir du fait qu'on ne pourrait pas observer de perception en visitant ce mécanisme. L'argument concerne en effet non ce que l'on peut observer, mais ce qui peut être expliqué à partir des raisons mécaniques. Une seconde erreur consisterait à croire que l'on ne peut observer de quoi expliquer la pensée. D'après cette lecture, l'argument du moulin consisterait à soutenir que les propriétés d'un système physique sont explicables exclusivement à partir des propriétés de ses constituants. Si tel était le cas, l'argument de Leibniz serait un exemple de paralogisme de la composition, exactement comme si l'on niait que l'eau ait la propriété d'être liquide du fait qu'en observant sa structure moléculaire H_2O on serait encore incapable d'expliquer sa propriété d'être liquide. Or la propriété d'être liquide n'appartient pas aux molécules prises séparément; mais il est possible d'expliquer les propriétés que nous associons à l'état liquide de l'eau à partir du comportement d'un ensemble de molécules.

En écartant ces erreurs interprétatives, on comprend du même coup que l'expérience de pensée du moulin n'est pas indispensable à l'argument mais revêt une fonction heuristique, offrant à l'imagination les ressources d'une explication strictement mécaniste. Dépouillé de l'image du moulin, l'argument a la structure suivante : 1) la perception est inexplicable mécaniquement, donc 2) la matière considérée en elle-même est dépourvue de la capacité de percevoir (conclusion); en outre 2') la perception appartient à une substance simple ou monade (corollaire). Le passage de la prémisse à la conclusion requiert un principe d'inférence, implicite seulement dans le § 17 de la *Monadologie*, mais qui apparaît explicitement dans d'autres textes. Il s'agit d'un principe de dépendance explicative selon lequel toutes les propriétés ou modifications d'une chose s'expliquent à partir de la nature de cette chose[1]. Les modes doivent en effet pouvoir s'expliquer

S. Duncan, « Leibniz's Mill Argument against Materialism », p. 250-272; M. Rozemond, « Mills Can't Think : Leibniz's Approach to the Mind-Body Problem », p. 1-28 et P. Lodge, « Leibniz's Mill Argument Against Mechanical Materialism Revisited ».

1. Voir Lettre à Bayle, GP III, 67 et *Essais de théodicée,* § 87 et 395, GP VI, 100 et 351.

entièrement par ce que Descartes appelait l'attribut principal de cette substance, ce que Leibniz nomme son essence ou nature, comme il s'en explique dans les *Nouveaux Essais* :

> Et toutes les fois qu'on trouve quelque qualité dans un sujet, on doit croire que, si on entendait la nature de ce sujet et de cette qualité, on concevrait comment cette qualité en peut résulter. Ainsi, dans l'ordre de la nature (les miracles mis à part), il n'est pas arbitraire à Dieu de donner indifféremment aux substances telles ou telles qualités, et il ne leur en donnera jamais que celles qui leur seront naturelles, c'est-à-dire qui pourront être dérivées de leur nature comme des modifications explicables [1].

Leibniz recourt à ce principe de dépendance explicative pour réfuter l'hypothèse matérialiste envisagée par Locke selon laquelle Dieu aurait pu surajouter la pensée à la matière [2]. D'après Locke, même si nous ne pouvons pas concevoir de quelle façon cela se ferait, parce qu'on ne peut l'expliquer mécaniquement, nous ne pouvons pas exclure une telle hypothèse car elle n'est pas contradictoire. Or d'après le principe de dépendance explicative, une telle hypothèse introduirait un miracle, incompatible avec la sagesse divine et l'ordre naturel.

Mais si l'on admet ce principe et avec lui l'inférence du caractère inexplicable mécaniquement de la pensée au fait que la matière ne pense pas, sur quoi la certitude du caractère inexplicable de la pensée repose-t-elle à son tour? Là aussi, la seule expérience de pensée du § 17 de la *Monadologie* ne permet pas de répondre. À cet effet, il faut se reporter à la définition de la perception, très abstraite à première vue, introduite au § 14 :

> L'état passager qui enveloppe et représente une multitude dans l'unité, ou dans la substance simple, n'est autre chose que ce qu'on appelle la *Perception*, qu'on doit bien distinguer de l'aperception ou de la conscience [...] [3].

La perception est une forme particulière de représentation ou d'expression et cette dernière notion est le véritable fondement de la de la philosophie de l'esprit de Leibniz. La perception « représente une multitude dans l'unité » [4]. L'unité en question est l'unité métaphysique de la substance. La perception est la forme d'expression qui a lieu lorsque

1. *Nouveaux Essais*, « Préface », A VI, 6, 66.

2. *Essai philosophique concernant l'entendement humain*, IV, VI, § 3, trad. fr. P. Coste, p. 796-798.

3. *Monadologie*, § 14, GP VI, 608.

4. *Cf.* Lettre à Bourguet de décembre 1741, GP III, 575; Lettre à Bourguet du 5 août 1715, GP III, 581; Lettre à Des Bosses du 11 juillet 1706, GP II, 311; *Principes de la nature*, GP VI, 598; *Specimen inventorum*, A VI, 4, 1625).

« ce qui est divisible et matériel… [est] exprimé dans un seul être indivisible, ou dans la substance qui est douée d'une véritable unité »[1]. La définition de cette notion d'expression est fixée dès sa première formulation en 1677 et reste fondamentalement inchangée jusque dans les derniers textes :

> Est dit exprimer une chose, ce en quoi il y a des rapports qui répondent aux rapports de la chose à exprimer […][2].
>
> Une chose exprime une autre (dans mon langage) lorsqu'il y a un rapport constant et réglé entre ce qui se peut dire de l'une et de l'autre. C'est ainsi qu'une projection de perspective exprime son géométral[3].
>
> Il suffit en effet pour l'expression d'une chose dans une autre qu'il existe une loi constante des relations par lesquelles les éléments singuliers de la première pourraient être rapportés aux éléments singuliers qui leur correspondent dans la seconde, tout comme un cercle peut être représenté par une ellipse, c'est-à-dire par une courbe ovale dans une projection en perspective, et même par une hyperbole bien que cette courbe lui soit plus dissemblable et qu'elle ne revienne pas sur elle-même, car à tout point de l'hyperbole peut être assigné par la même loi constante un point correspondant du cercle dont elle est le projeté[4].

L'expression est une relation entre deux choses en vertu de laquelle il y a une fonction qui nous fait passer de l'une à l'autre[5]. Un isomorphisme est un exemple de relation expressive, mais toute expression n'est pas un isomorphisme. Ainsi un planisphère selon une projection de Mercator conserve les angles entre les régions de la Terre, mais déforme les distances et les aires, en particulier vers les pôles. Il y a ainsi expression lorsque certaines structures de l'exprimé sont conservées dans l'exprimant[6]. Une projection perspective comme la formation de l'image d'un objet dans un miroir correspond exactement à cette définition de l'expression : il y a bien une « loi constante », qui coïncide ici avec les lois optiques, loi qui préserve certaines relations entre les parties de l'objet représenté dans les parties de son image. Toute expression n'est pas pour autant une perception : l'image réfléchie dans un miroir, un portrait, ou encore une image rétinienne ne sont pas des perceptions. Il s'agit en effet d'objets spatialement étendus

1. *Lettre à Arnauld*, A II, 2, 240-241.
2. *Quid sit Idea ?*, A VI, 4, 1370, R, 445.
3. *Lettre à Arnauld*, A II, 2, 240.
4. *Sur le principe de raison*, C 15, R 476-477.
5. Voir M. Kulstad, « La conception leibnizienne de l'expression », p. 149-176 (article original paru dans *Studia Leibnitiana* 9/1, 1977).
6. Voir C. Swoyer, « Leibnizian expression », p. 65-99, en part. p. 82 ; J.-B. Rauzy, *La doctrine leibnizienne de la vérité*.

et divisibles en parties. Et selon Leibniz, la représentation cognitive requiert une expression dans une unité indivisible : « la perception… est l'expression de la multitude dans l'unité, qui diffère beaucoup de l'expression dans un miroir ou dans un organe corporel »[1]. L'expression de la multitude dans l'unité est ainsi tout à la fois le critère de la représentation cognitive et la marque du mental[2]. Dès lors, il est impossible de trouver de la pensée dans une machine analogue à un moulin, puisqu'une telle machine est un mécanisme composé de parties multiples et non une unité indivisible. Cette impossibilité n'est pas seulement hypothétique et physique, mais conceptuelle et métaphysique.

Leibniz ne donne pas de justification de cette définition de la perception et de l'exigence d'unité indivisible. Il estime toutefois que cette unité peut être établie *a posteriori*, à partir de l'expérience même de la multiplicité dans l'unité de la conscience de soi. Au § 16 de la *Monadologie*, il affirme ainsi que « nous expérimentons nous-mêmes une multitude dans la substance simple, lorsque nous trouvons que la moindre pensée dont nous nous apercevons enveloppe une variété dans l'objet ». Nous avons conscience d'avoir des perceptions et ces perceptions impliquent une unité dans la multitude[3]. Cette expérience se rattache à une critique du caractère trop étroit du *cogito* cartésien : la certitude initiale ou « vérité première de fait » ne se limite pas au seul « Je pense », mais enveloppe également la variété de nos pensées[4]. Cette expérience d'une multiplicité dans nos perceptions est en même temps une perception consciente de l'unité indivisible de l'âme. Il y a ici une ambiguïté susceptible de conduire à une mésinterprétation de la position de Leibniz. L'unité expérimentée d'une perception peut en effet désigner ou bien l'unité de la conscience elle-même, ou bien l'unité du sujet de la perception, l'âme[5]. Mais la première interprétation doit être écartée du fait que cette unité caractérise toutes les perceptions et non les seules perceptions conscientes[6]. Ainsi l'unité de la perception est fondée dans l'indivisibilité

1. *Specimen inventorum*, A VI, 4, 1625.

2. Dans une lettre à Arnauld, Leibniz parle d'« expressions immatérielles » (A II, 2, 253). Nous reviendrons dans la dernière section sur les difficultés à concevoir précisément l'expression d'une multitude dans une unité indivisible.

3. *Cf.* P. Lodge et M. Bobro, « Stepping Back Inside Leibniz's Mill », p. 567.

4. C'est une constante depuis la *Lettre à Foucher* de 1675, A II, 1, 388 ; cf. *Remarques sur Descartes*, GP IV, 357 ; *Nouveaux Essais*, IV, II, § 2, A VI, 6, 367.

5. La première interprétation a été défendue par M. Wilson dans « Leibniz and Materialism », p. 396.

6. *Principes de la nature*, § 4, GP VI, 600 ; *cf.* Lettre à De Volder, GP II, 271 ; *Extrait du Dictionnaire de M. Bayle*, GP IV, 541 ; *Considérations sur les principes de vie*, GP VI, 543.

de la monade et justifie l'impossibilité d'expliquer mécaniquement la pensée. Mais l'argument du moulin ne permet pas de prouver une telle unité et sa valeur est ainsi avant tout illustrative[1].

LA PENSÉE : PERCEPTION, APERCEPTION ET CONSCIENCE

En comprenant par l'âme un être capable de perceptions, il faut dire qu'il y a partout des âmes. Toutes les monades sont pourvues de perception et d'appétition. La nature des monades est en effet d'être « représentatives »[2]. Toutefois, il faut encore distinguer plusieurs variétés de perception :

> L'expression est commune à toutes les formes et c'est un genre dont la perception naturelle, le sentiment animal et la connaissance intellectuelle sont des espèces[3].

Ces trois types d'expressions cognitives ou perceptions ne sont pas mutuellement exclusifs, mais toutes les substances ne sont pas capables d'avoir des sensations ou des sentiments et encore moins d'accéder à la connaissance rationnelle. Celles qui ne sont capables que d'une perception naturelle sont appelées des entéléchies[4] ou « monades toutes nues »[5] ou encore des âmes au sens large[6]. Une thèse centrale de Leibniz est que les monades ne sont jamais séparées, mais jointes à d'autres monades qui constituent le corps organique de cette monade ou encore une « machine de la nature »[7]. Les monades nues et leur corps organique forment ce que

1. L'exigence d'unité contenue dans la définition de la perception n'est pas la seule voie empruntée pour établir l'immatérialité du sujet percevant. Une seconde ligne d'argumentation met l'accent sur l'activité inhérente à la pensée plutôt que sur l'unité. Voir GP VII, 332 ; Frémont 3 p. 162 : « Du seul mécanisme, ou de la matière nue et de ses modifications, l'on ne peut expliquer la perception, non plus que le principe de l'action et du mouvement. Et partant il faut admettre quelque chose de plus que la matière, qui soit aussi bien le principe de la perception, ou action interne, que du mouvement, ou action externe ». *Cf.* Lettre à Bayle, GP III, 68-69 ; Lettre à Burnett, III, 227 ; *Initia scientia generalis*, VII, 530. Parmi les commentateurs, voir Y. Belaval, *Études leibniziennes. De Leibniz à Hegel*, p. 146-150 et M. Rozemond, « Mills Can't Think ».

2. *Monadologie,* § 60, GP VI, 617.

3. *Lettre à Arnauld,* 9 octobre 1687, A II, 2, 240.

4. *Monadologie,* § 18, GP VI, 609.

5. *Ibid.,* § 24, GP VI, 611.

6. Lettre à Wagner, GP VII, 529.

7. Cf. *Nouveaux Essais*, « Préface », A VI, 6, 58 ; Lettre à Sophie Charlotte, GP III, 344 ; *Réponse aux réflexions contenues dans la seconde édition du Dictionnaire critique de*

Leibniz appelle « un vivant » qui est un organisme analogue à un animal[1]. Ce corps organique doit disposer d'organes qui rendent possible la perception, ce qui confère une grande importance à l'observation anatomique à l'aide du microscope, susceptible d'apporter une confirmation empirique à la thèse leibnizienne[2].

Lorsqu'une substance est capable de sentiment, il s'agit d'une âme au sens étroit, douée d'une « vie sensitive ». Le sentiment, c'est-à-dire la capacité à avoir des sensations, requiert outre la perception l'attention et la mémoire[3]. Avec le corps organique auquel elle est unie, une telle âme forme un animal. Enfin, les monades capables de réflexion sur elles-mêmes et d'accéder au raisonnement et à la connaissance des vérités nécessaires sont des esprits. Les esprits humains n'en sont qu'une espèce, et il faut admettre selon Leibniz toute une gradation d'esprits plus parfaits[4]. Alors que les monades nues et les âmes expriment le monde, les esprits sont « des miroirs vivants de l'univers des créatures »; ils sont en outre des « images de la Divinité »[5].

Il n'est pas nécessaire qu'une monade ait toujours et exclusivement des perceptions distinguées ou des sensations pour appartenir à l'un ou l'autre de ces types. Il suffit qu'elle en soit capable ou plus précisément, qu'elle ait parfois de telles perceptions. Ainsi dans un profond sommeil ou un évanouissement, l'état d'un esprit ou d'une âme ne diffère pas de celui d'une simple monade[6]. La distinction entre les types de monades repose donc sur des capacités ou dispositions différentes, les monades simples étant incapables d'accéder aux perceptions plus distinctes. La distinction des types d'âmes selon leurs capacités perceptives marque une distinction de nature et pas seulement de degrés : un esprit n'est pas une âme ayant des sensations plus distinctes, mais possède une faculté d'un genre très différent qui lui permet à la fois de faire réflexion sur lui-même et de

M. Bayle, GP IV, 564; *Considérations sur les principes de vie*, GP VI, 545-46; Lettre à Wagner, GP VII, 530; *Essais de théodicée*, « Discours préliminaire », § 10, GP VI, 56; *Principes de la nature*, § 3, GP VI, 599; *Monadologie*, § 62-66, GP VI, 617-618.

1. Lettre à Arnauld, 9 octobre 1687, A II, 2, 253; *Lettre à Des Maizeaux*, GP VII, 535.

2. Lettre à Sophie Charlotte, 8 mai 1704, GP III, 344 : « chaque être vivant ou doué de perception le demeurera toujours, et gardera des organes proportionnés ». Sur cette question, voir F. Duchesneau, *Leibniz. Le vivant et l'organisme*.

3. Lettre à Wagner, GP VII, 530.

4. *Monadologie*, § 29 et 82-83, GP VI, 611 et 621.

5. *Ibid.*, § 83, GP VI, 621.

6. *Ibid.*, § 20-21, GP VI, 610; *Principes de la nature*, § 4, GP VI, 600.

raisonner, c'est-à-dire de former des inférences déductives, ce qui suppose de posséder le concept de nécessité [1].

Leibniz superpose à cette distinction des trois espèces fondamentales de perceptions et d'âmes une distinction entre perception et aperception. Cette dernière distinction s'inscrit dans le contexte d'une critique de la conception cartésienne de l'esprit et de la conscience comme critère du mental :

> Ainsi il est bon de faire distinction entre la *Perception* qui est l'état intérieur de la Monade représentant les choses externes, et l'*Aperception* qui est la *Conscience*, ou la connaissance réflexive de cet état intérieur, laquelle n'est point donnée à toutes les âmes, ni toujours à la même âme. Et c'est faute de cette distinction que les Cartésiens ont manqué, en comptant pour rien les perceptions dont on ne s'aperçoit pas, comme le peuple compte pour rien les corps insensibles. C'est aussi ce qui fait croire aux mêmes Cartésiens, que les seuls esprits sont des Monades, qu'il n'y a point d'Âme des Bêtes, et encore moins d'autres *Principes de Vie* [2].

La distinction est claire à première vue. Il y a deux actes de l'esprit : la perception et l'aperception. Cela permet de distinguer les perceptions conscientes (dont il y a aperception) et les perceptions inconscientes (dont on ne s'aperçoit pas). Les Cartésiens ont à la fois identifié l'ensemble des perceptions aux perceptions conscientes et restreint les substances immatérielles aux seuls esprits. En conséquence, les animaux n'ont pas d'âme et sont incapables de perceptions. Cette dernière thèse recèle un danger théologique, car en restreignant l'âme à un sujet de perceptions conscientes, on risque de confondre l'absence de perception consciente avec la destruction pure et simple de l'âme et de menacer ainsi l'immortalité de l'âme. Ces conséquences résultent de l'acceptation de deux thèses cardinales défendues par Descartes et la plupart des Cartésiens. La première d'entre elles est (A) que *toute pensée est consciente*. Il s'agit de la définition même de la pensée (*cogitatio*) pour Descartes [3]. En outre, la pensée est l'attribut

1. Voir *Nouveaux Essais*, « Préface », A VI, 6, 50-51 ; II, XXXIII, 270-271 ; *Monadologie*, § 26-29, GP VI, 611 ; *Principes de la nature*, § 5, GP VI, p. 600-601. La frontière entre les entéléchies et les âmes n'est pas du même ordre qu'entre les âmes et les esprits. Un simple vivant peut se développer en animal, et l'entéléchie devenir une âme au sens strict, ce qui se produit dans la génération animale qui obéit à un processus de préformation. Au contraire un esprit ne commence à exister que par un acte de création divine particulier, aussi appelé transcréation (*Essais de théodicée*, § 90-91, GP VI, 152-153).

2. *Principes de la nature*, § 4, GP VI, 600.

3. Descartes, *Secondes réponses*, « Exposé géométrique », déf. 1, AT IX-1, 124 : « Par le nom de pensée, je comprends tout ce qui est tellement en nous, que nous en sommes immédiatement connaissants (*ut ejus immediate conscii simus*). Ainsi toutes les opérations de la volonté, de l'entendement, de l'imagination et des sens, sont des pensées ». Cf. *Principes de la*

principal de l'esprit ou *res cogitans*, autrement dit constitue l'essence de celle-ci[1]. Leibniz en considère surtout un corollaire, à savoir (B) que *l'âme pense toujours*, puisque nulle chose ne peut exister sans son essence[2].

Leibniz n'est pas seul à juger que l'acceptation conjointe de (A) et (B) entraîne des conséquences paradoxales. Ainsi Locke partage avec les Cartésiens la thèse (A) mais, reconnaissant qu'il nous arrive de n'avoir aucune pensée consciente, il en conclut que l'âme ne pense pas toujours[3]. Leibniz prend l'exact contrepied de Locke en s'appuyant sur la thèse de l'activité monadique : chaque substance agit toujours. Comme la perception est l'action propre de l'âme, il s'ensuit que l'âme a toujours des perceptions ou pense toujours. Or c'est un fait que nous n'avons pas toujours conscience de nos pensées. Donc toute perception n'est pas consciente[4].

Si l'aperception distingue la perception en général de la perception consciente, le rapport de l'aperception à la notion de conscience reste toutefois ambigu. Cette ambiguïté se traduit par le fait que la dichotomie de la perception et de l'aperception ne permet pas de la situer clairement dans la hiérarchie tripartite des monades : l'aperception est-elle présente dans les âmes qui ont des sensations, ou bien appartient-elle seulement aux esprits qui sont capables d'une réflexion sur soi et d'accéder à la connaissance des vérités nécessaires ? Les quelques textes qui caractérisent l'aperception sont ambigus. Ainsi, au § 14 de la *Monadologie*, Leibniz écrit :

> L'état passager qui enveloppe et représente une multitude dans l'unité ou dans la substance simple n'est autre chose que ce qu'on appelle la Perception, qu'on doit bien distinguer de l'aperception ou de la conscience, comme il paraîtra dans la suite. Et c'est en quoi les Cartésiens ont fort manqué, ayant compté pour rien les perceptions dont on ne s'aperçoit pas[5].

philosophie, I, IX (AT VIII-1, 7 ; IX-2, 28). Cette conception est reprise chez les cartésiens ; *cf.* Malebranche, *Recherche de la vérité*, III-2, 1 (OCM I, 415) ; Arnauld, *Des vraies et des fausses idées*, chap. II, éd. D. Moreau, p. 53 et 73 ; A. Simmons, « Changing the Cartesian Mind », p. 34-35. Cependant Descartes distingue la conscience immédiate accompagnant chaque pensée de la conscience réflexive à l'œuvre dans l'introspection et par laquelle nous prenons une telle pensée comme un objet d'une pensée distincte d'ordre supérieur ; cf. *Lettre à Arnauld*, 29 juillet 1648, AT V, 220-221.

1. *Principes*, I, 63, AT VIII-1, 30-31.

2. Descartes, Lettre à Gibieuf, 19 janvier 1642, AT III, 478. Descartes s'efforce de dissiper l'apparence paradoxale de ces conséquences, en distinguant la conscience accompagnant toute pensée de la mémoire de cette pensée, laquelle n'est pas toujours remarquée ; cf. *ibid.*, AT III, 478-479 et AT V, 221-222.

3. Locke, *Essai philosophique concernant l'entendement humain*, II, I, § 9-11.

4. *Nouveaux Essais*, « Préface », A VI, 6, 53 ; II, I, § 9-11, A VI, 6, 112-113.

5. *Monadologie*, § 14, GP VI, 608-609.

L'aperception apparaît ici comme synonyme de conscience, ce qui paraît confirmé par l'usage du verbe « apercevoir » dans la phrase suivante : une perception inaperçue est une perception inconsciente, puisque pour les « Cartésiens » toute pensée est consciente. Le passage précédemment cité du § 4 des *Principes de la Nature et de la Grâce* apporte une caractérisation plus précise :

> Ainsi il est bon de faire distinction entre la *Perception* qui est l'état intérieur de la Monade représentant les choses externes, et l'*Aperception* qui est la *Conscience*, ou la connaissance réflexive de cet état intérieur [...] [1].

Tout le poids de l'interprétation repose sur le sens de la conjonction « ou ». Elle revêt vraisemblablement une valeur plutôt explicative que disjonctive : la conscience impliquerait dès lors une réflexion sur la perception initiale. Cette lecture est confortée par l'un des arguments mobilisés par Leibniz à l'encontre de la thèse (A) :

> Il est aisé de leur montrer le contraire, c'est-à-dire, qu'il n'est pas possible que nous réfléchissions toujours expressément sur toutes nos pensées; autrement l'Esprit ferait réflexion sur chaque réflexion à l'infini sans pouvoir jamais passer à une nouvelle pensée. Par exemple, en m'apercevant de quelque sentiment présent, je devrais toujours penser que j'y pense, et penser encore que je pense d'y penser, et ainsi à l'infini. Mais il faut bien que je cesse de réfléchir sur toutes ces réflexions et qu'il y ait enfin quelque pensée qu'on laisse passer sans y penser; autrement on demeurerait toujours sur la même chose [2].

La thèse cartésienne entraîne une régression à l'infini, car si toute pensée est consciente, il s'ensuit que chaque pensée implique une gradation infinie de pensées et empêche l'esprit de penser plus d'une chose. Pour être concluant, l'argument suppose que toute conscience exige qu'à une première perception s'ajoute une perception d'ordre supérieur ayant la première pour objet [3] :

> Cette pensée de moi qui m'aperçois des objets sensibles, et de ma propre action qui en résulte, ajoute quelque chose aux objets des sens. Penser à

1. *Principes de la nature*, § 4, GP VI, 600.

2. *Nouveaux Essais*, II, I, § 19, A VI, 6, 118.

3. Cette conception de la réflexion comme acte distinct de l'acte premier d'intellection est héritée de l'aristotélisme. Elle est notamment celle de Thomas d'Aquin; cf. *Summa theologiae* Ia, qu. 87, art. 3, in corp. et ad 2. Descartes affirme au contraire l'identité de la *cogitatio* et de l'acte réfléchi de conscience qui l'accompagne; cf. *Septièmes réponses*, AT VII, 559 et les remarques de Leibniz en A VI, 4, 1470-1471.

> quelque chose et considérer qu'on y pense, ce sont deux pensées très différentes [...] [1].

Dans une conception de la conscience impliquant l'existence de perceptions d'ordre supérieur, la mémoire joue un rôle central. En effet, l'acte réflexif n'est pas simultané avec la perception qui en est l'objet, mais se déploie dans le temps. C'est pourquoi, afin qu'une perception prenne pour objet une première perception, il faut que cette dernière soit remémorée :

> [L]e souvenir présent ou immédiat, c'est-à-dire la conscience ou la réflexion, qui accompagne l'action interne, ne saurait tromper naturellement : autrement on ne serait pas même certain qu'on pense à telle ou telle chose [...] [2].

La mémoire est ainsi requise pour la réflexion et l'aperception, ce que Leibniz illustre par le phénomène de l'attention rétrospective : je peux ne pas avoir prêté attention au bruit d'une chute d'eau mais, averti par quelqu'un, je m'en souviens en même temps que j'en prends conscience [3]. Le mécanisme semble être le suivant : une première perception d'un bruit, conservée par la mémoire est immédiatement suivie d'une réflexion sur cette perception ; grâce à cette réflexion, la première perception devient une expérience consciente [4].

L'aperception implique ainsi une forme de réflexion et avec elle une mémoire (immédiate) des perceptions passées. Lorsqu'une perception est accompagnée d'aperception, elle est consciente [5]. Mais toute perception réflexive n'est pas consciente, sous peine d'ouvrir la voie à la régression à l'infini décrite dans le passage cité plus haut. Tous ces éléments permettent ainsi de dégager une théorie de la conscience comme perception d'ordre supérieur [6].

1. *Lettre touchant ce qui est indépendant des sens*, GP VI, 501.

2. *Nouveaux Essais*, II, XXVII, § 13, A VI, 6, 238. Voir aussi *Divisio terminorum* A VI, 4, 562-563. Ce lien étroit entre esprit et mémoire apparaît très tôt chez Leibniz. Ainsi dans un texte de 1671, il définit le corps comme un esprit momentané (*mens momentanea*) du fait qu'il lui manque la mémoire (*Theoria motus abstracti*, A VI, 2, 266 ; cf. *De obligatione credendi*, Grua 181 ; *Table de définitions*, C 495).

3. Voir *Nouveaux Essais*, « Préface », A VI, 6, 53 ; *Monadologie*, § 23, GP VI, 610.

4. Plus exactement, la perception initiale telle qu'elle est conservée par ce que nous appellerions une mémoire de travail.

5. *Cf.* M. Kulstad, *Leibniz on Apperception, Consciousness, and Reflection*, en particulier p. 36-38. Selon Y. Belaval, *Études*, p. 126, les animaux ont une mémoire-écho, distincte de la mémoire des esprits. Elle n'implique pas de réflexivité.

6. Parmi les commentateurs qui attribuent à Leibniz une conception de la conscience comme pensée d'ordre supérieur (*higher-order theory of consciousness*), voir notamment

Il peut sembler que Leibniz identifie purement et simplement l'aperception, la réflexion et la conscience [1]. Cela impliquerait que seuls des êtres dotés de la faculté de réfléchir, de raisonner et d'accéder à la connaissance des vérités nécessaires seraient capables d'aperception, en sorte que la conscience serait le privilège des esprits, à l'exclusion des autres monades et des animaux en particulier [2]. Cette interprétation exclusive se heurte néanmoins au problème de la perception animale. Les animaux ne semblent pas disposer de la capacité à réfléchir et devraient donc être dépourvus d'aperception et de sensations conscientes [3]. Cependant, cette conséquence serait aussi contre-intuitive que la thèse cartésienne des animaux machines rejetée par Leibniz. En outre, certains textes semblent confirmer que Leibniz attribue une forme d'aperception aux animaux, notamment dans ce passage des *Nouveaux Essais :*

> Nous nous apercevons de bien des choses en nous en hors de nous que nous n'entendons pas, et nous les entendons, quand nous avons des idées distinctes, avec le pouvoir de réfléchir et d'en tirer des vérités nécessaires. C'est pourquoi les bêtes n'ont point d'entendement, au moins dans ce sens, quoiqu'elles aient la faculté de s'apercevoir des impressions plus remarquables et plus distinguées, comme le sanglier s'aperçoit d'une personne qui lui crie et va droit à cette personne, dont il n'avait eu déjà auparavant qu'une perception nue, mais confuse comme de tous les autres objets qui frappent son cristallin [4].

Le sanglier « s'aperçoit » de l'homme qui pousse un cri. Il y a en lui une différence entre la simple perception d'un homme devant lui, comparable à sa présence dans son champ visuel, et l'aperception, qui correspond à une attention particulière portée à cet objet présent dans son champ visuel.

M. Kulstad, *Leibniz on Apperception;* R. Gennaro, « Leibniz on consciousness and self-consciousness », p. 353-371 ; A. Simmons, « Changing the Cartesian Mind ». L. Jorgensen, « The Principle of Continuity and Leibniz's Theory of Consciousness », p. 223-248, critique cette interprétation.

1. C'est la thèse défendue dans R. McRae, *Leibniz : Perception, Apperception, and Thought*, p. 33. Voir aussi E. Naert, *Mémoire et conscience de soi selon Leibniz* et Y. Belaval, *Études*, p. 126-128.

2. Certains passages paraissent restreindre la conscience aux âmes raisonnables ou esprits. Voir Lettre à Arnauld, septembre 1687, A II, 2, 231 : « La notion de la pensée outre cela demande qu'il y ait une conscience, et c'est ce qui appartient à l'âme raisonnable » ; *cf.* Lettre à Arnauld, 9 octobre 1687, A II, 2, 241.

3. Cf. *Considérations sur les principes de vie*, GP VI, 542 : « … les bêtes autant qu'on en peut juger, manquent de cette réflexion, qui nous fait penser à nous-mêmes » ; voir aussi dans les textes antérieurs, *Discours de métaphysique,* § XXXIV ; *Specimen inventorum*, A VI, 4, 1625.

4. *Nouveaux Essais,* II, XXI, § 5, A VI, 6, 173.

Si les animaux sont effectivement capables d'aperception, alors celle-ci n'est pas le privilège des seuls esprits.

Cependant, l'attribution de la conscience aux animaux est-elle compatible avec la définition comme réflexion ? Il n'est pas question pour Leibniz d'attribuer aux animaux les mêmes capacités cognitives qu'aux esprits. D'un côté, la conscience implique une forme de réflexion. De l'autre, les sensations dans les animaux s'accompagnent de conscience et le sentiment, ou sensation consciente, requiert de l'attention et de la mémoire. Cette tension peut être résolue en distinguant deux types de réflexion et, conjointement deux formes d'aperception : d'une part une réflexion et une aperception simple, commune aux âmes et aux esprits; d'autre part la réflexion propre aux esprits.

Les perceptions animales s'accompagnent d'un type de réflexion qui produit une aperception simple ou ce qu'on peut appeler une conscience de l'acte. La conscience animale suppose une réflexion sur une perception en tant qu'elle est la représentation d'un état extérieur c'est-à-dire d'un « objet externe »[1]. Le sanglier a une perception consciente d'une personne qui crie. Mais cette conscience de l'acte n'implique pas que le sanglier possède une conscience de lui-même, en tant que conscience d'un objet particulier, le sujet de ces actes conscients. Les esprits sont en revanche des « Êtres réflexifs »[2]. Leur aperception peut également porter sur une perception en tant qu'elle est un objet interne ou une modification d'un sujet pensant. Il s'agit d'une « aperception de ce qui est en nous »[3]. Si j'aperçois quelqu'un criant en ma direction, outre la perception consciente de cette situation, je peux considérer mes propres sensations visuelle et auditive. Cependant, « cette réflexion ne se borne pas aux seules opérations de l'esprit [...], elle va jusqu'à l'esprit lui-même »[4]. En effet, à partir de cette conscience de l'objet interne, l'aperception peut prendre pour objet le moi qui est le sujet de ces actes mentaux :

> Ceux qui connaissent ces vérités nécessaires, sont proprement ceux qu'on appelle animaux raisonnables, et leurs âmes sont appelées Esprits. Ces âmes sont capables de faire des actes réflexifs et de considérer ce qu'on appelle Moi, Substance, Âme, Esprit, en un mot, les choses et les vérités

1. *Ibid.*, II, XIX, § 1, A VI, 6, 161.
2. Lettre à Sophie Charlotte, GP III, 345.
3. *Nouveaux Essais*, I, I, § 25, A VI, 6, 86.
4. *Échantillons de réflexions sur l'Essay*, A VI, 6, 14.

> immatérielles. Et c'est ce qui nous rend susceptible des sciences ou des connaissances démonstratives [1].

Ainsi, l'aperception comme réflexion sur un état interne ne concerne pas seulement les actes perceptifs, mais possède également un objet distinct, le Moi. Cette réflexion implique la faculté d'acquérir des connaissances ou des idées distinctes. La connexion entre l'aperception comme conscience de soi et la capacité à avoir une idée métaphysique comme celle de substance s'explique par le rôle de la réflexion : « la réflexion suffit pour trouver l'idée de la substance en nous-mêmes, qui sommes des substances » [2]. Elle est étroitement liée aussi à la rationalité et à nos « connaissances démonstratives », qui s'opposent aux simples « consécutions empiriques », communes aux bêtes et aux hommes. La conscience de soi propre aux êtres réflexifs est indissociable de la rationalité.

PETITES PERCEPTIONS, IDÉES INNÉES ET ANALYSE DES SENSATIONS

L'analyse leibnizienne de l'aperception suppose la possibilité de perceptions inconscientes. La simple possibilité théorique ouverte par l'analyse de l'aperception ne constitue cependant pas un motif suffisant pour affirmer l'existence de ces perceptions inconscientes ni *a fortiori* pour leur assigner un rôle central dans la philosophie de l'esprit. Leibniz affirme cependant l'existence dans l'âme à chaque instant d'une infinité de perceptions insensibles ou petites perceptions. Puisqu'elles sont inconscientes, leur existence ne peut être directement établie par l'observation mais inférée par le raisonnement. Elles découlent d'abord de certains principes de la métaphysique, en particulier du principe de continuité. Ce principe exclut qu'un changement dans la nature se produise par un saut :

> Rien ne se fait tout d'un coup, et c'est une de mes grandes maximes et des plus vérifiées que la nature ne fait jamais des sauts : ce que j'appelais la loi de la continuité [...] et l'usage de cette loi est très considérable dans la physique. Elle porte qu'on passe toujours du petit au grand et à rebours par le médiocre, dans les degrés comme dans les parties, et que jamais un

1. *Principes de la nature*, § 5, GP VI, 601 ; cf. *Monadologie*, § 30, GP VI, 612 ; *Nouveaux Essais*, II, I, § 2, A VI, 6, 111 ; XXI, § 5, A VI, 6, 137 ; GP VI, 578.

2. *Nouveaux Essais*, I, III, § 18, A VI, 6, 105. Cf. *Échantillons de réflexions sur l'Essay*, A VI, 6, 14 : « et c'est en s'apercevant de lui, que nous nous apercevons de la substance » ; *Nos esse substantias*, Grua 558.

> mouvement ne naît immédiatement du repos ni ne s'y réduit que par un mouvement plus petit [...]. Et tout cela fait bien juger que les perceptions remarquables viennent par degrés de celles qui sont trop petites pour être remarquées [1].

Le principe de continuité implique donc que nos perceptions conscientes ne peuvent pas surgir de nulle part, mais proviennent « par degrés » de petites perceptions inaperçues. La formulation employée ici pourrait laisser entendre qu'on a affaire à une variation continue du degré de conscience de nos perceptions, en sorte que les petites perceptions seraient encore conscientes, quoiqu'à un degré infime. En physique, Leibniz compare par exemple le repos à un mouvement infiniment lent, ce qui pourrait accréditer cette interprétation [2]. Il n'est pas du tout évident toutefois que les petites perceptions seraient des perceptions faiblement conscientes. En effet, Leibniz affirme que l'aperception n'est pas donnée pour toujours aux esprits comme nous pouvons en faire l'expérience dans un sommeil profond ou un évanouissement [3]. Le principe de continuité implique seulement qu'une perception consciente doit être fondée sur une transition continue à partir des caractéristiques de nos perceptions insensibles, comme Leibniz l'illustre avec l'exemple du bruit de la mer sur le rivage [4] :

> Et pour juger encore mieux des petites perceptions que nous ne saurions distinguer dans la foule, j'ai coutume de me servir de l'exemple du mugissement ou du bruit de la mer dont est frappé quand on est au rivage. Pour entendre ce bruit comme l'on fait, il faut bien qu'on entende les parties qui composent ce tout, c'est-à-dire le bruit que fait chaque vague, quoique chacun de ces petits bruits ne se fasse connaître que dans l'assemblage confus de tous les autres ensemble, et qu'il ne se remarquerait pas si cette vague qui le fait était seule. Car il faut qu'on en soit affecté un peu par le mouvement de cette vague et qu'on ait quelque perception de chacun de ces bruits, quelque petits qu'ils soient; autrement on n'aurait pas celle de cent mille vagues, puisque cent mille riens ne sauraient faire quelque chose [5].

1. *Nouveaux Essais*, « Préface », A VI, 6, 56-57 ; cf. *ibid.*, II, I, § 18, A VI, 6, 117.

2. Selon Russell, une perception inconsciente (au sens d'inaperçue) est un état de conscience, mais elle est inconsciente en ce sens qu'elle n'implique pas de conscience de soi ; *cf.* B. Russell, *La philosophie de Leibniz*, p. 175 ; N. Rescher, *Leibniz. An Introduction to His Philosophy*, p. 119-120.

3. *Principes de la nature*, § 4, GP VI, 600 ; *Monadologie*, § 20, GP VI, 610.

4. L'argument tiré du principe de continuité est discuté par A. Simmons, « Changing the Cartesian Mind », en particulier p. 45, et L. Jorgensen, « The Principle of Continuity ».

5. *Nouveaux Essais*, « Préface », A VI, 6, 54 ; cf. *Principes de la nature*, § 13, GP VI, 604.

La perception du bruit de l'ensemble provient de ce que le nombre de vagues qui produisent un son dépasse un seuil. Comme dans un sorite, une série continue (ici le nombre de vagues) s'accompagne d'effets discontinus en apparence, produisant un effet de seuil : en-deçà d'un certain nombre de vagues, le bruit quoique perçu, ne donne pas lieu à une expérience consciente, alors qu'au-delà il donne lieu à une expérience consciente. Le nombre est ici le facteur décisif, car il rend compte du caractère à la fois conscient et confus de notre perception, comme on le verra plus loin.

Cet exemple fait partie de tout un ensemble de cas évoqués par lesquels Leibniz établit l'existence des petites perceptions qui permettent de rendre compte d'un grand nombre de phénomènes. Leur existence est ainsi établie par une procédure hypothético-déductive d'inférence à la meilleure explication :

> D'ailleurs il y a mille marques qui font juger qu'il y a à tout moment une infinité de perceptions en nous, mais sans aperception et sans réflexion, c'est-à-dire des changements dans l'âme même dont nous ne nous apercevons pas, parce que ces impressions sont ou trop petites ou en trop grand nombre ou trop unies, en sorte qu'elles n'ont rien d'assez distinguant à part, mais jointes à d'autres, elles ne laissent pas de faire leur effet et de se faire sentir au moins confusément dans l'assemblage [1].

Les multiples phénomènes évoqués ont pour trait commun de requérir une représentation sans conscience. Certains sont purement cognitifs, par exemple l'effet d'accoutumance : celui qui vit près d'un moulin à eau ne prête plus attention au bruit de sa roue au bout d'un certain temps, mais il perçoit pourtant ce bruit comme en atteste le fait qu'il peut se souvenir de l'avoir entendu si on lui demande. Leibniz avance d'autres phénomènes cognitifs : le réveil à partir d'un profond sommeil [2], ou encore certains phénomènes liés à notre attention, comme le changement d'orientation de l'attention [3]. Les petites perceptions permettent aussi de rendre compte de phénomènes motivationnels, comme les cas d'indifférence apparente, dans lesquels nos décisions sont déterminées par des motifs cachés qui nous déterminent inconsciemment à choisir telle action plutôt que telle autre [4].

1. *Nouveaux Essais*, « Préface », p. 41.
2. *Ibid.*, II, I, § 13, A VI, 6, 115.
3. *Ibid.*, II, I, § 14, A VI, 6, 115.
4. Voir *ibid.*, « Préface », A VI, 6, 56; II, I, § 15; II, XXI, § 36, A VI, 6, 188-190. À proprement parler, il s'agit de perceptions insensibles de petites inclinations qui sont des appétits insensibles. Ce que Leibniz appelle l'inquiétude est l'expérience consciente d'une

Les perceptions insensibles sont également mobilisées dans la défense des idées et des principes innés. Contre l'empirisme de Locke, Leibniz soutient que l'esprit n'est pas à l'origine une *tabula rasa*, une tablette vide, pourvu de la simple faculté d'acquérir des idées. Il est au contraire comparable à un bloc de marbre dont les veines le disposent à être sculpté de telle façon plutôt que d'une autre :

> Hercule y serait comme inné en quelque façon, quoiqu'il fallût du travail pour découvrir ces veines, et pour les nettoyer par la polissure, en retranchant ce qui les empêche de paraître. C'est ainsi que les idées et les vérités nous sont innées, comme des inclinations, des habitudes, ou des virtualités naturelles, et non pas comme des actions, quoique ces virtualités soient toujours accompagnées de quelques actions souvent insensibles qui y répondent[1].

Dans ce passage, Leibniz paraît assimiler les idées innées à des dispositions mentales. L'esprit ne possède pas seulement une capacité indéterminée à former des idées ; il est disposé en outre à former telles idées plutôt que d'autres en vertu de sa nature, par exemple l'esprit possède l'idée de substance de manière innée, car il est naturellement disposé à rattacher les propriétés qu'il observe à des sujets de ces propriétés. Cette conception dispositionnaliste des idées innées est un leitmotiv chez Leibniz et s'accompagne d'une conception générale des idées comme dispositions mentales qui s'activent à l'occasion de l'expérience et qui existent virtuellement dans l'esprit auparavant[2]. Dans un certain nombre de passages, il semble cependant que cette identification des idées innées à des dispositions mentales ne constitue qu'un premier niveau d'analyse. À un second niveau en effet, ces dispositions ou « virtualités » sont à leur tour fondées dans la structure actuelle de l'esprit. Et c'est à ce second niveau que les petites perceptions jouent un rôle qui s'éclaire à partir de l'analogie étroite

pluralité de petites inclinations insuffisantes à constituer un motif suffisant pour agir (*ibid.*, II, XXI, § 36, A VI, 6, 188). A. Simmons, « Changing the Cartesian Mind », p. 61, évoque d'autres phénomènes susceptibles d'être expliqués par les petites perceptions : la vision aveugle (la capacité à réagir de manière appropriée à l'environnement, sans en être conscient) ; l'effet cocktail (le fait de reconnaître son nom prononcé au milieu d'une foule bruyante) ; ou encore le fait de remarquer la cessation d'un phénomène auquel on n'avait pas prêté attention (par exemple la perception de la cessation du bruit d'un réfrigérateur).

1. *Nouveaux Essais*, « Préface », A VI, 6, 52.

2. Pour l'idée en général comme disposition, cf. *Quid sit idea*, A VI, 4, 1360, R 445. La conception dispositionnaliste des idées et des vérités innées apparaît dans *Discours de métaphysique*, § XXVI-XXVII (A VI, 4, 1570-1572) et surtout dans *Nouveaux Essais*, I, I, § 1-27, *passim*. Il arrive à Leibniz de parler indifféremment de l'idée innée comme disposition et comme idée implicite ou latente, par contraste avec une idée aperçue, ce qui favorise en retour l'identification de l'idée innée à une petite perception.

entre le rôle des corpuscules dans l'explication des phénomènes physiques et celui des petites perceptions pour celle des phénomènes mentaux :

> En un mot, les perceptions insensibles sont d'un aussi grand usage dans la pneumatique que les corpuscules insensibles le sont dans la physique, et il est également déraisonnable de rejeter les uns et les autres sous prétexte qu'elles sont hors de portée de nos sens [1].

Ainsi, les dispositions des corps apparents sont fondées dans les propriétés et notamment la configuration des corpuscules. La fragilité est une propriété dispositionnelle du verre. Mais elle est fondée dans la structure corpusculaire du verre qui est la base catégorique de la disposition. Si l'on pousse à son terme l'analogie, les petites perceptions seront la base catégorique des idées innées comprises comme dispositions mentales[2]. Ces petites perceptions constituent ainsi ce qu'on pourrait appeler la structure interne de l'esprit[3].

L'analogie corpusculaire permet également d'éclairer la nature du rapport des petites perceptions à la conscience et de comprendre qu'une petite perception isolée n'est pas un objet aperceptible. Certains des exemples donnés par Leibniz, telle la perception rétrospective du bruit du moulin, pourraient laisser penser qu'il y a une perception du bruit de l'eau qui, jointe à l'aperception, accède au statut de perception consciente. Mais ce serait se méprendre sur le fait que Leibniz entend produire une *explication* de la perception consciente. Une telle explication demande notamment que, parmi nos perceptions, certaines possèdent des caractéristiques susceptibles de les distinguer comme objets d'une aperception. L'analogie corpusculaire implique que ces caractéristiques dépendent des petites perceptions entrant dans la composition de cette perception.

Leibniz propose une explication de cette nature dans le cas des sensations, c'est-à-dire des perceptions confuses des sens. Nos sensations sont des épisodes mentaux conscients. Une sensation est une perception distincte, distinguée, ou encore relevée[4]. La distinction d'une perception est ce en vertu de quoi cette perception est consciente. Elle dépend d'une série de facteurs dont les principaux sont la multitude et la variété des petites perceptions. Dans l'exemple du bruit de la mer, nous ne percevons

1. *Nouveaux Essais*, « Préface », A VI, 6, 56.

2. *Cf.* les « actions insensibles » qui « répondent » aux dispositions dans le passage précédent.

3. *Cf.* N. Jolley, *The Light of the Soul : Theories of Ideas in Leibniz, Malebranche, and Descartes*, p. 159-165 ; *id.*, *Leibniz*, p. 112-118.

4. *Specimen inventorum*, A VI, 4, 1625 ; *Nouveaux Essais*, II, I, § 9 et § 11, A VI, 6, 111 et 113 ; *Principes de la nature*, § 13, GP VI, 604.

que l'effet du mouvement de toutes les vagues au bord du rivage, car il contient un nombre suffisamment grand de perceptions pour atteindre le seuil d'une perception distinguée ou consciente. Une telle perception est cependant confuse, car elle résulte d'un ensemble de petites perceptions correspondant au bruit de chaque vague. La multitude rend ainsi compte à la fois de la confusion des sensations et du fait que nous pouvons en avoir conscience.

La variété est un autre facteur essentiel. Pour être consciente, une perception doit présenter une certaine nouveauté, susceptible d'attirer notre attention[1]. En témoigne l'exemple du bruit de l'eau du moulin qu'on ne remarque plus après un certain temps[2]. Cet exemple montre aussi que le caractère distingué d'une perception varie selon le contexte : le même bruit de l'eau du moulin est composé d'une multitude suffisante de petites perceptions pour être aperçu à tel moment, mais faute de nouveauté, il ne l'est plus au bout d'un certain temps. La variété compense également la confusion produite par un trop grand nombre d'impressions, car à l'inverse, « un trop grand nombre de petites perceptions peu distinguées comme qui suivent un coup de tête, nous étourdit »[3].

Le caractère distingué des sensations dépend ainsi de la multitude et de la variété des perceptions qui entrent dans leur composition. Ainsi les sensations, que nous expérimentons phénoménalement comme indivisibles, dépendent des petites perceptions qui semblent entrer dans leur composition comme le soulignent plusieurs passages :

> Ces petites perceptions [...] forment ce je ne sais quoi, ces goûts, ces images des qualités des sens, claires dans l'assemblage, mais confuses dans les parties[4].

> La perception de la lumière ou de la couleur par exemple, dont nous nous apercevons, est composée de quantité de petites perceptions, dont nous ne nous apercevons pas [...][5].

Leibniz généralise cette thèse à toutes nos perceptions distinctes, c'est-à-dire distinguées, ou susceptibles d'être conscientes :

> [C]haque perception distincte de l'âme comprend une infinité de perceptions confuses, qui enveloppent tout l'univers[6].

1. *Nouveaux Essais*, II, IX, § 1, 134.
2. *Ibid.*, « Préface », A VI, 6, 53-54.
3. Lettre à Sophie Charlotte, GP III, 346.
4. *Nouveaux Essais*, « Préface », A VI, 6, 54.
5. *Ibid.*, II, IX, § 4, A VI, 6, 134.
6. *Principes de la nature*, § 13, GP VI, 604.

La complexité des sensations permet à Leibniz de maintenir que chaque perception est essentiellement représentative alors que les sensations n'ont aucune ressemblance avec les mouvements corporels auxquels elles sont corrélées. Ainsi la douleur ne ressemble pas au mouvement de l'épingle s'enfonçant dans le bras. De même, la sensation de la lumière ne ressemble pas à ce qui se passe dans la flamme. Ceci conduit les cartésiens à soutenir que la relation entre une idée sensible et un état corporel est arbitraire et librement instituée par Dieu[1]. Leibniz défend une position intermédiaire en maintenant que « la représentation a un rapport naturel à ce qui doit être représenté »[2]. Cette ressemblance représentative n'est autre que l'expression :

> Je dirais plutôt qu'il y a une manière de ressemblance, non pas entière et pour ainsi dire *in terminis*, mais expressive, ou de rapport d'ordre, comme une ellipse et même une parabole ou hyperbole ressemblent en quelque façon au cercle dont elles sont la projection sur le plan, puisqu'il y a un certain rapport exact et naturel entre ce qui est projeté et la projection qui s'en fait, chaque point de l'un répondant suivant une certaine relation à chaque point de l'autre. C'est ce que les cartésiens ne considèrent pas assez [...][3].

La ressemblance expressive demande comme on l'a vu une correspondance entre les éléments du représenté et ceux du représentant. Dans la sensation, cette condition est satisfaite par l'isomorphisme entre les petites perceptions et les mouvements des corpuscules. Ainsi la ressemblance ne se situe pas au niveau global, aperceptible, de la sensation consciente, mais au niveau inférieur des petites perceptions entrant dans la composition de celle-ci.

Alors que les sensations se présentent comme des expériences premières, indivisibles ou simples, cette simplicité n'est donc qu'apparente. Comme le vert résulte du mélange de pigments bleus et jaunes, de même les sensations que nous avons du jaune ou du bleu ne sont simples qu'en apparence et sont en réalité composées d'une multitude de petites perceptions. L'apparence de simplicité résulte de la confusion de ces idées,

1. Voir en particulier Malebranche, *Recherche de la vérité*, I, 1, OCM I, 42-43; I, 13, OCM I, 154. L'arbitraire de la relation de la sensation aux mouvements corporels permet selon Malebranche d'établir que les sensations ne sont pas représentatives; cf. *Recherche de la vérité*, III-1-1, OCM I, 388. Tous les cartésiens n'en tirent pas la même conclusion et, sur cette question de la nature représentative de la sensation, Descartes lui-même adopte une position ambivalente qui se prête à des interprétations contraires. *Cf.* A. Simmons, « Changing the Cartesian Mind ».

2. *Essais de théodicée*, § 356, GP VI, 326.

3. *Nouveaux Essais*, II, VIII, § 13; cf. *Théodicée*, § 357.

elle-même due à la multitude des petites perceptions qui entrent en elles[1]. Le rapport des sensations aux petites perceptions qui la composent est comparé à l'illusion d'un disque diaphane produite par le mouvement d'une roue dentée :

> On ne saurait démêler l'idée des dents de la roue, c'est-à-dire de la cause dans la perception d'un transparent artificiel, que j'ai remarqué chez les horlogers, fait par la prompte rotation d'une roue dentelée, ce qui en fait disparaître les dents et paraître à leur place un transparent continuel imaginaire, composé des apparences successives des dents et de leurs intervalles, mais où la succession est si prompte que notre fantaisie ne la saurait distinguer. On trouve donc bien ces dents dans la notion distincte de cette transparence, mais non pas dans cette perception sensitive confuse, dont la nature est d'être et de demeurer confuse : autrement, si la confusion cessait (comme si le mouvement était si lent qu'on en pourrait observer les parties et leur succession), ce ne serait plus elle, c'est-à-dire : ce ne serait plus ce fantôme de transparence[2].

Aucune introspection, même à l'aide d'un hypothétique microscope mental, n'est capable de dissiper l'apparence phénoménale, ce « fantôme sensitif » pas plus qu'elle ne nous pourrait nous donner un accès direct aux petites perceptions correspondant aux mouvements de chacune des dents de la roue. La confusion est en effet un aspect essentiel et inéliminable de l'expérience phénoménale ou de nos idées confuses. Seul un détour par une analyse scientifique des phénomènes permet de construire un modèle de ces petites perceptions qui représentent les propriétés réelles des corps. On constate ainsi qu'en dépit du jugement de Kant, Leibniz n'a nullement cherché à « intellectualiser les apparences »[3].

CONCLUSION

L'analyse de la nature des sensations témoigne ainsi du rôle absolument central des petites perceptions dans la philosophie de l'esprit de Leibniz. En même temps, elle soulève une véritable difficulté pour celle-ci. D'un côté en effet nous avons vu que la distinction de l'âme et du corps reposait sur l'impossibilité d'expliquer la perception en termes

1. *Nouveaux Essais*, II, II, § 1, A VI, 6, 120.

2. *Ibid.*, IV, VI, § 7, A VI, 6, 403.

3. Kant, *Critique de la raison pure*, A 271/B 327. Sur l'analyse indirecte des qualités sensibles, qui suppose la construction d'un modèle explicatif formulé en termes mécanistes, voir C 190 et l'analyse de ce passage dans l'article de G. H. R. Parkinson, « The "Intellectualization of Appearences" : Aspects of Leibniz's Theory of Sensation and Thought », p. 3-20.

mécaniques. La définition de la perception comme représentation d'une multitude dans l'unité joue alors un rôle crucial, dans la mesure où aucun mécanisme corporel n'est en mesure de satisfaire cette condition d'unité. Mais d'un autre côté, l'analyse de l'esprit fait apparaître une multiplicité irréductible au sein des monades. Ainsi, l'explication du fait que certaines perceptions soient conscientes comme celle de la nature représentative des sensations reposent toutes deux sur l'hypothèse de l'existence d'une multitude de perceptions insensibles. Cette difficulté n'a pas échappé à Leibniz. Dans la *Monadologie*, il souligne même :

> Nous expérimentons nous-mêmes une multitude dans la substance simple, lorsque nous trouvons que la moindre pensée dont nous nous apercevons enveloppe une variété dans l'objet. Ainsi tous ceux qui reconnaissent que l'âme est une substance simple doivent reconnaître cette multitude dans la monade[1].

Chaque perception représente une variété sensible *dans* l'objet. La perception d'une feuille d'arbre par exemple contient la perception de sa couleur, figure, texture, etc. La multiplicité est donc compatible avec la simplicité de la monade, mais dans la mesure où il s'agit d'une multitude *représentée* qui contient les diverses modifications d'une même pensée ou perception. Nous avons toutefois rencontré de nombreux passages dans lesquels il est clair que la composition n'est pas seulement représentée. Les petites perceptions sont parfois présentées par Leibniz littéralement comme des parties de la sensation :

> Il y a des perceptions confuses, mais il y en a aussi de simultanées, car lorsqu'il y a perception d'un out, il y a tout à la fois perceptions des parties actuelles, et même chaque partie a plus d'une modification; et il y a perception tout à la fois non seulement de chaque modification, mais encore de chaque partie: *ces perceptions si multipliées sont différentes l'une de l'autre*, quoique notre attention ne puisse pas toujours les distinguer, et c'est ce qui fait les perceptions confuses[2].

Les perceptions confuses ou sensations sont effectivement complexes et composées de petites perceptions, distinctes les unes des autres, correspondant aux parties des objets perçus. La définition de la perception comme expression de la multitude dans l'unité devrait ainsi se comprendre comme l'expression par chaque perception insensible dans l'unité d'une substance métaphysiquement simple.

1. *Monadologie*, § 16, GP VI, 609; *cf.* GP VI, 627.
2. GP VI, 628, nous soulignons.

Le recours aux petites perceptions dans l'explication des phénomènes mentaux soulève une autre difficulté. Leibniz leur attribue en effet un rôle analogue à celui des corpuscules pour l'explication des propriétés des corps. Ces perceptions insensibles constituent en quelque sorte la micro-structure de l'esprit, qui permet de rendre compte de divers mécanismes mentaux, par exemple des idées innées. Mais le modèle causal approprié aux mécanismes est celui des causes efficientes. Or Leibniz affirme que la causalité efficiente ne s'applique qu'aux corps, tandis que les esprits sont soumis au règne des causes finales et à des lois « éthico-logiques ». L'explication appropriée aux esprits doit se faire en termes de raisons et d'intentions et non de mécanismes psychiques inconscients. Leibniz affirme cependant l'harmonie des deux règnes : celui des causes finales et celui des causes efficientes :

> Les âmes agissent selon les lois des causes finales, par appétitions, fins et moyens. Les corps agissent selon les lois des causes efficientes ou des mouvements. Et les deux règnes, celui des causes efficientes et celui des causes finales, sont harmoniques entre eux [1].

Aussi pourrait-on rétorquer qu'il s'agit d'un faux problème. Cependant Leibniz affirme que ces deux régimes de causalité régissent respectivement les corps et les esprits. Or l'explication par les petites perceptions reconduit la dualité des deux règnes au sein même des esprits, entre le niveau des perceptions et des appétits conscients et celui des perceptions et appétits insensibles. C'est là une conséquence inattendue de la principale innovation de la « pneumatique » leibnizienne.

Jean-Pascal ANFRAY
(ENS Ulm)

1. *Monadologie*, § 79, GP VI, 620; cf. *Principes de la nature*, § 3, GP VI, 599.

LEIBNIZ SUR L'HARMONIE PRÉÉTABLIE ET LA CAUSALITÉ [1]

Je vois le ballon de football devant moi. Je déplace intentionnellement ma jambe pour le frapper. Mon pied le frappe et il s'envole dans les airs. Mais le coup est raté. Le ballon va directement sur la gardienne. Il frappe ses mains et elle perçoit une sensation douloureuse dans son esprit. Elle aperçoit un coéquipier qui fonce vers la ligne de touche, décide d'agir et lance le ballon dans le champ. Le ballon atterrit juste devant lui et, quelques frappes plus tard, il retentit dans le but.

La théorie de l'harmonie préétablie de Leibniz est d'abord et principalement une explication de l'interaction (apparente) entre l'esprit et le corps. C'est une théorie expliquant ce qui arrive lorsque j'ai l'intention de déplacer ma jambe et ma jambe se déplace, et aussi ce qui arrive quand la gardienne de but l'attrape et ressent une sensation douloureuse dans son esprit. La première section ci-dessous expliquera la théorie de l'harmonie préétablie de Leibniz, la comparera avec les théories adverses, et montrera comment se développe l'idée leibnizienne selon laquelle il existe deux domaines, l'un des corps et de la causalité efficiente, l'autre des esprits et de la causalité finale.

La théorie de l'harmonie préétablie de Leibniz n'est cependant pas seulement une explication de l'interaction (apparente) entre l'esprit et le corps. Par conséquent, la deuxième section examinera de plus près la vision leibnizienne de la causalité au sein du domaine des corps – sa vision, par exemple, de l'interaction causale (apparente) entre mon pied et le ballon de football, entre le ballon et le filet du but. La troisième section fera de même concernant l'explication leibnizienne de la causalité au sein du domaine des esprits ou « monades » – son explication, par exemple, de la

1. Traduit de l'anglais par Christian Leduc.

manière dont je parviens à avoir une perception du ballon et à former le désir de le frapper.

Comme nous le verrons, la théorie de l'harmonie de Leibniz est beaucoup plus qu'une brillante solution à un ancien problème de la métaphysique moderne. Elle constitue, d'une certaine manière, le filon le plus manifeste de la conception leibnizienne de la causalité dans le monde créé, une conception riche, complexe et encore aujourd'hui sous-estimée.

UNE HARMONIE PRÉÉTABLIE : CORPS ET ESPRITS

Il paraît évident que l'esprit et le corps interagissent de manière causale. Je forme l'intention de déplacer ma jambe et ma jambe se déplace; le ballon frappe mes mains et je ressens une douleur dans mon esprit. Mais comment cette interaction causale fonctionne-t-elle exactement? Comment notre esprit peut-il causalement affecter notre corps, et notre corps causalement affecter notre esprit ? La solution novatrice de Leibniz à ce problème du rapport esprit-corps suggère qu'ils ne le peuvent tout simplement pas. L'interaction entre notre esprit et notre corps, laquelle nous semble si évidente, n'est en réalité qu'une illusion, quoique « bien fondée ». Selon Leibniz, dès le moment de la création, Dieu a coordonné les corps et les esprits de telle manière qu'ils interagissent de manière causale seulement en apparence. Au moment précis où je forme l'intention de déplacer ma jambe, mon esprit en vient, de façon indépendante, à l'expérience de la douleur. Mon esprit et mon corps sont, suggère Leibniz, comme deux horloges causalement indépendantes, mais synchronisées; l'apparence d'interaction causale entre elles est une illusion fondée sur l'harmonie préétablie par Dieu[1].

La théorie de l'harmonie préétablie de Leibniz est d'ailleurs plus audacieuse qu'elle n'y paraît. Car chaque esprit, selon Leibniz, est non seulement en harmonie avec son propre corps, mais aussi avec tous les autres corps existants. En s'appuyant sur des considérations théoriques générales, Leibniz insiste sur le fait que chaque esprit perçoit tout ce qui arrive dans son monde[2]. Je perçois non seulement le ballon devant moi, mais aussi – souvent seulement de manière inconsciente – les événements

1. *Éclaircissement des difficultés que Monsieur Bayle a trouvées dans le système nouveau de l'union de l'âme et du corps*, GP IV, 520.

2. Voir, par exemple, *Principes de la nature et de la grâce fondés en raison*, § 3, GP VI, 598-599.

qui se produisent à l'autre bout de la ville, à l'autre bout de la terre, et, d'ailleurs, à l'autre bout de l'univers. Lorsqu'un changement arrive dans un corps, peu importe lequel, et peu importe son lieu, un changement se produit dans mon esprit. Inversement, Leibniz maintient que tout esprit est associé à un corps, et que tous les corps sont « connectés ». De sorte que lorsqu'un changement arrive dans un quelconque esprit, en relation à un changement correspondant dans son corps, des effets de propagation se produisent dans les autres corps existants[1]. Ultimement, la théorie de l'harmonie préétablie de Leibniz exige ainsi non simplement la coordination divine de paires particulières esprits/corps, mais, de manière plus audacieuse, la coordination divine de chaque esprit avec tous les corps existants et de chaque corps avec tous les esprits existants.

Leibniz défend sa théorie de l'harmonie préétablie en soulignant ce qu'il considère comme étant ses nombreuses vertus. Il soutient qu'elle aide à concilier la métaphysique aristotélico-scolastique avec la science mécanique[2]; qu'elle attribue une « correspondance » entre les substances, ce qui est « une chose admirablement belle en elle-même et digne de son Auteur »[3]. Elle lui permet d'expliquer pourquoi, bien que les esprits et les corps ne puissent interagir de manière causale, ils semblent toutefois interagir causalement, et peuvent même être dits interagir ainsi, de la même manière que les coperniciens peuvent « véritablement » parler du lever du soleil[4]. Il soutient que sa théorie de l'harmonie préétablie fournit une nouvelle explication de l'union entre l'âme et le corps, puisque « c'est ce rapport mutuel réglé par avance dans chaque substance de l'univers [...] qui fait uniquement *l'union de l'âme et du corps* »[5]. Mais peut-être que sa plus grande vertu, du point de vue de Leibniz, est de ne faire face à aucun adversaire de taille. Leibniz croit que les principales théories alternatives à sa théorie de l'harmonie préétablie s'effondreraient après examen.

Leibniz surnomme l'une de ces solutions de rechange la théorie de l'influence physique (*influxus physicus*). La théorie de l'influence physique, selon la manière dont Leibniz la comprend, suggère que l'esprit et le corps interagissent de manière causale lorsque quelque chose – une

1. *Principia logica-metaphysica*, A VI, 4, 1646-1647.

2. *Système nouveau de la nature et de la communication des substances*, GP IV, 478-479.

3. *Éclaircissement du nouveau système de la communication des substances*, GP IV, 494.

4. « Éclaircissement du nouveau système de la communication des substances, pour servir de réponse à ce qui en a été dit dans le journal du 12 septembre 1695 », *Journal des savants*, 14, 2 avril 1696, p. 167.

5. *Système nouveau de la nature*, GP IV, 484-485. Voir également : *Remarques de l'Auteur du Système de l'Harmonie préétablie sur un endroit des Mémoires de Trévoux du Mars 1704*, GP VI, 595.

certaine forme d'être – passe d'une substance à une autre. Même si sur ce point précis ils furent souvent vagues, l'idée leibnizienne selon laquelle plusieurs de ses prédécesseurs adoptèrent une telle conception n'est pas sans fondement[1]. Dans sa discussion systématique, et qui a fait autorité en matière de causalité, le grand scolastique du XVIIe siècle, Francisco Suarez, écrit ceci :

> Une cause est un principe qui influence *per se* un autre être. [...] Par cette expression, influencer *per se*, on exclut la privation ou toutes les autres causes *per accidens* qui ne sont pas reliées *per se* ou n'influencent pas un autre être. Le verbe influencer devrait être pris [...] de manière plus générale comme l'équivalent d'être donné ou communiqué à un autre être[2].

La définition de Suarez suggère en effet que la véritable causalité se produit lorsqu'une cause transfère une certaine forme d'être à ses effets. Cela implique que mon pied est la cause du mouvement du ballon de football en lui transférant quelque chose – peut-être du mouvement ou de l'énergie – et que l'image, disons, de Pelé est la cause de ma représentation mentale de Pelé, puisque quelque chose est transféré de l'image de Pelé, ou de quelque chose de similaire, d'abord dans un milieu corporel, ensuite à mes organes sensoriels, et ultimement à mon esprit.

Leibniz rejette la théorie de l'influence physique autant comme théorie générale de la causalité que comme explication plus précise de l'interaction causale entre l'esprit et le corps. Il la rejette comme théorie générale de la causalité parce qu'il croit qu'il est simplement inconcevable que quelque chose puisse être transféré d'une substance à une autre. Par exemple, il écrit : « on ne saurait concevoir ni des particules matérielles, ni des espèces ou qualités immatérielles, qui puissent passer d'une de ces substances dans l'autre »[3]. Si elle prétend à une pleine généralité, la position de Leibniz n'est cependant pas extrêmement convaincante. Est-ce si difficile de concevoir, disons, des particules matérielles passant d'un corps matériel à un autre ? L'argument de Leibniz pourrait néanmoins sembler plus fort lorsqu'on le restreint à l'interaction causale entre l'esprit et le corps (ou entre les esprits). On sait que Leibniz soutient que les monades – qui sont des substances similaires à des esprits – « n'ont point de

1. Pour une discussion sur la théorie de l'influence physique, en particulier dans sa relation à Leibniz, voir E. O'Neill, « *Influxus Physicus* ». Pour une histoire de la théorie après Leibniz, voir E. Watkins, « The Development of Physical Influx in Early Eighteenth-Century Germany ».

2. Suarez, *Disputationes*, 25, 384b.

3. *Éclaircissement du nouveau système de la communication des substances, pour servir de réponse à ce qui en est dit dans le Journal du 12 septembre 1695*, GP IV, 499.

fenêtres, par lesquelles quelque chose y puisse entrer ou sortir »[1]. Si l'on accepte une telle idée, il est alors clair que les interactions causales entre l'esprit et le corps (ou entre les esprits) ne peuvent être comprises selon les termes de la théorie de l'influence physique. Car si rien ne peut aller à l'intérieur ou à l'extérieur des esprits, alors ceux-ci ne peuvent pas non plus recevoir quelque chose ou s'en départir, y compris des formes d'être, comme l'exige la théorie de l'influence physique.

Une deuxième solution de rechange à la théorie leibnizienne de l'harmonie préétablie est la théorie de l'occasionnalisme. La théorie de l'occasionnalisme jouissait déjà d'une longue histoire avant l'époque de Leibniz, et ce depuis la philosophie médiévale arabe et latine. Elle trouva cependant une nouvelle impulsion compte tenu de remarques suggestives de Descartes, et elle fut développée de différentes manières par des cartésiens de seconde génération, tels Géraud de Cordemoy, Louis de la Forge, Arnold Geulincx, Johannes Clauberg et, surtout, Nicolas Malebranche[2]. L'idée centrale de l'occasionnalisme est que Dieu est la seule véritable cause efficace dans le monde. Les créatures sont dépourvues de toute efficacité causale propre et ne servent que de simples occasions à l'intervention causale et directe de Dieu. Ma volonté de frapper le ballon ne cause ainsi pas le mouvement de ma jambe. Celle-ci sert simplement d'occasion pour Dieu de déplacer lui-même le ballon. L'impact du ballon sur mes mains ne cause pas en moi une sensation de douleur. Il sert plutôt d'occasion pour Dieu d'affecter directement mon esprit. Bien qu'elle ne soit pas populaire aujourd'hui, la théorie de l'occasionnalisme attirait de nombreux partisans à l'époque de Leibniz et était soutenue par un ensemble impressionnant d'arguments, dont certains continuent de motiver des considérations contemporaines au sujet de la causalité.

Leibniz rejette l'occasionnalisme pour une grande diversité de raisons. Une première ligne argumentative provient de sa conception de la nature des substances créées. Selon Leibniz, il est essentiel que les substances créées soient le lieu de l'activité causale[3]. Supposer que les créatures ne bénéficient d'aucune efficacité causale propre les réduirait à n'être que de simples modes de Dieu. D'après la conception que s'en fait Leibniz,

1. *Monadologie*, § 7, GP VI, 607.

2. Pour une vue d'ensemble du développement de la théorie de l'occasionnalisme, voir H. Gouhier, *La Vocation de Malebranche*; S. Nadler, *Occasionalism : Causation Among the Cartesians*; J. Prost, *Essai sur l'atomisme et l'occasionalisme dans la philosophie cartésienne*.

3. Voir *De ipsa natura*, GP IV, 515.

l'occasionnalisme se confond ainsi avec la doctrine de Spinoza, puisque « elle paraît faire de Dieu, d'accord avec Spinoza, la nature même des choses : car ce qui n'agit pas, ce qui est dépourvu de puissance active, de toute marque distinctive, en un mot ce qui est privé de toute raison de subsister, cela ne peut en aucune façon être une substance »[1]. Une autre ligne argumentative provient de la conception qu'a Leibniz de la perfection de Dieu. Leibniz maintient que sa théorie de l'harmonie préétablie, selon laquelle la création de Dieu est si parfaite qu'elle ne requiert pas d'intervention corrective subséquente, convient davantage à la perfection divine que la théorie de l'occasionnalisme, laquelle requerrait que Dieu joue constamment avec sa création.

En présentant sa théorie de l'harmonie préétablie, Leibniz discute souvent de l'existence de deux domaines, un domaine des corps et de la causalité efficiente, d'une part, et un domaine des âmes et de la causalité finale, d'autre part. Par exemple, dans la *Monadologie*, Leibniz écrit : « Les âmes agissent selon les lois des causes finales par appétitions, fins et moyens. Les corps agissent selon les lois des causes efficientes ou des mouvements. Et les deux règnes, celui des causes efficientes et celui des causes finales, sont harmoniques entre eux »[2]. De manière similaire, dans ses *Principes de la nature et de la grâce*, Leibniz nous dit que : « les changements des corps et les phénomènes au dehors naissent les uns des autres par les lois des causes efficientes, c'est-à-dire des mouvements », tandis que les « perceptions dans la Monade naissent les unes des autres par les lois des appétits, ou des causes finales du bien et du mal »[3]. De telles remarques suggèrent une vision intuitive, voire séduisante. Les esprits se développent de façon téléologique, c'est-à-dire qu'ils agissent selon certaines fins. Je veux, par exemple, frapper le ballon afin de marquer un but. Les corps se développent de manière efficiente, c'est-à-dire qu'ils sont déterminés par des causes efficientes en accord avec les lois de la nature. Le ballon de football, par exemple, voyage avec une vitesse donnée parce que mon pied l'a frappé avec une vitesse donnée. Cette vision intuitive – selon laquelle l'harmonie préétablie leibnizienne entre esprits et corps est simultanément une harmonie préétablie entre les causes finales et efficientes – est élégante et exacte en soi. Mais ce n'est pas la fin de l'histoire. Les deux prochaines sections montreront que l'harmonie préétablie de Leibniz entre l'esprit et le corps est étayée par deux autres

1. *De ipsa natura*, GP IV, 515, Schrecker, 233.
2. *Monadologie*, § 79, GP VI, 620.
3. *Principes de la nature et de la grâce*, § 3, GP VI, 599.

harmonies que l'on considère moins souvent, l'une au sein du domaine des corps, l'autre au sein du domaine des esprits.

LA CAUSALITÉ DANS LE DOMAINE DES CORPS

Mon pied frappe le ballon de football et il s'envole avec une vitesse et une direction données. Il ricoche sur le poteau du but avec une vitesse différente et une nouvelle direction. Il est possible qu'elle entre ensuite en collision avec un autre ballon sur la ligne de touche, ce qui les enverrait tous les deux dans des trajectoires prévisibles. Comment pouvons-nous donner la meilleure explication de telles interactions entre les corps matériels, à savoir entre le pied et le ballon, entre le ballon et le poteau, entre les ballons, etc. ? Leibniz est d'accord avec ses contemporains qui sont partisans de la nouvelle science et pour qui les comportements des corps doivent être expliqués, de manière paradigmatique, en faisant appel aux lois de la nature, comme la loi de Galilée de la chute des corps et la troisième loi du mouvement de Newton[1]. Leibniz contribua à ce projet de formulation et d'amélioration des lois de la nature. Il propose des critiques dévastatrices des lois cartésiennes du choc[2]. Il défend avec vigueur une série de lois de conservation, y compris, la plus célèbre, la conservation de la *vis viva*[3]. Il propose de nouvelles dérivations des principales lois de l'optique[4]. En ce qui nous concerne, cependant, Leibniz cherche à clarifier ce qu'il considère comme étant les implications philosophiques des lois de la nature, défendant, en particulier, trois thèses principales.

La première thèse concerne le statut modal des lois de la nature. Les lois, telle la loi galiléenne de la chute des corps, sont-elles nécessaires ou contingentes ? Descartes donna une description extrêmement influente des lois du mouvement et qui impliquait selon plusieurs que les lois de la nature devaient être nécessaires. Le même résultat semble suivre dans le système de Spinoza. Selon cette opinion, les lois doivent être ce qu'elles sont. On ne pourrait invalider la loi galiléenne de la chute des corps pas plus qu'on ne pourrait le faire pour les lois de la géométrie et de l'arithmétique. Une autre opinion, attribuée par Bayle à Leibniz, et qui domine toujours aujourd'hui,

1. Pour une vue d'ensemble utile de l'émergence des explications causales dans la science moderne, voir J. R. Milton, « Laws of Nature ».

2. *Lettre de M. L. sur un principe général utile à l'Explication des lois de la nature*, GP III, 53 ; Lettre à Bayle, GP III, 46.

3. *De legibus naturae*, GM VI, 226-231.

4. Voir en particulier : *Unicum opticae, catoptricae et dioptricae principium,* Dutens III, 145-150 ; *Tentamen Anagogicum*, GP VII, 270-279.

est que les lois de la nature sont contingentes et arbitraires[1]. Selon cette opinion, la loi de Galilée est vraie par hasard. Le monde aurait pu être bien différent en ce qui concerne la chute des corps : au lieu de tomber selon une accélération constante, les corps auraient pu tomber selon une vitesse constante ou une accélération variable. Par ailleurs, selon cette opinion, il n'y a aucune raison décisive qui serait favorable à la loi de Galilée. Si l'on imagine – comme le faisaient la plupart des philosophes modernes – que Dieu a créé le monde, on peut imaginer qu'il lui serait indifférent ou au moins qu'on ne s'en prenne pas à lui d'avoir créé un monde en accord avec la loi de Galilée.

Leibniz s'oppose à ces deux opinions qui – selon sa perspective – sont extrêmes. Il maintient que les lois de la nature ne sont ni nécessaires ni arbitraires. Elles sont plutôt contingentes, mais néanmoins déterminées par des considérations d'optimalité. Ainsi, dans les *Essais de théodicée*, il écrit :

> Ces considérations font bien voir que les lois de la nature qui règlent les mouvements ne sont ni tout à fait nécessaires, ni entièrement arbitraires. Le milieu qu'il y a à prendre, est qu'elles sont un choix de la plus parfaite sagesse. Et ce grand exemple des lois du mouvement fait voir le plus clairement du monde, combien il y a de différence entre ces trois cas, savoir premièrement une nécessité absolue, métaphysique ou géométrique, qu'on peut appeler aveugle et qui ne dépend que des causes efficientes ; en second lieu, une nécessité morale, qui vient du choix libre de la sagesse par rapport aux causes finales; et enfin en troisième lieu, quelque chose d'arbitraire absolument, dépendant d'une indifférence d'équilibre qu'on se figure, mais qui ne saurait exister, où il n'y a aucune raison suffisante ni dans la cause efficiente ni dans la finale[2].

En effet, Leibniz suggère que Descartes et Bayle ont tous les deux tort. Descartes a tort parce que dans un certain sens les lois de la nature sont contingentes. Si l'on fait abstraction de la sagesse de Dieu, on peut imaginer Dieu créant le monde avec des lois différentes. À cet égard, les lois de la nature ne sont donc pas comme les lois de l'arithmétique ou de la géométrie. Mais Bayle – du moins selon la manière dont Leibniz l'interprète – a également tort. Bien que les lois de la nature soient contingentes, elles ne sont pourtant pas arbitraires. D'après Leibniz, Dieu a choisi d'instancier les lois actuelles de la nature, non d'un coup de tête ou par

1. *Essais de théodicée*, § 340 et 344, GP VI, 316 et 318-319.

2. *Ibid.*, § 349, GP VI, 321. Voir également § 345, GP VI, 319 et *Principes de la nature et de la grâce*, § 11, GP VI, 603.

fantaisie, mais parce qu'elles sont essentielles au meilleur des mondes possibles[1].

La deuxième thèse de Leibniz concerne ce qu'on pourrait considérer comme la métaphysique des lois de la nature. Quelles sont les lois de la nature et comment gouvernent-elles le monde? Parler en termes de lois de la nature, de leur création, de leur découverte, etc. pourrait laisser entendre que les lois de la nature sont comme des choses, qu'elles sont des ingrédients indépendants du monde, à l'égal des esprits et des corps. Mais ce n'est pas le portrait que donne Leibniz. L'ontologie fondamentale leibnizienne relativement au monde créé se restreint aux seules substances, c'est-à-dire aux unités véritables, sous le modèle des esprits ou des organismes. N'étant pas des unités véritables – n'étant pas comme des esprits ou des organismes – les lois de la nature ne peuvent faire partie des ingrédients fondamentaux du monde créé. Elles doivent plutôt être identifiées, selon Leibniz, aux concepts ou abstractions dont bénéficient les esprits rationnels et qui sont applicables aux événements du monde. La loi galiléenne de la chute des corps n'est pas une chose, mais un modèle, une régularité ou une règle compris par Dieu et les autres esprits intelligents. Selon cette perspective, il est immédiatement clair que, pour Leibniz, les lois de la nature ne peuvent gouverner les corps, disons, en les poussant ou les tirant autour d'elles. Leibniz maintient plutôt que les corps sont déterminés dans leur comportement par des forces qui se situent à l'intérieur des corps eux-mêmes. Les corps lourds près de la surface de la Terre tombent selon une accélération constante non parce que les lois de la nature les poussent ou les tirent, mais plutôt parce qu'ils sont dotés de pouvoirs intrinsèques qui les dirigent à tomber selon une accélération constante. Pour Leibniz, les lois de la nature ont une puissance explicative dans la mesure où elles nous permettent de subsumer des phénomènes particuliers sous des régularités générales, mais elles n'ont pas de puissance causale au sens où elles provoqueraient directement les comportements qu'elles subsument.

Leibniz soutient que son explication de l'efficacité des lois de la nature est supérieure à celle que fournissent les occasionnalistes comme Malebranche. Malebranche identifie les lois de la nature à des décrets divins. Mais comment de tels décrets devraient-ils réguler le comportement des corps? Leibniz soutient que si les lois de la nature sont identifiées à des

1. Pour une discussion sur la conception leibnizienne de la contingence en relation avec les lois de la nature, voir K. Okruhlik, « The Status of Scientific Laws in the Leibnizian System » ; J. McDonough, « Leibniz's Optics and Contingency in Nature » ; C. Wilson, « Leibniz's Dynamics and Contingency in Nature ».

décrets généraux conçus dès le début de la création, et non fondés sur les pouvoirs intrinsèques des corps, alors elles ne peuvent être efficaces, car « le commandement fait dans le passé n'existe plus maintenant, il ne peut pas non plus avoir d'efficace actuelle, à moins qu'il n'ait laissé après lui quelque effet subsistant qui dure et qui opère maintenant encore »[1]. N'était-il pas possible que les lois de la nature soient tout de même identifiées à des décrets généraux et que leur efficacité soit fondée sur des volontés particulières de Dieu, des volontés conçues en accord avec ces décrets généraux[2] ? Leibniz ne croit pas qu'il s'agisse d'une meilleure solution. Car il soutient que des miracles se produiraient dès qu'une chose arriverait, « qui passe les forces des créatures », comme s'il arrivait, par exemple, que l'eau brûle ou que les cochons volent[3]. D'après cette compréhension des miracles, Leibniz soutient que si l'efficacité des lois de la nature était fondée sur les volontés particulières de Dieu, alors Dieu serait tenu d'accomplir des miracles constamment. Étant donné qu'une telle activité serait indigne de la sagesse divine, Leibniz en conclut que les occasionnalistes échouent à proposer une conception défendable de la nature et de l'efficacité des lois de la nature.

La troisième thèse centrale de Leibniz concerne le rôle des explications téléologiques dans les sciences naturelles. On sait que Descartes avait affirmé ne pas recourir aux causes finales dans sa physique[4]. Selon plusieurs, Spinoza semblerait faire un pas de plus en suggérant que les explications téléologiques prennent l'ordre d'explication dans le mauvais sens et que les causes finales ne sont « rien que des fictions humaines »[5]. Bien qu'il reconnaisse les limites des explications scolastiques antérieures, Leibniz soutient néanmoins qu'un rejet en bloc de l'explication téléologique n'est ni nécessaire ni prudent. Comme plusieurs partisans de la nouvelle science, Leibniz est disposé à reconnaître que nous ne pouvons espérer connaître toutes les fins de Dieu, mais il ne voit aucune raison de supposer que nous ne pouvons en discerner quelques-unes[6]. Il se plaint qu'« il est déraisonnable d'introduire une intelligence souveraine

1. *De ipsa natura*, GP IV, 507, Schrecker, 203-205.

2. Pour une discussion des idées de Malebranche quant à la nature et l'efficacité des lois de la nature, voir S. Nadler, « Occasionalism and General Will in Malebranche ».

3. *Éclaircissement des difficultés que Monsieur Bayle a trouvées dans le système nouveau de l'union de l'âme et du corps*, GP IV, 520.

4. Descartes, *Principia philosophiae*, AT VIII, 15-16; *Meditationes de prima philosophia*, AT VII, 55.

5. Spinoza, *Éthique* I, « Appendice ».

6. *Animadversiones circa assertiones aliquas Theoria Medica verae Clar. Stahlii*, Dutens, II/2, 132.

ordonnatrice des choses, et puis au lieu d'employer sa sagesse, ne se servir que des propriétés de la matière pour expliquer les phénomènes »[1]. Il soutient plus loin que « la voie des finales » est souvent utile pour faire des découvertes dans le domaine de la nature, et que l'étude de l'anatomie fournit un cas évident de son usage effectif[2].

Le travail de Leibniz sur les lois de l'optique lui fournit une autre voie, mais moins évidente, pour défendre les explications téléologiques. À la fin des années 1670, Leibniz en est venu à constater que la loi de réflexion pourrait être dérivée du principe selon lequel, comme il le dit : « la nature, se proposant une fin, choisit les moyens optimaux »[3]. Au début des années 1680, Leibniz put fournir une explication unifiée de deux lois centrales de la géométrie optique – la loi de réflexion et la loi de réfraction – en montrant que les deux suivent le principe suivant lequel la lumière voyage toujours selon les « chemins les plus faciles » (les chemins les plus faciles se définissant en l'occurrence avec rigueur en termes de distance et de résistances dans les milieux concernés)[4]. Leibniz continua de développer son approche des lois de l'optique dans les décennies qui suivirent en montrant, par exemple dans le *Tentamen Anagogicum* de 1696, comment les chemins optimaux pourraient être déterminés dans des cas plus difficiles impliquant des miroirs concaves et convexes[5]. Dans une série d'études innovantes, Leibniz montra comment des raisonnements similaires pourraient aussi être appliqués afin de résoudre des problèmes spécifiques de mécanique. Les techniques inventées par Leibniz dans ses études d'optique et de mécanique annoncèrent ce qu'on appelle maintenant les principes variationnels – des principes explicatifs puissants qui ressemblent à des lois et qui sont encore employés aujourd'hui dans l'étude du monde naturel[6].

Leibniz suggère que ce que l'on pourrait appeler ses « principes d'optimalité » appuie les explications téléologiques dans le monde naturel de deux manières différentes. D'abord, Leibniz croit que les principes

1. *Discours de métaphysique*, § 19, A VI, 4, 1561.

2. *Ibid.*, § 22, A VI, 4, p. 1565.

3. *Definitiones cogitationesque metaphysicae*, A VI, 4, 1404.

4. *Unicum opticae, catoptricae et dioptricae principium*, Dutens, III, 145-150.

5. *Tentamen Anagogicum*, GP VII, 270-279.

6. Pour une discussion sur l'histoire du développement des principes variationnels, voir H. Goldstine, *A History of the Calculus of Variations from the 17th through the 19th Century*; R. Woodhouse, *A History of the Calculus of Variations in the Eighteenth Century*. Pour une discussion chez Leibniz de l'application de raisonnement trouvé dans ses études d'optique à des problèmes spécifiques de mécanique, voir J. McDonough, « Leibniz and the Foundations of Physics : The Later Years » ; *id.*, « Leibniz on Monadic Agency and Optimal Form ».

d'optimalité – comme l'élégance des lois du mouvement ou la simplicité des principes de conservation – appuient les arguments téléologiques de planification en indiquant qu'elles « marquent que l'univers est l'effet d'une puissance intelligente universelle » et en révélant « la sagesse de l'auteur dans l'ordre et dans la perfection de l'ouvrage »[1]. Ensuite, Leibniz maintient également que les principes d'optimalité autorisent les explications téléologiques dans l'ordre de la nature. Ainsi, il nous dit que : « Les causes finales [...] sont souvent employées par les physiques spéciales pour leur grandeur et aussi leur fécondité, non seulement pour que nous admirions davantage le plus bel ouvrage de l'auteur suprême, mais aussi pour que nous devinions parfois la méthode de découverte d'une telle production qui ne le serait sinon que de manière hypothétique »[2]. Ici l'idée de Leibniz est que de la même manière qu'on pourrait expliquer la course d'un joueur sur le terrain pour empêcher un adversaire de compter, un philosophe naturel – en s'appuyant sur les principes d'optimalité – pourrait expliquer le comportement d'un rayon de lumière en s'appuyant sur son « but » de suivre un chemin optimal. Pour Leibniz, les principes d'optimalité appuient ainsi les explications téléologiques divines et naturelles.

Si l'on prend un peu de recul, on peut voir que l'explication leibnizienne de la causalité dans le monde naturel est plus compliquée qu'elle n'apparaissait au départ. À l'égard des corps dans le monde naturel, Leibniz accepte le cadre explicatif élargi suggéré par la nouvelle science. Les comportements des corps doivent être expliqués en s'appuyant sur les lois de la nature. Cependant, il propose un portrait distinct de la nature et de l'efficacité causale des lois de la nature. Les lois elles-mêmes sont des concepts ou abstractions correspondant aux événements dans le monde naturel. Ces événements sont provoqués par des forces intrinsèques aux corps eux-mêmes. À la manière de l'interaction apparente entre l'esprit et le corps, les interactions entre les corps sont pour Leibniz ultimement fondées sur l'harmonie préétablie. Par ailleurs, Leibniz ne défend pas seulement la conception des lois de la nature elles-mêmes, mais aussi les explications téléologiques dans le domaine de la nature, suggérant que les corps matériels pourraient être expliqués en s'appuyant sur les causes finales. Ce qui implique cependant que même parmi les corps eux-mêmes, il existe non seulement une harmonie préétablie entre les corps, mais aussi une harmonie entre les causalités finale et efficiente.

1. *Tentamen Anagogicum*, GP VII, 270 et 272.
2. *Essais de théodicée*, § 209, GP VI, 243.

LA CAUSALITÉ DANS LE DOMAINE DES ESPRITS

Les fondements de la métaphysique leibnizienne de la maturité se limitent aux monades, similaires aux esprits. On le sait, la *Monadologie* s'ouvra ainsi avec l'idée que « La *Monade*, dont nous parlerons ici, n'est autre chose, qu'une substance simple, qui entre dans les composés ... Et il faut qu'il y ait des substances simples, puisqu'il y a des composés; car le composé n'est autre chose, qu'un amas, ou *aggregatum* des simples »[1]. Dans un passage un peu plus instructif de la même période, Leibniz écrit :

> La substance est soit simple, comme l'âme qui n'a pas de parties, soit composée, comme l'animal qui consiste dans une âme et dans un corps organique. [...] on voit qu'il ne consiste qu'en substances simples et qu'en elles réside la source de toutes les choses et modifications qui leur adviennent[2].

Alors que les commentateurs sont toujours en désaccord concernant la nature exacte de la relation métaphysique entre les monades et les corps, la plupart sont d'accord pour dire que, dans la période de maturité, Leibniz croit que l'activité causale des créatures se fonde ultimement sur les monades, et non sur les corps.

Selon Leibniz, les monades contiennent des perceptions et des appétits. En vertu de leurs perceptions, les monades perçoivent le monde autour d'elles. En effet, Leibniz maintient qu'en vertu de leurs perceptions, chaque monade perçoit, depuis son propre point de vue, conscient ou inconscient, tout ce qui est arrivé, arrive et arrivera dans son monde[3]. D'après Leibniz, je ne perçois pas seulement le ballon en face de moi, mais aussi les choses qui arrivent au même moment à l'autre bout de la ville, les choses qui sont déjà arrivées à l'autre bout de la Terre et les choses qui arriveront à l'autre bout de l'univers. Et chacun d'entre nous, bien sûr, fait quelque chose de similaire à partir de notre propre point de vue distinct. En vertu de leurs appétits, les monades passent d'un état perceptuel à un suivant. Ainsi, les appétits constituent, comme il l'écrit : « L'action du principe interne, qui fait le changement ou le passage d'une perception à une autre »[4]. Comme c'est le cas des perceptions, chaque monade bénéficie de son propre ensemble d'appétits, qui, dans leur grande majorité, n'émergent pourtant pas au niveau de l'attention consciente. Je pourrais

1. *Monadologie*, § 1-2, GP VI, 607.

2. *Sur le principe de raison*, C, 13-14, R, 474-475.

3. *Principes de la nature et de la grâce*, § 3, GP VI, 598-599; *Monadologie*, § 60, GP VI, 617.

4. *Monadologie*, § 15, GP VI, 609.

porter consciemment attention à mon désir de marquer un but, mais être inconscient de mon désir faible de me gratter le bas de la jambe.

Plus loin, Leibniz fait la distinction entre trois genres de monades sur la base de leurs capacités représentationnelles. Le genre le plus bas de monade – ce que Leibniz appelle les « monades simples » – a des perceptions qui sont typiquement très confuses. Leibniz nous dit que « si nous n'avions rien de distingué et pour ainsi dire de relevé, et d'un plus haut goût dans nos perceptions, nous serions toujours dans l'étourdissement. Et c'est l'état des Monades toutes nues »[1]. Les « âmes » des plantes servent de modèle de ce que sont les monades simples. Les monades du niveau intermédiaire – ce que Leibniz appelle les monades « sensitives » – ont non seulement des perceptions confuses, mais aussi l'aptitude à porter consciemment attention aux entités distinctes en tant qu'entités distinctes[2]. Les âmes des animaux servent de modèle de ce que sont les monades sensitives. Le plus haut genre de monades – ce que Leibniz appelle les esprits – a des perceptions qui leur fournissent des pensées d'ordre supérieur – l'aptitude à réfléchir à leurs propres perceptions et à elles-mêmes. Leibniz maintient que parce qu'ils bénéficient de pensées d'ordre supérieur, les esprits sont capables de saisir des vérités nécessaires concernant la moralité, les mathématiques et la métaphysique[3]. Les âmes humaines servent d'exemple paradigmatique de ce que sont les esprits.

En considérant la théorie de l'harmonie préétablie de Leibniz, il est clair que les monades doivent se déployer de manière téléologique. Et il est assez facile de constater comment cela est possible dans le cas des esprits. Je suis aux prises avec un ensemble de perceptions, certaines claires et manifestes, d'autres confuses et faibles. Je vois un adversaire avec le ballon se diriger vers le but de mon équipe, je veux l'empêcher de marquer. Ces appétits déterminent ou aident à déterminer ce que je ressentirai par la suite. Bien qu'il n'existe pas d'interaction causale directe entre mon esprit et mon corps, mes appétits me conduisent d'un état perceptuel à un autre. Mon appétit – mon désir – d'empêcher l'adversaire de marquer un but contribue de manière causale à l'apparition de nouvelles perceptions, disons, de déplacer ma jambe, de me rapprocher de mon adversaire, etc. Bien que cette description nécessiterait d'entrer dans plus de détails, il est relativement facile de voir comment on pourrait comprendre le développement téléologique des monades dans les cas d'action intentionnelle et volontaire.

1. *Monadologie*, § 24, GP VI, 611.
2. *Nouveaux essais sur l'entendement humain*, II, chap. XXI, § 5, A VI, 6, 173.
3. *Principes de la nature et de la grâce*, § 5, GP VI, 600-601.

Il est moins clair d'expliquer comment on devrait comprendre le développement téléologique des monades dans les cas d'action non intentionnelle et involontaire. On sait que Pierre Bayle soulève précisément ce problème dans une note de son *Dictionnaire historique et critique*. Bayle note que, selon la théorie de l'harmonie préétablie de Leibniz, il existe un sens pour lequel l'âme d'un chien « sentirait la faim et la soif à telle et telle heure, quand même il n'y aurait aucun corps dans l'univers » puisque l'âme du chien se développe sans aucune intervention causale et directe avec son corps. Bayle objecte toutefois :

> [...] je ne saurais comprendre l'enchainement d'actions internes & spontanées, qui ferait que l'âme d'un chien sentirait de la douleur immédiatement après avoir senti de la joie, quand même elle serait seule dans l'Univers. Je comprends pourquoi un chien passe immédiatement du plaisir à la douleur, lors qu'étant bien affamé, et mangeant du pain, on lui donne subitement un coup de bâton; mais que son âme soit construite de telle sorte, qu'au moment qu'il est frappé il sentirait de la douleur, quand même il continuerait de manger du pain sans trouble ni empêchement, c'est ce que je ne saurais comprendre [1].

Bayle trouve la spontanéité de l'âme du chien, tel que l'exige la théorie de l'harmonie préétablie de Leibniz, « fort incompatible [...] avec les sentiments de douleur » [2]. Mais on pourrait y voir un problème encore plus général. Supposons qu'on accepte qu'il soit possible de comprendre comment les monades pourraient se développer de manière téléologique dans les cas impliquant des actions intentionnelles et volontaires. On pourrait toujours se demander si l'on peut vraiment comprendre comment les monades se développent de manière téléologique dans les cas où leurs états représentationnels successifs ne sont pas intentionnels ou volontaires, ou bien parce qu'ils ne sont pas du tout perçus comme étant bons, comme il semble être le cas du chien de Bayle, ou bien parce qu'ils ne sont pas du tout perçus de façon consciente, comme ce sera toujours le cas pour les monades simples (et de même la plupart du temps pour les monades plus élevées).

Les commentateurs ne sont pas d'accord quant à la manière dont ils croient que Leibniz répond ou devrait répondre aux inquiétudes de Bayle. Une première ligne interprétative suggère qu'on devrait toujours comprendre le développement téléologique des monades sur le modèle de

1. Bayle, *Dictionnaire historique et critique*, « Rorarius », note H.
2. *Ibid.*

l'action intentionnelle et volontaire[1]. Que Leibniz pensât lui-même adopter cette réponse est suggéré par l'une de ses lettres à Sophie Charlotte du 8 mai 1704. Il y écrit :

> Quand nous voyons [...] l'âme suivre les lois morales du bien et du mal apparent dans quelque délibération : disons des autres cas que nous ne voyons pas ou que nous ne démêlons pas si bien, qu'il en est de même, et que c'est tout comme ici. C'est-à-dire, expliquons les choses dont nous n'avons qu'une connaissance confuse, par celles dont nous en avons une distincte, et disons que [...] tout se fait moralement dans l'âme, ou suivant les apparences du bien et du mal, tellement que même dans nos instincts ou dans les actions involontaires où le seul corps paraît avoir part, il y a dans l'âme un appétit du bien ou une fuite du mal qui la pousse, quoique notre réflexion ne puisse point en démêler la confusion[2].

La réflexion de Leibniz suggère ici que même si le comportement des monades simples ne peut être exactement celui du comportement des esprits, néanmoins l'expérience de notre propre esprit nous donne la meilleure et la seule compréhension de ce qu'est une monade simple. De la même manière qu'on calque les appétits et perceptions inconscientes sur les appétits et perceptions conscientes, on devrait calquer le développement causal des monades simples – et de toutes les monades dans la mesure où elles sont comme des monades simples – sur notre propre développement causal. De cette façon, comme Leibniz le dit dans une autre lettre de 1704, mais cette fois-ci à Damaris Masham : « les actions internes dans l'âme : le tout ne consistant que dans l'état présent joint à la tendance aux changements, qui se font dans [...] l'âme suivant les perceptions du bien et du mal »[3].

Une autre ligne d'interprétation suggère que les monades bénéficient de plusieurs genres d'appétits[4]. Certains appétits sont des appétits intentionnels et volontaires, ce sont des appétits calqués sur les désirs et liés à la perception propre du bien de la monade. Lorsque je suis motivé à frapper le ballon, mon expérience est conduite par de tels appétits, par mon désir de frapper le ballon et par ma considération que frapper le ballon est une bonne chose. D'autres appétits sont des appétits non intentionnels et involontaires. Lorsqu'un chien est frappé par un bâton, il passe à des

1. *Cf.* M. B. Bolton, « Change in the Monad » ; J. Carriero, « Substance and Ends in Leibniz », p. 115-140 ; J. McDonough, « Leibniz on Monadic Agency and Optimal Form ».

2. GP III, 346-347.

3. GP III, p. 341.

4. J. Jorati, « Monadic Teleology Without Goodness and Without God », p. 43-72 ; M. Rozemond, « Leibniz on Final Causation » ; D. Rutherford, « Leibniz on Spontaneity », p. 156-180.

perceptions de douleur. Mais il n'est pas conduit à ces perceptions douloureuses par des appétits intentionnels et volontaires. Néanmoins, il doit être conduit à ces perceptions par certains appétits – comme on l'a vu, Leibniz maintient que chaque monade est causalement isolée aussi bien des corps que des autres monades. Or, selon cette ligne d'interprétation, les monades doivent être dotées non seulement d'appétits intentionnels et volontaires, mais aussi d'appétits non intentionnels et involontaires, des appétits qui ne sont pas guidés par la perception propre du bien de la monade. Bien qu'il existe peu d'évidences textuelles d'après lesquelles Leibniz pense adopter l'idée qu'il y ait des appétits non gouvernés par la perception propre du bien de la monade, cette proposition offre au moins une solution intuitive à l'objection de Bayle. Elle nous permet de supposer que le malheureux chien de Bayle est conduit de ses états perceptuels agréables à ses états perceptuels désagréables essentiellement par des appétits non intentionnels et involontaires. La supposition selon laquelle il y aurait plus d'un genre d'appétit offre ainsi un remplacement, au sein du système de Leibniz, aux influences causales qu'on attribuerait normalement aux causes externes.

Que les monades se développent de manière téléologique n'empêche pas, selon Leibniz, leur développement de manière efficiente. Et, en effet, il y a de bonnes raisons de supposer que Leibniz croit que les monades se développent également de manière efficiente. Il décrit les monades en tant qu'elles sont conduites par leurs perceptions et appétits passés selon leurs lois de série, et il nous dit explicitement que « la représentation de la fin dans l'âme est la cause efficiente de la représente des moyens dans cette même âme »[1]. La description leibnizienne de la causalité efficiente est d'une certaine manière compliquée par son soutien aux doctrines théologiques traditionnelles de la conservation divine et de la concomitance divine. Les philosophes et théologiens élaborèrent ces doctrines pour maximiser la dépendance des créatures à l'égard de Dieu, dans la mesure où cette dépendance est cohérente avec la responsabilité humaine. Certains commentateurs ont soutenu que l'engagement de Leibniz en faveur des doctrines de la conservation et de la concurrence ébranle ultimement son engagement en faveur de la causalité efficiente des monades[2]. Il semble toutefois plus vraisemblable que Leibniz croit, de la même manière que ses

1. *Unicum opticae*, Dutens, 2.2, p. 134.

2. *Cf.* S. Lee, « Leibniz on Divine Concurrence », p. 203-248 ; R. C. Sleigh, « Leibniz on Malebranche on Causality ».

prédécesseurs scolastiques, qu'il pourrait réconcilier de telles thèses traditionnelles avec un engagement favorable à une véritable causalité[1].

Si Leibniz maintient en effet que les monades se développent aussi bien de manière téléologique qu'efficiente, on reste avec une vision du domaine des âmes qui reflète le domaine des corps tel qu'étudié dans la section précédente. Dans l'articulation de sa théorie de l'harmonie préétablie, Leibniz met l'accent sur la causalité efficiente dans le domaine des corps et sur la causalité finale dans le domaine des esprits. Comme on l'a vu, cependant, un examen plus minutieux de la compréhension leibnizienne de la causalité dans le domaine des corps révèle une vision plus intéressante. Le comportement des corps, semble-t-il, peut être expliqué respectivement en termes de causalité efficiente ou finale. La situation est d'ailleurs similaire dans le domaine des âmes. Dans l'articulation de sa théorie de l'harmonie préétablie, Leibniz met l'accent sur le développement téléologique des esprits. Un examen plus minutieux relève de même une vision plus intéressante. Le développement téléologique des monades est parallèle à un développement causal efficient. La célèbre harmonie préétablie leibnizienne entre les esprits et les corps est ainsi étayée par une paire moins largement reconnue d'harmonies causales, l'une dans le domaine des corps, l'autre dans le domaine des esprits.

Jeffrey McDONOUGH
(Harvard University)

1. Voir J. McDonough, « Leibniz: Creation and Conservation and Concurrence », p. 31-60.

DEUXIÈME PARTIE

SCIENCES, MORALE ET THÉOLOGIE

MATHÉMATIQUE ET PHILOSOPHIE AU FIL DE L'ANALYSE DES NOTIONS

Leibniz ne fut pas seulement un des plus grands mathématiciens du XVIIe siècle, il fut aussi un des plus inventifs et des plus productifs. Calcul différentiel, *analysis situs*, déterminants, combinatoire, arithmétique binaire, calculs logiques : on ne compte plus les domaines où notre philosophe a fait œuvre de pionnier, souvent à l'insu de ses contemporains. Rendre compte des rapports entre ses mathématiques et sa philosophie s'avère donc une tâche ardue – d'autant qu'une grande part de sa production reste encore à ce jour mal connue, sinon inconnue[1]. La difficulté se redouble du fait que la place des mathématiques dans la pensée philosophique de Leibniz a été l'objet d'intenses discussions parmi les commentateurs. Dès la seconde « Renaissance Leibniz » – comme on a pu qualifier le moment de redécouverte du philosophe à la charnière des XIXe et XXe siècles – on vit ainsi s'opposer des évaluations contradictoires : pour certains, les mathématiques devaient être remises au cœur de la philosophie leibnizienne, quand d'autres la tenaient encore (comme cela avait été largement le cas dans les siècles précédents) pour peu importante – entendons : non pour la gloire de leur auteur, mais pour la compréhension de questions qui paraissaient le vrai cœur du système : individuation, liberté humaine ou existence du mal. Mais même dans le premier camp, les tensions étaient vives : d'un côté, on proposait de voir la logique comme le noyau méconnu du système (Russell, Couturat[2]), tandis que de l'autre on insistait sur les modèles dynamiques et qualitatifs, l'accent étant plutôt mis

1. Leibniz a peu publié de mathématiques de son vivant au regard de ce qu'il a produit. Mais il conservait avec soin ses recherches et jusqu'à ses moindres brouillons. Nous disposons donc d'une très grande quantité de manuscrits, dont plus de la moitié reste inédite à ce jour.

2. B. Russell, *A Critical Exposition*; L. Couturat, *La Logique de Leibniz*.

sur le calcul différentiel ou l'*analysis situs* (Cassirer, Brunschvicg[1]) – opposition où se reflètent, notons-le au passage, deux des grandes matrices de la métaphysique leibnizienne de la substance, soit l'inhérence du prédicat au sujet (*praedicatum inest subjecto*) et la promotion du concept de force[2].

Dès 1925, Dietrich Mahnke avait dressé un remarquable portrait de ce moment et de la question qu'il ouvrait : comment penser la coexistence de deux projets qui occupèrent Leibniz toute sa vie, mais semblent à première vue relever d'orientations divergentes, celui d'une « mathématique universelle » et celui d'une « métaphysique de l'individuation »[3] ? Nombreux sont ceux qui, depuis cette époque, ont cherché à relever un tel défi. Avec peu de succès, il faut bien l'avouer. Car nous manquons encore à ce jour d'une vue synthétique dans laquelle les différents aspects de la mathématique leibnizienne pourraient s'accorder et se relier clairement au reste de sa philosophie. Non que les liens manquent, bien au contraire ! Leibniz nous offre même un des rares exemples d'auteur chez qui mathématiques et philosophie se sont profondément nourries l'une l'autre[4]. Mais c'est plutôt que les fils sont trop nombreux et divers pour permettre de tisser une vue d'ensemble. Pis, comme on le voit remarquablement dans les différentes interprétations de la « mathématique universelle », ils tirent souvent en sens opposés.

Certes, il existe plusieurs propositions de synthèse, mais qui, quelles que soient leurs qualités intrinsèques, sont allés en direction contraire de l'évolution générale du commentaire leibnizien : tandis que l'on se débarrassait peu à peu de l'horizon d'un « système » de Leibniz[5], c'est précisément un tel système qu'on rêvait encore de reconstituer comme unifiant la diversité des « modèles » mathématiques[6]. Quand on était de plus en plus attentif aux détails de l'évolution de sa pensée, à ses revirements, à ses tensions, c'est *une* philosophie des mathématiques qu'on cherchait encore

1. E. Cassirer, *Leibniz' System*; L. Brunschvicg, *Les étapes de la philosophie mathématique*. Pour un aperçu des polémiques qui agitaient ces courants, je me permets de renvoyer à D. Rabouin, « Interpretations of Leibniz's *Mathesis universalis* ».

2. Voir le *De primae philosophiae emendatione, et de notione substantiae*, Schrecker, 161-167.

3. D. Mahnke, *Leibnizens Synthese von Universalmathematik und Individualmetaphysik*.

4. Voyez l'ouverture de G.-G. Granger, « Philosophie et Mathématique Leibnizienne ».

5. Voyez le bilan dressé par A. Heinekamp dans « L'État actuel de la recherche leibnizienne ». Selon l'auteur, la recherche leibnizienne a connu au cours du XXe siècle trois développements significatifs, qu'il a proposé de désigner ainsi : « à la recherche du vrai système leibnizien », « les interprétations structuralistes » et « refus du caractère systématique de la philosophie leibnizienne ».

6. M. Serres, *Le Système de Leibniz et ses modèles mathématiques*.

à reconstituer[1]. À cela s'ajoutait un autre défaut auquel l'histoire des sciences devenait de plus en sensible. La plupart de ces stratégies interprétatives, qui présentent assurément autant de jalons essentiels dans la compréhension de l'œuvre, avaient en commun de vouloir interpréter Leibniz à travers la figure, historiquement problématique, du «précurseur». Ainsi Leibniz se trouvait-il placé à l'origine de lignées conduisant tantôt à Boole (et aux tenants de l'algèbre universelle: Schröder, Whitehead), tantôt à Frege, tantôt à Hilbert, tantôt à Bourbaki, tantôt à René Thom ou à Benoît Mandelbrot, quand il n'était pas le grand-père d'une philosophie de la nature renouvelée, telle que pouvait encore en rêver un Hermann Weyl. Or s'il est vrai que Leibniz a été une influence importante, et souvent revendiquée, par nombre de programmes philosophiques et scientifiques du XXe siècle[2], la simple juxtaposition de ces lignées montre qu'il ne se réduit à aucune d'elles. C'est même un des intérêts que présente aujourd'hui sa position, de déjouer ainsi nombre d'oppositions installées. À lire le commentaire, on se convainc assez vite que Leibniz fut tout à la fois «logiciste», «formaliste», «structuraliste» aussi bien que «philosophe de la nature». Comme ces positions sont déclarées incompatibles, c'est qu'étant un peu de tout cela, il fut précisément autre et qu'étant autre, il nous permet justement de penser autrement.

Le versant négatif du tableau qui précède apparaît alors : à lire ces interprétations, on se trouve face à un recueil de déclarations contradictoires non seulement des interprètes, mais de Leibniz lui-même. Ainsi ne comprend-on plus si l'on doit considérer que toutes les notions mathématiques se ramènent au seul principe de non-contradiction et à un calcul purement logique (fût-il simplement rêvé)[3], ou s'il faut s'y laisser conduire par des principes qui, comme la fameuse Loi de continuité, ne sont vrais que « par tolérance »[4]. Le face à face du Leibniz logicien rêvant de ramener toutes les controverses à un simple *calculemus!*[5], et du Leibniz attelé à l'élaboration d'instruments nouveaux et ne se souciant pas nécessairement

1. Voir Y. Belaval, *Leibniz critique de Descartes*, dont une des lignes directrices est le portrait d'un Leibniz « formaliste » face à un Descartes « intuitionniste ».

2. Voir R. Krömer et Y. Chin-Drian, *New Essays on Leibniz Reception in Philosophy of Science.*

3. Sur le fait que le principe de non-contradiction « suffit pour démontrer toute l'Arithmétique et toute la géométrie », cf. *Second Écrit à Clarke*, § 1, 1715, GP VII, 355-356.

4. Sur le fait que «tout se fait dans la géométrie» selon la loi de continuité, *cf.* Leibniz à Varignon, 2 février 1702 (GM IV, 93-94). Pourtant une telle loi n'est vraie que «par tolérance» (Leibniz à Wolff, 1713, GM V, 385).

5. Voir, par exemple, *Ad constitutionem scientiae generalis* [*circa* 1682], A VI, 4, 450.

de les « charger de questions métaphysiques »[1] paraît subsister. C'est pourquoi on ne s'étonnera pas de lire sous la plume d'Enrico Pasini, à l'orée du XXIe siècle, un appel à ouvrir à nouveaux frais différentes « lignes d'investigation » pour comprendre l'interaction des mathématiques et de la philosophie chez Leibniz[2]. De même ne s'étonnera-t-on pas de constater que le commentaire récent s'est beaucoup attelé à réhabiliter des lectures « pragmatistes »[3] des mathématiques et de la logique leibnizienne, quand il ne s'agissait pas d'exhumer une pratique « irrationaliste »[4] – l'insistance étant mise sur son caractère exploratoire[5].

Or si cette dernière position est assurément plus satisfaisante au regard de l'inventivité leibnizienne, elle laisse les questions ouvertes largement en l'état. Il ne suffit pas de dire que les documents nous montrent un mathématicien au travail, qui explore, hésite, invente, car ceci est vrai de tous les mathématiciens. Leibniz fut un grand explorateur, c'est entendu : mais concevait-il cette exploration comme inhérente au déploiement de la vérité mathématique ou comme une voie d'accès vers un territoire où les vérités, inscrites dans l'entendement divin, relevaient d'un ordre immuable ? Bien plus, les approches récentes, moins systématiques et plus pragmatiques, laissent souvent dans l'ombre la nature même des relations que doivent entretenir mathématiques et philosophie, comme s'il suffisait d'avoir relâché les mailles de l'ordre géométrique pour que certaines frontières disparaissent. Or Leibniz n'a cessé de mettre en avant l'écart infranchissable qui séparait à ses yeux l'analyse des notions en métaphysique (où nous avons affaire, en dernière instance, à des substances singulières) et en mathématiques (où nous avons affaire à des notions incomplètes et

1. « Réponse aux réflexions contenues dans la seconde édition du *Dictionnaire Critique* de M. Bayle » (GP IV, 569).

2. E. Pasini, « La philosophie des mathématiques chez Leibniz ». En dépit du titre de l'article, on prendra garde que l'auteur y soutient : « les ingrédients d'une philosophie des mathématiques sont différents à différentes époques, et l'on doit admettre l'inexistence, en général, d'une accomplie philosophie des mathématiques, au sens d'aujourd'hui, chez Leibniz » (p. 956).

3. Voir V. Peckhaus, « Leibniz' Pragmatismus ».

4. Ainsi M. Serfati décrit-il le travail de l'*ars combinatoria*, jadis modèle d'un calcul logique, comme allant à l'occasion contre les exigences de la rationalité scientifique : « the combinatorial game may appear to run counter not only to habitual practices, but also, in a way, to rationality itself » (« Symbolic Inventiveness and "Irrationalist" Practices », p. 134).

5. Voyez notamment H. Sinaceur, « *Ars inveniendi* aujourd'hui » ; E. Grosholz et E. Yakira, *Leibniz's Science of the Rational* ; H. Breger, « The Art of Mathematical Rationality » ; E. Knobloch, « Leibniz between *ars characteristica* and *ars inveniendi* » ; N. Goethe, P. Beeley et D. Rabouin, *G. W. Leibniz, Interrelations between Mathematics and Philosophy*.

abstraites). La question persiste : comment concilier le rêve d'une mathématique *universelle* et une métaphysique de l'*individuation ?*

Mon but dans cet article sera de reprendre cette question en suivant l'évolution de la pensée leibnizienne. Nombre de contradictions apparentes proviennent, en effet, de ce que l'on reconstruit une « philosophie des mathématiques » de Leibniz en mettant bout à bout des déclarations et des programmes d'époques et d'intentions différentes. Sans pouvoir entrer dans les détails de ces programmes, je voudrais au moins en indiquer quelques lignes de force. On y verra les rapports des mathématiques et de la philosophie s'y dessiner (et souvent s'y redessiner) dans le cadre d'un dialogue constant qu'on étouffe à vouloir le faire entrer à toute force dans les rets d'un système.

MATHÉMATIQUES ET PHILOSOPHIE D'APRÈS LEIBNIZ

Mon fil directeur sera donné par la manière dont Leibniz lui-même présente régulièrement les rapports entre mathématiques et philosophie. Mais pour bien le saisir, nous devons commencer par mettre à distance certaines déclarations aussi fréquemment répétées que diversement interprétées et dont il apparaît vite que le principal intérêt est d'être suffisamment vagues pour être lues en des sens opposés par les interprètes. Ainsi en va-t-il du trop célèbre : « Ma métaphysique est toute Mathématique pour dire ainsi, ou la pourrait devenir »[1], que chacun interprète à l'aune de sa conception de ce que doit être la mathématique leibnizienne. Or, replacée dans son contexte, il apparaît que Leibniz ne veut rien dire d'autre sinon qu'il tâche de procéder en philosophie par définitions et axiomes – programme partagé par tant d'auteurs classiques, et en des sens si différents, qu'il nous donne peu d'indications sur les rapports effectifs de sa pratique de mathématicien et de sa pratique de philosophe[2].

On doit surtout rappeler d'emblée que Leibniz a établi des lignes de démarcation, qui sont très stables dans son œuvre et bloquent un certain nombre de rapprochements pourtant très répandus. Ainsi insiste-t-il dès la fin des années 1670 sur le fait que la physique ne peut pas se comprendre à partir des mathématiques et nécessite l'intervention de principes

1. Leibniz à L'Hospital, 27 décembre 1694, A III, 6, 253.

2. Sur le fait qu'il s'agit d'un programme répandu et indépendant des avancées mathématiques de tel ou tel auteur, voir les déclarations de Leibniz lui-même dans la *Recommandation pour instituer la science générale* [1686], A VI, 4, 705-706.

métaphysiques supérieurs[1]. Le formalisme mathématique échoue, en effet, à départager par lui-même l'approche des cartésiens, centrée sur la quantité de mouvement, et celle qu'il promeut, centrée sur la puissance et l'action. On fait donc fausse route à chercher dans l'invention du calcul différentiel la matrice d'une élaboration métaphysique, quand Leibniz n'aura cessé d'insister sur le fait que le trajet était inverse. C'est l'autonomisation de la réflexion physique, dans ses fondements, qui porte un des arguments pour le développement de la nouvelle analyse : « le Calcul infinitésimal est utile quand il s'agit d'appliquer la Mathématique à la Physique », rappelle-t-il à Masson en 1716, « *cependant ce n'est point par là que je prétends rendre compte de la nature des choses* »[2]. Parallèlement, il insiste régulièrement sur le fait que le calcul ne porte en lui-même aucun engagement métaphysique : « Les Mathématiciens cependant n'ont point besoin du tout des discussions métaphysiques, ni de s'embarrasser de l'existence réelle des points, des indivisibles, des infiniment petits, et des infinis à la rigueur »[3]. De toute évidence, quand Leibniz dit que les mathématiciens ont besoin d'être philosophes[4], ce n'est pas à cette philosophie-là qu'il pense.

Plus généralement, Leibniz parvient assez rapidement à la conviction, sur laquelle nous reviendrons par la suite, que la juridiction de la métaphysique et celle des mathématiques sont distinctes. Qui ne se souvient des feuilles du Jardin de Herrenhausen, dont la ressemblance n'est jamais parfaite et qui suffisent à établir la différence entre les êtres réels et les êtres mathématiques ? Car « c'est notre imperfection et le défaut de nos sens, qui nous fait concevoir les choses physiques comme des Êtres Mathématiques, où il y a de l'indéterminé ». À l'inverse, « la Nature ne peut point, et la sagesse divine ne veut point tracer exactement ces figures d'essence bornée, qui présupposent quelque chose d'indéterminé, et par conséquent d'imparfait, dans les ouvrages de Dieu »[5]. Nous devons donc être particulièrement

1. Voir M. Fichant, *La Réforme de la dynamique* – et encore en 1702, dans une lettre à Sophie-Charlotte : « Les Lois de la force dépendent de quelques raisons merveilleuses de la métaphysique ou des notions intelligibles sans pouvoir être expliquées par les seules notions matérielles ou de la mathématique, qui sont de la juridiction de l'imagination » (GP VI, 507 ; A I, 21, 335).

2. GP VI, 629 (nous soulignons).

3. Réponse à Bayle, GP IV, 569.

4. Leibniz à Malebranche, 13/23 mars 1699, A II, 3, 539.

5. Leibniz à la princesse Sophie, 31 octobre 1705, A I, 25, 202 ; GP VII, 563. Cette distinction apparaît dès la fin des années parisiennes (cf. *Meditatio de principio individui* [1676], A VI, 3, 490) ou les remarques métaphysiques de décembre 1676 (A VI, 3, 400) : « Tout Être complet ne peut être produit que d'une seule façon : ceci est un indice suffisant du fait que les Figures, puisqu'elles peuvent être produites de diverses manières, ne sont pas des Êtres complets » (notre traduction).

vigilants lorsqu'il s'agit de traiter des « modèles » mathématiques de la philosophie leibnizienne. Aussi loin que l'on puisse pousser certaines analogies, elles resteront des analogies et masquent parfois des différences essentielles[1].

Par contraste, on doit garder à l'esprit qu'il existe de nombreux textes où Leibniz établit une continuité forte entre les mathématiques et la philosophie. Ainsi une lettre célèbre de 1678 qu'on suppose écrite à la Princesse Élisabeth avance : « Mais pour moi je ne chérissais les Mathématiques, que par ce que j'y trouvais les traces de l'art d'inventer en général, et il me semble que je découvris à la fin que Monsieur des Cartes lui-même n'avait pas encore pénétré le mystère de cette grande science »[2]. Or l'art d'inventer est alors placé au cœur même de la philosophie : « Car j'ai reconnu que la Métaphysique n'est guère différente de la vraie Logique, c'est-à-dire de l'art d'inventer en général »[3]. C'est cette relation que je voudrais retracer en suivant le guide qui nous est donné par Leibniz lui-même : l'analyse des notions comme ars inveniendi, au croisement des mathématiques et de la philosophie.

DU *DE ARTE COMBINATORIA* À L'ARRIVÉE À PARIS : UN RÊVE DE JEUNESSE ET SA TRANSFORMATION

Il est bien connu que Leibniz a conçu un rapport intime entre mathématiques et philosophie dès le temps de sa Dissertatio de arte combinatoria, parue l'année de ses vingt ans, en 1666. Le simple fait qu'il n'ait alors eu qu'une éducation mathématique très limitée, n'ayant pas eu accès aux mathématiques qui se développent dans l'orbe de la géométrie cartésienne, tend à montrer que les mathématiques furent prises d'emblée dans un programme philosophique fort[4]. Mais l'argument se retourne tout aussi bien : quand on voit le détonateur que fut le séjour à Paris (1672-1676) et la découverte des nouvelles mathématiques de son temps, il paraît exagéré de vouloir trop accorder à l'orientation philosophique initiale. Ce serait manquer, en effet, la reconfiguration profonde à laquelle ce programme fut soumis lors de la confrontation avec des mathématiques plus élaborées.

1. Ainsi Leibniz, en *post-scriptum* à sa lettre à Des Bosses du 24 avril 1709, rappelle-t-il qu'il avait d'abord présenté les âmes comme des points (« métaphysiques »), mais qu'il ne soutient plus cette thèse qui évoque une spatialité des monades et lui paraît désormais constituer une *metabasis eis allo genos* (GP II, 372).

2. A II, 12, 662.

3. *Ibid.*

4. Comme il s'en explique très clairement à Jakob Bernoulli en 1703 (GM III, 71), ce n'est qu'à son arrivée à Paris, en 1672, qu'il fut initié aux mathématiques de son temps, sous la férule bienveillante de Huygens, *cf.* Hofmann, *Leibniz in Paris*.

Pour bien comprendre cette évolution, encore faut-il en saisir la formulation première. Leibniz lui-même en a retracé le cadre général à plusieurs reprises :

> Dès l'enfance, alors que j'apprenais la logique, j'ai pris l'habitude de rechercher en profondeur les raisons de ce qu'on me proposait; j'interrogeais déjà mes précepteurs : puisqu'on possédait les prédicaments des termes incomplexes, qui permettaient d'ordonner les notions, pourquoi n'aurait-on pas formé de la même manière les prédicaments des termes complexes, par lesquels on aurait ordonné les vérités ?
> J'ignorais que les géomètres ne font pas autre chose lorsqu'ils effectuent une démonstration et disposent les propositions selon qu'elles dépendent les unes des autres. Je pensais pour ma part que ceci serait universellement en notre pouvoir si l'on établissait d'abord les vrais prédicaments des termes simples en constituant à cette fin une sorte d'alphabet de la pensée ou de catalogue des genres les plus hauts (ou tenus pour les plus hauts) comme *a*, *b*, *c*, *d*, *e*, *f*, et si, à partir de là, on produisait les notions inférieures par combinaison[1].

Dans le vocabulaire de l'époque, il s'agissait donc de reconnecter deux parties séparées de la logique, « l'analyse des notions » et « l'analyse des vérités », et cela par une refonte des catégories (ou « prédicaments ») sous l'égide d'une approche combinatoire. Mais notons également que Leibniz rappelle avoir ignoré alors que ce rêve était déjà en partie *réalisé* par les mathématiciens. Ceci correspond très bien à l'évolution qu'on voit se dessiner jusqu'à l'arrivée à Paris.

De fait, si le programme du *De arte combinatoria* rapproche les combinaisons logiques d'une forme de calcul, c'est d'abord sous l'influence *philosophique* de Hobbes[2]. Dans le dixième chapitre du traité, un de ceux consacrés aux usages (*usus*) de l'art combinatoire, Leibniz rend plus explicite cette référence et se situe également dans l'héritage du « Grand art » de Raymond Lulle. C'est alors qu'il envisage un modèle numérique où la décomposition des termes pourrait être pensée sur le modèle de la décomposition d'un nombre en ses diviseurs[3] – programme qui reste alors à l'état de simple analogie et ne se développera que plus de dix ans après au titre des premiers échantillons de « caractéristique numérique »[4]. Cette ana-

1. *De Synthesi et Analysi universali* [entre 1683-1686 ?], GP VII, 292, trad. R, 135. Un tableau comparable est dressé dès 1679 dans le *De numeris characteristicis ad linguam universalem constituendam* (A VI, 4, 265).

2. GP IV, 46.

3. GP IV, 64-66.

4. Voyez les textes d'avril 1679 rassemblés sous ce titre en R, 39-75.

logie se transcrit également dans le projet d'une écriture universelle[1], fondée sur un alphabet des notions simples, première annonce du célèbre thème de la *caracteristica universalis*. Un peu auparavant, Leibniz s'était placé sous l'égide de la nouvelle algèbre symbolique, définie comme science générale des proportions entre quantités inconnues[2]. En mettant ces différents passages bout à bout, on peut voir s'esquisser les premiers contours de la « spécieuse universelle », conçue sur le modèle de l'algèbre des modernes, qu'il s'agirait de mener plus avant jusqu'à prendre la forme d'un calcul logique universel et à laquelle Leibniz se référera si souvent tout au long de sa vie. Mais gardons à l'esprit que le lien avec l'algèbre n'est pas fait explicitement en 1666[3]. C'est pourquoi il faut parler ici d'un programme, que Leibniz présentera d'ailleurs comme tel à son nouveau protecteur quelques années plus tard : fournir « un moyen qui permet de faire en philosophie ce qu'ont fait Descartes et d'autres par l'algèbre et l'analyse en Arithmétique et en Géométrie »[4]. Or ce programme, comme nous le verrons, ne conduisit pas Leibniz où il pensait arriver.

Que le rapprochement avec l'algèbre symbolique ne soit pas allé de soi ne doit pas nous surprendre. Nous ne devons pas oublier, en effet, que Hobbes avait été pris dans une querelle très vive avec le mathématicien John Wallis, dans laquelle c'était ce dernier qui défendait la primauté de l'algèbre symbolique[5]. Leibniz mentionne cette controverse en 1671 et y dessine sa propre voie, médiane :

> Si nous avions à chaque fois conscience d'avoir mis en ordre les mots distinctement et de manière constante, il suffirait d'avoir recours à des connaissances aveugles pour raisonner distinctement.
> Ainsi cette Analyse Symbolique des *Recentiores*, quelles que soient les critiques que Hobbes lui oppose, est d'un très grand usage pour raisonner vite et bien.

1. GP IV, 72.
2. GP IV, 35.
3. Voir également le passage suivant des *Elementa rationis* [1686] : « quant à moi, alors que j'étais encore un enfant, n'étudiais que les préceptes de la logique commune *et n'avais aucune connaissance de la mathesis*, la pensée m'est venue, sous je ne sais quelle impulsion que l'on pouvait inventer une analyse des notions, d'où par une certaine combinaison pourraient sortir des vérités que l'on pourrait évaluer comme par des nombres » (A VI, 4, 727, trad. R, 156, nous soulignons).
4. A II, 1, 261. Leibniz à Johann Friedrich, mi-octobre (?) 1671 (notre traduction).
5. D. Jesseph, *Squaring the Circle*.

> D'où il appert que ceux qui possèdent l'art d'user des mots adéquats de manière constante, ont coutume de raisonner adéquatement, c'est-à-dire d'ordonner leurs pensées[1].

Il s'agit donc de trouver un juste milieu entre la défense de la connaissance « aveugle » (ou « symbolique ») et la capacité à « user de mots adéquats de manière constante », ce qui suppose une analyse des notions rendant la caractéristique « réelle ». Leibniz n'aura d'ailleurs de cesse de reprocher aux projets existants de « caractéristique » ou bien de ne pas entrer dans l'analyse des notions ou bien de n'avoir pas su développer une symbolique efficace sur le modèle de l'algèbre et de l'arithmétique[2].

On trouve dans cette première formulation du projet l'essentiel des thèmes qui porteront l'idée d'une « caractéristique universelle » jusqu'au dernier moment de l'œuvre[3]. Mais on doit néanmoins être particulièrement attentif aux inflexions qui se manifestent dès les premières années. En rapprochant plus clairement la caractéristique de l'algèbre au début des années 1670, Leibniz ouvre en effet la possibilité de traiter des notions de manière « distincte » sans en avoir encore achevé l'analyse (du moment qu'on les a mises en ordre « de manière constante »). Cette possibilité va jouer un rôle crucial pour accompagner le développement des mathématiques leibniziennes. De fait, l'arrivée à Paris est marquée par un échange avec Huygens où le jeune homme va montrer l'étendue de ses capacités, mais qui va également jeter un doute profond sur le premier modèle combinatoire.

L'occasion en est donnée par une question portant sur la série des inverses des nombres triangulaires et a été rapportée par Leibniz dans un texte intitulé *Accessio ad arithmeticam infinitorum*[4]. Utilisant une méthode qu'il avait élaborée avant son arrivée à Paris, Leibniz a l'idée de voir cette somme infinie comme une série de différences, ce qui permet d'éliminer les termes intermédiaires (selon le procédé dit aujourd'hui des « séries télescopiques »). Plus généralement, il applique ce procédé à toutes les colonnes du triangle « harmonique » (constitué des inverses des nombres du triangle « arithmétique » de Pascal, voir fig. 1 et 2 ci-dessous). Il en tire la règle que la somme des termes d'une des colonnes est

1. A VI, 2, 481 (notre traduction).

2. *Zur Ars signorum von George Dalgarno* (A VI, 3, 170). Ce thème se poursuit après les années parisiennes *cf.* Leibniz à Gallois, 19 décembre 1678, A III, 2, 570.

3. Voyez encore la description donnée à Rémond le 10 janvier 1714 (GP III, 605).

4. Ce texte est contenu dans la lettre à Jean Gallois d'octobre 1672 (A II, 1, 342-356/A III, 1, 1-20). Les « nombres triangulaires » tirent leur nom du fait qu'on peut les représenter sous la forme de triangles de points (1, 3, 6, 10).

égale au rapport des « exposants » (des numéros) des lignes qui la précèdent[1].

Triangulum arithmeticum

1	1	1	1	1	1	etc.
2	3	4	5	6	etc.	
3	6	10	15	etc.		
4	10	20	etc.			
5	15	etc.				
6	etc.					
etc.						
Numeri Naturales	Trigonales	Pyramidales	Trigono-trigonales	Trigono-pyramidales	Pyramido-pyramidales	Trigono-trigono-trigonales

Triangulum harmonicum

$\frac{1}{1}$	$\frac{1}{1}$	$\frac{1}{1}$	$\frac{1}{1}$	$\frac{1}{1}$	$\frac{1}{1}$	etc.
$\frac{1}{2}$	$\frac{1}{3}$	$\frac{1}{4}$	$\frac{1}{5}$	$\frac{1}{6}$	etc.	
$\frac{1}{3}$	$\frac{1}{6}$	$\frac{1}{10}$	$\frac{1}{15}$	etc.		
$\frac{1}{4}$	$\frac{1}{10}$	$\frac{1}{20}$	etc.			
$\frac{1}{5}$	$\frac{1}{15}$	etc.				
$\frac{1}{6}$	etc.					
etc.						
Naturalium	Trigonalium	Pyramidalium	Trigono-trigonalium	Trigono-pyramidalium	Pyramido-pyramidalium	Reciproci

Figure 1 : en haut : une version du « triangle arithmétique » de Pascal. En bas : le « triangle harmonique » de Leibniz. La question posée par Huygens était de calculer la somme des termes de la deuxième colonne (source : A VII, 6, 607).

1. Il faut compter à partir de la colonne des « unités », non représentée dans la figure ci-dessus. Ainsi les inverses des nombres triangulaires constituent la *troisième* colonne. Leur somme vaut donc le rapport des numéros des lignes précédentes, la deuxième sur la première : soit 2 sur 1 (de même la somme de la quatrième colonne, celle des inverses des nombres « pyramidaux », vaudra 3/2, la cinquième 4/3, etc.).

Ce résultat simple et puissant, qui impressionne vivement Huygens, pose néanmoins un problème pour les premières lignes : celle des inverses des nombres entiers, pour lesquels le procédé de Leibniz donne 1/0. Bien plus, si l'on représente la première colonne, celle des unités, comme le fait Leibniz dans l'*Accessio*, on obtient le résultat : 0/0 (Leibniz ne s'autorise pas à compter des colonnes « en négatif » et s'arrête donc à 0). Leibniz interprète naturellement ces cas comme indiquant ce que nous appellerions la divergence de ces séries (ce qui est juste, même si le procédé qu'il utilise pour l'établir ne serait pas jugé comme valide aujourd'hui). Il considère donc qu'il a obtenu une démonstration du fait que le nombre infini ou « nombre de tous les nombres » (somme de toutes les unités) est impossible[1].

Ce résultat mathématique, d'apparence anodine, va jouer un rôle central dans la philosophie de Leibniz : d'un côté, il montre que nous devons refuser l'idée d'un nombre infini, une conception dont notre philosophe va progressivement réaliser qu'elle conduit *ipso facto* à refuser également l'existence d'infiniment petits en mathématiques et qu'elle pose à nouveaux frais la question de l'infini en métaphysique[2] ; de l'autre, elle indique que le premier modèle combinatoire était trop naïf : on peut, en effet, combiner des notions parfaitement « claires et distinctes » (comme les unités arithmétiques) sous la forme de relations non moins « claires et distinctes » (comme l'addition) et aboutir à une notion pourtant contradictoire (comme le plus grand de tous les nombres).

Par la suite, Leibniz précisera que la question n'est pas liée, comme on aurait pu le croire, à l'intervention de l'infini dans la synthèse. Ainsi on peut facilement donner des exemples de combinaison finie impossible comme il le fera avec le célèbre « décaèdre régulier ». Je peux, en effet, aisément former la notion « claire et distincte » d'un solide à dix faces régulières (un diamant à dix faces, comme on en trouve d'ailleurs dans la nature), objet pourtant « impossible » dans la géométrie euclidienne où est démontrée l'existence de cinq solides réguliers (les corps « platoniciens ») et de ces cinq seulement[3]. Cette remarque est à la source de ce que Leibniz expose à la Princesse Elisabeth en 1678 lorsqu'il explique que les mathématiques ont été pour lui le lieu d'exercice du véritable *ars inveniendi* et

1. Pour le détail des calculs, voir E. Hofmann, *Leibniz in Paris*.

2. Voir D. Rabouin, « Infini mathématique et infini métaphysique ».

3. *Nouveaux essais sur l'entendement humain*, III, chap. III, § 15, GP V, 272. Il va sans dire que cet objet n'est impossible que par rapport aux réquisits portés par la définition des solides réguliers, mais c'est précisément le point que Leibniz veut indiquer : si tous les réquisits n'ont pas été pensés, je peux produire un objet qui contredit une des conditions cachées.

l'occasion de réaliser la faiblesse de la méthode cartésienne. L'argument était déjà présenté de manière ramassée dans une lettre à Oldenburg en 1675 : « Il paraît que nous pensons beaucoup de choses (confusément s'entend), qui impliquent pourtant contradiction, comme par exemple : le nombre de tous les nombres. D'où il ressort que nous devons considérer avec suspicion la notion d'infini, de minimum, de maximum, du plus parfait et de la Totalité elle-même » [1]. C'est là le fondement de sa critique de la démonstration cartésienne *a priori* de l'existence de Dieu. Elle aurait, en effet, omis l'essentiel : attester la possibilité de la notion qu'elle formait. On y voit remarquablement le lien de l'*ars inveniendi*, tiré des mathématiques, à la vraie logique et à la métaphysique.

Je me suis attardé sur cet exemple inaugural non seulement parce qu'il a joué un rôle important dans la pensée de Leibniz, mais aussi parce qu'il nous montre clairement les dangers des lectures qui posent un lien de la philosophie aux mathématiques à sens unique. S'il est vrai que Leibniz dit s'être tourné vers les mathématiques parce qu'il y cherchait les traces du vrai « art d'inventer », on ne doit pas sous-estimer la manière dont la pratique mathématique a agi en retour sur ce programme. On pourrait en prendre bien d'autres exemples, à commencer par celui de la quadrature du cercle, également mentionnée dans la lettre à Elisabeth et sur laquelle Leibniz obtient ses premiers résultats en 1673, ou ses recherches sur les nombres premiers qui le conduisent progressivement à mettre en doute la possibilité d'en exhiber une structure régulière – ce qui rejaillit immédiatement sur la possibilité de représenter les notions simples par des nombres [2]. Tous ces exemples iraient dans le même sens : la remise en cause progressive d'un premier modèle « enfantin » [3] où il s'agissait de parvenir à un catalogue de notions absolument simples et de recomposer l'ensemble des vérités d'une manière purement combinatoire.

Leibniz multiplie les déclarations en ce sens à la fin des années parisiennes. La plus saisissante est certainement celle des *Elementa cogitandi* où la reconnaissance de son erreur première est particulièrement explicite :

> [S]'il est vrai qu'il y a une démonstration parfaite, à savoir qui ne laisse rien sans preuve, il est alors nécessaire qu'il existe des éléments de la pensée, car la démonstration sera parfaite seulement lorsque tout sera analysé. *Mais je m'aperçois maintenant que c'est faux, et que la démonstration est*

1. A II, 12, 393.
2. Voir D. Rabouin, « The Difficulty of Being Simple ».
3. Le mot est de Leibniz : *puerilis* (A VI, 4, 265).

parfaite dès que l'on est parvenu aux identiques, ce qui peut avoir lieu bien que tout n'ait pas été analysé[1].

Comprendre cette évolution paraît essentiel pour deux raisons : d'une part, on ne compte plus les références au projet d'une « caractéristique universelle » ou d'un *ars combinatoria* qui se contente de pointer la constance d'un programme sans s'intéresser aux détails de sa réalisation, aux difficultés que Leibniz y rencontre et aux amendements qu'il y opère ; d'autre part, on fait trop souvent de Leibniz un défenseur de la connaissance « aveugle » ou symbolique sans se rendre compte que cette connaissance est prise d'emblée dans une perspective critique. Si Leibniz constate, en effet, que la plupart de nos connaissances sont symboliques, et que c'est notamment le cas de toute l'arithmétique et l'algèbre[2], ce n'est pas pour s'en satisfaire benoîtement. Tout son argument, hérité de sa pratique mathématique, est qu'une telle connaissance est dangereuse si elle n'est pas accompagnée d'attestations de possibilité[3].

Cette première ligne d'évolution étant retracée, nous devons alors affronter une nouvelle question : puisque Leibniz semble s'être très tôt departi d'un modèle naïf d'alphabet des notions simples et de connexion directe de l'analyse des notions à l'analyse des vérités[4], comment se fait-il qu'il se soit pourtant toujours référé à son rêve de jeunesse de manière positive ? Ainsi peut-il encore avancer dans un texte de la fin des années 1680 :

> J'ai vu exposés les plus vrais et les plus beaux abrégés de cette analytique des pensées humaines, lorsque j'ai étudié de manière plus approfondie l'analyse mathématique, à laquelle j'ai tant consacré de mes soins studieux que je ne sais si l'on trouve beaucoup de gens à y avoir mis plus de travail de nos jours.
> Je fus certainement le premier à venir bout, sous les applaudissements des plus grands mathématiciens, de questions mathématiques parmi les plus

1. *De Elementis cogitandi*, avril 1676, A VI, 3, 504-507, trad. R, 21-22 (nous soulignons). Voir également, sur la difficulté d'atteindre aux simples, la lettre à Vaget de 1679, A II, 12, 772.

2. « J'ai l'habitude d'appeler aveugle ou encore symbolique cette pensée dont nous faisons usage en algèbre, en arithmétique, et presque partout » (*Meditationes de cognitione veritate et ideis*, 1683, A VI, 4, 587-588, trad. Schrecker, 19).

3. Voyez l'article de M. Picon dans ce recueil.

4. Voir notamment *Sur les premières propositions et les premiers termes* [1676], A VI, 3, 436 ; *De la sagesse* [1676], A VI, 3, 671, et encore dans les années 1680 l'*Introductio ad Encyclopaediam arcanam*, A VI, 4, 530-531.

reculées, et ce fait est établi aux yeux de deux qui prennent un plaisir assidu à ces études [1].

Que le programme initial ait été profondément reconfiguré et amendé ne signifie donc nullement qu'il ait été abandonné, ni qu'il ait été infructueux. Il fut même, comme le rappelle ici Leibniz, la matrice d'une réforme des mathématiques particulièrement féconde. C'est cet aspect qu'il nous faut donc maintenant éclaircir.

LES « NOUVELLES ANALYSES » ET LE PROGRAMME D'UNE « SCIENCE GÉNÉRALE »

Autant la pratique mathématique infléchit fortement le programme philosophique initial, autant il est indéniable que le programme philosophique continua d'exercer une influence décisive sur la pratique mathématique. Comme je voudrais essayer de le montrer dans ce qui suit, il contribua même à donner à la mathématique leibnizienne son tour si singulier. Le ressort de cette influence est clair et nous venons de le rappeler : si Leibniz est un grand défenseur de la fécondité des méthodes symboliques, à l'aide desquelles il parvient à étendre l'analyse cartésienne hors de son orbe, que ce soit du côté de l'algorithme différentiel (*analysis infinitorum*), d'une caractéristique géométrique (*analysis situs*) ou des calculs logiques (*analysis notionum et veritatum*), il ne faut pas oublier que l'approche « aveugle » qui guide ces « nouvelles analyses », et donc autant de nouveaux « calculs », n'avait de sens à ses yeux qu'accompagnée d'une analyse *conceptuelle* (*analysis cogitationum*). Sans cet ancrage dans des définitions, le calcul symbolique, appuyé sur la simple substitution des « identiques », se trouve en effet toujours susceptible de porter des contradictions cachées.

Parmi les différentes descriptions des mathématiques leibniziennes, on s'étonne d'ailleurs de ne pas le voir crédité plus souvent d'avoir inventé, selon une expression promise à un grand succès au XIXe siècle, la mathématique « conceptuelle ». Car c'est peut-être là la plus évidente source de son inventivité sans mesure (comme il l'a toujours lui-même clamé). Cet aspect apparaît aujourd'hui de plus en plus clairement à mesure que le détail de sa pratique est mieux connu. Il correspond d'ailleurs à une méthodologie parfaitement explicite. Ainsi un des grands fragments de l'année

1. *De arte characteristica ad perficiendas scientias ratione nitentes*, A VI 4, 911, trad. R, 160-161.

1679 sur la « caractéristique géométrique » nous rappelle que Leibniz a essayé plus de dix fois à différentes époques avant de parvenir « au plus simple », c'est-à-dire aux vrais « éléments » de la connaissance géométrique [1]. Or au vu du résultat auquel il parvient alors, il ne fait pas de doute que c'est bien l'analyse des notions qui lui a servi d'*ars inveniendi*. C'est elle qui lui a permis d'isoler un ensemble de relations fondamentales réglant les rapports entre points dans l'espace (ce vocabulaire d'apparence moderne est celui de Leibniz) [2] : la situation (ou distance), la congruence, la similitude, la coïncidence, le rapport, etc. Dans les *Elementa rationis* (1686), évoquant ce « nouveau genre d'analyse mathématique », Leibniz souligne que personne n'avait été capable de la développer avant lui, faute d'une compréhension adéquate de la notion de similitude [3].

De fait, Leibniz insiste à plusieurs reprises sur le tournant qu'a marqué la découverte de cette définition [4]. Elle repose sur le fait que deux entités sont semblables quand elles ne peuvent être distinguées (ou discernées) qu'en étant mises en présence l'une avec l'autre. Une de ses premières apparitions a lieu en 1677 dans une lettre à Gallois qui ne fut pas envoyée et qui témoigne remarquablement des rapports complexes reliant alors mathématiques et philosophie :

> Il n'est pas si aisé qu'on pense, de donner des véritables démonstrations en métaphysique. Cependant il y en a et de très belles. On n'en saurait avoir avant que d'avoir établi de bonnes définitions qui sont rares. Par exemple il n'y a personne qui ait bien défini ce que c'est que semblables. Et cependant avant que de l'avoir défini, on ne saurait donner des démonstrations naturelles de plusieurs propositions importantes de métaphysique et de mathématique. Après avoir bien cherché, j'ay trouvé que deux choses sont parfaitement semblables, lors qu'on ne les saurait discerner que *per compraesentiam*, par exemple deux cercles inégaux de même matière ne se sauraient discerner qu'en les voyant ensembles, car alors on voit bien que l'un est plus grand que l'autre [5].

Plusieurs points peuvent nous arrêter ici. Tout d'abord, l'analyse des notions mathématiques fondamentales est immédiatement (et explici-

1. Leibniz, *La Caractéristique Géométrique*, p. 150-151.

2. *Ibid.*, p. 149-153.

3. A VI 4, 722-723, trad. R, 152-153.

4. Sur le caractère central de la *similitudo* dans les projets leibniziens d'*analysis situs*, voir V. De Risi, *Geometry and Monadology*.

5. A II, 1, 568-569. Dans la suite du passage, Leibniz insiste sur le fait qu'il a obtenu des théorèmes concernant ces relations. La définition de la similitude apparaît également dans le fragment LH XXXV, 1, 11 fol. 25, daté par les éditeurs de Hanovre de janvier 1677 (*La Caractéristique Géométrique*, fgt. II, p. 57).

tement) prise dans un dialogue avec la métaphysique dont le ressort fondamental est la question de la discernabilité. Or les deux domaines vont y marquer leurs territoires respectifs. De fait, la similitude en mathématiques n'a de sens qu'appuyée sur une forme de co-présence, qui elle-même suppose qu'on se place dans un cadre sinon perceptif, du moins imaginatif : « s'il est possible que dans la nature soient données des choses différant seulement par le nombre, et que de cela seul découle qu'elles sont à la vérité non pas une mais plusieurs, ce n'est pas ici le lieu d'en traiter, car cela relève de la Métaphysique ; il nous suffit que l'on puisse trouver des choses telles qu'elles ne puissent être distinguées par l'imagination, c'est-à-dire par ce qui apparaît aux sens »[1]. Dès la fin des années 1670, on voit ainsi se dessiner une théorie des objets mathématiques comme prenant sens dans le cadre restreint du règlement des phénomènes ou de l'imagination – théorie qui sera ensuite régulièrement répétée jusqu'aux dernières années[2]. Bien plus, ces objets sont « abstraits » ou « incomplets » au sens où leur discernabilité n'est jamais complète et que les notions simples s'y résorbent inévitablement dans des classes d'objets équivalents (ceux que la relation ne peut justement pas discerner). C'est là le ressort de toute mise en calcul en tant qu'elle repose sur la célèbre formule : « *deux choses sont* ... (mettez ici la relation d'équivalence ou d'indiscernabilité que vous voulez) *lorsqu'elles peuvent être substituées l'une à l'autre en préservant*... (mettez ici le domaine d'objets abstraits qui résulte de cette identification) ». Ainsi, comme nous venons de le voir, deux choses sont *semblables* quand elles peuvent être substituées l'une à l'autre en préservant leur *forme*, *égales* quand on préserve leur *grandeur*, (logiquement) *identiques* quand on préserve leur *vérité*, etc.[3]. Le « calcul » n'est plus alors que le règlement de ces jeux de substitution entre « identiques ».

Il est remarquable que l'analyse des notions parvienne dans ce contexte à un répertoire de relations fondamentales qui partagent des traits formels communs que Leibniz isole comme tels (réflexivité, transitivité, stabilité

1. *Elementa nova matheseos universalis*, A VI, 4, 514 (notre traduction).

2. Pour trois caractérisations de la mathématique allant en ce sens à trois époques différentes, voir A VI, 4, 560 (1683-1685 ?) ; A IV, 4, 502 (1695) et la lettre à Sophie d'octobre 1705 déjà citée (A I, 25, 202).

3. Voir par exemple la liste de *Definitiones* proposée en 1680 :

« *Identique*, si l'un peut être partout substitué à la place de l'autre. Si l'un peut être partout substitué à l'autre, alors l'autre à l'un en retour.

Egales sont les choses qui ont même Quantité.

Semblables sont les choses qui peuvent être substituées en préservant la qualité, c'est-à-dire que l'on ne peut discerner si on ne les contemple pas en même temps », A VI, 4, 406 (notre traduction).

par correspondance fonctionnelle ou « détermination ») et qui correspondent très exactement à ce qu'il appelle des « identiques ». On voit donc que les déclarations maintes fois répétées sur le fait que les vérités mathématiques sont réductibles « aux identiques » sont faussées si l'on entend par là uniquement le « principe des identiques » (*A est A*) qui en délivre certes la forme logique épurée, mais en masque également la diversité (il y a plusieurs relations identiques au principe des mathématiques et toute la question est précisément de savoir comment elles se rapportent l'une à l'autre)[1]. Enfin, on voit que cette analyse conduit en droite ligne et à une refonte de la « mathématique universelle » et à sa subordination à un projet de science générale reposant sur une « analytique des pensées humaines »[2].

Cette stratégie se retrouve en fait dans tous les projets de réforme des mathématiques que Leibniz entreprend à cette époque. Grâce au travail d'Eberhard Knobloch, nous disposons notamment d'une édition complète d'un traité de quadrature du cercle de l'hyperbole et de l'ellipse, élaboré en 1675-1676[3] et dans lequel Leibniz a explicité les fondements de l'analyse infinitésimale (sans recourir pour autant à l'aspect algorithmique qu'il met au point à la même époque et qui pose des problèmes de fondements propres). Or on constate, ici aussi, la volonté de ramener les premières notions à des phénomènes d'indiscernabilité : deux grandeurs peuvent être dites égales, quand leur différence est inassignable, c'est-à-dire que cette dernière peut être rendue plus petite que toute grandeur donnée. Il devient alors possible d' « asseoir fermement les fondements de la Méthodes des indivisibles » sans accepter pour autant l'existence d'infinitésimaux réels. C'est la nouvelle définition de l'égalité (contextuelle) que Leibniz répètera mot pour mot dans sa querelle sur les fondements du calcul avec Nieuwentijt en 1695[4]. En algèbre, comme l'expliquent les *Elementa nova matheseos universalis*, Leibniz se rend compte que la « comparaison des équations » qui repose sur les diverses relations entre coefficients (identification, symétrie, homogénéité, etc.) s'inscrit dans le cadre d'une notion de similitude étendue aux formes symboliques (et non

1. Pour des exemples plus détaillés, voir D. Rabouin, « *Analytica Generalissima Humanorum Cognitionum* ».

2. Voir notamment le passage des *Elementa rationis* déjà cité, où Leibniz fait allusion à la science *de simili et dissimili*, elle-même soutien de la science « des formules et de la combinaison » (ailleurs nommée *ars combinatoria*) qui sert de guide à l'analyse des notions y compris en dehors des mathématiques (A VI 4, 723-724, trad. R, 152-153).

3. Leibniz, *Quadrature arithmétique du cercle, de l'hyperbole et de l'ellipse*.

4. *Responsio ad nonnullas difficultates a Dn. Bernardo Niewentiit circa methodum differentialem*, 1695, GM V, 322.

plus seulement géométriques)[1]. Pour faire apparaître ces relations, il met au point une caractéristique spécifique, à l'aide de « nombres fictifs » comme 10, 11, 12 qui correspondent à ce que nous indiquerions par une notation indicielle : a_{10}, a_{11}, a_{12}, et par où va se dégager, entre autres, la première théorie des « déterminants »[2]. C'était là, à ses yeux, une preuve manifeste du pouvoir de l'*ars combinatoria* comme « science des formes et des formules », dont on manque la réelle puissance d'*ars inveniendi* à méconnaître sa fécondité dans la réforme de l'algèbre elle-même[3]. Ainsi les plus grandes avancées mathématiques de Leibniz semblent toutes découler de cette pratique systématique de l'analyse conceptuelle qui consiste à se ramener à des « identiques » et qu'on comprend si mal en en faisant une simple profession de foi « logiciste ».

Sous ce point de vue, un autre fait doit particulièrement nous arrêter. La stratégie générale de réduction aux identiques que nous voyons se dessiner à partir des années parisiennes et qu'on a si souvent interprétée à tort comme une dérivation à partir de calculs logiques a fonctionné exactement en sens inverse : après avoir, dans un premier temps, maintenu le projet d'un calcul logique fondé sur des notions représentées par des nombres et donc sur une analyse des notions qu'on supposait achevée, Leibniz change d'approche au début des années 1680 et transfert à la logique la stratégie qui avait fonctionné avec un si grand succès dans les mathématiques. C'est ainsi qu'il élabore deux de ses plus beaux systèmes logiques : celui des *Recherches générales sur l'analyse des notions et des vérités*[4] et celui du *Non inelegans specimen demonstrandi in abstractis*[5]. Dans les deux cas, il s'agit d'*abandonner* le rêve d'une analyse complète des notions et de travailler avec des symboles d'indéterminés[6]. Cela permet dans le premier cas de représenter les notions par des variables et de mettre au point les premiers rudiments de ce que nous appellerions un calcul des prédicats, dans le second cas d'exhiber la structure opératoire propre au calcul propositionnel et de mettre en avant ce que nous appellerions les axiomes d'une algèbre booléenne.

1. A VI, 4, 515.

2. Voir E. Knobloch, *Die mathematischen Studien von G.W. Leibniz zur Kombinatorik* ; M. Serfati, « Mathématiques et pensée symbolique chez Leibniz ».

3. Voir *Matheseos universalis pars prior* (GM VII, 60-61) et *Nova algebrae promotio* (GM VII, 179).

4. A VI, 4, 739-788, trad. R, 200-303.

5. A VI, 4, 845-855, trad. R, 424-434.

6. Sur le fait que ces calculs supposent l'abandon du premier projet combinatoire, voyez l'introduction de J.-B. Rauzy, *in* R, 182-183.

Tout à son enthousiasme, Leibniz élabore alors un programme de « science générale » dans laquelle ces différentes entreprises pourraient converger vers une « nouvelle » *mathesis universalis*, elle-même mise sous la dépendance d'un « calcul universel » et dont l'efficace pourrait même s'étendre jusqu'à atteindre des notions métaphysiques [1]. C'est là la première réponse à la question de Mahnke sur les possibles voies d'une synthèse entre mathématique universelle et métaphysique de l'individuation : si, en effet, les mathématiques relèvent du domaine de l'imaginable, alors il est possible de constituer une mathématique universelle comme science générale des structures phénoménales, appuyée en dernière instance sur un sujet singulier percevant qui est à la source de ces points de vue sur le monde. Malheureusement, trop de commentateurs – Mahnke au premier chef – ont vu là le *dernier mot* du programme leibnizien en négligeant complètement sa localisation à un moment précis du développement. Or, comme nous allons l'évoquer en conclusion, ce programme élaboré à la fin des années 1680 ne fut pas plus stable que celui qui l'avait précédé.

CONCLUSION : VERS DE NOUVELLES SYNTHÈSES

De même qu'on constate une évolution significative des vues métaphysiques de Leibniz après son voyage en Italie (1689-1690) et l'élaboration du projet des *Dynamica*, de même voit-on une évolution concomitante des rapports entre mathématiques, logique et philosophie. Faute de place, je me contenterai de l'indiquer sur l'exemple qui m'a servi de fil directeur : la conception de la « mathématique universelle » et son lien à l'analyse des notions. Alors que le projet des années 1680 est celui d'une « logique de l'imagination », capable de traiter aussi bien de la grandeur que de la forme, de l'égalité que de la similitude (ou encore de la « quantité » que de la « qualité ») [2], il est tout à fait frappant de voir que les descriptions de la *mathesis universalis* dont nous disposons après 1690 se resserrent significativement autour de la seule quantité [3]. Il ne s'agit plus d'élargir les

1. *Initia scientiae generalis. Conspectus speciminum*, 1679, A VI, 4, 362) et surtout *Guilielmi Pacidii Plus Ultra*, 1686 (A VI, 4, 673).

2. *Elementa nova matheseos universalis*, A VI, 4, 514.

3. Voir D. Rabouin (éd.), *G. W. Leibniz. La Mathématique universelle*. On trouve une exception dans un passage des *Nouveaux essais*, très souvent cité sans qu'on perçoive toujours et son caractère isolé et le fait qu'il repose sur une analogie (IV, chap. XVII, § 4 ; GP V, 460-461).

mathématiques à une science de la forme, mais de la force. Or cette dernière relève d'une « estime » générale qui la met sous la dépendance de la seule science de la mesure et de la grandeur. Une évolution comparable se constate aussi bien du côté des projets d'*analysis situs*, resserrés sur la congruence et les aspects métriques [1], que des projets de calculs logiques qui se resserrent alors sur la syllogistique [2]. Par ailleurs, le projet même de *Scientia generalis* semble également se reconfigurer profondément à cette époque et prendre une importance beaucoup moins centrale dans l'organisation du savoir [3].

Même s'il est encore trop tôt pour pouvoir prétendre livrer tous les ressorts d'une telle évolution, on peut mentionner quelques pistes. Remarquons tout d'abord que le projet d'une subordination de la science des relations générales mathématiques sous un calcul universel s'avéra d'emblée très précaire. La grande avancée de Leibniz fut en effet de parvenir à une axiomatisation de l'algèbre logique qui supposait d'en isoler l'axiome caractéristique, dit aujourd'hui « d'idempotence » (A + A = A). Or cet axiome ne vaut pas dans le calcul des grandeurs [4]. Le calcul logique n'acquiert donc sa pleine puissance axiomatique, au milieu des années 1680, qu'à ne *plus* sursumer l'ensemble des mathématiques. On peut également remarquer, plus positivement, que Leibniz parvient avec la constitution de sa dynamique à un authentique système d'un genre complètement différent de celui esquissé dans les projets de *scientia generalis* des années 1680, mais beaucoup mieux articulé en ce qui concerne les rapports entre métaphysique, mathématiques et physique. Si ce système n'effaça pas totalement les projets anciens, c'est que les avancées conceptuelles des années 1680 étaient bien trop importantes pour pouvoir se résorber purement et simplement dans la nouvelle configuration. On le voit très bien dans le traité de *Mathesis universalis* que Leibniz entreprend d'écrire à la

1. Voir V. De Risi, *Geometry and Monadology*.

2. Comme le rappelle W. Lenzen : « Le grand but de Leibniz en logique était de construire un calcul général des concepts qui lui aurait permis de vérifier strictement la théorie traditionnelle du syllogisme. Il n'est pas aisé d'établir une chronologie de cette entreprise, mais on peut avancer avec un certain degré de certitude l'affirmation suivante : d'un côté, Leibniz s'est occupé de problèmes relevant de la théorie traditionnelle du syllogisme pratiquement tout au long de sa vie (d'adulte), c'est-à-dire de 1665, quand il compose la *Dissertatio* jusqu'en 1715, où furent écrits les *Schedae de novis formis et figuris syllogisticis* (C, 206-210). *Les différents brouillons d'un calcul général, de l'autre côté, date d'une période beaucoup plus brève, entre 1680 et 1690 à peu près* » (W. Lenzen, « Leibniz's Logic », p. 56, nous traduisons et soulignons).

3. A. Pelletier, « L'ordre des choses : catégories et définitions chez Leibniz » et « The *Scientia Generalis* and the *Encyclopaedia* ».

4. GP VII, 246, trad. R, 412.

fin des années 1690 [1]. Présentant l'analyse des notions, Leibniz échoue à exhiber une organisation claire comme il avait commencé à le faire dans les *Elementa nova*. Une des raisons de cette confusion provient du fait que l'approche des équations par la similitude et les « nombres fictifs » agit désormais de l'intérieur de la science universelle de la quantité et en perturbe jusqu'à l'idée de notion simple. Après avoir présenté l'importance des considérations combinatoires dans l'algèbre, Leibniz va même jusqu'à dire : « D'où il appert aussi combien l'Algèbre est restée jusqu'à présent dans un état d'imperfection : en effet, aucun moyen d'exprimer ne serait-ce que les termes simples n'a été bien établi » [2]. Ainsi Leibniz en est-il arrivé, à la fin des années 1690, à considérer que les notions de l'algèbre ne sont pas encore bien comprises.

Ceci s'accompagne naturellement d'une réflexion accrue pour fournir une axiomatique satisfaisante des opérations algébriques et des nombres entiers. La chose est remarquable car le fameux passage des *Nouveaux Essais* sur la démonstration « analytique » de $2 + 2 = 4$ [3] est très souvent pris comme point de départ des vues leibniziennes sur les objets mathématiques, alors qu'elle intervient au bout d'un long processus de maturation et dans un contexte où il ne s'agit nullement de tout ramener à cette définition simple du nombre. En témoigne d'ailleurs un autre passage du même ouvrage où Leibniz rappelle ses doutes anciens sur notre capacité à bien comprendre ce qu'est un nombre premier [4]. Un exemple du même genre est fourni par les tentatives pour ramener la géométrie à des démonstrations « analytiques », en particulier le fameux postulat des parallèles, dont Leibniz doit finalement concéder qu'il fait intervenir le principe de raison suffisante (et non de la seule contradiction) [5]. Ces éléments s'inscrivent dans une reconfiguration typique des dernières années dont témoigne à soi seul le titre des *Initia rerum mathematicarum metaphysica*. Il s'agit désormais d'exhiber les fondements *métaphysiques* des mathématiques. Ici encore, c'est dans le dialogue entre pratiques mathématiques et réflexions philosophiques que peut se comprendre une détermination qu'on écrase à vouloir la penser dans les termes d'*une* philosophie des mathématiques ou d'un système.

David RABOUIN
(CNRS, SPHERE, Université Paris Diderot)

1. GM VII, 53-76.
2. GM VII, 61.
3. *Nouveaux Essais*, IV, chap. VII, § 10, et A VI, 6, 413-414.
4. *Nouveaux Essais*, IV, chap. XVII, § 9, GP V, 470.
5. Voir V. De Risi, *Leibniz on the Parallel Postulate*.

LES FONDEMENTS DE LA PHYSIQUE SELON LEIBNIZ [1]

Pour paraphraser Locke[2], Leibniz peut figurer parmi les architectes (*master-builders*) de la science moderne, mais aussi parmi les artisans-philosophes (*under-labourers*) qui ont préparé le terrain pour la connaissance scientifique. Dans le champ de la philosophie naturelle, Leibniz contribua directement à l'avancement des sciences, mais ses réalisations, telles que l'invention du calcul infinitésimal et la création de la dynamique, témoignaient d'un esprit proprement philosophique et furent systématiquement exploitées à des fins épistémologiques. L'éventail des intérêts et contributions scientifiques de Leibniz était largement ouvert : il s'étendait de la médecine et de la physiologie à la mécanique et à la physique mathématique et englobait l'optique, l'acoustique, le génie, etc., sans oublier de substantiels développements en théorie du droit, en histoire et en linguistique qui marquèrent le développement ultérieur des sciences humaines. Or, fait sans doute plus important, Leibniz a réfléchi sur sa pratique scientifique et celles des savants, ses contemporains, et tiré de ces réflexions des analyses relatives à la découverte et à la justification en science. Ce processus s'est développé de double façon : l'œuvre scientifique de Leibniz s'est construite et a évolué en fonction, peut-on dire, de réquisits méthodologiques qui se sont déployés séquentiellement tout au long de sa carrière. Réciproquement, comme cette œuvre se développait, Leibniz en inférait des lignes directrices sur la constitution de la science et ses normes, sur les principes régulateurs et la façon dont ils pouvaient exprimer l'ordre architectonique impliqué dans les systèmes naturels, voire même sur le type de métaphysique qui pouvait se révéler conforme au nouveau savoir

1. Ce chapitre reprend avec modifications un texte précédemment publié : F. Duchesneau, « Leibniz's contribution to natural philosophy ».

2. Voir Locke, *An Essay concerning Human Understanding*, p. 9-10.

d'expérience. En ce qui concerne sa postérité, il serait particulièrement contestable de s'en tenir aux vues traditionnelles selon lesquelles la science leibnizienne céda le pas à la science newtonienne en raison de la supériorité conceptuelle de cette dernière au sujet de la mécanique et du système du monde. L'idée d'un triomphe inconditionnel du newtonianisme à compter du XVIIIe siècle doit être tenue pour un mythe historique. Toutefois, l'hypothèse selon laquelle la conception relativiste du temps et de l'espace selon Leibniz aurait préfiguré des développements centraux de la physique de la relativité au XXe siècle pourrait s'avérer également mythique. Je ne remets pas en cause le fait que les représentations et concepts de la science leibnizienne aient pu profondément influencer des générations de scientifiques jusqu'au temps présent. À mon avis, les méthodes de Leibniz relatives à la formation des modèles et des théories, ainsi que certains de ses concepts et hypothèses interprétatives, ont donné lieu, déformées et indirectement transmises, à des courants majeurs des sciences plus récentes. Mais ce serait là une histoire complexe à retracer. Mon propos est ici plus modeste : j'entends décrire et analyser quelques éléments de la science leibnizienne d'un point de vue philosophique. Ces éléments se signalent par leur pertinence et leur raffinement méthodologique, ainsi que par leur structure formelle progressivement acquise. Ils se sont construits sur la base de principes et de modèles. La façon dont ils combinent méthodes de découverte et de démonstration, stratégies analytiques et synthétiques pour l'explication des phénomènes, pourrait être à la limite schématisée par la formule « Je façonne des hypothèses » (*Hypotheses fingo*). Mais d'un tel point de vue méthodologique, ces éléments ont connu des phases d'évolution. D'où la nécessité d'adopter une approche conjointement analytique et diachronique pour en montrer et évaluer les principaux traits, pour établir comment les projets et réalisations de Leibniz auxquels j'ai choisi de me référer sont survenus en leur contexte et se sont développés en corrélation avec une métaphysique et une théorie de la connaissance, ellesmêmes en évolution.

LA MÉCANIQUE ABSTRAITE ET LE PREMIER SYSTÈME DE LA NATURE

La première phase de l'œuvre à considérer a pris racine, à la fin de la décennie 1660, dans le projet leibnizien de produire une nouvelle philosophie naturelle qui se conformât pleinement à la conception mécaniste du monde, tout en satisfaisant aux réquisits d'une métaphysique chrétienne[1]. Je réfère ici pour l'essentiel aux travaux de philosophie naturelle qui aboutirent aux deux traités que Leibniz publia en 1671, juste avant son séjour à Paris à compter de 1672 et avant sa première visite à Londres en 1673. La *Theoria motus abstracti*, dédiée à l'Académie royale des sciences à Paris et l'*Hypothesis physica nova*, dédiée à la Royal Society à Londres, se révélèrent décisives pour la réorientation et la maturation de son œuvre scientifique. La physique impliquée se fondait sur une conception analytique des éléments de mouvement, présentés comme déductibles de définitions *a priori*. Conformément aux implications de la géométrie des indivisibles, ces éléments étaient conçus comme des indivisibles de mouvement, des *conatus*, qui se combineraient de façon à rendre compte des changements résultant du choc de corps abstraits dénués de tout pouvoir de résister du fait de leur masse. Les inférences déduites de la théorie abstraite du mouvement devaient par suite être ajustées de façon à correspondre aux propriétés manifestées dans le système des phénomènes, c'est-à-dire aux combinaisons de *conatus* dont il était présumé qu'elles pourraient fournir un modèle explicatif applicable au monde des phénomènes. Les interactions régulières des corps qui se produisent en réalité résulteraient donc de séquences intentionnelles d'événements matériels : elles dépendraient de l'action d'un esprit, Dieu imposant une corrélation persistante et harmonique des mouvements qui surviennent entre les corps. Ainsi les régularités phénoménales ne sauraient être tenues pour réductibles aux implications causales strictes du modèle des indivisibles de mouvement et des combinaisons de *conatus :* elles requerraient un cadre d'explication physique qui leur fût propre. Le principal modèle physique auquel Leibniz eut recours dans l'*Hypothesis physica nova* était celui de bulles de diverses sortes, réagissant diversement à l'impulsion mécanique de particules d'éther et se combinant pour produire plusieurs types de structures emboîtées, fournissant le substrat requis afin de rendre compte des processus physiques et chimiques observés. Le statut hypothétique des bulles comme composants ultimes des corps, de même que le rôle régulateur de l'entendement divin harmonisant les effets des mouvements et

1. Sur cette première philosophie, voir P. Beeley, *Kontinuität und Mechanismus*.

préservant l'économie de la nature, impliquait un ajustement *ad hoc* de la théorie cinématique de façon à constituer une explication des réalités physiques.

Jamais par la suite Leibniz ne rejettera complètement les formes d'explications que l'on trouvait dans l'*Hypothesis physica nova*. À diverses occasions, il soulignera les limitations inhérentes à l'algorithme des indivisibles de mouvement dont il s'était servi dans la *Theoria motus abstracti* et les erreurs commises dans la formulation d'une mécanique abstraite qui ne pouvait satisfaire aux réquisits du système actuel de la nature. Les modèles explicatifs auxquels il avait référé manquaient de justification causale adéquate, même s'ils fournissaient un fondement théorique intéressant, s'agissant d'expliquer des caractéristiques du système matériel telles que l'émission et la transmission de lumière, l'élasticité, la gravité ou le magnétisme. Quoiqu'imparfait, le programme de recherche de 1671 constituait une tentative intéressante pour combiner et harmoniser deux aspects antagonistes du système de physique imaginé : d'une part, une théorie abstraite qui présentait de profondes affinités avec les concepts et déductions mécaniques du *De corpore* (1655) de Hobbes[1] ; d'autre part, une théorie concrète qui visait à systématiser les composantes plus empiriques d'un système mécaniste de la nature dans le style de Gassendi et de Boyle[2]. Une lettre à Honoré Fabri du début 1677 prônait encore une structure duale pour la théorie physique qui impliquât la déduction possible de tous phénomènes des lois de la mécanique pour autant que celles-ci fourniraient la raison unificatrice de leur production causale[3]. Mais ce qui s'affirme peu à peu, après 1676, c'est la nécessité de concevoir un système de la nature qui puisse se passer d'ajustement *ad hoc* tels ceux que requérait l'application de la première mécanique abstraite au monde des phénomènes.

1. Voir H. Bernstein, « Conatus, Hobbes, and the young Leibniz ».
2. Voir F. Duchesneau, *La Dynamique de Leibniz*, p. 16-18.
3. Lettre à Honoré Fabri, A II, 1, 447-448.

LA RÉFORME DE LA MÉCANIQUE

La période de maturité de la carrière scientifique de Leibniz débute par une réforme radicale de cette synthèse initiale, l'invention de la dynamique et les premiers échanges polémiques avec les Cartésiens. Elle s'étend de la fin du séjour à Paris en 1676 aux dernières années de la décennie 1680. L'invention d'un nouveau principe pour la mécanique – changement que Leibniz a lui-même qualifié de « réforme » (*reformatio*) – est survenue en janvier-février 1678, dans le *De corporum concursu*[1]. Durant son séjour parisien, Leibniz avait profité de l'influence de Christiaan Huygens et avait eu maints échanges avec des savants français tels qu'Edme Mariotte; il avait aussi à la même époque approfondi sa connaissance des contributions anglaises à la mécanique, notamment celles de John Wallis. En 1676, Leibniz entreprend de réexaminer en profondeur la question des lois du mouvement et de l'interaction des corps. Son objectif était de dépasser les conceptions relativistes reflétées dans les exposés de ces lois chez Huygens et Mariotte et de replacer tout le système mécanique sous l'égide d'une discipline formelle, la géométrie. Il estimait posséder la clé d'une conciliation possible entre les lois empiriques du choc et un principe empirique de conservation analogue au principe cartésien de conservation de la quantité de mouvement : cette clé consistait dans le principe d'équivalence de la cause pleine et de l'effet entier.

Il s'agissait de trouver le moyen de subsumer les règles du choc des corps en collision, à savoir des généralisations empiriques, sous des lois théoriques en déployant un système intégré d'équations susceptible d'exprimer les causes efficientes impliquées. Leibniz envisageait de formuler un système combinatoire d'équivalents définitionnels en termes de causes et d'effets qui pût fournir un moyen uniforme pour mesurer les forces mouvantes dans tous les cas. Il commença par présumer que cette mesure correspondrait à la quantité de mouvement selon Descartes, exprimée par le produit de la masse par la vitesse (mv). Dans cette perspective, le *Pacidius Philalethi*, un manuscrit daté de 1676, avait introduit une remarquable dissociation entre les *momenta* comme déterminations élémentaires au mouvement et les expressions géométriques susceptibles de traduire l'enchaînement de ces moments[2]. À cette époque, Leibniz n'avait pas encore trouvé comment échapper à la croyance selon laquelle une sorte de « transcréation » continue sous-tendait les séquences actuelles de changements physiques par-delà les éléments discrets du mouvement.

1. Leibniz, *La Réforme de la dynamique*.
2. *Pacidius Philalethi*, A VI, 3, 565-567.

Il ne possédait pas encore les concepts physiques appropriés pour contrer cette forme latente d'occasionnalisme, concepts qui pussent symboliser adéquatement la permanence d'un ordre causal substantiel entre et dans les sujets ou agents des interactions mécaniques.

Comme Michel Fichant l'a montré, le *De corporum concursu* forme un document épistémique unique en son genre[1]. Dans cet écrit, Leibniz entreprend une « déduction » systématique des lois du choc de façon à en établir la conformité avec un principe similaire au principe de conservation de la quantité de mouvement. Il compare les calculs théoriquement déduits avec les résultats obtenus d'une expérience fondée sur les propriétés des pendules et des corps en chute libre et destinée à mesurer les déplacements respectifs de corps inégaux en mouvement après le choc – les cas d'égalité étant tenus pour l'amorce de séries graduelles d'inégalités, et l'un des corps étant au repos au départ alors que le mouvement de l'autre était causé par la chute depuis des hauteurs variables. Leibniz ne pouvait pas ne pas reconnaître l'écart entre les inférences tirées du modèle et les données d'observation fournies par l'expérience. Il modifie alors et reformule ou « réforme » la déduction et il la fonde sur la conservation présumée du produit de la masse par la hauteur de chute avant l'impact. Cette fois-ci, l'accord des différents cas s'avère dans la série continue des variables de masse et de carré de la vitesse.

Dans le cas précis de notre univers physique, le système aurait été nécessairement organisé de telle manière que l'équivalence entre causes pleines et effets entiers ait lieu et se maintienne à travers les changements phénoménaux impliqués. Toutefois, même si la conservation de la force sera désormais mesurée par mv^2, et que l'explication sera présumée fondée conformément au principe de l'équivalence causale et suivant la règle méthodologique de continuité, la théorie n'a pas encore été formulée qui pût fournir une conceptualisation véritable relative aux forces sous-jacentes. La base « métaphysique » de la théorie est encore pour ainsi dire manquante, hormis une forme d'occasionnalisme similaire à celui que la *Pacidius Philalethi* avait évoqué. De ce point de vue, nous pouvons désormais soutenir que l'interprétation de Martial Gueroult de la façon dont la dynamique se serait constituée pour des raisons métaphysiques ne cadre plus avec ce que nous avons récemment appris sur le modèle théorique de 1678[2]. Ne connaissant pas le *De corporum concursu*, cet interprète tendait à projeter rétrospectivement un état de la question

1. M. Fichant, « Neue Einblicke in Leibniz' Reform seiner Dynamik (1678) ».
2. M. Gueroult, *Leibniz. Dynamique et métaphysique.*

contemporain du *Specimen dynamicum* (1695) sur l'acceptation initiale par Leibniz de la conservation de mv^2.

Au début des années 1680, Leibniz s'apprête à ajuster la mécanique réformée à un ensemble d'arguments et de concepts théoriques, mais cela ne pouvait dépendre que d'une recherche de formulations scientifiques maximisant la cohérence et la fonctionnalité de la nouvelle mécanique. Ces développements théoriques allaient susciter des distinctions conceptuelles à la frontière de la science et de la métaphysique proprement dite. Fait significatif : ce fut lorsqu'il atteignit une première formulation d'ensemble de sa métaphysique que Leibniz divulgua sa mécanique réformée. Ce fut le cas dans la *Brevis demonstratio erroris memorabilis Cartesii et aliorum circa legem naturalem* (1686)[1], dont les arguments se trouvèrent repris dans les articles 17 et 18 du *Discours de métaphysique*, écrit la même année[2]. À l'encontre de ceux qui tenaient la mécanique pour uniquement réductible à des lois empiriques, Leibniz s'accorde avec Descartes pour reconnaître qu'un principe de conservation de la « puissance motrice » (*potentia motrix*) doit figurer comme composante fondamentale des explications physiques. Mais, sur la base de la loi empirique de la chute des corps selon Galilée et d'axiomes accordés par les Cartésiens, il montre l'écart entre la mesure de la quantité de mouvement *mv* et les véritables réquisits du concept de force motrice. Suivant les implications de la loi de Galilée et donc suivant la leçon de l'expérience, il propose une mesure de la puissance conservée selon le produit mv^2.

À ce stade, il n'a pas encore pleinement déployé la structure de la dynamique proprement dite. De façon plus allusive qu'explicite, il suggère que la théorie devrait harmoniser des modèles empiriquement fondés et un substrat d'entités théoriques exprimant l'ordre immanent au système de la nature. Dorénavant, il est acquis qu'une entité théorique doit se conserver sous la désignation de force motrice. Et la définition de cette force doit surpasser l'intelligibilité abstraite de simples concepts géométriques. Le nouveau principe est aussi présumé posséder une fonction régulatrice pour la systématisation des diverses lois empiriques. Ceci est clairement signifié dans la controverse avec Malebranche et Catelan, alors que Leibniz montre que sa mécanique réformée se conforme au principe architectonique de continuité, principe fondé en métaphysique et d'application mathématique générale, mais particulièrement utile pour estimer la cohérence théorique et la valeur programmatique des hypothèses de

1. *Brevis demonstratio*, GM VI, 117-119.
2. *Discours de métaphysique*, A VI, 4, 1529-1588.

science[1]. Leibniz soutient en outre que ce principe peut servir de fil d'Ariane lorsqu'il s'agit d'atteindre le véritable niveau d'explication scientifique. Les caractéristiques de la théorie projetée requéraient certes d'être explicitées, mais il était présumé que les raisons causales à développer devaient être cherchées hors des limites de la simple formalisation géométrique et cinématique des phénomènes. Tel était le temps où Leibniz décida de restaurer les formes substantielles comme éléments conceptuels clés représentant les principes de détermination du changement au sein des substances corporelles ou de ce qui en tenait lieu.

La dynamique

Débutant en 1689, la phase suivante concerne l'invention de la dynamique proprement dite et se termine avec l'*Essay de dynamique* (c. 1700). Selon la perspective méthodologique de la science leibnizienne, le principe de conservation de la force vive, comme il sera plus tard désigné, avait été obtenu par des moyens d'analyse, à savoir des axiomes d'équivalence appliqués à des généralisations ou lois empiriques. Le système d'explications requérait d'être justifié par sa capacité à engendrer des déductions plus formelles des lois mécaniques, à savoir un système combinatoire d'équations suffisant à fonder la théorie. Cet objectif détermina la rédaction du *Phoranomus* (1689) durant le voyage de Leibniz en Italie[2]. Leibniz vise alors à constituer une science des puissances et des effets. Son objectif est d'échapper aux contraintes conceptuelles imposées à la théorie du mouvement par le recours aux seuls principes de la statique archimédienne sur lesquels Galilée et Descartes s'étaient tous deux appuyés afin de fonder leurs mécaniques.

Le *Phoranomus* tente d'appliquer le principe d'équivalence causale à l'analyse de mouvements non contraints, uniformes et constants, dans lesquels la force motrice (*vis motrix*) se conserve sans génération ni exhaustion[3]. Dans de tels cas, l'effet mesuré selon le ratio direct des masses et des distances parcourues et le ratio inverse des temps de translation doit être tenu pour équivalent à la mesure de la force vive dans les cas d'impacts. Le modèle combinatoire proposé pour ce calcul de l'effet demeurait problématique, car il combinait directement des éléments

1. *Réponse de M. L. à la remarque de M. l'abbé D. C., contenue dans l'article 1. de ces Nouvelles*, mois de juin 1687, GP III, 51-55.

2. Leibniz, *Phoranomus seu De potentia et legibus naturæ*, Rome, juillet 1689.

3. F. Duchesneau, « Leibniz's theoretical shift in the *Phoranomus* and *Dynamica de potentia* ».

« substantiels » et des éléments « modaux ». Mais il fournissait un cadre définitionnel pour représenter le système de causes sous-tendant des effets moteurs violents aussi bien que non contraints. Le modèle méthodologique mobilisé dans cette *mathesis mechanica* incitait Leibniz à rechercher les ratios inhérents à l'action formelle et leur congruence par rapport à ceux qui fournissaient un équivalent analytique de la force vive. La dynamique comme science et son identité conceptuelle émergeront lorsque cette méthodologie d'analyse combinatoire parviendra à surmonter les insuffisances du *Phoranomus*.

Cela se produira peu après dans la *Dynamica* (1689-1690), qui propose une théorie de la « puissance et de l'action » déductivement construite. Dans ce manuscrit d'importance majeure, Leibniz entreprend d'intégrer le théorème de conservation de la force vive au sein d'une véritable structure théorique : cette structure inclut les cas dans lesquels la force s'épuise en des effets qui servent à la mesurer selon le produit de facteurs mv^2; mais elle sert aussi à rendre compte des cas dans lesquels la force s'exprime en action non contrainte avec préservation d'un agent causal autonome sous-tendant son effet formel. La dynamique comme « science de la puissance et de l'action »[1] se révèle quand Leibniz établit que la théorie de la force peut intégrer de façon architectonique tant les mouvements contraints que non contraints[2].

À la suite de la *Brevis demonstratio*, Leibniz avait dû répondre aux critiques émanant des Cartésiens, en particulier de Catelan et de Malebranche. Parce que ses arguments semblaient dépendre de généralisations empiriques, à savoir de la loi de Galilée et de certaines propriétés contingentes attribuées aux réalités physiques, telles l'élasticité et la gravité, il avait été mis au défi de justifier son principe de conservation comme fondement possible d'un système des lois de la nature. Rappelons que l'un des principes de la méthodologie scientifique pour Leibniz tenait à la correspondance stricte entre analyse et synthèse ou combinatoire (*combinatoria*)[3]. Les procédés analytiques mis en œuvre pour prouver le théorème des forces vives ne pouvaient qu'inciter Leibniz à développer un système de raisons synthétiquement ordonnées et aptes à confirmer le principe de conservation comme pierre d'assise de la théorie physique.

1. *Dynamica*, GM VI, 287 et 464.
2. Voir F. Duchesneau, *La Dynamique de Leibniz*, p. 147-262.
3. Voir sur ce point F. Duchesneau, *Leibniz et la méthode de la science*, p. 55-86.

L'argument relatif à la force s'exerçant sans contrainte se fonde sur les définitions de l'effet formel et de l'action formelle :

> La quantité d'effet formel dans le mouvement est ce dont la mesure est constituée par le fait qu'une matière d'une certaine quantité (le mouvement étant équidistribué) est mue sur une certaine longueur[1].
>
> La quantité d'action formelle dans le mouvement est ce dont la mesure est constituée par le fait qu'une certaine quantité de matière est mue sur une certaine longueur (le mouvement étant uniformément équidistribué) à l'intérieur d'un certain temps[2].

Le terme « formel » désigne des propriétés qui sont estimées essentielles par contraste avec des caractéristiques modales qui dépendent de la position et de l'arrangement contingent (*situs*) des corps dans un système physique particulier. La distinction entre les deux types d'effets consiste en ce que les premiers se révèlent dans le mouvement non contraint et permettent par suite leur transposition en une appréhension rationnelle et « métaphysique » de la réalité corporelle, alors que les seconds ne deviennent manifestes que dans et par la résistance des corps au changement – suivant le concept leibnizien d'inertie[3] – et comportent une relation incontournable à l'expérience contingente des changements mécaniques affectant les corps. Les notions d'action formelle et d'effet formel sont distinctes, car elles correspondent à des relations quantitatives déterminées qui se combinent par la suite de façon à signifier les éléments substantiels de force par-delà le niveau de la réalité phénoménale. Ainsi la dynamique comme science satisferait-elle aux réquisits de complétude et de finalité impliqués dans la mise en œuvre de la procédure synthétique d'invention et de démonstration. On doit postuler cette relation architectonique au sein des réquisits, même si elle ne se révèle pas directement à l'analyse des notions visées, en raison des corrélations hypothético-déductives suivant lesquelles le modèle théorique est censé éclairer l'explication des phénomènes.

Du point de vue méthodologique, la stratégie consiste à construire en partant des définitions des systèmes d'équations qui puissent exprimer, par convergence, ce qui est causalement impliqué dans l'action motrice. L'axiome qui unifie le système d'équations se lit : « Le fait que la même quantité de matière se meuve sur la même longueur en un temps moindre

1. *Dynamica*, GM VI, 345.
2. *Ibid.*, GM VI, 346.
3. Voir H. Bernstein, « Passivity and inertia in Leibniz's dynamics ».

constitue une plus grande action »[1]. On obtient ainsi une détermination du « pouvoir d'agir » qui est directement proportionnelle à la combinaison de la quantité de matière et du déplacement dans l'espace et inversement proportionnelle au temps dépensé pour accomplir l'action.

L'argument démonstratif en faveur de cette thèse se formule soit en mode de syllogisme, soit de calcul opérant par substitution d'équivalents définitionnels. Ainsi trouve-t-on par exemple la forme syllogistique développée dans la lettre à De Volder du 23 mars/3 avril 1699[2]. Une lettre à Papin du 14 avril 1698 propose une formulation équivalente en forme de calcul par substitution d'équivalents :

> Dans les mouvements uniformes d'un même corps, soient les temps *t;* les espaces, *s*; les actions *a;* les puissances *p*. Nous aurons alors :
>
> 1) *s* comme *tv*; autrement dit, les espaces parcourus sont en raison composée des temps dépensés et des vitesses;
>
> 2) *a* comme *sv*; autrement dit, les actions sont en raison composée des espaces parcourus et des vitesses avec lesquelles ils ont été parcourus;
>
> 3) Donc, en substituant *tv* à *s* au point 2, selon le point 1, *a* sera comme *tvv*. Autrement dit, les actions sont en raison composée simple des temps et double des vitesses[3].

Pour dresser son système d'équivalences et combiner les réquisits de la notion d'action formelle, Leibniz recourt à une distinction qui implique la double signification du facteur *v* selon que l'on considère l'action à travers l'effet formel de déplacement dans l'espace, ou selon son ingrédient intensif lié à la promptitude d'accomplissement. Dans la *Dynamica*, une définition cruciale exprime cette double relation entre intensité (*intensio*) et extension (*extensio*) ou diffusion (*diffusio*) de l'action :

> La diffusion de l'action dans le mouvement ou l'extensio de l'action est la quantité d'effet formel dans le mouvement. L'intensio de la même action est la quantité de vitesse par laquelle l'effet se produit ou par laquelle la matière est transportée sur la longueur[4].

Leibniz combine un effet embryonné comme s'il devait s'actualiser dans l'instant (facteur *v*), avec un effet déployé dans l'espace de translation par un corps se mouvant sans contrainte (facteur *s*) : il présume ainsi que le facteur embryonné intervient constamment le long du parcours. Il s'agit de

1. *Dynamica*, GM VI, 349.
2. Lettre à De Volder du 23 mars/3 avril 1699, GP II, 173.
3. A. G. Ranea, « The *A priori* method and the actio concept revised. Dynamics and metaphysics in an unpublished controversy between Leibniz and Denis Papin », p. 53.
4. *Dynamica*, GM VI, 355.

la transposition de l'action motrice comme d'une sorte de forme active, d'agent causal impliquant à la fois une propension à agir et un effet moteur traduisant cette propension dans la durée. Comme toute résistance inertielle – au sens leibnizien d'un pouvoir de résister au fait d'être mu – est suspendue, la propension est présumée se conserver intégralement à travers l'effet formel, « de telle sorte qu'on pourrait l'ajouter à cet effet comme un gain permanent en termes de translation virtuelle »[1]. En combinant les ingrédients dynamiques extensif et intensif exprimés dans l'effet moteur et dans l'effet virtuel conservé, l'on forme un analogue théorique du pouvoir d'agir. Sur cette base, la *Dynamica* fait du concept d'action (*actio*) la pierre de touche de la dynamique : ainsi les théorèmes de conservation de l'action peuvent être réunis à ceux de la force vive qui impliquent une conservation de la force motrice à travers des alternances d'actualisation et d'exhaustion.

Le rôle nodal du couple intensité/extension (*intensio/extensio*) pour l'analyse de l'action renvoie à une construction théorique qui suppose la finalité immanente de centres de force; en retour, cette conception s'incarne dans des modèles mathématiques traduisant de telles raisons suffisantes causales et qui s'avèrent représentatifs des effets architectoniques dans la nature. Un bon exemple nous en est fourni dans la correspondance avec De Volder, lorsque Leibniz tente de répondre à l'interrogation du savant néerlandais au sujet du facteur d'efficience causale (*præstantia*) de l'action[2]. Le problème venait du fait que De Volder réduisait l'efficience de l'action, qui est due à un pouvoir réel, à la seule intensité de l'action mesurée par la vitesse instantanée. Selon Leibniz, l'intensité de l'action ne peut pas être supposée fournir seule une expression intégrale de la force : celle-ci ne peut être mesurée par le seul ratio de la vitesse dans l'instant. Il propose donc de combiner les paramètres extensif et intensif de la force, une fois réduits à leurs termes intelligibles et une fois qu'on a montré qu'ils consistent en combinaisons architectoniques de réquisits. D'où deux relations possibles qui en résulteraient : 1) les actions sont en raison combinée des puissances et des temps; 2) les actions sont en raison combinée des vitesses et des espaces parcourus. On peut résoudre la seconde relation en prenant en compte que l'espace est mesuré par le produit de la vitesse par le temps. Si l'on suppose que ces relations sont considérées dans l'unité de temps, les deux évaluations possibles de l'action se réduisent à l'équation de la puissance ou de la force selon le produit mv^2. C'est là, à mon avis, « la marque d'une

1. F. Duchesneau, *La Dynamique de Leibniz*, p. 186.
2. Lettre de Leibniz à De Volder du 9/20 janvier 1700, GP II, 204.

construction analytique répondant aux normes de la combinatoire architectonique »[1]. Cette interprétation est corroborée par le commentaire de Leibniz à De Volder au sujet de la résolution combinatoire du concept d'action formelle : « Ainsi peut-on voir comment toutes choses conspirent de nouveau avec beauté et se trouvent réunies par une raison indubitable »[2]. Concernant la même notion il avait écrit à Papin dans une lettre datée d'après mai 1699 :

> La perfection ou le degré de réalité dans les choses, et particulièrement dans le mouvement se peut estimer suivant deux raisons, savoir par l'extension, qui est ici la grandeur du lieu ou de l'espace changé, et par l'intension qui est ici la promptitude ou la vitesse du changement ou mouvement[3].

La stratégie de Leibniz semble consister à concentrer l'attention sur une correspondance expressive entre la symbolisation algébrique des paramètres pour une force qui persiste intacte à travers l'action, et la projection de raisons formelles relatives au fondement causal sous-jacent. En joignant les dimensions intensive et extensive de l'action, Leibniz vise une construction théorique de type combinatoire susceptible de symboliser l'ordre des causes efficientes fondant les effets relatifs à l'action non contrainte. La force conçue comme entité théorique se caractérise par l'action sur soi-même (*actio in se ipsum*), activité auto-reproductive immanente au corps en mouvement. Comme Leibniz l'écrivait à De Volder le 11 septembre 1699 :

> Dans l'action libre ou formelle elle-même de ce même mobile, aussi longtemps qu'on le conçoit comme agissant sur lui-même, nous pouvons analogiquement concevoir quelque effet réel qui ne sera pas un changement de lieu (que je considère plutôt comme quelque chose de modal), mais le mobile lui-même s'apprêtant à avancer avec une vitesse donnée au moment suivant, se produisant lui-même et avançant avec la même vitesse qu'au moment précédent[4].

1. F. Duchesneau, *La Dynamique de Leibniz*, p. 298.

2. Lettre de Leibniz à De Volder du 9/20 janvier 1700, GP II, 203 : « Ita vides quam pulchre rursus omnia conspirent indubitataque ratione colligantur ».

3. Leibniz à Papin, après le 7 mai 1699, LBr 714, f. 310r, d'après A. G. Ranea, « The *A priori* method and the actio concept revised. Dynamics and metaphysics in an unpublished controversy between Leibniz and Denis Papin », p. 56.

4. Lettre à De Volder du 11 septembre 1699, GP II, 191. Nous suivons ici la traduction d'A.-L. Rey, dans *Leibniz – De Volder. Correspondance*, p. 150.

Une telle construction théorique projetée ne peut être réalisée sans faire appel à des principes architectoniques. Ces principes guident la combinaison de notions « métaphysiques » avec des modèles hypothétiques formulés de façon à se conformer à l'ensemble le plus complet de données, soit que celles-ci soient présentement disponibles, soit qu'elles restent à découvrir par l'expérience suivant la délinéation de l'hypothèse proposée. Tel est le profil épistémologique d'une théorie de la force réalisée suivant le mode *a priori* de la dynamique leibnizienne.

Le *Specimen dynamicum*[1] dont la première partie paraît en 1695 dans les *Acta eruditorum* semble se conformer à un mode de présentation *a posteriori*, comme si Leibniz avait finalement décidé de ne pas révéler à un public plus large la structure géométrique et le style démonstratif *a priori* de sa dynamique. Toutefois, le texte présente le système de principes et de concepts théoriques qui justifie les lois et modèles de la nouvelle science. Leibniz réutilise le concept de *conatus*, mais en ajuste la signification et l'expression suivant un modèle analogique emprunté au calcul infinitésimal. Le nouveau concept de force donne lieu à la constitution d'une matrice à quatre termes et deux niveaux : il se décline en forces primitives active et passive et forces dérivatives active et passive. Le niveau des forces dérivatives est celui des lois empiriques et des modèles qui les représentent; quant au niveau des forces primitives, il semble combiner des principes et concepts théoriques qui possèdent divers liens analogiques avec l'ordre métaphysique des entéléchies représentant l'élément formel des composés dans la nature.

En reprenant l'argumentation *a posteriori* relative à la conservation de la force vive, Leibniz forme et combine les concepts requis pour expliquer la corrélation entre forces dérivatives et l'économie des changements phénoménaux qui en découlent. Ce procédé aboutit à une superposition d'instances : les *conatus* se combinent avec la masse pour engendrer l'*impetus;* l'*impetus* considéré dans l'instant de sa formation engendre la « force morte » (*vis mortua*); celle-ci engendre la « force vive » (*vis viva*) par sommation de *conatus* élémentaires dans la durée. Toutes ces instances, symbolisées par des formules inspirées du calcul infinitésimal, sont vues comme représentant les ingrédients formels, objets d'intégration et sous-tendant les propriétés qui en découlent comme de leur source. En même temps toutefois, ces formules analytiques requièrent des raisons suffisantes d'un autre ordre qui puissent signifier les composantes de la réalité au fondement des phénomènes. Ainsi Leibniz combine-t-il de diverses façons les relations analogiques signifiées par ses modèles

1. *Dynamica*, GM VI, 234-254.

physiques. Mais l'intelligibilité de telles constructions théoriques dépend de ce que l'on peut qualifier de « lois métaphysiques ». Ces lois dépendent de principes architectoniques qui structurent la connexion des forces dérivatives avec leurs raisons déterminantes dans les forces primitives. Ces principes spécifient le sens des entités formelles – entéléchies, monades – représentant le système endogène d'agents causaux sous-tendant l'interaction phénoménale des corps.

L'*Essai de dynamique* tardif, rédigé vers 1700, reflète à certains égards les discussions poursuivies par Leibniz avec certains correspondants privilégiés au sujet des preuves *a priori* et *a posteriori* de sa dynamique[1]. Il complète l'approche précédente, à savoir le traitement analytique des théorèmes et principes au fondement de la théorie de la force. Leibniz y propose l'intégration algébrique de deux principes de conservation relative – le principe de conservation des vitesses respectives des corps avant et après le choc (*vis respectiva*) et le principe de conservation de la quantité de progrès du centre de gravité du système dans un sens avant et après le choc (*vis progressiva*) – sous un principe de conservation absolue qui se décline de façon double comme conservation de la quantité d'action ou de la force vive. La combinaison des principes traduit analogiquement la nécessité de recourir à des raisons suffisantes métaphysiques pour rendre compte des phénomènes mécaniques, qui se trouvent par ailleurs expliqués, sur le plan physique, par un ensemble de paramètres expressifs de la force. Les modèles physiques ainsi proposés renvoient à un système plus profond de principes architectoniques et de formes substantielles qui rendent raison du *nexus* des phénomènes bien fondés.

En définitive, ce qui semble caractériser la dynamique consisterait en ceci : 1) la combinaison des modèles permet un ensemble d'équivalences analytiques sur le plan des lois physiques. 2) Des principes architectoniques interviennent dans l'édification d'une théorie unificatrice, soit positivement, en fixant le type d'ordre qui permet d'unifier les relations physiques sur le plan des phénomènes, et en fournissant des analogies formelles pour la construction de modèles explicatifs ; soit négativement, en provoquant l'élimination systématique des hypothèses inadéquates. 3) En ce qui concerne les raisons formelles sous-jacentes, il est fait appel à des entités théoriques fondant les séquences causales qu'expriment les interactions entre corps. À l'horizon de ce système explicatif, figurent certes des représentations de type métaphysique, mais, en même temps,

1. Pour ce texte voir *Dynamica*, GM VI, 215-231. Concernant les discussions au sujet des arguments en faveur de la dynamique, voir F. Duchesneau, *La Dynamique de Leibniz*, p. 263-340.

dans les limites de la pratique scientifique, les seules raisons à évoquer sont celles qui paraissent requises pour assurer la combinaison des lois de la dynamique et garantir l'explication progressive des effets empiriques issus de l'interaction de centres de force se déployant à l'infini.

LA THÉORIE DE LA GRAVITATION

Une autre phase importante de l'implication de Leibniz en physique concerne son opposition à ce qu'il considérait comme des déficiences du nouveau style d'explication introduit par Newton, style qui s'opposait à certains fondements de sa dynamique et de sa métaphysique de la nature. Comme il a été montré, la lecture des *Philosophiæ naturalis principia mathematica* (1687) de Newton induisit de notables réactions de la part de Leibniz qui s'affirmèrent dans la rédaction de la *Dynamica*, mais aussi dans une tentative subtile d'ajuster la théorie tourbillonnaire des mouvements planétaires de façon à englober les modèles dérivés de l'analyse newtonienne[1]. Or, de façon encore plus significative, Leibniz s'employa à articuler un cadre philosophique distinct concernant l'espace, le temps et ce qu'il tenait pour les concepts fondamentaux d'un système de la nature conforme à la méthodologie scientifique des modernes. La séquence de travaux répondant à cet objectif s'étend du *Tentamen de motuum cœlestium causis* (1689)[2] aux écrits de la controverse avec Samuel Clarke[3].

Parmi les hypothèses formulées ou révisées par Leibniz, la tentative pour assigner une cause mécanique à la gravitation apparaît paradigmatique. Le but poursuivi est ultimement d'unir en un même ensemble d'explications les phénomènes de circulation planétaire, de rayonnement lumineux, de gravité et de magnétisme terrestre. Par ailleurs, Leibniz envisage une approche synthétique qui pourrait inclure les analyses de Kepler et de Newton et compenser pour le choix de ce dernier de suspendre toute recherche causale concernant la gravitation, au-delà de la postulation de l'attraction comme propriété essentielle des corps en interaction, et de contester l'intelligibilité des hypothèses métaphysiques. L'argumentation antithétique développée par Leibniz est représentative d'un concept normatif d'explication scientifique.

1. Voir D. Bertoloni Meli, *Equivalence and Priority: Newton versus Leibniz. Including Leibniz's Unpublished Manuscripts on the* Principia.

2. *Tentamen de motuum cœlestium causis*, GM VI, 144-161.

3. *Correspondance entre Leibniz et Clarke*, GP VII, 352-440.

Les historiens des sciences ont souvent compté l'hypothèse harmonique selon Leibniz comme un échec de la science, ou du moins comme une spéculation immédiatement périmée. Comme l'un d'eux l'a soutenu : « Ainsi, partis du système de Newton, dont Huygens semble se rapprocher, nous retombons, pour ce qui concerne Leibniz, en pleine métaphysique »[1]. Certes, le profil méthodologique de la science newtonienne occultera rapidement le style leibnizien d'explication causale, reposant sur des hypothèses relatives aux entités théoriques. Mais certaines mises en garde sont appropriées à ce propos. Lorsqu'on considère le contexte épistémologique de la science newtonienne, l'on ne doit pas omettre l'insatisfaction théorique profonde engendrée par l'agnosticisme de Newton eu égard à une déduction mécanique possible de l'attraction comme propriété primaire de la matière. Newton lui-même a tenté plus d'une fois de construire des hypothèses en vue de fonder causalement la force de gravitation. Aussi son « Je ne fabrique pas d'hypothèses » (*Hypotheses non fingo*) pourrait avoir signifié un constat d'échec méthodologique avant de servir de maxime positive justifiant de sevrer la pratique scientifique inductive de tout présupposé métaphysique. Cette pratique newtonienne révisée devait par suite se limiter à rendre compte des phénomènes par des modèles conformes aux propriétés quantifiables et aux calculs *a posteriori :* d'où la notion de déduction présumée suffisante à partir des phénomènes sans interférence de constructions hypothétiques. Or, les successeurs de Newton ont souvent sous-estimé les insuffisances épistémologiques de leur pratique de réduction de l'explication causale aux seules corrélations mesurables entre phénomènes.

Au contraire, pour Leibniz, les raisons causales méritaient d'être recherchées de façon à produire un système cohérent de concepts théoriques. Telle lui semblait être la condition pour édifier une science démonstrative par-delà la simple collation raisonnée de données empiriques recommandée par les *experimental philosophers*, tels Boyle, Locke et Newton. La question théorique soulevée par Leibniz véhiculait une exigence théorique qui dépassait les insuffisances de ses propres modèles, comme Huygens l'a reconnu, alors même qu'il émettait des critiques radicales contre l'hypothèse leibnizienne du tourbillon harmonique[2]. Bien qu'imparfaite, la solution de Leibniz présentait une originalité et un intérêt spécifique que certains historiens des sciences ont soulignés[3]. Eric Aiton

1. R. Degas, *La Mécanique au XVIIe siècle*, p. 498.

2. Voir lettre de Huygens à Leibniz, du 12 janvier 1693, GM II, 150.

3. Outre D. Bertoloni Meli, cité *supra*, voir E. Aiton, « The mathematical basis of Leibniz's theory of planetary motion ».

affirme en particulier : « L'absence d'influence de cette théorie est à regretter : elle était mathématiquement sans faille et remarquable parmi les tentatives pour expliquer les mouvements planétaires par l'action de tourbillons fluides » [1].

En dépit de ses dénégations, par exemple dans sa correspondance avec Huygens [2], il ne fait pas de doute que la lecture des *Principia* de Newton ait incité Leibniz à présenter ses propres vues concernant la mécanique céleste dans le *Tentamen de motuum cœlestium causis* en février 1689 et dans le *De causa gravitatis* en mai 1690. En réponse aux diverses critiques émises contre ses modèles, incluant celles de Huygens et de Varignon, Leibniz prépara par la suite une nouvelle version du *Tentamen* qui cependant ne fut pas publiée. Les principales propositions de l'essai original se trouvent bien résumées dans le brouillon de la lettre à Arnauld du 23 mars 1690 [3]. La démonstration leibnizienne prend pour acquises les lois de la circulation planétaire selon Kepler, exposées dans l'*Epitome astronomiæ copernicanæ* (1618-1621) et dans l'*Harmonice mundi* (1619). La première loi – historiquement la seconde – spécifie la trajectoire elliptique des planètes ; la seconde loi – historiquement la première – est celle des aires : les aires balayées par les rayons s'étendant du Soleil à la planète sont égales pour des durées de parcours égales ; la troisième loi est celle du ratio sesquialtère : le carré de la période de révolution d'une planète est proportionnel au cube de sa distance moyenne (a) au Soleil, k représentant une constante pour le système solaire : $T^2 = k.a^3$. Ces lois renvoient à des déterminations observationnelles. Leibniz considérait qu'elles requéraient un fondement causal et que ce fondement ne pouvait être fourni par des qualités ou pouvoirs occultes.

Au-delà de Kepler, c'est évidemment la force newtonienne d'attraction qui est en question, Leibniz l'accepterait comme un simple paramètre quantitatif, mais il en rejette la notion comme entité théorique et propriété primaire des corps, notion qu'il assimile à celle des qualités ou pouvoirs occultes de la scolastique aristotélicienne : d'où, par exemple, les critiques radicales qu'exprime le manuscrit *Antibarbarus physicus pro philosophia reali contra renovationes qualitatum scholasticarum et intelligentiarum chimæricarum* [4]. De façon plus rigoureuse, Leibniz suppose que le modèle tourbillonnaire peut nous conduire à une explication réelle, puisqu'il satisferait à l'exigence d'intelligibilité causale : à défaut de cela, l'explication

1. E. Aiton, *The Vortex Theory of Planetary Motion*, p. 138.
2. Lettre à Huygens, GM VI, 189.
3. Lettre à Arnauld du 23 mars 1690, GP II, 138.
4. *Antibarbarus physicus*, GP VII, 337-344.

recherchée se réduirait à une simple représentation symbolique des phénomènes, sans fondement théorique, comme chez Newton[1].

Sans entrer dans les détails mathématiques et les modifications subséquentes, considérons les traits principaux de la démonstration. Leibniz présume que le mouvement des planètes autour du Soleil est déterminé par la conjonction de trois forces. En premier lieu, une force transradiale de vection du tourbillon qui emporte la planète selon une orbite elliptique, en accord avec les lois de Kepler. Mais, si l'on considère le rayon joignant la planète au foyer occupé par le Soleil, il faut envisager un déplacement « paracentrique » résultant de l'interaction de deux forces, l'une correspondant à une force centripète dirigée vers le Soleil, l'autre à une force centrifuge propulsant le mobile suivant la tangente à l'extrémité du rayon. L'exercice de la force centrifuge est provoqué par l'entraînement tourbillonnaire. Mais celui-ci doit en outre intervenir pour rendre compte de l'expansion elliptique transradiale. Le système dépend de postulats mécanistes, des lois empiriques de Kepler et, finalement, de l'algorithme infinitésimal que Leibniz applique aux composantes de *conatus* et d'*impetus* à la racine du déplacement des corps célestes.

Fondés sur les principes de l'inertie et de la transmission de l'impulsion par contact, les postulats impliquent que les mouvements des planètes sont déterminés par des orbes fluides déférents. La détermination motrice résulte de la circulation tourbillonnaire et du mouvement paracentrique, qui combine une force centrifuge provenant de cette circulation et une force de répulsion (*conatus excussorius*), produite par l'impact de parties matérielles repoussant le mobile vers le foyer central le long du rayon. Construisant un modèle mathématique pour les paramètres dynamiques impliqués, Leibniz établit que la trajectoire de circulation harmonique s'actualise conformément aux lois képlériennes. *De facto*, Leibniz compare les avantages de ce modèle à ceux du modèle de Newton pour l'avancement des explications physiques. L'alternative se présente comme suit : pour Newton, la trajectoire serait engendrée par des déterminations inertielles instantanées, une fois postulée la force de gravitation (*vis gravitationis*) qui ne fait que symboliser les phénomènes, à défaut de rendre compte de la détermination au mouvement circulaire (ou elliptique). Selon l'hypothèse leibnizienne, le mouvement des corps célestes résulte conjointement de la circulation tourbillonnaire de l'éther et de forces de percussion dont dépendraient les effets d'attraction. La question se pose de la notion causale correspondant à la force gravitationnelle. Leibniz part de quelques modèles *a priori* concernant la transmission lumineuse et l'attraction

1. Voir F. Duchesneau, *Leibniz et la méthode de la science*, p. 229-258.

magnétique qu'il transpose mathématiquement. Puis, il se sert de ces modèles mathématiques pour symboliser les lois empiriques dont il s'agit de rendre compte. Finalement, il vise à montrer l'accord des deux types de propositions impliqués sous l'égide de principes architectoniques qui incarnent l'exigence de raison suffisante.

Cette stratégie d'explication occasionne certaines réflexions épistémologiques dans la correspondance avec Huygens et dans l'*Illustratio tentaminis de motuum cœlestium causis*[1]. Les objections de Huygens émanaient d'un physicien soucieux d'appliquer le rasoir d'Occam aux entités théoriques postulées et sensible au risque d'apories dans les hypothèses leibniziennes sur la gravitation. Il était particulièrement insatisfait de l'explication suivant laquelle la théorie du tourbillon harmonique justifierait la figure elliptique des orbites planétaires et la trajectoire atypique des comètes. Ce dernier argument était aussi au cœur des objections formulées par David Gregory au nom de l'orthodoxie newtonienne[2]. En réplique, Leibniz entreprend de montrer que l'on peut déduire les modèles particuliers correspondant aux lois empiriques de modèles quantitatifs plus généraux, tels ceux de la dynamique. En outre, il fait appel à des considérations relatives aux raisons théoriques dont on ne saurait faire l'économie, s'agissant d'atteindre de réelles explications causales. L'objectif n'est-il pas celui de parvenir aux raisons mécaniques constantes des effets empiriques, raisons qui assureraient le maintien et l'ajustement du système physique en vertu de ses propres lois, plutôt que par quelque *fiat* divin? La théorie apparaît fondée, lorsqu'elle permet de concevoir l'accord des causes efficientes comme l'effet de raisons architectoniques représentant la formule la plus probable d'engendrement d'effets correspondant à ceux que l'expérience révèle. Ce point de vue rejoint la notion d'hypothèse telle que Leibniz l'avait développée, notamment dans la correspondance avec Hermann Conring[3].

1. *Illustratio tentaminis de motuum cœlestium causis*, GM VI, 254-276.

2. D. Gregory, *Astronomiæ, physicæ et geometriæ elementa.*

3. Voir Lettres de Leibniz à Conring du début mai et de juin 1678, A II, 1, 399-429; F. Duchesneau, *Leibniz et la méthode de la science*, p. 169-258; *id.*, « Leibniz et la méthode des hypothèses ».

LA MÉTHODE DE LA SCIENCE

Pour Leibniz, la science est affaire de méthode. Et, de fait, on peut lui attribuer une méthodologie très élaborée, peut-être la plus élaboré de l'époque moderne. Au-delà de ses propres contributions à diverses disciplines scientifiques, sa théorie de la méthode constitue une œuvre en soi.

En rapport étroit avec ses travaux proprement scientifiques, Leibniz a forgé une conception méthodologique comportant des schèmes analytiques et des processus de mise en forme rationnelle des connaissances. Ainsi propose-t-il de lier structures de démonstration et de découverte. Il inventorie les moyens de codifier, d'analyser et d'expliquer les phénomènes. Il promeut la recherche de raisons suffisantes théoriques de généralité croissante. Mais, loin de dépendre de postulats purement spéculatifs, l'approche leibnizienne favorise des inférences hypothétiques soumises à validation empirique et pragmatique tout autant que conceptuelle. En définitive, la méthodologie leibnizienne incarne l'idéal d'une science qui produit, révise et contrôle des « essais architectoniques » susceptibles de représenter les causes et structures de la réalité phénoménale. D'où l'image d'une science qui se construit et se réforme conformément à ses principes.

Leibniz a formulé les linéaments de son programme dans divers projets d'encyclopédie destinés à fournir les principes d'une « science générale » (*scientia generalis*). À travers ces esquisses, se profile l'objectif de placer la totalité des disciplines rationnelles et empiriques sous une même structure démonstrative et heuristique. L'analyse combinatoire des objets les plus complexes correspondant aux phénomènes se construirait conformément à une procédure hypothético-déductive reflétant l'arrangement architectonique des éléments définitionnels impliqués. Parallèlement à cette science générale prenant en compte les composantes formelles des phénomènes, une *mathesis*, conjoignant les modes de l'analyse et de la synthèse, assurerait le rattachement des connexions empiriques dûment fondées à des raisons causales établies de façon analogique et conditionnelle[1]. Une telle construction ne peut être réalisée sans règles. La science générale est appelée à fournir un cadre normatif permettant l'invention de démonstrations et d'explications. Ce cadre comprend des procédures logiques et des schèmes conceptuels ordonnés à la formulation de programmes de recherche. L'art de la découverte (*ars inveniendi*) spécifie comment l'analyse et la synthèse mèneront à des raisons suffisantes sous forme de chaînes de définitions conditionnelles. S'objectant à la

1. Voir H. P. Schneider, « Funktion und Grundlegung der *Mathesis Universalis* im Leibnizschen System ».

conception cartésienne de la méthode, perçue comme fondée sur la seule évidence psychologique, Leibniz évoque en contrepartie le pouvoir rationnel de fabriquer des modèles et des démonstrations en forme et de recourir à des hypothèses et à des synthèses provisoires. Ainsi l'analyse étendrait la portée de nos chaînes démonstratives en les prolongeant par le moyen d'expressions symboliques. Cela implique que l'on développe des modèles « mathématiques » sur la base d'analogies, pour représenter les connexions entre phénomènes, et se donner ainsi les moyens de les intégrer dans un cadre théorique. Afin de développer une science démonstrative portant sur des vérités de fait, l'on doit donc élaborer des schèmes analytiques hypothétiques et inventer les moyens appropriés pour les corroborer, notamment par l'extension des raisons explicatives obtenues à d'autres vérités de fait.

La théorie leibnizienne des hypothèses s'affirma à l'époque où Leibniz fonda sa mécanique réformée, comme cela s'avère dans la correspondance avec Hermann Conring en 1678[1]. La question concernait alors les moyens d'anticiper les raisons causales, s'agissant de rendre compte d'ensembles donnés de phénomènes. En forgeant des équivalents définitionnels, il est en effet possible de fournir des raisons causales de substitution qui soient valides, bien que fictives, pourvu qu'elles reflètent véritablement les corrélations observées entre phénomènes et que l'expérience confirme le potentiel heuristique et explicatif de ces hypothèses. Dans les *Nouveaux Essais sur l'entendement humain*, Leibniz donne encore plus de relief à cette doctrine[2]. Les hypothèses de science peuvent accéder au statut de savoir démonstratif lorsqu'elles fournissent une représentation cohérente pour le déchiffrement analytique des phénomènes et qu'il est possible de les traduire en modèles mathématiques adéquats. Certes, Leibniz est confronté à l'objection du cercle de Pappus puisqu'il tient l'analyse et la synthèse pour des procédés démonstratifs équivalents[3]. C'était précisément ce genre de cercle logique que Descartes avait tenté d'éviter en distinguant l'usage des hypothèses pour expliquer les faits et l'usage des faits pour prouver les hypothèses. Descartes avait d'ailleurs eu recours à l'argument subsidiaire selon lequel une hypothèse peut être fondée sur un ensemble de raisons théoriques qui suffisent à expliquer telle ou telle classe

1. Voir A II, 1, 385-389, 397-402.0

2. Voir en particulier *Nouveaux Essais*, 4.12.9, A VI, 6, 453-454.

3. Sur cette question, voir J. Hintikka et U. Remes, *The Method of Analysis, Its Geometrical Origin and Its General Significance* et I. Lakatos, *Philosophical Papers*, p. 70-103.

de phénomènes[1]. Quant à Leibniz, il interprète les relations conditionnelles impliquées dans l'hypothèse au moyen de modèles mathématiques qui impliquent des relations conditionnellement nécessaires. Il situe l'hypothèse comme partie d'un réseau de raisons théoriques qui traduisent les implications causales au sein de séquences données de phénomènes et orientent la recherche de nouveaux faits qui puissent la corroborer.

Une fois développée, la notion leibnizienne d'hypothèse remplit une fonction régulatrice lorsqu'il s'agit d'évaluer des schèmes généraux servant à l'explication des phénomènes. Ainsi Leibniz relativise-t-il le recours à l'hypothèse corpusculaire que les savants de son temps, en particulier les *experimental philosophers* dans le sillage de Robert Boyle, considéraient comme la pierre de touche de la « déduction à partir des phénomènes ». Selon lui, les représentations corpusculaires que l'on peut se donner des micro-dispositifs au sein des corps ne présentent qu'une valeur relative dans la mesure où elles ne peuvent fournir qu'un éclairage provisoire sur l'infrastructure des propriétés physiques observées et sur l'interconnexion de celles-ci. Mais de tels modèles ni ne signifient les ingrédients premiers de la réalité, ni ne fournissent l'explication causale la plus fondamentale des phénomènes. Ils expriment plutôt des relations de concomitance réglée, qui, jusqu'à un certain point mathématiquement formalisable, peuvent symboliser l'ordre des causes réelles et formelles, à savoir les forces primitives, les entéléchies ou monades[2].

Indiscutablement, la construction théorique constitue le procédé méthodique le plus fondamental pour les sciences de la nature. Ce procédé implique le recours à des principes architectoniques. Ceux-ci incarnent de façon diverse l'exigence de raison suffisante, appliquée à la recherche scientifique. Ils comportent trois formes principales que l'on peut rattacher aux principes de finalité, d'identité des indiscernables et de continuité. Ils jouent un rôle régulateur et critique, lorsqu'il s'agit d'écarter des hypothèses mal conçues ou inversement de déterminer le profil d'inférences causales valides. Mais ils servent tout particulièrement à façonner des modèles mathématiques et à atteindre les vraies raisons théoriques. Le recours aux principes architectoniques illustre précisément l'approche prospective visant des raisons suffisantes, approche intégrée à la structure même de la science leibnizienne. Les éléments de méthode si astucieusement assemblés par Leibniz surpassaient de loin la pratique scientifique de la plupart de ses contemporains.

1. Voir lettre de Descartes à Morin du 13 juillet 1638, AT II, 197-198.

2. Voir C. Wilson, *Leibniz's Metaphysics. A Historical and Comparative Study*, p. 138-157.

Certes, l'œuvre scientifique de Leibniz s'était conformée à ce modèle, mais elle n'avait épuisé ni le potentiel ni la valeur programmatique de sa méthodologie. Celle-ci peut encore aujourd'hui servir de pierre de touche pour nombre de constructions scientifiques en développement[1]. La notion d'une physique mathématique subordonnée à des principes architectoniques pour la formulation de ses modèles constitue de fait une part importante de l'héritage leibnizien. Sous un angle différent, Herbert Breger a pu d'ailleurs insister sur la relation à établir entre le principe de symétrie régissant la conception des transformations et des invariants dans une physique plus récente et les modèles analytiques que Leibniz a développés sur la base de sa notion de l'unité dans la diversité – en tout état de cause une notion régulatrice pour sa conception des lois de la nature[2]. Résumons : historiquement, les deux caractéristiques les plus centrales de la science leibnizienne de la nature ont sans doute été : 1) l'idée d'une stricte correspondance entre les modes analytique et synthétique (ou combinatoire) de formulation des hypothèses explicatives ; 2) le recours aux principes architectoniques pour produire des modèles mathématiques et théoriques. Dans les deux cas, nous semblons confrontés à des traits épistémologiques majeurs de ce que nous avons pris l'habitude de considérer comme la science en acte.

François DUCHESNEAU
(Université de Montréal)

1. F. Duchesneau, « Leibniz's models for a science of nature », p. 209.
2. Voir H. Breger, *Kontinuum, Analysis, Informales*, p. 13-27.

LEIBNIZ ET LA CONNAISSANCE DU VIVANT

L'œuvre de Leibniz est parsemée d'images d'étangs pleins de poissons, de jardins pleins de plantes, de vers à soie ensevelis et de mouches ressuscitées[1]. Leibniz repère des êtres vivants dans la moindre partie de la matière et construit une philosophie où la vie semble tenir une large place. Tout cela a conduit à le voir comme un penseur baroque, vitaliste et précurseur de la biologie à naître[2].

Il est vrai que Leibniz s'est constamment intéressé à ce que nous regroupons sous le label de « sciences de la vie » mais qui ne portait alors pas ce nom, à savoir l'anatomie, l'entomologie, la botanique et, plus généralement, toutes les observations relevant de l'histoire naturelle. Des manuscrits montrent qu'il a essayé de construire sa propre physiologie et l'on sait que certains naturalistes ont joué un rôle clé dans le développement de sa pensée. Cependant, contrairement à ce que l'on pourrait croire, Leibniz n'a rien d'un vitaliste. Quand il écrit « la nature est pleine de vie »[3], il ne désigne pas par vie les phénomènes aujourd'hui associés à ce mot. Quand il note « il y a de l'organisme partout », il n'insinue pas que chaque parcelle de matière soit en elle-même un corps vivant. Quand il reproche aux Cartésiens d'avoir été trop loin en réduisant les animaux à des machines, il considère pourtant que les corps animés fonctionnent bel et bien comme des machines.

S'il est facile de parodier l'opposition entre la théorie cartésienne de l'animal-machine, d'un côté, et le système leibnizien des monades, de l'autre, les choses sont de toute évidence plus nuancées. Pour les clarifier, nous montrerons la fonction du recours à l'expérience chez Leibniz : les observations anatomiques et microscopiques étayent des thèses qui ne

1. Pour ce dernier exemple, voir par exemple *Système nouveau de la nature*, GP IV, 480.

2. La lecture vitaliste de Leibniz a pu, en France, s'appuyer sur une lecture trop rapide de Deleuze, qui évoque un « animisme » et un « organicisme » leibniziens (G. Deleuze, *Le pli*, p. 16). Ces deux notions sont trompeuses : pour Leibniz l'âme n'est ni la source d'une force spécifiquement vitale, ni un principe organisateur du corps.

3. *Principes de la nature*, § 1, GP VI, 598.

portent justement pas sur les phénomènes physiques. L'extrapolation au-delà des faits d'expérience est surtout conduite par deux principes, celui d'uniformité de la nature et celui de continuité. Une fois cette extrapolation comprise, nous pourrons appréhender la double dimension des concepts de vie et d'organisme, irréductibles à l'histoire naturelle et pourtant alimentés par elle.

Un corpus hétérogène

Leibniz est un grand lecteur d'ouvrages médicaux et il a lui-même écrit sur la réforme des institutions médicales, engageant à développer l'observation clinique et l'expérimentation anatomique[1]. Il a laissé de courts textes sur le mouvement animal[2], sur la circulation du sang[3] ou encore la sécrétion[4]. Il a passé un certain temps à répondre point par point à Stahl qui, dans sa *Theoria medica vera,* estimait que la « vie » devait constituer l'objet spécifique du médecin[5]. Il s'est efforcé de donner à ses correspondants de nouvelles pistes de recherche, par exemple sur la classification botanique[6]. Il s'est intéressé aussi bien aux plantes thérapeutiques[7] qu'aux causes des maladies[8], aux réfutations de la génération spontanée[9] qu'à l'art d'élever les vers à soie[10]. On ne pourrait ici résumer la conception leibnizienne du corps humain ou même animal, tant les lettres et manuscrits sur le sujet sont épars, parfois légèrement discordants, souvent brefs ou inachevés, relevant de disciplines qui nous semblent hétérogènes mais qui étaient alors investies par les mêmes savants. Plusieurs ouvrages

1. *Directiones ad rem medicam pertinentes*, p. 40-68.

2. Notamment dans le *De scribendis novis Medicinae Elementis* [1682 ?], d'abord édité par Pasini, *Corpo e funzioni cognitive*, p. 212. Les manuscrits médicaux seront à l'avenir publiés systématiquement dans la série VIII de l'Akademie.

3. Manuscrit intitulé *Machina animalis* [1677 ?], Pasini, *Corpo e funzioni cognitive*, p. 210.

4. *De secretione animali*, Dutens II, 2, 89.

5. Texte central pour le vivant : *The Leibniz-Stahl Controversy*.

6. *Epistola ad Gackenholtzium, De methodo botanica*, Dutens II, 2, 164-172.

7. *De novo antidysenterico americano*, Dutens II, 2, 110-119.

8. *De causis et curatione febrium* [1705 ?], Pasini, *Corpo e funzioni cognitive*, p. 224, où est affirmé que les membranes propagent sensation et mouvement, comme chez Baglivi.

9. Leibniz mentionne les arguments de Redi contre la génération spontanée : LH 37, f. 7, 6-7, Ritter n° 42487.

10. Le projet d'une culture de vers à soie pour financer la Société des sciences de Berlin est notamment mentionné par M. R. Antognazza, *Leibniz*, p. 394.

récents ont fait le point sur cette question[1]. Il n'est pas davantage possible de repérer dans les œuvres leibniziennes une théorie de la vie explicite et unifiée. Si les termes « organisme », « vie » ou « vital » y sont très présents, en particulier dans les textes les plus tardifs, c'est surtout comme un élément intégré à la métaphysique, essentiel mais secondaire, non développé pour lui-même. Pour comprendre la fonction de ce vocabulaire, nous partirons plutôt du contexte scientifique : trois aspects de l'histoire naturelle et de l'anatomie ont vraisemblablement frappé Leibniz au point d'en imprégner toute sa philosophie.

DES CORPS ORGANIQUES ET ANIMÉS DANS CHAQUE PARCELLE DE MATIÈRE

En 1679, Leibniz évoque les « expériences du microscope », selon lesquelles il y a « jusqu'à 800 000 petits animaux visibles dans une goutte d'eau et chacun de ces animaux est [...] encore un corps qui a beaucoup de rapport aux animaux ordinaires »[2]. Antoni van Leeuwenhoek, le naturaliste sans doute le plus souvent cité par Leibniz, observait en effet un grand nombre d'animalcules dans des gouttes d'eau de pluie ou d'eau poivrée, si petits qu'un grain de sable pouvait en contenir plusieurs centaines[3]. Il trouvait également de tels « atomes vivants » dans le corps humain, comme l'atteste en 1677 sa description de la semence masculine où se mouvaient par milliers comme de minuscules anguilles[4]. Plusieurs ouvrages avaient déjà présenté au public une toute nouvelle réalité microscopique, corroborant les propos romanesques sur l'emboîtement à l'infini de minuscules mondes au sein de plus grands[5] : là où la matière semble le plus simple, uniforme et inerte, apparaît désormais une multitude de corps complexes, variés et mobiles. L'un des premiers pas est marqué par les *Observationum Microscopicarum Centuria* (1656) où Pierre Borel estime que la structure des « atomes animés » qu'il décrit pourrait convaincre un athée de vénérer « leur Architecte suprême »[6]. Un autre jalon important est

1. En particulier F. Duchesneau, *Leibniz. Le vivant*, et J. E. H. Smith, *Divine Machines*, contenant tous deux des traductions de plusieurs manuscrits.

2. À Malebranche, A II, 1, 719.

3. « Observations... 1676 », *Phil. Trans.*, 1677, p. 821-831 (« living atoms », p. 821).

4. « Observationes de Natis è Semine Genitali Animalibus », *Phil. Trans.*, 1677, p. 1042.

5. Ch. Sorel, *Histoire comique de Francion*, livre XI, p. 428.

6. *Observationum Microscopicarum Centuria* [*Centuries d'observations microscopiques*], « Senatui populoque Middelburgi », n. p., notre traduction (ouvrage cité par Leibniz, A VI, 3, 478). Ni ce motif théologique, ni les observations microscopiques ne sont alors

la publication, en anglais cette fois et richement illustrée, d'une nouvelle série d'observations microscopiques par Robert Hooke en 1665. Même le plus trivial est digne d'observation. À l'image du ciron, minuscule parasite, ce « raccourci d'atome »[1] selon le mot de Pascal, s'ajoute celle de jardins microscopiques. En 1669, Leibniz mentionne la *Micrographia* de Hooke au sujet de la rouille du fer qui serait en réalité un petit bosquet[2]. Une planche de l'ouvrage reproduisant les moisissures d'un livre suscite également dans le *Journal des sçavans* un commentaire enthousiaste : « On ne croirait jamais que ce fût un amas de petites plantes et que toutes les choses qui paraissent moisies fussent autant de petits prés émaillés de diverses fleurs »[3]. Convaincu que le microscope n'a montré qu'un échantillon de ce qu'on devrait pouvoir observer partout ailleurs, Hooke note : « dans chaque petite parcelle de [la] matière, nous contemplons désormais une variété de créatures presque aussi grande que celle qu'on était auparavant capable de dénombrer dans tout l'univers lui-même »[4].

Composés d'une multitude d'organes restés invisibles à nos yeux, les insectes microscopiques sont alors invoqués hors du champ de la science naturelle à la fois pour décentrer la position de l'homme dans l'univers et pour souligner la portée limitée de l'expérience humaine[5]. Selon Malebranche par exemple, « notre vue est très limitée ; mais elle ne doit pas limiter son objet [...]. Ce qu'un ciron est à notre égard, ces petits animaux le sont à un ciron ; et peut-être qu'il y en a dans la nature, de plus petits, à l'infini, dans cette proportion si étrange d'un homme à un ciron »[6]. L'infini s'illustre dans ce rapport de grandeur qu'on peut sans cesse redoubler. C'est parfois un moyen supplémentaire de réfuter l'existence d'atomes physiques, par définition insécables : les minuscules animaux, rebaptisés « atomes animés » ou « vivants », sont hautement composés et décomposables ; leur description persuade aisément qu'un élément physique est toujours divisible, aussi petit soit-il[7]. Leibniz paraît fidèle à ce type

inédites en tant que telles. Voir C. Wilson, *The Invisible World*, p. 183 et P. Hamou, *La mutation du visible* 2, p. 100.

1. Pascal, *Pensées*, fragment 230, p. 262.

2. GP I, 19.

3. Journal du lundi 20 décembre 1666, *Journal des sçavans*, I, 1665-1666, p. 499. Hooke compare les moisissures plutôt à des champignons qu'à des plantes.

4. R. Hooke, *Micrographia*, « Pref. » (notre traduction).

5. Notons l'usage très large du terme « insecte », incluant « la vermine », voire les serpents (cf. *Dictionnaire de Furetière*).

6. *De la recherche de la vérité*, I, VI, § I, OC I, 80-81.

7. Parmi d'autres, Grew fait des récits de Leeuwenhoek une illustration de la divisibilité de la matière pour les réfractaires aux preuves mathématiques (*Cosmologia sacra*, p. 11-12).

d'usage, quand il considère, selon l'un de ses leitmotivs, « qu'il n'y a point de portion de la matière où il n'y ait une infinité de corps organiques et animés »[1].

Cependant, Leibniz ne convoque pas seulement les images microscopiques pour relativiser la portée de nos sens, pour mieux réfuter l'atomisme ou pour glorifier la création divine comme d'autres l'ont fait avant lui. Il les utilise aussi pour accréditer sa propre métaphysique, c'est-à-dire pour corroborer la réalité d'éléments simples et indestructibles. Or ces éléments sont inobservables, à la fois intrinsèquement, parce qu'ils sont immatériels, et extrinsèquement, parce qu'il y en a une infinité, bien au-delà de la portée des expériences.

Détaillons cette spécificité leibnizienne à partir de sa première occurrence. Au cours de ses échanges avec Antoine Arnauld sur le *Discours de métaphysique* en 1686-1687, Leibniz envisage qu'il y ait dans la nature une multitude de « formes substantielles » dont les propriétés sont opposées à celles de la matière. Alors que la matière est pour Leibniz seulement un agrégat de parties, une multitude que l'on peut décomposer sans fin, les formes substantielles sont au contraire parfaitement indivisibles et incorruptibles. Assimilées à des sortes d'âmes, conçues à l'exemple de ce qu'on appelle *moi*, elles sont douées de perception : elles représentent les choses extérieures à leur façon. En bref, elles jouent pour les animaux, végétaux et peut-être d'autres choses encore, le rôle que joue l'esprit en nous. Or Arnauld ne voit pas l'intérêt d'introduire ces formes substantielles ou cette multitude d'âmes, « dont on n'a aucune idée claire et distincte », qu'on ne « peut prouver par leurs effets » et qui suscitent des questionnements embarrassants. Par exemple « si le feu prenait à une de ces maisons où on nourrit des cent mille vers à soie, que deviendraient ces cent mille âmes indestructibles »[2] ?

Leibniz allègue alors les observations microscopiques pour défendre une position bien étrange aux yeux d'Arnauld :

> Ceux qui conçoivent qu'il y a quasi une infinité de petits animaux dans la moindre goutte d'eau, comme les expériences de M. Leeuwenhoek ont fait connaître, et qui ne trouvent pas étrange que la matière soit remplie partout de substances animées, ne trouveront pas étrange non plus qu'il y ait quelque chose d'animé dans les cendres mêmes et que le feu peut transformer un animal et le réduire en petit, au lieu de le détruire entièrement[3].

1. *Considérations sur les principes de vie*, GP VI, 539.
2. A II, 2, 154.
3. A II, 2, 254.

Les faits récemment décrits par l'histoire naturelle ne prouvent aucune thèse en particulier. Ils sont employés plus généralement, pour faire accepter les arguments que l'expérience ne peut confirmer et qu'Arnauld juge invraisemblables. Rien n'interdit par exemple de penser qu'« un bloc de marbre n'est qu'un tas d'une infinité de corps vivants », comme un lac plein de poissons, ou que les vers à soie brûlés dans un incendie sont simplement repliés sur « un autre théâtre »[1].

Ainsi, pour Leibniz, les « substances animées » révélées par le microscope ne sont pas seulement à entendre en un sens faible ou métaphorique, comme de petits corps complexes et mobiles. Elles indiquent avant tout l'omniprésence des « âmes » invisibles qui animent toujours ces corps organiques. À l'inverse des atomes physiques dont Leibniz ne cesse de souligner le caractère contradictoire, ces âmes, formes ou « atomes de substance »[2] sont les véritables éléments indivisibles au fondement de la matière. Pour illustrer leur présence et leur pérennité, les textes leibniziens ne cesseront plus, à partir de 1687, de mentionner des lacs pleins de poissons ou des vers à soie ensevelis.

« Ce qui ne commence pas ne périt point non plus »[3]

Le deuxième élément que retient Leibniz dans le développement de l'histoire naturelle est la formation et croissance des animaux. Or dans ce domaine aussi l'expérience donne lieu à une extrapolation, c'est-à-dire à la formulation, à partir de faits réellement observés, d'assertions que l'expérience ne peut trancher. De l'idée que la génération apparente est le résultat d'un processus de déploiement continu, Leibniz en infère l'idée que la mort n'est qu'un enveloppement, non une destruction. Selon ses propres mots, il n'y a pas de « mort à la rigueur ». Comment, en invoquant l'appui de l'expérience[4], affirmer quelque chose d'apparemment aussi contraire à l'expérience ?

Leeuwenhoek, d'un côté, estime que les animaux qu'il observe dans la semence masculine se développent simplement pour devenir l'embryon lui-même. Il suppose que de la semence masculine à la naissance en passant par l'utérus, les petits animaux croissent et changent de forme

1. A II, 2, 173.
2. *Système nouveau*, GP IV, 482.
3. A II, 2, 236
4. *Système nouveau*, GP IV, 480.

extérieure; ils gardent notamment la même « âme vivante »[1]. Swammerdam, d'un autre côté, a consacré un ouvrage à l'étude des insectes, où il « expose clairement la manière lente et presqu'insensible de l'accroissement de leurs membres, où [il] découvre évidemment l'erreur où l'on tombe d'ordinaire au sujet de leur prétendue transformation ». Ce qui infirme en particulier les théories de la génération alors les plus répandues, qui voyaient dans les insectes une classe d'êtres à part, moins noble, s'engendrant par hasard et sujette à des métamorphoses (la chenille se changeant subitement en papillon). Quand les modifications paraissent soudaines, elles sont en réalité préparées doucement en amont, sous les enveloppes externes. Cette continuité de tous les changements est exprimée par l'idée d'un devenir insensible, que Swammerdam oppose à une transformation effective[2].

Voici ce que Leibniz a retenu de ces observations : tout ce qui s'apparente à une métamorphose, ou à une apparition sans précédent, est en réalité la manifestation de petites modifications continues. La génération ne serait elle-même que l'effet de l'accroissement d'un minuscule animal déjà existant. C'est là l'idée de la préformation de l'animal :

> Ce sont aussi les expériences des Microscopes, qui ont montré que le papillon n'est qu'un développement de la chenille, mais surtout que les semences contiennent déjà la plante ou l'animal formé, quoiqu'il ait besoin par après de transformation et de nutrition ou d'accroissement pour devenir un de ces animaux, qui sont remarquables à nos sens ordinaires[3].

Ce qui suggère d'abord qu'un même animal subsiste d'un bout à l'autre de son développement, même sous des formes radicalement distinctes, même lorsqu'il semble parfaitement immobile et qu'on le croit mort. Il y a en effet des cas de morts seulement « apparentes », par exemple quand les insectes sont immobilisés par le froid et semblent ensuite ressusciter sous l'action de la chaleur[4].

Que les insectes en général, et le ver à soie en particulier, aient joué un rôle notable dans la philosophie du XVIIe siècle est attesté chez d'autres auteurs. Malebranche, par exemple, qui soutient aussi l'idée d'une préformation des corps organiques, fait dire à l'un des personnages de ses *Entretiens sur la métaphysique et sur la religion :* « quand j'étais enfant,

1. « An abstract of a letter concerning generation by an insect », *Phil. Trans.*, 1685, p. 1129.

2. *Histoire générale des insectes* [orig. en néerlandais : 1669], sous-titre de l'ouvrage et p. 8.

3. *Considération sur la doctrine d'un esprit universel unique* [1702], GP VI, 534.

4. J. Swammerdam, *Histoire générale des insectes*, p. 150.

je me souviens d'avoir nourri des vers à soie. Je prenais plaisir à leur voir faire leur coque, et s'y enterrer tout vivants pour ressusciter quelques temps après»[1]. Mais Leibniz va plus loin pour répondre au problème soumis par Arnauld, à savoir le devenir des âmes présentes dans des animaux qui auraient péri : selon lui leurs corps eux-mêmes ne sont jamais engendrés et ne périssent pas davantage. Créés avec le monde, les animaux ne font ensuite que se développer ou s'envelopper. Ainsi, bien que Leibniz ne soit pas le seul alors à envisager que les corps organiques aient été préformés par Dieu, et comme emboîtés à l'infini dans les semences de leurs géniteurs avant de se modifier et de croître, il est en revanche le seul à affirmer que la mort elle-même est un simple repli[2].

Leibniz avait une raison particulière de donner crédit à cette idée que toute transformation est l'effet d'un déploiement ou d'un pliage de structures cachées. En 1687, il avait démontré publiquement que les règles du choc des corps, point central de la physique cartésienne, étaient incorrectes et en infraction avec le principe de continuité[3]. Dans sa formulation non technique, utilisée ultérieurement par Leibniz, ce principe stipule que dans la nature rien n'est produit par saut. Le passage du mouvement au repos suppose par exemple une série d'états intermédiaires, et implique de considérer le repos comme une vitesse infiniment petite. De façon comparable, l'histoire naturelle des insectes rétablit précisément les états intermédiaires qui rendent intelligibles leurs transformations les plus remarquables. Or non seulement ce type d'études qui montre

1. *Entretiens sur la métaphysique et sur la religion*, XI, § VI, OC XII, 258. Pour sa position sur la génération, voir X, § III, OC XII, 229 : « On peut bien croire que les lois générales des communications des mouvements suffisent, pour développer, et pour faire croître les parties des corps organisés. Mais on ne peut se persuader qu'elles puissent jamais former une machine si composée. On voit bien, si on ne veut avoir recours à une providence extraordinaire, que c'est une nécessité de croire que le germe d'une plante contient en petit celle qu'elle engendre, et que l'animal renferme dans ses entrailles celui qui en doit sortir ». Leibniz rapproche lui-même sa position de celle de Malebranche dans le *Système nouveau*, GP IV, 479.

2. Pour la diversité des conceptions usuellement regroupées sous la dénomination « préformationnisme », voir « Génération », dans R. Andrault *et al.*(dir), *Médecine et philosophie de la nature humaine*, p. 220-222, et P. Bowler, « Preformation and Pre-Existence », p. 221-244. Sur le détail de la position de Leibniz et certaines de ses indécisions sur la génération des animaux (par exemple sur le rôle respectif des deux géniteurs, ou encore sur la façon dont les âmes des animaux présents dans la semence peuvent devenir raisonnables), voir J. E. H. Smith, *Divine Machines*, p. 176 *sq.* et F. Duchesneau, *Leibniz. Le vivant*, p. 204 *sq.*

3. GP III, 52.

expérimentalement la « liaison des apparences »[1] confirme que la nature obéit au principe de continuité mais, réciproquement, toute idée de discontinuité est invalidée *a priori* au titre de simple illusion. De la sorte, la mort, discontinuité apparente, est requalifiée par Leibniz comme une diminution ou un enveloppement. Ce que les naturalistes eux-mêmes n'ont jamais affirmé.

Dans le *Discours de métaphysique* qui précède immédiatement la correspondance avec Arnauld, tous les événements vécus par un individu sont dits compris, ou inclus, dans la notion de cet individu. L'idée que le « passé est gros de l'avenir » doit d'abord s'entendre selon un modèle logique, celui de l'inclusion des prédicats dans la notion d'un sujet. Désormais, Leibniz dispose d'un modèle temporel, moins technique et plus imagé : celui du ver à soie, qui manifeste un changement dont l'issue, l'état présent, est comme contenue dans l'état antérieur. Selon les termes que l'on trouve dans les récits d'observation, en particulier chez Malpighi, le ver à soie prépare sous des membranes ses quatre mues à venir et demeure un temps en état d'assoupissement, de léthargie, voire de « demi-mort », avant de rejeter ses anciennes dépouilles dont les plis se sont entièrement resserrés[2]. Chez Leibniz on retrouve ce même vocabulaire de l'enveloppement, du pli, des dépouilles organiques, de la léthargie et de la demi-mort. S'il s'applique d'abord au corps de l'animal, il figure aussi la temporalité de l'âme, et partant de l'ensemble des substances, dont chaque perception garde des traces des perceptions précédentes et contient la suivante, qui en est le déploiement.

« PAR UNE EXCEPTION TOUT À FAIT ÉTRANGE ET BIEN ÉLOIGNÉE DE L'USAGE DE LA NATURE »[3]

Leibniz considère donc d'une part qu'il y a partout des animaux et des âmes – ou du moins des principes « analogues à l'âme » –, et d'autre part que ces âmes et animaux ne meurent jamais véritablement. C'est ce que signifie l'affirmation « la nature est pleine de vie » établie dans le

1. À Foucher, GP I, 373 : « Il est vrai que d'autant plus que nous voyons de la liaison dans ce qui nous arrive, d'autant plus sommes-nous confirmés dans l'opinion que nous avons de la réalité de nos apparences ; et il est vrai aussi que d'autant que nous examinons nos apparences de plus près, d'autant les trouvons-nous mieux suivies, comme les microscopes et autres moyens de faire des expériences font voir ».

2. Tous ces termes se trouvent chez Malpighi (y compris « demi-mort » [semi-mortuus]) dans *La structure du ver à soie* [trad. de *Dissertatio de bombyce* 1669], p. 30-32.

3. *Éclaircissement sur les principes de vie et les natures plastiques* [1705], GP VI, 547.

prolongement de l'histoire naturelle et par extrapolation à partir d'elle. Or Leibniz ne cesse de mettre en scène le caractère anti-cartésien d'une telle affirmation.

Pour Descartes, seuls les hommes ont des âmes et sont doués de pensée. Ce que Leibniz condamne comme une forme d'anthropocentrisme : « il est donc aussi ridicule d'attribuer à l'homme seul la forme substantielle et la perception ou l'âme que de croire que tout a été fait pour l'homme seul et que la terre est le centre de l'univers »[1]. Que l'homme constitue une telle « exception » serait « tout à fait étrange », car contraire à la raison et à l'expérience. À la raison, parce que l'univers opère par des lois simples et uniformes, sans anomalie ni complexité inutile, conformément à la sagesse de Dieu qui en est le créateur. À l'expérience, parce que l'ensemble des observations aussi bien que le sens commun plaident en faveur de l'uniformité de la nature. Il est par exemple difficilement acceptable que les bêtes n'aient pas d'âme et ne puissent à ce titre véritablement éprouver des sentiments à l'instar des hommes. Les observations, quant à elles, tout à la fois supposent et confortent l'idée que les mêmes lois de la nature s'appliquent partout. Nous l'avons vu avec Swammerdam : estimant que les ouvrages de Dieu ne dépendent que d'un très petit nombre de règles, il refuse de voir dans les insectes une forme d'exception à « l'ordre constant et immuable de la nature »[2] ; ce qui l'incite à nier la génération spontanée et les métamorphoses. En retour, ses observations sur la transformation des insectes favorisent de nouvelles analogies, par exemple entre le papillon de nuit et la grenouille, entre la grenouille et le fœtus humain.

Pour soutenir l'uniformité de la nature, un troisième aspect du développement des sciences médicales pouvait être allégué par Leibniz : l'anatomie comparée, non pas nouvelle en tant que telle, mais en plein essor, notamment parce qu'elle bénéficie des apports de l'anatomie fine ou subtile. Avec ou sans microscope, celle-ci s'attache désormais à résoudre les organes en unités structurelles ou fonctionnelles plus petites. Or la structure fine des organes semble confirmer une grande proximité entre les différents corps animés, des végétaux aux mammifères. Notamment pour la circulation ou la respiration, dont on peut observer des avatars dans les insectes et surtout les végétaux[3]. On réfléchit aussi au mouvement de la « plante sensitive » qui se rétracte lorsqu'on la touche et qui a donc, peut-

1. *Pensées sur l'instauration d'une physique nouvelle* [1679], trad. M. Fichant, p. 25-26 ; A VI, 4, 2009.

2. J. Swammerdam, *Histoire générale des insectes*, p. 26.

3. Leibniz évoque des poumons chez les végétaux dans la lettre à Gakenholz, Dutens II, 2, 172. Voir notamment N. Grew, *Anatomy of Plants*, p. 127.

être, une forme de perception naturelle. Si l'on admet que les animaux ont des âmes, pourquoi ne pas en attribuer aussi aux végétaux qui leur ressemblent en certains aspects ? On peut très bien concevoir qu'à chaque type de vivant corresponde un type de forme substantielle ou d'âme, c'est-à-dire une certaine faculté immatérielle plus ou moins grande à percevoir :

> Je souhaiterais de pouvoir expliquer les différences ou degrés des autres expressions immatérielles qui sont sans pensée, afin de distinguer les substances corporelles simples, les vivants, et les animaux autant qu'on les peut distinguer, mais je n'ai pas assez médité là-dessus, ni assez examiné la nature pour pouvoir juger des formes, par la comparaison de leurs organes et opérations. Monsieur Malpighi fondé sur des analogies fort considérables a beaucoup de penchant à croire que les plantes peuvent être comprises sous le même genre avec les animaux, et sont des animaux imparfaits[1].

Il est vrai que l'unité de la nature, et sa « marche graduelle » « des machines les plus simples aux machines plus complexes »[2], est l'un des grands principes qui guident les observations de Malpighi. Mais une fois encore, Leibniz se prononce par analogie sur ce qui dépasse doublement la portée des observations. Il envisage d'abord qu'au-delà des vivants déjà connus, il y en ait d'autres, plus rudimentaires encore, « qui nous sont entièrement inconnus »[3] : ceux-ci auraient un principe de vie analogue à l'âme, et à ce titre exerceraient une forme de perception. Ensuite, même pour les vivants déjà connus, qu'est-ce qui permet de dire qu'ils sont doués de perception ? Ce ne sont pas les observations, dans la mesure où pour Leibniz la perception, même si elle suppose à divers degrés des organes sensoriels plus ou moins complexes, est une action purement « interne » qui n'est pas forcément manifestée par les signes extérieurs de la sensibilité. Leibniz souligne par exemple auprès d'Arnauld qu'il « n'attribue pas pour cela toujours la volupté et la douleur »[4] à toutes les âmes qu'il imagine omniprésentes dans la nature. Si, par exemple, les végétaux sont bien des êtres animés et disposent d'un principe de vie percevant, ils ont probablement une perception non consciente, non distinguée, sans relief, qui ressemble peut-être à la perception d'un homme évanoui. Les animaux, pour leur part, peuvent éprouver plaisir et douleur ; ils jouissent d'une véritable sensibilité grâce à des organes plus développés, plus proches des nôtres. Leur perception des phénomènes n'est pas complètement

1. À Arnauld, oct. 1687, A II, 2, 253.
2. *Opera omnia*, I, p. 1.
3. *Considérations sur les principes de vie* [1705], GP VI, 539.
4. À Arnauld, avril 1687, A II, 2, 189.

indistincte car leurs organes sensoriels, par exemple l'oreille ou l'œil, concentrent les stimuli extérieurs[1]. Les hommes de leur côté ont des âmes qui sont de véritables esprits, exerçant une pensée et une réflexion dont les bêtes sont incapables. Les « expressions immatérielles » évoquées par Leibniz dans la citation ci-dessus constituent donc un genre dont perception naturelle, sentiment animal et connaissance intellectuelle sont autant d'espèces[2]. L'*expression* est une notion technique et cardinale dans la métaphysique leibnizienne. Mentionnons simplement ici qu'« expression » et « représentation » d'une part, « expression » et « perception » de l'autre, sont dans les lettres à Arnauld parfois utilisées comme des équivalents[3].

Le principe d'uniformité n'autorise à parler que par présomption de la perception des autres vivants. Leibniz mentionne parfois que nous ne saurions « dire en quoi consiste la perception des plantes, et [que] nous ne concevons pas bien même celle des animaux »[4]. Nous n'y avons pas accès comme nous avons accès, par « expérience interne », à nos propres perceptions; nous n'avons pas non plus « l'expérience intime » des autres corps comme nous avons celle du corps humain[5]. En explorant les organes sensoriels, l'anatomie permettra sans doute un jour d'affiner l'analogie entre le corps humain et les autres corps organiques et, de là, de préciser par extrapolation l'analogie entre la perception dont nous sommes conscients et celle des autres principes de vie. Leibniz connaissait par exemple les travaux de ses contemporains sur l'ouïe chez les animaux[6]. Lui-même s'est intéressé en détail à la façon dont l'oreille interne dans l'homme « exprime » les tons transmis par les vibrations de l'air[7]. Il n'en demeure pas moins que le support fourni par l'expérience à la thèse de l'omni-

1. *Principes de la nature*, GP VI, 599; *Monadologie*, § 25, GP VI, 611.

2. A II, 2, 240.

3. *Ibid.* : « Une chose exprime une autre (dans mon langage), lorsqu'il y a un rapport constant et réglé entre ce qui se peut dire de l'une et de l'autre, c'est ainsi qu'une projection de perspective exprime son géométral ». Voir C. Swoyer, « Leibnizian Expression », ainsi que le chap. III du présent ouvrage.

4. À Bourguet, 1715, GP III, 581. Voir aussi *Nouveaux Essais sur l'entendement humain*, II, 9, § 11, A VI, 6, 139.

5. À Fardella, 1690, A VI, 4, 1669.

6. En particulier J.-G. Duverney et E. Mariotte : Leibniz, « Cogitationes novae quomodo formetur sonus ... atque in organo auditus exprimatur », dans *Leibnizens nachgelassene Schriften physikalischen, mechanischen und technischen Inhalts*, hrsg. E. Gerland, Leipzig, Druck und Verlag von B. G. Teubner, 1906, réimp. : New York, Olms, 1973, p. 16-27 ; en part. p. 27.

7. À Schelhammer, A III, 3, 355. Mariotte utilise en premier le verbe « exprimer » dans ce contexte (A III, 3, 375); voir R. Andrault, *La vie selon la raison*, p. 285 et 327.

présence d'âmes percevantes est indirect. Il correspond au repérage de corps organiques qu'on estime comparables au corps humain, puis à la différenciation, à partir de la variété de ces corps et de leurs organes, de différentes capacités perceptives.

La critique de l'anthropocentrisme dont se serait rendu coupable Descartes admet donc deux facettes : elle implique de ne pas prêter à l'homme seul une âme, mais elle implique également de refuser l'assimilation de tout principe immatériel à l'âme et à la sensibilité humaines.

Dans l'univers cartésien, seuls les hommes disposent d'une âme susceptible de pensée, irréductible à une matière uniforme. Dans l'univers leibnizien, des principes de vie doués de perception animent des corps organiques omniprésents dans la nature. Conformément au principe du meilleur, la variété phénoménale de cet univers leibnizien est le pendant de la simplicité de ses principes : de la vie partout, mais des principes de vie divers, dotés de capacités différentes ; une matière dans laquelle il y a *in fine* partout des corps vivants, mais dont chaque petite partie n'est pas elle-même un vivant. C'est le cas d'un morceau de pierre, par exemple, qui est un corps non organique, et n'a à ce titre pas de principe de vie ou d'âme en propre. Car « il ne faut point dire pour cela, que chaque portion de la matière est animée, c'est comme nous ne disons pas qu'un étang plein de poissons est un corps animé, quoique le poisson le soit »[1]. En effet, au moins à partir du *Système nouveau de la nature et de la communication des substances,* en 1695, Leibniz établit une distinction très nette entre les corps organiques et animés d'un côté, et les simples agrégats ou masses de matière, de l'autre. Au titre d'agrégats, il mentionne le morceau de marbre, l'horloge, ou même le troupeau de moutons, dénués d'unité réelle, de vie et de perception. Cette distinction entre l'organique et l'inorganique est illustrée par l'impossibilité de la génération spontanée et par la nécessité de la préformation : un morceau de pierre ou de terre ne se transformera jamais en un corps animé et vivant, quelles que soient les modifications qu'on lui fasse subir[2]. Il faut donc parvenir à concevoir que pour Leibniz le moindre

1. *Considérations sur les principes de vie*, GP VI, 539-540.

2. « Les recherches des Modernes nous ont appris, et la raison l'approuve, que les vivants dont les organes nous sont connus, c'est-à-dire, les plantes et les animaux, ne viennent point d'une putréfaction ou d'un chaos, comme les anciens ont cru, mais de semences préformées, et par conséquent de la transformation des vivants préexistants », *Principes de la philosophie* § 6, GP VI, 601. Sur le net partage entre corps organiques et corps inorganiques, outre la réfutation de la génération spontanée, voir Leibniz, *Protogaea,* Dutens II, 2, 181, sur l'origine des fossiles, dont le *De solido intra solidum* de Nicolas Steno est une source d'inspiration. Notons que dans les lettres à Arnauld, en 1687, Leibniz laisse ouverte une possibilité qu'il refusera

caillou contienne à l'infini des corps organiques et animés sans être lui-même un tel corps organique.

EN QUOI LES CORPS ORGANIQUES SONT-ILS « ANIMÉS » ?

La difficulté de la position de Leibniz, c'est qu'elle s'appuie sur l'usage, ou le sens commun, pour critiquer l'idée cartésienne selon laquelle seul l'homme dispose d'une âme. Mais les notions d'âme et de principe de vie n'y correspondent pas au sens commun – pas plus d'ailleurs qu'aux théories héritées d'Aristote. Ce que Leibniz entend par vie, c'est uniquement la perception et l'appétit; et par principes de vie, les unités actives qui perçoivent. Or Leibniz se fait de la perception une idée très générale : elle est la représentation de la multitude dans l'unité[1] (comme la représentation de choses divisibles et matérielles dans un seul être indivisible à l'instar du moi)[2]. L'appétit est lui-même défini comme la tendance d'une perception à une autre. Il est possible que des êtres perçoivent sans que de l'extérieur on en repère des marques certaines. En outre, l'unité des principes de vie n'a rien à voir avec l'unité apparente ou empirique, à laquelle on pense quand on dit que le morceau de marbre est « un » ou même que le corps d'un mouton forme un tout intègre, qu'on ne peut diviser sans qu'il périsse. C'est au contraire une unité absolument indivisible, qui ne peut être matérielle. L'âme est aussi assimilée par Leibniz à ce qu'il appelle une « entéléchie » ou encore une « force primitive », source de ses propres actions. Mais ces actions sont purement internes : le principe de vie exerce une force, ou loi de changements, par laquelle il génère ses perceptions. Certes, cette force interne est à l'origine de toute force physique, et donc du mouvement. Néanmoins, si l'on s'en tient au niveau des phénomènes, aux corps et à la matière observables, toutes les choses naturelles obéissent aux mêmes types de mouvement. Rien ne justifie de voir dans les phénomènes vitaux des sortes d'exceptions aux lois mécaniques. C'est en cela qu'il convient d'expliquer les fonctions des corps vivants exactement comme on explique celles des machines : « tout ce qui se produit dans la matière provient de l'état de la matière qui

par la suite, à savoir l'existence de substances corporelles (un corps + une forme substantielle) qui ne soient pas animées, ni vivantes (voir A II, 2, 237).

1. M. Fichant relève le caractère « formel et universel » de la perception (Leibniz, *Discours de métaphysique. Monadologie*, n. 11 p. 472). Voir lettre à Bourguet, GP III, 581 : « il suffit qu'il y ait une variété dans l'unité, pour qu'il y ait une perception ».

2. À Arnauld, oct. 1687, A II, 2, 240.

précède, par les lois du changement. Et c'est cela que veulent, ou doivent vouloir, ceux qui disent que tout peut être expliqué mécaniquement dans les corps »[1], écrit-il en 1710 contre Stahl, qui voulait à l'inverse accorder un statut spécial au vivant. Dans tous ses textes, manuscrits, correspondances ou opuscules publiés, jamais Leibniz ne dément ce grand principe mécaniste. Il ne faut donc pas penser que l'âme exerce une action biologique sur le corps, qu'elle en assure la conservation ou l'unité fonctionnelle. L'idée d'une influence quelconque d'un principe vital sur la structure ou les mouvements corporels est radicalement étrangère à la pensée de Leibniz. Donc à proprement parler, l'âme, ou le principe de vie, et l'action qu'ils exercent en tant qu'unités véritables, se situent à un niveau métaphysique, extérieur au champ de la physiologie. Corollairement, les thèses sur les âmes et substances animées ne peuvent être déduites de l'observation des corps vivants.

Dans sa philosophie tardive, Leibniz utilise le terme générique de « monades » pour désigner toutes les unités actives et perceptives que sont dans d'autres textes les formes substantielles, les âmes ou encore, plus tardivement, les principes de vie[2]. En un sens, cela lève l'ambiguïté du vocabulaire de l'animation, qui pourrait faire croire que l'âme est directement source de la spontanéité animale pour Leibniz. Dans le mot « monade », c'est d'abord la notion d'unité que l'on entend (« *Monas* est un mot grec qui signifie l'unité, ou ce qui est un »)[3]. Or cette monade, il la décrit parfois comme un « miroir vivant », qui exprime tout l'univers en vertu de sa propre action interne. Il y a donc, progressivement chez Leibniz, une inversion du définissant et du défini : dans les lettres à Arnauld, c'est quelque chose d'analogue à l'âme, conféré présomptivement aux végétaux et animaux, qui explique la spécificité des vivants, en particulier leur unité; dans les années 1700-1710, les termes « vie », « vivant » et « vital » caractérisent désormais régulièrement ce qu'est une monade ou une âme[4].

1. *Animadversiones circa Assertiones aliquas Theoriae Medicae verae Stahlii*, Dutens II, 2, 131. Sur le mécanisme leibnizien, voir F. Duchesneau, notamment : « Leibniz et Stahl » et « Leibniz's model for analyzing organic phenomena ».

2. Selon plusieurs textes, la monade désigne l'ensemble âme – ou entéléchie première – + matière première passive. Notamment dans le *De ipsa natura* et les lettres à De Volder. Mais ce point doctrinal ne modifie pas notre propos.

3. *Principes de la nature*, § 1, GP VI, 598.

4. « Extrait du Dictionnaire de M. Bayle article Rorarius… avec mes remarques », GP IV, 532 : « chaque âme est un miroir vivant représentant l'univers suivant son point de vue et surtout par rapport à son corps ».

LES MACHINES DE LA NATURE : PLIS ET ROUAGES

Qu'est-ce qu'un animal, ou, plus généralement un être vivant? C'est une monade, une âme ou un esprit, associé à un corps organique dont il fait l'unité et qui constitue l'instrument de ses perceptions. Si les actions vitales de la monade ne sont pas directement accessibles par l'expérience externe, les corps organiques ont en revanche des propriétés par lesquelles ils diffèrent visiblement des corps non organiques. Pour les appréhender, Leibniz forge le concept apparemment oxymorique de « machines de la nature » dont la description est profondément originale[1].

À s'en tenir au *Système nouveau de la nature et de la communication des substances* (1695), on peut discerner quatre critères identifiant une « machine de la nature ». Selon le premier critère, elle a un nombre d'organes véritablement infini; ce qui la rend indestructible. Selon le second, elle est machine dans ses moindres parties, jusqu'à l'infini. Plus tard, dans la *Monadologie* (1714), Leibniz donne un exemple : « la dent d'une roue de l[ai]ton a des parties ou fragments qui ne nous sont plus quelque chose d'artificiel, et n'ont plus rien qui marque de la machine par rapport à l'usage où la roue était destiné[e] »[2]. Ce propos concorde avec les développements récents de l'anatomie : aussi loin que s'étend désormais la dissection, elle révèle au sein de chaque organe des parties encore complexes, structurées et adaptées à certains usages : le cœur est composé de fibres musculaires qui peuvent se contracter; ces fibres sont elles-mêmes composées de fibrilles; le foie est une glande conglomérée, composée à son tour de petites glandes, etc. Toute partie d'organe disséqué semble donc elle-même fonctionnelle : elle est encore un véritable instrument ou « machine » en vertu de sa propre structure. On ne parvient jamais par l'analyse matérielle à des parties homogènes comme peut l'être un bout de laiton, matériau brut, encore non travaillé, non adapté à un usage spécifique. Passons au troisième critère : une machine de la nature demeure « toujours cette même machine qu'elle a été, n'étant que transformée par des différents plis qu'elle reçoit, et tantôt étendue, tantôt resserrée et comme concentrée lorsqu'on la croit perdue »[3]. En partie appuyée sur

1. Voir M. Fichant, « Leibniz et les machines de la nature ». Sur la notion même de machines de la nature et l'idée d'emboîtement, voir R. Andrault, *La vie selon la raison*, p. 135 *sq*. Sur le sens extrêmement général du mot « machine » à l'époque, voir S. Roux, « Quelles machines pour quels animaux? Jacques Rohault, Claude Perrault, Giovanni Alfonso Borelli », p. 75.

2. GP VI, 618.

3. GP VI, 482.

l'observation des insectes, la pérennité des corps organiques implique qu'une fois préformés par Dieu, les transformations des vivants se réduisent à des modifications mécaniques d'accroissement, de diminution et de pliage[1]. Si les seules lois du mouvement ne peuvent expliquer la complexité et l'artifice des machines de la nature, dont Dieu est par conséquent nécessairement le créateur, du moins expliquent-elles toutes les modifications possibles des corps organiques une fois créés. En ce sens, la préformation soutenue par Leibniz n'apparaît pas tant comme une critique dirimante du mécanisme cartésien que comme sa correction, précisant ses conditions de validité[2]. Enfin, dernier critère, et non le moindre : il y a dans toute machine de la nature une véritable unité, conférée par « l'âme ou forme », « qui répond à ce qu'on appelle moi en nous »[3]. Nous avons déjà signalé plus haut l'aspect fondamental de cette analogie entre le « moi » et les autres vivants.

Tous ces critères ont partie liée avec l'expérience, interne (le « moi en nous »), et externe (l'anatomie, l'embryologie, l'entomologie) ; mais extrapolés à l'infini, ils lui sont nettement irréductibles. Ils sont systématisés en vertu de principes rationnels et interprétés en accord avec le principe d'uniformité de la nature, le principe du meilleur et le principe de continuité.

La combinaison de ces deux types de critères, internes et externes, est d'ailleurs subtile. Si l'on s'en tient à ses propriétés corporelles, la machine de la nature qu'est chaque corps organique n'a pas l'unité simple de l'âme à laquelle elle est associée. Au contraire, ce qui la caractérise est sa complexité. Mais elle présente tout de même une autre forme d'unité qui lui permet de former un vivant avec cette âme. D'une part une unité fonctionnelle, parce que chaque organe contribue au fonctionnement de la machine sans qu'il y ait, à un quelconque niveau de décomposition, de l'échelle macroscopique à l'échelle microscopique, un saut ou une discontinuité qui révèlerait une partie non intégrée. D'autre part une unité diachronique, la continuité des modifications au cours du temps par laquelle la machine subsiste sous ses différents plis. Dans les deux cas, la continuité, garante de l'unité indestructible de l'animal, est rendue possible par la complexité de l'arrangement organique (l'infinité des organes, la multiplicité des « enveloppes »).

1. Dès 1679, le pli est utilisé par Leibniz comme une forme de variation qui préserve l'unité, par opposition à la division (A VI, 4, 1401).

2. C'est d'ailleurs aussi le cas du préformationnisme de Malebranche, qu'il présente comme la conséquence d'un mécanisme conséquent. Voir *infra* la citation donnée n. 1 p. 178.

3. *Système nouveau*, GP IV, 482.

Cette théorie peut sembler difficile. Retenons un élément important, et constant : c'est le couplage, en tout être vivant, entre un principe immatériel qui perçoit et un corps organique qui est l'instrument de cette perception. Car si toute âme ou monade représente plus particulièrement son propre corps, à travers lui elle représente les modifications de tout l'univers, passé, présent et futur. Or à l'infinité de cette expression ou perception au sens large, doit répondre l'infinité des organes enveloppés dans toute machine de la nature[1]. De la sorte, « les corps organiques ne sont jamais sans âme » et « les âmes ne sont jamais séparées de tout corps organique »[2].

Il y a deux conceptions du corps vivant qui ont été souvent imputées à Leibniz sans qu'elles soient vraiment prescrites par les textes. La première, c'est l'idée que chaque partie d'un corps vivant est un corps vivant, comme dans les fictions de Cyrano de Bergerac, où un amas de petits hommes forme un grand jeune homme, unifié et animé par un petit roi[3]. Certes, il y a des vivants partout. À ce titre, il y en a dans les moindres parties d'un corps animal, par exemple dans les humeurs. Mais il y en a aussi dans l'étang, qui n'est en soi pas un vivant. Ce n'est pas l'inclusion de vivants qui fait la spécificité du vivant. Car n'importe quelle masse de matière implique à son fondement des monades avec leurs corps organiques. En outre, au cours de l'échange avec Stahl, Leibniz rappelle que « n'importe quelle partie d'un corps organique n'est pas un corps organique : même si le cœur retient assez longtemps son mouvement une fois qu'il est extrait du corps, il n'est pas prouvé par là que le cœur soit un corps animé »[4]. Au-delà de cet exemple nous disposons de peu d'éléments pour préciser la façon dont les petits animaux ou végétaux invisibles partout présents s'agencent spécifiquement ou non dans les vivants. On sait simplement qu'un même corps organique n'est pas toujours constitué par la même portion de matière, qui se renouvelle sans cesse. Par conséquent, il ne faut pas penser que l'âme de ce corps possède « d'autres vivants inférieurs, destinés toujours à son

1. À De Volder, GP II, 251 ; *Monadologie*, § 62 et § 63, GP VI, 618. Voir P. Phemister, *Leibniz and the Natural World*, p. 135.

2. GP VI, 545.

3. *États et empires de la lune et du soleil*, p. 240, cité dans les *Nouveaux Essais*, A VI-6, 220 : les génies auraient « le plaisant avantage, que l'imaginatif Cyrano attribue à quelques Natures animées dans le Soleil, composées d'une infinité de petits volatiles, qui en se transportant selon le commandement de l'âme dominante forment toutes sortes de corps ». Cyrano est également cité dans la *Théodicée*, § 343, GP VI, 318. Voir aussi Cyrano, *États et empires*, p. 116 : « peut-être que notre chair, notre sang et nos esprits ne sont autre chose qu'une tissure de petits animaux [poux, vers, cirons], qui [...] nous prêtent mouvement par le leur ».

4. *Responsiones ad Stahlianas observationes*, ad. obs. 21, § 17, Dutens II, 2, 157.

service »[1]. En tout cas, rien n'indique qu'un organe quelconque soit en lui-même un corps animé, c'est-à-dire un corps organique associé à une âme ou principe de vie[2].

La seconde interprétation s'appuie sur la notion tardive de monade dominante[3]. Car la monade (ou entéléchie, ou âme) qu'il faut concevoir dans les vivants par analogie avec le moi est parfois caractérisée comme dominante, ou encore « centrale » et « distinguée »[4]. Ces termes spécifient la monade qui fait l'unité d'un corps organique en son ensemble, par opposition aux monades subordonnées, unités dont procède la matière de ce corps, à leur tour associées à leurs propres corps organiques. Or on a parfois compris cette distinction ainsi : la monade dominante d'un animal donné régirait des monades subordonnées accomplissant des fonctions secondaires dans les organes de l'animal. Mais d'une part, jamais Leibniz n'explicite la domination autrement qu'en termes de degré de perfection des monades dont les perceptions peuvent être plus ou moins claires. À notre connaissance, aucun texte n'indique comment articuler subordination des monades et subordination des fonctions corporelles au sein d'un même animal[5]. D'autre part, dans la mesure où Leibniz écrit au moins une fois que le cœur n'est pas nécessairement animé, dans la mesure, surtout, où il exclut d'utiliser les âmes et monades dans l'explication des phénomènes, il invite plutôt à ne pas expliquer les relations monadiques à partir de la physiologie.

1. *Monadologie*, § 71, GP VI, 619

2. Et pour la réfutation de l'idée selon laquelle le corps animal a directement pour parties des substances corporelles, c'est-à-dire des vivants (*i.e.* monades + corps organiques), voir M. Fichant, « Leibniz et les machines de la nature » et P. Phemister, *Leibniz and the Natural World*, p. 98.

3. Notamment lettre à De Volder 1703, GP II, 252. Voir B. Look, « On Monadic Domination in Leibniz's Metaphysics ».

4. *Principes de la nature*, § 3, GP VI, 599.

5. Pas plus qu'il ne dit précisément comment la causalité finale dans l'âme répond concrètement à la causalité efficiente dans le corps organique (R. Andrault, *La raison des corps*, p. 144 *sq.*).

CONCLUSION : ORGANISME ET THÉOLOGIE PHYSIQUE

Les propriétés des corps organiques révélées par les sciences de la nature fournissent un motif d'admiration de la création divine et rencontrent l'ambition de la théologie physique : prouver et glorifier Dieu à partir de l'expérience du monde.

> Il n'y a point de chaos dans l'intérieur des choses, et l'organisme est partout dans la matière dont la disposition vient de Dieu. Il s'y découvrirait même d'autant plus qu'on irait plus loin dans l'anatomie des corps; et on continuerait de le remarquer quand même on pourrait aller à l'infini [1].

Le terme « organisme » n'a donc pas le sens qu'il aura par la suite, en particulier au XIXe siècle. L'organisme ici n'est pas une chose, un corps, ni une sorte de totalité. Il est une propriété de la matière : « son ordre et son artifice » [2], c'est-à-dire la subtilité de son arrangement et l'industrie dont elle témoigne. Dans certains textes de Leibniz cependant, organisme et machine naturelle sont présentés comme synonymes [3]. Cela signale l'ambiguïté tout autant que l'importance des considérations sur le vivant dans la philosophie leibnizienne : les machines de la nature sont d'abord des corps organiques, de ceux qu'étudie l'anatomie, et elles comportent des propriétés spécifiques. Mais parce qu'il y a des vivants partout, il y a des machines de la nature partout dans la matière. De la sorte, par métonymie, on peut dire que l'organisme est une propriété de la matière elle-même, et non seulement des corps vivants et de leurs organes.

Ainsi, le point de départ de Leibniz, à savoir la distinction entre corps organiques et simples masses avérée par l'expérience, est plutôt gommé lorsqu'il s'agit de souligner la perfection de l'auteur de la nature et l'uniformité de la création. Par extrapolation et inclusion, l'organisme, de propriété des organes, devient plus généralement l'ordonnancement divin de toute matière. C'est donc l'usage de l'anatomie au profit de la théologie naturelle, joint à la polémique contre les Cartésiens, qui conduit Leibniz à « vitaliser » toute la nature, c'est-à-dire à estimer que la nature est pleine de vie et la matière pleine d'organisme.

Raphaële ANDRAULT
(CNRS, IHRIM, ENS Lyon)

1. *Théodicée*, GP VI, 40.
2. A II, 2, 237.
3. À Lady Masham, 1704, GP III, 356 : « je définis l'Organisme, ou la Machine naturelle, que c'est une machine dont chaque partie est machine ». Sur les enjeux théologiques de l'organisme, voir R. Andrault, *La vie selon la raison*, p. 32 *sq.*

POLITIQUE ET ÉTHIQUE CHEZ LEIBNIZ

> [...] je tiens que la vertu ferait plus d'effet infiniment, accompagnée comme elle est, de tant de solides biens ; si quelque heureuse révolution du genre humain la mettait un jour en vogue et comme à la mode
>
> G. W. Leibniz, *Nouveaux Essais sur l'entendement humain* (II, XXI, § 37, A VI, 6, 190)

La réflexion politique leibnizienne présente un caractère instable, d'une part parce que ses implications philosophiques débordent des limites de la politique *stricto sensu* ; d'autre part, parce qu'elle ne peut être comprise sans référence aux événements de l'époque. La philosophie politique n'est jamais parfaitement « pure », étant toujours traversée par des éléments contingents. On ne peut donc pas interpréter la politique de façon immuable, indépendamment des développements historiques et politiques. Si cette observation vaut pour tout penseur politique, elle s'applique plus encore à Leibniz. Ayant reçu une formation de juriste, il n'a pas souhaité devenir professeur d'université, mais a préféré travailler pour des princes : avant d'être philosophe politique et philosophe du droit, il était diplomate, politicien et juriste [1]. En ce sens, il observait la politique de près, à partir de la « verità effettuale della cosa », pour reprendre la formule de Machiavel.

Cette particularité de la figure leibnizienne n'est pas sans effets sur la structure de ses écrits politiques. Si l'on trouve chez tout philosophe de fortes différences entre ses écrits plus systématiques et ceux qui répondent aux circonstances, cela est particulièrement vrai de Leibniz. Nombre de ses œuvres sont étroitement liées à des faits spécifiques, et ne peuvent donc être comprises par une théorie générale. Si d'autres écrits présentent un

1. Sur Leibniz comme politicien : *cf.* C. Haase, « Leibniz als Politiker » ; L. Stern, *Die politischen Ideen*.

caractère plus systématique, lié à la métaphysique et à l'éthique, il serait difficile de trouver chez Leibniz un texte équivalent, par exemple, au *Léviathan* de Hobbes ou au *Contrat social* de Rousseau, c'est-à-dire à des œuvres où se trouverait « synthétisée » la conception politique du philosophe. Cela ne signifie pas que la production politique leibnizienne ait été limitée. Actuellement, la série des *Politische Schriften* de l'*Akademie-Ausgabe* compte huit volumes, couvrant la période antérieure à 1700, et l'on attend encore des volumes pour les années suivantes, jusqu'en 1716, date de sa mort. Mais la structure de la pensée politique de Leibniz présente une grande diversité interne, sans véritable systématicité. Les spécialistes sont partagés quant à la possibilité d'appliquer à Leibniz l'expression de « philosophie politique »[1] : elle serait problématique, dans la mesure où la politique, étant liée à des événements contingents, serait interprétée comme un élément non susceptible d'une fondation philosophique. Une position particulièrement radicale à cet égard est celle de Bertrand Russell, qui a soutenu que le seul but politique de Leibniz a été de « servir » les princes. Mon essai s'efforcera de mettre en question une telle approche, sans soutenir la thèse d'une identité immédiate et d'une liaison non problématique entre philosophie et politique, mais en soulignant l'importance des liens qui existent entre ces domaines. Comme il s'agit d'un sujet très complexe, il est donc possible de soutenir la thèse de l'existence d'une philosophie politique leibnizienne, mais avec une sorte d'instabilité[2].

La politique n'est pas conçue par Leibniz en termes ascientifiques : elle possède un statut de vérité, mais d'une façon différente de la mathématique, parce qu'elle concerne des vérités de fait, et non des vérités de raison. En effet, elle ne se fonde pas sur une certitude entière ou métaphysique, mais plutôt sur un élément de probabilité. Toutefois, Leibniz a parfois tenté de « mathématiser » la politique. Par exemple, dans un texte de jeunesse, le *Specimen demonstrationum politicarum pro eligendo rege polonorum* (1669), Leibniz se sert d'une méthode mathématique afin de résoudre la question du choix du futur roi de Pologne. Même plus tard, par exemple dans des écrits où il cherche à peser les « raisons » de la paix et celles de la guerre, on peut repérer une approche « mathématisante ». En général, il y a des éléments *more geometrico demonstrata*, mais cela ne signifie pas que Leibniz établisse une sorte de mathématique politique. En effet, la politique, liée à la dimension de la contingence, ne peut pas

1. Voir H. Schepers, « Demonstrationes Catholicae », p. 3, qui soutient la thèse de la possibilité d'appliquer à Leibniz l'expression de « philosophie politique ».

2. Sur certaines des marques distinctives de la philosophie politique de Leibniz : L. Basso, *Individuo e comunità* ; *id.* (dir.), *Republic and Common Good*.

atteindre la certitude propre à la mathématique. En même temps, Leibniz insiste sur l'importance de donner un degré de scientificité même aux domaines fondés sur les vérités de fait. La compréhension de cette complexité du politique (et non pas seulement de la politique) a conduit à l'idée d'une logique de la probabilité. Celle-ci permettrait de tenir compte du statut propre de la politique par rapport à la mathématique. Mais Leibniz n'a développé que partiellement la science de la probabilité. Il s'agit d'une sorte de tentative, seulement commencée : en ce sens, la question reste inachevée.

Il faut aborder le sujet du rapport entre politique, d'un côté, et théologie et métaphysique, de l'autre. Cette problématique est très importante parce que Leibniz soutient souvent que l'on ne peut pas fonder la politique *iuxta propria principia*, indépendamment de la structure générale des choses. En outre, la critique qu'il adresse à Hobbes (et à Pufendorf) part justement de l'idée que ces penseurs auraient conçu un droit naturel détaché de la théologie et de la métaphysique. Selon Leibniz, cette conception politique, fondée sur des conventions, conduit à la pleine justification de la souveraineté et à l'élimination de tout espace de liberté des individus et des groupes. La référence à la théologie et à la métaphysique présente donc une fonction stratégique pour la constitution du corps politique. Quand on fait référence au bien commun et à la justice, on ne peut pas oublier que, dans l'ontologie leibnizienne, toutes les choses tendent au bien commun selon une loi de justice. Le bien commun et la justice ne constituent pas un « produit » de la politique. Par exemple, dans l'*Origine radicale des choses*, le monde n'est pas seulement interprété comme une *machina*, mais aussi comme une *optima respublica* ayant pour fin la félicité des individus : « [...] le monde n'est pas seulement la machine la plus admirable, mais, en tant qu'elle est composée d'âmes, c'est aussi la meilleure république, où il est pourvu à toute la félicité et à toute la joie possible qui constitue leur perfection physique »[1]. Et cette conception constitue aussi une critique des philosophes comme Hobbes, qui réactiveraient la position de Thrasymaque en réduisant le juste à ce qui est utile au plus fort, et en niant la possibilité d'un espace de justice qui ne soit pas l'effet de la décision du pouvoir constitué. Précisons deux aspects.

Le premier de ces aspects concerne le rôle de la souveraineté. Il est vrai que Leibniz ne conçoit pas le corps politique à la manière contractualiste de Hobbes et de Pufendorf. Il est également vrai que l'élément de la souveraineté, fondée sur le consensus, n'est pas aussi central. Mais cela ne signifie pas que Leibniz élimine la dimension de la souveraineté. On pourrait

1. *De rerum originatione radicali*, 1697, GP VII, 306, Schrecker, 185.

soutenir la thèse selon laquelle Leibniz présente des aspects prémodernes, parce que la domination politique ne fonctionne pas à partir des règles modernes de la légitimation. Il s'agit d'une *auctoritas* qui n'est pas vraiment fondée sur le consensus et qui n'est donc pas dotée des marques distinctives du contractualisme. Cette image de Leibniz, répandue[1], ne permet cependant pas de comprendre plusieurs éléments de l'approche leibnizienne et de son développement interne. En effet, dans les premiers écrits jusqu'au *Caesarinus Fürstenerius* (1677) on constate la présence d'une sorte de modèle médiéval, proche de celui de Dante – un modèle qui tourne autour des deux « soleils » de l'Empereur et du Pape. Plus tard, en revanche, la pensée leibnizienne est moins caractérisée par cette sorte de « nostalgie » du Moyen Âge. Par exemple, dans les *Observations sur le projet d'une paix perpétuelle de M. l'Abbé de Saint-Pierre* (1715) on revient aussi au modèle médiéval, mais l'enjeu de la réflexion est d'interpréter la balance entre les différentes puissances (sans réduire ces dernières à un schéma unique) à l'intérieur du scénario européen de l'époque.

Leibniz s'efforce plutôt d'interpréter la dynamique moderne avec plus de complexité que Hobbes et Pufendorf, mais non de « restaurer » le passé. En outre, il faut souligner que Leibniz se trouvait dans une conjoncture, après la paix de Westphalie, où l'Empire Germanique était lui-même en phase de transformation, avec une coexistence entre l'« ancien », c'est-à-dire la persistance des éléments féodaux, et le « nouveau », c'est-à-dire l'introduction d'éléments de *Verstaatlichung*, en commençant à posséder certaines marques distinctives de l'État moderne[2]. On rencontre donc des ambivalences à cet égard. Par conséquent il serait faux d'affirmer que Leibniz refuse entièrement la dimension moderne de la souveraineté : s'attachant aux cas concrets de l'Empire germanique, des Provinces Unies, de la Confédération helvétique, pays très différents les uns des autres, qui sont dotés de souveraineté, mais de manière décentralisée et divisée, Leibniz préfère un système fédéraliste, et met en doute le modèle centraliste français. En tout cas, la question de la *summa potestas* n'est pas abordée à partir de l'élément du contrat social, à la différence de Hobbes, Pufendorf, Locke, en étant conçue à travers les formes concrètes d'association qui opèrent dans la *societas*, avec les hiérarchies existantes. Même s'il y a des ambivalences à cet égard, et l'on peut repérer aussi des aspects

1. Par exemple, selon des différentes interprétations, on peut voir J. Baruzi, *Leibniz et l'organisation* ; N. Bobbio, « Leibniz e Pufendorf », *Rivista di filosofia*, 1, 1947, p. 118-129 ; W. Schneiders, « *Vera politica* ».

2. Voir M. Stolleis, *Geschichte des öffentlichen Rechts*.

contractuels, chez Leibniz le contrat social ne joue pas une fonction de fondation du corps politique.

Le deuxième aspect qui rend la question plus compliquée, en lien avec le premier, concerne la question centrale de la justice et le fait qu'elle ne se réduit pas à des considérations de pouvoir. En particulier, il faut aborder son rapport avec la réflexion de Hobbes et de Pufendorf (surtout de Hobbes, parce que Leibniz considère Pufendorf comme une sorte de mauvais imitateur de Hobbes). Or, critiquer la neutralisation hobbesienne de la justice et sa subordination à une souveraineté absolue, ne signifie pas oublier la question du pouvoir, selon une vision idéalisée de la politique. En effet, Leibniz reconnaît à Hobbes le mérite d'avoir compris l'importance de l'unité de la *summa potestas*, sans laquelle la sûreté de l'État est mise en péril. Leibniz remarque à plusieurs reprises que les deux buts de la république sont la félicité et la sûreté. Si la félicité joue un rôle stratégique, en continuité avec l'aristotélisme politique, on ne peut pas oublier l'importance de la question de la *securitas publica*. Ces deux problématisations peuvent compliquer l'image de Leibniz, souvent présenté comme un critique absolu de Hobbes et de Pufendorf, en mettant en évidence son rapport complexe à ces penseurs [1].

Ayant jusqu'à maintenant surtout insisté sur le schéma binaire métaphysique-politique, il faut introduire un troisième élément crucial : l'éthique. Très souvent, on sous-estime l'éthique de Leibniz, en maintenant qu'il n'y aurait pas chez lui de véritable reconnaissance de ce domaine puisqu'il ne jouerait qu'un rôle secondaire dans la structure générale de sa pensée. Cette position a ses raisons. En effet, il ne semble pas que l'éthique a une place autonome. Et l'on ne trouve pas chez Leibniz un œuvre semblable à l'*Éthique* de Spinoza, au *Traité de la nature humaine* de Hume, ou, plus tard, à la *Critique de la raison pratique* de Kant – un ouvrage qui permettrait d'appréhender de façon systématique sa réflexion sur la morale. La place de l'éthique est en outre étroitement limitée par la métaphysique, d'un côté, et par le droit, de l'autre, si bien qu'elle risque de ne pas avoir un espace propre. Ces observations nous permettent de comprendre certains aspects de la question, mais ne sont pas suffisantes.

1. Voir, selon des différentes interprétations, E. Ruck, *Die Leibniz'sche Staatsidee*, p. 38-55 ; G. Grua, *La justice humaine*, p. 367 ; C. J. Friedrich, « Philosophical Reflections », p. 62-63 ; H.-P. Schneider, « Leibniz Gedanken », p. 21 ; F. Sturm, *Das römische Recht* ; R. J. Mulvaney, « The Early Development » ; H. Schiedermair, *Das Phänomen der Macht*, p. 183-185 ; N. Jolley, « Leibniz on Hobbes » ; P. Riley, *Leibniz' Universal Jurisprudence* ; T. J. Hochstrasser, *Natural Law Theories*, p. 72-110 ; I. Hunter, *Rival Enlightenments* ; U. Goldenbaum, « "All you need is Love, Love" » ; D. Döring, « Leibniz's Critique of Pufendorf ».

En effet, remarquer la singularité du statut de l'éthique ne signifie pas en nier l'importance, comme l'a montré l'étude classique d'Albert Heinekamp[1]. Ici on fera référence surtout à l'éthique dans son rapport avec la politique, afin de mettre en évidence les points de contact et de séparation entre ces domaines.

Il semblerait d'abord que l'éthique leibnizienne soit très liée à une conception classique, surtout aristotélicienne. En effet, Leibniz insiste dès ses notes de jeunesse sur le lien entre éthique et politique. Mais une réponse à cette question n'est pas facile à donner. Premièrement, comme on l'a souligné, on peut repérer les racines grecques de l'éthique leibnizienne. Cette dernière est également liée à la dimension de la félicité, en présentant une signification non seulement éthique mais aussi politique : Leibniz reprend l'idée selon laquelle le but de la *polis* est la félicité conçue en termes non individualistes. De ce point de vue, il y a une sorte de priorité du bien commun par rapport au bien individuel ; ou plutôt, il s'agit de penser ensemble le bien individuel et le bien commun. En résulte une conception éthique très différente de celle de Kant[2]. En effet, Leibniz ne conçoit pas l'éthique par référence à un individu autonome. Deuxièmement, il serait vraiment difficile de repérer le concept du devoir, au sens du *Sollen* kantien, à l'intérieur de l'éthique leibnizienne. Il semblerait que l'éthique ne constitue pas un domaine isolé, séparé des autres éléments, parce qu'elle est liée, d'un côté, à la théologie et la métaphysique, de l'autre, à la politique. En effet, il n'y a pas de scission entre la métaphysique et la morale, entre l' « être » et le « devoir être », mais il n'y a pas pour autant d'identité entre ces dimensions. Précisons que l'on peut aussi bien employer le mot « morale » que le mot « éthique » : il n'y a pas une distinction claire, chez Leibniz, à cet égard. Même si la distinction hégélienne entre la morale comme élément propre à l'individu singulier et l'éthique comme élément propre à un contexte plus étendu et donc supérieur à la morale « kantienne » en étant irréductible à un individu singulier, ne s'applique pas à la réflexion de Leibniz, on parlera ici d' « éthique » plutôt que de « morale », parce que la référence n'est pas à un agir purement individuel.

1. A. Heinekamp, *Das Problem des Guten*. Voir aussi L. Le Chevallier, *La morale de Leibniz* ; G. H. R. Parkinson, *Leibniz on Human Freedom* ; J. Hostler, *Leibniz'Moral Philosophy* ; G. Brown, « Leibniz' Moral Philosophy » ; M. J. Seidler, « Freedom and Moral Therapy » ; P. Rateau, *Leibniz et le meilleur des mondes possibles*.

2. Selon une interprétation différente, fondée sur l'idée de la continuité entre Leibniz et Kant à cet égard : Ch. Johns, *The Science of Right*.

Il faut fournir d'autres déterminations à l'éthique, dans sa liaison avec la politique. Les écrits leibniziens donnent d'abord l'impression d'une pleine homologie entre théologie, métaphysique, éthique et politique. En témoigne par exemple l'idée, qui revient souvent, du bien commun comme étant ce vers quoi toutes les choses tendent selon une loi de justice. Il est impossible d'analyser ici tous les aspects de la question complexe de l'harmonie chez Leibniz. Nous nous contenterons donc de rappeler son caractère crucial, qui s'étend à ses implications politiques : il s'agit de « l'harmonie des peuples satisfaits »[1]. Mais il n'y a pas harmonie sans dissonances, sans ombres[2]. On peut certainement repérer, à l'intérieur de cette harmonie, des éléments classiques, en particulier aristotéliciens, où l'expérience joue un rôle crucial. Il s'agit d'une « pratique de la vertu »[3], cette dernière étant conçue non pas selon une idée abstraite et moraliste du devoir, mais selon la capacité à comprendre la situation dans sa contingence. Au-delà de l'image harmonisante, qui n'exclut pas les dissonances, la pensée éthique et politique leibnizienne n'est pas réductible à une pensée de l'harmonie. Le développement du bien commun, comme il est évident par exemple dans le *De summa juris regula*[4], présente une ambivalence entre cette position plutôt classique, et une idée « moderne » de la « maximisation » du bien, conçue presque comme une sorte d'accumulation capitaliste[5]. Je ne pense pas que l'on puisse faire de Leibniz un proto-utilitariste, suivant l'interprétation de René Sève[6]. En tout cas, les deux éléments ne se trouvent pas nécessairement en contradiction. Dans cette liaison entre la justice et le bien commun, plus on est juste, plus on est content du bien commun : est juste ce qui est utile à la communauté (*public*

1. Lettre à Sophie de Hanovre du 4 décembre 1697, A I, 14, 849. Voir R. W. Meyer, *Leibniz und die europäische Ordnungskrise*, p. 211-213 ; H. H. Holz, *Leibniz*, p. 130.

2. Voir *Elementa juris naturalis* [1670-1671 ?], A VI, 1, 484 ; *De Schismate* [1683], A IV, 3, 259 ; *Essais de théodicée*, §145 et §147, GP VI, 196 et 198. Sur la centralité de l'harmonie : D. Mahnke, *Leibnizens Synthese*, p. 13-16 ; Y. Belaval, « L'idée d'harmonie » ; M. Serres, *Le système de Leibniz*, I, p. 93-121 ; W. Schneiders, « *Harmonia universalis* ».

3. Lettre à Sophie de Hanovre du 6 février 1706, GP VII, 569.

4. Voir *De summa juris regula*, [1678-1680/81 ?], A VI, 4, 613.

5. Voir J. Elster, *Leibniz et la formation*, qui interprète la conception économique leibnizienne, entre mercantilisme et capitalisme, à partir d'une originelle confrontation avec Marx, mais surtout avec Weber et Schumpeter, p. 181 : « La difficulté fondamentale nous semble être la suivante. D'une part il y a chez Leibniz une économie morale, qui insiste sur la maximisation de la différence entre le bien et le mal dans l'univers [...]. D'autre part il propose une économie physique, dont le problème est de maximiser le rendement de ces ressources rares que sont l'espace et le temps ».

6. Voir R. Sève, *Leibniz et l'école moderne*.

interest)[1], de sorte que la félicité soit étendue le plus possible[2]. La centralité de la justice, conçue comme charité du sage (*caritas sapientis*), met en place une perspective qui réunit l'éthique et la politique, sans distinction nette entre ces domaines. Dans son interprétation de la philosophie politique, Patrick Riley souligne sa double origine : celle classique, grecque, surtout platonicienne, et celle chrétienne, paulinienne[3]. Dans les *Essais de théodicée*, par exemple, on remarque que « Saint Paul lui-même dit que [...] la *justice* est comprise dans la bonté du sage »[4]. Selon Riley, cette conception leibnizienne est très critique à l'égard de la gnoséologie et de la politique modernes de Descartes et de Hobbes.

On peut certainement repérer des accents classiques dans le traitement leibnizien de la justice : cette dernière, conçue d'après Aristote comme une vertu, concerne l'*habitus* du *vir bonus*. L'élément aristotélicien est ici interprété à travers l'élément chrétien, parce que cet homme *amat omnes* : la justice est liée à l'amour, avec son substrat théologique[5]. Dans les *Nouveaux essais*, la justice universelle est définie comme « une vertu morale entière »[6], témoignant là encore de la liaison structurelle entre éthique et politique. En considérant l'idée de la justice comme *caritas sapientis*, il faut remarquer l'importance de la référence à la singularité du *sapiens*, l'« incarnation » de la *sapientia* d'après son caractère pratique[7]. Par exemple, même dans des textes politiques, il est possible de trouver beaucoup de références à la sagesse : cette dernière est vue, dans le

1. Voir *Initium Institutionum iuris perpetui*, 1695, M, 1. Voir É. Naërt, *Leibniz et la querelle*, p. 157-160 ; H. H. Holz, *Leibniz. Das Lebenswerk eines Universalgelehrten*, p. 99-114.

2. Voir *Initium Institutionum iuris perpetui*, 1695, M, 2.

3. Voir P. Riley, « Introduction » dans *id.*, *Leibniz' Universal Jurisprudence*.

4. *Essais de théodicée*, § 179, GP VI, 221. Voir *Mars Christianissimus* [1683], A IV, 2, 455.

5. *Elementa juris naturalis*, A VI, 1, 465 et 481-482.

6. *Nouveaux Essais*, IV, VIII, A VI, 6, 432. Voir *Praefatio Codicis juris gentium diplomatici* [1693], A IV, 5, 63.

7. Voir *De justitia et jure* [1679-1680 ?], A VI, 4, 2777 ; *ibid.*, A VI, 4, 2777 ; *Aphorismi de felicitate, sapientia, caritate, justitia*, « Erste Fassung » [1678-1679 ?], A VI, 4, 2792 ; *Juris naturalis principia* [1678-1679], A VI, 4, 2809 ; *Tentamina quaedam ad novum codicem legum condendum* [1680], « Zweiter Ansatz », A VI, 4, 2854 ; *De justitia ac amore voluntateque Dei* [1680-1688 ?], A VI, 4, 2890 ; *De libero territorio* [1682], A IV, 2, 401. Voir G. Grua, *La justice humaine*, p. 400 : « La formule définitive de 1677, la justice charité du sage [...] concilie spontanéité et calcul, sagesse pour soi et pour tous [...]. La justice universelle est bien définie par la piété utilitaire ou mieux désintéressée au sens hédoniste, déduite sous tous ses aspects positifs et polémiques de l'optimisme » ; G. Grua, *Jurisprudence universelle*, p. 164-238 ; H. Schiedermair, *Das Phänomen der Macht*, p. 225 ; R. J. Mulvaney, « The Early Development », p. 72.

Specimen polonais, comme *scientia optimi*[1], dans le *Consilium Aegyptiacum*, comme *scientia felicitatis*[2]. Mais il faut préciser que c'est surtout à partir de 1670 que la sagesse, auparavant liée à la *prudentia*, est définie comme *scientia felicitatis*. De nombreux plans portant sur le droit naturel commençaient avec la sagesse en tant que science de la félicité[3]: cet élément ne peut être réduit à la dimension pratique, étant parfois presque identifié avec la science générale, avec la métaphysique ou théologie naturelle, selon une connexion entre éthique et métaphysique.

La conception de la *justitia* comme *caritas sapientis* se définit dans la continuité de l'enseignement de Socrate (et de Platon) où la justice jouait un rôle crucial à partir de la liaison entre *honestas* et *utilitas*[4]. Il s'agit d'une correspondance biunivoque : d'un côté, la politique présente un caractère moral, de l'autre, l'éthique n'est pas conçue en référence à l'individu isolé, mais toujours selon une réciprocité entre le « propre » et l' « autrui ». À cet égard, la référence polémique est constituée par la position du sophiste, et en particulier par celle de Thrasymaque, qui définit le juste comme ce qui est utile au plus fort, en présentant une fonction purement instrumentale. Dans la *Méditation sur la notion commune de la justice* cette idée revient avec force. À l'intérieur de cette vision, Hobbes, souvent loué au début, devient une sorte de Thrasymaque « moderne » qui élimine ou neutralise la justice, avec ses racines dans la structure des choses, en la réduisant à l'*arbitrium potentis*[5].

La polémique avec Hobbes doit être comprise à l'intérieur de la structure leibnizienne tripartite du droit naturel qui dérive du schéma d'Ulpien. Le premier degré est le *jus strictum*, le droit *stricto sensu*, qui concerne le rapport entre individus privés. Il peut être assimilé, à certains égards, à la justice commutative aristotélicienne. Le deuxième degré, l'*aequitas*, va au-delà du droit *stricto sensu*, en ajoutant une dimension plus grande, publique, et donc apparaît semblable à la justice distributive aristotélicienne. Ici on peut repérer une référence à l'éthique grecque dans son rapport étroit avec l'élément de la politique. Enfin, le troisième degré, *honeste* ou *pie vivere*, ouvre le scénario métaphysique et théologique de la république des esprits, dont Dieu est le monarque[6] : cette perspective est

1. *Specimen demonstrationum politicarum pro eligendo rege Polonorum* [1669], Prop. XXXVIII, A IV, 1, 36.

2. *Consilium Aegyptiacum*, « De eo quod Franciae interest », A IV, 1, 249-250.

3. Voir G. Grua, *La Justice humaine*, p. 34-36.

4. Voir *De justitia ac amore voluntateque Dei* [1680-1688 ?], A VI, 4, 2891.

5. Voir *Praefatio annotatoris* [1701], Grua, 472.

6. H. Rudolph, « Einleitung », p. 15, utilise l'expression « christlicher Universalismus », afin d'indiquer les marques distinctives de la position leibnizienne.

supérieure à la justice distributive. Il faut alors souligner que, d'un côté, le degré suivant n'élimine pas le précédent, mais l'intègre, pour ainsi dire, de l'autre, que le degré suivant est plus important que le précédent. Ainsi le troisième constitue le niveau le plus haut, la *justitia universalis*. En reprenant la thèse classique de Gaston Grua, on peut soutenir que toute la philosophie leibnizienne (et pas seulement sa pensée politique) peut être conçue comme une jurisprudence universelle. Les *Essais de théodicée*, comme l'indique le terme même de « théodicée », relèvent eux aussi de ce caractère juridique de la réflexion.

Il faut encore ajouter deux observations à propos des trois degrés du droit naturel. La première concerne l'éthique, laquelle est cruciale à l'intérieur de l'*aequitas* mais aussi de la *justitia universalis* [1], relativement à son substrat théologique et métaphysique. La deuxième concerne le rapport avec Hobbes. Leibniz accuse Hobbes (et Pufendorf) d'avoir fondé le discours sur le *jus strictum*, et de ne pas avoir fait référence aux deux autres degrés. Si on se limite au premier degré, se réalise le principe latin selon lequel *summum ius summa est iniuria* [2]. Et cet élément revient à plusieurs reprises quand l'on développe des sujets politiques spécifiques, par exemple le droit de résistance [3]. Donc la division du droit naturel en trois niveaux, avec la centralité de la question de la justice met elle aussi en place le lien entre éthique et politique. À cet égard il faut remarquer l'efficacité de l'expression « véritable politique », qui « consiste dans la justice et dans la charité, et [...] un grand Prince ne saurait être mieux servi que lorsque le bonheur des peuples fait le sien [...] » [4].

La centralité de la catégorie de félicité met également en évidence le lien indiqué, souvent sans une claire distinction de rôles entre éthique et politique. Mais la question se révèle plus compliquée. Premièrement, on n'insistera jamais assez sur l'importance de la dimension pratique, et le lien entre théorie et pratique. Comme Leibniz le souligne dans la conclusion des *Nouveaux Essais* : « Et même dans les arts manuels plus nobles, le savoir a été fort bien allié avec l'opération, et pourroit l'être d'avantage [...] Mais il faudroit changer en bien des choses l'état present de la littérature et de l'éducation de la jeunesse, et par conséquent de la

1. *Méditation sur la notion commune de la justice* [1702-1705], M, 65. Voir P. Riley, « Leibniz "Méditation sur la notion commune de la justice" ».

2. Voir *Praefatio annotatoris* [1701], Grua, 472.

3. *Méditation sur la notion commune de la justice*, M, 66.

4. Leibniz für Eberhard von Danckelmann. *Vorschlag zur Errichtung einer Akademie der Wissenschaften und Künste* [01/1685 ?], A I, 11, 166. Sur la « véritable politique » : É. Naërt, *La pensée politique*, p. 34-35 ; X. Schneiders, « *Vera politica* ».

police »[1]. Il s'agit d'un *cogitare practice*, d'une pensée utile à la vie, dans la singularité de chaque situation. La morale ne peut donc être conçue de façon abstraite, mais elle doit être interprétée selon des conditions concrètes. Deuxièmement, on doit reprendre l'idée, non pas de la déduction de l'éthique à partir de la politique, mais certainement de son lien avec la politique. Dans la *Lettre sur l'Education d'un Prince,* Leibniz remarque l'importance de la réflexion sur la morale et sur la politique : « La Philosophie Morale est entrée dans la Politique et dans le droit [...] »[2].

Afin de comprendre ce problème, la notion de la « place d'autrui » joue un rôle stratégique :

> La place d'autrui est le vrai point de perspective en politique aussi bien qu'en morale. Et le précepte de Jésus Christ, de se mettre à la place d'autrui ne sert pas seulement au but dont parle notre Seigneur, c'est-à-dire à la morale pour connaître notre devoir envers le prochain ; mais encore à la politique pour connaître les vues que notre voisin peut avoir contre nous[3].

Cet élément constitue la juste perspective, en politique comme en morale, en nous faisant découvrir des aspects que, autrement, nous n'aurions pas compris. À la base de la question est la recherche de la co-implication entre le bien individuel et le bien commun, le propre et l'autrui : il ne s'agit pas seulement d'une médiation, mais d'une réciprocité entre eux. À cet égard Gilles Deleuze a écrit des pages très précises, en refusant l'image d'un Leibniz *sic et simpliciter* penseur de l'équilibre[4]. La même idée, énoncée auparavant, de la « maximisation » du bien met en évidence qu'il ne s'agit pas seulement d'un équilibre entre des éléments différents, parce que l'on peut repérer, plus qu'un équilibre, un mouvement vers une direction précise, le bien. Un passage des *Essais de théodicée* est très clair à cet égard :

> [...] comme bien souvent il y a plusieurs partis à prendre, on pourrait au lieu de la balance comparer l'âme avec une force qui fait effort en même temps de plusieurs côtés, mais qui n'agit que là où elle trouve le plus de facilité ou le moins de résistance [...] C'est ainsi que les inclinations de l'âme vont sur tous les biens qui se présentent [...][5].

1. *Nouveaux Essais*, IV, XXI, A VI, 6, 527. Voir G. Friedmann, *Leibniz et Spinoza*, p. 252 ; R. T. W. Arthur, *Leibniz*, p. 185-189.
2. *Lettre sur l'Éducation d'un Prince* [1685-1686], A IV, 3, 554.
3. *La place d'autrui* [1679 ?], A IV, 3, 903. Voir F. Gil, « Leibniz, la place d'autrui » ; A. Cardoso, « La place d'autrui » ; Q. Racionero, « El principio de la "place d'autrui" ».
4. Voir G. Deleuze, *Le Pli*.
5. *Essais de théodicée*, § 325, GP VI, 309.

Dans un autre texte, *Sur la générosité*, ces aspects reviennent en force, parce que l'expression « place des autres » dénote la dimension publique, où la félicité commune n'est pas conçue en opposition à notre propre félicité :

> Nous devons avoir égard à la dignité de notre nature dont l'excellence consiste dans la perfection de l'esprit, ou dans la plus haute vertu. Nous devons prendre part au bonheur de ceux qui nous environnent, comme au nôtre, ne cherchant pas nos aises ni nos intérêts, dans ce qui est contraire à la félicité commune, enfin nous devons songer à ce que le public souhaite de nous et que nous souhaiterions nous mêmes si nous nous mettions à la place des autres, car c'est comme la voix de Dieu et la marque de la vocation [1].

Dans les *Elementa juris naturalis* Leibniz souligne que la différence entre *aestimare* et *amare* est que, dans le deuxième élément, se développe une pleine « fusion des horizons », où le « moi » et le « toi » n'existent plus comme des sujets séparés et isolés [2]. Le bien général devient progressivement le bien particulier de chacun : l'intérêt particulier plus grand consiste dans le *conatus* vers le bien général [3]. Par opposition aux lectures « monastiques » de la monadologie, on peut repérer une dimension « solidaire » de la conception leibnizienne : « *Monadae, non Monachae* » [4].

En approfondissant cet argument, on reconnaît l'existence d'une approche optimiste chez Leibniz, surtout si on tient compte d'une certaine réception à partir du *Candide* de Voltaire où le leibnizianisme se présente sous la figure caricaturale de Pangloss. Naturellement il est nécessaire de souligner que cette co-implication du moi et d'autrui est très éloignée de l'interprétation simpliste de Voltaire. Mais la question de la « place d'autrui » pourrait à bon droit s'interpréter en des termes très différents, c'est-à-dire, en termes « stratégiques » [5]. Il ne s'agit pas d'être bons, mais de se mettre à la place des autres, en cherchant à comprendre la façon dont les autres agissent, et en se donnant la possibilité de les devancer. Donc la place d'autrui révèle une fonction cruciale, une sorte de « balance » continue aussi dans les questions militaires, quand on doit choisir entre la guerre et la paix. Il serait problématique de penser qu'il existe chez Leibniz des influences machiavéliennes. La manière dont Leibniz relie éthique et politique s'oppose à la séparation machiavélienne de ces domaines, et donc à l'interprétation de la politique *iuxta propria principia*. Toutefois, on peut

1. *Sur la générosité* [1686-1687], A VI, 4, 2723.
2. Voir *Elementa juris naturalis*, A VI, 1, 464.
3. Voir, par exemple, *Essais de théodicée*, « Préface », GP VI, 27-28.
4. Discussion avec Gabriel Wagner du 3 mars 1698, Grua, 395-396.
5. Voir M. Dascal, « Strategies of Dispute ».

qualifier de machiavélienne cette recherche stratégique de se mettre à la place des autres, et donc de les comprendre, afin de pouvoir les attaquer ou se défendre. Et, en cela, on peut repérer un autre élément provenant de Machiavel, apprécié par Leibniz, en considérant son *Arte della guerra*, à savoir le lien étroit entre la politique et la guerre [1]. Sans pouvoir développer ici la question de la guerre, il faut seulement préciser que la position leibnizienne est très éloignée de toute forme d'utopisme. Il remarque avec réalisme la centralité de la dynamique de la guerre et de la paix, sans exclure la première. Quant à la référence à Machiavel, il faut souligner que, dans les *Essais de théodicée*, Leibniz fait un éloge plutôt surprenant de l'anthropologie de Machiavel, à partir de la prise de conscience de la médiocrité humaine: «À l'égard de la vertu et du vice, il y règne une certaine médiocrité. Machiavel a déjà remarqué qu'il y a peu d'hommes fort méchants et fort bons, et que cela fait manquer bien de grandes entreprises» [2]. En effet, la plupart des hommes ne sont ni bons ni mauvais, et se montrent donc incapables d'accomplir des entreprises importantes: on peut repérer, chez Leibniz, une anthropologie moins idéaliste qu'on ne le pense habituellement.

Après avoir mis en évidence les implications de la question de la «place d'autrui», il faut finalement approfondir le rapport entre politique et éthique [3]. Le passage cité sur la «place d'autrui» présente presque une identité entre les éléments indiqués: «ainsi en politique comme en morale», «en morale comme en politique». Il semblerait presque impossible de différencier l'éthique de la politique. Dans un petit texte de jeunesse, *Note sur Aristote. «Éthique et politique»*, Leibniz souligne que, chez Aristote, la politique n'est rien d'autre que l'éthique, le sujet est constitué par la communauté politique, la *polis*, et l'éthique contient la doctrine civile ou politique [4]. Au-delà de la question de la coïncidence seulement partielle entre éthique et politique chez Aristote (en termes différents que chez Platon), il est évident que Leibniz semble ici concevoir

1. Voir G. Gerber, «Leibniz' Beziehung zu Machiavelli».

2. *Essais de théodicée*, § 148, GP VI, 198.

3. Sur le rapport entre politique, éthique et métaphysique, voir É. Naërt, *La pensée politique*, p. 8: «[...] il arrive encore à Leibniz de définir la politique, d'une part, comme la science de l'utilité publique et de l'État, d'autre part, comme l'art ou la science de l'utilité privée dans nos rapports avec autrui et le droit montre comment, en procurant le bien de l'autre, nous trouvons le nôtre. Les mêmes termes n'ont pas toujours sous la plume de Leibniz la même signification et leur équivocité empêche de distinguer d'une manière absolue, chez notre auteur, morale, jurisprudence et politique»; J. Salas, *Razón y legitimidad*; T. Guillén Vera, «Bases filosoficas»; C. Roldán, «Estudios leibnizianos», p. 175-177.

4. Notes sur Aristote. «Éthique et politique» [1662-1664], Grua, 563-564.

éthique et politique comme identiques. Toutefois, dans d'autres passages, on peut repérer des distinctions Par exemple, dans les *Elementa juris naturalis*, la politique est définie *scientia utili* et l'éthique *scientia justi*, mais avec la précision que l'*utile* et le *juste* s'impliquent réciproquement, parce qu'on ne peut pas être heureux au milieu d'une foule de misérables[1]. Dans la définition de la politique comme science de l'utile, on trouve des éléments encore hobbesiens, comme c'est souvent le cas dans les écrits de jeunesse de Leibniz. En même temps, Leibniz commence à développer l'idée d'une connexion étroite entre l'éthique et la politique, entre le juste et l'utile, mais d'une manière très différente que celle de Hobbes.

La centralité de la question du bien ne doit pourtant pas être interprétée en termes statiques, comme une sorte de possession durable : au contraire, dès les *Elementa juris naturalis*, le bien est conçu de manière dynamique, comme but d'un *progressus in infinitum*[2]. À propos de cette sorte de « morale de progrès »[3], il faut préciser que le progrès leibnizien ne peut être conçu, *sic et simpliciter*, comme une anticipation des Lumières, selon un horizon sans ombres, en étant doté d'un substrat théologique et métaphysique, comme le montre bien, par exemple, le *Fragment sur l'Apocastase* : il s'agit d'une dimension qualitative et intensive, non purement quantitative et cumulative[4]. Dans ce contexte, le lien entre bonté et progrès joue un rôle décisif. À cet égard la question du progrès des sciences est très importante, la science étant conçue non seulement comme activité « technique », mais aussi comme douée d'une signification éthique et politique. Le but des études consiste dans la félicité des hommes ou, au moins, dans une satisfaction constante[5], afin de promouvoir le bien public. D'ailleurs, dans une lettre à Burnett, Leibniz valorise l'« Empire de la raison », par opposition au « pouvoir arbitraire »[6]. Ce dernier est critiqué surtout parce qu'il tend à la destruction de la dimension rationnelle, sans laquelle un corps politique juste ne peut pas exister. Il ne s'agit pas de faire de Leibniz un démocrate : au contraire, on peut repérer dans ses écrits une critique sévère, d'inspiration aristotélicienne, de la démocratie. Il ne s'agit pas non plus d'une approche proto-libérale : la notion de liberté n'est pas

1. *Elementa juris naturalis*, A VI, 1, 459-460. Voir M. Gaudemar, « Éthique et morale ».

2. Par exemple, *Elementa juris naturalis*, 1669-1670 ?, A VI, 1, 483. Voir L. Basso, « Félicité commune et inquiétude ».

3. G. Deleuze, *Le Pli*.

4. Voir M. Fichant, « Postface », p. 199.

5. Par exemple, *Concept einer Denkschrift von Leibniz (für den Czaaren Peter)* [1708], FC VII, 468.

6. Lettre à Thomas Burnett du 18 juillet 1701 ?, « Beilage », GP III, 277-278.

conçue de façon proto-libérale, mais à partir de l'élément de la raison[1]. Le savoir et la raison jouent un rôle décisif dans la réflexion politique leibnizienne. À cet égard, importante est la question de la fondation des Académies des Sciences : les savants ne sont pas seulement des érudits, mais doivent chercher d'apporter une contribution au bien commun.

En conclusion, comme on l'a remarqué à plusieurs reprises, la philosophie pratique leibnizienne ne présente pas un caractère systématique : on y trouve une oscillation entre des textes plus contingents et des textes plus « généraux ». Le rapport entre politique et éthique n'est pas non plus déterminé une fois pour toutes : son statut est en partie provisoire, « inachevé ». Mais, au-delà de cela, on peut faire deux remarques ouvertes. La première concerne le rôle de la politique à l'intérieur de la réflexion leibnizienne. Même si la pensée politique de Leibniz n'a pas été valorisée par la plupart des spécialistes leibniziens, la question de la politique est décisive dans la vie et dans l'œuvre du philosophe allemand. On pourrait considérer tout l'itinéraire leibnizien comme traversé par la référence à la politique. Le mot « politique » s'entend en un sens aussi bien strict que large : « strict », parce que Leibniz a écrit un grand nombre de textes politiques, et que la plupart sont liés à des événements spécifiques. « Large » parce que même les écrits métaphysiques, par exemple le *Discours de métaphysique* et la *Monadologie* comportent des références à la politique : les métaphores politiques qu'on y trouve, comme la cité, la république, le prince, ne sont pas purement décoratives. On peut repérer aussi une sorte de « politique » du savoir, comme on l'a souligné au sujet des Académies scientifiques. La signification politique de la réflexion émerge pleinement si l'on assume jusqu'au bout le lien entre théorie et pratique : Leibniz conçoit un savoir qui n'est pas seulement érudition, mais savoir utile à la vie, capable de changer les situations des individus et des groupes, y compris dans leurs aspects matériels. Et, même si l'on n'a pas analysé l'élément du droit, les questions juridiques y jouent un rôle remarquable[2].

1. Lettre à Thomas Burnett du 18 juillet 1701 ?, *op. cit.*, p. 278-279. Voir T. Dagron, *Toland et Leibniz*, p. 28-38.

2. Voir, selon des questions et des interprétations juridiques différentes, entre les autres, G. Hartmann, *Leibniz als Jurist* ; G. Grua, *Jurisprudence universelle* ; E. Wolf, « Leibniz als Rechtsphilosoph » ; A. Bayart, « Leibniz et les antinomies » ; H. P. Schneider, *Justitia universalis* ; Y. Belaval, « Religion et fondement du droit chez Leibniz » ; G. Kalinowski, « La Logique juridique de Leibniz » ; J.-L. Gardies, « La rationalité du droit » ; G. Otte, « Leibniz und die juristische Methode » ; K. Luig, « Die Privatrechtsordnung » ; P. Landau, *Stufen der Gerechtigkeit* ; P. König, « Das System des Rechts » ; K. Luig, « Leibniz und die Prinzipien » ; Boucher, « La logique du droit positif » ; Armgardt, *Das rechtslogische System* ; Buschmann,

La deuxième (et dernière) observation concerne l'éthique et sa liaison avec la politique. Ici, l'éthique a surtout été conçue par rapport à la politique, à une dimension qui n'est pas réductible à un individu isolé, en dehors d'un contexte social et communautaire. En tout cas, l'éthique leibnizienne se fonde sur une connexion entre soi et autrui, où la division entre ces domaines n'est pas claire. D'un côté, Leibniz refuse la séparation moderne entre éthique et politique, et l'idée d'analyser cette dernière *iuxta propria principia*, indépendamment de la métaphysique et de l'éthique. On a remarqué l'importance structurelle de la tripartition ulpienne du droit naturel, et de la définition de la justice comme charité du sage. Mais, d'un autre côté, l'existence d'éléments grecs et chrétiens ne doit pas faire oublier qu'il y a aussi des écarts entre l'éthique et la politique, et cette dernière ne peut être interprétée en termes seulement « harmonisants », et sans référence à des structures d'autorité, selon une vision « idéalisée » et « éthique » de la politique. On peut aussi repérer un Leibniz réaliste, qui procède à une critique immanente de Hobbes et de Pufendorf, mais sans nostalgie des paradigmes du passé, à partir d'une tentative pour concevoir un corps politique qui possède la stabilité recherchée par Hobbes, mais où la stabilité ne signifie pas immobilité, mais ouverture au changement.

Luca BASSO
(Università degli Studi di Padova)

« Leibniz als juristischer Reformer » ; P. Boucher, « Leibniz : What Kind of Legal Rationalism ? ».

LA THÉOLOGIE DE LEIBNIZ

> « Je commence en philosophe ;
> mais je finis en théologien »[1].

Dans son *Eloge de M. Leibnitz*, Bernard de Fontenelle présentait le penseur de Hanovre comme un « Théologien, non seulement en tant que Philosophe et Métaphysicien, mais Théologien dans le sens étroit »[2], appréciation confirmée par la recherche actuelle montrant que les investigations de Leibniz en matière de théologie représentent un aspect aussi décisif qu'original de sa pensée[3]. L'ampleur du corpus leibnizien consacré à des thématiques religieuses, doctrinales ou ecclésiales, est tout à fait significative, de même que la constance de cette préoccupation qui se déploie, parfois de façon fragmentaire, des premiers aux derniers écrits. Il est dès lors pertinent de parler de « la vocation religieuse » de Leibniz, selon les termes mêmes de Michel Fichant, qui rappelle qu'il y a « dans la *conjonction* du plan religieux, du projet d'institution de la science et de l'entreprise politique, une ligne forte et structurante de la pensée de Leibniz »[4]. S'il est indéniable que la théologie n'est pas une préoccupation marginale dans l'œuvre de Leibniz, encore convient-il de cerner en quoi son approche revêt des aspects originaux. La théologie, qui se définit comme l'étude ou le discours (*logos*) portant sur Dieu (*theos*), constitue effectivement une voie d'entrée privilégiée dans la pensée philosophique de Leibniz, assimilable à une vaste méditation sur l'idée de Dieu et sur ses conséquences. Dans sa diversité encyclopédique, l'œuvre de Leibniz,

1. Cité par J. Baruzi, *Leibniz et l'organisation religieuse de la terre*, n. 1 p. 507.
2. De Fontenelle, *Œuvres Complètes*, p. 244.
3. Voir en particulier W. Li, « Leibniz im Lichte der Theologien ».
4. M. Fichant, « L'Invention métaphysique », p. 25.

accorde un traitement central à la notion de Dieu, fondement premier, qu'elle s'emploie longuement à définir et à étudier au moyen des « lumières internes naturelles (c'est-à-dire la raison) »[1]. Désigné comme le « père des lumières »[2], Dieu surpasse certes la rationalité, mais en garantit la validité. Dès lors la théologie leibnizienne, associant théologie naturelle et théologie révélée, se présente comme une *théologie de la lumière*, dont l'étude constituera le premier temps de cet exposé. Le travail théologique de Leibniz, à visée apologétique, revêt de plus la forme d'une plaidoirie bien construite pour défendre la cause de Dieu contre ses détracteurs, il se décline donc en autant d'échantillons de *Théodicée*. Néanmoins la théologie leibnizienne ne saurait se concevoir sans « christologie philosophique »[3], car l'universalité de la Grâce accordée par un Dieu aussi juste que bon ne peut s'actualiser sans la médiation de Jésus-Christ, *Theoanthropos*, mort pour le rachat de *tous*. Le sacrifice universellement rédempteur consenti par le Christ fonde une conception de la prédestination ainsi qu'une interprétation eucharistique relevant d'une *théologie de l'amour*, dont l'analyse sera développée dans le deuxième temps de cette étude. Enfin, nous verrons, dans un troisième temps, que la théologie de Leibniz, qui entre-implique épistémologie de la lumière et éthique de la charité, aboutit à une visée pratique : instaurer « une organisation religieuse de la terre », selon l'expression de Jean Baruzi. Autrement dit, la pensée théologique de Leibniz est fondamentalement *irénique*, au sens où elle devrait servir d'instrument de pacification des Églises. En effet, l'ecclésiologie leibnizienne a pour visée idéale d'instaurer une Église universelle, dont l'unité riche de diversité (principe d'harmonie), serait source de paix. Le théologien philosophe estime que la *pax Dei*, résultant d'un dénouement philosophique des controverses doctrinales, est essentiellement tributaire d'une clarification du sacrement eucharistique, véritable *sacramentum unionis*, instauré par le Christ.

1. Grua, 139.
2. *Essais de théodicée*, GP VI, 121.
3. X. Tilliette, *L'Église des philosophes*, p. 10, 41-54.

UNE THÉOLOGIE DE LA LUMIÈRE

« Dieu est le soleil et la lumière des âmes »[1].

La théologie est présentée par Leibniz tantôt comme un champ de la métaphysique, tantôt comme la métaphysique elle-même, ce qui met l'accent sur la centralité de l'idée de Dieu. L'approche logique de la théologie que Leibniz met en œuvre conduit à une théologie naturelle, qui s'accorde avec la théologie révélée. En posant « la conformité de la Foi avec la Raison »[2] au principe de sa théologie, Leibniz fait l'apologie d'une religion intelligente où « la véritable raison [...] s'accorde toujours avec la véritable révélation »[3]. La métaphore classique de la lumière, constamment employée par Leibniz en matière de théologie, reçoit une double origine : elle résulte d'une raison bien conduite, procédant par ordre et preuves décisives, mais il importe de souligner que son activité prend racine dans l'intelligence de Dieu. Distincte de la vaine érudition, inutile et querelleuse, la véritable raison donne accès à des vérités qui sont source de félicité, puisqu'elle est une faculté dont l'activité émane d'un Dieu bienveillant, origine de toutes clartés, naturelles ou révélées. *A contrario* une raison obscurcie entraîne inévitablement des distorsions théologiques : « il n'est aucune erreur si minime qu'en fin de compte elle ne mène nécessairement à l'athéisme, à cause de la connexion de toutes les vérités »[4]. Ainsi, dénouer les controverses théologiques, au moyen des deux grands principes de non-contradiction et de raison suffisante, revient à promouvoir une foi éclairée. Le fil d'Ariane d'une méthode logique, procédant à une mise en forme des arguments, ainsi qu'à un travail de définition de la terminologie utilisée, s'avère indispensable pour dépasser les mésententes ou réfuter les sophismes occasionnant des disputes théologiques, voire des schismes.

En appréhendant la religion au moyen de lumières clarificatrices, Leibniz fait de la théologie un champ de savoir ouvert à l'investigation philosophique, caractérisé par la conjonction d'une présentation d'enseignements sur les mystères chrétiens (création, trinité, incarnation ou personne du Christ, rédemption, prédestination, eucharistie, résurrection des corps...) et d'un travail critique mettant à distance les thèses erronées. Ce faisant, Leibniz donne accès, si ce n'est à l'intelligibilité

1. *Discours de métaphysique*, § 28.
2. *Discours préliminaire sur la conformité de la Foi avec la Raison*, GP VI, 49-101.
3. Grua, 126.
4. C. Rösler-Le Van, *Negotium Irenicum*, p. 989.

complète des mystères chrétiens qui surpassent la raison humaine, à tout le moins à la présomption de vérité qu'on peut légitimement leur accorder tant que le contraire n'est pas prouvé. Autrement dit, les mystères demeurent en partie incompréhensibles pour l'entendement limité des hommes, mais démontrer leur possibilité en prouvant qu'ils ne contiennent pas de contradiction, et les éclairer de manière analogique, est chose faisable. Au sujet de la trinité[1], il s'agit de montrer qu'il est possible de penser une substance absolument unique, néanmoins composée de trois personnes, ce qui permet d'éviter de tomber dans l'erreur unitariste des sociniens. Leibniz recourt à une analogie explicative : de même que l'esprit qui réfléchit sur soi renvoie à un seul individu dans lequel on peut distinguer « celui qui pense » de « celui qui est pensé », de même Dieu est une unité indivisible triplement composée. Héritier d'Augustin, Leibniz établit un lien analogique entre les trois principales facultés de l'esprit (*posse-scire-velle*) et les personnes de la trinité.

L'usage de la lumière rationnelle en théologie permet non seulement d'éclaircir les mystères chrétiens, de façon à tout le moins présomptive, mais de plus d'établir des connexions fructueuses entre doctrines religieuses et découvertes scientifiques. Religion et science sont deux aspects d'une même vérité, tantôt révélée, tantôt naturelle. En intégrant ses connaissances considérables en patristique, théologie médiévale, histoire des Églises et théologie des controverses dans son projet de savoir encyclopédique, Leibniz décloisonne la théologie en lui assignant la possibilité : 1) d'être un terrain d'application de thèses scientifiques, 2) de bénéficier d'images explicatives propres aux sciences, et 3) de conférer un sens apologétique aux progrès scientifiques.

1) Le travail philosophique renouvelé sur le mystère eucharistique, qu'il soit appréhendé sur le mode catholique de la transsubstantiation, ou sur les modes protestants de la présence réelle, spirituelle ou symbolique, ne se restreint pas à une explication strictement doctrinale, mais reçoit un traitement scientifique qui permet d'arbitrer entre les différents énoncés. L'explication leibnizienne de la présence hyperphysique, adimensionnelle ou substantielle, du corps du Christ dans les espèces sacramentelles sert à la fois de caution et de critère discriminant en science. Dès les œuvres de jeunesse, il y a convergence entre le traitement philosophique du problème théologique de l'eucharistie et l'élaboration des

1. M. R. Antognazza, « Leibniz *De Deo Trino :* Philosophical Aspects of Leibniz's Conception of the Trinity », p. 1-13.

fondements conceptuels de la science des corps[1]. Leibniz veut en effet « démontrer que la nature du corps consiste en autre chose qu'en étendue selon les Cartésiens, ou en impénétrabilité selon les Gassendistes [ce qui pourrait] être de grand usage pour la religion »[2]. Il s'agit pour Leibniz d'invalider le dualisme substantiel de Descartes qui rend inintelligible le mystère, en montrant l'insuffisance du mécanisme qui doit être fondé sur la dynamique.

2) Leibniz transpose des paradigmes scientifiques sur des questions théologiques afin de les clarifier. Ainsi, pour expliquer « l'imperfection naturelle des créatures », il recourt de façon récurrente à une analogie portant sur « l'inertie naturelle des corps »[3] selon Kepler. Le positif des créatures, *i.e.* le bien et les perfections qui leur sont donnés par Dieu, est comparé au mouvement d'entraînement qu'un fleuve exerce sur des embarcations, et le privatif en elles (leur résistance au bien qui cause le péché) s'apparente à la limitation de leur vitesse par leur inertie. Le bien est dynamique, il est mouvement vertueux, effort, action, dont l'énergie s'origine en un Dieu cause motrice. *A contrario*, le mal est statique, il renvoie à l'inertie du mobile, à sa lenteur ou engourdissement, il est privation (non être), défaut ou passion, limitation de la créature. L'explication métaphysique de la racine du mal ou du péché trouve ainsi un éclairage rationnel grâce aux enseignements de la science physique.

3) Aux yeux de Leibniz, les découvertes scientifiques, qui honorent certes l'intelligence humaine, manifestent avant tout la gloire de Dieu, ce qui leur assigne une finalité apologétique. Ainsi, la contemplation des vérités scientifiques permet non seulement de mieux comprendre l'agencement du monde (les lois physiques ou le règne de la nature), mais aussi de tout rapporter à Dieu, auteur de l'harmonie du monde (des lois métaphysiques ou du règne de la grâce). « Plus on connaît la nature et les vérités solides des sciences réelles, qui sont autant de rayons de la perfection divine, plus on est capable d'aimer Dieu véritablement »[4]. La métaphore solaire utilisée par Leibniz dans sa présentation de l'argument téléologique

1. M. Fichant, *Science et métaphysique dans Descartes et Leibniz*, p. 202 : dès 1668, « justification rationnelle de la foi et construction de la science relevaient d'un même projet et mettaient en œuvre la même méthode d'analyse des notions et de synthèse démonstrative, *la question centrale de la transsubstantiation formant trait d'union entre la pensée de la réalité physique et l'exigence religieuse* » (nous soulignons).

2. A I, 16, 376.

3. *Unvorgreiffliches Bedencken*, 228v, in *Negotium Irenicum*, p. 1028-1030. Voir aussi *Essais de théodicée*, § 30, *Causa Dei*, § 70-73.

4. Grua, 91.

ou physico-théologique (la beauté et l'ordre du monde, tels que la science les fait découvrir, résultent de l'action suprêmement intelligente d'un Dieu lumineux, organisateur ultime et bienveillant du cosmos) met l'accent sur la perfection de Dieu et de son œuvre.

Dans la théologie leibnizienne, clarifier l'idée de Dieu constitue un point de départ nécessaire, tant du point de vue ontologique que méthodologique : « Dieu est le premier et le plus facile à connaître par la voie de la lumière [*Lichtweg*] »[1]. Ainsi, l'ordre logique du raisonnement veut que Dieu, dernière raison des choses ou souveraine cause, soit le premier objet appréhendé par l'intelligence. Dieu est non seulement la première vérité éternelle qui conditionne toutes les autres, mais il est également le fondement de l'accès au vrai : « Seule la lumière intérieure, que Dieu Lui-même allume en nous, a le pouvoir de donner une juste connaissance de Dieu »[2]. La connaissance *de* Dieu s'entend ici en deux sens : objet d'étude (connaissance *sur* Dieu) et processus d'intelligibilité (connaissance *initiée par* Dieu). Dans cette lumineuse dynamique circulaire, Dieu est instigateur : pour obtenir une claire représentation de son idée, l'âme doit recevoir de Lui Ses clartés. Selon les textes et les contextes, Leibniz recourt à l'une ou l'autre des deux approches possibles de la notion de Dieu : soit immédiate par son essence (preuve ontologique), soit médiate par ses effets (preuve cosmologique).

Concernant son essence, l'Être premier se caractérise comme une substance absolument parfaite, unique mais tri-composée, éternelle, continuellement créatrice du plus parfait des mondes possibles, omniprésente, omnisciente, toute-puissante, suprêmement juste et bonne, souverainement sage, sainte… En Dieu, ces attributs, en nombre infini, qui sont autant de perfections, ne sauraient se juxtaposer sans s'accorder, autrement dit « les *attributs divins* doivent nécessairement être compatibles, ou comme le disent nos théologiens, être *harmoniques* »[3], ce qui revient à revisiter la preuve ontologique de l'existence de Dieu, car l'existence découle certes de la perfection, ainsi que l'affirme Descartes reprenant la preuve de saint Anselme, mais Leibniz pose comme condition *sine qua non* que l'infinité des attributs parfaits qui, de ce fait, ne sont pas pleinement compréhensibles, demeurent toutefois non-contradictoires. Pouvoir concilier rationnellement les perfections divines est un critère décisif permettant de distinguer les conceptions théologiques acceptables des

1. *Von den wahren Theologia Mystica* [vers 1698], trad. C. Rösler, p. 279-300, ici p. 283.
2. *Ibid.*, trad. cit., p. 281.
3. *Negotium Irenicum*, p. 992.

conceptions fautives, critère dont Leibniz va user pour sortir du labyrinthe de la nécessité : c'est ainsi qu'il pourra réfuter Hobbes, Newton, et Samuel Clarke, dont les concepts de Dieu mènent à des thèses théologiques aux conséquences irrecevables [1].

La théologie leibnizienne, vaste entreprise de justification de la grandeur de Dieu, mais aussi de sa suprême bonté, a pour objectif d'expliquer la juxtaposition de trois affirmations qui semblent difficilement compatibles : « Dieu est bon, l'homme est libre et le mal existe » [2]. Dès le *Von der Allmacht* [3], écrit de jeunesse, Leibniz pose les jalons de cette réflexion qui traversera toute son œuvre : comment un Dieu bienveillant, tout aussi puissant (*Allmacht*) que clairvoyant (*Allwissenheit*), peut-il vouloir le mal, et plus précisément le mal de la faute (le péché), qui conduit à la damnation ? De plus, comment concevoir un homme libre, vu qu'il s'insère dans un monde créé et ordonné continuellement par un Dieu omniscient pouvant dès lors prévoir tout ce qui arrivera ? Le providentialisme semble mener au fatalisme, à une « nécessité absolue ». Or, condamner sans raison certains hommes à la réprobation et en élire d'autres au salut (double prédestination) revient à imposer un décret arbitraire (*decretum absolutum*), ce qui apparente Dieu à un tyran, conséquence inacceptable. Leibniz va donc entreprendre à la fois de clarifier la notion de nécessité, en montrant qu'une « nécessité hypothétique » garantit la liberté de l'homme, et expliquer que Dieu « permet le mal sans le vouloir », ce qui préserve la bonté et la justice du Créateur. Il en résulte une conception optimiste du monde créé « le meilleur possible », où le bien du tout l'emporte sur le mal particulier, où les créatures grâce à la « lumière innée de leur entendement » [4] peuvent opter pour des actes vertueux et où les maux rehaussent l'harmonie du tout. Dieu est comparé à un Monarque d'une « cité parfaite », où « les lois [y] sont réglées suivant la plus parfaite raison » [5]. La justice universelle, dont Dieu assure le respect, garantit donc le droit naturel. Dès ses premiers écrits, Leibniz établit un parallélisme fécond entre théologie et jurisprudence : la théologie est la science de la félicité éternelle (*felicitas aeterna*) distincte de la félicité temporelle (*felicitas temporalis*), dont se préoccupe la jurisprudence séculière.

1. I. Backus, « Leibniz's Quarrel on Necessity with Hobbes, Newton and Clarke », p. 119-136.

2. P. Rateau, *La Question du mal chez Leibniz*, p. 28.

3. *Von der Allmacht und Allwissenheit Gottes und der Freiheit des Menschen*, trad. C. Rösler, p. 66-88.

4. *Causa Dei*, § 98.

5. Grua, 114.

L'analogie récurrente d'un Dieu solaire, cause souveraine d'un monde empli de merveilles, dont les perfections sont assimilables à des rayons, revient sous la plume de Leibniz lorsqu'il s'emploie à clarifier la relation de la création vis-à-vis de son Créateur :

> Ainsi pour bien aimer Dieu il faut connaître ses perfections que les vérités éternelles nous représentent, lorsqu'en pénétrant dans le fonds des choses nous y voyons le grand ordre et l'harmonie universelle toute merveilleuse, qui est a l'égard de la divinité ce que le rayon est au soleil [1].

En effet, Dieu conserve les êtres par une création continuée que Leibniz compare à l'émission continue des rayons provenant du soleil[2]. Sans adopter une théorie cosmologique strictement émanatiste, ni limiter Dieu à une comparaison réductrice (Dieu est davantage que le soleil, vu qu'Il est à l'origine de plusieurs systèmes solaires), Leibniz fait néanmoins usage de cette métaphore, d'inspiration platonicienne, pour expliquer que les possibles (qui n'impliquent pas de contradiction) comme les actuels (qui, assemblés, forment le monde) entretiennent une relation de dépendance perpétuelle à Dieu, origine des essences comme des existences.

Tout ce qu'il y a de parfait dans la série du monde actualisée, série choisie la meilleure parmi une infinité d'autres possibles, provient du concours de Dieu. Le bien suprême de Dieu, conjugué à son omnipotence, se manifeste sous forme d'une force motrice qui attribue de la perfection aux créatures, mais une perfection relative à leur degré de réceptivité. Tout ce qui est bon, parfait et positif, dans les choses, la nature ou les esprits, dérive de Dieu, « père des lumières et dispensateur de tout bien »[3]. La métaphore solaire se retrouve également pour caractériser les justes qui sont à l'image de Dieu[4]. Notons que Leibniz utilise une autre comparaison pour décrire la nature de la relation des esprits à Dieu qui appartient également au champ lexical de la lumière : en tout homme, même non baptisé (non régénéré), « les étincelles de l'image divine [...] ne sont pas complètement éteintes »[5], et il précise que ces « vestiges de l'image divine consistent d'une part en la lumière innée de l'entendement, de l'autre en la liberté native de la volonté »[6]. Les termes utilisés (étincelle, image, vestige) viennent préciser la situation ontologique de l'homme : ils

1. Grua, 89.
2. *Causa Dei,* § 9.
3. *Ibid.*, § 12 ; voir aussi *Théodicée,* § 31 : « tout don parfait venant du père des lumières ».
4. *Discours de métaphysique,* § 37 : « Les justes seront comme des soleils » (*Matthieu*, 13, 43).
5. *Causa Dei,* § 89.
6. *Ibid.*, § 98.

expriment une similitude entre l'homme et Dieu (tous les esprits sont des unités et Dieu est l'unité primitive) corrélée à une déficience de la créature par rapport à son Créateur. Mais l'homme miroir de Dieu, s'il en est une copie imparfaite – ce qui l'éloigne de son modèle –, connaît néanmoins une proximité si étroite à Dieu que ce dernier « fait partie de [lui] plus intimement que le corps » (*Gott ist mir näher angehörig als der Leib*)[1]. En son fond propre, l'homme peut retrouver Dieu. Cette relation d'appartenance à Dieu, intime et indistante, relève de ce que Jean Baruzi a qualifié, de façon paradoxale mais appropriée, de « mysticisme rationnel »[2], où raison et amour entrent en correspondance. L'homme créé par Dieu, à son image, possède une « portion de raison » qui ne diffère de celle de Dieu « que comme une goutte d'eau diffère de l'Océan, ou plutôt comme le fini de l'infini »[3].

Cette présence de clartés rationnelles dans l'entendement humain est corrélée à une essence primitive (ou force) propre à chaque substance, et à la volonté qui permet d'effectuer des choix. Ces trois formalités, à savoir la force (*posse*), la lumière (*scire*), l'amour (*velle*), qui se trouvent en Dieu comme en tout autre esprit avec des différences de perfection ou de degré, devraient s'harmoniser de sorte que la puissance éclairée par la lumière engendre de l'amour. Pour parvenir à cette cohérence des facultés, les hommes doivent laisser la « lumière innée de l'entendement » les conduire, en évitant d'avoir l'esprit obscurci par les passions ou le manque d'attention :

> [Dieu] dispense la lumière de la Raison pour gouverner les âmes aussi généralement qu'il répand celle du soleil pour guider les corps. Mais comme il est dans le pouvoir des hommes de fermer les yeux pour ne pas recevoir l'éclat de ce grand luminaire, ou de se laisser couvrir le visage, il en est de même à l'égard de la raison lorsqu'on s'abandonne à des préjugés ou lorsque l'on s'obstine à refuser des bonnes instructions[4].

Il convient dès lors que les hommes soient à l'écoute de la loi éternelle que Dieu a inscrit dans leurs cœurs et qu'ils pratiquent « cette adoration en esprit et vérité que Dieu demande »[5], à savoir aimer Dieu plus que toute autre chose. Ainsi, connaître l'idée de Dieu, qui reste toutefois en partie inconnaissable en raison de son infinité, n'équivaut pas à une

1. *Von den wahren Theologia Mystica*, trad. cit., p. 291.
2. J. Baruzi, *Dialogues mystiques*, p. 1. Voir C. Rösler « Leibniz et la mystique », p. 303-305.
3. *Discours préliminaire*, § 61.
4. Grua, 47.
5. Grua, 195.

compréhension strictement théorique, mais implique une union à Lui, d'où résulte une clarification intérieure, manifestée non seulement par un don de lumière et d'intelligence, mais aussi par la mise en mouvement d'une capacité à agir pour contribuer à l'instauration du bien commun. L'action de Dieu en l'homme, qui suppose de la part de l'âme une réception passive, est un octroi de lumière ou de sagesse, qui fait « naître en nous un effort pour agir sur nous et sur les autres choses conformément à cette lumière, cet effort d'un esprit éclairé qui va à exprimer le bien et l'amour »[1]. Remarquons que pour Leibniz, l'amour pour Dieu n'est pas « antérieur à la lumière », mais qu'il en découle sous forme d'une capacité à agir de façon vertueuse. Dans le contexte de ce mouvement unitif à Dieu, Leibniz procède à une inversion des catégories classiques en faisant de la raison une passion et de l'amour une action : « Ainsi la lumière est notre passion, l'amour est le plaisir qui en résulte, et qui consiste dans une action sur nous mêmes, dont provient un effort d'agir encore sur les autres pour contribuer au bien en tant qu'il dépend de nous » (*ibid.*). La fameuse maxime leibnizienne : *theoria cum praxi*, trouve un domaine d'application en théologie[2] dans la jonction de la lumière à la charité : « Et lorsque [le Christ] nous recommande d'aimer sur toutes choses ce grand Dieu qu'il a dépeint si aimable et si bon ; et notre prochain après lui, il comprend en même temps et la théorie et la pratique »[3]. Notons au passage que l'articulation théologique entre théorie et pratique, ou lumière et charité, repose *in fine* sur l'enseignement du Christ, ce qui permet d'affirmer que si l'idée de Dieu est centrale dans la pensée leibnizienne, la figure du Fils, qui est l'une des expressions de ce Dieu trinitaire infiniment aimable, joue un rôle tout aussi décisif : il enseigne une doctrine claire et donne l'exemple d'une action irréprochable ou pure, car aussi serviable qu'aimante.

UNE THÉOLOGIE DE L'AMOUR

Leibniz ne peut consentir à une piété aveugle, fondée sur le *credo quia absurdum est*, car à ses yeux « la foi sans la lumière n'éveille pas l'amour »[4]. Conformément aux enseignements de Jésus-Christ, la théologie leibnizienne de la lumière répond à une exigence d'intelligibilité, mais elle est en même temps une théologie de l'amour. Méditer sur l'idée

1. Grua, 87.
2. M. R. Antognazza, « Theory and Praxis in Leibniz's Theological Thought », p. 35-57.
3. Grua, 91.
4. *Von den wahren Theologia Mystica*, trad. cit., p. 413.

de Dieu induit des progrès cognitifs, mais aussi éthiques, ce qui revient à associer connaissance et sagesse. « Il y a peu de gens qui sachent ce que c'est que l'amour de Dieu sur toutes choses, qui est pourtant le principe de la vraie religion. Cet amour est plus grand à mesure qu'on est plus éclairé »[1]. Ainsi, une théologie de la lumière « véritable » ne saurait être dissociée d'un amour de prédilection pour Dieu : étant infiniment parfait, Dieu est infiniment aimable. Par suite, une restriction dans l'amour envers Dieu constitue tout autant une erreur de raisonnement qu'une incroyance cachée. Concevoir véritablement les infinis perfections du Créateur devrait « enflammer les âmes d'un amour divin »[2], et les conduire à « un progrès perpétuel de joies provenant de l'amour céleste »[3]. Réfléchir à l'idée de Dieu suppose non seulement de respecter les lois de la logique (les attributs divins doivent entrer en harmonie) tout en donnant accès au bonheur véritable (aimer Dieu comble l'âme de félicité), mais aussi et nécessairement d'entrer dans un perfectionnement moral, où il convient d'agir charitablement envers autrui, signe distinctif de la véritable piété. « La règle principale de la religion chrétienne : nous devons aimer Dieu sur toutes choses et les autres hommes comme nous-mêmes »[4]. Amour de Dieu et philanthropie universelle vont de pair, car aimer le Créateur, c'est agir pour Sa gloire, et donc s'engager au service du bien commun :

> La pierre de touche de l'amour de Dieu est celle que S. Jean nous a donnée. Et lorsque je vois qu'on a une véritable ardeur pour procurer le bien général, on n'est pas loin de l'amour de Dieu[5].

Aimer Dieu de façon privilégiée résulte de la connaissance de l'excellence de Sa nature, et par voie de conséquence de l'excellence de Ses œuvres. Même si le détail de l'organisation parfaite du monde dépasse l'entendement limité de la créature, l'homme peut avoir confiance que Dieu fait tout « pour le mieux et que rien ne saurait nuire à ceux qui l'aiment »[6], car Il gouverne les esprits en entrant en société avec eux, à la manière du plus magnanime ou débonnaire des Monarques. Le dessein premier de ce bienveillant Prince est d'offrir le plus de félicité possible à ses sujets : dans la cité de Dieu, monde moral qui est « la plus noble partie de l'univers »[7], tout concourt au bien des esprits qui, par leur nature, sont

1. Grua, 161.
2. *Discours de métaphysique*, § 33.
3. Grua, 92.
4. Grua, 585.
5. Grua, 107.
6. *Discours de métaphysique*, § 4-5.
7. *Ibid.*, § 36.

proches de la divinité. Concevoir les infinies perfections de l'Etre le plus adorable qui soit procure une félicité radieuse, dont la marque distinctive est un état d'esprit empli de contentement et d'une ardeur à procurer le bien général. Dès lors, il convient de considérer les évènements passés et présents non avec résignation, à la manière des stoïciens, mais avec entière satisfaction vu qu'ils sont l'expression de la bienveillante volonté divine. En revanche, en ce qui concerne le futur, l'homme doit faire effort pour contribuer au bien général, ce qui exclut l'oisiveté fataliste fondée sur l'argument paresseux (*logos argos*), mais aussi l'indifférence quiétiste, dont la passivité est fautive.

Dès la Préface du *Codex Juris gentium* (1693), Leibniz définit l'amour comme le fait de prendre plaisir à la félicité d'autrui. Cet altruisme intéressé, car réjouissant, équivaut à vouloir en un même mouvement le bien d'autrui et le sien propre. En aimant l'autre, l'individu s'attache à son bonheur qu'il fait sien, mais aussi à son malheur, dont il souffre. Cet amour aussi bienveillant qu'intéressant, n'est ni cupide, ni mercenaire, il ne se fonde pas sur l'utilité ou l'intérêt égoïste (amour de concupiscence). Il n'est pas désintéressé pour autant, puisqu'il est source de plaisir. La définition leibnizienne de l'amour implique la réciprocité : l'amant et l'aimé partagent un même bonheur qui se renforce en spirale[1], vu que la joie de l'un conforte la joie de l'autre. Pour Leibniz, l'amour entre humains et l'amour envers le divin sont de nature identique (univocité de l'amour), mais se distinguent par la perfection de l'objet aimé, et par suite par l'intensité de la plénitude ressentie par l'amant. Qu'il s'agisse de l'amour humain ou divin, une conception de l'amour entièrement désintéressée est exclue, ce qui permet de mettre un terme à la querelle théologique du « pur amour »[2]. Madame Guyon défendait une vision mystique du « pur amour », détaché au point de devenir indifférence au péché et au salut. Dans cet état de contemplation désintéressé, supposé accessible à tous, tout acte est inutile, fût-il de foi ou de charité : la prière, les œuvres, voire les sacrements, finissent par perdre leur utilité, conséquences que Leibniz ne saurait admettre, d'où sa critique en règle du quiétisme. Fénelon, archevêque de Cambray, pensait pouvoir affirmer, à la suite de Madame Guyon, qu'il est possible d'aimer Dieu en se détachant de toute satisfaction, sans se soucier de son salut, ce qui revient à opposer amour de soi (naturel) et amour pur (envers Dieu). Or, pour Leibniz, il convient non de les opposer, mais de les concilier : « comme le véritable amour de Dieu fait la perfection

1. P. Rateau, *Leibniz et le meilleur des mondes possibles*, p. 225 *sq*.
2. É. Naërt, *Leibniz et la querelle du pur amour*.

et la félicité de l'âme, son vrai intérêt est d'aimer Dieu sur toutes choses »[1]. À trop vouloir préconiser le désintéressement, on tombe dans une chimère, voire un athéisme subtil : « la supposition qu'un amateur de Dieu pourrait être content quand il serait damné, est une fiction d'un cas impossible » (*ibid.*). Se quereller au sujet du pur amour, c'est méconnaître que l'amour peut réjouir de façon pure, à la manière du plaisir esthétique : « Si j'achetais un beau tableau de Raphaël pour le revendre avec gain, je serais intéressé, mais si c'était seulement pour le plaisir que je trouverais à le voir, cela répondrait au pur amour »[2]. Aimer Dieu ne saurait mener ni à un anéantissement de soi, ni à une contemplation oisive, mais doit conduire à une union de volonté[3] source d'un contentement actif, au service du bien commun. Dieu, soucieux que son empire soit heureux et florissant, veut la félicité de ceux qui l'aiment. De son côté, l'homme de bonne volonté, aussi vertueux que sage, qui s'attache à Dieu comme à un « Maître »[4] ou à un « Père »[5], tâche de se conformer à la volonté divine, en prenant part à Son Royaume par de bonnes pensées et de bonnes actions, conformément aux enseignements de Jésus-Christ.

La théologie leibnizienne assigne un rôle important à la figure du Christ, qui est lumière et amour assemblés : ses enseignements sont éclairants et édifiants, il est caractérisé comme le fondateur d'une religion lumineuse, comparé à un législateur, présenté comme rédempteur, ses fonctions sotériologique et eschatologique sont mises en avant. L'Évangile de Jésus-Christ, « divinement bien exprimé », « a changé entièrement la face des choses humaines »[6]. Le Christ est celui qui a le mieux expliqué le fonctionnement de la cité de Dieu et « lui seul a fait voir combien Dieu nous aime, et avec quelle exactitude il a pourvu à tout ce qui nous touche »[7]. La bonté de Dieu ne saurait se concevoir sans la thèse d'une grâce universelle qui suppose l'incarnation du Fils, puisque son sacrifice rédempteur permet aux hommes d'être sauvés, son sang étant versé *pour tous*[8], ce qui revient à rejeter les thèses des particularistes. Par ailleurs, Leibniz rappelle à de multiples reprises dans ses négociations iréniques, en particulier interprotestantes, que le sacrement eucharistique possède une vertu unitive à la substance du Christ, qui nourrit (naturellement) et restaure

1. Grua, 125.
2. Grua, 142.
3. M. De Gaudemar, *Leibniz, de la puissance au sujet*, p. 243.
4. *Discours de métaphysique*, § 4-5.
5. *Monadologie*, § 84.
6. *Discours de métaphysique*, § 37.
7. *Ibid.*
8. *Von den wahren Theologia Mystica*, trad. cit., p. 294.

(surnaturellement) le communiant. Dans le *Tentamen Expositionis Irenicae trium potissimarum inter Protestantes Controversiarum* (Essai d'exposition irénique des trois principales controverses entre les protestants) de 1698 [1], Leibniz indique que la nature duale du Christ, Dieu-homme (*Théo-anthropos*), est substantiellement absorbée lors de la manducation des espèces consacrées : sa présence « hyperphysique » se manifeste sous forme d'une « force » (*vis*, *conatus*) régénérante. L'union du communiant au Christ est salvifique.

La réception substantielle du corps et du sang du Christ unit les croyants au Christ, et par le Christ, les unit à Dieu et entre eux. La communion partagée fonde donc la communauté ecclésiale (union externe) par adhésion substantielle des communiants au Christ et donc à Dieu (union interne). Jésus-Christ ne saurait s'identifier à Dieu (il n'*est* pas Dieu, même s'il *a* les attributs divins), ni n'est un milieu entre l'homme et Dieu (car il n'y a pas de milieu entre l'absolu et le limité [2]). Dans la personne de Jésus-Christ sont unies, sans être confondues, la nature absolue de Dieu et la nature limitée de l'homme : l'incarnation est l'union la plus étroite qui puisse exister entre le Créateur et la créature. Ainsi, la réception réelle et substantielle lors de la célébration eucharistique, en unissant le communiant à la personne de Jésus-Christ, l'unit en même temps à sa limitation humaine et à son absoluité divine. Leibniz insiste sur l'importance des termes : Jésus-Christ *est* une « personne » qui *a* deux « natures ». De même que le Christ est consubstantiel au pain, de même le Fils est consubstantiel au Père [3]. S'unir au Christ par la communion, c'est en même temps s'unir à Dieu par l'union personnelle. L'union eucharistique est donc redoublée, ou plus exactement portée à l'absolu : elle permet à la créature limitée de s'unir avec l'illimité, ce qui a pour effet d'octroyer au communiant une lumineuse force d'action, aux effets charitables, et par suite irénistes : « la charité nous doit éloigner de tout ce qui sent la secte, et qui augmente les divisions » [4]. *Sacramentum caritatis*, la Cène est aussi *sacramentum unitatis*.

La théologie leibnizienne de la charité, reposant sur l'amour de Dieu sur toutes choses, a pour corollaire une ecclésiologie irénique : « [...] on peut être sauvé par l'amour sincère de Dieu sur toutes choses, de quelque

1. Trad. et commentaire dans *Negotium Irenicum*, p. 755-856. Cet opuscule est un excellent résumé des thèses de Leibniz en matière irénique.

2. A I, 11, 21.

3. A I, 15, 602.

4. Grua, 93.

communion qu'on puisse être »[1]. C'est dans la charité, qui prime sur la foi, que « consiste l'âme de l'unité »[2]. En effet, la charité, qui évite soupçons et querelles, dispose à la conciliation, et par suite à l'union des confessions. Reconnaître que les torts sont partagés (« On peut avouer qu'il y a de la coulpe de part et d'autre quant au schisme »[3]), c'est adopter une théologie modérée, encline à adoucir les propos, renoncer à l'esprit guerrier en comparant le mal à une maladie : « Je voudrais qu'on approuvât partout ce qui est bon, sans faire la guerre à ceux qui y mêlent du mal, à peu près comme les saints ne font point la guerre aux malades »[4]. En préconisant de chercher partout ce qui est bon, Leibniz se prémunit contre les attitudes hostiles, empressées à censurer, excommunier ou condamner. Lors des négociations iréniques interprotestantes (*negotium irenicum*), le philosophe formule une « loi d'humanité ou de charité »[5], afin de ne pas réprouver des auteurs dont les thèses aboutissent, sans qu'ils en soient conscients, à des hérésies. Ainsi, l'erreur involontaire doit être corrigée avec bienveillance, et non susciter l'anathème. L'entre-implication de la justice et de la charité[6] chez Leibniz est le reflet de l'imbrication réciproque de la théologie et de la politique au sein de l'échiquier européen tributaire des préoccupations hégémoniques et dynastiques des souverains. Dès lors, la charité qui fonde la théologie leibnizienne ne conduit pas à se contenter d'une simple « tolérance » mutuelle (civile ou ecclésiastique), mais doit parvenir à une « union véritable » ou à une « vraie concorde », dont la solidité repose sur des articles de foi réellement unifiés, car philosophiquement harmonisés.

Pour transcender les clivages confessionnels, Leibniz se fait l'architecte d'un édifice de paix qui a pour clef de voûte « l'amour de Dieu sur toutes choses ». En aimant Dieu, les créatures sont portées « à la perfection dont elles sont capables par l'union avec lui, qui ne peut consister que dans l'esprit »[7]. Leibniz assigne à la théologie de faire converger clartés rationnelles et charité dans un projet politique et religieux où prévaut l'harmonie[8], conçue comme unité dans la diversité.

1. Grua, 103.
2. A I, 11, 439.
3. Grua, 188.
4. Grua, 144.
5. *Negotium Irenicum*, p. 986.
6. R. Sève, *Leibniz. Le droit de la raison*, p. 105.
7. Grua, 580.
8. J.-B. Neveux, *Vie spirituelle et vie sociale*, p. 691-692 : « [I]l paraît établi que si [Leibniz] a mis sa plume au service du Hanovre, ce n'est pas seulement parce qu'il avait

UNE THÉOLOGIE IRÉNIQUE

> « Qu'est-ce donc que la correspondance sur l'union des Églises sinon une vaste théorie de l'amour de Dieu ? » [1]

Fondé sur une théologie de la lumière et de l'amour assemblés, l'irénisme[2] rationnel de Leibniz a pour visée idéale l'instauration d'une Église universelle. Le remarquable ouvrage de Jean Baruzi, *Leibniz et l'organisation religieuse de la terre*, publié en 1907, met en avant la volonté de Leibniz de donner à son projet d'unification des Églises une dimension universelle, et donc œcuménique au sens étymologique du terme (*oikouménê gê*, terre habitée)[3]. En effet, Leibniz envisage une union possible des religions chrétiennes, sans exclure de retrouver des fondements communs entre le christianisme de l'Occident et les croyances de l'Orient (en particulier celle des chrétiens orthodoxes et des Chinois). Il a appliqué son schème d'harmonie à sa conception ecclésiale. Ainsi, on peut considérer comme deux aspects d'une même entreprise d'un côté ses projets de *réunion* avec les catholiques (envisagés dès les *Démonstrations catholiques* vers 1668[4], puis menés avec de nombreux partenaires et correspondants, dont nous ne mentionnerons que les évêques Jacques-Bénigne Bossuet, Royas y Spinola et Franz Anton von Buchhaim), et d'un autre côté ses projets d'*union* entre les protestants (lors d'un *negotium irenicum* devant rapprocher tout d'abord la Cour luthérienne de Hanovre et la Cour réformée de Berlin qui a eu lieu de 1697 à 1706, avec une brève

besoin de la faveur du prince, mais bien parce que les idées qu'il eut à exposer correspondaient à ce qui est sans doute le fond de sa spiritualité, le désir, la passion même de l'harmonie ».

1. J. Baruzi, *Leibniz et l'organisation religieuse de la terre*, p. 244.

2. Le concept d'irénisme (de *eïrênê*, la paix) est problématique et les spécialistes s'interrogent quant à sa définition. Ils vont parfois jusqu'à nier la possibilité de l'élaborer puisqu'elle dépend de contextes historiques toujours variables et, de plus, est porteuse d'un projet considéré comme irréalisable. Que le concept d'irénisme relève partiellement de l'utopie n'invalide toutefois pas la possibilité de le penser, au moins à titre d'idéal régulateur. En revanche, parler d'un irénisme générique semble hypothétique. Aussi est-il plus exact d'évoquer des tentatives iréniques plurielles, au nombre desquelles appartient l'engagement spécifique de Leibniz. Voir P. O. Léchot, « Irénisme », p. 633-634.

3. Il faut se garder de l'anachronisme qui consisterait à attribuer sans précaution à la philosophie leibnizienne de la religion ce concept apparu au XIXe siècle et qui a reçu une certaine effectivité ecclésiale seulement au XXe siècle. L'irénisme de Leibniz, de portée universelle, pourrait être qualifié d'œcuménique, à la condition de se référer au sens antique du terme (terre habitée, sens repris par les chrétiens). Voir H. Rudolph, « Bemerkungen zur Kirchengeschichtlichen Einordnung des Leibnischen Ökumenismus », p. 35-45.

4. *Demonstrationes catholicae*, A VI, 1, 489-548.

reprise en 1716). Le principal interlocuteur berlinois de Leibniz était le prédicateur réformé de la Cour Daniel Ernst Jablonski, théologien érudit, auteur en 1697 d'un écrit irénique remarquable : *Kurtze Vorstellung der Einigkeit und des Unterscheides im Glauben beyder Evangelischen so genandten Lutherischen und Reformirten Kirchen*... (Brève présentation de l'accord et du désaccord dans la foi des deux Églises évangéliques, nommées luthérienne et réformée...)[1]. Le philosophe iréniste a entretenu une riche correspondance avec Jablonski et rédigé en réponse deux écrits iréniques majeurs : en 1698, le *Tentamen Expositionis Irenicae*, et à partir de 1698, secondé par l'Abbé luthérien de Loccum, Gerhard Wolter Molanus, l'*Unvorgreiffliches Bedencken über eine Schrifft genandt Kurtze Vorstellung*... (Modeste considération sur un écrit intitulé «Brève présentation... »)[2].

L'irénisme chez Leibniz est un concept complexe, aux facettes multiples mais convergentes : il se définit *négativement* comme volonté d'éviter de nouveaux schismes ainsi que d'écarter les clivages religieux déjà existants fixés dans des positions dogmatiques antagoniques, et *positivement*, comme dessein de clarifier et unifier les doctrines, inscrites dans des confessions de foi faisant autorité, afin de réunir les Églises et les États en tenant compte de l'échiquier politique. L'irénisme leibnizien provient d'un engagement personnel sincère, qui n'a rien d'opportuniste, car il est aussi profond que constant. Il s'exprime théoriquement par l'élaboration d'une méthode philosophique mettant en lumière les convergences doctrinales entre les confessions, afin de trouver pratiquement des procédés liturgiques partageables, le rite eucharistique dessinant la pierre angulaire de cet édifice de paix. Mais ce travail de clarification doctrinale à visée unitive, recourant à un mode de communication spécifique, faisant alterner le secret et la publication, doit pour Leibniz être corrélé à une *praxis* diplomatique : sa politique ecclésiale emploie des stratégies adaptées à ses différents interlocuteurs, qu'ils soient représentants des institutions religieuses, des facultés de théologie, des académies des sciences ou des corps diplomatiques, ou encore membres des familles régnantes des différentes Cours européennes. La finalité de ce travail théologico-philosophique, mené au nom de l'amour de Dieu sur toutes choses, corrélé à un

1. H. Rudolph, «Zum Nutzen von Politik und Philosophie für die Kirchenunion», p. 108-127 ; avec, en appendice : D. E. Jablonski, *Kurtze Vorstellung*, p. 128-166.

2. Pour une trad. commentée de ces textes et de cette correspondance, *cf.* C. Rösler-Le Van, *Negotium Irenicum*. Pour une brève vue d'ensemble : *id.*, «*Negotium Irenicum*. Les tentatives d'union des Églises protestantes de G. W. Leibniz et D. E. Jablonski», p. 35-56.

pragmatisme politique et ecclésial, a pour visée idéale l'instauration d'une Église universelle.

Le mode d'exposition irénique que Leibniz adopte se fonde sur une transposition en philosophie des problématiques théologiques et implique un mode de communication empreint de modération, contrairement aux théologiens schismatiques qui se reconnaissent à leur outrance, leurs vues partisanes, leur propension à anathématiser, bref, leur manque de lumière et de charité : « Ceux qui sont d'humeur sectaire ou schismatique... ne sauraient avoir ni la charité ni la lumière... » [1]. Ainsi, à leur mauvaise foi, s'ajoute leur foi mauvaise. Autant de passions qui les privent des lumières d'une raison éclairée par les rayons du soleil divin [2] et les empêchent d'accéder à la « véritable théologie, que souvent les Théologiens ne connaissent guère » [3] ou à la vraie religion qui, parce qu'elle est naturelle, embrasse l'universel : « La raison est le principe d'une religion universelle et parfaite » [4]. Dans la question du religieux, comme dans l'ensemble de l'œuvre de Leibniz, ainsi que le rappelle Michel Fichant, « l'universel [...] est à la fois fin et moyen » [5]. De fait, la philosophie leibnizienne procède par un mouvement de décentrement qui conduit à penser le particulier à partir du point de vue idéal du tout. Leibniz soutient que ce point de vue, réservé à Dieu seul, n'est certes que très partiellement partageable par les créatures limitées, toutefois le chemin de perfectionnement qu'il propose à l'intelligence tend à l'infini vers ce point ultime.

Voyons à titre d'exemple significatif comment il applique ce schème d'universalité lors des tentatives d'union des Églises protestantes, menées avec le prédicateur de la Cour de Berlin Jablonski à partir de 1697. D'un côté, Jablonski et surtout Leibniz pensaient qu'il fallait instaurer un axe solide entre Berlin et Hanovre, avant d'espérer pouvoir gagner d'autres États protestants à la cause irénique, d'un autre côté aussi bien Leibniz que Jablonski raisonnaient dès le début en termes de relation triangulaire (en incluant l'Église anglicane), voire multi-polaire (en ouvrant l'échiquier politique à des constellations plus larges). De fait, l'Angleterre était un allié indispensable pour renforcer le bloc des puissances protestantes contre l'hégémonie catholique, en particulier gallicane, la France s'étant rendue tristement célèbre par la persécution des huguenots. De plus,

1. Grua, 105.

2. A. Robinet, *Le Meilleur des mondes*, p. 153-160 : « Le soleil de justice : la religion naturelle ».

3. Grua, 102.

4. Grua, 49.

5. M. Fichant, *Science et Métaphysique*, p. IX.

l'éventualité que la maison de Hanovre puisse obtenir la couronne d'Angleterre situait les négociations iréniques dans la perspective d'une politique dynastique où prévalait la raison d'État. Enfin, le culte anglican était considéré par Leibniz et Jablonski comme pouvant servir à la fois de modèle et de garde-fou à l'union des luthériens et des réformés d'Allemagne. L'ouverture internationale de ces transactions était donc bien le signe de la volonté des deux négociateurs de ne pas s'en tenir à la particularité des deux Cours de Hanovre et Berlin. Voulant échapper aux enfermements particularistes, leur projet avait une portée européenne[1] et idéalement universelle. Mais leur marge de manœuvre était restreinte non seulement du fait de leur position respective dans les deux Cours, mais aussi en raison de la nature même de leur projet qui impliquait nécessairement la collaboration des hommes politiques et des ecclésiastiques (dont les perspectives et les intérêts n'étaient que partiellement compatibles), d'où le double échec de ces transactions iréniques (en 1706 et 1716). Soulignons qu'en même temps que Leibniz et Molanus agissaient pour l'*union* des protestants, ils contribuaient aussi aux tentatives de *réunion* avec les catholiques. L'année 1698 avec l'*Additionale Responsum*, ainsi que les années 1700-1701 où Leibniz se rend à Vienne, en constituent des points culminants (les tentatives de *réunion* n'aboutiront pas davantage). Cela montre, premièrement, que leur visée était plus universelle que le seul souhait de constituer une Église protestante unifiée[2]; deuxièmement, qu'ils ne considéraient pas les entreprises d'*union* et de *réunion* comme concurrentielles, mais comme potentiellement complémentaires, même s'ils n'en ont pas informé Jablonski, afin de ne pas risquer d'être mal perçus de lui, vu que l'irénisme protestant de ce dernier se constituait dans une opposition au catholicisme de la Contre-Réforme; troisièmement, que même lorsque la succession à la couronne d'Angleterre nécessite que la politique hanovrienne devienne très protestante, et donc ne soutienne plus les transactions avec les catholiques, Leibniz quant à lui n'y renonce pas pour autant, ce qui témoigne d'une liberté d'action qui est la marque de la force de sa conviction religieuse universaliste. Sans méconnaître le particulier, ni vouloir l'abolir, le philosophe irénique Leibniz pense et agit *sub specie universalitatis*.

1. J. Baruzi, *Leibniz et l'organisation religieuse de la terre*, p. 204, 235, 265.

2. *Ibid.*, p. 264-265 : « Leibniz semble avoir compris dès l'origine que deux unions doivent se superposer. [...] il rapprochera les Protestants, afin que, si quelque accord se produisait jamais avec l'Église romaine, les Églises protestantes fussent capables de s'insérer, sans désordre, en la communion générale ».

La théologie irénique leibnizienne, rationnellement apologétique, est associée à une théologie sacramentelle ou à une métaphysique eucharistique, accordant un rôle éminent à la figure du Christ, *Théo-anthropos*, véritable trait d'union entre Dieu et les hommes. En effet, le sacrement eucharistique revêt une importance majeure aux yeux du philosophe : il permet d'accorder la physique (étude des corps) à la métaphysique (étude de la substance), et ce faisant, la naturalité du pain à la grâce de la présence réelle du Christ, dont les effets sont salvifiques. Si la théologie sacramentelle revêt une importance centrale aux yeux de Leibniz, c'est parce qu'elle s'accorde aux sciences, à ses projets iréniques, ainsi qu'à sa théologie de la lumière et de l'amour en l'inscrivant dans sa conception sotériologique, tant individuelle (pour le communiant) que collective (pour l'humanité). Ainsi, expliquer le mystère de la transsubstantiation[1], c'est à la fois répondre à une exigence d'intelligibilité, à l'affirmation d'une régénération intérieure et à une volonté d'union ecclésiale. Non seulement l'*union* des Églises protestantes, mais aussi leur *réunion* à l'Église catholique, sont conditionnées selon Leibniz par l'union des chrétiens au Christ lors du sacrement. Il est donc justifié de soutenir, avec Christiane Frémont, que pour Leibniz, « la christologie est la condition de la réunion des Églises »[2]. La Cène est véritablement un *sacramentum universalis* ou un pain universel, car elle permet dans l'idéal de rallier toutes les confessions chrétiennes. En effet, dès les *Démonstrations catholiques*, Leibniz affirme que sa définition de la substance corporelle permet d'éclairer la présence réelle des luthériens, et de démontrer sa compatibilité non seulement avec la présence spirituelle des réformés, mais aussi avec la conception transsubstantialiste des catholiques depuis le IVe concile de Latran (1215). Leibniz démontre que la « communion » ne saurait être « sacrement de la division »[3], puisqu'une approche éclairée de ce point de doctrine, source de schismes et de conflits, de polémiques et de condamnations pour hérésie, permet de dénouer les divergences théologiques, ce qui rend possible (de droit mais pas nécessairement de fait) la réconciliation des Églises chrétiennes ou la communion ecclésiastique.

Lors du *negotium irenicum*, la fin visée par Leibniz se présente sous la forme complexe d'une échelle à trois degrés, dont le premier est « la tolérance civile », le second « la tolérance ecclésiastique » et le dernier

1. C. Frémont, *L'être et la relation*, p. 47-69 : exposé d'une grande clarté sur le traitement philosophique de la transsubstantiation.

2. *Ibid.*, p. 31.

3. A. Gounelle, *La Cène, Sacrement de la Division*.

« l'union complète »[1]. Les deux premiers échelons mènent à une union seulement « virtuelle », pouvant servir de masque à des abus. Seul le dernier échelon permet d'obtenir une « union réelle », définie comme la possibilité pour les luthériens et les réformés de communier ensemble. Leibniz ne se contente pas de définir « l'union complète » comme la simple participation commune des fidèles au culte eucharistique, mais il souligne la nécessité de l'établir solidement sur une explication philosophique du mystère qui, sans prétendre tout clarifier, puisse permettre d'éviter les reproches d'incohérence, voire d'absurdité. Le philosophe de Hanovre démontre qu'une conception du corps caractérisée par la seule étendue cartésienne, ou la stricte localité, en restant uniquement dimensionnelle, ne permet pas de concevoir le mode de présence du Christ dans les espèces sacramentelles. Selon Leibniz, la multilocalisation de la force d'action eucharistique du Christ implique une explication « hyperphysique »[2] de la nature de son corps éminemment glorieux, dont la modalité de donation est « adimensionnelle »[3], c'est-à-dire immédiate et indistante. L'hyperphysique sacramentelle de Leibniz reconduit à l'universel : l'ubiquité de Jésus-Christ, ou sa présence hyperphysique universelle, se fonde sur la toute-puissance divine et prend corps, dans la célébration de la Cène.

CONCLUSION

> « Les idées que Jésus-Christ nous donne de Dieu
> sont grandes en même temps qu'elles sont claires »[4].

La théologie de Leibniz résulte de la convergence de plusieurs finalités : un engagement de foi protestant philosophiquement assumé (son luthéranisme modéré est empreint de liberté) ; une insertion de la théologie dans un système encyclopédique du savoir (lumières théologiques et lumières naturelles ou scientifiques s'accordent) ; la volonté d'établir à partir de la connaissance de Dieu une coopération des esprits au sein d'une monarchie universelle ; l'articulation de la théorie à la pratique (au moyen d'une conception éthique et jurisprudentielle de la charité enseignée par le Christ) ; une volonté forte et constante d'œuvrer à la paix des Églises (clarifier autant que possible les doctrines ou les mystères revient à

1. *Negotium Irenicum*, p. 379.
2. *Tentamen*, § 5, in *Negotium Irenicum*, p. 813.
3. *Negotium Irenicum*, p. 249.
4. Grua, 90.

promouvoir la *pax Dei*). La spiritualité de Leibniz, à visée apologétique, résulte donc tout autant d'une authentique adhésion de foi que d'une recherche de la vérité aux effets édifiants et conciliateurs. Méditer sur l'idée de Dieu et ses infinies perfections donne accès à une certaine intelligibilité des mystères chrétiens, et se manifeste principalement par le fait de susciter de l'amour pour le Créateur, et par suite, pour ses créatures. La théologie leibnizienne est éthique à sa racine, puisque penser véritablement à Dieu, être le plus parfait donc le plus aimable, revient à vouloir le servir en œuvrant au bien commun ou à la célébration de Sa gloire. Caractérisée par une compréhension philosophique de la lumière et de l'amour qui se renforcent et se complètent réciproquement, la théologie leibnizienne aboutit à une conception politico-ecclésiale irénique, dont l'idéal recteur est l'instauration progressive d'une religion universelle, unifiée mais riche de diversité. Il est dès lors paradoxalement cohérent que Leibniz puisse soutenir que ses démonstrations iréniques des doctrines religieuses, du fait qu'elles soient « purement philosophiques », n'appartiennent de ce fait à « aucune confession »[1]. Il s'agit pour lui de retrouver, derrière la diversité des Églises effectives, catholique, luthérienne ou réformée, l'unité idéale et fondamentale de « l'Église chrétienne primitive »[2], ce qui suppose de penser une Église universelle *une*, mais dont l'unicité pour ainsi dire « surconfessionnelle » (rationnelle), respecte la diversité des Églises particulières. Voilà pourquoi Leibniz, qui affirme appartenir à la confession modérée d'Augsbourg[3], dit aussi être catholique « *in foro interno* »[4]. Il n'y a là nulle contradiction. La pensée de Leibniz n'est pas binaire (ou bien protestant, ou bien catholique), mais elle est intégrative et situationnelle : luthérien modéré face aux luthériens orthodoxes et aux réformés, protestant vis-à-vis des catholiques de Rome, mais universellement catholique, si le pléonasme est permis, face à toutes les positions particularistes. De plus, la « catholicité universelle » de Leibniz, fondée sur l'idée d'un Dieu trinitaire, aussi bienveillant que puissant et savant, suppose une christologie philosophique. Ainsi, la théologie leibnizienne se caractérise par une contemplation des attributs et des perfections de Dieu,

1. *Negotium Irenicum*, p. 252.

2. *Ibid.*, p. 362.

3. Leibniz ne renie jamais son identité confessionnelle protestante, malgré les propositions qui lui ont été faites de conversion au catholicisme. Toutefois, il ne se qualifie pas de « luthérien », mais revendique sa fidélité à la « Confession d'Augsbourg ». C'est dire qu'il n'adhère pas inconditionnellement à la doctrine du réformateur Luther (dont il ne partage pas toujours les idées et dont il critique le manque de modération), mais qu'il est fidèle à l'esprit de la Réforme luthérienne marquée par la modération de Melanchthon.

4. J. Baruzi, *Leibniz et l'organisation religieuse de la terre*, p. 288, note 3, et A I, 6, 234.

évoquée tout au long de son œuvre, mais aussi par une vénération du Père à travers son Fils : « la contemplation des bienfaits de Dieu qu'il nous a donné en Jésus-Christ est le plus grand préparatif de la grâce du divin amour »[1]. En effet, Leibniz assigne un rôle majeur à l'incarnation[2], à la personne de Jésus-Christ, ainsi qu'à l'eucharistie, rôle trop souvent minimisé dans les interprétations du leibnizianisme. Les commentateurs ont à raison thématisé l'importance centrale, radicale et première, de Dieu dans la métaphysique optimiste et justificatrice du philosophe, mais insuffisamment le rôle du Christ, qui incarne la jonction de la lumière et de l'amour divins, en particulier par le don d'une grâce universelle qu'il actualise par son incarnation et sa passion, ainsi que par sa présence régénérante dans le sacrement eucharistique. Notre étude vient donc confirmer le constat de Christiane Frémont : « On a trop souvent lu le dix-septième siècle comme le siècle du Père, peut-être faudrait-il *aussi* le lire comme celui du Fils. À côté du Dieu garant des vérités éternelles, il y a le Verbe fait chair, ou le savoir fait chair »[3]. Et effectivement, dans sa *Théodicée*, Leibniz va jusqu'à soutenir que Jésus-Christ est le *summus philosophus*.

Claire RÖSLER-LE VAN
(Docteur de l'Université de Paris-Sorbonne)

1. Grua, 80.
2. M. R. Antognazza, *Leibniz on the Trinity and the Incarnation*.
3. C. Frémont, *L'être et la relation*, p. 31-32.

TROISIÈME PARTIE

LA CONNAISSANCE

LES FORMES DE LA PENSÉE
LOGIQUE ET LANGAGE CHEZ LEIBNIZ

MISOSOPHE. Nous pouvons nous sauver sans la logique.

THÉOLOGIEN. Je l'admets, car nous pouvons même nous sauver sans raisons et nous pouvons raisonner sans syllogismes ; mais nous ne pouvons pas soutenir et sauvegarder les fondements de la foi sans raisons, ni trouver facilement la vérité dans des choses bien difficiles ou convaincre un adversaire opiniâtre sans les arts logiques[1].

NATURE ET FONCTION DE LA LOGIQUE

Qu'est-ce que la logique et à quoi doit-elle servir ? Bien que Leibniz n'ait composé aucun traité systématique de logique, il a pourtant laissé plusieurs indications sur la façon dont il concevait la nature et la fonction de cette discipline[2]. Dans les *Nouveaux essais*, il écrit que « la *Logique* est l'art, qui enseigne l'ordre et la liaison des pensées »[3]. À son correspondant Gabriel Wagner, il explique que « par la logique ou art de penser j'entends l'art d'utiliser l'entendement, donc non seulement de juger ce qui est proposé, mais aussi de découvrir ce qui est caché »[4]. À Koch, il demande si par logique il entend « tout l'art de penser », y compris les arts de l'imagination et de la mémoire, ou seulement « celui qui consiste dans l'usage de la raison »[5]. La logique est donc premièrement un art, selon une caractérisation standard à l'époque. Alors que la science au sens strict n'a qu'un but purement théorétique, le propre de l'art est d'être orienté vers la praxis. Présenter la logique comme un art revient à en souligner l'orientation

1. A VI, 4, 2217.

2. *Cf.* R. Kauppi, *Über die Leibnizsche Logik*, p. 14-34 ; H. Burkhardt, *Logik und Semiotik*, p. 386-395 ; H. H. Knecht, *La Logique chez Leibniz*, p. 55-74. Dans ce qui suit, les passages cités sont traduits par l'auteur de l'article.

3. A VI, 6, 342-343.

4. GP VII, 516.

5. GP VII, 476.

pratique et la fonction prescriptive : elle nous apprend à faire quelque chose comme il faut, et précisément à utiliser correctement nos facultés intellectuelles en introduisant de l'ordre et de la liaison dans nos pensées.

En revanche, du point de vue de son statut épistémique, la logique partage le degré suprême de certitude qui est propre à la connaissance scientifique. C'est ce que Leibniz fait valoir contre Locke lorsque ce dernier soutient l'identification de la logique et des arts de la parole. Leibniz s'y oppose en caractérisant la première comme « la science de raisonner, de juger, d'inventer »[1]. Car en tant que science, la logique ne saurait se confondre avec « la connaissance des étymologies des mots et de l'usage des langues, qui est quelque chose d'indéfini et d'arbitraire »[2] (nous verrons néanmoins que Leibniz est loin de couper tout rapport entre logique et linguistique).

Le passage de la lettre à Wagner assigne à la logique la double fonction de juger et découvrir, selon une distinction provenant de la tradition ramiste. En tant qu'art de la découverte et non seulement du jugement, cette logique excède les bornes que nous lui assignons aujourd'hui et se caractérise plutôt comme une méthodologie scientifique générale contenant soit une heuristique (dérivée de la topique aristotélicienne), soit une méthode expérimentale ou « art d'interroger la nature »[3]. La possibilité d'une logique de la découverte était pourtant controversée. Aux yeux de plusieurs, la découverte de la vérité apparaissait comme une activité qui échappe à toute réglementation et qui dépend des ressources cognitives individuelles : pour ceux qui en sont doués, le seul « entendement naturel »[4] est suffisant pour faire progresser la connaissance sans le secours de l'art, alors que pour ceux qui en sont dépourvus, les règles de l'art se révèlent inefficaces. La réponse est typiquement leibnizienne : les lignes tracées par un enfant se servant d'une petite règle sont plus droites que celles tracées à main libre par un maître.

1. A VI, 6, 522.
2. *Ibid.*
3. GP VII, 518.
4. *Ibid.*

LOGIQUE NATURELLE ET LOGIQUE ARTIFICIELLE

Cette image exprime bien la fonction que Leibniz assigne à la logique et la façon dont il conçoit l'opposition entre l'entendement naturel et l'art de s'en servir. Car outre le fait de distinguer la science de l'art, les philosophes ont aussi l'habitude d'opposer l'art à la nature. La description de la logique en termes d'art évoque alors son caractère d'artifice et met en cause la distinction entre logique naturelle et logique artificielle : la logique est un art au sens où elle dépasse l'organisation spontanée et irréfléchie de la pensée pour lui imposer des règles issues d'un travail de réflexion. Cela pose une autre question très débattue à l'époque moderne, celle de l'utilité ou inutilité de la logique en général : est-il vraiment avantageux, voire nécessaire de connaître les règles logiques pour bien conduire sa raison ? Comme les détracteurs de la logique font régulièrement remarquer, il y a même des analphabètes qui savent très bien raisonner sans avoir la moindre notion de ces règles, jugées donc superflues.

La réponse de Leibniz consiste, en premier lieu, à accorder l'existence d'une « logique naturelle »[1] qui explique les capacités inférentielles préthéorétiques, c'est-à-dire indépendantes de toute réflexion sur les lois du raisonnement. C'est quelque chose d'analogue à l'« arithmétique naturelle » dont se servent les gens qui n'ont pas appris l'« art de calculer »[2]. Leibniz soutient pourtant, en deuxième lieu, l'unité profonde entre logique naturelle et logique artificielle. Il n'y a au fond qu'une seule logique, car le « bon sens naturel », que tout homme possède, obéit (sans le savoir) aux mêmes lois universelles que les logiciens tirent au clair : les lois énoncées par la logique artificielle « ne sont autres que celles du *bon sens*, mises en ordre et par écrit » ; donc le passage du naturel à l'artificiel est comparable au passage de la « coutume [...] non-écrite » à la loi écrite[3]. Or, comme une loi écrite se laisse envisager et appliquer plus aisément qu'une coutume[4], cela suffit pour défendre l'utilité du travail des logiciens : « Au reste de ce que le vulgaire des hommes ignore la Logique artificielle, cela n'en prouve pas l'inutilité, non plus qu'on prouverait celle de l'Arithmétique artificielle, parce qu'on voit quelques personnes bien compter dans les rencontres ordinaires sans avoir appris à lire ou à écrire »[5]. L'art de penser

1. GP VII, 523.
2. *Ibid.*
3. A VI, 6, 480.
4. *Ibid.*
5. A VI, 6, 482.

aide « le bon sens naturel » à ne pas se tromper sur « la force des conséquences »[1].

Si l'analogie entre logique et arithmétique chez Leibniz n'a rien de surprenant, il propose dans la lettre à Wagner une autre analogie plus remarquable : celle entre la logique et l'art du langage (*Sprachkunst*). Du point de vue pédagogique, la préséance temporelle de la logique naturelle sur la logique artificielle correspond au rapport entre l'exercice pratique et la grammaire : « dans l'apprentissage d'une langue, il faut s'en tenir plutôt à l'exercice qu'à la grammaire, mais si l'on est déjà assez expert dans la langue, alors la grammaire sert pour monter plus haut »[2]. Le côté normatif et « artificiel » de toutes ces disciplines – l'ensemble codifié des règles logiques, arithmétiques et grammaticales – repose donc sur des fonctions naturelles de l'esprit qui s'exercent avant tout apprentissage, car elles ne sont que des spécifications de la rationalité elle-même.

TRADITION ET INNOVATION

Chez Leibniz, la distinction entre art du jugement et art de la découverte s'accompagne souvent d'une autre distinction : celle entre la logique traditionnelle issue de l'aristotélisme scolastique et la « vraie logique » qui attend de voir le jour, et dont la première n'est qu'un échantillon ou « une ombre »[3]. Cet écart est regretté déjà dans une note de 1677-1678 : « Après tant de logiques, la Logique que je souhaite n'a pas encore été écrite »[4].

Il faut pourtant éviter toute opposition simpliste entre tradition et innovation, surtout en raison de l'attitude complexe de Leibniz envers la logique traditionnelle. D'un côté, il est toujours prêt à la défendre contre ses détracteurs. De l'autre, il n'hésite jamais à dénoncer son insuffisance et ses limites. Cette double perspective est explicitement assumée par rapport à la syllogistique, noyau de la logique traditionnelle. Le défaut que plusieurs textes imputent à cette logique est justement la place centrale ou presque exclusive qu'elle accorde au syllogisme, au détriment des autres formes d'inférence – ce qui exclut notamment la possibilité de traiter les « conséquences asyllogistiques », qui ne se laissent pas reconduire au syllogisme canonique[5]. Le syllogisme présente aussi des limites

1. A VI, 6, 480-481.
2. GP VII, 523.
3. GP VII, 516.
4. A VI, 4, 8.
5. *Cf.* A VI, 6, 479.

importantes sur le plan pragmatique. Sa structure est étrangère aux pratiques discursives ordinaires, car s'il fallait expliciter chaque passage et exprimer chaque raisonnement par deux prémisses et une conclusion, tout discours deviendrait prolixe[1]. La pensée et la parole humaine, selon Leibniz, procèdent le plus souvent par enthymèmes – ce que fait aussi la démonstration euclidienne, qui présente donc une structure déductive proche des procédés naturels de l'esprit, mais capable aussi d'atteindre une parfaite rigueur, grâce au recours aux lemmes : « Car quand [Euclide] fait des *Enthymèmes* en apparence, la proposition supprimée et qui semble manquer, est suppléée par la citation à la marge, où l'on donne le moyen de la trouver déjà démontrée. Ce qui donne un grand abrégé sans rien déroger à la force »[2]. Cependant, loin de rejeter le syllogisme en tant qu'exercice stérile de l'école, Leibniz tient sa forme pour « une des plus belles [inventions] de l'esprit humain, et même, des plus considérables » ; ou encore, pour « une espèce de *Mathématique universelle* » qui contient aussi « un *art d'infaillibilité* »[3]. Il refuse même de nier « absolument » que le syllogisme puisse servir de « moyen pour découvrir la vérité »[4].

Parfois, chez Leibniz, les deux distinctions que nous venons de considérer (jugement/découverte, logique traditionnelle/logique nouvelle) se superposent. Certains textes identifient la « vraie logique » à « l'art d'inventer »[5], alors que la logique traditionnelle se trouve souvent réduite à un art de juger. Ces distinctions semblent pourtant renvoyer à une distinction plus profonde qui concerne l'essence même de la logique : la distinction entre la matière et la forme du raisonnement. Si les opérations du jugement diffèrent de celles de la découverte, la différence ne concerne pas simplement le statut épistémique des leurs objets respectifs, c'est-à-dire des vérités en tant que déjà connues ou à connaître. La différence essentielle est que, dans le premier cas, on envisage les vérités en tant que conclusions de raisonnements et on se demande si l'inférence est correcte, c'est-à-dire si telle conclusion suit de telles prémisses ; car si elle suit et que les prémisses sont vraies, la conclusion sera également vraie. Dans le second cas, ce qui importe surtout c'est la valeur de vérité des propositions qu'on avance, non pas la validité d'un certain schéma déductif. Car l'art du jugement envisage les vérités en tant que conclusions de

1. *Cf.* A VI, 4, 230 ; A VI, 6, 478.
2. A VI, 6, 479.
3. A VI, 6, 478.
4. Leibniz à Wolff, 21 février 1705, *in* Gerhardt (éd.), *Briefwechsel zwischen Leibniz und Christian Wolff*, p. 18.
5. GP VII, 172 ; GP IV, 292.

raisonnements pour établir si l'inférence est correcte ; il s'occupe donc prioritairement de la forme du raisonnement en faisant abstraction de sa matière, c'est-à-dire des contenus déterminés de la pensée, alors que l'art de la découverte thématise justement cette matière, qui pour Leibniz consiste essentiellement dans les concepts de l'esprit.

MATIÈRE ET FORME

Le rapport entre la matière et la forme de la pensée est capital pour comprendre non seulement la conception leibnizienne de la logique mais aussi la façon dont il a cherché à réaliser son projet de réforme de la discipline. L'insistance sur l'art de la découverte et donc sur la reconnaissance d'une sorte de logique matérielle, laquelle porte sur les contenus et non les structures du raisonnement, implique que la logique ne se borne pas à l'étude des conditions de validité des raisonnements. C'est surtout pour cette raison qu'on a pu contester l'attribution à Leibniz d'une conception purement formelle de la logique[1]. Pourtant, Leibniz n'a jamais confondu la logique au sens strict d'une discipline qui concerne la forme de la pensée avec la logique au sens large d'une méthode scientifique générale. Des textes qui réservent le nom de « logique » à la seule discipline formelle en témoignent[2].

En 1679[3], Leibniz part du constat que dans tout argument ou raisonnement il est possible de distinguer forme et matière[4]. Il désigne par ailleurs la forme par les mots de « structure » ou « disposition »[5], qui font penser, selon l'acception courante, à l'ordre des termes dans le syllogisme. Ailleurs, il précise pourtant qu'il entend « la forme un peu autrement que le

1. *Cf.* J. MacFarlane, *What Does It Mean to Say that Logic Is Formal ?*, p. 102-110.

2. *Cf.* A VI, 4, 344-345 : la logique est « l'Art des inférences, c'est-à-dire l'art de juger ce qui est proposé », tout à fait distinct de l'art de la découverte, appelé « topique ».

3. On peut regrouper les essais de calcul en deux grandes périodes, 1679-1680 et 1686-1690, à leur tour différemment sous-divisées par les spécialistes (voir p. ex. la tripartition par M. Mugnai, « Introduzione », p. 15). Bien que les calculs du deuxième groupe soient les plus développés et célèbres (notamment les *Generales inquisitiones* de 1686 : A VI, 4, 739-788), je ferai référence plutôt aux calculs de 1679, en raison de la centralité qu'ils accordent à la question de la forme (*cf.* M. Mugnai, « Introduzione », p. 26 et *id.*, *Introduzione alla filosofia di Leibniz*, p. 260-261). Sur ces premiers calculs, voir le bilan de M. Capozzi et G. Roncaglia, « Logic and Philosophy of Logic », p. 115-116. Pour une reconstruction systématique de l'ensemble des calculs leibniziens, voir W. Lenzen, *Das System der Leibnizschen Logik* et « Leibniz's Logic ».

4. A VI, 4, 222.

5. A VI, 4, 718 ; GP IV, 363.

vulgaire »[1], donc autrement que ce qu'on fait dans les écoles, où « on ne considère pas assez que la forme ne consiste pas dans cet ennuyeux *quicunque, atqui, ergo* »[2]. La forme logique ne se réduit pas au seul syllogisme parce qu'il s'agit d'un concept plus général que celui de telle ou telle forme spécifique. Tout raisonnement, syllogistique ou non, a une certaine forme ou structure, qu'il peut partager avec d'autres raisonnements, par ailleurs tout à fait différents. La forme telle que Leibniz l'entend correspond donc plutôt à ce que nous appelons un schéma d'inférence. Bien que Leibniz ne le dise pas explicitement, plusieurs textes suggèrent clairement que la forme est ce qui reste d'un raisonnement si l'on fait abstraction de sa matière, c'est-à-dire du contenu particulier des propositions qui le composent.

Leibniz confirme l'interprétation de la forme en termes de schéma inférentiel par l'argument justifiant la distinction entre le matériel et le formel du raisonnement. Il considère les deux syllogismes suivants :

> Tout triangle est un trilatère
> Quelque triangle n'est pas un équilatère
> Donc, quelque Équilatère n'est pas un trilatère.
>
> Tout métal est minéral[3]
> Quelque métal n'est pas or
> Donc, quelque or n'est pas minéral[4].

Les deux raisonnements suivent évidemment le même chemin pour atteindre leurs conclusions ; et tous les deux partent de prémisses vraies. Pourtant, la conclusion de l'un est vraie, alors que la conclusion de l'autre est manifestement fausse. Cela indique que la vérité de la première conclusion ne dépend pas du chemin suivi pour la déduire – car le même chemin a conduit, dans l'autre cas, à une fausseté. Elle ne dépend donc pas de ce qui est commun aux deux raisonnements, mais bien de ce qui est propre au premier, c'est-à-dire de son contenu, des choses dont il est question. Ce fait nous force à distinguer deux niveaux d'évaluation différents. Un argument peut « réussir dans une certaine matière », bien qu'il échoue si on l'applique « aux autres exemples de la même forme »[5]. C'est ce qui arrive dans le premier syllogisme, dont la conclusion « est

1. A VI, 4, 2264.
2. A VI, 4, 2260.
3. « Minéral » est à entendre ici dans le sens général de « inanimé ».
4. A VI, 4, 222.
5. *Ibid.*

bonne mais en vertu de la matière et non de la forme, car on peut porter des exemples de forme semblable qui ne réussissent pas »[1].

La distinction entre matière et forme est donc étroitement liée à l'intuition que, dans tout raisonnement, il faut évaluer séparément la valeur de vérité des propositions et la validité de l'inférence. En effet, en ce qui concerne les conditions de « légitimité » des arguments, Leibniz observe que la matière et la forme peuvent l'une et l'autre être bonnes ou mauvaises, ce qui rend l'argument, à son tour, bon ou mauvais dans la matière, ou dans la forme, ou dans l'une et l'autre – auquel cas l'argument est « légitime », ne contenant aucun vice matériel ni formel[2]. Un argument est bon par sa matière si la conclusion est vraie et bon dans sa forme si la conclusion est « prouvée à partir des prémisses »[3].

Est correcte toute forme « prédémontrée, qui conclut en vertu de sa disposition »[4]. Même « un compte bien dressé, un calcul d'Algèbre [...] seront à peu près des arguments en forme »[5]. Il y a donc une pluralité de formes logiques légitimes, ayant pourtant différents degrés de généralité ; et c'est en fonction de ces degrés que les formes tendent à s'organiser selon une hiérarchie où les formes les plus générales sont celles qui peuvent s'appliquer indistinctement à toute matière, puisqu'elles en sont complètement abstraites. La hiérarchisation implique que les formes logiques spéciales sont à démontrer à partir des formes plus générales. Par exemple, les procédés déductifs utilisés par Euclide « ne sont que des espèces de formes d'argumenter particulières et propres aux Mathématiciens et à la matière qu'ils traitent. Et ils démontrent ces formes avec l'aide des formes universelles de la Logique commune »[6]. Du point de vue formel, la géométrie se trouve subordonnée à la logique, ce qui renverse la supériorité accordée par l'opinion vulgaire à la démonstration mathématique. Il n'est donc pas vrai qu'au dehors des mathématiques on ne saurait atteindre la certitude démonstrative : au contraire, « la Logique est aussi susceptible de démonstrations, que la Géométrie, et l'on peut dire que la Logique des Géomètres, ou les manières d'argumenter [c'est-à-dire, les formes de raisonnement] qu'Euclide a expliquées et établies en parlant des propositions, sont une extension ou promotion particulière de la Logique

1. A VI, 4, 222 ; *cf.* A VI, 4, 718.
2. GP IV, 363.
3. A VI, 4, 231.
4. GP IV, 363.
5. A VI, 6, 478.
6. A VI, 6, 479.

Générale »[1]. S'il y a une primauté des mathématiques, c'est dans le sens historique où elles ont fourni « les modèles de l'art de démontrer »[2].

LES ÉLÉMENTS DU CALCUL

Une bonne partie des efforts que Leibniz consacre à l'étude des formes logiques vise précisément à repérer les lois et les fondements de cette logique générale qui gouverne tous les raisonnements humains. En fait, il ne faudrait pas en restreindre la portée à la seule cognition humaine : autant Leibniz est pluraliste en ce qui concerne la variété des formes logiques qu'on peut tenir pour correctes, autant il est moniste en ce qui concerne la validité de la logique elle-même. Dans un dialogue daté entre 1678 et 1679, il distingue les principes physiques, c'est-à-dire les lois naturelles qui s'imposent à l'homme mais que la puissance absolue de Dieu pourrait enfreindre, des principes métaphysiques valables au même titre pour les créatures et pour le créateur, « car ils traitent de la Vérité et de l'Être en général, qui est commun à Dieu et aux créatures »[3]. Tels sont le principe de non-contradiction et le principe que le tout est plus grand que la partie, mais aussi « les *Principes logiques* ou formes syllogistiques que même Dieu et les anges admettent comme vrais »[4]. À l'objection que ni Dieu ni les anges n'ont besoin de la logique, Leibniz répond que même s'ils n'utilisent pas les syllogismes, ils ne les rejettent non plus[5]. La validité des schémas d'inférence est indépendante de leur utilité pratique et repose sur les lois de la logique incréée, lesquelles ont le même statut que les principes métaphysiques. Il n'y a au fond qu'une seule logique et ses lois sont valables pour tout être rationnel : c'est ce que Leibniz répète sans cesse contre la théorie cartésienne de la création des vérités éternelles et contre l'écart qu'elle avait creusé entre la logique humaine et la logique divine. Ce qui est intéressant dans le passage cité, c'est qu'ici l'univocité de la logique[6] est affirmée, à la fois, à propos des lois telles que le principe de non-contradiction et des formes du raisonnement. Cette distinction invite à préciser la notion de « matière » à l'œuvre dans la logique leibnizienne.

1. A VI, 6, 370.
2. A VI, 6, 371.
3. A VI, 4, 2215.
4. *Ibid.*
5. *Ibid.*
6. *Cf.* H. H. Knecht, *La Logique chez Leibniz*, p. 69.

Leibniz identifie parfois la matière avec les prémisses dont on tire la conclusion par l'application d'une certaine forme. C'est ainsi qu'il caractérise le vice matériel comme la faute qui consiste à assumer « autre chose que les principes ou ce qui a été prouvé à son tour à partir des principes par un argument légitime »[1]. La légitimité matérielle du raisonnement dépend de la vérité des prémisses et relève donc du choix des principes, ce qui soulève la question traditionnelle de l'évidence première : quelles sont les vérités que l'on peut assumer en tant que principes premiers et indémontrables ? Car s'il n'y a pas de tels principes, comment évitera-t-on la régression à l'infini dans la chaîne des démonstrations ?

La stratégie générale de Leibniz consiste à faire l'économie des principes ; elle s'articule pourtant en deux volets différents. D'une part, il faut chercher à démontrer tous les axiomes qui n'ont pas la forme expresse de l'identité (A = A) : ils seront donc traités comme des théorèmes et réduits aux axiomes identiques[2]. Les axiomes identiques ne sont évidemment que des instances du principe d'identité, que Leibniz couple souvent avec le principe de non-contradiction comme composant un seul principe. Ailleurs, il distingue les « vérités identiques » en affirmatives (« A est A », « Chaque chose est ce qu'elle est ») et négatives, dont la première est le principe de non-contradiction formulé dans les termes du principe de la bivalence (« une proposition est ou vraie ou fausse ») et de façon à inclure aussi la loi du tiers exclu (« il n'y a point de milieu entre le vrai et le faux »)[3]. À ces vérités, qui sont premières parmi les vérités dites « de raison » et qui sont reconnues comme vraies par la seule considération des termes, Leibniz ajoute une autre classe de principes évidents en soi : les vérités premières de fait, qui énoncent l'immédiateté de la perception interne[4]. Tous les principes sont donc réduits à ces deux (classes de) vérités indémontrables qui sont le fondement de toute démonstration et de toute connaissance[5].

D'autre part, la réduction du nombre des principes est opérée par la distinction entre « principes matériels » ou « directs » et « principes formels » ou « réflexifs »[6], c'est-à-dire, entre les vérités qu'on assume

1. GP IV, 363.

2. Voir par ex. A VI, 4, 506.

3. A VI, 6, 361-362. *Cf.* H. Ishiguro, *Leibniz's Philosophy*, p. 49-50.

4. A VI, 4, 135.

5. A VI, 4, 124. Sur l'usage des axiomes identiques dans la démonstration, *cf.* A VI, 6, p. 363.

6. Un passage des *Generales inquisitiones*, affirmant la coïncidence (ou équivalence logique) entre « l'énonciation (directe) *L* et l'énonciation (réflexive) *L est vraie* » (A VI, 4, 748), suggère que « réflexif » renvoie, pour Leibniz, à des énoncés métalinguistiques.

comme prémisses du raisonnement et les règles d'inférence qu'on applique pour en tirer une conclusion[1]. Dans un fragment daté entre 1679 et 1685, Leibniz indique comme paradigme de la démonstration le procédé de réduction à l'absurde, où il n'existe comme « matière » que les assomptions qu'on veut réfuter. La *reductio* procède donc par la seule force de la forme : « Je n'assume donc que des principes réflexifs [*principia reflexa*] c'est-à-dire indirects ou formels, *primo* que la forme syllogistique soit bonne, *secundo* que la contradiction soit absurde ; par contre, je n'emploie d'autres principes matériels [...] que ces hypothèses mêmes de l'adversaires dans lesquelles je montre qu'il y a de la fausseté »[2]. Le principe de contradiction joue ici le rôle de principe formel parce qu'il permet d'inférer, d'une contradiction, la fausseté de la prémisse dont elle découle. Or, comme « toute démonstration est en réalité une réduction à l'absurde » et n'a donc besoin « d'aucune supposition ou principe direct, mais seulement de principes réflexifs », Leibniz observe que son approche, en privilégiant la forme, fait cesser la difficulté, notoire, qui consiste à savoir d'où vient la certitude des principes eux-mêmes[3].

S'il y a chez Leibniz une approche formaliste de la logique, elle consiste avant tout à vider le raisonnement de son contenu afin d'envisager les procédures inférentielles indépendamment de tout principe matériel. Leibniz est assez explicite à ce propos. Dans ses réflexions plus avancées au moins, il se montre capable de maîtriser la distinction entre la structure formelle du calcul, définie par certaines opérations avec leurs propriétés, et ses interprétations possibles, qui varient selon les différents domaines d'objets auxquels on l'applique[4]. Mais déjà dans le *Calculus consequentiarum* de 1679, c'est la possibilité de distinguer entre la matière et la forme du raisonnement qui permet de les étudier séparément : « Dans toute argumentation deux sont les choses qu'il faut juger : la Forme et la Matière. [...] Par conséquent, le calcul qui touche la Matière peut être séparé du calcul formel »[5]. Nous allons voir que cette distinction entre deux espèces de calcul, l'un incluant la matière et l'autre portant exclusivement sur

1. Sur la présence de cette distinction chez Leibniz, voir N. Rescher, « Leibniz's Interpretation », p. 2 n, 3 n.

2. A VI, 4, 125.

3. *Ibid.*

4. Je dois cette remarque ainsi que l'indication des sources suivantes à Massimo Mugnai, que je remercie. *Cf.* A VI, 4, 834 ; et *Sur la calculabilité du nombre de toutes les connaissances possibles* [1693-1694], éd. P. Beeley, *The Leibniz Review*, p. 93-97, en particulier p. 93-94.

5. A VI, 4, 222.

la forme, est cruciale pour comprendre comment s'articulent les deux projets logico-symboliques de Leibniz : la caractéristique universelle et le calcul général.

CONCEPT, PROPOSITION, RAISONNEMENT

Dans le texte cité ci-dessus, le rôle de la matière ou du contenu de la pensée est attribué aux concepts alors qu'ailleurs on le trouve attribué à des propositions : les prémisses du raisonnement. Cette variation met en cause la question du rapport entre concept et proposition, un point très délicat de la logique leibnizienne.

L'arrière-fond des réflexions que Leibniz y consacre est la doctrine traditionnelle des trois opérations de l'esprit : concevoir, juger (c'est-à-dire, affirmer ou nier), et raisonner[1]. Cette division du domaine noétique est conçue sur le modèle des trois niveaux de complexité des expressions linguistiques : les expressions sub-énonciatives (et précisément les termes catégorématiques, qui peuvent faire fonction de sujet ou prédicat), les énoncés et les groupes d'énoncés structurés par l'emploi de certaines particules. Non sans ambiguïté, Leibniz utilise souvent le mot « terme » pour indiquer tantôt les entités noétiques, tantôt leurs expressions linguistiques[2]. Il distingue principalement entre « ce que les Logiciens appellent un Terme incomplexe » (le concept, la notion[3]) et le terme complexe (vérité, proposition, ou énoncé). Le second contient, outre les termes incomplexes, une affirmation ou négation, et a donc la propriété d'être vrai ou faux[4]. Or, si les vérités sont la matière du raisonnement, les idées ou concepts sont en revanche « la matière des vérités »[5] : chaque opération de l'esprit fournit la matière à l'opération de niveau supérieur. Cela montre que les différentes caractérisations de la matière logique que nous avons rencontrées sont donc tout à fait compatibles entre elles ; mais aussi que les

1. *Cf.* A VI, 4, 272.

2. Par exemple, dans le *Specimen calculi universalis* on lit soit que « Le nom est un terme signifiant une chose, assumé arbitrairement » soit, peu après, que « Par *Terme* je n'entends pas le nom mais bien le concept c'est-à-dire ce qui est signifié par le nom » (A VI, 4, 287-288 ; *cf.* A VI, 4, 288 et 558). Une ambiguïté semblable affecte les termes « proposition » (*propositio*) et « énonciation » (*enuntiatio*) : *cf.* G. H. R. Parkinson, *Logic and Reality*, p. 5-9.

3. A VI, 6, 12.

4. Sur les propositions comme porteurs de vérité, voir le *Dialogus* de 1677 (A VI, 4, 21).

5. A VI, 4, 973.

concepts ou termes incomplexes sont les éléments de base de la logique leibnizienne[1].

Selon un récit autobiographique célèbre, lorsque le jeune Leibniz commence à étudier à l'école la « logique vulgaire », il est frappé par l'ordre que les prédicaments ou catégories de la tradition aristotélicienne étaient capables d'introduire dans le domaine des termes incomplexes, mais constate que l'intérêt des logiciens pour les « connexions des termes incomplexes » ne s'étendait pas aux connexions des termes complexes[2]. L'idée lui vient alors qu'il faut « inventer des prédicaments nouveaux pour les termes complexes, dans lesquels les propositions seraient coordonnées pour constituer des syllogismes tout comme les termes incomplexes sont coordonnés dans les prédicaments vulgaires pour constituer des propositions »[3]. Il s'aperçoit pourtant que pour y arriver il faut réformer les prédicaments traditionnels, car la possibilité d'ordonner les propositions en séries dépend de la disposition correcte des notions : l'ordre des termes complexes ne peut découler que d'une catégorisation satisfaisante des termes incomplexes.

À partir de cette intuition, une autre idée lui vient aussi, l'idée qu'une « analyse des notions » permettrait de construire un calcul des vérités : car « si l'on avait des notions correctement résolues et ordonnées, on pourrait les représenter par des nombres, et par conséquent il deviendrait possible d'examiner les vérités [...] en calculant, dans la mesure où elles dépendent de la raison »[4]. On disposerait alors d'un calcul touchant la matière, pour revenir à la distinction tracée ci-dessus : grâce aux « notes caractéristiques » il serait possible de « juger si un argument est bon en vertu de la matière, si non de la forme »[5]. Cette prise en charge de la dimension matérielle par l'analyse des notions permet de faire la distinction entre ce projet, aboutissant à l'invention d'une caractéristique universelle, et le projet d'un calcul universel établissant les règles pour raisonner correctement.

1. Leibniz reconnaît pourtant que certains termes incomplexes (par exemple une description comme « la rationalité de l'homme ») ne peuvent être analysés sans avoir recours à des énoncés (« l'homme est rationnel »), car ils en impliquent – dirions-nous – la vérité : GP II, 472. *Cf.* M. M. Mugnai, *Introduzione alla filosofia di Leibniz*, p. 63-64.

2. A VI, 4, 727 ; *cf.* A VI, 4, 265, 494, 538 et GP VII, 517. *Cf.* W. Kabitz, *Die Philosophie des jungen Leibniz*, p. 14-16.

3. A VI, 4, 727. Ailleurs, Leibniz rapproche ce projet de jeunesse à la méthode des géomètres, qui disposent les propositions selon leurs relations de dépendance (A VI, 4, 538). Pour se faire une idée de ces prédicaments que le jeune philosophe voulait inventer, on peut donc songer au classement des propositions en définitions, axiomes, théorèmes, etc.

4. A VI, 4, 727.

5. A VI, 4, 242.

La mise en œuvre de ce deuxième projet – précurseur de la logique symbolique développée à partir du dix-neuvième siècle – est présentée par Leibniz comme une étape provisoire. On laisse de côté la matière du raisonnement parce qu'on n'a pas encore l'instrument pour la traiter, c'est-à-dire un système de notation formé de caractères qui expriment adéquatement les contenus de la pensée : les concepts simples et leurs combinaisons. Car Leibniz pense avoir trouvé le moyen de réduire tout raisonnement à une espèce de calcul : il a « découvert qu'à chaque Terme ou notion peut être assigné son nombre caractéristique, moyennant quoi calculer et raisonner seront la même chose »[1]. Toutefois, la « complexité des choses » est si extraordinaire qu'il n'a pas encore été possible au philosophe d'indiquer « les vrais nombres caractéristiques »[2]. Pour atteindre ce résultat, il faudra auparavant rassembler et ordonner toutes les connaissances disponibles et remonter, par voie d'analyse conceptuelle, à leurs éléments premiers. L'introduction de caractères qui ont entre eux la même relation subsistant entre les notions[3] présuppose l'analyse des pensées, et ce jusqu'au repérage des concepts simples ou primitifs constituant une sorte d'alphabet des pensées humaines, dont toutes les autres notions dérivent par composition.

Par contre, l'étude des formes du raisonnement peut avancer indépendamment : il suffit d'adopter des caractères provisoires. Leibniz s'est rendu compte « que la forme des conséquences peut néanmoins être saisie par le calcul et démontrée au moyen de nombres fictifs, qu'on emploie entre temps à la place des vrais nombres caractéristiques »[4]. En ce sens, les différents calculs logiques construits par Leibniz à partir de l'hiver 1678/1679 ne considèrent que la dimension formelle du calcul, abstraction faite de la matière de la pensée[5]. En termes de procédés cognitifs, cette mise entre parenthèses du contenu du raisonnement s'effectue par ce que Leibniz appelle la pensée *aveugle* ou *symbolique*[6], qui consiste à remplacer les idées des choses par des signes dont l'interprétation est suspendue tout au long du calcul.

1. A VI, 4, 222.
2. *Ibid.*
3. A VI, 4, 272.
4. A VI, 4, 222.
5. Il est donc correct de dire que Leibniz concevait ses calculs comme « une théorie générale des structures qui pouvait fournir la syntaxe pour sa *characteristica universalis* » (W. Kneale et M. Kneale, *The Development of Logic*, p. 336).
6. *Cf.* A VI, 4, 587.

LES CARACTÈRES DU CALCUL

Le recours à la notation arithmétique caractérise les calculs logiques d'avril 1679, dont la sémantique est déjà dominée par les idées typiquement leibniziennes que toute proposition concerne une relation entre concepts et que la relation fondamentale entre deux concepts est celle de l'inclusion[1]. Dans la langue ordinaire, cette relation s'exprime par la copule – tout verbe incluant, selon Leibniz, le verbe être[2]. Une proposition de forme canonique *A est B* signifiera donc que le concept *A* contient le concept *B*. Cette approche intensionnelle domine la théorie leibnizienne de la proposition et de la vérité[3] : « Dans toute proposition le prédicat est dit être contenu (*inesse*) dans le sujet, c'est-à-dire, la notion du prédicat est enveloppée dans la notion du sujet. Car dans une proposition universelle affirmative, quand je dis : *Tout homme est animal*, je veux dire que le concept d'*animal* est enveloppé dans le concept d'*homme* »[4]. Comme toute proposition peut être réduite à la forme canonique, cela fournit un critère de vérité valable pour toute proposition (pas seulement pour les universelles affirmatives), qui sera donc vraie si et seulement si le concept du prédicat est contenu dans le concept du sujet.

C'est à cette conception que se rattache, dès son origine, l'idée d'employer, même en dehors des mathématiques, des procédures computationnelles, moyennant une notation numérique. « J'observais – raconte Leibniz à propos de ses premières intuitions de logicien – que la notion qui est prédiquée d'une notion est contenue en elle tout comme le nombre facteur est contenu dans le produit »[5]. Leibniz entrevoit une analogie entre la façon dont le concept d'homme est constitué par les concepts d'animal et de raisonnable, et la façon dont le nombre six est divisible par les nombres deux et trois[6]. Il comprend que la relation d'inclusion exprimée par la copule a pour équivalent mathématique la relation de divisibilité : *b est a* équivaut à dire que *b* est divisible par *a*[7]. Si on trouvait le moyen d'assigner à chaque concept son nombre caractéristique, cela ouvrirait la voie à la possibilité non seulement d'exprimer la composition des concepts par les opérations de multiplication et division, mais aussi de calculer tout rapport

1. *Cf.* A VI, 4, 135. Sur la sémantique des calculs voir les considérations de C. Swoyer, « Leibniz's Calculus », en particulier p. 18.

2. *Cf.* A VI, 4, 112.

3. Voir notamment S. Levey, « Logical Theory in Leibniz », p. 110-117.

4. A VI, 4, 223.

5. A VI, 4, 727.

6. *Ibid.*

7. A VI, 4, 120.

d'inclusion entre concepts et, par conséquent, la valeur de vérité de toute proposition formulable dans ce langage. Mais même faute des nombres caractéristiques, Leibniz pense que le principe découvert lui fournit le moyen de « démontrer toutes les formes des logiciens » et d'appliquer « le même artifice à toutes les notions distinctes »[1].

Peu après, dans les calculs du début d'été 1679, l'abandon de la notation arithmétique et l'adoption d'une notation d'inspiration algébrique faite de lettres arbitrairement choisies permet d'atteindre un degré supérieur de généralité et d'abstraction formelle : « Pour comprendre la nature de ce calcul, il faut noter que tout ce que nous énonçons par certaines lettres que nous avons assumées à notre gré (*pro arbitrio*), doit s'entendre comme pouvant s'énoncer de la même façon par n'importe quelles autres lettres assumées »[2]. Dans cette notation, le produit logique de plusieurs termes s'exprime par juxtaposition des lettres désignant les termes : si a désigne le concept d'animal et b le concept de raisonnable, ab désignera le concept composé d'animal raisonnable. Et c'est grâce à cette notation que Leibniz arrive à formuler le principe d'idempotence : $aa = a$[3].

CALCUL ET SUBSTITUTION

Les calculs de ce deuxième type abordent la prédication non pas directement à partir des relations d'inclusion entre concepts mais bien du point de vue, plus opératoire, des relations de substituabilité entre les termes[4]. Car tout processus inférentiel, tout raisonnement ou démonstration consiste, selon Leibniz, dans une série de substitutions. Le progrès scientifique ne fait qu'établir des relations d'équivalence qui autorisent les « substitutions des pensées » : les sciences « montrent que dans une proposition nécessaire on peut substituer sans danger le prédicat à la place du sujet [...] et que, en démontrant, on peut substituer sans danger certaines vérités qu'on appelle prémisses avec une autre vérité appelée conclusion »[5]. La substitution d'un terme par un autre devient ainsi l'opération fondamentale du calcul logique ; et les principes du calcul ont

1. A VI, 4, 727.
2. A VI, 4, 289. *Cf.* L. Couturat, *La Logique de Leibniz*, p. 342 : « Ce principe fait ressortir [...] le caractère *formel* du calcul ».
3. A VI, 4, 274.
4. Sur substitution et substituabilité, *cf.* R. Kauppi, *Über die Leibnizsche Logik*, p. 72-73 ; H. Ishiguro, *Leibniz's Philosophy*, p. 17-34 ; H. Burkhardt, *Logik und Semiotik*, p. 230-231, 330-332.
5. A VI, 4, 102-103.

justement la fonction de déterminer les substitutions légitimes. Ils comprennent, outre les axiomes identiques ou « propositions vraies par soi » (*a est a*, *ab est a*, *ab est b*), une règle d'inférence primitive présentée comme « conséquence vraie par soi »[1] :

Si *a est b* & *b est c*, alors *a est c*.

De cette proposition conditionnelle, Leibniz tire un schéma d'inférence qui correspond évidemment au syllogisme Barbara (par transposition des prémisses) :

Tout homme est animal
Tout animal est substance
Ergo, tout homme est substance.

Selon l'interprétation que Leibniz en donne, la règle implique que « le sujet peut toujours être substitué à la place de son prédicat lorsque ce dernier joue le rôle de sujet dans une autre proposition »[2]. Toute prédication ayant la forme *a est b* revient donc à poser une relation de substituabilité du sujet au prédicat. Si cette relation est réciproque, elle équivaut à la relation d'identité, caractérisée en termes d'inter-substituabilité *salva veritate* : « Est *le même* ce qui peut partout être substitué à la place de l'autre *salva veritate* » ; et « Si *a* est *b* et *b* est *a*, alors *a* et *b* seront *le même* »[3].

Par ailleurs, un postulat du calcul prévoit l'introduction de termes par définition, ce qui revient à assumer une relation d'identité, donc de substituabilité réciproque, entre le terme définissant et le terme défini. Leibniz tient à remarquer que l'arbitraire des définitions n'implique nullement l'arbitraire de la déduction que l'on fait en assumant les définitions comme prémisses, car « la connexion entre les conclusions ou théorèmes, et les définitions ou hypothèses arbitraires est absolument vraie »[4]. Au fond, c'est une autre façon d'exprimer l'indépendance de la forme, dont la validité absolue n'est pas touchée par la contingence de la matière à laquelle on l'applique.

1. A VI, 4, 275, 281, 293.
2. A VI, 4, 275.
3. *Ibid.*
4. A VI, 4, 281. L'indépendance des relations logiques et donc des vérités qui en découlent par rapport au choix arbitraire du système d'expression justifie aussi l'emploi de caractères arbitrairement choisis dans la démonstration des théorèmes. Cette position réaliste et anti-relativiste sur la vérité est soutenue notamment dans le *Dialogus* de 1677 (A VI, 4, 20-25). Elle oriente aussi les réflexions de Leibniz sur la traduction et l'inter-traductibilité des langues : *cf.* M. Favaretti Camposampiero, « Leibniz et la traduction universelle ».

Il est difficile, à vrai dire, de déterminer si la procédure de définition porte directement sur les éléments du langage ou bien sur les termes entendus comme concepts[1]. C'est que la liaison entre la pensée et le langage est pour Leibniz si étroite que les opérations de l'entendement semblent parfois se réduire sans reste à leur expression linguistique ou symbolique. Si les *Fundamenta calculi ratiocinatoris* s'ouvrent par l'affirmation que « Tout raisonnement humain s'accomplit *par le moyen de* certains signes ou caractères » employés comme des abrégés à la place des choses ou de leurs idées[2], le *De modis combinandi characteres* fait même consister le raisonnement dans la manipulation des signes : « Tout raisonnement fait par nous *n'est rien d'autre* qu'une connexion et substitution de caractères – qu'ils soient des mots, ou des notations, ou même des images. Or toute substitution naît d'une certaine équivalence »[3].

Certainement, dans la langue parfaite que Leibniz envisage, les substitutions des pensées seraient entièrement remplaçables par les substitutions de caractères sémantiquement équivalents. Dans cette langue, toutes les vérités portant sur des choses exprimables pourraient être démontrées «*par le seul calcul*, c'est-à-dire par le seul traitement des caractères selon une certaine forme, sans aucun travail de l'imagination ou effort de l'esprit»[4]. Qu'en est-il pourtant des langues naturelles ? Ont-elles une fonction dans l'étude de la logique et des formes du raisonnement ?

LANGAGE ET COMPOSITIONNALITÉ

Si l'on peut, en effet, envisager les travaux leibniziens sur la caractéristique universelle et le calcul dans le cadre du projet d'un langage artificiel, plusieurs études ont aussi montré qu'on ne peut séparer entièrement ces travaux des recherches linguistiques, historiques, étymologiques et proprement philosophiques conduites par Leibniz sur les langues naturelles[5]. En réalité, pour Leibniz, la construction de la caractéristique et du calcul logique doit être précédée par un travail d'analyse qui porte nécessairement sur une langue en usage (préférablement le latin, en tant que langue officielle de la communauté scientifique) :

1. *Cf.* par ex. A VI, 4, 294-295.
2. A VI, 4, 918 (je souligne).
3. A VI, 4, 922 (je souligne).
4. A VI, 4, 272.
5. Voir A. Heinekamp, « Ars characteristica » ; M. Mugnai, *Astrazione e realtà* ; D. Rutherford, « Philosophy and Language ». Sur les langues naturelles, voir S. Gensini, *Il naturale e il simbolico*.

> Pour la découverte et la démonstration des vérités il est besoin de l'analyse des pensées : et comme elle correspond à l'analyse des caractères que nous utilisons pour signifier les pensées, car à chaque caractère correspond une certaine pensée, c'est pour cela que nous pouvons rendre sensible l'analyse des pensées et la diriger comme par un fil mécanique : car l'analyse des caractères est quelque chose de sensible[1].

Pourquoi le logicien, avec ses projets de calcul, doit-il s'intéresser à cette analyse du langage ? C'est que la distinction entre la matière et la forme logique a son corrélat linguistique dans la distinction entre les termes catégorématiques, qui expriment des concepts (donc la matière des pensées), et les termes syncatégorématiques ou particules[2], qui servent à structurer le discours et reflètent donc l'organisation formelle de la pensée[3].

Du côté matériel, il s'agit de produire, par une application répétée de la procédure de définition par substitution d'expressions équivalentes, une analyse sémantique du vocabulaire qui aboutisse au catalogue des notions simples dont nous avons parlé. On définit la signification des mots d'une langue pour atteindre les éléments de la pensée, car « comme les vocables sont inventés pour la désignation des pensées, nous pourrons utiliser leur tracé »[4].

Du côté formel, ce sont les structures du discours ordinaire qui fournissent un répertoire des schémas d'inférence : la logique, en tant que « Art des inférences [...], doit être tirée de l'usage des hommes qui parlent et écrivent »[5]. Nous savons pourtant que, au lieu de suivre les schémas du syllogisme, les hommes abrègent souvent leurs raisonnements au moyen de certaines particules, qui fonctionnent donc comme des raccourcis inférentiels[6]. Ces inférences asyllogistiques « sont à démontrer non à partir des principes logiques, mais à partir des principes grammaticaux, c'est-à-dire de la signification des flexions et des particules »[7]. Aux particules appartient, écrit Leibniz, « presque toute la force logique »[8]. Et dans un écrit au titre programmatique de *Analysis particularum*, il affirme que « comme

1. A VI, 4, 102.
2. *Cf.* A VI, 4, 742.
3. Le *De lingua philosophica* distingue les vocables en mots (noms, verbes, adverbes) et particules : « Les mots [*Voces*] constituent la matière, les particules la forme du discours » (A VI, 4, 882).
4. A VI, 4, 595.
5. A VI, 4, 344.
6. *Cf.* A VI, 4, 132 et 345 ; A VI, 6, 480.
7. A VI, 4, 344.
8. A VI, 4, 719.

tous les rapports des Notions sont exprimés par des particules, l'Analyse des particules sera de grande importance pour comprendre les notions qui impliquent des rapports »[1].

Pour ces raisons, dans le plan des sciences, la logique doit être précédée par l'exposition d'une grammaire rationnelle ou philosophique « dont les Grammaires régulières [c.-à-d., normatives], ne sont que des parties ou des échantillons »[2]. La tâche du grammairien est d'étudier la « Signification Régulière de toutes les flexions, particules et dispositions »[3], pour discriminer entre les traits particuliers de quelque langue, tels que la division des genres, et les traits universels et essentiels qui seuls concernent la grammaire philosophique. Donc, comme tous les vocables, les particules doivent elles aussi faire l'objet d'une analyse sémantique conduite jusqu'aux éléments primitifs – en ce cas, jusqu'aux particules « qui ne peuvent être éliminées par aucune explication, telles que *est, et, non* »[4], et qui sont celles que Leibniz va utiliser encore dans ses calculs logiques[5]. Le projet d'une analyse des particules est donc fonctionnel dans l'étude des formes. Cet espoir de constituer la vraie logique à travers l'analyse grammaticale conduit Leibniz, par exemple, à considérer la règle inférentielle de la double négation comme relevant de la signification de la particule « non »[6]. D'ailleurs, c'est au fil d'une analyse grammaticale de la particule disjonctive latine *vel* que Leibniz donne sa formulation la plus claire de la loi (dite de De Morgan) selon laquelle la disjonction de deux propositions est équivalente à la négation de la conjonction des négations des mêmes propositions[7].

Le fondement théorique de ce projet analytique leibnizien (analyse des concepts et de la structure des pensées, appuyée sur l'analyse des langues) est une conception compositionnelle soit du langage soit de la pensée elle-même, comme en témoigne l'*Analysis linguarum* de 1678. Nous savons que l'analyse des caractères procède par substitution : on remplace un caractère (ou en général une expression) par plusieurs caractères (ou expressions) équivalents, qui en forment la définition. On constatera alors, dit Leibniz, « que même les pensées qui correspondent aux caractères substitués équivalent à la signification du caractère de départ, qu'on

1. A VI, 4, 647. *Cf.* les considérations de M. Dascal, « Leibniz on Particles », p. 44-49.

2. A VI, 4, 117.

3. A VI, 4, 344 ; *cf.* A VI, 4, 106.

4. A VI, 4, 344 ; *cf.* A VI, 4, p. 104.

5. *Cf.* A VI, 4, 147.

6. A VI, 4, 146.

7. *Cf.* A VI, 4, 899. J'ai insisté sur cette fonction des particules dans M. Favaretti Camposampiero, « Il significato di "non" ».

proposait de résoudre »[1]. Pour comprendre la légitimité de ces substitutions, il faut considérer que les expressions linguistiques de tout niveau (vocables, syntagmes, énoncés, périodes) « se comprennent une fois qu'on a compris les parties dont elles sont composées » ; par conséquent, « il suffit d'avoir une analyse des vocables primaires, c'est-à-dire qui ne tirent pas entièrement leur signification de leur étymologie, [et une analyse] des locutions, des proverbes, des formules »[2]. C'est une formulation assez claire du principe sémantique de compositionnalité : la signification d'une expression composée est entièrement déterminée par la signification des expressions composantes – y compris (comme spécifié dans la suite du texte) les éléments morphologiques et syntactiques (flexions, particules, etc.), qui définissent la structure du composé. Mais le passage cité contient aussi une limitation de la validité du principe : Leibniz s'est aperçu que les langues ordinaires abondent en expressions idiomatiques (locutions, proverbes, formules) dont la signification n'est pas compositionnelle dans le sens indiqué, et qui doivent donc être analysées à l'instar des vocables primaires[3].

L'analyse grammaticale des langues naturelles prépare donc l'analyse logique : si la première porte sur la substituabilité réciproque des expressions, la seconde montre « comment des propositions peuvent être substituées à la place de propositions »[4], ce qui revient à l'opération fondamentale du raisonnement. Le propre de la langue artificielle construite sur la base de ces analyses sera, par contre, de combler l'écart entre grammaire et logique, pour unifier finalement les règles morpho-syntactiques qui gouvernent les substitutions grammaticales, donc aussi la construction des expressions linguistiques, avec les règles d'inférence qui gouvernent les substitutions logiques et au final tout processus de déduction rationnelle.

Matteo FAVARETTI CAMPOSAMPIERO
(Università Ca' Foscari Venezia)

1. A VI, 4, 102.
2. A VI, 4, 104.
3. Je ne partage pas l'avis de D. Rutherford, « Philosophy and Language », p. 249, selon qui Leibniz soutient ici la nécessité d'éliminer toute expression qui ne respecte pas la compositionnalité.
4. A VI, 4, 104.

L'ENCYCLOPÉDIE

INTRODUCTION

Leibniz envisage dès son plus jeune âge la rédaction d'une encyclopédie[1]. C'est un projet qu'il conçoit notamment sous l'influence des travaux des encyclopédistes de Herborn, Johann Heinrich Alsted et son élève Johann Bisterfeld, dont il reprend une conception néo-platonicienne, « pansophiste », des sciences comme miroir cyclique de l'univers et un projet d'éducation universelle dont l'encyclopédie fait partie intégrante[2]. Il présente même parfois son projet comme destiné à parachever le travail déjà accompli par Alsted dans le *Cursus philosophica Encyclopaedia*

1. Pour des commentaires généraux, voir L. Couturat, *La Logique de Leibniz*, p. 119-174; R. McRae, *The Problem of the Unity of the Sciences*, p. 69-88; L. E. Loemker, *The Struggle for Synthesis*, p. 32-36; H. H. Knecht, *La Logique chez Leibniz*, p. 273-278; F. Duchesneau, *Leibniz et la méthode de la science*, p. 18-55; C. Vasoli, *L'Enciclopedismo del Seicento*, p. 71-90; M. Lærke, « *More mathematico demonstrata, ordine naturali exposita* », p. 233-249; *id.*, « Leibniz, the Encyclopedia, and the Natural Order of Thinking », p. 233-255; *id.*, *Les Lumières de Leibniz*, p. 205-284; M. R. Antognazza, *Leibniz. A Very Short Introduction*, chap. III.

2. Voir L. E. Loemker, « Leibniz and the Herborn Encyclopedists », p. 323-338; C. Mercer, *Leibniz's Metaphysics*, p. 40-41; K. Moll, « Der Enzyklopädiredegedanke bei Comenius und Alsted », p. 1-30; I. Valbusa, « Leibniz on Alsted's Encyclopaedia », p. 1084-1090; M. R. Antognazza, *Leibniz. An Intellectual Biography*, p. 32-46. Spécifiquement sur Leibniz et Alsted, voir M. R. Antognazza et H. Hotson (éd.), *Alsted and Leibniz on God, the Magistrate and the Millenium*. Sur Leibniz et Bisterfeld, voir Leibniz, *Notae ad Joh. Henricum Bisterfeldium* [1663-1666 ?], A VI, 4, 157, 159, 161; M. R. Antognazza, *Leibniz on the Trinity and the Incarnation*, p. 9-11; id., « Immeatio and Emperichoresis », p. 41-64; *id.*, « Debilissimae Entitates ? », p. 1-22; M. Picon, *Normes et objets du savoir dans les premiers essais Leibniziens*, vol. I, chap. II, p. 79-106; H. Hotson, *Johann Heinrich Alsted*.

de 1620 et l'*Encyclopaedia septem tomis distincta* de 1630[1]. Selon la définition que Leibniz donne dans le *Consilium de encyclopaedia nova conscribenda methodo inventoria* de 1679, « l'essence du projet consiste en l'organisation, d'une manière qui soit propice à l'invention, des connaissances humaines disponibles les plus importantes et les plus utiles pour la vie »[2]. D'autres textes proposent des définitions semblables : « un inventaire qui contient, ou renvoie à, une histoire complète de la nature et des arts, ainsi que tout ce qui mérite d'être gardé en mémoire en vertu de son sens ou de ses rapports »[3]; « un inventaire exact de toutes les connaissances acquises mais dispersées et mal rangées »[4]. Elle doit « mettre l'ensemble de l'expérience humaine à l'écrit »[5], en ordonnant ses éléments selon un ordre rationnel. L'encyclopédie constitue ainsi l'interface entre l'*historia* au sens large (l'observation et l'expérience comprises) et une organisation formelle des sciences conçue « par le haut », pour ainsi dire.

Leibniz, bien entendu, ne publia jamais un tel inventaire. Faut-il alors reléguer l'encyclopédie au tiroir déjà bien rempli des ébauches de projet irréalisables conçus par l'esprit prolixe du philosophe de Hanovre? Ce serait se tromper sur la nature même de l'entreprise. Tout d'abord, l'inachèvement permanent de l'édifice fait partie de sa construction profonde, car l'encyclopédie est conçue comme une structure essentiellement ouverte, faite pour pouvoir toujours intégrer des nouvelles découvertes et inventions[6]. Ensuite, Leibniz n'envisage jamais de réaliser à lui seul l'encyclopédie : « ce n'est pas l'entreprise d'un seul homme, ni même de peu de personnes »[7]. Il s'agit d'un projet collectif, « un travail divin des gens savants »[8]. Il ne peut se réaliser qu'avec l'assistance de toutes ces « personnes éclairées et de bonne intention » à qui Leibniz dédie un mémoire tout entier en 1692 en les incitant à se rassembler autour du projet

1. Voir *De ratione perficiendi* et *emendandi Encyclopaediam Alstedii* [1669-1671 ?], A VI, 2, 394-97; *Collectanae de inventione* et *studiis generalibus* [août 1676], A VI, 3, 335; *De republica literaria* [mai 1681], A VI, 4, 430; Leibniz à Lange, 5 juin 1716, Dutens V, 404.

2. *Consilium de encyclopaedia nova conscribenda methodo inventoria* [juin 1679], A VI, 4, 340 (nous traduisons; de façon générale, et sauf indication contraire, les traductions sont les nôtres).

3. *Praefatio operis ad instaurationem scientiarum* [début 1682], A VI, 4, 440. Voir aussi *Semestria literaria* [1679], A IV, 3, 789.

4. *Nouvelles ouvertures*, 1686, A VI, 4, 690-91.

5. *Semestria literaria*, A, IV, 3, 784.

6. Voir H. H. Knecht, *La Logique chez Leibniz*, p. 273-78.

7. *Nouvelles ouvertures*, A VI, 3, 691.

8. *Aufzeichnung für die Audienz bei Kaiser Leopold I*, août-septembre 1688, A IV, 4, 22.

commun de faire avancer les sciences[1]. Le projet encyclopédique est également inséparable de l'établissement des institutions scientifiques et des académies permettant de coordonner les collaborateurs et de mettre en place les structures matérielles nécessaires pour sa réalisation. La création des académies de ce type était pour Leibniz une affaire politique[2].

LE BUT DE L'ENCYCLOPÉDIE

Théoriquement, dans la forme que Leibniz dit «démonstrative», l'encyclopédie se forme par l'ensemble des connaissances qui découlent de la *scientia generalis*, une théorie générale de la vérité et des idées ainsi que de leurs principes à la fois logiques et métaphysiques. La science générale, quant à elle, est formellement régie par la *characteristica universalis*, conçue comme une langue formelle «qui rapporte parfaitement les relations de nos pensées»[3]. Elle est couronnée par une métaphysique qui, chez Leibniz, se confond avec la théologie naturelle[4]. En menant à bien la science, et en faisant des découvertes qui viennent constamment s'y ajouter, on glorifie ainsi la création divine par accumulation. Selon une métaphore récurrente, «le corps entier des sciences peut être considéré comme l'océan, qui est continué partout, sans interruption ou partage, bien que les hommes y conçoivent des parties, et leur donnent des noms selon leur commodité»[5]. Dans les *Essais de théodicée*, Leibniz emploie cette même métaphore pour décrire l'unité du monde: «Car il faut savoir que tout est lié dans chacun des mondes possibles: l'univers, quel qu'il puisse être, est tout d'une pièce, comme un océan [...]»[6]. Le parallèle est significatif: le corps entier des sciences reflète en effet l'ordre de la création tout entière et un ouvrage qui en fait l'état démontre la présence de la main de Dieu:

1. *Mémoire pour des personnes éclairées et de bonne intention* [vers 1692], A IV, 4, 612-21. Voir aussi *Semestria literaria*, A IV, 4, 792.

2. Voir par exemple *Entwürff gewisser Staats-Tafeln* [début 1680], A VI, 3, 342. Pour des commentaires, voir O. Klopp, *Leibniz der Stifter gelehrter Gesellschaften*; H. Rudolph, « Scientific Organizations and Learned Societies ».

3. Leibniz à Gallois, 19 décembre 1678, A II, 1, 669.

4. Il s'agit là d'une manière parmi d'autres de construire le rapport entre la science générale, caractéristique, métaphysique et encyclopédie, toutes présentes chez Leibniz dans des textes différents et à des époques différentes. Pour une discussion plus approfondie, voir A. Pelletier, « The *Scientia Generalis* and the *Encyclopaedia* ».

5. Phil. VIII, 94-95, *in* C, 530-31.

6. *Essais de théodicée*, 1710, § 9, GP VI, 107. Sur l'usage de l'image de l'océan chez Leibniz, voir C. Marras, « The Role of Metaphor in Leibniz's Epistemology », p. 199-212.

> Je tiens les arts et les sciences en plus haut estime parce que la gloire de Dieu et l'avantage de l'humanité tout entière y sont toujours promus. Car la merveille de Dieu, de sa puissance, de sa sagesse et de sa bonté, se manifeste particulièrement dans les sciences et dans la connaissance de la nature et de l'art[1].

L'encyclopédie se présente comme une cartographie exacte de la création reflétant l'ordre total que Dieu y a mis, un vaste édifice qui reflète la providence divine par l'harmonie des choses[2]. La référence à la totalité, à l'ordre global, est ici essentielle pour bien saisir en quel sens l'encyclopédie se fait *ad majorem Dei gloriam*. Comme chacun sait, la théodicée de Leibniz repose en grande partie sur l'idée d'une justification des maux apparents et ponctuels, perçus d'un point de vue singulier, par la considération de la totalité d'un point de vue global. Celui qui possèderait l'encyclopédie complète – ce qui, soit dit en passant, n'arrive jamais car elle va à l'infini – tiendrait également tous les éléments requis pour justifier l'ordre divin.

En même temps, l'encyclopédie est conçue comme un outil pratique, *ad usum vitae*[3] :

> [...] on peut dire hardiment que les connaissances solides et utiles sont le plus grand trésor du genre humain et le véritable héritage que nos ancêtres nous ont laissé, que nous devons faire profiter et augmenter, non seulement pour le transmettre à nos successeurs en meilleur état que nous ne l'avons reçu, mais bien plus pour en jouir nous-mêmes autant qu'il est possible pour la perfection de l'esprit, pour la santé du corps, et pour les commodités de la vie[4].

Leibniz compare souvent l'encyclopédie à un entrepôt de marchandises organisé de façon pratique et commode, une économie familiale bien gérée, une bibliothèque bien cataloguée, etc.[5]. Elle doit être confectionnée d'une façon telle qu'elle facilite l'usage des connaissances. Leibniz s'inscrit sur ce point directement dans la lignée du programme scientifique de l'*Instaurantia magna* (1620) de Francis Bacon : l'encyclopédie doit

1. Leibniz pour Pierre le Grand [1712], *in* W. Guerrier, *Leibniz in seinen Beziehungen zu Russland und Peter dem Grossen*, p. 206.

2. Y. Belaval, *Leibniz critique de Descartes*, p. 109-25.

3. Voir par exemple *Consultatio de naturae cognitione* [1679], A IV, 3, 872.

4. *Discours touchant la méthode de la certitude, et l'art d'inventer pour finir les disputes, et pour faire en peu de temps des grands progrès* [août 1688-Octobre 1690], A VI, 4, 952.

5. Voir A VI, 4, 440, 615 ; A I, 2, 122, 157 ; A I, 8, 205-206 ; GP VII, 58, 157, 162-163, 178, 29 ; C, 30, 214.

servir à augmenter notre pouvoir et notre maîtrise de la nature[1]. En même temps qu'elle « consigne à leur registre » l'ensemble des connaissances déjà acquises, elle fournit aussi de nouveaux points de départ, en indiquant des lacunes à remplir et des pistes possibles à suivre[2]. Afin de donner à l'encyclopédie une forme qui permet ainsi de l'assimiler à l'*ars inveniendi*, Leibniz propose notamment une classification des sciences en *loci*, une topologie des « lieux communs » scientifiques enracinée dans une conception réformée de la logique aristotélicienne, et qui cherche un point de médiation entre les traditionnelles catégories aristotéliciennes et la « dialectique » conçue par le philosophe français Pierre de la Ramée[3].

Finalement, on peut assigner à l'encyclopédie un rôle didactique ou éducatif, conformément à l'idéal d'éducation universelle que Leibniz hérite aussi des encyclopédistes de Herborn. Selon le *Mémoire pour des personnes éclairées et de bonne intention*, « pour contribuer véritablement au bonheur des hommes, il faut leur éclairer l'entendement, il faut fortifier leur volonté dans l'exercice des vertus, c'est-à-dire dans l'habitude d'agir suivant la raison »[4]. L'encyclopédie occupe un rôle central dans l'acquisition d'une telle « habitude d'agir suivant la raison ». L'organisation nécessaire de l'encyclopédie contraint en effet celui qui voudrait y contribuer à « progresser de façon continue en suivant une série déterminée » dans ses propres travaux[5]. Celui qui opère dans l'espace de l'encyclopédie apprend alors du même coup à s'orienter dans les connaissances humaines selon en certain ordre. L'ordre encyclopédique sert à inculquer un certain comportement scientifique, un certain *habitus*. Comme Leibniz écrit à Pierre le Grand à propos du projet, « une telle méthode d'enseignement [*Lehrart*] serait celle qui montrerait le chemin [*der Wegweiser*] vers l'augmentation des sciences et des nouvelles inventions »[6]. Cet *habitus*, comportement ou attitude scientifique, est essentiellement gouverné par des idéaux de modération et de non-sectarisme : en cherchant toujours à compléter l'encyclopédie plutôt que de le réécrire toujours

1. Voir par exemple *Discussion d'une question utile* [1687], A IV, 3, 492 : « L'avantage du genre humain en général est l'augmentation de son pouvoir ». Sur le contexte allemand, voir H. Hotson, « The Instauration of the Image of God in Man », p. 1-21.

2. *Nouvelles ouvertures*, A VI, 4, 691.

3. Voir par exemple Leibniz à Wagner, 27 février 1697, GP VII, 514-27. Sur Leibniz et Ramus, voir A. Blank, « Ramus and Leibniz on Analysis », p. 155-166. Sur le ramisme en Allemagne, voir H. Hotson, *Commonplace Learning*.

4. *Mémoire pour des personnes éclairées*, A IV, 4, 615.

5. *De arte characteristica ad perficiendas scientias ratione nitentes* [été 1688], A VI, 4, 915.

6. Voir *Concept einer Denkschrift*, in *Œuvres de Leibniz*, VII, p. 593.

à nouveau, le scientifique qui y collabore ne cherche jamais juste à détruire ce qui a été bâti avant, mais il se sert de façon constructive du travail accompli par ses prédécesseurs en faisant seulement de petits pas, toujours en avant et en proposant seulement « quelques nouvelles vérités » sans jamais tout renverser d'un coup[1]. L'encyclopédie se présente alors aussi comme un projet « didactique ou méthode d'enseignement et d'apprentissage » construite d'une manière telle qu'elle « stimule des esprits éclairés à entreprendre des [projets] audacieux similaires, pour qu'ils puissent apprendre non seulement de leurs prédécesseurs illustres, mais également des nouveaux arts utiles pour la vie »[2].

L'ORGANISATION DE L'ENCYCLOPÉDIE

Venons plus précisément aux principes d'organisation auxquels la construction de l'encyclopédie doit obéir afin de pouvoir remplir le rôle à la fois théologique, scientifique, moral et didactique auquel elle est destinée. Il convient de distinguer d'abord les perspectives théoriques et pratiques. Théoriquement, l'encyclopédie doit organiser les différents éléments de nos connaissances selon un ordre qui représente directement et de façon transparente les rapports conceptuels qui existent entre eux, en rendant apparente la structure logique des connaissances et l'ordre des choses selon l'harmonie des choses, pour la gloire de Dieu. D'un point de vue pratique, en revanche, pour le bien public et l'usage du genre humain, elle doit s'exposer d'une manière qui rend manifeste les implications et les usages de ces éléments de la manière la plus commode. Les diverses formulations que Leibniz donne de son projet vont révéler des tensions importantes entre ces deux points de vue, avec des conséquences importantes pour la manière dont il projette d'organiser l'encyclopédie concrètement, c'est-à-dire pour son mode d'exposition.

Le texte le plus connu sur l'organisation de l'encyclopédie se trouve dans les *Nouveaux essais sur l'entendement humain*, dans la partie 4, chapitre XXI, d'ailleurs le dernier chapitre de l'ouvrage. Ici, Leibniz s'oppose à une classification traditionnelle des sciences selon la logique, la théorie et la pratique, censées constituer des domaines du savoir parfaitement séparés. En réalité, maintient Leibniz, ces domaines se superposent

1. Voir Leibniz à Arnauld, 12 avril 1686, A II, 2, 20. Voir aussi M. Lærke, *Les Lumières de Leibniz*, chap. III.

2. *Consilium de literis instaurandis condendaque Encyclopaedia* [automne 1679], A VI, 3, 791.

largement, à un point tel que l'ensemble des savoirs peuvent être envisagés des trois points de vue à la fois. Par conséquent, cette division ne peut pas, ou du moins pas sous cette forme, servir de façon efficace à classer les sciences, car elle donne lieu à ce qu'on appellerait aujourd'hui un « inventaire à la Prévert ». Il envisage alors comme un meilleur alternatif une double organisation, synthétique et analytique :

> Je trouve deux dispositions principales de toutes les vérités doctrinales, dont chacune aurait son mérite, et qu'il serait bon de joindre. L'une serait *synthétique* et *théorique* rangeant les vérités selon l'ordre des preuves, comme font les mathématiciens : de sorte que chaque proposition viendrait après celles dont elle dépend. L'autre disposition serait *analytique* et *pratique*, commençant par le but des hommes, c'est-à-dire par les biens dont le comble est la félicité, et cherchant par ordre les moyens qui servent à acquérir ces biens ou à éviter les maux contraires. Et ces deux méthodes ont lieu dans l'encyclopédie en général comme encore quelques-uns les ont pratiquées dans les sciences particulières. Car la géométrie même traitée synthétiquement par Euclide comme une science, a été traitée par quelques autres comme un Art, et pourrait néanmoins être traitée démonstrativement sous cette forme, qui en montrerait même l'invention[1].

À ces deux dispositions principales, Leibniz ajoute une troisième, prenant la forme d'un « répertoire » systématique ou alphabétique permettant de suivre un terme ou une proposition à travers l'ensemble de l'ouvrage; bref, une sorte d'*index rerum*[2]. La disposition théorique est celle, synthétique, qui suit « l'ordre des preuves » comme les « mathématiques » et elle est « démonstrative ». La disposition « analytique », plus mystérieuse, « commence par le but », à savoir quelque « bien » pour les hommes, pour ensuite exposer les « moyens » permettant de l'obtenir. La suite du texte note également que la disposition synthétique est « selon l'origine » alors que l'analytique est « selon l'usage ». La conception de cette disposition selon deux ordres principaux remonte loin : Leibniz explique déjà dans un texte de 1679 que l'encyclopédie universelle « contient deux parties, l'une théorique, l'autre pratique. La [partie] théorique procède selon l'ordre synthétique; [la partie] pratique selon l'ordre analytique »[3].

Mais comment faut-il comprendre plus précisément cette double disposition? Selon la tradition cartésienne, en suivant la formulation canonique qu'elle reçoit dans *Logique de Port-Royal* d'Arnauld et Nicole[4],

1. *Nouveaux Essais*, IV, 21, § 4, A VI, 6, 524.
2. *Ibid.*
3. *Consilium de literis instaurandis condendaque Encyclopaedia*, A IV, 3, 793.
4. Voir Arnauld et Nicole, *La Logique ou l'art de penser*, IV, chap. II.

la différence entre une organisation analytique et synthétique est celle-ci : une organisation analytique « cherche les causes par les effets », c'est-à-dire, elle commence par les choses complexes qu'elle décompose conceptuellement en remontant vers les choses plus simple qui en sont les constituants ; une organisation synthétique, en revanche, procède dans le sens inverse en « cherchant les effets par les causes », à savoir, en commençant par les éléments les plus simples pour aller, en les recomposant conceptuellement, vers les choses plus complexes. L'ordre analytique est celui que Descartes favorise pour exposer sa philosophie et qu'il adopte dans les *Méditations métaphysiques*. Le paradigme de l'ordre géométrique est celui d'Euclide, le *mos geometricus*, et que Spinoza adopte quand il rédige son introduction à Descartes (1663) et, ensuite, quand il entreprend d'écrire son *Éthique* (posth. 1677). Dans les deux cas, il s'agit d'exporter une distinction provenant des mathématiques vers la philosophie. On pourrait alors penser que, chez Leibniz, dans la manière dont il envisage l'organisation de son encyclopédie, analytique et synthétique, il s'agit également de se servir de cette manière « des mathématiques hors des mathématiques » [1]. Ce serait une conclusion exacte qu'il faut pourtant adopter avec un peu de prudence car Leibniz est en réalité à cheval sur deux traditions distinctes. L'usage de la distinction analytique-synthétique en philosophie n'est pas seulement d'origine cartésienne mais cette même dichotomie fut également employée par les représentants de la tradition de l'*historia literaria* en Allemagne – une tradition bien connue par Leibniz – justement pour désigner deux types d'organisation des connaissances humaines : l'une, analytique, selon l'ordre chronologique ; l'autre, synthétique, selon l'ordre des disciplines [2]. Les *Nouveaux essais* semblent ici distinguer assez clairement l'exposition synthétique de l'organisation selon les disciplines, en indiquant qu'il existe en outre « une division civile des sciences selon la faculté et les professions » [1], tout en rattachant la disposition synthétique assez clairement

1. *Nouveaux Essais*, II, XXIX, § 12, A VI, 6, 260-61.

2. Sur ce point, voir M. C. Carhart, « *Historia Literaria* », p. 184-206. Sur cette tradition du XVIe au XVIIIe siècle en Allemagne, voir F. Grunert et F. Vollhardt (dir.), *Historia literaria*. L'*historia literaria* désigne à la fois une manière d'organiser les connaissances et une discipline universitaire. Pour l'exemple paradigmatique des travaux faits dans cette tradition – souvent des grandes sommes de connaissances destinées à servir dans l'enseignement universitaire – on peut consulter le *Polyhistor, Literarius, Philosophicus et Practicus* [1688] de D. G. Morhof. Un des premiers représentants est Christophe Milieu (Christophus Mylaeus) dont le *De Scribenda Vniversitatis rervm historia fibri qvinqve* date de 1551 (voir D. R. Kelley, « Writing Cultural History », p. 342-65). Pour Leibniz et l'*historia literaria*, voir *Contemplatio de historia literaria statuque praesenti eruditionis* [1682 ?], A VI, 4, 451-89. Voir aussi A VI, 4, 972. Pour une référence à Mylaeus, voir A VI, 4, 679.

1. *Nouveaux Essais*, IV, 21, § 4, A VI, 6, 524.

au paradigme démonstratif de la géométrie euclidienne. En ce qui concerne la disposition analytique, la situation est plus compliquée. Car Leibniz présente la disposition analytique de l'encyclopédie d'une manière qui fait bien plus penser à la tradition l'*historia literaria*, car il s'agit d'une approche plus chronologique que conceptuelle relative aux « moyens », c'est-à-dire à la genèse, d'une découverte : c'est ainsi que l'analyse « devrait nous permettre d'entrevoir l'origine des découvertes, à savoir, comment les gens sont arrivés à leurs découvertes et à leurs sciences, ou comment on peut y arriver »[1]. Au lieu d'exposer l'origine de quelque connaissance en montrant ses réquisits logiques, à savoir, les notions qui entrent dans sa composition conceptuelle, Leibniz semble plutôt vouloir proposer des récits qui relatent les procédures concrètes ayant permis aux scientifiques de parvenir à cette connaissance, en se faisant ainsi une conception de l'analyse qu'on peut dire « historique » qui se confond avec la recherche de l'« origine des découvertes ». Nous verrons dans la section suivante pourquoi.

Il y a enfin un critère économique qui s'applique, à la fois, à la disposition analytique et à la disposition synthétique. Selon le *Concilium de encyclopaedia nova* de 1679, « les choses sont le plus claires [...] quand elles sont présentées nues et simples, et avec tout le superflu enlevé »[2]. Leibniz prône souvent les avantages de cette « vérité toute nue » qui permet de retrouver rapidement l'information voulue[3]. En critiquant un projet comparable, le *Dictionnaire historique et critique* (1697) de Pierre Bayle, Leibniz reprend ainsi son homologue français pour confectionner des entrées de dictionnaire qui sont d'une « trop grande prolixité »[4] :

> Peut-être ne serait-il pas mauvais aussi de garder un certain ordre constant dans chaque titre, car ces discours libres et vagabonds, où les connexions naissent par hasard, comme dans une conversation, sont bons dans quelque petit ouvrage galant, fait plutôt pour plaire que pour profiter, mais ils ne sont pas bons à éclaircir les choses, dont le bon arrangement tient souvent lieu de commentaire et sert à épargner les paroles[5].

1. *Concept einer Denkschrift*, p. 593.

2. *Consilium de encyclopaedia nova*, A VI, 4, 340.

3. *Essais de théodicée*, « Préface », GP VI, 38 ; voir aussi le « Discours préliminaire », § 30, GP VI, 68, et *Essais sur un nouveau plan d'une science certaine* [1688-1690 ?], A VI, 4, 948.

4. *Commentaire sur le projet* [fin septembre 1692], GP VI, 17.

5. *Ibid.*, GP VI, 18. Il s'agit, *stricto sensu*, non pas d'un commentaire sur le *Dictionnaire historique et critique* [1697] mais sur le pré-projet que Bayle publie en 1692, le *Projet et fragmens d'un Dictionnaire critique*. Pour une lecture approfondie de la confrontation Leibniz-Bayle sur ce point, voir M. Lærke, *Les Lumières de Leibniz*, p. 205-84.

En faisant preuve d'un même souci d'économie, Leibniz envisage également deux versions distinctes de l'« encyclopédie réelle », d'une part, un *atlas universalis major* « avec beaucoup des figures et des descriptions précises des choses » ; et, d'autre part, un *atlas universalis minor* qu'il présente comme un « petit manuel *ad usum communem vitae* » ou un « petit *Enchiridion Humanae Cognitionis* » dans lequel est contenu uniquement le « noyau » ou ce qui est « le plus utile » [1].

Dans l'encyclopédie, il ne s'agit donc pas simplement d'accumuler des informations et de les remettre en ordre, mais également d'en faire l'économie et d'y opérer un tri, afin de ne pas s'y perdre :

> Ce qui se trouve de bon dans les auteurs est tellement couvert et obscurci par le désordre, par la répétition, et par la multitude des inutilités qu'il en faut acheter trop chèrement la jouissance au prix de son temps qui est la plus précieuse des choses dont nous pouvons disposer. Et c'est ce qui fait qu'ordinairement on n'écrit et on ne lit que pour paraître et pour se divertir, le nombre des livres et la confusion des choses nous effraye, et nous ôte toute espérance d'en tirer une science solide [2].

Il faut des incisions précises dans le flux d'informations car « par ce seul moyen serait réduit à un étroit passage l'immense océan, où autrement la curiosité du genre humain sera finalement engloutie » [3]. On peut sur ce point également faire une comparaison avec les réflexions de Leibniz sur « l'horizon de la doctrine humaine » dans un ensemble de textes rédigés en 1693 [4] où il envisage avec consternation une situation où, comme le formule déjà le *Consilium de encyclopaedia nova*, « le trop grand nombre des choses et des livres annule tout espoir d'en jouir, et recouvre ce qui est solide et utile par une masse de choses creuses » [5]. Pour éviter une telle confusion, écrit Leibniz dans *Recommandation pour instituer la science générale* de 1686, à propos des propositions scientifiques vraies : « On n'aurait donc qu'à les dépouiller des vains ornements, de les énoncer d'une manière nette et simple comme les géomètres ont coutume de faire : et puis de les ranger selon l'ordre de leur dépendance et des sujets. Leur

1. *Aufzeichnung für die Audienz*, A IV, 4, 25.

2. *Recommandation pour instituer la science générale* [1686], A VI, 4, 697.

3. Leibniz cité *in* L. Davillé, *Leibniz historien*, p. 450 n. 5. Voir sur ce thème aussi M. Fichant, « Postface : *Plus ultra* », p. 125-210 ; D. Selcer, « The Uninterrupted Ocean », p. 25-50.

4. Ces textes sont édités par M. Fichant dans Leibniz, *De l'horizon de la doctrine humaine*, p. 39-60.

5. A VI, 4, 338.

liaison y paraîtrait d'elle-même bientôt, et l'une se démontrerait par l'autre, pourvu qu'on se gardât de faire des sauts »[1].

L'ORDRE NATUREL DE LA PENSÉE

Selon le mémoire à Pierre le Grand déjà mentionné plus haut, l'encyclopédie devrait être exposée selon un « ordre droit et commode », une formulation qui évoque vivement un critère de facilité d'usage[2]. Mais en quoi consiste une telle organisation « commode », exactement? Comment se présente-t-elle concrètement? La plupart des commentateurs, tel Louis Couturat, Robert McRae ou encore François Duchesneau, estime que l'encyclopédie est essentiellement conçue sur le modèle des mathématiques et présentée selon un ordre strictement déductif. Pour Couturat, par exemple, l'« encyclopédie devait être le recueil de toutes les connaissances humaines, tant historiques que scientifiques, disposées dans un ordre logique et suivant une méthode démonstrative »[3]. De même, dans *The Problem of Unity in the Sciences*, Robert McRae place les mathématiques à la base même du projet[4]. François Duchesneau, comme Couturat[5], insiste sur le fait que l'encyclopédie devait être organisée *more geometrico* selon un ordre déductif[6]. Sur ce point, le passage des *Nouveaux essais* déjà cité plus haut, selon lequel l'encyclopédie « rang[e] les vérités selon l'ordre des preuves, comme font les mathématiciens », fournit une preuve importante. Mais ce n'est pas le seul texte allant en ce sens. Ainsi, dans un texte qui porte sur ce que Leibniz lui-même désigne comme une « encyclopédie démonstrative », il maintient que « si cette Encyclopédie était faite comme je la souhaite, on pourrait donner le moyen de trouver toujours les conséquences des vérités fondamentales ou des faits donnés par une manière de calcul aussi exact et aussi simple que celui de l'Arithmétique et de l'Algèbre »[7]. De même, selon le *Semestria literaria* de 1679, dans l'encyclopédie, « les pensées humaines ou notions [...] sont résolues et ordonnées, et [...] toutes les vérités principales découlant de la

1. A VI, 4, 695.
2. *Concept einer Denkschrift*, p. 593.
3. L. Couturat, *La Logique de Leibniz*, p. 119.
4. R. McRae, *The Problem of the Unity of the Sciences*, p. 86-88.
5. F. Duchesneau, *Leibniz et la méthode de la science*, p. 18.
6. *Ibid.*, p. 25-26, 46, 49 et 51.
7. *Recommandation pour instituer la science générale*, A VI, 4, 708.

raison sont démontrées selon leurs fondements, et mathématiquement ordonnées »[1].

Il faut pourtant se garder d'en conclure qu'une organisation strictement démonstrative des connaissances est à tous égards propice à l'invention ou qu'elle représente toujours pour Leibniz l'option la plus « commode ». En réalité, il ne faut pas surestimer l'aspect synthétique de l'encyclopédie au point de négliger la disposition analytique qui est d'une importance capitale pour que l'encyclopédie puisse servir de façon efficace *ad usum vitae*. En réalité, d'un point de vue à la fois pratique et didactique, la disposition strictement démonstrative n'est pas seulement insuffisante mais même en une certaine façon contre-productive. On peut sur ce point se rapporter à un passage dans le *Consilium de encyclopedia nova* où Leibniz discute « l'ordre de positionnement » de l'encyclopédie, à savoir, son mode concret d'exposition :

> L'ordre de positionnement doit être mathématique, quoique différent de celui d'Euclide. Certes, les géomètres démontrent avec une certaine exactitude, mais ils forcent l'esprit bien plus qu'ils ne l'éclairent. Ce faisant, ils obtiennent beaucoup d'admiration, en extorquant du lecteur réticent son assentiment et en le cernant au moyen d'artifices inattendus; mais ils ne tiennent pas assez compte de la mémoire et du génie du lecteur, puisqu'ils cachent en quelque sorte les raisons et les causes naturelles des conclusions, et rendent ainsi difficile la saisie de la manière dont ils sont parvenus à leurs découvertes. Et pourtant il est de la plus grande importance pour toute science de connaître non seulement les conclusions et leurs démonstrations, mais également l'origine des découvertes, ce qu'il suffit à la mémoire de retenir, car tout le reste peut en être dérivé. La lumière des découvertes doit donc être couplée avec la rigueur démonstrative, et les éléments de chaque science doivent être rédigés d'une telle manière que le lecteur ou l'élève voie toujours les connections, qu'il devienne en quelque sorte un partenaire du maître dans l'invention, et qu'il l'accompagne plutôt que de le suivre [...]. Il s'ensuit encore clairement qu'il ne sera pas nécessaire de donner d'abord des définitions et des axiomes, des phénomènes ou expériences, mais qu'ils peuvent être introduits au fur et à mesure que l'ordre naturel de la pensée demande leur usage[2].

La forme géométrique extorque de l'esprit du lecteur son consentement par la force de la logique mais sans l'engager véritablement dans la démonstration, c'est-à-dire, sans l'engager au niveau de ce que Leibniz désigne comme l'*ingenium lectoris*. Or, pour se montrer efficace au niveau pratique, l'encyclopédie doit tenir compte des capacités naturelles des

1. *Semestria literaria*, A, IV, 3, 784.
2. *Consilium de encyclopaedia nova*, A VI, 4, 341-42.

scientifiques qui vont s'en servir : elle doit s'adapter à leurs besoins et à leurs capacités intellectuelles pour qu'ils puissent mieux assimiler et utiliser les connaissances en question. Il faut donc présenter l'encyclopédie d'une manière qui permette au lecteur d'assimiler naturellement, c'est-à-dire au niveau psychologique, les informations qu'elle contient. Or, cet effet ne se produit pas quand elles sont présentées *more geometrico*, de façon strictement démonstrative[1]. Leibniz suit sur ce point les recommandations fournies par Platon dans un dialogue qu'il admire : le *Ménon*[2]. Comme dans ce dialogue où Socrate enseigne des rudiments des mathématiques à un jeune garçon-esclave, le lecteur de l'encyclopédie doit être guidé doucement plutôt que forcé vers la connaissance et il doit parvenir à saisir la signification des démonstrations par ses propres moyens. Or, de ce point de vue, la forme strictement démonstrative, géométrique, est très défectueuse car elle « force l'esprit bien plus qu'[elle] ne l'éclaire ». Pour cette raison, poursuit Leibniz :

> [D]e la même façon que les autres sciences doivent aborder la vérité en suivant l'exemple des mathématiques, l'aspérité des mathématiques doit à son tour être réduite par une manière plus douce de procéder en suivant l'exemple des autres sciences, pour que nous puissions à la fois tirer la foi de la volonté et satisfaire l'esprit avide de connaître les causes[3].

L'ordre d'exposition que Leibniz envisage pour l'encyclopédie est sur ce point conforme à ce qu'il écrit sur sa propre pratique d'écriture : « Je n'écris jamais rien en philosophie que je ne le traite par définitions et par axiomes, quoique je ne lui donne pas toujours cet air mathématique qui rebute les gens, car il faut parler familièrement pour être lu des personnes ordinaires »[4]. Loin d'adopter une forme exposition purement déductive, l'encyclopédie doit chercher un équilibre entre exactitude et lisibilité, un équilibre dont la difficulté est bien mise en évidence dans *Projets et essais pour avancer l'art d'inventer* où Leibniz oppose Euclide et Ramus, coupables des vices contraires sur ce point :

> Ramus a repris Euclide de ce qu'en suivant la rigueur des démonstrations, il a abandonné la méthode qui parait plus propre à éclairer l'esprit, mais le bon Ramus qui avait voulu changer la méthode d'Euclide, n'a pas seulement perdu la rigueur mais encore la vérité et l'exactitude[5].

1. Voir M. Lærke, « Leibniz : lire les géomètres », p. 79-94.
2. Voir *Nouveaux essais*, I, I, § 5, A VI, 6, 77 ; *Rationale fidei catholicae* [1685 ?], A VI, 4, 2316-17 ; *Discours de métaphysique*, art. XXVI, A VI, 4, 1571.
3. *Consilium de encyclopaedia nova*, A VI, 4, 342.
4. Leibniz à Burnett, 10 décembre 1705, GP III, 302.
5. *Projet et essais pour avancer l'art d'inventer* [1688-1690], A VI, 4, 968.

C'est dans ce contexte qu'on doit comprendre les formulations ambiguës que Leibniz propose sur la disposition analytique de l'encyclopédie. Pour Leibniz, comme nous l'avons déjà constaté, la disposition analytique de l'encyclopédie ne consiste pas, ou pas toujours, à reconstruire la genèse conceptuelle des connaissances en exposant les éléments conceptuels plus simples dont elles dérivent, en suivant la conception cartésienne de l'analyse. Il s'agit plutôt de remonter aux « origines des découvertes » en proposant des récits de la manière dont elles ont été faites, des « histoires naturelles » des découvertes, permettant aux aspirants scientifiques de voir comment la recherche scientifique se fait réellement dans les laboratoires mentaux ou concrets des savants. Cette stratégie correspond, il nous semble, à un tel effort d'éclairer l'esprit et de faire du lecteur *quasi socius inveniendi*, « comme un partenaire dans l'invention ».

Conclusion

L'encyclopédie forme, à la fois, un recensement général des connaissances humaines et un instrument de travail dont on doit se servir pour inventer et faire avancer les sciences, pour la gloire de Dieu et la félicité des hommes. D'un point de vue théorique, l'encyclopédie doit être organisée d'une manière telle qu'elle rend manifeste l'ordre divin du monde qu'explorent les sciences; d'un point de vue pratique, en revanche, l'encyclopédie doit être exposée d'une manière telle que les informations qu'elle contient soient facilement utilisables pour les savants engagés dans la réalisation collective des sciences.

Le projet vient s'ajouter à tout un programme intellectuel de redressement du monde intellectuel, conçu à partir d'un diagnostic général de ce qu'il appelle « l'état actuel de l'érudition », une notion qui recouvre, à la fois « toutes les connaissances humaines » et « la République des lettres »[1]. Leibniz lance ainsi le projet sur le fond d'une évaluation plutôt sombre : actuellement, les savants, cherchant la gloire plus que les connaissances, se sont perdus dans la confusion des disputes. Ils démolissent encore et encore ce qui a été bâti mais sans jamais progresser :

1. *Guiliemi Pacidii plus ultra* [1686 ?], A VI, 4, 675 : « *De statu praesenti eruditionis, seu Reipublicae literariae* », et A VI, 4, 681 : « *De statu praesenti eruditionis, omnisque cognitionis humanae.* » Pour cette expression, voir aussi *Contemplatio de historia literaria statuque praesenti eruditionis* [début 1682 ?], A VI, 4, 451-490; *Initia et specimina scientiae novae generalis* [1682 ?], A VI, 4, 442; *Relation de l'état présent de la république des lettres* [1675 ?], A IV, 1, 568-571. Pour un commentaire, voir M. Lærke, *Les Lumières de Leibniz*, p. 60-61.

> [...] ils entrent en guerre avec les autres, et font tort aux bonnes choses qu'ils disent, comme aussi aux vérités anciennes dont ils ébranlent les fondements dans l'opinion des hommes amateurs de nouveautés. Les hommes ayant la tête remplie de subtilités creuses et sans démonstration, et se battant par caprice et par passion, perdent misérablement le temps précieux qu'ils pourraient employer à avancer les connaissances solides [1].

Au lieu de s'appuyer sur les connaissances déjà acquises pour faire quelques pas en avant, les intellectuels s'emploient à critiquer leurs prédécesseurs afin de pouvoir se vanter d'innover. Le cartésianisme avec son ambition de balayer le champ intellectuel pour recommencer de nouveau est sur ce point le paradigme d'une philosophie animée par les pires ambitions : la recherche de la gloire aux dépens des prédécesseurs[2]. En même temps, Leibniz dénonce des savants désorganisés qui ramassent du savoir sans égard pour leurs rapports et leur usage précis, tel un père de famille « dévoué mais peu judicieux » qu'il décrit dans la *Praefatio operis ad instaurationem scientiarum* qui, faute de bien s'y prendre, se trouve dans l'obligation d'inventorier et de réorganiser chaque soir son ménage entier[3]. Afin de remédier à ces malheurs, Leibniz s'imagine alors une communauté de savants dont les connaissances sont « unies en un corps d'une seule science »[4], dans laquelle chaque membre contribue à la découverte et à la sauvegarde des connaissances humaines, pour la gloire de Dieu et le bien public ; où chacun s'applique, dans son domaine, à faire avancer les sciences en s'appuyant sur les résultats déjà obtenus par d'autres. En consignant ainsi chaque science à sa place précise dans le cercle des connaissances et « en tirant des données ce qu'on peut en tirer, [...] nous allons utiliser et profiter [...] de ces trésors déjà trouvés ainsi que de leurs bénéfices divins »[5], l'encyclopédie serait alors une sorte de machine à produire des nouvelles découvertes à partir des anciennes, en conformité avec l'éthique savante de modération et de collaboration qui anime de façon générale le projet intellectuel de Leibniz[6].

Mogens LÆRKE
(CNRS, IHRIM, ENS Lyon)

1. *De la philosophie cartésienne*, A VI, 4, 1482. Voir aussi A I, 5, 11 ; A VI, 4, 613 et 619.

2. Voir par exemple Leibniz à Nicaise, 5 juin 1692, A II, 2, 532-38 ; Leibniz à Wagner, 27 février 1697, GP VII, 515. Voir aussi M. Lærke, *Les Lumières de Leibniz*, p. 322-29.

3. *Praefatio operis ad instaurationem scientiarum*, A VI, 4, 440.

4. *Concilium de encyclopaedia nova*, A VI, 4, 349.

5. *De arte characteristica ad perficiendas scientias ratione nitentes*, A VI, 4, 915. Voir aussi L. Couturat, *La Logique de Leibniz*, p. 150-51.

6. Voir M. Lærke, *Les Lumières de Leibniz*, chap. III.

THÉORIE DE LA CONNAISSANCE ET MÉTHODE

La théorie de la méthode connaît au début du XVIIe siècle de profondes transformations du fait de son rapprochement avec la doctrine des facultés et des opérations de l'esprit humain : la méthode est désormais conçue comme l'ensemble des règles nécessaires au bon usage des facultés. Par rapport à cette évolution, l'œuvre de Leibniz constitue une singularité. La préoccupation des méthodes est certes omniprésente dès ses premiers écrits : formé au contact des controverses qui opposaient sur ce sujet les partisans de l'aristotélisme renaissant à ceux de Ramus, il s'est bientôt rallié aux promesses liées à la généralisation de la procédure démonstrative des géomètres, avant d'élaborer son propre projet d'une « vraie méthode » appuyée sur l'invention de symboles adéquats aux concepts qu'ils représentent[1]. En revanche, les processus psychologiques qui concourent à la formation de la connaissance ne figurent pas parmi les thèmes majeurs dont on peut suivre les transformations tout au long de son œuvre. Si bien que l'existence même d'une théorie leibnizienne de la connaissance, constituée pour elle-même indépendamment des autres domaines de sa philosophie, fait encore débat entre ses commentateurs[2].

Sans prétendre trancher leurs divergences, nous partirons de deux points avérés :

– contrairement aux auteurs pour lesquels l'entreprise de constitution du savoir doit commencer par s'assurer des capacités de l'esprit qui lui serviront d'instruments, Leibniz considère que « la question de l'origine de nos idées et de nos maximes n'est pas préliminaire en philosophie »[3]. Comme l'écrit François Duchesneau, « la préoccupation de Leibniz est d'abord relative au fondement de toute connaissance démonstrative :

1. A VI, 4 A, 7.
2. C. Leduc, *Substance, individu et connaissance chez Leibniz*, p. 10-20.
3. A VI, 6, 6.

ce fondement ne peut se situer que dans l'appréhension des vérités nécessaires découlant de principes comme ceux d'identité et de non-contradiction »[1].

– N'appelant pas un traitement prioritaire, la question de la connaissance a principalement été abordée par Leibniz à l'occasion de deux grandes controverses. La première l'occupe entre le milieu des années 1670 et celui des années 1680. Elle vise ces composantes essentielles du cartésianisme que sont la théorie de l'idée et la démonstration de l'existence de Dieu que Descartes fait reposer sur elle. La seconde controverse, bien différente à tous égards, commence lorsque Leibniz prend connaissance de l'*Essai concernant l'entendement humain* de Locke (1690), puis de l'usage de certaines de ses thèses par le libre penseur John Toland[2]. Il renverse alors ses batteries : après avoir, au milieu des années 1680, intégré des éléments de noétique et de logique élaborés dans ses écrits antérieurs et leur avoir donné la forme d'une doctrine propre à répondre aux prétentions d'un rationalisme fort, il est conduit vingt ans plus tard à revendiquer – en les réinterprétant – certaines des positions cartésiennes qu'il avait attaquées, afin de défendre contre l'empirisme de Locke ses propres conceptions de la substance et de l'âme[3]. Dans le contexte de cette seconde controverse, les facteurs psychologiques sur lesquels repose, selon Leibniz, notre capacité à atteindre des connaissances démonstratives deviennent des arguments mobilisables en faveur de l'immatérialité de l'âme.

Entre ces deux époques, Leibniz a créé une apparence de continuité en renvoyant fréquemment les lecteurs de ses écrits tardifs à ses *Méditations sur la connaissance, la vérité et les idées* de 1684. Il sera particulièrement instructif de comparer le contenu de ce texte avec l'usage qu'en fait Leibniz vingt ans plus tard. Nous verrons comment cette première composition doctrinale, nourrie d'éléments tirés des logiques scolastiques du premier XVIIe siècle, puis systématisés sans référence à une quelconque topique des facultés, a pu être présentée rétrospectivement, au tournant du XVIIIe siècle, comme contenant « les fondements [...] de la doctrine qui regarde l'entendement »[4]. Avant d'en venir aux grands textes de ces deux époques, nous commencerons par rappeler les données fondamentales du

1. F. Duchesneau, « Les *Nouveaux Essais* : l'harmonie des perspectives », p. 308.

2. M. R. Antognazza, *Leibniz*, p. 409-410 ; T. Dagron, *Toland et Leibniz*.

3. « Vous savez, Philalethe [...] que j'ai toujours été comme je suis encore pour l'idée innée de Dieu, que M. des Cartes a soutenue » (*NE* I, 1, 1 ; A VI, 6, 74).

4. *Nouveaux Essais* III, 4 ; A VI, 6, 297.

problème du savoir tel qu'il s'est d'abord présenté à Leibniz, et les réponses qu'il lui a apportées.

LE PROBLÈME DU SAVOIR : DIMENSION MODALE, DIMENSION NOÉTIQUE, RÔLE DES DÉFINITIONS

Bien avant les grands affrontements à l'occasion desquels il développera sa théorie de la connaissance, Leibniz a toujours envisagé la question générale du savoir selon deux distinctions majeures : la première, logique et théologique, oppose le nécessaire et le contingent, la « raison » et le fait; la seconde, noétique, oppose les notions confuses ou encore « simples à notre égard » aux notions distinctes, c'est-à-dire susceptibles de définition.

L'un des traits les plus constants de la pensée de Leibniz est la distinction fondamentale qu'il pose entre deux types de propositions. Elle apparaît dès le *De Arte combinatoria* de 1666, où elle est rapportée à son fondement théologique : Leibniz y oppose « les théorèmes, ou propositions de vérité éternelle, c'est-à-dire qui reposent non sur l'arbitre de Dieu, mais sur sa nature » à celles « dont la vérité n'est pas fondée dans l'essence mais dans l'existence » et qui « sont toutes vraies comme par hasard, c'est-à-dire par l'arbitre de Dieu » [1]. La « nature » de Dieu constitue le fondement des vérités éternelles parce qu'elle contient les idées divines sur le modèle desquelles tout ce qui existe a été créé. Le fait que telle ou telle chose existe – par exemple, le fait qu'« il y a un monde » [2] – est toujours le résultat d'une décision divine; mais cette décision a elle-même été précédée par la connaissance qu'a Dieu des essences des choses. Sont ainsi fondés l'ordre du nécessaire et celui du contingent.

La distinction de ces deux types de propositions détermine la partition fondamentale – la seule véritablement indépassable – de l'ensemble du savoir [3]. À chacun de ces domaines s'appliquent des procédures épistémologiques propres. Les propositions nécessaires, bientôt dites « de raison »

1. A VI, 1, 199.

2. Selon l'exemple de proposition contingente donné par Leibniz en 1669 (A VI, 1, 398).

3. « L'orbe tout entier des sciences a, de sa nature même, cette division certaine que notre connaissance porte soit sur des concepts purs et des vérités éternelles, soit sur des perceptions confuses des faits dont on observe qu'ils se produisent. [...] Une fois les sciences divisées en expérimentales et intellectuelles, les autres subdivisions n'ont pas des limites aussi fixes, pas plus que l'océan germanique n'est séparé de la mer atlantique [...] par une ligne certaine, parce que l'Océan est un et continu » (1683-1685 ? A VI, 4 A, 524, notre trad.).

sont « vraies par leurs termes »[1] : leur prédicat est au nombre des concepts élémentaires dont la combinaison produit le concept du sujet, cette composition étant pensée par Leibniz d'après celle des facteurs arithmétiques d'un nombre[2]. Ces propositions sont donc susceptibles d'une *démonstration* consistant à définir leurs termes, c'est-à-dire à en analyser la composition jusqu'à ce que l'appartenance de l'un à l'autre devienne manifeste[3]. Leibniz définit ainsi, dès 1671, la démonstration comme un « enchaînement de définitions »[4]. Des propositions contingentes ou « de fait », en revanche, « il n'y a pas de démonstration, mais une induction »[5].

Aussi originelle que la partition des champs du savoir, mais indépendante d'elle, la catégorie du « sensible » apparaît dès les premiers écrits de Leibniz. Elle y englobe tout ce qui peut être nommé, mais non défini, ou encore ce que « l'on ne peut expliquer par des termes mieux connus » que son nom même. En ce sens, un tel nom est un « terme simple »[6]. Car les sensibles sont donnés dans une expérience insubstituable : « nous ne saurions expliquer à un aveugle ce que c'est que le rouge »[7]. Il s'agit là d'une thèse proprement phénoménologique, dans la mesure où elle décrit une modalité de notre expérience indépendamment de toute démarche tendant à expliquer la constitution de l'objet senti ou le processus de la perception. L'une des premières listes de « qualités sensibles » dressées par Leibniz énumère ainsi « 1. la pensée 2. la causalité », perçues en

1. Le terme *ratio* recouvre, pour Leibniz comme pour ses prédécesseurs, une multitude de sens : contentons-nous de signaler ici que, s'il désigne la faculté de raisonner, il est également synonyme de *conceptus*. Une « proposition de raison » est ainsi celle qui énonce un rapport entre des *concepts*, indépendamment de l'existence des objets correspondants.

2. Leibniz réinterprète par là, à la lumière de la logique hobbesienne, la caractérisation scolastique des principes indémontrables des sciences comme des propositions dont la vérité s'impose à quiconque saisit la signification de leurs termes. Oubliant la distinction traditionnelle entre ces principes et les propositions démontrables, Leibniz étend cette acception sémantique de la nécessité à toutes les propositions démontrables (*cf.* Hobbes, *De Corpore* I, 3, 10 et M. Picon, « Leibniz, Hobbes et les principes des sciences »).

3. « Dans toute démonstration, il y a résolution soit du seul sujet, soit du sujet et du prédicat ensemble. Résoudre est substituer à un terme sa définition, ou une partie de sa définition, ou encore un autre terme préalablement démontré du présent terme par une telle résolution » (A VI, 4 F, 2786 ; trad. fr. M. Parmentier, *L'estime des apparences*, p. 64 mod.).

4. Lettre à Conring (A II, 1, 153) ; pour le développement de cette thèse, voir la lettre au même de mars 1678 (A II, 1, 599-600), trad. fr. *in* C. Frémont, *Discours de métaphysique*, p. 138-140.

5. A VI, 1, 199. Sur les propositions « mixtes » et les procédures qui leur sont applicables, voir M. Mugnai, *Introduzione*, p. 81-82.

6. A VI, 1, 285.

7. A VI, 4, 586, Schrecker, 15. *Cf.* F. de Buzon, « Réduction et irréductibilité du sensible », p. 541-42.

nous-mêmes « par l'esprit seul », puis, conformément à la théorie aristotélicienne des objets communs à plusieurs sens[1], « le nombre [...], l'étendue [...], le mouvement » ; enfin les « qualités propres à un seul sens » comme les couleurs et les sons, dont la sensation ne peut être réduite à plusieurs autres plus élémentaires, même si la physique a pour tâche d'en fournir une explication causale, en les traitant comme les effets de mouvements dans la matière[2]. Cette liste évoluera, Leibniz distinguant bientôt, parmi ces « termes primitifs », ceux qui ne sont simples qu'« à notre égard », c'est-à-dire dont la simplicité apparente résulte de notre incapacité à en discerner les composants (couleurs, sons, plaisir, douleur...) ; ceux dont la signification donne prise à l'analyse, et qui, étant ainsi susceptibles de définition, seront dits « distincts » (étendue, nombres, mouvement)[3] ; ceux enfin qui seraient intrinsèquement inanalysables. Quant à ces derniers, Leibniz doute dès 1677 que nous parvenions jamais à les discerner[4]. Mais il persistera, tout au long de son œuvre, à penser ensemble l'irréductibilité d'expériences qu'aucun discours ne peut expliciter, et la possibilité pour l'analyse physique d'en distinguer les facteurs[5].

La définition occupe ainsi le centre de la théorie leibnizienne de la connaissance. Dans le domaine du savoir démonstratif, Leibniz considère avec Hobbes que les définitions sont les seuls principes indémontrables[6]. C'est en outre, comme on l'a vu, par la définition des termes d'une proposition, puis des éléments dégagés par ces premières définitions, que l'on parvient à la démonstration de la proposition.

1. Aristote, *De Anima* 425 a.

2. A VI, 1, 286-288.

3. Pour la distinction entre ces deux types d'attributs physiques en 1679, voir A VI, 4, 2003, traduit par M. Fichant sous le titre « Pensées pour l'instauration d'une nouvelle physique », *Philosophie* 39, 1993, p. 7-26.

4. « Nous ne pensons rien de parfaitement simple », A VI, 4, 26 ; *cf.* A VI 4, 159, 529, R 132.

5. À Vagetius, 1679 : « Toutes les [choses] qui ne s'expliquent pas par une définition, mais qu'il faut faire voir par un exemple, ou qui doivent être senties pour être connues, comme la chaleur, le froid, les couleurs, sont des premiers-connus [*protonoemata*] à notre égard ; mais en réalité ils peuvent être analysés, car ils ont leurs causes » (A II, 1, 497, notre trad.). À Sophie-Charlotte, 1702 : « Nous ne saurions comprendre comment ce tournoiement, ces tourbillons, et ces cercles, quand ils seraient vrais, feraient justement ces perceptions que nous avons du rouge, du chaud, du bruit [...] comment la perception que nous avons du vert résulte de celles que nous avons des deux couleurs qui le composent et comment une telle réfraction fait de ce[s] trois couleurs une seule. Cela va si loin que nous ne saurions même y donner des définitions nominales pour expliquer les termes » (A I, 21, 330). Voir C. Leduc, « Leibniz and Sensible Qualities ».

6. A II, 1, 190, 351, 599-600; A VI, 4, 2787, trad. fr. M. Parmentier, *L'estime des apparences*, p. 64-65.

Dans le domaine de la connaissance en général, la possibilité de définir un terme marque la frontière entre la part *confuse* de notre expérience et sa part *distincte*. Dès lors que pouvons décomposer la signification d'un mot en d'autres plus simples, ou que nous pouvons énumérer les propriétés d'une chose, en avons une connaissance *distincte :* « Nous avons [des choses] des notions distinctes en tant que nous connaissons certains de leurs caractères, grâce auxquels [...] nous pouvons les distinguer de toutes les autres, autrement dit, en tant que nous pouvons leur assigner une définition »[1]. La distinction sera plus ou moins parfaite selon que ces caractères distinctifs seront à leur tour distinctement connus.

Mais la définition reçoit à partir des dernières années 1670 un rôle plus important encore. Les travaux de mathématiques conduits par Leibniz durant son séjour à Paris (1672-1676) lui ont découvert que certaines notions, quoiqu'elles semblent se présenter à l'esprit de manière claire et distincte, sont en réalité contradictoires[2]. Ces contradictions nous sont dissimulées du fait que notre pensée, tacite ou énoncée, est dépendante des mots : ceux-ci opèrent une fonction d'abréviation qui supplée à notre incapacité à penser simultanément plusieurs idées. De sorte que « nous avons les idées des simples, nous n'avons que les caractères des composés »[3]. De ses premiers écrits jusqu'à la fin de son œuvre, Leibniz qualifie d'« aveugle » ou « suppositive » la pensée qui porte ainsi sur des truchements verbaux ou symboliques[4].

Pour nous assurer que ces expressions désignent bien des réalités, deux types d'expérience sont possibles : soit nous constatons que ce qu'elles désignent existe effectivement; soit nous nous représentons distinctement la manière dont la chose désignée peut être produite. Dans ce second cas, c'est une définition génétique, du type de celles employées par les géomètres depuis l'Antiquité, qui atteste la possibilité (c'est-à-dire le caractère

1. A VI, 4, 196. Sur les sources scolastiques de cette notion de distinction et sur la médiation décisive entre ces sources et Leibniz que représente la *Logica Hamburgensis* de Joachim Jungius [1638], voir M. Picon, « Vers la "doctrine de l'entendement en abrégé" », p. 109-110.

2. « Il paraît que nous pensons beaucoup de choses (confusément s'entend), qui impliquent pourtant contradiction, comme par exemple : le nombre de tous les nombres. D'où il ressort que nous devons considérer avec suspicion la notion d'infini, de minimum, de maximum, du plus parfait et de la Totalité elle-même » (A II, 1, 393; passage traduit et commenté *in* D. Rabouin, « Idée, représentation et correspondance mathématique chez Leibniz », p. 114-115. Voir l'article du même auteur dans le présent volume.

3. A VI, 3, 462; M. Mugnai, *Introduzione*, p. 39-40; M. Picon, « On the Constitution of Leibniz's Formalism ».

4. A VI, 1, 170, 551; A VI, 2, 481; A II, 1, 353-54; A VI, 4, 587-88; *Discours de métaphysique*, art. 24; *Nouveaux Essais*, II, 21 (A VI, 6, 185).

non contradictoire) du terme défini : « Démontrer la possibilité de quelque chose, c'est expliquer une hypothèse, ou un mode possible [de construction] [...] lequel étant posé, il s'ensuit que la chose est produite »[1]. À partir de 1677, Leibniz reprend l'expression scolastique de « définition réelle » pour désigner celles qui manifestent la possibilité de leur objet, en particulier les définitions génétiques qui nous en donnent une connaissance dite *a priori*[2]. Il importe de garder à l'esprit qu'il emploie cette expression latine en son sens traditionnel, désignant ce qui précède dans l'ordre de la nature, autrement dit la cause d'un fait donné (de même qu'*a posteriori* qualifie la connaissance par les effets). Ces qualifications sont donc relatives, la cause d'un fait étant en général l'effet d'un autre. Si Leibniz qualifie fréquemment d'*a posteriori* la connaissance d'expérience, c'est parce que celle-ci porte par définition sur ce qui existe, et que l'existence est naturellement postérieure à la possibilité. L'opposition aristotélicienne entre *a priori* et *a posteriori* ne correspond pas encore pour lui, comme ce sera le cas pour la plupart de ses successeurs, à celle de l'intellectuel et du sensible[3].

LES GRANDES SYNTHÈSES DES ANNÉES 1680 ET LA NOTION D'IDÉE

Ces divers éléments doctrinaux – distinction du confus et du distinct, thèse de la confusion inéliminable d'une part de notre rapport au monde et à nous-mêmes, dépendance de notre pensée à l'égard des mots, rôles des définitions – sont réunis par Leibniz en 1684 dans ses *Meditationes de cognitione, veritate et ideis*[4]. Ils y sont présentés sous la forme d'une hiérarchie des types de connaissance qui, tout en paraissant reprendre les étapes du traitement de l'idée et des définitions au premier livre de la *Logique* de Port-Royal, s'ordonne en réalité en fonction des différents degrés de la *distinction*, telle que la définissaient les logiques

1. A VI, 1, 515.

2. Leibniz envisage encore un autre type de connaissance *a priori* de la possibilité : celle que nous donnerait une définition « essentielle », qui « pousse l'analyse à bout jusqu'aux notions primitives » (*Discours de métaphysique*, art. 24) ; ces notions n'étant pas à la portée de la connaissance humaine, une telle connaissance n'appartient qu'à Dieu, exception faite des définitions des premiers nombres par sommation d'unités (*Nouveaux Essais*, IV, 2, 1 ; A VI, 6, 366).

3. R. M. Adams, *Leibniz*, p. 109-110.

4. *Acta Eruditorum* [novembre 1684], A VI, 4, 585-592, Schrecker 13-29.

scolastiques[1]. Cette typologie ascendante, partant des significations obscures pour culminer dans la connaissance adéquate, demeure ainsi bien plus proche du traitement par Joachim Jungius des « Différences entre notions »[2] que des grands traités contemporains qui, comme la *Recherche de la Vérité* de Malebranche, s'attachent successivement aux opérations des sens, puis de l'imagination, enfin de l'entendement. Les impressions des sens, par exemple, ne sont évoquées par Leibniz que comme un cas parmi d'autres de connaissance claire mais encore confuse, également illustrée par l'appréciation esthétique[3]. Quant à la connaissance des nombres, qui représente le plus haut degré de distinction dont nous soyons capables, elle n'est rapportée ni à l'entendement ni à la raison : pas plus que l'imagination, ces facultés ne sont nommées dans l'opuscule de 1684[4].

Dans quelle intention Leibniz a-t-il donné cette présentation des thèses épistémologiques qu'il avait élaborées au cours de la décennie précédente ? Les *Meditationes* se présentent d'abord comme une contribution à la « querelle des vraies et des fausses idées » qui oppose en France les partisans de Malebranche à ceux d'Arnauld : pour les premiers, une idée est un archétype intelligible subsistant dans l'entendement divin, où nous l'appréhendons immédiatement; pour les seconds, elle est l'acte même de l'esprit visant un objet, ou encore, en termes leibniziens, une « forme ou différence de nos pensées »[5]. Leibniz admet les deux acceptions, qui se rencontrent tour à tour dans ses écrits, mais il tient à proscrire leur confusion. Ainsi dans une note du printemps 1676, un peu postérieure à sa première lecture de Malebranche :

1. Sur cette classification, sa genèse et son rôle dans l'argumentaire leibnizien sur le statut de l'idée, voir M. Picon, « Vers la "doctrine de l'entendement en abrégé" ».

2. Voir en particulier sa *Logica Hamburgensis* [1638], L. I, chap. XV. Si ce chapitre n'est pas cité dans les *Meditationes*, Leibniz y fait référence dans un texte un peu postérieur (A VI, 4, 726).

3. « De même nous voyons que les peintres et les autres artistes reconnaissent très bien ce qui est bien fait et ce qui est mal fait, mais que souvent ils ne peuvent donner les raisons de leurs jugements et répondent, lorsqu'on les questionne, que dans l'œuvre qui leur déplaît il manque un je ne sais quoi » (A VI, 4, 586, sch. 15). La perception sensible disparaîtra même entièrement de la nouvelle version de cette classification donnée à l'article 24 du *Discours de métaphysique*. Leibniz déclare fréquemment s'accorder avec Descartes sur la différence entre clair et distinct, mais cet accord, résultat d'une lecture superficielle des *Principes de la philosophie*, masque une nette divergence entre les deux auteurs (voir M. Picon, « Vers la "doctrine de l'entendement en abrégé" », p. 105-107).

4. A VI, 4, 587, Schrecker 17. Leibniz reproche simplement à certains auteurs d'abuser du terme d'*idée* « pour donner du poids à certaines de leurs imaginations » (A VI, 4, 590, Schrecker 25).

5. *Discours de métaphysique*, art. 26 (A VI, 4, 1570).

> L'idée peut être prise de deux façons savoir *pour la qualité ou forme de la pensée,* comme la vélocité et la direction le sont du mouvement ou bien *pro objecto immediato sive proximo perceptionis.* Et de cette manière l'idée ne serait pas une façon d'être de notre âme. Et cela est apparemment le sentiment de Platon ou de l'auteur de la *Recherche*. Car quand l'âme pense à l'être, à l'identité, à la pensée, à la duration, elle a un certain objet immédiat ou cause prochaine de sa perception. Et de cette manière il se peut que nous voyions tout en Dieu [...]. Ces formules ou façons de parler ont quelque chose de vrai, mais pour parler juste, il faut donner des significations constantes aux termes [1].

Le même souci de distinguer entre ces acceptions de l'idée inspirera la rédaction des *Meditationes* et de l'article 26 du *Discours de métaphysique* [2]. Car leur confusion est pour Leibniz le défaut rédhibitoire de la preuve cartésienne de l'existence de Dieu, véritable cible de l'opuscule de 1684. Lorsque Descartes écrit « je ne puis rien exprimer par des paroles, lorsque j'entends ce que je dis, que de cela même il ne soit certain qu'il y a en moi l'idée de la chose qui est signifiée par ces paroles » [3], il suppose l'acception intentionnelle de l'idée dont Arnauld se fera le défenseur [4]; mais il prête également à l'idée « claire et distincte » de Dieu une « réalité objective » propre à fonder la démonstration de l'existence de ce dont elle est l'idée [5]. Encore eût-il fallu, objecte Leibniz, qu'aient été définis les critères de la clarté et de la distinction. Une fois cette lacune comblée par la classification des notions des *Meditationes,* il en infère que l'appréhension de l'idée, au sens objectif où elle est autre chose qu'une simple pensée, ne pourrait être le fait que d'une pensée « intuitive » qu'il juge hors de notre portée (voir *infra*). Si bien que, lorsque l'objet d'un raisonnement n'est pas donné empiriquement, seule une définition réelle peut garantir qu'il n'est pas contradictoire, autrement dit que ce raisonnement a bien un objet : une idée, dont la réalité ne nous est connue que moyennant ce procédé indirect [6].

1. A VI, 3, 315-316.
2. « Pour bien concevoir ce que c'est qu'idée, il faut prévenir une équivocation... » (A VI, 4, 1570).
3. AT VII, 160.
4. *Logique* de Port-Royal, I, 1.
5. AT VII 40-41, 161.
6. « Il arrive assurément que nous croyons souvent à tort avoir dans l'esprit les *idées* des choses, lorsque nous supposons faussement que nous avons déjà expliqué certains termes dont nous nous servons. Et il n'est pas vrai, ou il prête certainement à équivoque de dire avec certains que nous ne pouvons parler d'une chose, en comprenant ce que nous disons, que nous n'ayons l'idée de cette chose » (A VI 4, 588, Schrecker 19 ; critique reprise dans le *Discours de métaphysique,* art. 23). *Cf.* les lettres à Burnett de l'été 1698 (GP III, 224) et janvier 1699 :

Car Leibniz ne croit plus à la possibilité, brièvement envisagée en 1676, que nous « voyons tout en Dieu », ni même que les idées les plus simples soient, d'une manière ou d'une autre, les « objets immédiats de la perception »[1]. Pour être intuitive, la pensée devrait non seulement être entièrement distincte (c'est-à-dire adéquate), mais également affranchie de l'abréviation opérée par les signes. Or Leibniz maintient sa thèse de 1675 selon laquelle des signes nous sont indispensables pour penser toute notion composée[2], et il ne revient pas sur ses doutes quant à notre capacité d'atteindre les notions « distinctes primitives » ou absolument simples. Le *Discours de métaphysique* les confirmera, « la plupart des connaissances humaines n'étant que confuses ou bien suppositives »[3].

Si Leibniz ne partage pas la thèse malebranchienne de la vision en Dieu, il ne se range pas pour autant à la conception de l'idée d'Arnauld. C'est une troisième acception de l'idée, inspirée du néo-platonisme de la Renaissance, qu'il évoque aux dernières lignes des *Meditationes :* elle n'est ni l'objet de la pensée, ni son acte intentionnel, mais une faculté ou disposition, inscrite dans notre esprit, que présuppose tout acte de pensée. Cette faculté innée constitue une médiation entre l'idée divine, d'après laquelle toute chose existante a été créée, et les connaissances que nous sommes capables de prendre de ces choses. Leibniz l'avait ainsi définie en 1677 :

> Qu'il y ait en nous une idée des choses n'est donc rien d'autre que ceci : Dieu, auteur des choses et de l'esprit, a imprimé à celui-ci une faculté de penser telle qu'il puisse tirer de ses opérations des [conclusions] correspondant parfaitement à celles qui suivent des choses[4].

« ceux qui décident sur la prétention de leurs idées, ne disent rien, s'ils ne les expliquent, et s'ils ne viennent au raisonnement suivant les règles de la Logique » (A I, 16, 511).

1. *Cf.* passage de 1676 cité *supra* p. 270. Vers 1685, Leibniz notera en marge d'une lettre de Malebranche : « Il explique ici que, comme je le croyais moi-même autrefois, l'idée est l'objet immédiat de l'esprit » (A VI, 4, 2651, notre traduction).

2. « Le plus souvent [...] nous n'embrassons pas toute la nature de la chose à la fois, mais nous substituons aux choses des signes [...]. J'ai l'habitude d'appeler aveugle ou encore symbolique cette pensée dont nous faisons usage en algèbre, en arithmétique, et presque partout » (A VI, 4, 587-88, Schrecker 17-19). Sur la continuité entre ces deux époques, voir M. Mugnai, *Astrazione e realtà*, p. 33-34.

3. *Discours de métaphysique,* art. 24. L'article 25 en tire cependant, quant à la « vision » de l'idée, une conclusion un peu différente de celle des *Meditationes* (voir M. Picon, « Vers la "doctrine de l'entendement en abrégé" », p. 126-128).

4. A VI, 4, 1371 ; *TLM* 446. Sur l'origine de cette conception de l'idée chez Marcile Ficin, voir T. Dagron, *Toland et Leibniz*, p. 136-139.

Les *Meditationes* ajoutent que ces connaissances virtuelles « correspondent à cela même que nous percevrions en Dieu » si, comme le voulait Malebranche, nous saisissions les idées par une perception transitive[1].

L'idée ainsi conçue réapparaît dans le *Discours de Métaphysique*, comme un cas particulier du rapport d'expression qui lie chaque substance à son créateur : « cette qualité de notre âme en tant qu'elle exprime quelque nature, forme, ou essence, est proprement l'idée de la chose [...]. Car notre âme exprime Dieu et l'univers, et toutes les essences aussi bien que toutes les existences » (art. 26).

À la différence des *Meditationes*, l'article 27 du *Discours* rattache à ce thème la question traditionnelle de la théorie de la connaissance : celle de l'origine de nos notions. À s'en tenir à l'« exactitude des vérités métaphysiques » exposées aux articles précédents, la question ne se pose plus : toutes les connaissances sont innées à l'âme à titre virtuel, et celle-ci n'est affectée immédiatement par aucun objet extérieur[2]. Ce point détermine le statut de toutes les discussions ultérieures sur l'origine, innée ou empirique, de nos connaissances : il s'agit de « doxologies ou practicologies », autrement dit de concessions faites à l'usage, ou de façons de parler pour se faire entendre du plus grand nombre[3]. Mais un point doit être défendu : renouant avec des réflexions anciennes qui n'avaient pas trouvé place dans l'argumentaire anti-cartésien des *Meditationes*, Leibniz conclut l'article 27 en soulignant le statut particulier de certaines notions :

> de quelque manière qu'on le prenne, il est toujours faux de dire que toutes nos notions viennent des sens qu'on appelle extérieurs, car celle que j'ai de moi et de mes pensées et par conséquent de l'être, de la substance, de l'action, de l'identité, et de bien d'autres, viennent d'une expérience interne[4].

Ces dernières lignes contiennent l'un des points essentiels que Leibniz s'efforcera de faire valoir, près de vingt ans plus tard, contre Locke. Mais la doctrine de l'innéité, dans les termes de laquelle il le reformulera, sera porteuse de nouvelles difficultés.

1. A VI, 4, 591, Schrecker, 29.

2. Comme Leibniz l'écrira encore dans les *Nouveaux Essais* : « toutes les pensées et actions de notre âme viennent de son propre fonds, sans lui pouvoir être données par les sens » (VI, 6, 74).

3. Cf. *Nouveaux Essais*, 1, 1, 1 ; A VI 6 74.

4. A VI, 4, 1572.

Le défi lockien

Parmi les évolutions majeures de la pensée de Leibniz au cours de la décennie qui suit la rédaction du *Discours de Métaphysique,* deux affectent particulièrement les thèses dont nous venons de retracer les premières systématisations. Poursuivant les réflexions sur l'union de l'âme et du corps exposées à l'article 33 du *Discours*, il élabore d'une part la doctrine de ce qu'il appellera à partir de 1696 « l'harmonie pré-établie » [1], selon laquelle « le corps exprime par ses propres lois tout ce qui se passe dans l'âme » [2]; il rencontre d'autre part, vers 1695, les thèses empiristes exposées par Locke dans son *Essai concernant l'entendement humain* (1690). Les questions noétiques ne représenteront que l'un des aspects de leurs divergences, dont les principaux enjeux auront trait à la notion de substance et à l'immortalité naturelle de l'âme [3]. La défense de celle-ci amènera Leibniz à reprendre, en les transformant, les éléments de noétique exposés dans les années 1680, et à leur surimposer des motifs nouveaux, principalement groupés autour de deux thèmes : l'innéité et l'intelligible pur.

Au premier livre de l'*Essai*, Locke dénonce la thèse des idées innées comme le refuge des préjugés. Leibniz lui oppose une théorie alternative de l'innéité, fondée sur sa propre conception des idées comme facultés ou dispositions qui s'actualisent à l'occasion des expériences [4]. Mais il invoque en outre les notions énumérées à l'article 27 du *Discours de métaphysique* comme provenant d'une « expérience interne » [5]. Il leur confère désormais le statut, autrefois refusé aux idées, d'« objets immédiats de l'esprit » :

> [...] peut-on nier qu'il y ait beaucoup d'inné en notre esprit, puisque nous sommes innés à nous-mêmes pour ainsi dire, et qu'il y a en nous : Être, Unité, Substance, Durée, Changement, Action, Perception, Plaisir, et mille autres objets de nos idées intellectuelles ? Et ces objets étant immédiats et

1. *Éclaircissement du nouveau système de la communication des substances,* GP IV 496.

2. Bodemann LH, p. 96; *cf.* annotation à la *Recherche de la vérité* [entre 1686 et 1699] : « Je ne crois pas qu'il y ait une intellection pure, à laquelle rien ne réponde dans le corps » (A VI, 4, 1815).

3. Lettre à Burnett, déc. 1703 (A I, 22, 708-709); N. Jolley, *Leibniz and Locke*, chap. II et VI; M. Parmentier, *Leibniz-Locke*, p. 246-248.

4. A VI, 6, 52, 106; M. Parmentier, *Leibniz*-Locke, p. 134 *sq.* Cela n'empêche pas Leibniz d'employer couramment *idée* au sens lockien, selon lequel ce terme désigne les perceptions occurrentes de l'esprit.

5. Ce point est justement noté par N. Jolley, *The Light of the Soul*, p. 181-185.

toujours présents à notre entendement [...] pourquoi s'étonner que nous disons que ces idées nous sont innées avec tout ce qui en dépend ?[1]

Nous sommes ainsi en présence de deux acceptions différentes de l'innéité : selon la première, toutes les idées nous sont innées à titre de dispositions, dont certaines seront actualisées par l'expérience; selon la seconde, un certain nombre d'idées nous sont innées en tant qu'objets immédiats découverts en nous-mêmes par la réflexion. L'équivoque vient à son comble lorsque Leibniz écrit : « je voudrais bien savoir, comment nous pourrions avoir l'idée de l'être, si nous n'étions des Êtres nous mêmes, et ne trouvions ainsi l'être en nous »[2]. Selon les différentes composantes de sa doctrine dégagées jusqu'ici, les thèses sous-jacentes à cette interrogation sont les suivantes :

– nos âmes comportent, parmi leurs caractères constitutifs (que l'on peut dire « innés »), une disposition ou tendance à former la notion abstraite d'*être* (de même que celles de « toutes les essences et toutes les existences » – cf. *DM* art. 26).

– cette tendance est actualisée par ceci que nous éprouvons réflexivement que nous sommes des êtres, au sens concret de substances qui sont les sujets de changements, d'actions, de perceptions...

– à partir de cette notion de substance que nous formons lorsque l'expérience interne actualise une disposition constitutive de notre esprit, nous organisons les données de notre expérience externe autour de sujets que nous supposons semblables à nous[3].

Contre la comparaison empiriste de l'esprit à une *tabula rasa*, Leibniz fait ainsi valoir deux argumentaires concurrents : l'un correspond à son acception propre de l'idée comme virtualité, solidaire de sa métaphysique de l'expression; l'autre à la thématique de l'expérience interne (*idée* étant alors pris non plus au sens de virtualité, mais au sens de *notion*)[4]. Ces arguments ne sont pas inconciliables entre eux, mais Leibniz semble ne s'être jamais soucié d'expliciter leur cohérence.

1. « Préface », A, VI, 6, 51-52.

2. A VI, 6, 86; commenté par N. Jolley, *The Light of the Soul*, p. 185.

3. Pour les premières formulations de cette thèse vers 1677, voir M. Picon, « Vers la "doctrine de l'entendement en abrégé" », p. 110-111 n. 24.

4. Ce second argument, plus exotérique, offre en outre l'avantage rhétorique de pouvoir être rattaché, au moins apparemment, au traitement par Locke de la réflexion : « Il est très vrai que nos perceptions des idées, viennent ou des sens extérieurs, ou du sens interne, qu'on peut appeler réflexion; mais cette réflexion ne se borne pas aux seules opérations de l'esprit, comme il est dit chap. premier, § 4. Elle va jusqu'à l'esprit lui-même, et c'est en s'apercevant de lui, que nous nous apercevons de la substance » (A VI, 6, 14).

Plus délicat encore est le problème que pose la notion, apparue notamment dans l'extrait de la *Préface* cité *supra*, d'« idée intellectuelle ». Au livre II, Leibniz définira l'intellect ou entendement par son opération propre :

> Ainsi dans mon sens l'entendement répond à ce qui chez les Latins est appelé *intellectus*, et l'exercice de cette faculté s'appelle intellection, qui est une perception distincte jointe à la faculté de réfléchir [...]. Toute perception jointe à cette faculté est une pensée [...] de sorte qu'on peut dire que l'intellection a lieu lorsque la pensée est distincte [1].

Selon les *Meditationes*, la distinction admettait divers degrés, depuis celui d'une simple description jusqu'à celui des notions mathématiques [2]. En était en revanche exclu le *plaisir*, exemple canonique de notion claire-confuse. Comment expliquer qu'il figure désormais au nombre des « objets de nos idées intellectuelles » (cf. *supra*)? Comment la hiérarchie des notions des *Meditationes*, auxquelles Leibniz renvoie incessamment le lecteur des *Nouveaux Essais*, s'accorde-t-elle avec sa nouvelle psychologie des facultés ? Nous tenterons de le comprendre en examinant, dans ses trois versions successives, un texte un peu antérieur aux *Nouveaux Essais :* la lettre « sur ce qui passe les sens et la matière ».

Quelques mois avant de commencer à rédiger ses commentaires à l'*Essai* de Locke, Leibniz consigne dans une lettre à la reine de Prusse Sophie Charlotte les réponses que lui inspirent les questions « s'il y a quelque chose dans nos pensées, qui ne vienne point des sens; et s'il y a quelque chose dans la nature qui ne soit point matériel » [3]. L'interrogation est ancienne, mais la menace matérialiste qu'incarne à ses yeux le philosophe irlandais John Toland, alors admis dans le cercle de la reine, lui confère une urgence nouvelle [4].

De même qu'en 1684, Leibniz donne à ses réflexions la forme d'une hiérarchie ascendante des types de connaissance, mais il la rapporte cette fois aux facultés de l'esprit. La description du premier degré de la

1. A VI, 6, 173.

2. A VI, 4, 587.

3. Ces questions formaient le sujet d'une lettre reçue de France par l'électrice Sophie, dont l'auteur et la date de composition demeurent obscurs. Peu satisfait des réponses apportées par l'auteur, Leibniz propose les siennes (A I, 21, 328-346).

4. L'enjeu du débat avec Toland est l'immortalité de l'âme, et plus particulièrement la question de savoir si elle lui appartient comme un attribut naturel, ou si elle lui est conférée par grâce divine. Voir T. Dagron, *Toland et Leibniz*, chap. V.

connaissance, *claire* mais *confuse*[1], présente une remarquable stabilité par rapport aux exposés précédents (à ceci près que Leibniz en situe désormais la source dans les seuls sens externes, sans reprendre – et pour cause, nous le verrons – les exemples du jugement esthétique, du plaisir ou de la douleur qui l'illustraient autrefois).

C'est encore aux cinq sens – lorsque leurs données ne sont plus prises séparément, mais collectivement, et unifiées par le « sens commun »[2] – que nous sommes redevables d'un grand nombre de notions que la première version de la lettre qualifie d'abord de « plus intelligibles », les suivantes de « distinctes ». Comme dans les *Meditationes*, Leibniz donne pour critère de cette distinction la possibilité de définir l'objet perçu. Mais, tandis que le texte de 1684 envisageait une progression continue de la distinction des notions, culminant dans la connaissance adéquate que nous avons des nombres, la lettre de 1702 manifeste, en ses rédactions successives, l'effort de Leibniz pour subordonner cette hiérarchie continue à la défense d'une dichotomie radicale : celle de l'imaginable et de l'intelligible[3].

Dans la première version de la lettre, le qualificatif d'*intelligible* est encore susceptible de degrés, les notions mathématiques fournies par le sens commun étant « plus intelligibles » que les sensibles propres. La seconde version met fin à cet usage, *intelligible* étant pris désormais en un sens absolu où il désigne proprement ce qui n'est pas imaginable. La troisième version confirme cette transformation :

> Il y a donc encore des objets d'une autre nature, qui ne sont point du tout compris dans ce qu'on remarque dans les objets des sens en particulier ou en commun, et qui ne sont point non plus des objets de l'imagination. Ainsi outre le *sensible* et l'*imaginable*, il y a ce qui n'est qu'*intelligible*, comme étant l'objet du seul *entendement*, et tel est l'objet de ma pensée, quand je pense à moi-même. Cette pensée de *moi*, qui m'aperçois des objets sensibles, et de ma propre action qui en résulte, ajoute quelque chose aux

1. Nous laissons de côté le cas marginal des notions « obscures » brièvement évoquées en 1684, mais disparues dès la reprise de la classification dans le *Discours*, et dont il n'est plus question ici.

2. Sur cette faculté de la psychologie aristotélicienne et sa réapparition chez Leibniz, voir F. de Buzon, « Réduction et irréductibilité du sensible ».

3. Cette dichotomie était elle aussi apparue dans certains écrits leibniziens à partir de 1676 (notamment en A VI 3 528-74) et avait pris une importance croissante dans les années 1680. Mais, tandis que la hiérarchie des notions visait à récuser l'invocation cartésienne des idées « claires et distinctes », l'opposition de l'imaginable et de l'intelligible intervenait quant à elle dans des contextes argumentatifs différents, critiquant en particulier les physiques exclusivement mécanistes et les menaces qu'elles recelaient pour l'immortalité de l'âme (ainsi en A VI, 4, 722). La lettre de 1702 se distingue par son effort pour intégrer les acquis de ces deux réflexions.

> objets des sens. [...] Et comme je conçois que d'autres êtres peuvent aussi avoir le droit de dire *moi*, ou qu'on pourrait le dire pour eux, c'est par là que je conçois ce qu'on appelle la *substance* en général, et c'est aussi la considération de moi-même qui me fournit d'autres notions de *métaphysique*, comme de *cause, effet, action, similitude*, etc., et même celles de la *Logique* et de la *Morale*[1].

Ces notions d'un troisième ordre, dont l'appréhension est l'opération propre d'une faculté appelée d'abord *intelligence* puis *entendement*, ne forment cependant pas un groupe homogène :

– celles de *moi*, de *substance* et d'*action* provenaient, selon le *Discours de Métaphysique*, de l' « expérience interne ». Qu'elles échappent à l'imagination était une thèse défendue de longue date par Leibniz[2], mais il avait fréquemment insisté sur leur caractère *confus*. C'était justement pour le faire comprendre au sujet de la substance qu'il avait fréquemment renvoyé ses correspondants à la définition du clair-confus donnée dans les *Meditationes*[3]. Dans la première des trois versions de la lettre de 1702, ces notions étaient encore réputées provenir d'un « sens interne »[4] ; à partir de la deuxième version, elles sont assignées au seul entendement (le sens interne étant désormais assimilé à l'imagination)[5] ;

– mais ce n'est que dans la troisième version du texte que Leibniz adjoint à ces notions formées par réflexion sur nous-mêmes les concepts abstraits de la métaphysique, de la logique et de la morale. Parmi eux, ceux de *cause*, d'*effet* et d'*action* sont des catégories fondamentales de la théorie leibnizienne de la substance, élaborée depuis la fin des années 1670 en fonction de sa découverte des vraies lois du mouvement. Ces notions relèvent ainsi de la métaphysique traditionnellement dite « spéciale » ou théologie naturelle, définie par Leibniz dès les premières années 1680 comme « la science des choses intellectuelles » ou « qui peuvent seulement

1. A I, 2, 339.

2. Notes sur Foucher [1676], A VI, 3, 319-21) ; lettre à Elisabeth, nov. 1678, A II, 1, 663.

3. À Burnett, janv. 1699, A I, 16, 510. Même thèse au sujet de la *pensée* dans les lettres à Arnauld d'oct. 1687 : « je demeure d'accord avec le père Malebranche que nous n'avons point d'idée distincte de la pensée, non plus que de la couleur. Ce n'est donc que par sentiment confus que nous en avons quelque notion » (A II, 2, 235 ; *cf.* A II, 2, 252). Sur ce point, et en général sur le rôle de l'expérience réflexive de l'*ego*, voir C. Leduc, *Substance, individu et connaissance*, p. 224-236.

4. *GP* VI 489. De même, dans l'*Échantillon des réflexions* sur l'*Essai* de 1698, la réflexion de l'esprit sur lui-même, d'où proviennent ces notions, est identifiée à l'opération du « sens interne » (A VI, 6, 14).

5. Dans les *Nouveaux Essais*, la distinction entre « sens interne » et « entendement pur » se brouillera à nouveau (A VI, 6, 128), confirmant le caractère instable de cette topique.

être conçues [*quae tantum intelligi possunt*] »[1], par opposition à celles qui peuvent être imaginées. La *similitude* en revanche est un concept traditionnel de la théorie générale de l'étant ou métaphysique « générale », en charge des objets les plus abstraits de la pensée[2]. Leibniz se félicitait depuis 1677 d'avoir donné de la similitude une définition suprêmement générale, et pour cela particulièrement féconde en géométrie[3]. Écrire qu'elle provient de notre réflexion sur nous-mêmes ne peut se justifier qu'en supposant d'une part la doctrine scolastique qui fait de la similitude l'une des « affections » qui « dérivent » du concept général d'étant, d'autre part la thèse, que développeront les *Nouveaux Essais*, selon laquelle nous ne trouvons qu'en nous-mêmes ce concept d'étant.

Une fois constitué ce domaine propre au seul entendement, Leibniz ajoute, dans la dernière version du texte, cette récapitulation :

> Il y a donc trois rangs de notions : les *sensibles* seulement, qui sont les objets affectés à chaque sens en particulier, les *sensibles et intelligibles à la fois*, qui appartiennent au sens commun, les *intelligibles* seulement, qui sont propres à l'entendement. Les premières et les secondes ensemble sont imaginables, mais les troisièmes sont au-dessus de l'imagination. Les secondes et les troisièmes sont intelligibles et distinctes ; mais les premières sont confuses, quoi que claires et reconnaissables.

La transformation opérée au fil des rédactions de cette lettre a ainsi consisté à soustraire les données de notre réflexion sur nous-mêmes à la faculté sensitive et à les présenter désormais comme exemptes de la confusion caractéristique de l'expérience : agrégées aux notions abstraites de la métaphysique, elles forment désormais l'apanage de l'entendement. L'autonomie de cette faculté par rapport au corps est ainsi attestée, et avec elle le caractère immatériel de l'âme qui en est le sujet[4].

La hiérarchie de la lettre de 1702, reconduite avec plus ou moins de constance dans les *Nouveaux Essais*, n'est donc plus celle des *Meditationes* de 1684 : elle est dominée par la catégorie nouvelle des idées intellectuelles, dont il importe de reconnaître le caractère équivoque :

1. A VI, 4, 510 ; 514. *Cf.* lettre au Landgrave de décembre 1686, A II, 2, 129.

2. Pour cette définition de la métaphysique, voir A VI, 1, 171 ou VI 2, 408. Sur l'appartenance de la notion de similitude à cette discipline, *De Analysi Situs* [1693], GM V 179-180, trad. angl. G. H. R. Parkinson, *Philosophical Papers and Letters*, p. 254-255.

3. Lettre à Gallois, A II, 1, 568 ; *cf.* A VI 4, 723.

4. Sur cet argument traditionnel en faveur de l'immortalité naturelle de l'âme, voir T. Dagron, *Toland et Leibniz*, p. 145.

– en un sens large, correspondant à la définition de l'entendement que nous avons rencontrée au livre II des *Nouveaux Essais*, les idées intellectuelles sont les notions distinctes en général, au premier rang desquelles se trouvent les notions suprêmement abstraites de la métaphysique dite *générale*. En ce sens, la similitude en fait partie, mais le plaisir, la douleur et les autres affections de l'âme devraient en être exclus.

– en un sens restreint, *intelligible* désigne ce qui n'est pas imaginable ou figurable; au premier rang de ces notions se trouvent celles, éminemment concrètes, mais données jusque-là par Leibniz pour confuses, que nous livre l'expérience interne; puis celles de la métaphysique *spéciale*, dont une connaissance distincte n'est possible que de manière médiate, moyennant des procédures discursives mettant en œuvre des systèmes de signes[1].

Leibniz réunit donc ici sous la catégorie de l'intelligible deux types de notions, dont il étend à chacun le statut noétique de l'autre: les notions abstraites sont désormais réputées être au-delà de l'imagination[2], tandis que celles tirées de l'expérience interne sont données pour distinctes[3].

Le corpus leibnizien comporte donc bien une théorie de la connaissance, bâtie autour de la description de ce que Leibniz appelle d'abord le « sensible », puis le « simple à notre égard ». C'est de ce registre que relève, dans la plupart de ses écrits, l'apport fondamental de l'« expérience interne » ou réflexion[4]. Ce corpus comporte, *par ailleurs,*

1. Un exemple éminent du rôle indispensable des signes pour penser ce qui n'est pas imaginable avait été donné à Leibniz en 1678 par l'ensemble de ses calculs qui avaient abouti à l'établissement des vraies lois du mouvement en fonction du concept métaphysique de force.

2. Selon la psychologie d'inspiration aristotélicienne que Leibniz présupposait encore en 1677, en revanche, l'abstraction des concepts généraux était l'opération propre de l'imagination (A VI, 4, 58).

3. Que cet apparent renversement doctrinal ne soit en réalité qu'un ajustement tactique de vocabulaire, c'est ce qu'incite à penser la suite de la lettre à Burnett de janvier 1699 citée *supra* n. 6 p. 279 : « [J]e crois qu'on a une idée claire, mais non pas une idée distincte de la substance, qui vient à mon avis de ce que nous en avons le sentiment intérieur en nous-mêmes qui sommes des substances. [...] Cependant il dépend de chacun de prendre les termes comme bon lui semble, et il est vrai qu'on a coutume de dire avec M. Locke, qu'on entend distinctement un son; aussi crois-je en ce sens que M. de Worcester aurait raison de dire qu'on connaît distinctement, c'est-à-dire clairement ce que c'est que la substance » (A I, 16, 511).

4. Cette thèse, contredite en 1702 pour les besoins de l'argumentaire anti-matérialiste, sera reprise ultérieurement. Ainsi dans cette note postérieure à 1704 : « Que nous ne soyons

une théorie de la science ou savoir démonstratif, développée dans le prolongement de relectures modernes de la logique aristotélicienne, au premier rang desquelles celles de Jungius et de Hobbes. La question des fondements de ce savoir trouve sa réponse dans la doctrine des définitions et des principes. La théorie de la connaissance et celle de la science se sont ainsi constituées chez Leibniz au fil d'élaborations relativement indépendantes, la première n'ayant pas été conçue par lui comme un préalable pour la seconde. C'est le sens de son affirmation selon laquelle « la question de l'origine de nos idées et de nos maximes n'est pas préliminaire en philosophie » [1].

Certains de ses écrits postérieurs à 1690 se caractérisent toutefois par un effort pour faire valoir entre ces deux versants, noétique et épistémologique, un rapport de fondement : si nous sommes capables de démonstrations, c'est, déclare alors Leibniz, parce que notre rapport à nous-mêmes, actualisant nos dispositions innées à concevoir ce qui n'est pas imaginable, en constitue la condition de possibilité [2]. Locke se serait ainsi formé une conception plus juste de l'âme s'il avait mieux compris la nature des démonstrations mathématiques [3]. Peu importe alors à Leibniz que cet argumentaire contredise la distinction entre le clair et le distinct qu'il avait constamment défendue jusque-là. Il s'agit désormais pour lui de conforter le statut de notre âme comme substance immatérielle, sujet d'une connaissance réflexive distincte parce que supra-sensible, afin d'apporter la preuve de son immortalité naturelle. Une épistémologie bâtie à partir des années 1670 autour d'une théorie des définitions et de l'opposition entre le sensible et le discursif fait ainsi place,

pas des substances, voilà qui est contraire à l'expérience, car nous n'aurions aucune connaissance de la substance si nous ne la tirions de notre expérience intime de nous-mêmes, lorsque nous percevons l'*Ego* et que, d'après cet exemple, nous attribuons à Dieu et aux autres monades l'appellation de substance » (Grua II, 558, notre traduction).

1. A VI, 6, 6.

2. Ce rapport de conditionnement entre connaissance réflexive et savoir démonstratif présentera cependant, jusqu'aux derniers écrits, un caractère instable : on confrontera sur ce point les *Principes de la grâce* (§ 5) et la *Monadologie* (art. 30). Selon les premiers, « les Ames sont capables de faire des actes réflexifs, et de considérer ce qu'on appelle moi, substance, âme, esprit, en un mot, les choses et les vérités immatérielles. Et c'est ce qui nous rend susceptibles des sciences ou des connaissances démonstratives » (GP VI, 600); selon la seconde, « c'est aussi par la connaissance des vérités nécessaires et par leurs abstractions, que nous sommes élevés aux Actes réflexifs » (GP VI, 612).

3. A I, 22, 708; GP III 473.

sans disparaître entièrement[1], à une théorie de la connaissance dominée par l'opposition entre l'imaginable et l'intelligible.

Marine PICON
(ENS Lyon)

1. Dans un passage remarquable du livre II des *Nouveaux Essais,* Leibniz retrouve la conception des fondements de la science qui soutenait depuis toujours ses espoirs pour son avancement. Il n'est plus alors question d'innéité, ni des prérogatives d'une faculté incorporelle : « Et il faut que ces deux géométries, celle de l'aveugle et celle du paralytique, se rencontrent et s'accordent et même reviennent aux mêmes idées, quoiqu'il n'y ait point d'images communes. Ce qui fait encore voir combien il faut distinguer les images des idées exactes *qui consistent dans les définitions* » (A VI, 6, 137 ; nous soulignons).

QUATRIÈME PARTIE

LA RÉCEPTION

LA RÉCEPTION DE LEIBNIZ EN FRANCE ET EN ANGLETERRE AU XVIIIe SIÈCLE

LA RÉCEPTION FRANÇAISE

Présenter les principales perspectives de la réception de Leibniz en France au XVIIIe siècle suppose certainement de prendre ses distances avec deux grandes images dominantes. L'une qui fait de l'institution d'un empirisme enfin débarrassé de ses oripeaux métaphysiques l'identité des Lumières spécifiquement françaises, l'autre qui considère que la preuve de ce triomphe peut être administrée grâce à l'évaluation du rapport de force entre Cartésiens et Newtoniens d'une part, et grâce, d'autre part, à la lecture du manifeste empiriste que constituerait l'*Encyclopédie*. Dans ce cadre de pensée, Leibniz serait immanquablement situé du côté des Cartésiens, ces philosophes métaphysiciens qui résistent à l'avènement d'une science et d'une philosophie modernes. C'est bien en ce sens que Voltaire s'évertue à moquer, dans son *Candide*, le meilleur des mondes possibles grâce à la figure de Pangloss qui enseigne la « métaphysico-théologo-cosmolonigologie », l'enjeu est alors clairement de ridiculiser la théodicée en réponse sans doute, pour une part, à la diffusion de la pensée de Leibniz à laquelle Émilie du Châtelet procède dans ses *Institutions de physique* de 1740. Émilie du Châtelet (1706-1749), grande connaisseuse de Leibniz et de Newton, auteure des *Institutions de Physique* de 1740, traductrice de la *Fable des Abeilles* de Mandeville et des *Principia mathematica philosophiae naturalis* de Newton, est souvent présentée comme l'introductrice en France des idées de Leibniz. Il n'y a qu'à lire la « Lettre critique » que La Mettrie[1] fait figurer dans la deuxième édition de son *Histoire naturelle de l'âme* en 1747 pour mesurer l'importance de la

1. La question de l'attribution de ce texte à La Mettrie est actuellement discutée même si elle n'est pas, aujourd'hui, absolument remise en cause.

Marquise du Châtelet pour la diffusion des idées leibniziennes et la reconnaissance dont elle jouit.

> Je n'hésite pas, Madame, de soumettre mes réflexions à votre jugement, la justesse de votre esprit et l'étendue de vos connaissances semblent déjà me promettre votre suffrage. Vous connaissez parfaitement les Monades de Leibniz, vous êtes même le premier des philosophes français qui nous ait développé son système avec toute la clarté dont il est susceptible : mais, Madame, vous avez eu la sagesse de n'en parler que par rapport à la Physique des Mixtes, et d'abandonner les idées de ce Philosophe sur les perceptions qu'il attribue à ses Etres simples. Tant cette dernière partie de l'Hypothèse Leibnizienne vous a paru au-delà des bornes mêmes de la Philosophie[1].

Elle est l'une des sources privilégiées de l'*Encyclopédie* pour un certain nombre d'entrées qui présentent la pensée de Leibniz : pensons simplement à « Contradiction » ou « Raison suffisante » qui sont des reprises de certains passages de ses *Institutions de physique* au cœur même de l'*Encyclopédie*.

Il est ainsi possible de nuancer la lecture que Voltaire fait de Leibniz et de montrer comment Leibniz vient troubler le jeu des antinomies rassurantes (métaphysique rationaliste contre *experimental philosophy*, Cartésiens contre Newtoniens, etc.), et cela est possible grâce à quelques décisions historiographiques. 1) La *République des Lettres* qu'elle soit un idéal plus ou moins utopique ou une réalité aux multiples facettes[2] rend mal aisé de consacrer un chapitre à la réception exclusive de Leibniz en France. Les réseaux de correspondants, les Académies de Paris, de Berlin et de Londres, mais aussi les Académies de province (Dijon, Lyon etc), leurs journaux savants (Le *Journal des Savants*, *The Philosophical Transactions*...)[3] conduisent à nuancer doublement tout propos de portée générale sur la réception de Leibniz en France. Il suffit de mentionner le rôle complexe de Maupertuis entre l'Académie royale des sciences de Paris et l'Académie des sciences de Berlin. 2) Dans l'historiographie des Lumières, il est souvent d'usage de considérer que la marque distinctive du XVIIIe siècle français, peut se réduire à un affrontement entre deux courants de pensée : les Cartésiens et les Newtoniens. Ces deux courants ont d'illustres représentants. Pour les Newtoniens français, il s'agit principalement de Voltaire, Maupertuis, Clairaut, Bouguer ; pour

1. La Mettrie, *Histoire naturelle de l'âme*, 2e éd., Lettre critique de M. de La Mettrie à Émilie du Châtelet, 1747, p. 2-3.

2. Voir H. Bots et F. Waquet, *La République des Lettres*.

3. Voir Y. Belaval, « Leibniz et l'Europe », p. 212.

les cartésiens : de Fontenelle et en théorie de Dortous de Mairan. Dans ce cadre, l'adhésion au newtonianisme, sous les différentes modalités d'appropriation qu'elle a pu prendre, est souvent comprise comme une conversion à l'empirisme, sans que soit toujours précisé s'il s'agit d'un empirisme épistémologique qui ferait droit à l'*experimental philosophy* comme canon de l'institution et des normes d'une théorie scientifique ou d'un empirisme épistémique qui nous reconduit à une théorie de la connaissance et à une métaphysique singulières et prend alors davantage Locke comme référence. Ce « triomphe du newtonianisme » se situe dans une anthropodicée qui serait la marque du siècle des Lumières. Newton serait alors un allié précieux dans le combat que les philosophes et savants empiristes mènent contre l'emprise de la tutelle métaphysique et religieuse sur la science et sur les objets mêmes de la philosophie. Naturellement cette interprétation revient à méconnaître ou minorer la dimension métaphysique et religieuse de la pensée de Newton, mais surtout cela conduit à interpréter la présence et l'influence des thèses empiristes au XVIIIe siècle sous le signe d'une émancipation à l'égard de ces tutelles. Or, on sait aujourd'hui grâce au travail historique précieux de C. Borghero[1] que la restitution du contexte se doit d'être beaucoup plus subtile que cela pour rendre compte de la complexité des positions. On peut en effet distinguer des auteurs qui voient entre Descartes et Newton une solution de continuité[2]. En un sens l'article « Newtonianisme » de l'*Encyclopédie* est là pour en attester et ceux qui font du combat contre le matérialisme la pierre de touche de leur engagement philosophique (dans le sillage du *Journal de Trévoux*). C'est certainement dans ce contexte qu'il faut comprendre l'interprétation et les usages de la pensée de Leibniz. J. B. Shank a, de son côté, montré comment la centralité des débats autour de l'opposition entre Cartésiens et Newtoniens s'est façonnée. C'est-à-dire comment une décision à la fois philosophique et institutionnelle (la décision de Fontenelle de soutenir les *Leçons de physique* de Privat de Molières dans les *Mémoires de l'Académie Royale des Sciences* de 1729) a conduit à orchestrer une opposition qui n'avait pas d'évidence : ni pour sa centralité, ni pour la restriction qu'elle imposait à la richesse des débats

1. Voir C. Borghero, *Les Cartésiens face à Newton*.

2. En un sens, c'est ce qu'a montré Ellen McNiven Hine en travaillant sur Dortous de Mairan. Elle a forgé le concept de « cartonian » pour remettre en cause le clivage entre Cartésiens et Newtoniens. Voir E. McNiven Hine, « Dortous de Mairan, the Cartonian », p. 163-179. Elle a ainsi montré qu'il n'était pas nécessaire de cesser d'être Cartésien pour devenir newtonien. Rupert Hall écrivait à propos du Père Sébastien Truchet qui était membre honoraire de l'Académie des Sciences « to become a Newtonian required that one ceased to be a Cartesian » (R. Hall, « Newton in France : A New View », p. 246).

philosophiques de cette époque. Mais l'Épitre d'un texte de Privat de Molières ultérieur (publié en 1742) a surtout montré que l'enjeu de l'opposition porte sur l'interprétation correcte du mécanisme[1] et de l'explication des phénomènes naturels qu'il introduit. Suivant cette perspective, Shank a cherché à « provincialiser » Newton[2], c'est-à-dire à relativiser la portée de son implantation en France au XVIIIe siècle et c'est dans ce contexte que la référence à Leibniz prend tout son sens. 3) Il faut ajouter que, jusqu'à la publication de l'édition de Louis Dutens en 1768, peu de textes de Leibniz sont effectivement disponibles en français au XVIIIe siècle et qu'il y a souvent une indistinction entre la pensée de Leibniz et celle de Wolff, particulièrement et tragiquement illustrée par le terme de « système leibnizo-wolffien » élaboré par Bilfinger en 1720. En effet, outre les articles publiés par Leibniz dans les journaux savants[3] qui peuvent être connus par les philosophes des Lumières (mais ne sont pas toujours tous accessibles), il faut mentionner naturellement et presque au premier chef les *Essais de théodicée* dès 1710 et ses nombreuses rééditions, la *Protogée* citée dans les articles « Licorne » et « Montagnes »[4] de l'*Encyclopédie*. Il semble qu'une source importante de l'*Encyclopédie* soit l'*Historia critica philosophia* de Brucker[5]. Ajoutons également la correspondance avec Clarke publiée en français en 1720[6] par Des Maizeaux, ainsi que les *Principes de la nature et de la grâce* qui figurent dans le même recueil, ou encore la version latine de la *Monadologie*, mais par exemple, les *Nouveaux Essais* achevés en 1704

1. Voir Privat de Molières, *Leçons de Phisique*, 1742. Voir l'Épitre au Chancelier, p. VI : « Mon dessein est de fixer, s'il est possible, les principes d'une Science où presque tout semble encore être incertain, & de donner ainsi des éléments à la Physique. Descartes avait prévalu sur les Anciens, et ses Disciples croyaient s'être justement acquis cette espèce de sécurité, où ils vivaient à l'ombre de sa Méthode ; le célèbre Newton est venu troubler leur repos. »

2. Voir J. B. Shank, *The Newton Wars and the Beginning of the French Enlightenment*. Le titre de son introduction est « Provincializing Newton », *cf.* p. 1-35.

3. Dans le livre de W. H. Barber, *Leibniz in France from Arnauld to Voltaire*, figure un appendice qui fait la liste de tous les articles publiés en français.

4. Voir K. Dao Duc, « Leibniz dans l'*Encyclopédie* », p. 125. Il mentionne également la vie de Leibniz que le chevalier de Jaucourt, grand contributeur de l'*Encyclopédie*, ajoute à l'édition de la *Théodicée* publiée à Amsterdam en 1734.

5. Sur cette question, voir J. Proust, *Diderot et l'Encyclopédie*.

6. Clarke et Leibniz, *A Collection of Papers which passed between the late learned Mr. Leibniz and Dr. Clarke in the years 1715 and 1716 related to the Principles of Natural Philosophy and Religion ;* éd. fr. publiée par P. Des Maizeaux, *Recueil de diverses pièces sur la philosophie, la religion naturelle, l'histoire, les mathématiques etc., par Mrs. Leibniz, Clarke, Newton et autres auteurs célèbres*.

ne paraissent que dans l'édition Raspe de 1765[1]. C'est donc un Leibniz partiel, mais aussi un Leibniz souvent wolffien qui est connu et diffusé, parfois au risque de la vulgarisation. Il faut ici mentionner le texte de Samuel Formey, *La Belle wolffienne*[2], qui, parce qu'il est écrit en français fait connaître, en France, la pensée de Wolff à partir de 1741. Formey prend explicitement pour modèle les *Entretiens sur la pluralité des mondes* de Fontenelle. Le motif de l'entretien galant entre une belle marquise désireuse de savoir et un philosophe prêt à accéder à ses demandes, également présent dans *Il Newtonianismo per le dame* d'Algarotti de 1737 verra le stéréotype de genre retourné par Émilie du Châtelet dans la préface de ses *Institutions de physique* de 1740 lorsqu'elle présente à son fils la métaphysique de Leibniz[3] et la physique de Newton. 4°/ La controverse est moins l'occasion de mesurer le rapport de force entre deux positions théoriques à l'occasion d'un affrontement public que le moyen de circonscrire des espaces théoriques de discussion et d'en identifier les enjeux. Il s'agit du vivant de Leibniz, mais également durant tout le XVIIIe siècle, d'une modalité importante de présentation de la pensée de Leibniz. On discute Leibniz, on conteste ses positions métaphysiques, mais on l'introduit aussi ainsi, dans la dispute[4]. En faisant cela, les philosophes du XVIIIe siècle, en un sens, ne font que répondre aux disputes suscitées par la publication d'un certain nombre de textes par Leibniz lui-même de son vivant dans des journaux savants. Ces disputes ont porté a) sur une critique du mécanisme cartésien : de son anti-finalisme avec l'*Unicum Opticae, catoptricae et dioptricae principium* de 1682 publié dans les *Acta Eruditorum*, de son principe de conservation avec la *Brevis demonstratio* de 1686 suivie de la dispute avec l'Abbé Catelan dans le *Journal des Savants*, de sa définition de la matière avec sa *Lettre sur la question si l'essence du corps consiste dans l'étendue* (1691), et donc de sa définition de la substance (voir le *Système nouveau de la nature et de la communication des substances* de 1695 et le *De ipsa natura* de 1698); b) sur la théorie des idées, via son intervention dans la querelle entre

1. Leibniz, *Œuvres philosophiques latines et françoises du feu Mr de Leibniz tirées de ses manuscrits qui se conservent dans la bibliothèque royale à Hanovre* [1765], puis *Gothofridi Guillemi Leibnitii opera omnia*. (6 vol.), éd. L. Dutens, 1768.

2. Formey, *La Belle wolffienne ou Abrégé de la philosophie wolfienne* [1741]. Dans la 2e édition de 1752, Formey adjoint deux lettres : l'une sur l'immortalité de l'âme et l'autre sur l'harmonie préétablie.

3. « Avant-propos », *Institutions de physique*, éd. 1740, p. 13.

4. Y. Belaval « Questions sur l'influence de Leibniz » : « Une influence s'établit souvent avec des polémiques, et Leibniz n'a pas cessé de polémiquer. » p. 230. Voir plus récemment et selon une perspective différente, M. Lærke, *Les Lumières de Leibniz*.

Malebranche et Arnauld avec les *Meditationes de Cognitione, Veritate et ideis* de 1683; c) sur l'explication des rapports entre l'âme et le corps contre les attaques de l'harmonie préétablie, à la fois dans les échanges avec Foucher (1693-1696) mais aussi dans les échanges avec Bayle (autour de l'article Rorarius du *Dictionnaire historique et critique*); c) sur le calcul infinitésimal et la définition de l'espace et du temps, il s'agit alors de discuter les thèses de Newton (pour le calcul, l'enjeu est celui d'une querelle de priorité; pour la correspondance avec Clarke qui présente les thèses newtoniennes, les enjeux sont épistémologiques).

Il faudrait donc distinguer deux formes de réception: une réception critique (Voltaire, D'Alembert, parfois Maupertuis et même Condillac, etc.) et une présentation générale des thèses leibniziennes (Samuel Formey, Fontenelle, Émilie du Châtelet, Diderot, etc...). Mais comme l'écrit Belaval: « Lorsqu'on suit une transmission d'héritage, on est obligé de tenir compte de deux facteurs: la *confusion* et la *diffusion*. C'est dans la confusion qu'un auteur se diffuse. On le trouve partout et on ne peut le saisir nulle part. [...] On recrée sans cesse Leibniz. On invente un leibnizianisme et c'est ce leibnizianisme qui féconde les esprits » [1]. Autant dire que plutôt que d'analyser la présence de Leibniz en France au XVIIIe siècle à l'aune de la fidélité aux textes de Leibniz (en récusant les écarts, malentendus ou mécompréhensions), il s'agit ici de comprendre quels sont les besoins épistémiques des philosophes du XVIIIe siècle. Que trouvent-ils dans les textes de Leibniz qui leur permet de répondre aux problèmes qu'ils rencontrent lorsqu'ils veulent rendre compte de la liberté, du mouvement, de Dieu ou encore du rapport entre l'âme et le corps? Autrement dit, on présentera les usages de Leibniz plutôt que son influence. Que dit ainsi l'*Éloge* que Fontenelle [2], secrétaire de l'Académie royale des sciences, cartésien affiché, écrit à la mort de Leibniz en 1716? Comment présente-t-il la philosophie de Leibniz au public français? On peut en retenir essentiellement trois choses: 1) En mentionnant la *Préface à Nizolius*, Fontenelle expose le travail de conciliation entrepris par Leibniz pour accorder Aristote (et non les Scolastiques) à Descartes [3], il présente également les critiques que Leibniz formule à l'encontre de la mécanique cartésienne, grâce à sa dynamique, mais conclut par la supériorité de la physique

1. Y. Belaval, *Études leibniziennes*, p. 221.
2. Voir *Histoire de l'Académie royale des sciences* pour l'année 1716, p. 94-128.
3. Voir Fontenelle, « Éloge de Leibniz », in *Histoire de l'Académie royale des sciences*, pour l'année 1732, p. 106.

cartésienne[1]; 2) Il présente l'invention du calcul infinitésimal, la querelle de priorité lancée par les sectateurs de Newton et considère que l'accusation de plagiat « établie » par le *Commercium epistolicum* de 1712 n'est pas fondée; 3) Il donne les grands principes qui régissent la nouvelle métaphysique[2] élaborée par Leibniz : principe de raison suffisante, principe de continuité, principe du meilleur (avec le rêve de Théodore), harmonie préétablie[3]. Il présente enfin les substances simples ou Monades de manière assez juste « qui sont les Vies, les Âmes ou les Esprits, qui peuvent dire Moi, [...] qui ne sont pas seulement des Miroirs de l'Univers des Créatures, mais des Miroirs ou Images de Dieu même »[4].

Les usages de Leibniz sont multiples au XVIIIe siècle : chez Buffon, Maupertuis ou Bonnet (dans l'explication du vivant), Maupertuis (dans la critique du recours aux causes finales), La Mettrie (dans sa conception d'une force motrice appliquée à l'âme), Voltaire (dans sa critique de la théodicée), Émilie du Châtelet (dans sa reprise des principes métaphysiques nécessaires à la fondation de la physique moderne), D'Alembert (dans l'organisation du système des savoirs plus que dans la querelle des forces vives)[5], Diderot (pour sa conception, en apparence critique, de la théorie de la connaissance, de l'épistémologie ou pour sa théorie de la perception)[6], ou encore Condillac (dans sa défense et démonstration des monades). Si l'on voulait proposer une vue schématique des thèses leibniziennes qui sont discutées, reprises ou contestées au XVIIIe siècle, il faudrait mentionner : 1) la querelle des forces vives à la suite de la controverse lancée par la publication dans les *Acta Eruditorum* en 1686 de la *Brevis demonstratio erroris mirabilis Cartesii*, 2) la conception de la substance simple comme monade avec une discussion qui portera principalement, dans l'héritage que l'interprétation wolffienne en proposera, sur la physicalisation ou non de la monade, sur la possibilité ou non d'attribuer la perception à toutes les formes de monades; 3) la critique de l'harmonie

1. Il est ainsi intéressant de voir que Fontenelle fait une présentation très informée de la dynamique leibnizienne tout en maintenant l'idée d'une prééminence de l'explication cartésienne du mouvement des corps sur les autres.

2. Même si le commentaire qui suit immédiatement la formulation de ces principes laisse dubitatif : « Ces principes si nobles et si spécieux ne sont pas aisés à appliquer, car dès qu'on est hors du nécessaire rigoureux et absolu, qui n'est pas bien commun en Métaphysique, le suffisant, le convenable, un degré ou un saut, tout cela pourrait bien être un peu arbitraire, et il faut prendre garde que ce ne soit le besoin du Système qui décide » (« Éloge de Leibniz », p. 116).

3. *Ibid.*, p. 117.

4. *Ibid.*, p. 117-118.

5. Voir V. Le Ru, *Jean Le Rond D'Alembert, philosophe.*

6. Voir C. Leduc *et al.* (éd.), *Leibniz et Diderot. Rencontres et transformations.*

préétablie, et avec elle, celle de la théodicée, avec un enjeu central : celui de la définition de la liberté humaine.

Belaval souligne que « le travail de l'histoire » ne fait pas la part belle à la pensée de Leibniz et fonde cette interprétation sur un choix de thèmes artificiellement isolés et sur le contexte de l'accusation de plagiat formulée par Newton à l'égard du calcul infinitésimal. Il faut ajouter que l'un des enjeux importants est sans doute celui mis en scène de manière caricaturale par Voltaire : celui de la liberté humaine. L'harmonie préétablie ne conduit-elle pas à nier la liberté de l'homme ? Cette question permet aisément aux détracteurs de Leibniz de disqualifier sa philosophie, néanmoins un certain nombre de conceptions métaphysiques de Leibniz, relatives en particulier à ses définitions de la matière et de la substance seront régulièrement reprises et discutées durant tout le XVIIIe siècle. Si l'*Éloge* de Fontenelle semble laisser croire que la dispute sur le principe de conservation entre Leibniz et les Cartésiens est close au bénéfice des Cartésiens, il n'en est rien et, à partir de 1728, la « véritable » querelle des forces vives éclate.

Les forces vives

La querelle est réactivée par la publication en 1728 du texte de Dortous de Mairan, *Dissertation sur l'estimation et la mesure des forces motrices des corps*[1]. Pour De Mairan, la controverse avec Leibniz porte sur trois points : il s'agit de la discussion sur la place du temps dans l'estime de la force, de la nécessité de recourir ou non aux expériences dans les procédures de validation du principe de conservation leibnizien, enfin de la discussion sur la notion de force : en un mot, la contestation de l'existence d'un concept de force dédoublé en force morte et force vive. Et cela, alors même qu'il récuse une approche métaphysique de la question[2]. Et c'est bien là l'un des enjeux de la querelle des forces vives au XVIIIe siècle : étant donné que la conception leibnizienne s'appuie sur une définition de la matière qui suppose une force interne de mouvement dans les corps et qui se dédouble en une force dérivative et une force primitive, l'un des enjeux est de déterminer jusqu'à quel point l'adhésion au principe de conservation suppose conjointement une adhésion à ses présupposés métaphysiques. Une controverse éclatera entre Dortous de Mairan et Émilie du Châtelet à la suite des commentaires ironiques et critiques que Madame

1. Voir Fontenelle, « Éloge de Leibniz », p. 135, même si certains historiens considèrent que c'est le texte du chevalier de Louville de 1721 qui relance la polémique.

2. *Dissertation*, chap. I, § 1 : « Je ne prétends point traiter en Métaphysicien de la Force des corps ».

du Châtelet formule dans la première édition de ses *Institutions* en 1740[1]. Émilie du Châtelet non seulement adhère à la conception leibnizienne de la matière et la dote d'une force[2] mais elle va également prouver expérimentalement la validité du principe de conservation leibnizien en s'appuyant sur les expériences réalisées par Jacob Hermann ou Willem's Gravesande. En faisant cela, elle donnera une assise métaphysique[3] et expérimentale au principe de conservation des forces vives. Dans le prolongement de ces questionnements, il faut certainement mentionner le principe de moindre action de Maupertuis[4] qui constitue indéniablement une référence à Leibniz. À cet égard, il n'est pas inutile de rappeler que Maupertuis, considéré comme l'un des principaux newtoniens français utilise un certain nombre de principes métaphysiques leibniziens. Mary Terral montre bien l'importance de ces principes leibniziens pour celui qui a aplati la terre[5].

La substance

Il faut souligner que si Fontenelle présente de manière assez complète la conception leibnizienne de la substance, c'est aussi souvent la conception wolffienne qui est mobilisée pour parler de la monade. Il est donc intéressant de voir que, malgré une connaissance partielle qui produit parfois un visage wolffien de la monade, un certain nombre de philosophes

1. Dans l'édition de 1742, elle fera figurer les lettres échangées avec De Mairan.

2. *Institutions de physique*, chap. VII, § 126, 131 et chap. VIII, § 141, 142.

3. Contrairement aux tentatives de Johann Bernoulli de ne s'en tenir qu'à un traitement mathématique de la querelle. Voir Costabel, *La Signification d'un débat sur trente ans (1728-1758)*, sur la « tentative illusoire » de Johann Bernoulli de traiter de la question des forces vives en mathématicien et non en philosophe.

4. Voir Maupertuis, « Accord de différentes lois de la nature », *Mémoires de l'Académie royale des sciences de Paris*, 1744, p. 417 *sq.* On trouve aussi une formulation explitice dans l'*Essai de cosmologie :* « L'action est proportionnelle au produit de la masse par la vitesse et par l'espace. Maintenant, voici ce principe si sage, si digne de l'Être suprême : lorsqu'il arrive quelque changement dans la Nature, la quantité d'Action employée dans ce changement est toujours la plus petite qu'il soit possible », *Œuvres*, Lyon, 1768, IV, p. 16. Voir aussi Martin-Robine, *Histoire du principe de moindre action, trois siècles de principes variationnels de Fermat à Feynman.*

5. M. Terrall, *The Man who Flattened the Earth*, p. 289. Voir aussi E. Cassirer, *La philosophie des Lumières*, p. 112 : « Sa position personnelle à l'égard de Leibniz n'est du reste pas exempte de toute contradiction mais la dépendance effective de sa métaphysique, de sa philosophie de la nature et de sa théorie de la connaissance à l'égard des principes leibniziens n'en est pas moins indéniable. Il recourt aux idées leibniziennes aussi bien pour démontrer son principe de moindre action que pour établir et prouver son principe de continuité ».

français du XVIIIe siècle ont bien perçu la différence entre Leibniz et Wolff et ont choisi de puiser dans la conception leibnizienne de la substance pour élaborer leur propre philosophie. Lorsque, dans les *Institutions de physique*, Émilie du Châtelet présente la conception leibnizienne de la substance, elle introduit le concept de monade au § 119 pour expliquer l'étendue de la matière : « M. de Leibniz qui ne perdait jamais de vue le principe de raison suffisante, trouva que ces Atomes ne lui donnaient point la raison de l'étendue de la Matière, et cherchant à découvrir cette raison, il crut voir qu'elle ne pouvait être que dans des parties non étendues et c'est ce qu'il appelle *des Monades* ». Mais le plus souvent Émilie du Châtelet utilise le terme wolffien d'être simple et elle préfère lui attribuer une activité dynamique, plutôt qu'une capacité perceptive, car il lui semble difficile de concevoir que toutes les substances puissent percevoir[1].

Émilie du Châtelet joue habilement des différences entre les conceptions leibnizienne et wolffienne de la substance en récusant la distinction wolffienne entre monades brutes et être simple et en préservant un seul et même principe d'intelligibilité pour toutes les formes de substance.

Un exemple des relations étroites existant entre Berlin et Paris qui témoigne de la présence de Leibniz dans ce contexte intellectuel peut se trouver dans le texte que Condillac choisit de rédiger en réponse à une question mise au concours à l'Académie de Berlin proposée pour la classe de philosophie spéculative en 1745 et adoptée en 1746. La question mise au concours était la suivante :

> On demande, qu'en commençant par exposer d'une manière exacte et nette la doctrine des Monades, on examine si d'un côté elles peuvent être solidairement réfutées et détruites par des arguments sans réplique ou si de l'autre on est en état, après avoir prouvé les Monades, d'en déduire une explication des principaux phénomènes de l'Univers et en particulier de l'origine et du mouvement des corps[2].

Il peut sembler étonnant que Condillac soit l'auteur de ce texte intitulé *Les Monades* puisqu'il a longtemps été considéré, par les philosophes des Lumières eux-mêmes, comme celui qui donnait un coup d'arrêt aux systèmes (que l'on pense que seulement un an plus tard, il rédige le *Traité*

1. Comme elle l'écrit au § 132 : « C'est encore un des sentiments de Mr de Leibniz, qui a le plus besoin d'être éclairci, que cette représentation de l'Univers et de tous ses changements, dans laquelle il prétend que l'essence de notre âme consiste. »

2. A. Harnack, *Geschichte der Königlich Preussischen Akademie der Wissenschaften zu Berlin*, II, p. 305.

des systèmes), ou encore celui qui voyait dans la définition leibnizienne de la monade des termes vagues et imagés »[1].

Mais *a contrario* de tout cela, un passage du texte *Les Monades* de Condillac est particulièrement éloquent :

> J'ai démontré qu'il y a des monades, qu'elles diffèrent nécessairement entre elles, et qu'elles produisent les phénomènes de l'étendue et des corps, qui n'en sont que des agrégats. J'ai prouvé qu'elles n'agissent point les unes sur les autres, et que, par conséquent elles ne concourent à former l'univers qu'en vertu de l'harmonie qui a été préétablie[2].

Comment expliquer des textes, en apparence, à ce point contradictoires ? Condillac est-il si hostile à Leibniz que l'histoire des Lumières l'a souvent admis ? S'agit-il simplement d'un texte de circonstance, d'un exercice rhétorique d'autant plus aisé à conduire que le texte est anonyme ? Récemment, Laurence L. Bongie a proposé de considérer que, à y regarder de près, un certain nombre des thèses leibniziennes formulées par Condillac dans *Les Monades* se trouvent de manière discrète présentes dans les textes ultérieurs de Condillac et que cet intérêt pour la métaphysique leibnizienne peut se comprendre puisqu'il était un préalable nécessaire « avant de pouvoir construire une métaphysique nouvelle, *une monadologie qui lui fût propre* »[3].

Il faut aussi dire un mot de l'article « Leibnizianisme », non signé, mais rédigé par Diderot dans l'*Encyclopédie* et plus généralement des rapports complexes que Diderot entretient avec la pensée de Leibniz. Commençons par rappeler le jugement que Diderot porte sur Leibniz :

> Un homme montre quelque fois plus de génie dans une erreur qu'un autre dans la découverte d'une vérité. Je vois plus de tête dans l'*Harmonie préétablie* de Leibniz ou dans son *Optimisme* que dans tous les ouvrages des théologiens du monde, que dans les plus grandes découvertes, soit en géométrie, soit en mécanique, soit en astronomie[4].

1. Condillac, *Essai sur l'origine des connaissances humaines* [1746], I. 131 : « En effet, ces termes [miroir, image], en passant du propre au figuré, n'ont plus qu'un rapport vague avec le premier sens qu'ils ont eu. Ils signifient qu'il y a des représentations toutes différentes de celles que nous connaissons, c'est-à-dire des représentations dont nous n'avons pas d'idée. Dire que les perceptions sont des états représentations, c'est donc ne rien dire. »

2. Condillac, *Les monades*, chap. IX : « De la monade première ou de Dieu », p. 235.

3. L. L. Bongie, « Introduction », *Les Monades*, p. 18.

4. Diderot, *Réfutation de l'ouvrage d'Helvétius intitulé l'Homme* [1774], in *id.*, *Œuvres*, t. II, p. 348, cité par Y. Belaval dans son introduction aux *Études leibniziennes*, « Pourquoi Leibniz ? », p. 15.

Il est désormais connu que l'article « Leibnitzianisme » reprend des éléments de l'*Éloge* de Fontenelle, comporte une traduction et une présentation des *Méditations sur la connaissance, la vérité et les idées* de 1684 ainsi qu'une traduction de la *Monadologie* et utilise le texte de Brucker déjà cité. Cela permet de comprendre l'importance stratégique de cette entrée de l'*Encyclopédie* pour la diffusion de la pensée de Leibniz auquel Diderot veut « rendre justice ». Même si Diderot reprend l'antienne jésuite d'un Leibniz, « fondateur de l'optimisme ou de ce système qui semble faire de Dieu un automate dans ses décrets et dans ses actions », il faut ajouter que Diderot souligne à plusieurs reprises l'actualité des thèses leibniziennes que ce soit sur le projet encyclopédique ou sur la sensibilité entendue comme propriété générale de la matière qui est sans doute une reformulation de la perception leibnizienne.

L'harmonie préétablie (et avec elle, l'optimisme) au prisme de ses détracteurs : Voltaire et D'Alembert

D'Alembert, pour qualifier la pensée de Leibniz, utilise le néologisme d'optimisme, présent pour la première fois en 1747 dans les *Mémoires de Trévoux*. C'est aussi sur le plan de la physique que la divergence avec Leibniz s'affirme. Au principe de conservation de la quantité de force vive, D'Alembert avait préféré le principe de conservation cartésien de la quantité de mouvement, mais conclut qu'il ne s'agit en définitive que d'une « querelle de mots » [1]. Rien d'étonnant à ce qu'on retrouve quelques années plus tard, en 1759, sous la plume de Voltaire ce terme d'optimisme comme sous-titre de *Candide*. L'harmonie préétablie de Leibniz y est alors ridiculisée sous les traits du précepteur Pangloss, et ce, dès le premier chapitre : « Pangloss [...] prouvait admirablement qu'il n'y a point d'effet sans cause, et que, dans ce meilleur des mondes possibles, le château de monseigneur le baron était le plus beau des châteaux et madame la meilleure des baronnes possibles » [2]. Voltaire choisit d'interpréter l'harmonie préétablie comme une justification, au nom du principe du meilleur, de tout ce qui est. Mais il faut préciser que Voltaire plus de vingt ans plus tôt avait forgé dans ses *Lettres philosophiques* de 1734 une histoire de la philosophie et des Lumières fondée, principalement, sur trois

1. D'Alembert, *Traité de Dynamique*, p. XXI : « Néanmoins comme nous n'avons d'idée précise et distincte du mot de force, qu'en restreignant ce terme à exprimer un effet, je crois qu'on doit laisser chacun le maître de se décider comme il voudra là-dessus ; et toute la question ne peut plus consister, que dans une discussion Métaphysique très futile, ou dans une dispute de mots plus indigne encore d'occuper des Philosophes. »

2. Voltaire, *Candide*, p. 3.

auteurs anglais (Bacon, Locke et Newton). L'un des enjeux de cette histoire de la pensée remodelée par Voltaire était précisément d'exclure Descartes de la philosophie des Lumières. Et cette interprétation aura une grande postérité non seulement au XVIIIe siècle avec D'Alembert et Condorcet, mais aussi dans l'historiographie des Lumières du XXe siècle. Si Voltaire, dans un premier temps, au moment de la rédaction des *Lettres philosophiques*, conserve encore une place de pionnier à Descartes[1], comme le souligne C. Borghero[2], Voltaire achève Descartes dans *Le Siècle de Louis XIV* en parlant de « philosophie chimérique » et en pointant dans l'article « Cartésianisme » vingt-sept de ses « erreurs », en particulier dans le domaine de la philosophie naturelle. Si Voltaire a d'abord cru que Newton, symbole de la philosophie des Lumières, réalisait un projet amorcé par Descartes, dans l'article « Cartésianisme », il fait désormais de Galilée le pionnier de la philosophie expérimentale. Cette éviction est certainement liée à une interprétation de Descartes qui en fait un matérialiste et un athée[3], c'est donc aussi pour des raisons métaphysiques que Newton est préféré à Descartes. Rappelons, dans ce cadre, que Voltaire dans ses *Eléments de philosophie de Newton* moque l'hypothèse de l'harmonie préétablie[4]. C'est dans ce contexte que l'on doit mentionner l'utilisation des thèses leibniziennes que font les rédacteurs du *Journal de Trévoux* qui disputent aux cartésiens le territoire de la République des lettres et qui sont plutôt hostiles à un Descartes qui a voulu se débarrasser des formes substantielles et des qualités occultes. Leibniz y est utilisé pour critiquer le supposé matérialisme déguisé de Descartes et Newton. Ce sont des réquisits liés à la préservation de la liberté et au refus du matérialisme qui guident leurs choix et leurs critiques des thèses de Descartes et de Newton. À cet égard, la critique que Leibniz entreprend de Descartes lorsqu'elle parvient à se diffuser en France conduit les Jésuites[5] à élaborer une pensée éclectique qui fait aussi une place à la physique expérimentale anglaise (et donc à certains aspects de la pensée de Newton). D'après Clarke l'argument permettant de disculper Newton de tout soupçon de matérialisme est de bien comprendre que les *Principes Mathématiques de la Philosophie Naturelle* sont « les seuls qui combattent directement le matérialisme, puisqu'ils font voir que la matière est la plus petite,

1. Voltaire, *Lettres philosophiques*, Lettre XIV « Sur Descartes et Newton », 1734, II, p. 6.

2. C. Borghero, *Les Cartésiens face à Newton*, p. 28.

3. *Ibid.*, p. 29-30.

4. Voltaire, *Éléments de philosophie de Newton*, partie I, chap. VI.

5. Voir par exemple le compte-rendu de l'édition de Des Maizeaux de 1720, publié par le *Journal de Trévoux*, 21, juillet 1721, p. 1234-1235.

et la moins considérable partie de cet univers »[1]. Pour le père Louis-Bertrand Castel (1688-1757), rédacteur principal des Mémoires de Trévoux sur ces questions c'est une preuve supplémentaire du matérialisme de Newton, car tous les matérialistes se sont limités à une explication mathématique du monde et ont admis le vide. Et, d'après lui, Leibniz ne s'y est pas trompé, c'est bien plutôt sur le versant métaphysique qu'il faudrait répondre à ce soupçon[2]. Mais cela ne conduit pas pour autant Castel à « succomber » au leibnizianisme car il lui semble que la pensée de Leibniz par la place qu'elle donne au principe de raison suffisante et au principe du meilleur, porte à son tour atteinte à la liberté et conduit à une sorte de fatalisme. Condorcet, lorsqu'il rédige son *Esquisse d'un tableau historique des progrès de l'esprit humain* (1793-1794), signale, dans la Neuvième époque (« Depuis Descartes jusqu'à la formation de la République française »), l'influence du principe du meilleur en France et en Angleterre, mais indique qu'il a « retardé les progrès de la philosophie »[3].

Autant dire que suivre la présence de Leibniz au XVIIIe siècle, revient à écrire une autre philosophie des Lumières françaises que celle qui verrait simplement s'opposer Cartésiens et Newtoniens. Autant dire également que la pensée de Leibniz est souvent utilisée pour donner une assise métaphysique à une philosophie et à une science renouvelées. Ainsi plutôt que de ne voir dans le XVIIIe siècle français que l'imposition progressive d'une hégémonie de l'empirisme et de figures multiples du matérialisme, l'analyse des usages de Leibniz permet de comprendre les fonctions qu'il occupe pour beaucoup d'auteurs des Lumières : rempart contre l'athéisme, source théorique permettant de penser l'animation de la matière, substrat métaphysique pour la science moderne.

La réception anglaise

La réception des idées de Leibniz en Angleterre est évidemment affectée par un certain nombre d'éléments contextuels déjà mentionnés : au premier titre, la querelle de priorité concernant l'invention du calcul infinitésimal et les échanges avec Clarke. Ces deux éléments vont orienter significativement et d'une manière assez négative la réception de Leibniz en Angleterre. Comme il est bien connu grâce à l'analyse approfondie qu'a

1. *Journal de Trévoux*, 21, juillet 1721, p. 1234.
2. *Ibid.*, p. 1234-1235.
3. Condorcet, *Ésquisse d'un tableau historique des progrès de l'esprit humain* [1793-1794], p. 159-160.

menée D. B. Meli[1], les relations de Leibniz avec la *Royal Society* sont bonnes jusqu'à la publication en octobre 1684 dans les *Acta Eruditorum* de sa *Nova methodus pro maximis et minimis*. Fatio de Duillier est le premier à formuler publiquement l'accusation de plagiat et à déclencher ainsi une longue controverse qui culminera dans un texte que John Keill publiera en 1710 dans les *Philosophical Transactions* en affirmant que Leibniz s'est contenté d'utiliser un nouveau formalisme pour exprimer le calcul qui avait en réalité été élaboré par Newton. S'ensuivent des échanges tendus, des demandes de réparation puis l'administration de la « preuve » de la préséance du calcul par Newton dans un texte à charge contre Leibniz, le fameux *Commercium epistolicum*. À partir de là, Meli propose une lecture de la controverse à la lumière de ce qu'il appelle la « violation d'un code de bonne conduite ». Il faut ajouter, dans la même perspective, tout le travail de construction de l'orthodoxie newtonienne mené par Samuel Clarke et Roger Cotes qui va les conduire à instituer la « bonne lecture » de Newton et consécutivement l'idée qu'être un bon newtonien suppose de se prononcer contre le principe de conservation leibnizien. Parmi d'autres, Willem 's Gravesande, introducteur des idées newtoniennes en Hollande, en fait les frais, lorsque Clarke lui reproche d'avoir ainsi « obscurci » la philosophie de Newton. Dans la charge qu'il lance contre W.'s Gravesande[2], il englobe G. W. Leibniz, J. Herman ou encore J. Bernoulli. La charge est si violente que 's Gravesande la mentionne dans le titre même du texte qui se veut une réponse : *Remarques sur la force des corps en mouvement, et sur le choc précédées de quelques réflexions sur la manière d'écrire de Mr le Docteur Samuel Clarke* (1729). Il s'agit d'expliquer que le principe de conservation des forces vives défendu par G. W. Leibniz, J. Herman, W.'s Gravesande et J. Bernoulli est contraire à la méthode newtonienne : celle qui applique l'abstraction mathématique aux vrais phénomènes de la nature. Ce texte qui délimite le cadre de l'orthodoxie newtonienne est significatif de l'attitude d'un cercle de newtoniens qui a élaboré une lecture autorisée et désormais officielle de la philosophie et de la méthodologie de Newton[3]. Ainsi, on comprend pourquoi Catherine Wilson peut écrire : « À sa mort, Leibniz, en Angleterre, devint un peu plus qu'un nom et un symbole, une menace pour l'honneur de Newton ainsi que pour l'honneur national »[4].

1. D. Bertoloni Meli, *Equivalence and Priority. Newton versus Leibniz*, p. 6-7.

2. S. Clarke, *Philosophical Transactions*, n° 401.

3. Voir C. Iltis, « The Leibnizian-Newtonian Debates : Natural Philosophy and Social Psychology », p. 343-377.

4. C. Wilson, *Leibniz's Metaphysics*, p. 443-444.

Malgré cela, il faut dire qu'il y a des raisons philosophiques qui rendent possible la réception de Leibniz en Angleterre, c'est l'importance et la présence d'un certain nombre de philosophes anglais dans la réflexion et la construction de sa pensée. En effet, lorsque dans les années 1660, Leibniz prend connaissance et adhère à la philosophie moderne, les auteurs qu'il ne cesse de citer sont, naturellement Galilée et Descartes, mais aussi Bacon, Hobbes et Digby[1]. Comme G. Brown et P. Phemister[2] le soulignent dans leur introduction à *Leibniz and the English-Speaking World*, Leibniz a lu un texte[3] de John Wilkins en 1676; un livre important[4] de Boyle, en 1689; il a rédigé différentes notes sur le livre de Cudworth, *True Intellectual System of the Universe* en 1690, il a naturellement lu et discuté l'*Essay* de Locke dans les *Nouveaux essais*. Il a également lu le texte de John Toland, *Christianity not Mysterious*, et les *Principles* de Berkeley. Il connaît Henry More (grâce surtout à l'édition de ses *Opera omnia* de 1679) et échange des lettres avec John Wallis. Il faut également dire un mot de ses relations étroites avec la *Royal Society* non seulement avec son secrétaire, Oldenburg avec qui il entretint une correspondance, mais aussi avec Locke et Newton qui étaient déjà « fellows » lorsque Leibniz vint la première fois à la Royal Society (rappelons l'envoi qu'il fit de son *Hypothesis physica nova* à la Royal Society). Il faut aussi faire référence à la pensée de certains Platoniciens de Cambridge (More et Cudworth ont déjà été évoqués, mais Anne Conway et Lady Masham, fille de Cudworth, doivent également figurer parmi ces interlocuteurs immédiats ou médiats) et aux interprétations qui ont pu conduire à considérer que ce contexte intellectuel pouvait être important pour comprendre l'élaboration du concept de monade[5]. Wilson considère même que l'adoption de ce terme par Leibniz « vient presque certainement » de ce groupe des Platoniciens de Cambridge. Une fois ces différents points rappelés, on peut distinguer trois cas différents de la réception de Leibniz en Angleterre au XVIIIe siècle : il s'agit de celle d'Alexander Pope autour de la théodicée, de celle de George Berkeley et de la place des monades sans porte ni fenêtre pour comprendre ce que l'on considérera comme son « idéalisme » et enfin de la présence d'un certain nombre de thèmes leibniziens majeurs (à la fois en métaphysique et dans sa théorie de la connaissance) dans la pensée de David Hume.

1. Leibniz, *Confessio naturae contra atheistas*, A, VI, 1, p. 489-90.

2. G. Brown et P. Phemister (ed.), *Leibniz and the English-Speaking World*, « Introduction », p. 1-18.

3. J. Wilkins, *Essay Towards a Real Character and a Philosophical Language*.

4. R. Boyle, *Some Physico-Theological Considerations About the Possibility of the Resurrection*.

5. C. Wilson, *Leibniz's Metaphysics*, en particulier p. 181.

Pope et la Théodicée

Il est d'usage de considérer que l'*Essay on Man* de Pope est une version poétique de la *Théodicée*. L'avantage de cette interprétation est qu'elle témoigne d'une exportation des thèses leibniziennes en Angleterre. En un sens, cette interprétation a été renforcée par la lecture qu'en propose Voltaire, en 1733, dans ses *Lettres philosophiques*, la vingt-deuxième :

> Comme tout ce qui tient à la métaphysique a été pensé de tous les temps et chez tous les peuples qui cultivent leur esprit, ce système tient beaucoup de celui de Leibnitz, qui prétend que de tous les mondes possibles Dieu a dû choisir le meilleur, et que, dans ce meilleur, il fallait bien que les irrégularités de notre globe et les sottises de ses habitants tinssent leur place.

Il est aisé de montrer que le texte de Pope tient sans doute davantage de Shaftesbury et de Bolingbroke que de Leibniz lui-même. Mais il est aussi possible de pointer les proximités apparentes de la *Théodicée* et de l'*Essay on Man* qui ont accrédité la thèse d'une réception de Leibniz par Pope. En un sens, restituer historiquement et philosophiquement la méprise puis ses raisons n'épuise pas les enjeux historiques de ce rapprochement. Même si certains ont pu affirmer que Pope ignorait tout de Leibniz[1], c'est bien l'optimisme supposément leibnizien que l'on croit reconnaître dans ce texte. De quoi s'agit-il exactement ?

Sous la figure de l'optimisme, il s'agit de distinguer un « tout est bien » en réalité introuvable chez Pope (puisque l'expression traduit : « One truth is clear, whatever is, is right »), d'un « meilleur des mondes possibles ». Et Pope fait de ce monde le résultat d'un choix divin entre plusieurs mondes possibles)[2]. Dans ce cadre, c'est le statut du mal qui fait sans doute le mieux voir la différence. Pour Pope, le mal, à un certain niveau de généralité, se révèle être un mal apparent en vue d'un bien réel. *A contrario*, pour Leibniz le mal moral dérivant du mal métaphysique « consiste dans le péché » mais reste imputable à l'homme dans la mesure où il n'est pas nécessaire, mais contingent, l'homme aurait pu faire un autre choix. Il y a là une vraie divergence qui se trouve encore accrue par la comparaison des démarches de Pope et de Leibniz : pour Pope, nous ne pouvons prétendre accéder aux raisons de Dieu, ce serait une forme d'orgueil que de croire cela, mais pour Leibniz, le principe de raison est, au contraire, une

1. E. de Silhouette, traducteur de l'*Essay*, contrairement à ce qu'affirme J.-P. de Crousaz, considère que « M. Pope, bien loin d'épouser le système de M. Leibniz ne l'a jamais lu : et il était si éloigné de vouloir justifier l'*harmonie préétablie*, qu'il n'en avait jamais entendu parler ».

2. Pope, *Epist.* I, II, 43f : « Of systems possible, if t'is confest / That Wisdom Infinite must form the best ».

contribution « à la gloire de Dieu en comprenant la rationalité du monde qui se manifeste, entre autres, par les lois qui le gouvernent »[1]. On peut conclure sur ce point comme le faisait Barber[2] en disant qu'en un sens, le poème de Pope relance l'intérêt pour des questions qui avaient été soulevées par la *Théodicée* et redonne une forme d'actualité à la pensée de Leibniz.

Berkeley, quelle homologie ?

Il faut rappeler que l'on pouvait déjà noter des mentions de la conception de la force physique dans le *De Motu* ainsi que dans l'*Alciphron*. Dans le *De Motu*, publié en 1721, Berkeley cherche à dissocier la mécanique de la métaphysique dans un dialogue serré avec les thèses leibniziennes et en particulier avec les textes portant sur la dynamique (au premier titre desquels figurent le *Specimen dynamicum* et le *De ipsa natura*). Pour y parvenir, il interroge la pertinence du couple conceptuel leibnizien de la force primitive et de la force dérivative. L'opération consiste à casser le lien par lequel Leibniz pense la réalité de la force dérivative : c'est-à-dire son rapport à la force primitive. En refusant de concevoir la force primitive (et avec elle, selon les époques, la forme substantielle puis l'entéléchie) comme le garant métaphysique de la réalité de la force dérivative, Berkeley démolit le dispositif leibnizien par lequel l'ambivalence de la force permettait à la métaphysique de fonder la mécanique[3]. L'enjeu est d'importance, car cette déconstruction de l'édifice épistémique suppose une connaissance et une discussion extrêmement fine de la dynamique leibnizienne qui conduit Berkeley à proposer non pas des lois causales de la mécanique mais des lois qui décrivent les régularités des phénomènes tout en accordant à la métaphysique un rôle régulateur.

Est-ce que voir une proximité entre Leibniz et Berkeley ne revient pas à basculer du côté d'une interprétation « idéaliste » de la pensée de Leibniz ? Le problème ne se pose pas avec la même acuité pour la théorie des idées, la distinction entre qualités premières et qualités secondes ou encore l'affirmation du caractère relatif de l'espace et du temps, mais bien plutôt pour tous les développements qui ont trait à la réalité des corps et plus

1. M. Parmentier, « Voltaire et l'optimisme leibnizien », p. 143.

2. W. H. Barber, *Leibniz in France*, p. 112 (nous traduisons) : « Ainsi le poème de Pope, avec son élégance et sa clarté a du relancer l'intérêt pour les problèmes présents dans la Théodicée et raviver de nombreux échos mourants de la pensée de Leibniz. »

3. Voir L. Peterschmitt, « La critique du réalisme leibnizien dans le *De Motu* de Berkeley ».

spécifiquement à la question de l'interprétation de cette phrase centrale dans la pensée de Berkeley : « exister, c'est percevoir ou être perçu. »

La question de la proximité philosophique entre Leibniz et Berkeley se formule bien souvent à partir de la reconnaissance d'une parenté sur le statut des phénomènes, de la matière et de la notion de perception [1]. Même si, dans le cadre de ce chapitre, la question de savoir si Leibniz connaissait et appréciait les thèses de Berkeley se pose de manière marginale, on peut toutefois rappeler, grâce à G. Brykman [2], que dans une lettre à Des Bosses du 5 mars 1715 [3], Leibniz mentionne Berkeley, et surtout qu'il annote un exemplaire des *Principes de la connaissance humaine* (1710) en 1714-1715. Dans ces annotations il indique les points communs et les différences entre la pensée de Berkeley et la sienne :

> Il y a beaucoup de vues justes et proches des miennes. Mais exprimées de façon paradoxale. Car on n'a pas besoin de dire que la matière n'est rien; mais seulement que c'est un phénomène, tel que l'arc-en-ciel; de dire que ce n'est pas une substance, mais le résultat de substances; et de dire que l'espace n'est pas plus réel que le temps, c'est-à-dire que l'espace est l'ordre des coexistants comme le temps est l'ordre des successifs (*sub-existentia*). Les véritables substances sont les monades ou êtres percevants. Mais l'auteur aurait du aller plus loin, jusqu'à l'infinité des monades et leur harmonie préétablie. C'est en vain et sans y réussir qu'il refuse les idées abstraites, réduit les idées aux images et méprise les subtilités de l'arithmétique et de la géométrie. Le pire est qu'il ait repoussé la division de l'étendue à l'infini, même s'il avait raison de repousser les quantités infiniment petites [4].

Ce passage est particulièrement intéressant car il permet d'identifier des proximités thématiques et des divergences conceptuelles sur la définition de la matière et de la substance en particulier, sur le statut des idées également. En effet, comme le souligne S. Daniel, on peut identifier au moins deux proximités : le statut des corps ou plutôt des agrégats comme phénomènes perçus, et le statut de la perception de la réalité [5].

Si Berkeley peut sembler proche à certains égards de la pensée de Leibniz, en particulier autour d'un « phénoménisme théocentrique » [6]

1. Voir C. Wilson, « The Phenomenalisms of Leibniz and Berkeley », p. 3-22.

2. G. Brykman, « Leibniz et les paradoxes de Berkeley », p. 97-114.

3. « Cet Irlandais qui attaque la réalité des corps ne semble pas avancer des arguments appropriés et il ne s'explique pas non plus suffisamment. Je suppose qu'il appartient à cette catégorie d'hommes qui souhaitent être connus pour leurs paradoxes » (GP II, 492).

4. Trad. fr. G. Brykman, « Leibniz et les paradoxes de Berkeley », p. 100, du texte donné par W. Kabitz dans « Leibniz und Berkeley », p. 636.

5. S. Daniel, « The Harmony of the Leibniz-Berkeley Juxtaposition », p. 179.

6. G. Brykman, « Leibniz et les paradoxes de Berkeley », p. 112.

partagé, leur conception de Dieu est différente : « la préséance logique de l'entendement sur la volonté de Dieu » insiste sur la sagesse d'un Dieu qui choisit parmi les possibles présents dans son entendement, le meilleur; *a contrario*, Berkeley fait de Dieu un Acte pur et le choix divin procède des vérités qui sont « au-dessus de la raison » [1].

Hume, un anti-leibnizien ?

Kant a posé un cadre de lecture des rapports entre les philosophies de Leibniz et de Hume en affirmant que ce dernier l'aurait « réveillé de son sommeil dogmatique », sommeil dans lequel l'aurait plongé Leibniz. Il a ainsi contribué à construire l'image d'une opposition entre deux figures antinomiques : celle du rationaliste dogmatique et celle de l'empiriste. Nous connaissons aujourd'hui les limites de ces constructions historiographiques sous lesquelles il est désormais possible d'identifier des points de discussion et des rapprochements. Pas plus qu'une histoire de la réception ne cherche à identifier des influences, elle ne s'emploie à trouver des précurseurs. C'est la raison pour laquelle ce n'est pas sous ce régime explicatif que l'on cherche à penser le statut de l'identité personnelle, le rapport entre la substance monadique et la fameuse « *bundle theory of the mind* » [2] de Hume ou encore la distinction entre les vérités de fait et les vérités de raison. La divergence porte pour l'essentiel sur la causalité et le refus de la nécessité causale.

La comparaison des systèmes philosophiques à laquelle on procède ne cherche pas à établir des liens de causalité, ni de manière prioritaire à identifier les chemins philologiques et historiques qui mènent de l'un à l'autre. On peut toutefois rappeler que Hume a lu Leibniz et connait dès 1739 la *Théodicée* puisqu'il la cite dans son *Traité de la Nature humaine* en mentionnant des critères permettant de distinguer le vrai du faux, les types de connaissance, la distinction entre le nécessaire et le certain et donc entre la nécessité métaphysique et la nécessité morale. Or, il semble clair que Hume montre les limites du principe de non-contradiction lorsqu'il s'agit de justifier l'existence des choses :

> Il n'est pas possible de rien démontrer, à moins de prouver que le contraire implique contradiction. Rien de ce que l'on conçoit clairement n'implique contradiction. Tout ce que nous concevons existant, nous pouvons aussi le

1. Berkeley, *Alciphron or the Minute Philosopher*, p. 182, cité par G. Brykman, « Leibniz et les paradoxes de Berkeley », p. 114.

2. Cette expression renvoie à une conception ontologique de l'objet uniquement caractérisé par un faisceau ou une collection de propriétés, relations ou tropes (cf. *Traité de la Nature Humaine*, livre I, chap. IV).

> concevoir comme non-existant. Il n'est donc aucun être dont la non-existence implique contradiction. Il n'est donc aucun être dont l'existence puisse être démontrée[1].

Comme le souligne V. Vasilyev, même si Hume reprend la distinction entre les deux types de connaissance, il faut dire que Leibniz et Hume ne s'accordent pas sur le traitement des principes mathématiques : Leibniz pense pouvoir les réduire et les déduire analytiquement selon le principe d'identité, là où Hume considère cela comme impossible[2]. Ce qui soulève la question de leurs rapports différents à la causalité.

La conception humienne de la connaissance est bien connue, il est inutile de rappeler qu'elle s'appuie sur l'impossibilité dans laquelle nous nous trouvons de faire de l'expérience le lieu de constitution d'une inférence de la cause à l'effet. Il n'est pas non plus possible de donner un fondement rationnel à cette corrélation dans la mesure où l'identité entre le présent et le futur ne peut être fondée en raison. Il n'est donc pas possible de faire de la corrélation constante une corrélation nécessaire et ni l'expérience, ni la raison ne peuvent faire de cette relation une nécessité. Elle s'est établie par l'habitude, mais c'est précisément ce que Hume doit alors tenter d'expliquer. C'est à cette étape de son cheminement qu'il convoque l'analogie avec le système de l'harmonie préétablie pour justifier et fonder l'accord entre la succession de nos idées et l'ordre du monde. La correspondance entre ces deux ordres s'effectue par l'habitude :

> Ici il y a une sorte d'harmonie préétablie entre le cours de la nature et la succession de nos idées … L'habitude est le principe par lequel cette correspondance s'est effectuée. [C'est-à-dire que la Nature a] implanté en nous un instinct qui transmet la pensée dans un mouvement correspondant à ce qu'elle a établi entre les objets extérieurs[3].

Et Hume semble, conséquemment, accepter que nous soyons dans le meilleur des mondes possibles :

> Il est très sûr pour nous d'affirmer que tout ce que nous savons que la Divinité a réellement fait est ce qu'il y a de meilleur, mais il est très dangereux d'affirmer qu'elle doit toujours faire ce qui nous semble le mieux[4].

1. Hume, *Dialogues concerning Natural Religion*, p. 171.

2. V. Vasilyev, « Hume : Between Leibniz and Kant », p. 22.

3. Cité par V. Vasilyev, *ibid.*, p. 23. Voir Hume, *Enquiries Concerning Human Understanding*, p. 54-55.

4. Hume, *Essays Moral, Political and Literary*, p. 400.

À la différence de Leibniz, Hume considère que c'est dans la nature que nous devons découvrir cette harmonie sans tenter de la saisir a priori [1].

Cet exemple montre bien que s'interroger sur la réception de Leibniz dans les textes de Hume ne conduit pas à comparer les systèmes en faisant abstraction du contexte historique dans lequel ils prennent place et d'où ils émergent, mais plutôt à identifier les éléments que Hume puise dans la philosophie de Leibniz pour élaborer sa propre pensée et pour, parfois, répondre à des problèmes théoriques qui ont une forme de proximité.

Ce que révèlent ces trois brèves études de cas, c'est la prégnance des enjeux théologiques non seulement dans la réception de Leibniz au XVIIIe siècle en Angleterre mais peut-être plus fondamentalement et de manière sans doute plus surprenante la persistance des thématiques propres à la théologie physique au cœur des Lumières. On voit comment la référence à Leibniz garantit une transition philosophique au cœur du XVIIIe siècle : que ce soit sur le chemin d'une autonomisation de la mécanique à l'égard de la métaphysique (Berkeley) ou à l'appui d'une réflexion sur l'impossibilité de rapporter la question de la causalité à une nécessité mathématique, autrement dit sur le chemin qui conduit à identifier les enjeux de la certitude morale (Hume).

Anne-Lise REY
(Université de Lille)

1. Voir V. Vasilyev, « Hume : Between Leibniz and Kant », p. 25.

LA RÉCEPTION ALLEMANDE DE LEIBNIZ AU XVIIIe SIÈCLE

UN DESTIN AVANT TOUT ALLEMAND

Il est sans doute paradoxal qu'un auteur ayant écrit en latin et en français, et fort peu dans la langue de son pays natal[1], ait connu une réception avant tout allemande. Ce fut pourtant le cas au XVIIIe siècle, où Leibniz devint très tôt une référence incontournable outre-Rhin. De quel Leibniz s'est-il agi, cependant; de quoi le philosophe fut-il alors le nom? Il nous appartiendra de reconstituer la figure que le philosophe a prise dans l'historiographie de l'époque. Plusieurs périodes devront être dégagées, qui mettront, chacune, l'accent sur tel pan de doctrine. À une époque où nulle édition d'envergure de Leibniz n'existe, où, en outre, ce sont souvent certaines traductions qui en présentent la pensée, la réception ne peut être que tronquée, voire biaisée. Yvon Belaval a vu dans la mécompréhension de la monadologie leibnizienne l'un de ces biais de réception. Il n'en a pas pour autant balayé l'interprétation que les Lumières allemandes ont donnée du penseur comme nulle et non avenue, puisque c'est aussi à partir d'elle que s'est construite la tradition d'analyse postérieure :

> D'un mot : au XVIIIe siècle, on a moins affaire à Leibniz qu'à son reflet plus ou moins déformant. Se tourne-t-on vers les Lumières, l'influence de notre philosophe demeure faible, superficielle. Se tourne-t-on vers l'*Aufklärung*, cette influence est permanente, mais le rejet, par Wolff, de la perception pour toutes les monades conduit à une monadologie physique que l'on croit mieux adaptable à Newton et qui n'en est pas moins un contresens de la monadologie leibnizienne. Cependant, c'est dans le monde de

1. Sur Leibniz et la langue allemande, voir Leibniz, *L'harmonie des langues*.

l'*Aufklärung* que se propage le plus sérieux de la pensée de Leibniz, et c'est à travers l'Allemagne qu'elle est parvenue jusqu'à nous [1].

La question de la substance est l'un des fils conducteurs de la réception de Leibniz durant le siècle, de Wolff à Boscovich, Kant ou même Herbart[2]. Elle n'est pourtant pas la seule, puisque d'autres thématiques y seront également prégnantes, comme celles de l'espace et du temps, de la justice de Dieu ou des degrés de clarté et de distinction que possèdent nos idées. Tous ces objets feront l'objet d'une réappropriation par Wolff et son école, qui apparaissent comme un passage obligé pour la reconstitution de la fortune connue par Leibniz au XVIIIe siècle. Même si la dernière étape de la réception, relative à l'origine de nos connaissances, ne portera pas cette empreinte, ses prémisses le font, quant à elles. Débutons donc avec la controverse sur l'idéalisme de Leibniz, controverse dans laquelle Wolff a joué un rôle décisif dans son effort pour l'en dédouaner.

LE PRISME WOLFFIEN

Ainsi que le rappellera Pfaff en 1722 dans son discours sur l'égoïsme[3], les termes d'égoïste et d'idéaliste ont été précisés par Wolff dans la seconde préface à la *Métaphysique allemande* parue en 1721. Qu'est-ce qu'un égoïste? Un idéaliste outré, pour lequel n'existe que lui-même, en tant qu'âme d'ailleurs. Un simple idéaliste n'aurait pas poussé jusqu'à la négation de l'existence d'autrui, en tant qu'esprit. Pour Pfaff, le terme d'idéalisme n'est point une arme à brandir contre Leibniz, mais plutôt contre des Français, au premier chef desquels Malebranche, et des penseurs d'expression anglaise, au premier rang desquels Berkeley (les Hobbes, Coward et Toland étant, quant à eux, les porte-parole du matérialisme, les négateurs d'une substantialité psychique). S'il ne nomme pas ces penseurs dans la seconde préface de sa *Métaphysique allemande*, Wolff a certainement dû les avoir en vue. Ce qui est sûr, en tout cas, c'est que Leibniz n'était pas du nombre. Son système de l'harmonie « prédéterminée »[4] présente en effet l'avantage de ne pas être unilatéral mais de concilier les points de vue extrêmes.

1. Y. Belaval, *Études leibniziennes. De Leibniz à Hegel*, p. 227.
2. Voir J. Croizer, *Les héritiers de Leibniz*.
3. Ch. Pfaff, *Oratio de egoismo, nova philosophica haeresi*.
4. *Vernünfftige Gedancken von Gott, der Welt und der Seele des Menschen, Gesammelte Werke* I, 2, p. 13* (nous paginons).

> Monsieur de Leibniz a aperçu que l'affaire du comment le corps et l'âme s'accordent l'un l'autre se laisse entendre lorsque l'on prend ensemble, l'un et l'autre, ce qu'enseignent les idéalistes et les matérialistes[1].

Leibniz adopterait donc une position moyenne, renvoyant dos à dos les sectateurs en conflit. Certes, il n'aurait jamais exposé cela, en aurait seulement pensé les prémisses[2], mais son intention serait claire : l'idéaliste et le matérialiste souffrent d'unilatéralité, et leurs doctrines doivent être cousues ensemble pour y remédier. On voit ici un Wolff fidèle à l'esprit conciliateur de Leibniz. Son devancier aurait souhaité proposer une solution meilleure que celles que l'on avait avancées jusque-là, une solution qui leur rendrait justice tout en les portant à un niveau d'intelligibilité supérieur. On trouve également un Wolff cantonnant la question de l'harmonie au niveau local, celui du commerce entre corps et âme, et ne poussant pas le propos jusqu'à la considération de l'harmonie générale. N'aurait-il donc eu connaissance que des horloges que l'on synchronise; aurait-il donc tout ignoré du règne de la nature et de la grâce en son ensemble? Nous allons voir que non. La lecture wolffienne de Leibniz se fait sous bénéfice d'inventaire et ne s'opère pas dans l'ignorance de grands points de doctrine. Considérons ainsi la reprise personnelle qu'il fait de la *Théodicée*[3].

Dès 1711, on trouve une recension wolffienne de la *Théodicée* dans les *Acta eruditorum*[4]. En 1720, dans la préface d'une traduction allemande de certains passages de Leibniz[5], on découvrira de même un renvoi explicite à cette œuvre-phare. Wolff avait été, par ailleurs, l'unique dépositaire du manuscrit pendant quelques mois, ce qui montre et sa connaissance de

1. *Vernünfftige Gedancken von Gott, der Welt und der Seele des Menschen, Gesammelte Werke* I, 2, p. 12* (nous paginons).

2. *Ibid.*

3. Remarquons en passant qu'une traduction allemande de la *Théodicée* a paru en 1720, avec en annexe un cahier de seize pages détaillant les publications de Leibniz, de la main de Johann Georg Eckhart, son successeur comme bibliothécaire au service du prince électeur de Hanovre. Voir S. Lorenz, « "Auferstehung eines Leibes dessen Glieder wunderbahrlich herum zerstreuet sind". Leibniz-Renaissancen und ihre editorischen Reflexe », p. 65-92, ici p. 71.

4. Voir A. Lalanne, « La recension *des Essais de Théodicée* dans les *Acta Eruditorum* par Wolff : une reconstruction systématique ? Traduction inédite et présentation de la recension à l'occasion du tricentenaire de sa publication », http://www.philosophiedudroit.org/lalanne,%20leibniz.htm, mis en ligne le 7 mai 2011.

5. *Merckwürdige Schrifften*, 113.

l'œuvre, quand bien même il l'aurait parcourue «*oculo fugitivo*»[1], et la confiance que Leibniz avait placée en lui.

Que ressort-il de la reprise wolffienne de la *Théodicée?* Certains silences sont éloquents : Wolff ne souhaite ainsi nullement s'égarer dans le labyrinthe de la continuité et des indivisibles, et n'en souffle mot. La question de la substance n'est ainsi pas son interrogation première. La liberté, quant à elle, se voit bien mieux traitée et fait l'objet d'un résumé concis mais fidèle. Des points précis de l'héritage leibnizien sont ainsi mis en lumière quand d'autres, avec lesquels ils conspirent pourtant, ne sont pas relevés.

C'est que Wolff, en fait, entend reprendre dans ses propres chaînes de raison le fonds doctrinal étranger susceptible d'y entrer. Le puîné ne fait pas que sélectionner dans les dires de l'aîné, il entend donner une assise plus profonde et unitaire à ce qui paraissait sans raison ni liaison. La préface de 1720 le donne clairement à lire :

> Puisque, dans mes pensées raisonnées sur Dieu, le monde et l'âme de l'homme, comme de toutes les choses en général [= *Métaphysique allemande*], j'ai en même temps déduit de leurs premiers principes les vérités métaphysiques de M. de Leibniz, on comprendra alors bien mieux et solidement tant la Théodicée que le présent écrit [= traduction allemande de quatre pièces] lorsqu'on aura consacré le zèle et le temps appropriés à ma métaphysique[2].

Ainsi, Wolff lui-même a donné raison par anticipation à ceux qui parleront de philosophie leibniziano-woffienne ou emploieront à cet effet quelque équivalent. Il aurait fondu puis enchaîné dans son plan personnel certaines séquences que Leibniz lui aurait léguées.

Le cercle autour de Wolff n'a pas été en reste dans la première diffusion du fonds leibnizien. Le philosophe et juriste Heinrich Köhler (1685-1737)[3], élève de Wolff à Halle et proche de Leibniz à Vienne à l'époque de la confection de la *Monadologie*, a joué un rôle prépondérant dans l'affaire. C'est à ce dernier que l'on doit la première traduction allemande du texte, parue en 1720, et sous ce titre, dont il l'a baptisé. En 1721, les *Acta eruditorum* donneront une version latine du texte, version que certains attribuent

1. Sur le sens de cette expression, voir G. Tognon, «Christian Wolff e gli "Essais de Théodicée"», p. 961-971.

2. Wolff, GW III, 113, feuillet (a)4 (non paginé).

3. Sur ce personnage, voir l'introduction de S. Carboncini-Gavanelli à Wolff, GW II, 114, 2010 : Leibniz, *Kleinere Philosophische Schriften mit einer Vorrede Herrn Christian Wolffs, ehedem von dem Jenaischen Philosophen Herrn Heinrich Köhler teutsch übersetzet, nun auf das neue übersehen von M. Caspar Jacob Huth* [original : Iéna, 1740].

à Wolff lui-même, même si ce point est controversé[1]. Quoi qu'il en soit, les versions allemande et latine présentent des écarts significatifs par rapport au texte français qui leur a servi de support, notamment en ce qui concerne l'existence d'une substance composée.

Ainsi qu'Antonio Lamarra l'a relevé[2], trois paragraphes dans la version latine de la *Monadologie* laissent entendre l'existence, non pas du composé, mais de la substance composée. Plutôt que d'aller dans le sens d'un phénoménalisme, cette traduction, de manière subtile mais significative, orienterait le regard vers les corps en tant qu'agrégats d'êtres subsistant par soi. Remarquons au passage que la version allemande, antérieure d'un an, sans être équivalente au latin à tous les endroits, introduit en son § 62, un accord entre « choses composées » et « substances simples »[3], substantivant donc grammaticalement et ontologiquement l'agrégat. En plus d'être dualiste, ou justement en raison de son dualisme[4], Wolff semble mêler des considérations cartésiennes au fonds leibnizien : le monde serait toujours une connexion de choses, comme les choses, considérées en elles-mêmes, seraient à leur tour toujours un *nexus;* dans tous les cas, la notion de parties l'une à l'extérieur de l'autre serait fondamentale.

Wolff ne reconnaîtra plus inconditionnellement à la substance corporelle la capacité de percevoir, d'avoir des idées. Dans la *Métaphysique allemande*[5], il laissera simplement de côté la question de savoir si les « unités naturelles leibniziennes »[6] sont comme un miroir de l'univers; il importait seulement de remarquer qu'il n'y avait pas de contradiction entre ces monades et les choses simples, agissant sans cesse pour changer leur limitation, mais dont on ne disait rien quant à leur force représentative! La suite de l'œuvre, notamment la *Psychologia rationalis*, ne laissera pourtant plus planer de doute sur la rupture réelle avec Leibniz. La succession des représentations en notre âme se doublera, de manière harmonique, de mouvements d'idées matérielles dans nos nerfs et notre cerveau, de nature différente[7]. L'influence cartésienne se fera donc encore sentir sur

1. Voir J. Park, « Le débat wolffien sur l'idéalisme de Leibniz lors de la première diffusion de la Monadologie latine », p. 325-339.

2. Voir A. Lamarra, « Le traduzioni settecentesche della Monadologie. Christian Wolff e la prima recezione di Leibniz », p. 1-117.

3. Voir § 62, p. 27 et *ibid.*, p. 101.

4. Ce dualisme a déjà été souligné par Ch. A. Corr dans son introduction à la *Métaphysique allemande*, en GW I, 2.1.

5. *Vernünfftige Gedancken von Gott, der Welt und der Seele des Menschen*, GWI, 2.1 et 2.2.

6. GW I, 2.2, § 598 *sq.*, p. 368 *sq.*

7. Voir par exemple la définition de l'idée matérielle en GW II, 6, § 112, p. 88.

la doctrine propre. Puisque Wolff avait présenté Leibniz comme un dualiste, et qu'il mettait en scène une convergence avec lui plutôt qu'une divergence de vue, il pouvait aisément se produire que ses nombreux lecteurs et auditeurs prêtent à ce dernier ce qu'il n'avait pas dit en fait.

L'harmonie leibnizienne, avec ce qu'elle comportait de causalité idéale entre les monades, apparaissait sous un jour trouble. Leibniz n'aurait certes pas dénié les qualités prêtées par Wolff aux éléments de la nature, mais il aurait assurément fait remarquer que ce dernier n'en disait pas assez à leur sujet : tout ce que Wolff en disait, Leibniz l'aurait dit aussi, mais la réciproque n'était pas vraie. L'auteur de la *Métaphysique allemande*, en mettant l'accent sur l'absence de conscience de soi chez beaucoup d'unités, laissait entendre qu'une absence d'idée tout court chez elles serait la bienvenue. À l'autre bout de l'échelle des êtres, toutefois, pour ce qui est des esprits appelés à un plus grand théâtre, eux qui ne disposent pas uniquement de la consécution empirique des bêtes mais peuvent pleinement posséder l'usage de la raison, l'accord se montre beaucoup plus important. Tant la psychologie latine wolffienne que l'allemande reprendront à leur compte l'exemple du chien réagissant par expérience lorsqu'on brandit un bâton devant lui[1]. Sur le registre de l'âme des bêtes, comme sur celui de la communauté pneumatologique entre Dieu et les hommes, le legs leibnizien passe dans la doctrine wolffienne.

DE LA MÉTAPHYSIQUE LEIBNIZIENNE À LA MÉTAPHYSIQUE LEIBNIZIANO-WOLFFIENNE

Tant Leibniz que Wolff ont affirmé n'avoir jamais parlé de métaphysique dans leur correspondance, laquelle a couru pendant plus de dix ans, avec une fréquence moyenne d'une lettre par mois pourtant[2]. La correspondance partielle éditée au dix-neuvième siècle[3] corrobore ces dires. Même si l'absence totale de conversation métaphysique semble peu

1. Voir par exemple la *Psychologia rationalis*, GW II, 6, § 765, p. 678-679 (laquelle s'appuie sur de nombreux paragraphes de la *Psychologia empirica*, GW II, 5), et la *Métaphysique allemande*, GW I, 2.2, § 870, p. 538. L'original leibnizien se trouve dans la *Monadologie*, au § 26 Voir Leibniz, *Discours de métaphysique* suivi de *Monadologie* et autres textes, p. 226.

2. Voir l'introduction de S. Carboncini-Gavanelli à Wolff, GW II, 113, p. 2*-3*.

3. *Briefwechsel zwischen Leibniz und Christian Wolff*. C. I. Gerhardt (Hrsg.), Hannover, H. W. Schmidt, 1860.

probable[1], le fait que les échanges épistolaires n'ont jamais touché de front les sujets de fond l'est bien davantage. Wolff ne peut donc être tenu pour le dépositaire d'un savoir leibnizien qu'il aurait dû communiquer tel quel à la postérité; la sentence souvent entendue de nos jours «Wolff n'a pas compris Leibniz» ne présente pas grand sens. Penseur se voulant autonome, il s'est bien plutôt défendu d'avoir été le simple élève du maître. L'entrelacs des propos a été revendiqué par le cadet; l'a été également le fait d'avoir confectionné ses propres chaînes de raison et de n'y avoir retenu que ce qui laissait démontrer le moment venu.

Wolff, inlassable commentateur de lui-même, est revenu dans une recension des *Acta eruditorum* sur la traduction par Köhler de la correspondance Leibniz/Clarke et d'autres pièces[2]. Son propos roule sur trois points: le traducteur aurait communiqué fidèlement sur la philosophie leibnizienne et wolffienne (où l'on voit qu'il n'y a qu'un pas à franchir pour parler de philosophie leibniziano-wolffienne); Leibniz aurait dispersé sa métaphysique dans divers écrits sans en livrer de présentation systématique (où l'on voit que la notion de système ne revêt pas le même sens chez les deux philosophes); la philosophie wolffienne serait à antéposer, au titre de présupposé, pour entendre les pensées leibniziennes (où l'on voit qu'une inversion de l'origine conceptuelle et de l'origine temporelle est tentée, à son profit, par le cadet). Comme il l'écrira plus tard à Manteuffel, le système de Leibniz «commence là où cesse le mien»[3]. L'harmonie préétablie, point focal de la philosophie leibnizienne, n'interviendra en effet plus chez Wolff que comme une hypothèse probable, et ce tardivement dans l'économie de l'enchaînement propre des raisons, dans la psychologie rationnelle ou la théologie naturelle. Pour l'amour de la vérité, il faudrait donc parcourir dans l'ordre souhaité les vérités wolffiennes pour ne toucher qu'en toute fin l'harmonie préétablie, dans son rapport à l'influx physique ou à l'occasionnalisme.

1. Wolff écrit à Manteuffel le 19 décembre 1746 que Leibniz lui aurait lui-même dit un jour être du même avis que Platon sur les monades ou l'immortalité de l'âme (*Der Briefwechsel zwischen Christian Wolff und Ernst Christoph von Manteuffel 1738 bis 1748; Teil 2*, http://slub.qucosa.de/api/qucosa%3A2850/attachment/ATT-0/, lettre n° 294, p. 236 – consulté le 21/04/2017).

2. Voir S. Carboncini-Gavanelli, « Introduction » à Wolff, GW II, 113, p. 8*.

3. Voir *ibid.*, p. 11*-12*. Voir la lettre n°242 du 11 mai 1746, dans laquelle Wolff se plaint de la confusion opérée par G. B. Bilfinger lorsque ce dernier a le premier parlé de «philosophie leibniziano-wolffienne», *Der Briefwechsel zwischen Christian Wolff und Ernst Christoph von Manteuffel 1738 bis 1748*; Teil 2, p. 159.

Wolff, pris dans des polémiques virulentes dès le début de sa carrière académique à Halle, peu après la mort de Leibniz, marque parfois ses distances avec ce dernier. Contre Lange notamment, qui l'accuse de se contenter de reprendre les thèses leibniziennes dans sa métaphysique, tout entière fondée sur l'harmonie préétablie, il déclare qu'il ne se trouve en fait que peu de choses leibniziennes dans son propos. Jean École a plutôt montré qu'il se trouvait en fait beaucoup de choses leibniziennes chez Wolff, mais de façon si personnelle qu'on ne peut parler de simple travail épigonal, ni de pure mise en forme[1]. Wolff n'a certes retenu de Leibniz que ce qui lui agréait, peu de chose dans chaque philosophème, mais il a mis à profit de nombreux philosophèmes leibniziens; le peu et le beaucoup s'entendent en fait de manière différente. *Non multum, sed multa*, pourrait-on dire si l'on regrettait que le sel leibnizien manquât aux propositions wolffiennes.

Les allégations personnelles de Wolff, celles de ses opposants mais également celles de ses partisans ont ainsi concouru à la formation précoce d'un monstre à deux têtes assez inouï dans l'histoire de la philosophie. En 1725, J. S. Billebius parle d'« harmonia praestabilita Leibnitio-Wolffiana », tandis que J. W. Feuerlin emploie le terme de « Metaphysica Leibnitio-Wolffiana ». Et il ne faut que peu d'années pour que ce type d'expressions n'entre dans la dénomination d'ouvrages et ne prenne une consistance plus ferme. 1738 voit ainsi la parution d'une *Anleitung zur Historie der Leibnitzisch– Wolffischen Philosophie*, les années suivantes donnant également, par la plume de C. G. Ludovici notamment, des ouvrages de ce type[2]. L'amalgame des deux penseurs a donc été de règle pendant une très large part du dix-huitième.

La collusion entre fonds leibnizien et wolffien n'a pas empêché des inflexions personnelles notables dans les exposés métaphysiques de l'*Aufklärung*. Baumgarten, qui signe en 1739 la première version de sa *Metaphysica*, affiche une parenté plus grande avec Leibniz sur des points de doctrine importants, la monadologie et l'harmonie préétablie :

> [C]ontre l'affirmation wolffienne selon laquelle les éléments ultimes du monde, des substances mondaines, sont des êtres simples, il reprend la thèse leibnizienne selon laquelle l'être réel est seulement et toujours monade, selon laquelle semblables monades seraient également les éléments ultimes de l'univers et de tous les êtres, du plus infime à Dieu[3].

1. Voir J. École, « Des rapports de Wolff avec Leibniz dans le domaine de la métaphysique », p. 88-96.
2. Voir *Ibid.*, p. 89.
3. Voir M. Casula, *La metafisica di A. G. Baumgarten*, p. 22-23.

Tous les êtres, par leur nature propre, sont dotés d'une force représentative, laquelle, par ailleurs, commence avec la sensation et monte jusqu'aux facultés supérieures de connaître. L'apport wolffien, revisité quant au nombre des facultés et relativement à la place et à la nature de la sensibilité dans l'économie de la connaissance[1], continue de se faire sentir, en parallèle, dans la structuration de la métaphysique baumgartenerienne. La philosophie leibniziano-wolffienne n'est dès lors nullement monolithique mais prend des figures différentes, selon les générations d'auteurs et leur talent propre.

La diffusion des idées leibniziennes s'est poursuivie grâce aux philosophes nourris de philosophie wolffienne. L'année 1744, pour ne parler que d'elle, a vu Johann Christoph Gottsched signer la préface à la quatrième édition de la *Théodicée* et traduire en allemand l'article « Rorarius » du *Dictionnaire* de Bayle[2]. Les problèmes touchés par Leibniz, concernant la liberté de la volonté, l'athéisme ou le problème de l'union de l'âme et du corps ont continué d'alimenter le débat de langue allemande. Celui de l'optimisme et de la justice de Dieu fut également relancé à cette occasion. Il est malgré tout fort probable que l'arrière-fond d'une question posée sur l'optimisme par l'Académie de Berlin en 1753, alors présidée par Maupertuis, ait porté autant sur Pope que sur Leibniz, peu apprécié. C'est du moins ainsi que l'a comprise le métaphysicien qu'était alors Immanuel Kant lorsqu'il a conçu par distinction ses propres thèses physico-théologiques.

Regardons justement de plus près aux dires du Kant précritique. La doctrine leibnizienne comporterait plusieurs erreurs fondamentales, ce qui la ferait manquer d'unité, si l'on suit le commentaire de Robert Theis[3]. La première viendrait du fait que « le plan du meilleur des mondes possibles est placé d'une part dans une *dépendance* et d'autre part dans une *indépendance* par rapport à la volonté divine »[4]; la volonté de Dieu serait par nature orientée vers le meilleur, tandis que son choix, les possibles étant coéternels à son entendement, serait en quelque sorte contraint. La seconde viendrait quant à elle de la déconnexion entre les preuves *a priori* et *a posteriori* de l'existence de Dieu, telles qu'exposées dans la *Monadologie*, avec la thèse du meilleur des mondes possibles. En rupture avec

1. Sur Baumgarten, voir par ex. S. Buchenau, *The Founding of Aesthetics in the German Enlightenment*.

2. Voir W. Ch. Zimmerli, « Von der Verfertigung einer philosophiehistorischen Größe : Leibniz in der Philosophiegeschichtsschreibung des 18. Jahrhunderts », p. 148-167, ici p. 149-150.

3. R. Theis, « La question de l'optimisme dans la première pensée de Kant », p. 157-164.

4. *Ibid.*, p. 160.

Leibniz, le Kant précritique voit, comme on le sait, dans la preuve physico-théologique la meilleure preuve de l'existence de Dieu : les choses forment en elles-mêmes un tout ordonné et bon, un plan harmonieux.

Alors que c'est le nom de Pope qui est principalement associé au *Poème sur le désastre de Lisbonne* de 1755, c'est celui de Leibniz qui apparaît dans *Candide*, publié en 1759. Même si Voltaire a reconnu en ce dernier quelqu'un qui fut sans doute le savant européen le plus universel, il n'en a pas moins critiqué de manière acerbe son prétendu optimisme, en y voyant une sorte de fatalisme. Bien que Voltaire ait bien compris que le bien et le mieux n'étaient nullement identifiables, que le mieux, en outre, ne se limitait pas au présent mais valait pour l'ensemble du monde considéré dans sa sommation historique, il lui semble que Leibniz a fait preuve de présomption en se confrontant à cette question métaphysique. Ainsi que Marc Parmentier le résume[1], « Leibniz fait trop confiance à la portée de sa raison en s'attaquant à un problème qui dépasse l'entendement humain ». Le conte philosophique servira d'expérience de pensée montrant l'inanité de la tentative faite pour restituer la justice de Dieu.

Un jalon important de la réception de Leibniz en ce début de seconde moitié du dix-huitième siècle est fourni par les travaux historiographiques de Brucker. Dans l'*Historia Critica Philosophiae* (seconde édition en 1766), on trouve un écho précis des débats ayant eu lieu autour de Leibniz les décennies précédentes. La controverse entre Bayle et Leibniz figure ainsi en bonne part (Brucker donne ici une interprétation du commerce des substances comme pacte entre elles), comme le font des passages très célèbres de Ludovoci, retraçant la polémique entre Wolff et Lange autour de l'harmonie préétablie (donnée, à la manière leibnizienne et wolffienne, comme une hypothèse), de même que le début de la *Métaphysique allemande*. Même si Brucker rend à Leibniz ce qui lui appartient, il ne laisse pas d'être tributaire d'un horizon interprétatif wolffien. Walter Ch. Zimmerli résume ainsi la position de l'historiographe, position qui connaîtra un retentissement important sur les travaux postérieurs allemands dans ce champ :

> Chez Brucker, partant, – quoique sans doute aussi contre l'intention de l'auteur – se montre déjà clairement la tendance à identifier la philosophie de Leibniz et de Wolff, et ce, de sorte que Wolff ait présenté la version plus systématiquement prégnante et dépourvue d'erreur des pensées conçues isolément par Leibniz. Leibniz demeure le génie, mais la haute estime dans laquelle on tient la procédure « démonstrative », la manière déductive et

1. M. Parmentier, « Voltaire et l'optimisme leibnizien », p. 149.

systématique de procéder, conduit à ce qu'on aperçoive en Leibniz comme la forme imparfaite, et en Wolff, en revanche, sa systématisation « mathématique » parfaite [1].

Sur la scène allemande, ce jugement continuera de retentir longtemps. La vive discussion autour de l'emploi de la méthode mathématique en philosophie, attestée par la mise au concours en 1761 par l'Académie de Berlin d'une question sur l'évidence (ou distinction, *Deutlichkeit*) de la théologie et de la doctrine morale, aura toutefois pour conséquence de polariser autrement les apports de Leibniz et de Wolff. Si la méthode mathématique n'est plus de mise en philosophie, on ne peut plus valoriser ainsi la mise au pas démonstrative de pensées originales. Friedrich Schlegel s'amusera ainsi de ce que certains aiment les systèmes comme ils le feraient de troupes en parade. Plus loin, d'un trait de plume, il inversera les valeurs du génie et de la mise en forme réglée, et marquera par là un tournant décisif dans l'histoire de la philosophie, celle de l'encensement de Leibniz et du mépris conjoint de Wolff : « Leibniz a affirmé, et Wolff démontré. En voilà assez dit » [2].

Mais un mot encore sur l'influence de Brucker, avant d'en revenir à la question de la distinction. Diderot, lorsqu'il a fait paraître en 1765 l'article « Leibnitzianisme » dans son *Encyclopédie*, a certainement relu plusieurs textes-clefs du philosophe, les *Meditationes de cognitione, veritate et ideis*, les *Essais de Théodicée* et la *Monadologie*. Il apparaît toutefois que cet article reprend un éloge de Fontenelle et traduit des passages de Brucker, tout en ajoutant, supprimant ou modifiant les sources. Malgré des divergences fondamentales entre un matérialisme athée et une métaphysique monadiste et finaliste, un empirisme et une défense des idées innées, une orientation aux savoirs empiriques et un positionnement plus logico-mathématique, on trouve des points de convergence entre Leibniz et Diderot : « l'idée d'encyclopédie et des sociétés savantes, une pratique philosophique plurielle, voire par moments éclectique, l'accent mis sur certaines questions comme le rapport entre l'inerte et le vivant, la modalité des lois de la nature et le statut des unités ultimes de la matière » [3].

1. *Ibid.*, p. 157.

2. Schlegel, *Charakteristiken und Kritiken I [1796-1801]*, *in* H. Eichner (Hrsg.), *Kritische Friedrich-Schlegel-Ausgabe*, Bd. I, 2, München/Paderborn/Wien, Schöningh, 1967, p. 177.

3. *Leibniz et Diderot*, « Avant-propos », p. 11-12.

L'INFLUENCE LEIBNIZIENNE SUR LES DÉBATS RELATIFS À LA CONNAISSANCE

L'opuscule leibnizien dénommé *Meditationes de cognitione, veritate et ideis* a connu une réception précoce. Il est ainsi par exemple déjà mentionné dans la *Logique allemande*[1] de Wolff comme un texte-clef. Le cadet, comme à l'accoutumée, ne reprend pas telle quelle l'échelle leibnizienne des notions mais la modifie à sa main. On voit ainsi apparaître par exemple une différence entre un concept distinct complet et un concept distinct incomplet, lequel comporte encore un peu de confusion[2]. Toutefois, les changements ne concernent pas uniquement la nomenclature. La réception wolffienne engage en fait une autre notion de la connaissance, avec un type d'analyse et un recours à l'abstraction qui lui sont propres. La cible visée se déplace également : ce n'est pas tant l'individuel dont on doit esquisser la notion qu'une certaine forme de généralité, conquise à partir de données individuelles sensibles. Derrière ces changements logiques se cachent ainsi des options ontologiques précises. C'est à partir des ressemblances qui nous sont livrées dans des jugements intuitifs, singuliers, que l'esprit va se mettre en branle pour fournir des concepts à proprement parler. Jean-Paul Paccioni résume ainsi le déplacement important s'étant opéré :

> Wolff situe ici d'emblée son analyse des notions au niveau de l'espèce, il ne s'agit pas d'envisager la notion complète d'un individu. La chose que l'on reconnaît chaque fois c'est l'usufruit, la colique, la rosée *dans leur généralité*, telles que l'on est ensuite capable de les reconnaître dans des circonstances singulières. Mais surtout, la complétude en jeu suppose qu'on puisse énumérer une quantité de caractères constituants, ceux-ci étant considérés comme des parties constitutives d'un concept, qui s'agrègent, s'additionnent de telle sorte qu'à la fin ils nous permettent de reconnaître la chose[3].

Les conséquences de ce déplacement wolffien se feront encore ressentir dans l'esthétique transcendantale de la *Critique de la raison pure*[4]. Lorsque Kant s'en prend au point de vue tout à fait faux de Leibniz et

1. Voir Wolff, *Vernünfftige Gedancken von den Kräfften des menschlichen Verstandes und ihrem richtigen Gebrauche in Erkenntnis der Wahrheit*, GW I, 1, 1978, avant-propos à la première édition, p. 109.

2. *Ibid.*, chap. I, § 16, p. 130-131.

3. J.-P. Paccioni, *Cet esprit de profondeur. Christian Wolff, l'ontologie et la métaphysique*, p. 91.

4. Kant, *Critique de la raison pure*, A 44/B 61-62 (les lettres A et B désignent respectivement la première et la seconde édition ; le nombre qui les accompagne indique la page).

de Wolff consistant à faire de la différence entre sensible et intellectuel une différence d'ordre logique[1], il souscrit en fait à une vision très wolffienne de ce qu'est un concept, à savoir une simple représentation de la conscience, prétendant avoir une valeur objective et ne pouvant être établi que dans un rapport à la sensibilité. On n'a donc aucunement affaire à une critique fondée de Leibniz, lequel n'a pas réellement traité de la sensibilité dans ses *Meditationes*.

Un autre point d'importance est à relever relativement à la discussion post-leibnizienne des degrés de distinction. Dans le commentaire wolffien, une analyse exhaustive des notions, allant jusqu'aux entités primitives et simples, se révèle possible. Là où Leibniz réservait cela à un entendement divin, son successeur ne pose aucune réserve de la sorte. Ainsi que Christian Leduc[2] le relève, plusieurs logiciens allemands du dix-huitième siècle adopteront la même position que Wolff relativement à l'analyse. Lambert, par exemple, défend également la thèse selon laquelle la décomposition d'un concept conduit à l'intuition de notions simples; son *Organon* exprimera cette position, tandis que son *Anlage zur Architektonik* produira une liste de pareilles notions, ne possédant qu'elles-mêmes comme marque distincte, telles l'extension ou la force.

Que la réélaboration des *Meditationes* ait accordé une place importante à l'intuition, sensible notamment, ne laisse pas d'étonner. On aurait très bien pu en tirer la leçon contraire de la limite de l'intuition simultanée pour un entendement fini, partant la nécessité d'avoir recours, notamment dans une longue analyse, à une connaissance aveugle, ou symbolique. « Des idées possédées distinctement peuvent ne pas être des objets de perception », comme le résume Matteo Favaretti[3]. Et toutes les fois que l'esprit ne parvient pas à concevoir une idée complètement distincte, pour ne pas l'avoir analysée ou parce qu'elle est trop complexe pour être intuitionnée, la pensée qui en résulte est aveugle. Selon Leibniz, le symbolisme

1. Dans le second tome de sa *Psychologie comme science*, qu'il a achevé de rédiger après avoir relu la *Critique de la raison pure*, Herbart a bien vu que Kant avait en partie fait sa différence entre facultés passive (sensibilité) et active (entendement) parce qu'il semblait ne pas avoir suffisamment fait la différence entre Leibniz et Wolff; l'autre raison de ce choix aurait été une compréhension de Leibniz trop lockéenne, trop marquée par l'accommodement à la doctrine d'autrui qu'il aurait pratiqué dans ses *Nouveaux Essais*. *Cf.* J. F. Herbart, *Psychologie als Wissenschaft, neu gegründet auf Erfahrung, Metaphysik und Mathematik, zweyter analytischer Theil*, Königsberg, Unzer, 1825, § 118, p. 167 n.

2. Voir C. Leduc, « Les *Meditationes* de Leibniz dans la tradition wolffienne », p. 295-317, plus particulièrement p. 307-308.

3. Voir M. Favaretti Camposampiero, *Filum cogitandi. Leibniz e la conoscenza simbolica*, préface de L. Perissinotto, p. 24.

ne présente donc rien d'un mode intrinsèquement défectif de connaissance, il est plutôt un secours qui se présente très fréquemment à l'esprit fini.

Il ne faudrait pourtant pas en conclure que Wolff a tenu pour rien l'usage des signes. Les facultés supérieures de connaître, en effet, opèrent avant tout de manière symbolique. Ces signes ne sont pas innés mais conventionnels, appris par le commerce avec des êtres parlants. L'usage de la raison, en effet, ne se développe qu'avec l'usage de la langue, la vie en communauté. Wolff, grâce à sa théorie linguistique, trace une voie moyenne entre l'innéisme et l'empirisme de la sensation, pour le dire avec l'interprète précédemment cité[1]. Cette réélaboration de l'apport leibnizien ne constitue pas un retour en arrière mais ouvre au contraire largement sur des productions novatrices du dix-huitième siècle. Les thèses sur les hiéroglyphes dans la *Psychologia empirica* influenceront la discipline nouvelle de l'esthétique; les sémiotiques de Lambert ou de Hoffbauer se ressentiront également de la forte élaboration que Wolff a faite de l'usage des signes; enfin, la matrice wolffienne continuera de se déployer dans les théories de Herder et de Humboldt sur la constitution linguistique de la pensée humaine[2]. La grande lumière reçue par les *Meditationes* de Leibniz a certes pu passer par de nombreux miroirs, mais elle n'en a pas moins éclairé toute une époque.

1765 représente une année importante dans la réception de Leibniz. C'est en effet à cette date que Raspe publie pour la première fois les *Nouveaux Essais*[3] et ouvre ainsi une nouvelle époque de commentaire (la version allemande datera, quant à elle, de 1778-1780). Le portrait de Leibniz deviendra également plus adéquat[4] lors de la parution par Dutens en 1768 de six volumes de ses œuvres, portant sur tous les domaines que le philosophe avait touchés. Max Wundt[5], qui insiste sur les traductions du français et, davantage, de l'anglais durant cette fin d'*Aufklärung*, voit surtout l'influence de Leibniz dans un renouveau du platonisme, par

1. Voir M. Favaretti Camposampiero, *Conoscenza simbolica. Pensiero e linguaggio in Christian Wolff e nella prima età moderna.*

2. Voir la conclusion de l'ouvrage précédemment cité.

3. Sur l'importance de l'édition par Raspe des *Œuvres latines et françaises de feu Mr de Leibnitz*, voir F. Duchesneau et J. Griard (dir.), *Leibniz selon les Nouveaux essais sur l'entendement humain.*

4. Sur ce portrait de Leibniz, voir par ex. *Leibnizbilder im 18. und 19. Jahrhundert*, A. Lewendoski (Hrsg.), *Studia-Leibnitiana SH-33*, Stuttgart, Franz Steiner, 2004; l'article de H. Busche, « *Wie triftig ist Kants Kritik des Metaphysikers Leibniz?* », p. 171-182, plus particulièrement p. 173, revient sur les différentes éditions de Leibniz à la fin de l'*Aufklärung*, avant de donner des clefs pour comprendre la lecture kantienne de Leibniz.

5. M. Wundt, *Die deutsche Schulphilosophie im Zeitalter der Aufklärung.*

opposition au psychologisme, devenu dominant depuis son importation, et à l'aristotélisme, dominant dans la scolastique allemande et dans le wolffianisme. Les *Nouveaux Essais* et leur célèbre opposition à la théorie de l'esprit comme table rase n'ont pas ressuscité l'innéisme cartésien ; au contraire, ils ont rappelé comment les occasions sensibles pouvaient réveiller les notions, lesquelles apparaissaient ainsi comme devant trouver une forme d'accomplissement dans l'expérience[1]. La Renaissance leibnizienne, avant de donner naissance à la fin du siècle à une Renaissance platonicienne, a du moins mis l'accent sur la question de la connaissance d'une manière déterminante.

On n'a nullement attendu Leibniz pour connaître quelque chose de la philosophie de Locke. Des essais de ce dernier étaient connus depuis longtemps, comme le texte posthume *Sur la conduite de l'entendement*, ainsi que l'atteste une recension très précoce par Wolff dans les *Acta eruditorum*[2]. Vers le milieu du siècle, Meier se voit chargé par le roi de Prusse de faire un cours sur Locke à Halle[3]. Le rationalisme commence à voir son hégémonie disputée : on reconnaît désormais, en plus des préjugés des sens, des préjugés de la raison, et on met toujours davantage l'accent sur les limites de notre entendement[4]. Avec la parution des *Nouveaux Essais*, le siècle commence à poser clairement la question de l'origine de nos connaissances, des sources de nos notions. Le grand connaisseur de l'époque qu'a été Giorgio Tonelli[5] a retracé deux grands débats du second dix-huitième siècle allemand : après une interrogation serrée sur la validité de la méthode mathématique en philosophie, un questionnement assidu a commencé de poindre concernant la question de la connaissance[6]. L'Académie de Berlin, notons-le au passage, a également joué un rôle notable dans la montée en puissance de ce dernier questionnement.

L'influence des *Nouveaux Essais* se retrouve par exemple sous la plume d'un auteur important de cette dernière période de l'*Aufklärung*, le médecin et philosophe de Leipzig Ernst Platner. Dans la première

1. *Ibid.*, p. 318-319.

2. Voir *Nova acta eruditorum Lipsiae*, janvier 1708, p. 40-44. La correspondance avec Leibniz, en 1705, montrait déjà du reste l'importance du philosophe anglais pour Wolff.

3. Voir par ex. l'article sur Georg Friedrich Meier dans *The Bloomsbury Companion to Kant*, p. 142-144, ici p. 142.

4. Sur les préjugés, voir P. Rumore, « Un wolffiano diffidente : Georg Friedrich Meier e la sua dottrina dei pregiudizi », p. V-XXXVI.

5. Voir G. Tonelli, *Da Leibniz a Kant. Saggi sul pensiero del Settecento*.

6. Voir l'article « La disputa sul metodo matematico nella filosofia della prima metà del Settecento e la genesi dello scritto kantiano sull' "evidenza" », p. 79-107.

mouture de ses *Aphorismes philosophiques*, datée de 1776[1], on voit clairement le retentissement de l'édition des *Nouveaux Essais* par Raspe, doublant celui de la *Monadologie*. Le § 21, p. 8, mentionne déjà en remarque ces deux œuvres pour appuyer l'existence de pensées obscures, l'âme, qui pense toujours, ne pouvant en être dépourvue. Le débat entre partisans de la philosophie de Locke et ceux de Leibniz est ensuite retranscrit durant de longues pages. L'éclectisme de Platner se nourrit ainsi des derniers apports en matière de philosophie de la connaissance.

Dans la seconde version, sortie en 1784, des *Aphorismes philosophiques*[2], on retrouve encore un exposé de points de doctrine prêtés à Leibniz. Alors que le § 92 déclare qu'il existe des concepts innés, ou principes de la raison, contenant en eux le fondement de toutes les sciences purement démonstratives, le § 93 rétablit une sorte d'équilibre en orientant l'*a priori* vers le sensible :

> Les concepts primitifs, ou principes de la raison, ne sont pas une simple faculté inefficace mais sont toujours prêts et dispos à s'appliquer et s'exprimer, dans les idées présentées par les sens ou la mémoire[3].

En cette année 1784, l'éclectisme de Platner continue de s'appuyer, entre autres, sur Leibniz, et il ne manque pas d'intégrer à sa revue de la pensée du temps quelques innovations issues de la philosophie transcendantale, en n'y voyant pas la rupture fondamentale que Kant leur prêtait.

KANT CRITIQUE ET SUCCESSEUR DE LEIBNIZ

La confrontation kantienne avec Leibniz n'avait toutefois pas attendu la première parution de la *Critique de la raison pure*, en 1781, pour se montrer en plein jour. La *Dissertation* de 1770[4], qui constitue un jalon important dans le parcours du philosophe, montre déjà à quel point la maturation du système personnel se fait dans une explication serrée avec le célèbre devancier. Et ce sont alors encore largement les thèses de la *Monadologie* ou de la correspondance entre Leibniz et Clarke qui sont discutées : l'inapplicabilité de la résolution en simples du composé, soit l'inanité *in concreto* de cet axiome ; l'erreur qu'il y a à traiter des choses sensibles

1. Platner, *Philosophische Aphorismen : nebst einigen Anleitungen zur philosophischen Geschichte*. En frontispice est imprimé un portrait de Leibniz.

2. *Ibid.*, Erster Theil. Le même portrait est reproduit.

3. *Ibid.*, p. 31.

4. Sur la position-charnière du texte intitulé *De mundi sensibilis atque intelligibilis forma et principiis*, voir déjà M. Gueroult, « La dissertation kantienne de 1770 », p. 3-25.

comme si elles étaient intelligibles; la faute commise dans la conception de l'espace et du temps. Pour le dire avec Émile Bréhier, en effet :

> L'espace et le temps [...] ne sont pas, comme l'a cru Leibniz, un ordre des choses successives et coexistantes, mais des formes *a priori* de la sensibilité, des manières d'être affecté[1].

Il faut porter le regard sur la *Critique de la raison pure* pour voir poindre ce qui serait, en sus, une influence de la discussion autour des *Nouveaux Essais*. Dans l'ultime section de l'ouvrage, relatif à l'histoire de la raison pure, Kant introduit une opposition entre deux courants, relativement à la question de l'origine des pures connaissances d'entendement[2]. À l'empirisme d'un Locke, venu en droite ligne de celui d'Aristote, s'opposeraient les « noologistes »[3], dont Leibniz (puisant chez Platon mais sans en reprendre le mysticisme), sans qu'aucun n'ait pu emporter la décision. On comprend en creux que c'est justement la tâche que Kant s'est lui-même proposée : donner droit à la raison, dans les limites de son usage correct, tout en affirmant par ailleurs que toute connaissance commence avec l'expérience.

L'explication la plus serrée et la plus longue avec Leibniz figure dans l'Amphibologie (ou Amphibolie) des concepts de la réflexion[4]. Kant se sert de la notion de « noogonie »[5], combat contre l'esprit, pour désigner la position de Locke. Cette dernière ne prend donc ainsi sens que dans sa tension avec celle qui lui fait face, à savoir celle de Leibniz. Locke aurait sensibilisé les concepts d'entendement tandis que Leibniz aurait intellectualisé le sensible. Le lien avec la section sur l'histoire de la raison[6] se dessine en creux. Comment ces deux positions dogmatiques en opposition frontale n'auraient-elles pas pu alimenter le scepticisme? Il serait maintenant temps que la raison entre comme dans son troisième âge, celui du criticisme. Les pouvoirs de connaître se verraient alors reconnaître leur juste emploi, leur domaine d'application légitime, la question de l'origine des connaissances consonnant avec celles de leurs limites.

1. É. Bréhier, *Histoire de la philosophie, II/XVIIe-XVIIIe siècles*, p. 458.
2. Voir Kant, *Critique de la raison pure*, A 854/ B 882.
3. *Ibid.*
4. *Ibid.*, à partir de A 271/B 327.
5. *Ibid.*, A 271/B 327.
6. *Ibid.*, à partir de A 852/B 880.

En 1790, pressé par Johann August Eberhard, Kant reviendra une nouvelle fois de manière synoptique sur sa compréhension de la philosophie de Leibniz[1]. Trois doctrines caractériseraient cette dernière : le principe de raison suffisante, la doctrine des monades et celle de l'harmonie préétablie. Manfred Kühn résume de la manière suivante la défense kantienne :

> Eberhard prétend concevoir le principe de raison suffisante en tant qu'objectif, lequel était cependant subjectif pour Leibniz, et il semble qu'il l'expose « à la moquerie, tandis qu'il pensait lui faire un éloge ». Eberhard comprend également de travers la monadologie alors qu'il essaie de montrer que les corps se composent de substances simples. Ce ne sont pas, pour Leibniz, les corps eux-mêmes qui se composent de substances simples, mais leur substrat intelligible[2].

Pour ce qui est du troisième point, l'accord entre règne de la nature et de la grâce, c'est bien ce que la critique de la raison a voulu promouvoir, se montrant en cela la véritable apologie de Leibniz. La philosophie transcendantale serait par conséquent l'héritière du leibnizianisme, et Kant un philosophe de même stature que son illustre devancier.

De la vision éclairée de Leibniz à l'historiographie leibnizienne contemporaine

Jusque dans sa conception de la philosophie comme développement d'un fonds déjà présent, Kant se montre leibnizien[3]; tant dans la thématique déployée que dans le geste de pensée, le maître de Königsberg dépose ses pas dans les traces de son aîné. En se faisant l'apologète de Leibniz, Kant ouvre la voie à une vaste tradition de commentaire, qui passera aisément de l'un à l'autre, en oubliant les médiations sans lesquelles pourtant le lien aurait été rompu, ou sans lesquelles, du moins, la relation aurait pris un autre visage.

À côté d'une ligne interprétative gnoséologique, liant Kant à Leibniz, comme à Locke et à Hume d'ailleurs, subsiste encore de nos jours un schéma heuristique davantage métaphysique, lequel tient ensemble

1. Les pièces de cette controverse figurent dans M. Lauschke, M. Zahn (Hrsg.), *Kant. Der Streit mit Johann August Eberhard*, Hamburg, Meiner, 1998.

2. M. Kühn, *Kant. Eine Biographie*, p. 410.

3. Voir M. Gueroult, *Dianoématique*, livre I, *Histoire de l'histoire de la philosophie*, t. 2, En Allemagne de Leibniz à nos jours, p. 330 : avec le leibnizianisme, « les conceptions de devenir, de développement, de genèse, sont dominantes ».

Leibniz et Spinoza. La controverse entre Kant et Eberhard, pour importante qu'elle se montra, ne fut en effet nullement la plus déterminante en cette fin de dix-huitième siècle. On doit en particulier à Jacobi d'avoir inauguré la querelle du panthéisme par la publication de textes de Lessing favorables au spinozisme[1]. Leibniz lui-même, indique Jacobi, aurait fort bien pu être en son cœur un partisan du philosophe hollandais. La proximité thématique, voire l'identité doctrinale des deux penseurs étaient avancées. Ce point interprétatif allait marquer très fortement le postkantisme et, au-delà, quand même ce serait sur un mode réactif, l'historiographie philosophique.

Herbart, successeur de Kant à Königsberg, revient dans la préface du second tome de sa *Psychologie comme science* sur l'impact qu'a eue, depuis quarante ans déjà, la publication d'un texte posthume de Lessing par Jacobi.

> Lorsque *Jacobi* se résolut à faire connaître son célèbre dialogue avec *Lessing*, il lui fallait s'attendre à ce que les lecteurs se scindent en deux partis, selon que son autorité, ou celle de Lessing, serait pour eux plus grande, et selon qu'ils inclinent davantage à la pensée qu'au sentiment. Les deux partis se sont constitués, et ils se font face aujourd'hui encore. Il faut maintenant à chaque nouvelle doctrine, chez ceux qui en entendent parler, souffrir de rencontrer quelque parti-pris dans cette querelle[2].

Contre l'identification de Leibniz à Spinoza, présente par exemple chez un Fichte[3] ou un Hegel[4], a fortement réagi toute une tradition de commentateurs. Trendelenburg, s'inscrivant en faux contre l'hégélien Erdmann, de même que Gerhardt ou Kabitz ont soutenu au dix-neuvième siècle ou au début du vingtième que le système philosophique de Leibniz s'était développé continûment depuis ses débuts et qu'il n'avait donc pas pu être influencé par la lecture de l'*Éthique*, intervenue au début des années 1670. Ursula Goldenbaum, qui refuse ce déni de l'influence exercée par Spinoza sur Leibniz, montre comment ce point de commentaire s'est maintenu jusqu'à nos jours dans quelques publications[5]. Il ne s'agit bien sûr plus pour l'interprète d'identifier massivement les positions de Leibniz

1. Sur cette querelle, voir H. Tavoillot, *Le Crépuscule des Lumières. Les documents de la querelle du panthéisme. 1780-1789*, et Herder, *Dieu. Quelques entretiens*.

2. H. Tavoillot, *Le Crépuscule des Lumières*, p. IV.

3. Voir R. Lauth, « Leibniz im Verständnis Fichtes », p. 396-422.

4. Sur le reproche de ne pas avoir compris correctement la nature de la réflexion que la doctrine de l'essence de la *Science de la logique* fait conjointement à Leibniz et Spinoza, voir H. W. Schmidt, *Georg W. F. Hegel. Wissenschaft der Logik – Die Lehre vom Wesen : Ein einführender Kommentar*, p. 190.

5. Voir U. Goldenbaum, « Leibniz's Fascination with Spinoza », p. 53.

et de Spinoza mais de montrer comment un accord a pu se faire sur certains points, malgré des différences doctrinales profondes, notamment eu égard au legs cartésien.

Les débats de la fin de l'*Aufklärung* ont ainsi continué de peser sur la conception que l'on s'est fait des classiques de la philosophie, ainsi que des rapports qu'ils ont entretenus entre eux. La querelle du panthéisme a cristallisé des positions contraires, pour un Dieu personnel transcendant ou un Dieu consubstantiel à la nature, et elle a transmis à la postérité l'image d'un Leibniz proche de thèses spinozistes. Ce rapprochement, notons-le bien, n'a pu se faire que parce qu'en parallèle une interprétation idéaliste de Spinoza a commencé d'émerger avec J. G. Wachter, un contemporain de Leibniz, et Mendelssohn, l'auteur des *Dialogues philosophiques*[1]. Le soupçon d'idéalisme dont Wolff avait essayé de dédouaner Leibniz a longtemps continué de planer sur ce dernier. La lecture idéaliste de Leibniz a certainement d'autant mieux pu prévaloir qu'elle a su ignorer ses sources, taire sa genèse, et se donner par suite comme un fait quasi-naturel. Contre une vision anhistorique, c'est sans doute l'un des mérites de l'historiographie contemporaine que de prendre en compte l'histoire de la réception de Leibniz depuis l'origine et de se situer, par le fait même, de manière déterminée dans la succession des générations.

Jean-François GOUBET
(Université d'Artois)

1. Voir M. Lærke, « Mendelssohn, Wachter et les origines du Spinoza idéaliste ».

LEIBNIZ ET LA PHILOSOPHIE FRANÇAISE AU XIXe SIÈCLE [1]

Dans ce chapitre, je montre le rôle central qu'a joué la philosophie de Leibniz dans le développement de la philosophie du XIXe siècle en France. Son œuvre philosophique n'y fut pas seulement l'objet d'études savantes. Elle fut également reçue comme présentant des hypothèses vivantes, susceptibles d'être développées et défendues afin d'aider au progrès de la pensée spiritualiste. Dans la première section, je rappellerai comment Madame de Staël réintroduisit la figure de Leibniz dans la pensée française au début du siècle. Dans la seconde section, je montrerai que les deux Leibniz de Madame de Staël devinrent les figures tutélaires de deux courants distincts de la « philosophie spiritualiste » : le premier, revendiqué par Victor Cousin, qui devint philosophie d'État, et le second revendiqué par Maine de Biran. Dans la troisième section, je discuterai les critiques que les membres de la deuxième école portèrent contre la première et dans la quatrième section, je me concentrerai sur l'entreprise d'un Charles Renouvier, cherchant à élaborer une nouvelle monadologie en dehors des milieux académiques français. La cinquième section sera consacrée à la tentative de Ravaisson pour faire d'un Leibniz plus introspectif la nouvelle philosophie d'État et la sixième étudie certaines tentatives pour réconcilier cette philosophie avec l'évolution darwinienne.

1. Traduit de l'anglais par David Rabouin.

LES DEUX LEIBNIZ DE MADAME DE STAËL

En 1813, Madame de Staël (1766-1817) publia son *De l'Allemagne* (un panorama de la culture allemande), après que la première édition du texte fut détruite pour n'être « point français », ce qui conduisit à son exil hors de France[1]. Cet ouvrage s'avéra de la plus grande importance pour la réception de la philosophie allemande en France au début du XIXe siècle – et en particulier pour ce qui concerne Leibniz. Elle y soutenait que la philosophie allemande avait progressé selon des voies bien plus prometteuses que la philosophie française. Ceci était dû au fait que la pensée française, au lieu de continuer dans la voie tracée par les grands esprits du XVIIe siècle, un Descartes ou un Malebranche, vers le « successeur naturel » qu'était Leibniz[2], avait opéré, sous l'influence d'Étienne Bonnot de Condillac (1714-1780), un détour regrettable par l'immoral empirisme anglais de Locke. Le problème dans cette opération était, aux yeux de Staël, que Locke et Condillac avaient remplacé la conscience et la liberté par l'intérêt égoïste et le déterminisme. Ceci avait fait de la philosophie une ennemie de l'humanité, puisque cela lui aliénait les croyances les plus profondes sises en son cœur. Ceci provenait, d'après elle, du fait qu'aussi bien Locke que Condillac avaient entrepris de réduire l'esprit à une *tabula rasa* passive, qui n'aurait obtenu ses traits que de la réception des sensations externes. En conséquence, il ne restait plus de place pour le libre arbitre[3]. Mais la découverte la plus profonde des philosophes allemands, aux yeux de Staël, était d'avoir saisi qu'il ne saurait y avoir de moralité digne de ce nom sans une métaphysique de l'esprit qui laisserait de la place pour le caractère indépendant de l'âme et le fonctionnement de sa volonté. Pourquoi ? parce que l'âme est la source de nos idées sur le vrai, le beau et le bien, et que de telles idées, combinées avec notre libre arbitre, forment les conditions de la moralité. C'est la raison pour laquelle la métaphysique devrait être étudiée par tout esprit éduqué[4].

Dans sa discussion de Leibniz, elle soutenait qu'il y a deux orientations de sa pensée. D'un côté, il y avait le Leibniz rationaliste, défenseur de l'harmonie préétablie et des substances simples. Ce Leibniz-là, d'après elle, avait poussé ses abstractions trop loin et nous présente des

1. M. Staël, *Dix années d'exil*, p. 227-229.

2. M. Staël, *De l'Allemagne*, p. 426.

3. Aussi bien Condillac que Locke auraient rejeté une telle description de leur compréhension de l'esprit humain.

4. *De l'Allemagne*, p. 412.

spéculations exagérées et gratuites[1]. Son harmonie préétablie, bien qu'elle soit fondée dans la décision de Dieu, nous jetait dans une fatalité aussi forte que celle des matérialistes. Or la fatalité sape les fondements de la moralité. De l'autre côté, il y avait le Leibniz introspectif dont les réflexions concrètes sur le travail intérieur de l'âme furent parmi les plus perspicaces de l'histoire de la philosophie. Le Leibniz rationaliste fut celui que connut le XVIIIe siècle français et qui fut le sujet des critiques aiguës de Condillac dans son *Traité des systèmes*[2]. Une bonne connaissance du Leibniz introspectif ne fut cependant pas rendue possible avant la publication de ses *Nouveaux Essais sur l'entendement humain*, qui fut rendu finalement disponible par Rudolf Erich Raspe, dans son édition des *Œuvres philosophiques* de 1765. C'est dans ce texte que Leibniz, d'après Staël, défend contre les empiristes l'existence d'une âme libre, en ajoutant au *Nihil est in intellectu quod fuerit in sensu* ce qu'elle appelle une « sublime restriction » : *excipe nisi ipse intellectus* (A VI, 6, 110). Cette restriction est « sublime » parce qu'elle nous encourage à réfléchir sur notre sens interne plutôt que sur nos sensations externes. Or c'est dans le sens interne que l'activité de l'âme est révélée et c'est par elle, selon Staël, que nous est donné un témoignage véridique de notre liberté. Ceci forme donc la base d'une métaphysique capable de fonder proprement la moralité.

La séparation par Staël de deux figures de Leibniz dresse le cadre de sa réception en France tout au long du XIXe siècle. Mais il s'agit d'un cadre qui tourna rapidement au champ de bataille. Comme nous le verrons, défendre un côté ou l'autre de la philosophie de Leibniz, voire les deux, devint une affaire politique. L'école de philosophie qui domina au XIXe siècle en France fut le « spiritualisme », mais c'était une école qui comprenait une certaine variété et des divisions. Il y eut un effort tout au long du siècle pour parvenir à définir la « vraie doctrine spiritualiste » par référence aux auteurs classiques comme Descartes, Malebranche et Leibniz[3]. Le développement des doctrines spiritualistes françaises se produisit en même temps que l'élaboration de nouvelles éditions, interprétations et présentations des textes de ces grands maîtres. De fait une interprétation favorable de l'un de ces géants de la philosophie classique, dont on aurait

1. *Ibid.*, p. 439.

2. Bien que Condillac ait été plus en accord avec la monadologie leibnizienne qu'il est trop souvent reconnu. En 1747, il soumit sa propre version révisée de la monadologie pour le prix offert au concours par l'Académie de Berlin au sujet des monades. Voir Condillac, *Les Monades*.

3. Je renvoie le lecteur à P. Vermeren, « Les aventures de la force active en France », p. 167, P.-F. Moreau, « *In Naturalismo* » et D. Antoine-Mahut, « Reviving Spiritualism with Monads », pour une discussion détaillée et fascinante de ces questions.

montré qu'il était le père « naturel » de sa propre perspective philosophique, pouvait agir comme une légitimation très significative de ses vues et, en conséquence, pouvait devenir une arme dans le combat philosophique. La manière dont les deux « pères » de la philosophie spiritualiste, Maine de Biran (1766-1824) et Victor Cousin (1792-1867), se dirigèrent l'un et l'autre vers la pensée de Leibniz l'indique très clairement.

BIRAN ET COUSIN : LES PÈRES FONDATEURS DU SPIRITUALISME FRANÇAIS

Quand Maine de Biran écrivit ses premières œuvres, il était un disciple de l'école de Condillac. Pourtant, il devint progressivement plus influencé par la philosophie de Leibniz à mesure qu'il y fut plus exposé. Il était particulièrement convaincu par l'argument de Staël selon lequel l'aspect le plus important de la philosophie de Leibniz était ses analyses introspectives sur le travail interne de l'âme; la raison en était que c'est là que se révèle le lien inextricable de la métaphysique à la morale[1]. Pour Biran, l'œuvre de Leibniz n'était pas totalement étrangère à l'empirisme, mais à une forme supérieure d'empirisme qui reconnaîtrait l'importance non seulement de ce qui est présenté aux sens externes, mais aussi de l'activité du sens interne. Néanmoins Biran et Staël se séparaient sur un point crucial. Staël affirmait que pour résister aux divagations métaphysiques, on devait restreindre la possibilité d'une métaphysique à la seule métaphysique de l'esprit et elle soutenait que les questions concernant la nature de Dieu, des substances spirituelles, et de la relation de l'esprit et du corps dépassaient les limites de l'intelligence humaine[2]. À la fin de sa vie, Biran devint de plus en plus convaincu de la possibilité d'une métaphysique spéculative et trouva un soutien à cette conception dans l'œuvre de Leibniz. Comme Staël, Biran voyait dans la pensée leibnizienne une métaphysique capable de soutenir une défense de la liberté, mais il croyait également que cela

1. Madame de Staël s'avéra tout à fait consciente du lien intime qui unifiait la métaphysique et la morale dans un « principe commun » (Maine de Biran, *Journal Intime*, p. 84).

2. En dépit de ses protestations contre les restrictions apportées par les « empiristes » à la métaphysique, cette vue est à certains égards une restriction plus grande que ce que l'on trouve chez Condillac qui, lui aussi, défendait une version de la méthode introspective. Dans son *Traité des sensations*, il écrivait : « il y a en nous un principe de nos actions, que nous sentons, mais que nous ne pouvons définir, on l'appelle *force*. Nous sommes également actifs par rapport à tout ce que cette force produit en nous, ou au dehors... Par analogie nous supposons dans tous les objets qui produisent quelque changement » (Condillac, *Œuvres philosophiques*, I, p. 226).

dépendait de la métaphysique pluraliste fondée sur des forces substituant partout dans la nature, qu'avait également soutenue Leibniz. Cette métaphysique était, à ses yeux, un « spiritualisme universel et absolu » et son développement allait être une source d'inspiration pour l'une des orientations majeures du spiritualisme au XIXe siècle, celle qui conduisit finalement à la tradition vitaliste d'un Bergson (1859-1941).

Dans l'une des rares œuvres que Biran publia de son vivant (anonymement toutefois), son *Exposition de la doctrine philosophique de Leibniz* parue en 1819, il soutient que le spiritualisme de Leibniz est la seule métaphysique susceptible de soutenir la liberté humaine. Ceci est lié au fait qu'il évite le panthéisme auquel toutes les versions de la métaphysique cartésienne (qu'elle soit de Descartes lui-même, de Malebranche ou de Spinoza) doivent inévitablement conduire. Mais pourquoi Biran croyait-il que le cartésianisme mène au panthéisme ? Parce que les substances créées de Descartes sont purement passives. Alors que Descartes est explicite à ce propos en ce qui concerne les substances étendues – les seules qualités qui appartiennent à leur essence sont l'étendue, la flexibilité et le changement (AT VII, 31) – il suit de cette thèse que la distinction entre création et préservation est purement « conceptuelle » et que, au final, la substance pensante doit elle aussi être passive. Si la même force nécessitée au départ pour créer le monde (la force infinie de Dieu) est requise à chaque moment pour le préserver (AT VII, 48-49), alors chaque fois que j'ai l'impression de commettre une action volontaire, ce ne peut être moi qui la veux, mais Dieu. J'ai le désir (lui-même causé par Dieu), mais je ne suis pas responsable de l'action causale. Comme « il est logiquement certain que tous les effets sont éminemment ou formellement enfermés dans leur cause »[1], si Dieu est la seule cause, il suit que chaque être créé est compris en Dieu et qu'il n'y a pas de réelle distinction entre Dieu et la nature.

Le grand mérite de Leibniz, insistait Biran, était d'avoir été le philosophe classique capable de présenter une authentique métaphysique de la personnalité dans laquelle l'individualité et la liberté n'avaient pas à être sapées par le pouvoir de Dieu :

> À quoi a-t-il [donc] tenu que Leibniz ne se soit pas laissé aller à cette pente dangereuse qui, depuis l'origine de la philosophie entraîne les spéculateurs les plus profonds et les plus hardis vers ce concept vide de grand tout, néant divinisé, gouffre dévorateur où vient s'absorber toute existence individuelle ? Nous sommes pressés de le dire ; l'auteur du système des monades ne fut préservé de cette funeste aberration, que par la nature ou le caractère propre du principe sur lequel il basa son système ; principe vraiment un et

1. *Œuvres de Maine de Biran* XI-I, p. 142.

> individuel, à titre de fait primitif de l'existence du moi, avant d'avoir acquis la valeur d'une notion universelle et absolue. Un système qui multipliait et divisait les forces vivantes à l'égal des éléments intelligibles ou atomes de la nature, devait, ce semble, prévenir ou dissiper pour toujours ces tristes et funestes illusions du spinozisme, trop favorisées par le principe de Descartes [1].

Tandis que toutes les créatures cartésiennes sont, en dernière analyse, passives, Leibniz propose une métaphysique où toutes les créatures sont fondamentalement actives : « toute substance est complètement et essentiellement *active*… Toute substance est force *en soi*, et toute force ou être *simple* est substance » (XI-1, p. 144). Le point crucial pour Biran est qu'il n'est besoin de rien d'autre pour être une substance sinon d'être une force active, c'est-à-dire d'être le principe de sa propre activité. Contrairement à Leibniz, il ne croyait pas que l'on devait poser en plus une unité substantielle.

Leibniz affirme que nous découvrons la force active par une réflexion sur notre expérience interne [2]. Biran le suit sur ce point. Cependant, Leibniz raisonne également à partir de la réflexion sur notre propre activité interne pour établir l'existence de telles forces partout dans la nature [3]. Biran rejoint Leibniz dans cette seconde étape. Il le fait au moyen du « principe d'uniformité » leibnizien, qui établit que « c'est toujours et partout en toutes choses tout comme ici » (GP III, 343).

Bien que Biran ne suive pas Staël sur la possibilité d'une métaphysique au-delà de la métaphysique de l'esprit, il est d'accord avec elle sur le fait qu'il y a deux côtés de la métaphysique de Leibniz. Bien plus, il affirme que le côté introspectif, qui nous présente un fondement dynamique de la liberté et de la personnalité, est incompatible avec le côté rationaliste, qui sape les deux. C'est parce que, selon Biran, l'introspection nous fournit une preuve indubitable de notre liberté et de notre activité, tandis que le côté rationaliste de la philosophie de Leibniz – sa défense de l'harmonie préétablie – les sape. À proprement parler, cela ne pointe pas vers une incohérence leibnizienne, puisque Leibniz ne croit pas que l'attestation introspective de notre activité interne soit une attestation de notre liberté. En fait, il cite en l'approuvant l'argument de Bayle selon lequel une girouette qui désirerait bouger dans la direction où se trouve la pousser le

1. *Œuvres de Maine de Biran* XI-1, p. 140.
2. Voir GP IV, 510.
3. Sur l'usage par Leibniz de la méthode introspective, voir P. Phemister, « "All the time and everywhere everything's the same as here" » et P. Lodge, « Leibniz on Created Substance and Occasionalism ».

vent par coïncidence « serait persuadée qu'elle se mouvrait d'elle-même pour exécuter les désirs qu'elle formerait » (GP VI, 295). De manière cruciale, cependant, comme nous le verrons, cela pointait vers une incohérence dans la philosophie de l'autre père du courant spiritualiste : Victor Cousin, père du spiritualisme *éclectique* et philosophe d'État.

Biran eut très peu d'influence de son vivant et publia très peu. L'influence de Cousin, au contraire, fut grande. Entre 1830 et 1848, il gagna un contrôle presque complet sur la direction de l'éducation philosophique en France. Comme Jules Simon le rapporte de première main : « La Révolution de 1830 qui avait fait Louis-Philippe roi des Français, avait fait M. Cousin roi des philosophes. Mais Louis-Philippe n'était qu'un roi constitutionnel, M. Cousin était un roi absolu »[1]. Cousin avait une « autorité despotique » dont Hegel, Leibniz ou Descartes n'aurait jamais pu rêver[2]. Il se référait aux professeurs de philosophie comme à son « régiment » et c'était un régiment sur lequel il avait un contrôle complet. Comme membre de ce régiment, Simon avance : « on n'était libre que nominalement. On n'avait que la liberté de se casser le cou »[3]. Pourtant, avant de gagner un tel pouvoir, Cousin donna une série de cours en 1817 et 1818 qui allaient former la base de son ouvrage le plus important *Du vrai, du beau et du bien*. Biran aurait suivi et discuté ces cours avec Cousin avant l'écriture de son *Exposition* de 1819 et l'on a des raisons de croire que l'argument touchant l'incohérence systématique était en fait dirigé vers Cousin plutôt que vers Leibniz[4].

Résumant ses cours de 1817 et 1818, Cousin nous dit que son but principal était d'établir l'existence de faits *volontaires* aussi bien que *rationnels*, en plus des faits *sensuels* à l'existence déjà bien établie[5]. Une analyse psychologique complète devait montrer, à ses yeux, la nécessité de ces trois classes de faits, dont aucun ne peut être réduit à l'autre. Condillac et Locke avaient défendu les faits sensuels. Biran défendait les faits volontaires. Cousin insistait en plus sur les faits rationnels. Un exemple de « fait rationnel », d'après lui, était que tout effet doit avoir une cause. Il était révélé à nous par la lumière naturelle de la raison. De manière cruciale, nous pouvons raisonner à partir des faits rationnels pour établir l'existence de Dieu. La psychologie est le commencement nécessaire de la philosophie

1. *La philosophie et l'enseignement officiel de la philosophie*, archives privées, fonds Jules Simon 87 AP 16. Cité dans P. Vermeren, *Victor Cousin*, p. 176.

2. J. Simon, *Victor Cousin*, p. 117.

3. *Ibid.*, p. 116.

4. Je défends cette position dans J. Dunham, « A Universal and Absolute Spiritualism ».

5. V. Cousin, *Fragments philosophiques*, p. XIII-XIV.

– elle nous révèle des faits indubitables, mais à partir de ces faits nous pouvons procéder avec l'aide de la raison d'une manière purement intellectuelle. La réflexion sur notre raison nous montre que ces faits rationnels sont des vérités *absolues*, c'est-à-dire universelles et nécessaires. Comme nos esprits sont finis et contingents, ils ne peuvent pas servir de fondement à ce qui est universel et nécessaire. Des vérités absolues réclament un fondement absolu, c'est-à-dire universel et nécessaire, comme elles. Cet absolu, toutefois, dépasse et se tient au-dessus des esprits individuels. Il est leur cause ultime. « Les lois de l'intelligence constituent donc un monde à part, qui domine le monde visible, préside à ses mouvements, le soutient et le porte, mais n'en dépend pas »[1].

La théorie de l'absolu, selon Cousin, est la théorie platonicienne du monde intelligible, mais, comme il l'écrit dans sa révision du texte en 1854, c'est cette théorie couronnée et complétée par Leibniz[2]. Dans l'interprétation de Cousin, la théorie platonicienne des Idées suggère une série de formes reliées entre elles, unifiées par un centre commun qui agit comme le principe de raison suffisante pour l'unité du monde. C'est ce que Platon appelle « l'Idée du Bien », mais, Cousin y insiste, nous devons l'entendre avec Leibniz comme Dieu ou l'Absolu. L'idée du Bien est la source de tout ce qui est beau et bon. En conséquence, Cousin s'interroge : « Qui peut produire directement, d'un côté le soleil et la lumière, de l'autre la vérité et l'intelligence, sinon un être réel ? »[3]. Bien qu'il soit parfois considéré que l'usage que Cousin fait du terme Absolu pour désigner Dieu suggère qu'il est hégélien, il est clair que cette terminologie est en fait empruntée à Leibniz. Comme Manns et Madden l'affirment à juste titre, l'absolu idéaliste n'influence Cousin que de la « plus superficielle des façons » et « le philosophe allemand par rapport auquel sa dette est la plus considérable était sans conteste ni Schelling ni Hegel, mais Leibniz »[4]. Cousin ne fait rien pour cacher cette situation. Ce sont les mots de Leibniz sur l'absolu que Cousin cite dans ses cours : « L'idée de l'absolu est en nous intérieurement comme celle de l'Être. Ces absolus ne sont autre chose que les attributs de Dieu ; et on peut dire qu'ils ne sont pas moins les sources des idées que Dieu est en lui-même le principe des Êtres »[5]. Leibniz utilise le terme « absolu » pour en référer à Dieu comme le *vrai infini*, ce qui n'est

1. V. Cousin, *Fragments philosophiques*, p. XXIII.

2. V. Cousin, *Du vrai, du beau, et du bien*, p. 71 et 97-99.

3. *Ibid.*, p. 73.

4. E. H. Manns et J. W. Madden, « Victor Cousin : Commonsense and the Absolute », p. 577.

5. A VI, 6, 158.

pas fait de parties et n'est pas une modification : « Le vrai infini à la rigueur n'est que dans l'absolu qui est antérieur à toute composition, et n'est point formé par l'addition des parties » [1].

La raison pour laquelle l'argument de Biran affecte le système de Cousin et non celui de Leibniz est que Cousin doit défendre deux thèses : 1) nous avons une preuve indubitable de notre liberté par l'intermédiaire de ce qu'il appelle des faits volontaires; et 2) Dieu, ou l'Absolu, est la source ou cause de toutes choses. Au mieux, la défense de (2) semble saper (1), au pire elle conduit tout droit au panthéisme. Il serait difficile de pointer les erreurs dans l'argument de Biran et, au premier abord, Cousin ne semble pas avoir essayé. Plutôt, comme il fut celui qui hérita des manuscrits de Biran après sa mort en 1824, il les tint cachés. Malgré les richesses connues pour être contenues dans ces manuscrits, il retarda la publication de dix ans et publia alors seulement, dans un premier temps, un volume – volume dont il affirma (à tort) qu'il contenait la pensée de Biran dans sa totalité[2]. P. Vermeren offre deux explications à ce retard[3]. D'abord, Cousin voulait conserver pour lui seul la gloire d'avoir été le philosophe qui dépassa le sensualisme du XVIIIe siècle; ensuite, il craignait que le spiritualisme de Biran menace l'hégémonie du sien[4]. Comme nous l'avons vu, Cousin avait de bonnes raisons d'avoir peur et quand il commença finalement à publier ces œuvres, il s'assura que l'*Exposition* de Biran fut assortie d'un traitement critique particulier, qu'il rédigea en introduction à son édition des *Œuvres posthumes*. Le développement de Cousin procède en trois étapes. Tout d'abord, il montre que Biran a eu tort d'affirmer que la philosophie de Leibniz était fondamentalement incohérente. Il insiste sur le fait que quand Biran présente un spiritualisme absolu et universel, libéré des principes universels et nécessaires de la raison qui soutient aussi bien son spiritualisme que celui de Leibniz, il professe une philosophie incomplète. C'est le commencement d'un système, mais pas un système à proprement parler. Ensuite, Cousin défend le fait que sa philosophie est plus leibnizienne que celle de Biran. C'est parce que l'aperception leibnizienne conduit non seulement à la conscience du Moi en tant que force, mais aussi à l'attention au non-Moi. Ainsi l'attention aux faits rationnels, qui sont

1. *Ibid.*

2. V. Cousin, *Fragments philosophiques*, t. II, p. 63.

3. P. Vermeren, « Les aventures de la force active en France », p. 159.

4. Cousin en avait été accusé dès 1842 par Pierre Leroux : « Est-ce bien parce que la publication de ceux-ci lui auraient fait de l'ombre, atténuant sa propre gloire d'avoir ruiné le XVIIIe siècle et présentant en outre le danger qu'on puisse trouver dans Maine de Biran le germe d'un autre spiritualisme, plus rigoureux et plus conséquent que l'éclectisme » (« De la mutilation d'un écrit posthume de M. Jouffroy », p. 293).

aussi partie du non-Moi nous conduit, via la méthode de Cousin, à la cause des causes. Ici nous atteignons : « non seulement le fondement de la monadologie, mais la monadologie tout entière, et peut-être aussi l'harmonie préétablie » – Cousin ajoutant néanmoins ici une réserve importante : « bien comprise » [1]. Mettant ensemble les deux premières étapes, Cousin soutient que l'harmonie préétablie du rationaliste Leibniz ne conduit pas à une dénégation de l'action des monades et au panthéisme, bien au contraire, il objecte que le Moi et le non-Moi agissent ensemble et se modifient l'un l'autre selon leurs propres actions gouvernées par des lois [2]. Chaque être agit sur tout autre être à l'intérieur de certaines limites. Cet accord universel bien gouverné est tout ce qu'est censée suggérer l'harmonie préétablie [3]. La scène est alors prête pour que Cousin puisse proprement réclamer l'héritage de Leibniz pour son école éclectique :

> J'avoue encore qu'il m'a fallu l'éclectisme pour reconnaître et goûter la direction éclectique répandue dans tous les ouvrages de Leibnitz. À mesure que j'avance, ou crois avancer en philosophie, il me semble que je vois plus clair dans la pensée de ce grand homme, et tout mon progrès consiste à le mieux comprendre. M. de Biran, au point où il s'est arrêté, n'a bien saisi du système entier de Leibnitz que la partie qu'éclairait à ses yeux sa propre théorie [4].

Cette réappropriation opérée, il avance vers sa troisième et dernière étape et tente de renverser la critique de Biran en montrant que c'est en fait la philosophie de Biran et non la sienne qui conduit au panthéisme [5]. L'argument de Cousin est peu prometteur. Il prétend que Biran a dangereusement sur-animé la nature. Si nous partons de notre causalité libre interne et argumentons que nous pouvons inférer l'existence de substances actives du même type partout dans la nature, notre causalité unique finit par n'être en rien différente dans son genre que l'activité de n'importe quelle substance corporelle, et au bout du compte la liberté humaine se voit réduite à la destinée naturelle. Comme toute causalité se trouve alors réduite à un même niveau, c'est le système de Biran, selon Cousin, et non le

1. V. Cousin, *Fragments philosophiques*, t. II, p. 80.

2. Bien que le langage du « Moi » et du « non-Moi » soit clairement influencé par la tradition idéaliste allemande, Cousin est en général un lecteur de l'idéalisme allemand tellement pauvre que les tentatives pour comprendre son œuvre en relation avec cette tradition sont habituellement de peu d'aide. L'usage de son langage n'indique que la plus superficielle ressemblance entre leurs philosophies.

3. V. Cousin, *Fragments philosophiques*, t. II, p. 81.

4. *Ibid.*, p. 82-83.

5. Sur la « La cousinianisation du biranisme », voir D. Antoine-Mahut, « Reviving Spiritualism with Monads ».

sien qui porte avec lui la vraie menace du panthéisme. Pour autant, malgré cette tentative futile de le remettre dans la boîte, le génie de Leibniz-Biran avait bel et bien été mis à découvert....

UNE NOUVELLE PHASE DANS LA PHILOSOPHIE SPIRITUALISTE

Sans surprise, les arguments de Cousin ne convainquirent pas tout le monde qu'il était le vrai Leibnizien et Biran le réel panthéiste. À la fin des années 1830, il avait attiré lui-même des critiques féroces qui opposèrent la forme dynamique du spiritualisme contre sa propre forme « éclectique ». Biran était certes mort en 1824, mais Pierre Leroux [1] (1797-1871) et Félix Ravaisson (1813-1900) défendirent avec talent son héritage comme « un vrai et profond métaphysicien » opposé à Cousin. Dans le livre de Leroux, *Réfutation de l'éclectisme* (1839) et la *Philosophie contemporaine* de Ravaisson, ils offraient en gros le même argument : la philosophie de Cousin était superficielle parce qu'elle recourrait à la méthode expérimentale de Bacon et des empiristes, sans reconnaître la supériorité de la nouvelle méthode introspective que Biran avait trouvée dans Leibniz. Leroux écrivait à ce sujet :

> M. de Biran [...] se servait de l'observation psychologique pour établir une grande vérité ontologique. M. Cousin, qui a emprunté les idées de Maine de Biran sans bien les comprendre, a vu là une méthode, non seulement pour la psychologie, mais pour la philosophie tout entière. Il a ainsi été confirmé dans son choix de la méthode expérimentale à la façon du XVIIIe siècle. Tandis que, par son inspiration, Maine de Biran tendait à sortir de cette fausse méthode, Cousin y est rentré. *O imitatores!* [2]

Le point crucial est, d'une part, la manière dont l'« expérience » est comprise dans la tradition empiriste du XVIIIe siècle et, d'autre part, la nouvelle philosophie de l'expérience développée par Leibniz. Dans la tradition empiriste, « expérience » est utilisée comme un nom – c'est ce par quoi nous recevons passivement les idées, mais ce sont les idées elles-mêmes, plus que l'expérience en tant que telle qui intéressaient les membres de cette école [3]. Par contraste, Leibniz et Biran utilisent

1. Sur Leroux et Leibniz, voir L. Rey, *Les enjeux de l'histoire de la philosophie en France au XIXe siècle*, p. 410-421 et D. O. Evans, *La Socialisme romantique. (1797-1871).*

2. P. Leroux, *Réfutation de l'éclectisme*, p. 101.

3. Ceci n'est probablement pas vrai de tous ses membres. Condillac, par exemple, était certainement intéressé par l'expérience en tant que telle, mais il était alors souvent lu à tort

« expérience » comme un verbe à la voie active. Comme Phemister l'a fait remarquer : « le point focal de Leibniz est [...] la nature même de l'expérience ». Et cet état expérientiel est celui dans lequel la sensation et la réflexion sont combinées de sorte que, à travers la conscience de soi, il peut se comprendre lui-même comme un être pensant et percevant qui est incarné et a une expérience sensible du monde extérieur »[1]. C'est un geste radical auquel, en effet, on ne rend pas justice si on le reconduit à une simple réforme de l'empirisme. C'est bien plutôt une authentique « philosophie de l'expérience » qui tente de dépasser aussi bien le rationalisme que l'empirisme pour rendre justice et au témoignage de nos sens externes, le *non-moi*, et à l'activité interne de l'esprit, le *moi* (dans la manière dont Leroux et Ravaisson lisent Leibniz, le premier est la perception et le second l'aperception). La connaissance achevée, nous dit Ravaisson, est la « perception réfléchie » ou « l'*aperception* de Leibniz : *apperceptio est perceptio cum reflexione conjunctu* »[2]. De telles perceptions réflexives nous révèlent notre nature comme être spontané et actif, incarné dans un monde matériel gouverné par des lois mécaniques. Pour Ravaisson, le point important est que nous n'avons pas *une* expérience de l'activité, mais plutôt que notre expérience même est activité, efficacité, ou encore cette causalité que les empiristes ont déclarée inconnaissable. Au moyen de l'approche de Leibniz-Biran, Ravaisson prétendait que le vrai objet de toute philosophie digne de ce nom lui était rendu, car la philosophie est « la science par excellence des causes et de l'esprit de toutes choses, parce que c'est avant tout la science de l'Esprit intérieur dans sa Causalité vivante »[3].

Le grand succès de la méthode de Leibniz-Biran, aux yeux de Ravaisson, était d'avoir montré que l'hypothèse empiriste selon laquelle « l'expérience n'atteint jamais ni les causes ni les substances » – était fausse. Néanmoins il est important de remarquer que, à l'inverse de Ravaisson, Biran aurait été en accord avec la seconde partie de l'axiome.

comme un simple disciple de Locke et son propre empirisme supérieur était ignoré. Cela dit, l'idée générale est assez claire. Les spiritualistes pensaient que les empiristes, comme Hume et Locke, étaient intéressés par les idées considérées de façon atomistes et leurs différents arrangements dans des composés, tandis que Leibniz nous a conduits à comprendre l'expérience comme un processus actif. Les empiristes, d'un côté, se concentraient d'après eux sur les contenus liés à *une* expérience ; Leibniz, de l'autre côté, se concentrait sur la nature de ce qu'est faire l'expérience de quelque chose. Pour une discussion plus détaillée de cette distinction, voir P. Phemister « "All the time and everywhere everything's the same as here" ».

1. P. Phemister, « "All the time and everywhere everything's the same as here" », p. 207.

2. F. Ravaisson, « Philosophie contemporaine », p. 419.

3. *Ibid.*, p. 420.

Bien que Biran ait cru que l'introspection nous fournissait un accès à la force et à la causalité, il ne croyait pas pour autant que le concept de substance n'ait aucun sens au-delà de ces forces. Il concevait la substance comme « sujet passif des modifications » et rejetait l'existence de toute entité passive de sa métaphysique. Ravaisson, au contraire, pensait que le rejet de la substance conduisait à une métaphysique de l'âme dans laquelle, au-delà de la connaissance de nos volontés immédiates, nous étions laissés dans un abîme impénétrable. Quand la volonté est séparée de la réalité substantielle, affirmait-il, « elle n'est qu'une abstraction »[1]. La volonté n'est pas sans fondement, mais est le produit de tendances antérieures fondées dans une unité substantielle véritable. Ravaisson appuyait ce point sur deux citations de Leibniz qui sont très parlantes. La première est tirée du *De Ipsa Natura :*

> Il doit donc s'ajouter [...] une âme ou une forme analogue à l'âme, ou une entéléchie première, c'est-à-dire une certaine tendance (*nisus*) ou force primitive d'agir, qui est la loi inhérente (*lex insita*) à cette substance et lui a été imprimée par le décret de Dieu[2].

La seconde est tirée d'une lettre à Bayle où Leibniz avance que « la nature de la substance consistant à mon avis dans cette tendance réglée, de laquelle les phénomènes naissent par ordre »[3]. Ces deux passages sont cruciaux car ils clarifient exactement ce que Ravaisson considère comme manquant dans l'interprétation de Biran et ceci est nécessaire puisque Leibniz lui-même suggère effectivement parfois que la substance n'est rien en dehors de la force. Il écrit ainsi : « je considère [*scil.* la force] comme le constitutif de la substance, étant le principe de l'action, qui en est le caractère »[4]. Pourtant, Leibniz fait une distinction entre force primitive et force dérivative, qui constituent les aspects respectivement temporels et atemporels de la substance. La force active primitive, limitée par la force passive primitive, forment à elles deux la monade complète[5]. Si une monade était une pure force active primitive, elle serait exactement comme Dieu. La force passive primitive limite la nature d'une monade et est la raison pour laquelle elle est distincte et inférieure à Dieu. À elles deux, nous dit Leibniz, elle forme la « monade complète » parce qu'elle constitue le fondement non-temporel d'où émerge la série temporelle des perceptions. La relation entre les forces primitives dans la monade ne

1. *Ibid.*, p. 425.
2. GP IV, 512, Schrecker 221
3. GP III, 58.
4. GP IV, 472.
5. GP II, 250 et 252.

change pas : « l'âme reste la même »[1]. Comme l'écrit Leibniz : « la force primitive est comme la loi d'une série, et la force dérivative est comme la détermination qui désigne certains termes dans la série »[2]. Pour Ravaisson, Biran élimine la force primitive, nous laissant avec les seules forces dérivatives, mais il laisse alors les secondes sans fondement. Néanmoins, Ravaisson argumente que ce qui change doit avoir un fondement qui ne change pas, les forces primitives de Leibniz, ce dont les forces dérivatives, que Biran reconnaît pleinement, tiennent leur être. Ici Ravaisson paraît plus fidèle à l'original Leibniz qu'aucun de ses contemporains.

Après le coup d'État de 1851

La révolution de 1848 et le coup d'État de 1851 mirent un terme non seulement à la domination de Cousin sur la communauté philosophique française, accompagnée du démembrement de son régiment, mais aussi, plus généralement, à l'enseignement de la philosophie, puisque Napoléon III suspendit le concours de l'*agrégation*. C'est en partie pour cette raison que le système philosophique le plus impressionnant de la seconde moitié du XIXe siècle fut développé en dehors des milieux universitaires. Déçu par la naissance du Second Empire, Charles Renouvier (1815-1903) s'installa chez lui comme un *ermite de la philosophie*, dans la forêt de Fontainebleau, et se consacra à l'établissement de sa propre philosophie originale que l'on pourrait appeler une *monadologie phénoméniste*. Il publia son système en treize volumes sous le titre *Essais de Critique générale*, le premier paraissant en 1854. Renouvier rejetait férocement la thèse de Cousin selon laquelle on pouvait acquérir une connaissance à partir de « faits rationnels », et il soutenait que tout ce que nous pouvons connaître consiste en phénomènes. Une fois cela accepté, nous sommes confrontés à un choix : nous pouvons ou bien devenir sceptique, prisonnier du voile des phénomènes, ou nous pouvons postuler que la réalité est connaissable. Mais puisque la seule chose qu'on puisse connaître, ce sont les phénomènes, c'est donc que la réalité doit être phénoménale. Bien plus, puisque nous sommes confrontés à ce choix, cela signifie que toutes nos croyances sont délibérées. Nous faisons le choix de ne pas être sceptique et de croire, ou encore nous avons *foi,* dans le fait que la réalité est connaissable.

1. A II, 3, 548.
2. GP II, 262.

Renouvier soutient que la poursuite de la connaissance doit commencer avec la *foi philosophique*, appuyée sur quatre hypothèses. Ces hypothèses sont l'objet d'un acte de foi parce qu'elles ne peuvent pas être *démontrées* avec certitude sans circularité et doivent être crues par un acte de la volonté libre. Pour autant, il est *subjectivement nécessaire* que nous croyons en elles si nous désirons nous engager dans une recherche scientifique. Premièrement, nous affirmons la « réalité de la conscience » : l'identité personnelle (l'unité centralisée d'une série indéfinie de phénomènes, la plupart non actuellement présents à la conscience), ainsi que les règles et le fonctionnement de l'intellect. Cependant, comme Renouvier croyait qu'il était impossible d'affirmer la réalité du subjectif sans affirmer en même temps celle de l'objectif, nous devons affirmer du même pas une seconde hypothèse : le monde extérieur correspond à nos phénomènes objectifs. La troisième est qu'il existe dans ce monde extérieur des êtres individuels gouvernés par des lois et caractérisés par des fonctions *analogues* aux nôtres. « Nous entendrons par groupes de phénomènes pour soi des existences relatives et que nous ne pouvons exprimer ni concevoir que relativement (les unes par rapport aux autres, et toutes par rapport aux données de la conscience). Ces existences se développent sans notre existence propre, et se développeraient quand même telle conscience individuelle, soit la mienne, ne serait point »[1]. La quatrième est l'affirmation de la rectitude naturelle des facultés humaines que nous exerçons dans nos recherches scientifiques. Toutes ces hypothèses *peuvent être mises en doute* et, par conséquent, le fait de les soutenir est un acte libre. Cependant, leurs effets positifs justifient de les postuler. Rien ne nous empêche d'imaginer le monde d'une manière irréconciliable avec nos formes de penser. Néanmoins, procéder ainsi reviendrait à le considérer d'un point de vue dépassant la connaissance et rendrait donc la recherche scientifique impossible.

La position de ces quatre hypothèses est liée à la métaphysique des monades. Ceci est dû au fait que quelles que soient les réalités les plus fondamentales, si nous voulons qu'elles soient comprises par nous, elles doivent être compréhensibles par analogie avec notre propre existence : « L'Hypothèse d'une pluralité primitive de consciences distinctes, dans le monde, semble donc la seule rationnelle, et la donnée des consciences actuelles s'y trouve conforme »[2]. De même que notre identité personnelle est constituée d'une série de représentations changeant de l'une à la

1. C.B. Renouvier, *Essai de Critique générale*, II.II. 38.
2. *Ibid.*, II.II. 379.

suivante selon les lois de la pensée, de même se comportent tous les êtres dans notre monde. Tous les êtres sont donc des monades :

> Les monades sont de véritables êtres ; on conçoit à la ressemblance de ceux qu'il est le mieux donné d'observer, et comme composés des mêmes éléments que ceux-ci, mais avec divers degrés d'atténuation ou d'intensité : une certaine force, une certaine perception, un certain appétit. Ces êtres sont en un mot des centres de représentation. Il est vrai que Leibniz les nomme encore des substances, il les qualifie de simples, et sur cette simplicité il raisonne [1].

Renouvier insiste sur le fait que les atomes des matérialistes ne sont que des abstractions mathématiques, faites à partir des phénomènes et à usage de la science, mais non pas pour identifier des êtres réels. Ces atomes ne peuvent être compris qu'en relation aux phénomènes et ne peuvent pas être conçus en dehors de cette relation sous peine d'engendrer des contradictions :

> Il n'est en pas de même du concept de la monade, dans lequel on fait entrer un faisceau de qualités où rien ne manque d'essentiel de ce qui constitue l'existence complète au point de vue de la conscience, et où rien ne prend place de ce dont l'existence en soi serait contradictoire. Quand nous imagions, dans la monade, une puissance appétitive, ou faculté de désirer, pouvant aller jusqu'à la poursuite réfléchie des fins; une puissance perceptive, qui comprend la représentation des choses dans le temps et dans l'espace, et peut s'étendre jusqu'à l'entendement et au jugement formel de toutes les sortes de relations; et une puissance active, ou pouvoir de modifier par ses déterminations certaines déterminations extérieures, et enfin même de disposer librement des premières, c'est une idée totale d'être ou exister que nous avons [2].

Pour une part à cause de la suspension de l'enseignement de philosophie et pour une autre parce que son œuvre était en complet décalage avec les vues de l'école cousinienne alors dominante, la production philosophique de Renouvier sortie morte née des presses. Néanmoins, vers la fin du siècle, les conditions devinrent bien plus favorables pour la réception de sa pensée et en 1899, il reçut le prix de l'*Académie des Sciences morales et politiques* pour la présentation systématique et magistrale de sa philosophie qu'il intitula, bien sûr, *La Nouvelle Monadologie* [3].

1. C.B. Renouvier, *Essai de Critique générale,* II.II. 22.
2. *Ibid.*, II.II. 392.
3. Voir A. Gunn, *Modern French Philosophy,* p. 65; P. Phemister, *Leibniz and the Environment*, fournit une brève discussion de traits leibniziens dans ce dernier ouvrage.

LA RÉINSTAURATION DE L'AGRÉGATION ET LE NOUVEAU PHILOSOPHE ROI

L'*agrégation* fut réinstituée en 1863. Ravaisson fut nommé président de la commission responsable de mettre en place le concours et on lui demanda, pour célébrer l'événement, d'écrire un rapport sur la philosophie française au XIXe siècle. Ce travail, le *Rapport sur la philosophie en France au XIXe siècle*, fut publié en 1867, l'année même où mourut Victor Cousin. Le *Rapport* est souvent vu comme sonnant le glas de l'école éclectique de Cousin et marquant le commencement du développement prospère de la tradition spiritualiste sous sa forme biranienne. Il est également difficile de sous-estimer l'importance de cette œuvre pour la compréhension de la réception de Leibniz dans la seconde moitié du dix-neuvième siècle. Cela est dû au fait que Ravaisson utilise le dernier chapitre de son œuvre pour donner un aperçu des doctrines philosophiques vers lesquelles se dirigeait (et *devait* se diriger) la philosophie française de son temps. Or les doctrines clefs qu'il proposait de distinguer étaient explicitement leibniziennes. Décrivant l'influence de ce chapitre, Bergson écrivit :

> Nulle analyse ne donnera une idée de ces admirables pages. Vingt générations d'élèves les ont sues par cœur. Elles ont été pour beaucoup dans l'influence que le *Rapport* exerça sur notre philosophie universitaire, influence dont on ne peut ni déterminer les limites précises, ni mesurer la profondeur, ni même décrire exactement la nature, pas plus qu'on ne saurait rendre l'inexprimable coloration que répand parfois sur toute une vie d'homme un grand enthousiasme de la première jeunesse [1].

Mais pourquoi Ravaisson croyait-il que les philosophes français de la fin du dix-neuvième siècle devaient continuer à suivre Leibniz? C'est parce que Leibniz est le philosophe qui reconnaît : 1) que l'explication philosophique doit être synthétique plutôt qu'analytique ; et 2) qu'il y a une harmonie entre la nécessité et la liberté, de sorte que le dépliement nécessaire de notre réalité n'est pas incompatible avec notre libre volonté qu'il en soit ainsi.

Dans le premier cas, Ravaisson soutient qu'aussi bien les matérialistes que les idéalistes procèdent par une méthode analytique. Ils essayent d'expliquer la réalité en la découpant dans ces parties les plus fondamentales, mais finalement les plus insignifiantes. Les matérialistes réduisent tout à des atomes, les idéalistes réduisent tout à des formes abstraites, mais dans l'un et l'autre cas, ils nous laissent avec « un même

1. H. Bergson, *Notice sur la vie et les œuvres de Félix Ravaisson-Mollien.*

abîme de vide et de nullité »[1]. Leibniz est le héros de l'histoire, car il montre la voie hors de ce dilemme par une philosophie de la synthèse. Ravaisson admet volontiers qu'on pourra être surpris qu'il ait choisi Leibniz comme authentique philosophe de la synthèse étant donné que ce dernier rêvait de découvrir le vrai alphabet de la nature en réduisant tout dans ses éléments les plus fondamentaux. Néanmoins, soutient Ravaisson, cela était important pour Leibniz seulement en ce qui concerne le *jugement*, tandis que la synthèse joue un rôle beaucoup plus important tant dans la logique que dans la métaphysique leibnizienne. Dans le processus de raisonnement inductif, nous ne faisons pas que découper les choses dans leurs éléments les plus fondamentaux (analyse), mais ces éléments sont dans le même temps *synthétisés*. Nous avons recours à des hypothèses ou à des analogies pour assembler, combiner et composer ces éléments et ceci est le cœur de la méthode synthétique appliquée à la logique[2]. Kant a très bien reconnu que l'objet offert à nos sens doit être synthétisé selon les lois de l'espace et du temps, mais Leibniz a vu plus loin que lui parce qu'il a reconnu qu'il y a une loi fondamentale, plus élémentaire encore et cruciale pour la synthèse, dont les lois pour l'espace et le temps sont dérivées. Quelle est cette loi ? C'est ce que Ravaisson appelle la « loi universelle » : *toutes les choses doivent s'efforcer à la perfection*. Mais pourquoi cette loi ultime est-elle *synthétique ?* Parce que tandis que l'analyse découpe les choses dans les parties élémentaires et procède ainsi vers le néant, la synthèse, au moyen de la loi ultime, procède vers plus de complexité et de plénitude. Pour Ravaisson, ce principe synthétique est notre nature volontaire – notre esprit ne reçoit pas passivement les impressions, mais forme plutôt activement son propre monde à partir de sa propre source interne. C'est ainsi, d'après lui, qu' « on comprend cette sentence d'Aristote selon laquelle l'âme est le lieu de toutes les formes » et que l' « on comprend cette sentence de Leibniz, que le corps est un esprit momentané… La nature, pourrait-on dire, est comme une réfraction ou dispersion de l'esprit »[3].

Le second aspect central que Ravaisson trouva dans la doctrine leibnizienne était l'idée qu'il était possible de combiner le règlement divin par des lois et la liberté individuelle : « Tout est réglé, constant, et pourtant radicalement volontaire »[4]. Le progrès de la nature n'est pas celui d'une nécessité *absolue*, car il y a une nécessité *morale* qui règle ses mouvements du plus simple au plus complexe et du plus imparfait au plus parfait.

1. H. Bergson, *Notice sur la vie et les œuvres de Félix Ravaisson-Mollien*, p. 258.
2. *Ibid.*, p. 252.
3. *Ibid.*, p. 271.
4. *Ibid.*, p. 271.

La nécessité morale assure que nous choisissons le meilleur parmi toutes les options disponibles à nous à la lumière de notre savoir présent. La différence entre le sage et l'ignorant, pour Ravaisson, est que « le sage, en choisissant le bien, le choisit infailliblement, et en même temps avec la volonté la plus libre »[1]. Bien que nous choisissions librement, il y a une « géométrie morale » par laquelle un esprit infini pourrait prédire ce que nous allons choisir.

Après le succès du *Rapport*, Ravaisson devint le chef d'une nouvelle école spiritualiste, une école qui allait obtenir nombre des positions les plus importantes dans la philosophie française et maintint pendant la moitié d'un siècle des pouvoirs comparables à ceux de Cousin pendant la Monarchie de Juillet. Néanmoins, pendant que Cousin cherchait à inciter et influencer de jeunes esprits, cette influence était dominatrice. L'influence de Ravaisson était différente. Il est vrai que certains membres de l'école défendaient des thèses très proches des siennes – voyez la *Psychologie et métaphysique* de Jules Lachelier (1885), qui contient une version plus serrée de l'argument déployé dans le chapitre final du *Rapport*. Néanmoins, comme Paul Janet le rapporta, il n'y avait pas de crainte que l'influence de Ravaisson dégénérât en domination[2].

ÉVOLUTION ET SPIRITUALISME

Quelques une des œuvres les plus créatives de la dernière école spiritualiste se développèrent en réponse aux vues nouvelles introduites dans le domaine biologique par la théorie de l'évolution darwinienne. La thèse d'Émile Boutroux (1845-1921), publiée en 1874 sous le titre *De la contingence des lois de la nature* suit les pas de Ravaisson et Lachelier en tentant également une réconciliation de la liberté d'êtres individuels et la nécessité des idéaux divins, mais cette fois à la lumière de la popularité renouvelée de la théorie de l'épigenèse. L'argument principal prend la théorie de l'évolution darwinienne et l'étend au-delà du domaine biologique. Ce ne sont pas seulement les espèces qui évoluent, mais également les structures fondamentales de la nature, et même ses lois. Au niveau le plus fondamental de la nature, il y a des puissances internes premières (les monades) s'efforçant spontanément (autant qu'elles le peuvent) vers Dieu. C'est par l'intermédiaire des efforts de ces agents que finalement, mais de manière contingente, les structures stables de la nature que nous prenons pour des

1. *Ibid.*, p. 268.
2. P. Janet, « Une nouvelle phase de la philosophie spiritualiste », p. 369-370.

lois nécessaires sont formées. Les lois ne sont pas séparées ontologiquement des agents ou quoi que ce soit au-dessus ou au-delà d'eux, mais plutôt des formes habituelles réalisées par les agents individuels eux-mêmes. « L'instinct des animaux, la vie, les forces physiques et mécaniques sont », soutient Boutroux, « en quelque sorte, des habitudes qui ont pénétré de plus en plus profondément dans la spontanéité de l'être. Par là ces habitudes sont devenues presque insurmontables. Elles apparaissent, vues du dehors, comme des lois nécessaires. Toutefois cette fatalité n'est pas de l'essence de l'être; elle lui est accidentelle »[1]. Boutroux s'accorde avec Leibniz que tous les êtres à tous les niveaux de la grande chaîne des êtres ressemblent à Dieu à un certain degré. Néanmoins, dans un contexte où c'est l'épigenèse plutôt que la préformation qui est désormais le cadre théorique dominant, Boutroux soutient que ces êtres peuvent progressivement s'améliorer et devenir plus ressemblants à Dieu, *individuellement* par leur interaction les uns avec les autres et *générationnellement* par l'hérédité. La manière dont ce progrès arrive est le produit de leurs actions contingentes, mais l'effort vers le progrès lui-même est nécessaire et assuré par l'idéal divin.

Comme nous l'avons vu, il était commun parmi les spiritualistes de la tendance Leibniz-Biran de soutenir qu'on acquiert par introspection une idée de l'individu comme action et ensuite d'argumenter par analogie pour conclure à l'existence de forces dans toute la nature. Assurément Boutroux part de la même position[2]. Pour autant, nous trouvons un développement notable de cette méthode introspective dans une œuvre de 1895 intitulée *Monadologie et sociologie*, écrite par l'un des pères fondateurs de la sociologie : Gabriel Tarde (1843-1904). Tarde soutenait que par l'introspection, nous faisons l'expérience de nous-mêmes non seulement comme étant actifs et incarnés (comme Biran l'avait soutenu), mais aussi comme socialement intégrés. De manière semblable, il conduit son raisonnement par analogie, mais cette fois pour soutenir que tous les êtres ne sont pas seulement actifs et incarnés, mais intégrés à l'intérieur d'une société. Pour Tarde, il n'est pas possible d'être sans faire partie d'une société. Ou encore, pour rendre plus sensibles les implications de cette vue : tout ce qui *est* est une société de monades. Ceci signifiait, par contraste avec un Herbert Spencer soutenant que nous devons comprendre la société comme un *organisme*, que nous devons, selon Tarde, comprendre l'organisme *comme une société*. En accord avec Boutroux, Tarde croyait qu'une monadologie renouvelée doit voir les structures et les lois comme des résultats achevés,

1. É. Boutroux, *De la contingence des lois de la nature*, p. 167.
2. *Ibid.*, p. 166.

nous pourrions dire comme des habitudes, de sociétés de monades. L'évolution elle-même, poursuivait-il, est le produit de telles sociétés : « Et que peut être cette transformation *directe, régulière*, rapide, imaginée par d'autres, si ce n'est l'œuvre d'ouvriers cachés qui collaborent à la réalisation de quelque *plan de réorganisation spécifique* conçu et voulu premièrement par l'un d'entre eux ? » [1]. À la fin du dix-neuvième siècle, il n'était donc pas rare parmi les philosophes de croire que les développements de la science moderne étaient en train de confirmer la grande hypothèse leibnizienne des monades. Le futur de la monadologie semblait de fait très lumineux [2].

Jeremy DUNHAM
(University of Durham)

1. G. Tarde, *Monadologie et sociologie*, p. 43.

2. Cette recherche a bénéficié du soutien d'une Bourse Early Career du Levehulme Trust et de l'Université de Sheffield. Je voudrais remercier les éditeurs de ce volume pour leurs commentaires sur ce chapitre, qui m'ont aidé à l'améliorer.

BIBLIOGRAPHIE

ADAMS, R. M., *Leibniz. Determinist, Theist, Idealist*, Oxford, Oxford University Press, 1994.

AITON, E., *The Vortex Theory of Planetary Motion*, New York, American Elsevier, 1972.

– « The Mathematical basis of Leibniz's theory of planetary motion », *Leibniz' Dynamica, Studia Leibnitiana Sonderheft* 13, Stuttgart, F. Steiner Verlag, 1984, p. 209-222.

– *Leibniz. A Biography*, Bristol/Boston, Adam Hilger, 1985.

ANDRAULT, R., *La Vie selon la raison. Physiologie et métaphysique chez Spinoza et Leibniz*, Paris, Honoré Champion, 2014.

– *La Raison des corps. Mécanisme et sciences médicales*, Paris, Vrin, 2016.

—, BUCHENAU, S., CRIGNON, C. et REY A.-L. (dir.), *Médecine et philosophie de la nature humaine de l'âge classique aux Lumières. Une anthologie*, Paris, Classiques Garnier, 2014.

ANTOGNAZZA, M. R. et HOTSON H. (éd.), *Alsted and Leibniz on God, the Magistrate and the Millenium*, Wiesbaden, Harrasowitz Verlag, 1999.

– *Leibniz on the Trinity and the Incarnation. Reason and Revelation in the Seventeenth Century*, New Haven, Yale University Press, 2007.

– *Leibniz. An Intellectual Biography*, Cambridge, Cambridge University Press, 2011.

– *Leibniz. A Very Short Introduction*, Oxford, Oxford University Press, 2016.

– « Immeatio and Emperichoresis : The Theological Roots of Harmony in Bisterfeld and Leibniz », dans S. Brown (ed.), *The Young Leibniz and His Philosophy, 1646-1676*, Dordrecht, Kluwer, 1999, p. 41-64.

– « Debilissimae Entitates? Bisterfeld and Leibniz's Ontology of Relations », *The Leibniz Review* 11, 2001, p. 1-22.

– « Leibniz's *De Deo Trino* : Philosophical Aspects of Leibniz's Conception of the Trinity », *Religious Studies* 37, 2001, p. 1-13.

– « Theory and Praxis in Leibniz's Theological Thought », dans W. Li et H. Rudolph (Hrsg.) *Leibniz im Lichte der Theologien, Studia Leibnitiana Supplementa* 40, Stuttgart, F. Steiner Verlag, 2017, p. 35-57.

ANTOINE-MAHUT, D., « Reviving Spiritualism with Monads : Francisque Bouiller's Impossible Mission (1839-64) », *British Journal for the History of Philosophy* 23/6, 2015, p. 1106-1127.

ARMGARDT, M., *Das rechtslogische System der « Doctrina conditionum » von Gottfried Wilhelm Leibniz*, Marburg, Elwert, 2001.

ARNAULD, A. et NICOLE, P., *La Logique ou l'art de penser*, Paris, Gallimard, 1992.

ARTHUR, R. T. W. *Leibniz*, Cambridge-Malden (MA), Polity, 2014.

BACKUS, I., « Leibniz's Quarrel on Necessity with Hobbes, Newton and Clarke », dans Li W. et Rudolph H. (Hrsg.) *Leibniz im Lichte der Theologien, Studia Leibnitiana Supplementa* 40, Stuttgart, F. Steiner Verlag, 2017, p. 119-136.

BARBER, W. H., *Leibniz in France from Arnauld to Voltaire*, Oxford, Clarendon Press, 1955.

BARUZI, J., « Dialogues mystiques », *Revue de Métaphysique et de Morale* 13, 1905, p. 15-38 [puis, Paris, Vrin, 1985].

– *Leibniz et l'organisation religieuse de la terre* [1907], Aalen, Scientia Verlag, 1975.

BASSO, L., *Individuo e comunità nella filosofia politica di G. W. Leibniz*, Soveria Mannelli, Rubbettino, 2005.

– « Félicité commune et inquiétude dans la pensée politique de Leibniz », *Les Études Philosophiques* 3, 2016, p. 443-454.

– (ed.), *Republic and Common Good in Leibniz's Political Thought, Studia Leibnitiana Themenheft* 1, Stuttgart, F. Steiner Verlag, 2011.

BAYART, A., « Leibniz et les antinomies en droit », *Revue Internationale de Philosophie* 2/3, 1966, p. 257-263.

BAYLE, P., *Projet et fragmens d'un Dictionnaire critique*, Rotterdam, Reiner Leers, 1692.

BEELEY, P., *Kontinuität und Mechanismus. Zur Philosophie des jungen Leibniz in ihrem ideengeschichtlichen Kontext, Studia Leibnitiana Supplementa* 30, Stuttgart, F. Steiner Verlag, 1996.

BELAVAL, Y., *Leibniz critique de Descartes*, Paris, Gallimard, 1960.

– *Leibniz. Initiation à sa philosophie*, Paris, Vrin, 1962.

– *Études leibniziennes. De Leibniz à Hegel*, Paris, Gallimard, 1976.

– *Leibniz, de l'Âge classique aux Lumières*, Paris, Beauchesne, 1995.

– « L'Idée d'harmonie chez Leibniz », *Studium generale* 9, 1966, p. 558-568.

– « Religion et fondement du droit chez Leibniz », *Archives de philosophie du droit* 18, 1973, p. 85-92.

– « Leibniz et l'Europe », dans Y. Belaval, *Leibniz, de l'Âge classique aux Lumières*, Paris, Beauchesne, 1995, p. 209-224.

– « Questions sur l'influence de Leibniz », dans Y. Belaval, *Leibniz, de l'Âge classique aux Lumières*, Paris, Beauchesne, 1995, p. 225-235.

BERGSON, H., « Notice sur la vie et les œuvres de Félix Ravaisson-Mollien ». Discours prononcé lors des séances des 20 et 27 février 1904 de l'Académie des sciences morales et politiques, 1904 [en ligne : http://www.asmp.fr/travaux/notices/ravaisson_bergson.htm].

BERKELEY, G., *Alciphron or the Minute Philosopher, in seven dialogues containing An Apology for the Christian Religion, against those who are called free-thinkers*, 3 e éd., London, J. & R. Tonson and S. Draper, 1752.

BERNSTEIN, H., « Conatus, Hobbes, and the young Leibniz », *Studies in History and Philosophy of Science* 11, 1980, p. 25-37.

– « Passivity and inertia in Leibniz's dynamics », *Studia Leibnitiana* 18, 1981, p. 97-113.

BERTOLONI MELI, D., *Equivalence and Priority : Newton versus Leibniz. Including Leibniz's Unpublished Manuscripts on the* Principia, Oxford, Clarendon Press, 1993.

BLANK, A., « Ramus and Leibniz on Analysis », dans M. Dascal (ed.), *Leibniz. What Kind of Rationalist ?,* Dordrecht, Springer, 2008, p. 155-66.

BOBBIO, N., « Leibniz e Pufendorf », *Rivista di filosofia*, 1, 1947, p. 118-129.

BOLTON, M. B., « Change in the Monad », dans E. Watkins (ed.), *The Divine Order, the Human Order, and the Order of Nature : Historical Perspectives*, Oxford, Oxford University Press, 2013, p. 175-194.

BOREL, P., *Observationum Microscopicarum Centuria*, Hagae Comitis, Vlacq, 1656.

BORGHERO, C., *Les Cartésiens face à Newton. Philosophie, science et religion dans la première moitié du XVIII e siècle*, Turnhout, Brepols, 2011.

BOTS, H. et WAQUET, F., *La République des Lettres*, Paris/ Bruxelles, Belin/De Bœck, 1997.

BOUCHER, P., « La Logique du droit positif romain chez le jeune Leibniz », dans D. Berlioz et F. Nef (dir.), *L'Actualité de Leibniz : les deux labyrinthes*, *Studia Leibnitiana Sonderheft* 34, Stuttgart, F. Steiner Verlag, 1999, p. 207-222.

– « Leibniz : What Kind of Legal Rationalism ? », dans M. Dascal (ed.), *Leibniz : What Kind of Rationalist ?,* Berlin, Springer, 2009, p. 231-249.

BOUTROUX, É., *De la Contingence des lois de la nature*, 3 e éd., Paris, Felix Alcan, 1898.

BOWLER, P., « Preformation and Pre-Existence in the Seventeenth Century », *Journal of the History of Biology* 4/2, 1971, p. 221-244.

BOYLE, R., *Some Physico-Theological Considerations About the Possibility of the Resurrection*, London. Printed by T.N. for H. Herringman, 1675.

BREGER, H., *Kontinuum, Analysis, Informales – Beiträge zur Mathematik und Philosophie von Leibniz*, Berlin, Springer Spektrum, 2016.

– « The Art of Mathematical Rationality », dans M. Dascal (ed.), *Leibniz : What Kind of Rationalist ?,* Dordrecht, Springer, 2008, p. 141-152.

BRÉHIER, É., *Histoire de la philosophie,* t. II, XVII e-XVIII e siècles, édition revue, corrigée et mise à jour par P.-M. Schuhl et A.-P. Leroy, Paris, P.U.F., 1981.

BROWN, G., « Leibniz' Moral Philosophy », dans N. Jolley (ed.), *The Cambridge Companion to Leibniz*, Cambridge, Cambridge University Press, 1995, p. 411-441.

— et PHEMISTER, P. (eds.), *Leibniz and the English-Speaking World*, The New Synthese Historical Library, Dordrecht, Springer, 2007.

BRUNSCHVICG, L., *Les Étapes de la philosophie mathématique*, Paris, Félix Alcan, 1912.

BRYKMAN, G., « Leibniz et les paradoxes de Berkeley », dans R. Bouveresse (dir.), *Perspectives sur Leibniz*, Paris, Vrin, 1999, p. 97-114.

BUCHENAU, S., *The Founding of Aesthetics in the German Enlightenment : The Art of Invention and the Invention of Art*, Cambridge, Cambridge University Press, 2013.

BURKHARDT, H., *Logik und Semiotik in der Philosophie von Leibniz*, München, Philosophia Verlag, 1980.

BUSCHE, H., « Wie triftig ist Kants Kritik des Metaphysikers Leibniz? », dans A. Lewendoski (Hrsg.), *Leibnizbilder im 18. und 19. Jahrhundert*, *Studia Leibnitiana Sonderheft* 33, Stuttgart, F. Steiner Verlag, 2004, p. 171-182.

BUSCHMANN, A., « Leibniz als juristischer Reformer in Mainz 1667-1672 », dans P. C. Hartmann (Hrsg.), *Die Mainzer Kurfürsten des Hauses Schönborn als Reichserkanzler und Landesherren*, Frankfurt am Main, Peter Lang, 2002.

BUZON, F. DE, « Réduction et irréductibilité du sensible : l'élision du sens commun chez Leibniz », *Revue de Métaphysique et de Morale* 4, 1991, p. 531-50.

CAPOZZI, M. et RONCAGLIA G., « Logic and Philosophy of Logic from Humanism to Kant », dans L. Haaparanta (ed.), *The Development of Modern Logic*, Oxford, Oxford University Press, 2009, p. 78-158.

CARDOSO, A., « La Place d'autrui dans la détermination de l'identité européenne », *Synthesis philosophica* 2, 1987, p. 479-485.

CARHART, M. C., « *Historia Literaria* and Cultural History from Mylaeus to Eichhorn », dans Miller P. N. (ed.), *Momigliano and Antiquarianism. Foundations of the Modern Cultural Sciences*, University of Toronto Press, Toronto, 2007, p. 184-206.

CARRIERO, J., « Substance and Ends in Leibniz », dans P. Hoffman, D. Owen et G. Yaffe (ed.), *Contemporary Perspectives on Early Modern Philosophy, Essays in Honor of Vere Chappell*, Peterborough, Broadview Press, 2008, p. 115-140.

CASSIRER, E., *Leibniz' System in seinen wissenschaftlichen Grundlagen* [1902], rééd. *Gesammelte Werke*, t. I, Hamburg, F. Meiner, 1998.

– *La Philosophie des Lumières*, Paris, Fayard, 1966.

CASULA, M., *La Metafisica di A. G. Baumgarten*, Milano, Mursia, 1973.

CHALMERS, D., *The Problem of Consciousness*, New York-Oxford, Oxford University Press, 1996.

CICÉRON, *Traité du destin*, trad. fr. A. Yon, Paris, Les Belles-Lettres, 1964.

CLARKE, S. et LEIBNIZ, G. W., *A Collection of Papers which passed between the late learned Mr. Leibniz and Dr. Clarke in the years 1715 and 1716 related to the Principles of Natural Philosophy and Religion*, Londres, J. Knapton, 1717 ; trad. fr. P. Des Maizeaux, *Recueil de diverses pièces sur la philosophie, la religion naturelle, l'histoire, les mathématiques etc., par Mrs. Leibniz, Clarke, Newton et autres auteurs célèbres*, 2 vol., Amsterdam, H. du Sauzet, 1720.

CONDILLAC, E. B., *Essai sur l'origine des connaissances humaines* [1746], éd., présentation et notes J.-Cl. Pariente et M. Pécharman, Paris, Vrin, 2014.
– *Les Monades*, éd. L. L. Bongie, Grenoble, Jérôme Millon, 1994.
CONDORCET, N., *Esquisse d'un tableau historique des progrès de l'esprit humain* [1793-1794], nouvelle éd. par Y. Belaval, Paris, Vrin, 1970.
COSTABEL, P., « La Signification d'un débat sur trente ans (1728-1758) : la question des forces vives », *Cahiers d'histoire et de philosophie des sciences* (Paris), Nouvelle série, 8, 1984.
COUTURAT, L., *La Logique de Leibniz d'après des documents inédits*, Paris, Alcan, 1901.
COUSIN, V., *Fragments philosophiques*, Paris, Ladrange, 1826 (3 e édition, 1838).
– *Du Vrai, du beau, et du bien*, 18 e édition, Paris, Didier et cie, 1873.
CROIZER, J., *Les Héritiers de Leibniz*, Paris, L'Harmattan, 2001.
CYRANO DE BERGERAC, S., *États et empires de la lune et du soleil*, éd. M. Alcover, Paris, Honoré Champion, 2004.
DAGRON, T., *Toland et Leibniz. L'invention du néo-spinozisme*, Paris, Vrin, 2009.
D'ALEMBERT, J. L. R., *Traité de Dynamique*, Paris, David, 1743.
DANIEL, S., « The Harmony of the Leibniz-Berkeley Juxtaposition », dans G. Brown et Phemister P. (eds.), *Leibniz and the English-Speaking World*, Dordrecht, Springer, 2007, p. 163-180.
DAO DUC, K. « Leibniz dans l'Encyclopédie », *Recherches sur Diderot et l'Encyclopédie* 48, 2013, p. 123-142.
DASCAL, M., « Leibniz on Particles, Linguistic Form and Comparatism », dans T. De Mauro et Formigari L. (eds.), *Leibniz, Humboldt, and the Origins of Comparativism*, Amsterdam-Philadelphia, John Benjamins, 1990, p. 31-60.
– « Strategies of Dispute and Ethics : "Du tort" and "La place d'autrui" », dans *Leibniz und Europa. VI. Internationaler Leibniz-Kongress*, Hannover, Leibniz-Gesellschaft, 1994, vol. II, p. 108-115.
DAVILLÉ, L., *Leibniz historien. Essai sur l'activité et la méthode historiques de Leibniz*, Paris, Félix Alcan, 1909.
DELEUZE, G., *Le Pli. Leibniz et le baroque*, Paris, Minuit, 1988.
DE RISI, V., *Geometry and Monadology. Leibniz's Analysis Situs and Philosophy of Space*, Basel, Birkhäuser, 2007.
– *Leibniz on the Parallel Postulate and the Foundations of Geometry*, Basel, Birkhaüser, 2016.
DIDEROT, D., *Réfutation de l'ouvrage d'Helvétius intitulé* L'Homme [1774], dans D. Diderot, *Œuvres*, vol. II, éd. Assézat-Tourneux, Paris, Garnier, 1875, p. 263-456.
DÖRING, D., « Leibniz's Critique of Pufendorf. A Dispute on the Eve of the Enlightenment », dans M. Dascal (ed.), *The Practice of Reason. Leibniz and his Controversies*, Amsterdam-Philadelphia, Andrew Benjamins, 2010, p. 245-272.
DORTOUS DE MAIRAN, J.-J., *Dissertation sur l'estimation et la mesure des forces motrices dans les corps*, Paris, C.-A. Jombert, 1741.

DU CHÂTELET, E., *Institutions de physique*, Paris, Prault, 1740 (1re éd.), Amsterdam, aux dépens de la compagnie, 1742 (2e éd.).
– *Lettres*, éd. par T. Besterman, Genève, Institut et Musée Voltaire, 1958.
DUCHESNEAU, F., *Leibniz et la méthode de la science*, Paris, P.U.F., 1993.
– *La Dynamique de Leibniz*, Paris, Vrin, 1994.
– *Leibniz. Le vivant et l'organisme*, Paris, Vrin, 2010.
– « Leibniz et Stahl : Divergences sur le concept d'organisme », *Studia Leibnitiana* 27, 1995, p. 185-212.
– « Leibniz's theoretical shift in the *Phoranomus* and *Dynamica de potentia* », *Perspectives on Science* 6, 1998, p. 77-109.
– « Leibniz's models for a science of nature », dans K. Nowak et H. Poser (Hrsg.), *Wissenschaft und Weltgestaltung*, Hildesheim, Georg Olms, 1999, p. 187-210.
– « Leibniz's model for analyzing organic phenomena », *Perspectives on Science* 11/4, 2003, p. 318-409.
– « Leibniz et la méthode des hypothèses », dans F. Duchesneau et J. Griard (dir.), *Leibniz selon les* Nouveaux Essais sur l'entendement humain, Montréal/Paris, Bellarmin/Vrin, 2006, p. 113-127.
– « Les *Nouveaux Essais* : l'harmonie des perspectives », dans F. Duchesneau et J. Griard (dir.), *Leibniz selon les* Nouveaux Essais sur l'entendement humain, Montréal/Paris, Bellarmin/Vrin, 2006, p. 305-334.
– « Leibniz's contribution to natural philosophy », dans B. Look (ed.), *The Continuum Companion to Leibniz*, London-New York, Continuum International Publishing Group, 2011, p. 239-258.
— et J. GRIARD (dir.), *Leibniz selon les* Nouveaux essais sur l'entendement humain, Montréal/Paris, Bellarmin/Vrin, 2006.
DUGAS, R., *La Mécanique au XVIIe siècle*, Neuchâtel, Éditions du Griffon, 1954.
DUNCAN, S., « Leibniz's Mill Argument against Materialism », *The Philosophical Quarterly* 62, 247, 2011, p. 250-272.
DUNHAM, J. « From Habit to Monads : Félix Ravaisson's Theory of Substance », *British Journal for the History of Philosophy* 23/6, 2015, p. 1085-1105.
– « A Universal and Absolute Spiritualism : Maine de Biran's Leibniz », dans D. Meacham et Spadola J. (eds.), *The Relationship between the Physical and the Moral in Man : The Philosophy of Maine de Biran*, London, Bloomsbury, 2016.
ÉCOLE, J., « Des Rapports de Wolff avec Leibniz dans le domaine de la métaphysique », dans *Leibniz, Werk und Wirkung : IV. Internationaler Leibniz-Kongreß, Vorträge*, Hannover, Leibniz Gesellschaft, 1983.
ELSTER, J., *Leibniz et la formation de l'esprit capitaliste*, Paris, Aubier, 1975.
EVANS, D. O., *Le Socialisme romantique : Pierre Leroux et ses contemporains*, Paris, L'Harmattan, 2013.
FAVARETTI CAMPOSAMPIERO, M., *Filum cogitandi. Leibniz e la conoscenza simbolica*, Milan, Mimesis, 2007.
– *Conoscenza simbolica. Pensiero e linguaggio in Christian Wolff e nella prima età moderna*, Hildesheim, Olms, 2009.

– « Leibniz et la traduction universelle », dans C. Le Blanc et L. Simonutti (dir.), *Le Masque de l'écriture. Philosophie et traduction de la Renaissance aux Lumières*, Genève, Droz, 2015, p. 563-582.

– « Il Significato di 'non': negazione e doppia negazione in Leibniz », *Verifiche,* à paraître.

FICHANT, M., *Leibniz. La Réforme de la dynamique*, textes inédits, Paris, Vrin, 1994.

– « Introduction », in G. W. Leibniz, *La Réforme de la dynamique.* De corporum concursu *et autres textes inédits*, éd. M. Fichant, Paris, Vrin, 1994.

– *Science et métaphysique dans Descartes et Leibniz*, Paris, P.U.F., 1998.

– « Neue Einblicke in Leibniz' Reform seiner Dynamik (1678) », *Studia Leibnitiana* 22, 1990, p. 38-68.

– « Postface : "Plus ultra" », dans G. W. Leibniz, *De l'horizon de la doctrine humaine (1695). Apokatastasis panton (La Restitution universelle)* [1715], trad. fr. M. Fichant, Paris, Vrin, 1991, p. 125-210.

– « Leibniz et les machines de la nature », *Studia Leibnitiana* 35, 2003, p. 1-28.

– « L'Invention métaphysique », dans G. W. Leibniz, *Discours de métaphysique* suivi de *Monadologie et autres textes*, Paris, Gallimard, 2004, p. 7-147.

FONTENELLE, B. LE BOVIER DE, « Éloge de Leibniz », *Histoire de l'Académie Royale des sciences. Année 1716*, Paris, 1718, p. 94-128.

FORMEY, H. S., *La Belle wolffienne ou Abrégé de la philosophie wolfienne*, La Haye, 1741.

FRIEDMANN, G., *Leibniz et Spinoza*, Paris, Gallimard, 1962 (2e éd.).

FRIEDRICH, C. J., « Philosophical Reflections of Leibniz on Law, Politics and the State », dans H. G. Frankfurt (ed.), *Leibniz. A Collection of Critical Essays*, Notre Dame-London, University of Notre Dame, 1966, p. 47-68.

FURETIÈRE, A., *Dictionnaire universel,* La Haye/Rotterdam, Arnout/Reinier Leers, 1690.

GARBER, D., *Leibniz: Body, Substance, Monad*, Oxford-New York, Oxford University Press, 2009.

GARDIES, J.-L., « La Rationalité du droit chez Leibniz », *Archives de philosophie du droit* 23, 1978, p. 115-129.

GAUDEMAR, M. DE, *Leibniz, de la puissance au sujet*, Paris, Vrin, 1994.

– « Éthique et morale chez Leibniz », *Philosophie* 39, 1993, p. 60-82.

GENNARO, R. J., « Leibniz on consciousness and self-consciousness », dans C. Huenemann et R. J. Gennaro (ed.), *New Essays on the Rationalists*, Oxford, Oxford University Press, 1999, p. 353-71.

GENSINI, S., *Il Naturale e il simbolico. Saggio su Leibniz*, Roma, Bulzoni, 1991.

GERBER, G., « Leibniz' Beziehung zu Machiavelli », *Der Staat* 3, 1967, p. 367-376.

GIL, F., « Leibniz, la place d'autrui, le principe du pire et la politique de la monadologie », *Passé Présent* 3, 1984, p. 147-164.

GOETHE, N. B., BEELEY, P. et RABOUIN, D. (eds.), *G. W. Leibniz, Interrelations between Mathematics and Philosophy*, Dordrecht, Springer Verlag, 2015.

GOLDENBAUM, U., « "All you need is Love, Love…" : Leibniz' Vermittlung von Hobbes' Naturrecht und christlicher Nächstenliebe als Grundlage seiner Definition der Gerechtigkeit », dans G. Abel, H.-J. Engfer et C. Hubig (Hrsg.), *Neuzeitliches Denken. Festschrift für Hans Poser zum 65. Geburtstag*, Berlin, De Gruyter, 2002, p. 209-231.

– « Leibniz's Fascination with Spinoza », dans B. Look (ed.), *The Continuum Companion to Leibniz*, London/New York, Continuum, 2011, p. 51-67.

GOLDSTINE, H., *A History of the Calculus of Variations from the 17th through the 19th Century*, Berlin, Springer, 1980.

GOUHIER, H., *La Vocation de Malebranche*, Paris, Vrin, 1926.

GOUNELLE, A., *La Cène, sacrement de la division*, Paris, Les Bergers et les Mages, 1996.

GRANGER, G.-G., « Philosophie et mathématique leibnizienne », *Revue de Métaphysique et de Morale* 86/1, 1981, p. 1-37.

GREGORY, D., *Astronomiæ, physicæ et geometriæ elementa*, Oxford, E Theatro Sheldoniano, 1702.

GREW, N., *The Anatomy of Plants*, s. l., W. Rawlins, 1682.

– *Cosmologia Sacra, or a Discourse of the Universe as it is the Creature and Kingdom of God*, London, W. Rogers, S. Smith and B. Walford, 1701.

GROSHOLZ, E. et YAKIRA, E., *Leibniz's Science of the Rational*, *Studia Leibnitiana, Sonderheft* 26, Wiesbaden, F. Steiner Verlag, 1998.

GRUA, G., *Jurisprudence universelle et théodicée selon Leibniz*, Paris, P.U.F., 1953.

– *La Justice humaine selon Leibniz*, Paris, P.U.F., 1956.

GRUNERT, F. et VOLLHARDT, F. (Hrsg.), *Historia literaria. Neuordnungen des Wissens im 17. und 18. Jahrhundert*, Berlin, Akademie Verlag, 2007.

GUEROULT, M., *Leibniz. Dynamique et métaphysique*, Paris, Aubier-Montaigne, 1967.

– « La Dissertation kantienne de 1770 », *Archives de philosophie* 41, 1978, p. 3-25.

– *Dianoématique. Histoire de l'histoire de la philosophie*, t. 2 : *En Allemagne de Leibniz à nos jours*, Paris, Aubier, 1988.

GUERRIER, W., *Leibniz in seinen Beziehungen zu Russland und Peter dem Grossen*, St. Petersburg und Leipzig, Kaiserlichen Akademie des Wissenschaften, 1873.

GUHRAUER, G. E., *Gottfried Wilhelm Freiherr von Leibnitz. Eine Biographie*, 2 vol., Breslau, Hirt, 1842.

GUILLÉN VERA, T., « Bases filosoficas para la ética y la política de Leibniz », *Revista de estudios politicos* 83, 1994, p. 273-312.

GUNN, A., *Modern French Philosophy*, New York, Dodd, Mead and Company, 1922.

HAASE, C., *Leibniz als Politiker und Diplomat*, dans C. Haase et W. Totok (Hrsg.), *Leibniz. Sein Leben-Sein Wirken-Seine Welt*, Hannover, Verlag für Literatur und Zeitgeschehen, 1966, p. 195-226.

HALL, R. « Newton in France : A new view », *History of Science* 13, 1975, p. 233-250.

HAMOU, P., *La Mutation du visible 2. Microscopes et télescopes en Angleterre de Bacon à Hooke*, Villeneuve d'Ascq, Presses Universitaires du Septentrion, 2001.

HARNACK, A., *Geschichte der Königlich Preussischen Akademie der Wissenschaften zu Berlin*, Hildesheim, Olms, 1970.

HARTMANN, G., *Leibniz als Jurist und Rechtsphilosoph*, Tübingen, Laupp, 1892.

HARTZ, G., *Leibniz's Final System. Monads, Matter and Animals*, Londres, Routledge, 2007.

HEINEKAMP, A., *Das Problem des Guten bei Leibniz, Kant-Studien*, Ergänzungsheft, Bonn, Bouvier, 1969.

– « Ars characteristica und natürliche Sprache bei Leibniz », *Tijdschrift voor Filosofie* 34, 1972, p. 446-488.

– « L'État actuel de la recherche leibnizienne », *Études philosophiques* 2, 1989, p. 139-160.

HERBART, J. F., *Psychologie als Wissenschaft, neu gegründet auf Erfahrung, Metaphysik und Mathematik, zweyter analytischer Theil*, Königsberg, Unzer, 1825.

HERDER, J. G., *Dieu. Quelques entretiens*, trad. fr. M. Bienenstock, Paris, P.U.F., 1996.

HESS, H. J., « Die unveröffentlichten naturwissenschaftlichen und technischen Arbeiten von G. W. Leibniz aus der Zeit seines Parisaufenthaltes. Eine Kurzcharakteristik », dans *Leibniz à Paris 1672-76, Studia Leibnitiana Supplementa* 17, Wiesbaden, F. Steiner Verlag, 1978, p. 183-217.

HINTIKKA, J. et REMES, U., *The Method of Analysis, Its Geometrical Origin and Its General Significance*, Dordrecht, Reidel, 1974.

HIRSCH, E. C., *Der Berühmte Herr Leibniz : Eine Biographie*, Munich, Beck, 2000.

HOCHSTRASSER, T. J., *Natural Law Theories in the Early Enlightenment*, Cambridge, Cambridge University Press, 2000.

HOFMANN, J. E., *Leibniz in Paris 1672-1676. His growth to mathematical maturity*, Cambridge, Cambridge University Press, 1974.

HOLZ, H. H., *Leibniz*, Stuttgart, Kohlhammer, 1958.

– *Leibniz. Das Lebenswerk eines Universalgelehrten*, hrsg. von J. Zimmer, Darmstadt, Wissenschaftliche Buchgesellschaft, 2013.

HOOKE, R., *Micrographia*, London, Martyn and Allestry, 1665.

– « Le journal du lundy 20 Decembre 1666 », *Journal des sçavans*, 1666, p. 491-501 : *Micrographia or Some physiological descriptions of minutes bodies made by magnifying glasses : with observations and inquiries thereupon by Robert Hooke fellow Royal Society, In fol.* London.

HOSTLER, J., *Leibniz' Moral Philosophy*, London, Duckworth, 1975.

HOTSON, H., *Johann Heinrich Alsted 1588-1638. Between Renaissance, Reformation and Universal Reform*, Oxford, Clarendon Press, 2000.

– « The Instauration of the Image of God in Man : Humanist Anthropology, Encyclopaedic Pedagogy, Baconianism, and Universal Reform », dans M. Pelling and S. Mandelbrote (ed.), *The Practice of Reform in Health, Medicine, and Science 1500-2000 : Essays for Charles Webster*, Ashgate, Aldershot, 2005, p. 1-21.

– *Commonplace Learning : Ramism and its German Ramifications, 1543-1630,* Oxford, Oxford University Press, 2007.

HUME, D., *Dialogues Concerning Natural Religion* [1779], ed. N. Kemp Smith, Indianapolis, Bobbs-Merrill, 1947.

– *Enquiries Concerning Human Understanding and Concerning the Principles of Morals*, ed. L. A. Selby-Bigge, 3 e éd. revue, Oxford, Oxford University Press, 1975.

– *Essays Moral, Political and Literary*, éd. T. H. Green et T. H. Grose, 2 vol., London, Longmans, Green, and co., 1898.

HUNTER, I., *Rival Enlightenments : Civil and Metaphysical Philosophy in Early Modern Germany*, Cambridge, Cambridge University Press, 2001.

ILTIS, C., « The Leibnizian-Newtonian Debates : Natural Philosophy and Social Psychology », *The British Journal for the History of Science* 6/4, 1973, p. 343-377.

ISHIGURO, H., *Leibniz's Philosophy of Logic and Language*, London, Duckworth, 1972.

JABLONSKI, D. E., *Kurtze Vorstellung…*, appendice de H. Rudolph, « Zum Nutzen von Politik und Philosophie für die Kirchenunion. Die Aufnahme der innerprotestantischen Ausgleichsverhandlungen am Ende des 17. Jahrhunderts », *Studia Leibnitiana Sonderheft* 29, 1999, p. 128-166.

— et LEIBNIZ, G. W., *Negotium Irenicum, L'union des Églises protestantes selon G. W. Leibniz et D. E. Jablonski*, éd. et trad. C. Rösler-Le Van, Paris, Classiques Garnier, 2013.

JANET, P., « Une Nouvelle phase de la philosophie spiritualiste », *Revue des Deux Mondes*, 2 e période, 108, 1873, p. 363-388.

JESSEPH, D., *Squaring the Circle. The War between Hobbes and Wallis*, Chicago, The University of Chicago Press, 1999.

JOHNS, Ch., *The Science of Right in Leibniz' Moral and Political Philosophy*, London-New Delhi-New York-Sydney, Bloomsbury, 2013.

JOLLEY, N., *Leibniz and Locke : A Study of the* New Essays on Human Understanding, Oxford, Clarendon Press, 1984.

– *The Light of the Soul : Theories of Ideas in Leibniz, Malebranche, and Descartes*, Oxford, Clarendon Press, 1990.

– *Leibniz*, London, Routledge, 2005.

– « Leibniz on Hobbes, Lockes's "Two Treatises" and Sherlock's "Case of Allegiance" », *The Historical Journal* 1, 1975, p. 21-35.

JORATI, J., « Monadic Teleology Without Goodness and Without God », *The Leibniz Review* 23, 2013, p. 43-72.

JORGENSEN, L., « The Principle of Continuity and Leibniz's Theory of Consciousness », *Journal of the History of Philosophy* 47/2, 2009, p. 223-248.

KABITZ, W., *Die Philosophie des jungen Leibniz. Untersuchungen zur Entwicklungsgeschichte seines Systems*, Heidelberg, Winter, 1909.

– « Leibniz und Berkeley », *Sitzungsberichte der Preussische Akademie der Wissenschaften, Philosophische-Historische Klasse* 24, Berlin, De Gruyter, 1932.

KALINOWSKI, G., « La Logique juridique de Leibniz, conception et contenu », *Studia Leibnitiana* 9/2, 1977, p. 168-189.

KANT, I., *Der Streit mit Johann August Eberhard*, éd. M. Lauschke, M. Zahn, Hamburg, Meiner, 1998.

– *Critique de la raison pure* [1781/1787], trad. fr. A. Renaut, Paris, Flammarion, 2006.

KAUPPI, R., *Über die Leibnizsche Logik. Mit besonderer Berücksichtigung des Problems der Intension und der Extension*, Helsinki, Acta Philosophica Fennica, 1960.

KELLEY, D. R., « Writing Cultural History in Early Modern Europe : Christophe Milieu and his Project », *Renaissance Quarterly* 52/2, 1999, p. 342-365.

KLOPP, O., *Leibniz der Stifter gelehrter Gesellschaften*, Leipzig, B. G. Teubner, 1864.

KNEALE, W. et KNEALE, M., *The Development of Logic*, Oxford, Oxford University Press, 1962.

KNECHT, H. H., *La Logique chez Leibniz. Essai sur le rationalisme baroque*, Lausanne, L'Âge d'Homme, 1981.

KNOBLOCH, E., *Die mathematischen Studien von G.W. Leibniz zur Kombinatorik*, *Studia Leibnitiana Supplementa* 16, Wiesbaden, F. Steiner Verlag, 1976.

– « Leibniz between *ars characteristica* and *ars inveniendi* : Unknown news about Cajori's "master-builder" of mathematical notations », dans A. Heeffer et M. van Dyck (ed.), *Philosophical Aspects of Symbolic Reasoning in Early Modern Mathematics*, London, College Publications, 2010, p. 289-302.

KÖNIG, P., « Das System des Rechts und die Lehre von den Fiktionen bei Leibniz », dans J. Schröder (Hrsg.), *Entwicklung der Methodenlehre in Rechtswissenschaft und Philosophie vom 16. bis zum 18. Jahrhundert*, Stuttgart, F. Steiner Verlag, 1998, p. 137-161.

KÜHN, M., *Kant. Eine Biographie*, München, Beck, 2003.

KULSTAD, M., *Leibniz on Apperception, Consciousness, and Reflection*, Munich, Philosophia, 1991.

– « La Conception leibnizienne de l'expression », trad. fr. dans *Les cahiers philosophiques de Strasbourg* 18, 2004, p. 149-176 (article original paru dans *Studia Leibnitiana* 9/1, 1977, p. 55-76).

LÆRKE, M., *Leibniz lecteur de Spinoza. La genèse d'une opposition complexe*, Paris, Honoré Champion, 2008.

– « Leibniz, the Encyclopedia, and the Natural Order of Thinking », *Journal of the History of Ideas* 75/2, 2014, p. 233-255.

– « *More mathematico demonstrata, ordine naturali exposita*. Leibniz sur l'organisation de l'encyclopédie », dans A. Pelletier (ed.), *Leibniz's Experimental Philosophy*, *Studia Leibnitiana Sonderheft* 46, Stuttgart, F. Steiner Verlag, 2015, p. 233-249.

– « Leibniz : lire les géomètres », dans J. Boulad-Ayoub, D. Antoine-Mahut, A. Torero-Ibad (dir.), *Les arts de lire des philosophes modernes*, Québec, Presses de l'Université Laval, 2015, p. 79-94.

– *Les Lumières de Leibniz. Controverses avec Huet, Bayle, Regis et More*, Paris, Classiques Garnier, 2015.

– « Mendelssohn, Wachter et les origines du Spinoza idéaliste », dans P. Girard, C. Leduc et M. Rioux-Beaune (dir.), *Les Métaphysiques des Lumières*, Paris, Classiques Garnier, 2016, p. 135-153.

LACHELIER, J., « Psychologie et métaphysique », *Revue philosophique de la France et de l'Étranger* 19, 1885, p. 481-516.

LAKATOS, I., *Philosophical Papers*, Cambridge, Cambridge University Press, 1978.

LALANNE, A., « La Recension des *Essais de Théodicée* dans les *Acta Eruditorum* par Wolff : une reconstruction systématique ? Traduction inédite et présentation de la recension à l'occasion du tricentenaire de sa publication », http://www.philosophiedudroit.org/lalanne, %20leibniz.htm, mis en ligne le 7 mai 2011.

LAMARRA, A., « Le Traduzioni settecentesche della *Monadologie*. Christian Wolff e la prima recezione di Leibniz », dans A. Lamarra, R. Palaia, P. Pimpinella (ed.), *Le prime traduzioni della* Monadologie *di Leibniz (1720-1721)*, Firenze, Olschki, 2001.

LA METTRIE, J. O., *Histoire naturelle de l'âme, augmentée par Lettre critique de M. de La Mettrie à Émilie du Châtelet*, Oxford, 1747.

LANDAU, P., *Stufen der Gerechtigkeit. Zur Rechtsphilosophie von Gottfried Wilhelm Leibniz und Karl Christian Krause*, München, Verlag der Bayerischen Akademie der Wissenschaften, 1995.

LAUTH, R., « Leibniz im Verständnis Fichtes », *Kant-Studien* 7, 1996, p. 396-422.

LE CHEVALLIER, L., *La Morale de Leibniz*, Paris, Vrin, 1933.

LÉCHOT, P. O., « Irénisme » dans P. Gisel (dir.), *Encyclopédie du protestantisme*, Paris, P.U.F., 2006, p. 633-634.

LEDUC, C., *Substance, individu et connaissance chez Leibniz*, Montréal/Paris, Presses de l'Université de Montréal/Vrin, 2009.

– « Leibniz and Sensible Qualities », *British Journal for the History of Philosophy* 18/5, 2010, p. 797–819.

– « Les *Meditationes* de Leibniz dans la tradition wolffienne », *Archives de philosophie* 73, 2013, p. 295-317.

– « Introduction », dans Leibniz, *Discours de métaphysique. Correspondance avec Arnauld*, Paris, Vrin, 2016, p. 7-62.

LEDUC C., PÉPIN, F., REY, A.-L. et RIOUX-BEAULNE, M. (dir.), *Leibniz et Diderot. Rencontres et transformations*, Montréal/Paris, Presses de l'Université de Montréal/Vrin, 2015.

LEE, S., « Leibniz on Divine Concurrence », *Philosophical Review* 113, 2004, p. 203-248.

LEIBNIZ, G. W., *Merckwürdige Schrifften : welche zwischen dem Herrn Baron von Leibnitz und dem Herrn D. Clarcke über besondere Materien der natürlichen Religion in Frantzös. und Englischer Sprache gewechselt, Gottfried Wilhelm Leibniz, Samuel Clarke; mit einer Vorrede Herrn Christian Wolffens, nebst einer Antwort Herrn Ludwig Philipp Thümmigs auf die fünffte Englische Schrifft; wegen ihrer Wichtigkeit in teutscher Sprache heraus gegeben worden von Heinrich Köhlern,* Iena, 1720, repris dans Ch. Wolff, *Gesammelte Werke* III, 113, Hildesheim, Olms, 2008.

– *Kleinere Philosophische Schriften mit einer Vorrede Herrn Christian Wolffs, ehedem von dem Jenaischen Philosophen Herrn Heinrich Köhler teutsch übersetzet, nun auf das neue übersehen von M. Caspar Jacob Huth* [Iena, 1740], Hildesheim, Olms, 2010.

– *Œuvres philosophiques latines et françoises du feu Mr de Leibniz tirées de ses manuscrits qui se conservent dans la bibliothèque royale à Hanovre*, éd. R. E. Raspe, Amsterdam-Leipzig, J. Schreuder, 1765.

– *Deutsche Schriften*, éd. G. E. Guhrauer, Berlin, Veit-Sittenfeld, 1838-1840, 2 vol.

– *Opera philosophica quae exstant omnia*, éd. J. E. Erdmann, Berlin, G. Eichler, 1839-1840, 2 vol.

– *Leibnizens gesammelte Werke : aus den Handschriften der Königlichen Bibliothek zu Hannover*, éd. G. H. Pertz, Hannover, Hahnsche-Hof Buchhandlung, 1843-1847.

– *Briefwechsel zwischen Leibniz, Arnauld und dem Landgrafen Ernst von Hessen-Rheinfels*, éd. C. L. Grotefend, Hannover, Verlage der Hanshen Hof-Buchhandlung, 1846.

– *Lettres et opuscules inédits de Leibniz, extraits des ms. de la Bibliothèque royale de Hanovre*, éd. L. A. Foucher de Careil, Paris, Ladrange, 1854.

– *Nouvelles lettres et opuscules inédits de Leibniz*, éd. L. A. Foucher de Careil, Paris, A. Durand, 1857.

– *Œuvres de Leibniz publiées pour la première fois à partie des manuscrits originaux*, éd. L. A. Foucher de Careil, Paris, Firmin Didot, 1859-1887, 7 vol.

– *Philosophiche Werke. Hauptschriften zur Grundlegung der Philosophie*, éd. E. Cassirer, trad. all. A. Buchenau, Leipzig, Meiner, 1904-1906.

– *Elementa philosophiae arcanae de summa rerum*, éd. I. Jagodinski, Kazan, Université Impériale de Kazan, 1913.

– *Confessio philosophi, la profession de foi du philosophe*, éd. et trad. Y. Belaval, Paris, Vrin, 1970.

– « Cogitationes novae quomodo formetur… atque in organo auditus exprimatur », dans *Leibnizens nachgelassene Schriften physikalischen, mechanischen und technischen Inhalts,* éd. E. Gerland, Leipzig, Teubner, 1906, rééd. New York-London, Johnson Reprint, 1973.

– « *Directiones ad rem medicam pertinentes* », éd. F. Hartmann et M. Krüger, *Studia leibnitiana* 8, 1976, p. 40-68.

– *Discours sur la théologie naturelle des Chinois, plus quelques écrits sur la question religieuse de la Chine*, éd. et trad. C. Frémont, Paris, L'Herne, 1987.

– « *Phoranomus seu De potentia et legibus naturæ, Rome, juillet 1689* », éd. A. Robinet, *Physis* 38, 1991, p. 429-541, p. 797-885.
– *De quadratura arithmetica circuli ellipseos et hyperbolae*, éd. E. Knobloch, Göttingen, Vandenhoeck & Ruprecht, 1993.
– « Pensées sur l'instauration d'une physique nouvelle, 1679 », trad. fr. M. Fichant, *Philosophie* 39, 1993, p. 7-26.
– *La Réforme de la dynamique.* De corporum concursu *et autres textes inédits*, éd. M. Fichant, Paris, Vrin, 1994.
– *Le Droit de la raison*, éd. et trad. R. Sève, Paris, Vrin, 1994.
– *La Caractéristique géométrique*, éd. J. Echeverría et M. Parmentier, Paris, Vrin, 1995.
– *Correspondence Leibniz – Castel de Saint Pierre*, éd. A. Robinet, Paris, Centre de philosophie de droit, 1995.
– *L'Harmonie des langues*, texte bilingue, trad. fr. M. Crépon, Paris, Seuil, 2000.
– *Von der Allmacht und Alwissenheit Gottes und der Freiheit des Menschen*, trad. fr. C. Rösler, *Philosophie* 68, 2000, p. 66-88.
– *Des conditions* (*De conditionibus*), éd. et trad. P. Boucher, Paris, Vrin, 2002.
– *Quadrature arithmétique du cercle, de l'ellipse et de l'hyperbole et la trigonométrie sans tables trigonométriques qui en est le corollaire*, trad. fr. M. Parmentier, Paris, Vrin, 2004.
– *Discours de métaphysique. Monadologie,* éd. M. Fichant, Paris, Gallimard, 2004.
– *Von den wahren Theologia Mystica*, trad. fr. C. Rösler, *Revue de Théologie et de Philosophie* 142, 2010, p. 279-300.
– *Leibniz – De Volder. Correspondance*, trad. fr. A.-L. Rey, Paris, Vrin, 2016.
– *The Leibniz-Stahl Controversy*, éd. et trad. F. Duchesneau et J. E. H. Smith, New Haven, Yale University Press, 2016.
– *Discours de métaphysique. Correspondance avec Arnauld*, éd. C. Leduc, Paris, Vrin, 2016
– *Mathesis universalis*, éd. et trad. sous la direction de D. Rabouin, Paris, Vrin, 2017.
— et WOLFF, C., *Briefwechsel zwischen Leibniz und Christian Wolff*, éd. C. I. Gerhardt, Hannover, H. W. Schmidt, 1860.
— et THOMASIUS, J., *Correspondance, 1663-1672*, éd. et trad. par R. Bodéüs, Paris, Vrin, 1993.
LENZEN, W., *Das System der Leibnizschen Logik*, Berlin-New York, De Gruyter, 1990.
– « Leibniz's Logic », dans D. M. Gabbay, J. Woods et A. Kanamori (eds.), *Handbook of the History of Logic.* Vol.3 : *The Rise of Modern Logic : from Leibniz to Frege*, Amsterdam, Elsevier, 2004, p. 1-83.
LEROUX, P., *Réfutation de l'éclectisme*, Paris, Librairie de Charles Gosselin, 1839.
– « De la Mutilation d'un écrit posthume de M. Jouffroy », *Revue indépendante*, 1er novembre 1842.
LE RU, V., *Jean Le Rond D'Alembert, philosophe*, Paris, Vrin, 1994.

LEVEY, S., « Logical Theory in Leibniz », dans B. Look (ed.), *The Continuum Companion to Leibniz*, London-New York, Continuum, 2011, p. 110-135.

LOEMKER, L. E., « Leibniz and the Herborn Encyclopedists », *Journal of the History of Ideas* 22/3, 1961, p. 323-38.

– *The Struggle for Synthesis. The Seventeenth Century Background of Leibniz's Synthesis of Order and Freedom*, Cambridge, Mass., Harvard University Press, 1972.

LOCKE, J., *An Essay Concerning Human Understanding*, éd. P. H. Nidditch, Oxford, Clarendon Press, 1975.

LODGE, P., « Leibniz's Mill Argument Against Mechanical Materialism Revisited », *Ergo* 1, 2014, p. 79-99.

– « Leibniz on Created Substance and Occasionalism », dans P. Lodge et T. Stoneham (ed.), *Locke and Leibniz on Substance*, London, Routledge, 2014, p. 186-202.

— et M. BOBRO, « Stepping Back Inside Leibniz's Mill », *The Monist* 81/4, 1998, p. 553-572.

LOOK, B., « On Monadic Domination in Leibniz's Metaphysics », *British Journal for the History of Philosophy* 10/3, 2002, p. 379-399.

LORENZ, S., « "Auferstehung eines Leibes dessen Glieder wunderbahrlich herum zerstreuet sind". Leibniz-Renaissancen und ihre editorischen Reflexe », dans A Sell. (éd.), *Editionen – Wandel und Wirkung*, Tübingen, Max Niemeyer Verlag (de Gruyter), 2007.

LUIG, K., « Die Privatrechtsordnung im Rechtssystem von Leibniz », dans G. Birtsch (Hrsg.), *Grund- und Freiheitsrechte von der ständischen zur spätbürgerlichen Gesellschaft*, Göttingen, Vandenhoeck & Ruprecht, 1987, p. 347-374.

– « Leibniz und die Prinzipien des Vertragsrechts », dans J.-F. Kervégan et H. Mohnhaupt (Hrsg.), *Gesellschaftliche Freiheit und vertragliche Bindung in Rechtsgeschichte und Philosophie*, Frankfurt am Main, Klostermann, 1999.

MACFARLANE, J., *What Does It Mean to Say that Logic Is Formal?*, PhD Dissertation, University of Pittsburgh, 2000.

MAHNKE, D., *Leibnizens Synthese von Universalmathematik und Individual-metaphysik*, Stuttgart-Bad Cannstatt, Friedrich Frommann, 1925.

MAINE DE BIRAN, *Journal Intime*, 3 vol., éd. H. Gouhier, Neuchatel, Éditions de la Baconnière, 1954.

– *Œuvres de Maine de Biran*, 20 vol., éd. F. Azouvi *et al.*, Paris, Vrin, 1984-2001.

MALPIGHI, M., *Dissertatio epistolica de Bombyce, Societati Regiae Londini ad Scientiam Naturalem promovendam Institutae dedicata,* Londini, apud Joannem Martyn et Jacobum Allestry, 1669.

– *Opera omnia,* Londini, apud Robertum Scott, 1686.

– *La Structure du ver à soie,* Paris, Maurice Villery, 1686.

MANNS, J. W. et MADDEN, E. H., « Victor Cousin : Common Sense and the Absolute », *The Review of Metaphysics* 43/3, 1990, p. 569-589.

MARRAS, C., « The Role of Metaphor in Leibniz's Epistemology », dans M. Dascal (ed.), *Leibniz. What Kind of Rationalist?*, Dordrecht, Springer, 2008, p. 199-212.

MARTIN-ROBINE, F., *Histoire du principe de moindre action, trois siècles de principes variationnels de Fermat à Feynman*, Paris, Vuibert, 2006.

MAUPERTUIS, P. L. M., « Accord de différentes lois de la nature », *Mémoires de l'Académie royale des sciences de Paris*, Paris, Imprimerie Royale, 1744.

MCDONOUGH, J., « Leibniz : Creation and Conservation and Concurrence », *The Leibniz Review* 17, 2007, p. 31-60.

– « Leibniz's Optics and Contingency in Nature », *Perspectives on Science* 18/4, 2010, p. 432-455.

– « Leibniz and the Foundations of Physics : The Later Years », *The Philosophical Review* 125/1, 2016, p. 1-34.

– « Leibniz on Monadic Agency and Optimal Form », dans A. Pelletier (ed.), *Leibniz's experimental philosophy*, *Studia Leibnitiana Sonderheft* 46, Stuttgart, F. Steiner Verlag, 2016, p. 93-118.

MCNIVEN HINE, H., « Dortous de Mairan, the Cartonian », *Studies on Voltaire* 266, 1989, p. 163-179.

MCRAE, R., *The Problem of the Unity of the Sciences*, Toronto, University of Toronto Press, 1961.

– *Leibniz : Perception, Apperception, and Thought*, Toronto, University of Toronto Press, 1976.

MERCER, C., *Leibniz's Metaphysics*, Cambridge, Cambridge University Press, 2001.

MEYER, R. W., *Leibniz und die europäische Ordnungskrise*, Hamburg, Hansischer Gildenverlag, 1948.

MILTON, J. R., « Laws of Nature », dans D. Garber et M. Ayers (ed.), *The Cambridge History of Seventeenth Century Philosophy*, Cambridge, Cambridge University Press, 1998, p. 680-701.

MOLL, K., « Der Enzyklopädiegedanke bei Comenius und Alsted, seine Übernahme und Umgestaltung bei Leibniz – neue Perspektiven der Leibnizforschung », *Studia Leibnitiana* 34/1, 2002, p. 1-30.

MOREAU, D., *Deux Cartesiens La polémique entre Antoine Arnauld et Nicolas Malebranche*, Paris, Vrin, 1999.

MOREAU, P.-F., « "In Naturalismo". Leibniz, Spinoza et les spiritualistes français », dans R. Andrault, M. Lærke et P. F. Moreau (dir.), *Spinoza/Leibniz. Rencontres, controverses, réceptions*, Paris, Presses Universitaires de Paris Sorbonne, 2014.

MUGNAI, M., *Astrazione e realtà. Saggio su Leibniz*, Milano, Feltrinelli, 1976.

– *Introduzione alla filosofia di Leibniz*, Torino, Einaudi, 2001.

– « Introduzione », dans G. W. Leibniz, *Ricerche generali sull'analisi delle nozioni e delle verità*, trad. it. M. Mugnai, Pisa, Edizioni della Normale, 2008, p. 1-57.

MÜLLER, K. et KRÖNERT, G., *Leben und Werk von Gottfried Wilhelm Leibniz. Eine Chronik*, Frankfurt am Main, Klostermann, 1969.

MULVANEY, R. J., « The Early Development of Leibniz's Concept of Justice », *Journal of the History of Ideas* 29, 1968, p. 53-72.

NADLER, S., « Occasionalism and General Will in Malebranche », *Journal of the History of Philosophy* 31/1, 1993, p. 31-47.

– *Occasionalism : Causation Among the Cartesians*, Oxford, Oxford University Press, 2011.

– *Le Meilleur des mondes possible. La rencontre entre Leibniz, Malebranche et Arnauld*, Paris, Bayard, 2011.

NAERT, É., *Leibniz et la querelle du pur amour*, Paris, Vrin, 1959.

– *Mémoire et conscience de soi selon Leibniz*, Paris, Vrin, 1961.

– *La Pensée politique de Leibniz*, Paris, P.U.F., 1964.

NEVEUX, J. B., *Vie spirituelle et vie sociale entre Rhin et Baltique au* XVIIe *siècle*, Paris, Klincksieck, 1967.

OKRUHLIK, K., « The Status of Scientific Laws in the Leibnizian System », dans K. Okruhlik et J. R. Brown (ed.), *The Natural Philosophy of Leibniz*, Dordrecht, Reidel, 1995, p. 183-206.

O'NEILL, E., « *Influxus Physicus* », dans S. Nadler (ed.), *Causation in Early Modern Philosophy*, University Park, PA, Pennsylvania State University Press, 1993, p. 27-55.

OTTE, G., « Leibniz und die juristische Methode », *Geschichte für Neuere Rechts-Geschichte* 1-2, 1983, p. 1-21.

PACCIONI, J.-P., *Cet esprit de profondeur. Christian Wolff, l'ontologie et la métaphysique*, Paris, Vrin, 2006.

PARK, J., « Le Débat wolffien sur l'idéalisme de Leibniz lors de la première diffusion de la *Monadologie* latine », dans J.-P. Paccioni (dir.), *Leibniz, Wolff et les monades. Science et métaphysique*, *Revue de synthèse* 128/3-4, 2007, p. 325-339.

PARKINSON, G. H. R., *Logic and Reality in Leibniz's Metaphysics*, Oxford, Oxford University Press, 1965.

– *Leibniz on Human Freedom*, *Studia Leibnitiana Sonderfheft* 2, Wiesbaden, F. Steiner Verlag, 1970.

– « The "Intellectualization of Appearences" : Aspects of Leibniz's Theory of Sensation and Thought », dans M. Hooker (ed.), *Leibniz. Critical and Interpretive Essays*, Minneapolis, University of Minnesota Press, 1982, p. 3-20.

PARMENTIER, M., *Leibniz-Locke, une intrigue philosophique : les* Nouveaux essais sur l'entendement humain, Paris, Presses de l'Université Paris-Sorbonne, 2008.

– « Voltaire et l'optimisme leibnizien », *Atlante. Revue d'études romanes* 1, 2014, p. 137-165.

PASCAL, B., *Pensées, opuscules et lettres,* éd. Ph. Sellier, Paris, Classiques Garnier, 2011.

PASINI, E., *Corpo e funzioni cognitive in Leibniz,* Milano, Franco Angeli, 1996.

– « La Philosophie des mathématiques chez Leibniz. Lignes d'investigation », dans H. Poser (Hrsg.), *Nihil sine ratione. Mensch, Natur und Technik im Wirken von*

G.W. Leibniz, Akten des VII. Internationalen Leibniz-Kongreß, Berlin, Leibniz-Gesellschaft, Hanovre, 2001, p. 954-963.

PECKHAUS, V., « Leibniz' Pragmatismus », dans H. Poser (dir.), *Nihil sine ratione. Mensch, Natur und Technik im Wirken von G. W. Leibniz*, Akten des VII. Internationaler Leibniz-Kongreß, Berlin, Leibniz-Gesellschaft, Hanovre, 2001, p. 967-972.

PELLETIER, A., « L'Ordre des choses : catégories et définitions chez Leibniz ». Thèse de doctorat, Université Paris IV, 2009.

– « The *Scientia Generalis* and the *Encyclopaedia* », dans M. R. Antognazza (ed.), *Oxford Handbook to Leibniz*, Oxford, Oxford University Press, 2013.

PETERSCHMITT, L., « La Critique du réalisme leibnizien dans le *De Motu* de Berkeley », *Asterion* 1, 2003, p. 112-126.

PFAFF, Ch. M., *Oratio de egoismo, nova philosophica haeresi*, Tübingen, Pflick, 1722.

PHEMISTER, P., « "All the time and everywhere everything's the same as here" : The Principle of Uniformity in the Correspondence Between Leibniz and Lady Masham », dans P. Lodge (ed.), *Leibniz and His Correspondents*, Cambridge, Cambridge University Press, 2004, p. 193-213.

– *Leibniz and the Natural World, Activity, Passivity and Corporeal Substances in Leibniz's Philosophy*, Dordrecht, Springer, 2005.

– *Leibniz and the Environment*, London, Routledge, 2016.

PICON, M., « Vers la "doctrine de l'entendement en abrégé" : éléments pour une généalogie des *Meditationes de cognitione, veritate et ideis* », *Studia Leibnitiana* 35/1, 2003, p. 102-132.

– « On the Constitution of Leibniz's Formalism », dans M. Kulstad, M. Lærke, D. Snyder (ed.), *The Philosophy of the Young Leibniz*, Stuttgart, F. Steiner Verlag, 2009, p. 139-146.

– *Normes et objets du savoir dans les premiers essais Leibniziens*. Thèse de doctorat, ENS de Lyon, 2015.

– « Leibniz, Hobbes et les principes des sciences », dans É. Marquer et P. Rateau (dir.), *Leibniz et Hobbes*, Montréal/Paris, Presses de l'Université de Montréal/Vrin, 2017.

PLATNER, E., *Philosophische Aphorismen : nebst einigen Anleitungen zur philosophischen Geschichte*, Leipzig, Schwickert, 1776, nouvelle éd. : 1784.

PRIVAT DE MOLIÈRES, J., *Leçons de Physique, contenant les élémens de la physique déterminés par les seules lois de la mécanique*, Paris, chez Guillaume Desprez et Guillaume Cavelier, 1742.

PROST, J., *Essai sur l'atomisme et l'occasionalisme dans la philosophie cartésienne*, Paris, Paulin, 1907.

PROUST, J., *Diderot et l'Encyclopédie*, Paris, A. Colin, 1967.

RABOUIN, D., « Idée, représentation et correspondance mathématique chez Leibniz », dans K. S. Ong-Van-Cung (dir.), *La Voie des idées ? Le statut de la représentation, XVIIe-XXe siècles*, Paris, CNRS Éditions, 2006.

– « Infini mathématique et infini métaphysique », *Revue de Métaphysique et de Morale* 70, 2011, p. 203-220.
– « Interpretations of Leibniz's *Mathesis universalis* at the Beginning of the XXth Century », dans R. Krömer et Y. Chin-Drian (ed.), *New essays on Leibniz Reception in Philosophy of Science 1800-2000*, Basel, Birkhäuser, 2011, p. 187-201.
– « *Analytica Generalissima Humanorum Cognitionum*. Some reflections on the relationship between logical and mathematical analysis in Leibniz », *Studia Leibnitiana* 45/1, 2013, p. 109-130.
– « The Difficulty of Being Simple. Interactions between Mathematics and Philosophy in Leibniz's Analysis of Notions », dans N. Goethe, P. Beeley et D. Rabouin (ed.), *G.W. Leibniz. Interrelations between Mathematics and Philosophy*, Dordrecht, Springer, 2015, p. 49-72.
RACIONERO, Q., « El principio de la "place d'autrui" y la racionalidad de la politica », dans I. Murillo (ed.), *La filosofia ante la encrucijada de la nueva Europa*, Colmenar Viejo, Diálogo filosófico, 1994, p. 583-611.
RANEA, A. G., « The *A priori* method and the *actio* concept revised. Dynamics and metaphysics in an unpublished controversy between Leibniz and Denis Papin », *Studia Leibnitiana* 21, 1989, p. 42-68.
RATEAU, P., *La Question du mal chez Leibniz*, Paris, Champion, 2008.
– *Leibniz et le meilleur des mondes possibles*, Paris, Classiques Garnier, 2015.
RAUZY, J.-B., *La Doctrine leibnizienne de la vérité*, Paris, Vrin, 2001.
RAVAISSON, F., « Philosophie contemporaine (1840) », dans F. Ravaisson, *Métaphysique et morale*, Paris, Vrin, 1986, p. 396-427.
– *La Philosophie en France au XIXe Siècle*, 4e éd., Paris, Librairie Hachette, 1895.
RENOUVIER, C. B., *Essai de Critique générale*, 1912 ; Premier Essai : *Traité de logique générale et de logique formelle*, 3 vol., Paris, Librairie Armand Colin ; Deuxième Essai : *Traité de psychologie rationnelle d'après les principes du criticisme*, 2 vol., Paris, Librairie Armand Colin ; Troisième Essai : *Principes de la nature*, Paris, Librairie Armand Colin.
— et PRATT, L., *La Nouvelle monadologie*, Paris, Armand Colin et Cie, 1899.
RESCHER, N., « Leibniz's Interpretation of His Logical Calculi », *Journal of Symbolic Logic* 19, 1954, p. 1-13.
– *Leibniz. An Introduction to his Philosophy*, Oxford, Blackwell, 1979.
REY, L., *Les Enjeux de l'histoire de la philosophie en France au XIXe siècle*, Paris, L'Harmattan, 2012.
RILEY, P., « Introduction », dans G. W. Leibniz, *Political Writings*, trad. angl. P. Riley, Cambridge, Cambridge University Press, 1972, p. 1-44.
– *Leibniz' Universal Jurisprudence. Justice as the Charity of the Wise*, Cambridge, Harvard University Press, 1996.
– « Leibniz's "Méditation sur la notion commune de la justice" », *The Leibniz Review* 13, 2003, p. 67-82.
ROBINET, A., *Malebranche et Leibniz. Relations personnelles*, Paris, Vrin, 1955.

– *G. W. Leibniz : le meilleur des mondes par la balance de l'Europe*, Paris, P.U.F., 1994.

ROLDÁN, C., « Estudios leibnizianos sobre etica : un bien tan prometedor como escaso », dans M. Luna, C. Roldán et J. Arana (ed.), *Treinta años de estudios leibnizianos*, numéro thématique de la *Revista de filosofia* 29, 2002, p. 171-183.

RÖSLER, C., « *Negotium Irenicum*. Les tentatives d'union des Églises protestantes de G. W. Leibniz et D. E. Jablonski », *Bulletin annuel de l'Institut d'histoire de la Réformation* 30, 2009, p. 35-56.

– « Leibniz et la mystique », *Revue de Théologie et de Philosophie* 142, 2010/III-IV, p. 301-319.

ROUX, S., « Quelles machines pour quels animaux ? Jacques Rohault, Claude Perrault, Giovanni Alfonso Borelli », dans A. Gaillard, J.-Y. Goffi, B. Roukhomovsky et S. Roux (dir.), *L'Automate. Machine, métaphore, modèle, merveille*, Pessac, Presses Universitaires de Bordeaux, 2013, p. 69-113.

ROZEMOND, M., « Leibniz on Final Causation », dans S. Newlands et L. M. Jorgensen (eds.), *Metaphysics and the good : themes from the philosophy of Robert Merrihew Adams*, Oxford, Oxford University Press, 2009, p. 272-294.

– « Mills Can't Think : Leibniz's Approach to the Mind-Body Problem », *Res Philosophica* 91/1, 2014, p. 1-28.

RUCK, E., *Die Leibniz'sche Staatsidee* [1909], Tübingen, Mohr, 1969.

RUDOLPH, H., « Zum Nutzen von Politik und Philosophie für die Kirchenunion. Die Aufnahme der innerprotestantischen Ausgleichsverhandlungen am Ende des 17. Jahrhunderts », dans M. Fontius, H. Rudolph, G. Smith (Hrsg.) *Labora diligenter*, *Studia Leibnitiana Sonderheft* 29, Stuttgart, F. Steiner Verlag, 1999, p. 108-127.

– « Bemerkungen zur Kirchengeschichtlichen Einordnung des Leibnischen Ökumenismus », dans A. Lewendoski (Hrsg.) *Leibnizbilder im 18. und 19. Jahrhundert*, *Studia Leibnitiana Sonderheft* 33, Stuttgart, F. Steiner Verlag, 2004, p. 35-45.

– « Einleitung », dans W. Li, H. Poser et H. Rudolph (Hrsg.), *Leibniz und die Ökumene*, *Studia Leibnitiana Sonderheft* 41, Stuttgart, F. Steiner Verlag, 2013, p. 9-16.

– « Scientific Organizations and Learned Societies », dans M. R. Antognazza (ed.), *The Oxford Handbook to Leibniz*, Oxford, Oxford University Press, 2013.

RUMORE, P., « Un Wolffiano diffidente : Georg Friedrich Meier e la sua dottrina dei pregiudizi », dans H.-P. Delfosse, N. Hinske, P. Rumore (Hrsg.), *G. F. Meier. Beyträge zu der Lehre von den Vorurtheilen des menschlichen Geschlechts*, Pisa, ETS, 2005.

RUSSELL, B., *A Critical Exposition of the Philosophy of Leibniz*, London, Allen and Unwin, 1900, rééd. Londres, Routledge, 1997, trad. fr. J. Ray et R. Ray, *La philosophie de Leibniz*, Paris, Alcan, 1908.

– « Recent work on the philosophy of Leibniz », *Mind* 12/46, 1903, p. 177-201.

RUTHERFORD, D., « Philosophy and Language in Leibniz », dans N. Jolley (ed.), *The Cambridge Companion to Leibniz*, Cambridge, Cambridge University Press, 1995, p. 224-269.

– « Leibniz on Spontaneity », dans D. Rutherford et J. A. Cover (eds.), *Leibniz : Nature and Freedom*, Oxford, Oxford University Press, 2005, p. 156-180.

SALAS, J. DE, *Razón y legitimidad en Leibniz*, Madrid, Tecnos, 1994.

SASAKI, C., *Descartes's Mathematical Thought*, Dordrecht, Kluwer, 2004.

SCHEPERS, H., « Demonstrationes Catholicae – Leibniz' großer Plan. Ein rationales Friedensprojekt für Europa », dans F. Beiderbeck et St. Waldhoff (Hrsg.), *Pluralität der Perspektiven und Einheit der Wahrheit im Werk von G. W. Leibniz. Beiträge zu seinem philosophischen, theologischen und politischen Denken*, Berlin, Akademie Verlag, 2011, p. 3-14.

SCHIEDERMAIR, H., *Das Phänomen der Macht und die Idee des Rechts bei G. W. Leibniz*, *Studia Leibnitiana Supplementa* 7, Wiesbaden, F. Steiner Verlag, 1970.

SCHLEGEL, F., *Charakteristiken und Kritiken I (1796-1801)*, vol. I/2 de H. Eichner (Hrsg.), *Kritische Friedrich-Schlegel-Ausgabe*, éd. H. Eichner et E. Behler, München-Paderborn-Wien, Schöningh, 1967.

SCHMIDT, K. J., *Georg W. F. Hegel. Wissenschaft der Logik – Die Lehre vom Wesen : Ein einführender Kommentar*, Paderborn-München-Wien-Zürich, Schöningh, 1997.

SCHNEIDER, H. P., *Justitia universalis. Quellenstudien zur Geschichte des christlichen Naturrechts bei Leibniz*, Frankfurt am Main, Klostermann, 1967.

– « Leibniz' Gedanken zur Ordnung von Kirche und Staat », *Zeitschrift für evangelisches Kirchenrecht* 1-2, 1967-1968, p. 18-31.

SCHNEIDER, M., « Funktion und Grundlegung der *Mathesis Universalis* im Leibnizschen System », dans A. Heinekamp (dir.), *Leibniz. Questions de logique*, *Studia Leibnitiana Sonderheft* 15, Stuttgart, F. Steiner Verlag, 1988, p. 62-182.

SCHNEIDERS, W., « *Vera politica*. Grundlagen der Politiktheorie bei G. W. Leibniz », dans F. Kaulbach et W. Krawietz (Hrsg.), *Recht und Gesellschaft. Festschrift für Helmut Schelsky zum 65. Geburtstag*, Berlin, Duncker & Humblot, 1978, p. 589-604.

– « Harmonia universalis », *Studia Leibnitiana* 16, 1984, p. 27-44.

SEARLE, J., « Minds, Brains, and Programs », *Behavioral and Brain Sciences* 3, 1980, p. 417-424.

SEIDLER, M. J., « Freedom and Moral Therapy in Leibniz », *Studia Leibnitiana* 17, 1995, p. 15-35.

SELCER, D., « The Uninterrupted Ocean : Leibniz and the Encyclopedic Imagination », *Representations* 98/1, 2007, p. 25-50.

SERFATI, M., « Mathématiques et pensée symbolique chez Leibniz », *Revue d'Histoire des Sciences* 54-2, 2001, p. 165-222.

– « Symbolic Inventiveness and "Irrationalist" Practices in Leibniz's Mathematics », dans M. Dascal (ed.), *Leibniz : What Kind of Rationalist ?*, Dordrecht, Springer, 2008, p. 125-139.

SERRES, M., *Le Système de Leibniz et ses modèles mathématiques*, Paris, P.U.F., 1968.

SÈVE, R., *Leibniz et l'école moderne du droit naturel*, Paris, P.U.F., 1989.

SGARBI, M., « G. F. Meier », dans G. Banham, D. Schulting et N. Hems (eds.), *The Bloomsbury Companion to Kant*, London/New Delhi/New York, Sydney, Bloomsbury, 2015, p. 142-144.

SHANK, J. B., *The Newton Wars and the Beginning of the French Enlightenment*, Chicago, The University of Chicago Press, 2008.

SIMMONS, A., « Changing the Cartesian Mind : Leibniz on Sensation, Representation and Consciousness », *The Philosophical Review* 110/1, 2001, p. 31-75.

SIMON, J., *Victor Cousin*, 3 e éd., Paris, Librairie Hachette, 1891.

SINACEUR, H., « Ars inveniendi aujourd'hui », *Les Études Philosophiques* 2, 1989, p. 201-214.

SLEIGH, R. C., « Leibniz on Malebranche on Causality », dans J. Cover et M. Kulstad (eds.), *Central Themes in Early Modern Philosophy*, Indianapolis, Hackett Press, 1990, p. 161-193.

SMITH, J. E. H., *Divine Machines. Leibniz and the Life Sciences*, Princeton, Princeton University Press, 2011.

SOREL, Ch., *Histoire comique de Francion,* éd. É. Roy Colombey [1909], Paris, Gallimard, 1996.

STAËL, M., *De l'Allemagne*, Paris, Charpentier, 1841.

– *Dix années d'exil*, Paris, Charpentier, 1845.

STENO, N., *De solido intra solidum naturaliter contento dissertationis prodromus,* Florentiae, ex typographia sub signo Stellae, 1669.

STERN, L., *Die politischen Ideen und die diplomatischen Aktionen von Gottfried Wilhelm Leibniz*, Berlin, Akademie Verlag, 1968.

STOLLEIS, M., *Geschichte des öffentlichen Rechts in Deutschland.* Erster Band : *Reichspublizistik und Policeywissenschaft : 1600-1800*, München, Beck, 1988, p. 126-267.

STURM, F., *Das römische Recht in der Sicht von G. W. Leibniz*, Tübingen, Mohr, 1968.

SUAREZ, F., *Disputationes metaphysicae*, Hildesheim, Olms, 1965.

SWAMMERDAM, J., *Historia Insectorum Generalis, ofte Algemeene Verhandeling van de Bloedeloose Dierkens,* Utrecht, Meinardus van Dreunen, 1669.

– *Histoire générale des insectes*, Utrecht, Guillaume de Walcheren, 1682.

SWOYER, C., « Leibniz's Calculus of Real Addition », *Studia Leibnitiana* 26, 1994, p. 1-30.

– « Leibnizian Expression », *Journal of the History of Philosophy* 33/1, 1995, p. 65-99.

TARDE, G., *Monadologie et sociologie* [1893], Paris, Institut Synthélabo, 1999.

TAVOILLOT, P.-H., *Le crépuscule des Lumières. Les documents de la querelle du panthéisme, 1780-1789*, Paris, Cerf, 1995.

TERRALL, M., *The Man Who Flattened the Earth*, Chicago, Chicago University Press, 2002.

THOMAS D'AQUIN, *Somme théologique*, trad. collective en 4 vol., Paris, Cerf, 2004.

TILLIETTE, X., *L'Église des philosophes, de Nicolas de Cuse à Gabriel Marcel*, Paris, Cerf, 2006.

THEIS, R., « La question de l'optimisme dans la première pensée de Kant », dans P. Rateau (dir.), *L'Idée de théodicée de Leibniz à Kant : héritage, transformations, critiques, Studia Leibnitiana Sonderheft* 36, Stuttgart, F. Steiner Verlag, 2009, p. 157-164.

TOGNON, G., « Christian Wolff e gli "Essais de Théodicée" », dans I. Marchlewitz und E. Albrecht (Hrsg.), *Leibniz, Tradition und Aktualität. V. Internationaler Leibniz-Kongreß. Vorträge*, Hannover, Leibniz Gesellschaft, 1988, p. 117-131.

TONELLI, G., *Da Leibniz a Kant. Saggi sul pensiero del Settecento*, éd. C. Cesa, Napoli, Prismi, 1988.

VALBUSA, I., « Leibniz on Alsted's *Encyclopaedia* : A formal analysis », dans H. Breger, J. Herbst et S. Erdner (Hrsg.), *Einheit in der Vielheit. VIII. Internationaler Leibniz-Kongreß. Vorträge*, Hannover, Gottfried-Wilhelm-Leibniz-Gesellshaft, 2006, p. 1084-1090.

VAN LEEUWENHOEK, A., « Observations communicated to the Publisher by M. Antony van Leewenhoeck, in a Dutch Letter of the 9 th of Octob. 1676 », *Philosophical Transactions* 7, 1677, p. 821-831.

– « Observationes D. Anthoni Leewenhoek, de Natis è Semine Genitali Animalibus », *Philosophical Transactions* 7, 1677, p. 1040-1046.

– « An abstract of a letter of M. Leewenhoeck… March 30 th 1685 to the R.S. concerning generation by an insect », *Philosophical Transactions* 15, 1686, p. 1120-1134.

VASILYEV, V., « Hume : Between Leibniz and Kant (The role of prestablished harmony in Hume's philosophy) », *Hume Studies* 19/1, 1993, p. 19-30.

VASOLI, C., *L'Enciclopedismo del Seicento*, Napoli, Bibliopolis, 2005.

VERMEREN, P., « Les Aventures de la force active en France : Leibniz et Maine de Biran sur la route philosophique menant à l'éclectisme de Victor Cousin », *Exercices de la patience* VII, 1987, p. 147-168.

– *Victor Cousin : Le jeu de la philosophie et de l'État*, Paris, L'Harmattan, 1995.

VIEHWEG, T., « Die juristischen Beispielsfälle in Leibnizens Ars combinatoria », dans G. Schischkoff (Hrsg.), *Beiträge zur Leibniz Forschung*, Reutlingen, Gryphius Verlag, 1947, p. 88-95.

VOLTAIRE, *Éléments de philosophie de Newton*, Paris, Prault, 1738.

– *Lettres philosophiques*, Amsterdam, chez E. Lucas, 1734.

– *Candide ou l'optimisme*, traduit de l'allemand de Mr le Docteur Ralph, Paris, Éditions de la Sirene, 1759.

WATKINS, E., « The Development of Physical Influx in Early Eighteenth-Century Germany », *Review of Metaphysics* 49/2, 1995, p. 295-339.

WILKINS, J., *Essay Towards a Real Character and a Philosophical Language*, London, S. Gellibrand, 1668.

WILSON, C., *Leibniz's Metaphysics. A Historical and Comparative Study*, Princeton, Princeton University Press, 1989.

– *The Invisible World. Early Modern Philosophy and the Invention of Microscope*, Princeton, Princeton University Press, 1997.

WILSON, M., « Leibniz's Dynamics and Contingency in Nature », dans *Ideas and Mechanism*, Princeton, Princeton University Press, 1999, p. 421-441.

– « Leibniz and Materialism », dans *Ideas and Mechanism*, Princeton, Princeton University Press, 1999, p. 388-406.

– « The Phenomenalisms of Leibniz and Berkeley », dans E. Sosa (ed.), *Essays on the Philosophy of George Berkeley*, Boston, D. Reidel, 1987, p. 3-22.

WOLFF, C., *Gesammelte Werke*, éd. J. Ecole, H. W. Arndt, Ch. A. Corr, J. E. Hofmann et M. Thomann, New-York-Hildesheim, Olms, 1962-1983.

– *Vernünfftige Gedancken von den Kräfften des menschlichen Verstandes und ihrem richtigen Gebrauche in Erkenntnis der Wahrheit*, dans *Gesammelte Werke* I, 1, 1978.

– *Vernünfftige Gedancken von Gott, der Welt und der Seele des Menschen*, dans *Gesammelte Werke* I, 2, 1983.

WOLF, E., « Leibniz als Rechtsphilosoph », dans C. Haase et W. Totok (Hrsg.), *Leibniz. Sein Leben-Sein Wirken-Seine Welt*, Hannover, Verlag für Literatur und Zeitgeschehen, 1966, p. 465-488.

WOODHOUSE, R., *A History of the Calculus of Variations in the Eighteenth Century* [1810], réimp. : Providence, Ams Chelsea, 2001.

WUNDT, M., *Die deutsche Schulphilosophie im Zeitalter der Aufklärung*, Hildesheim, Olms, 1992.

ZENZ-KAPLAN, J., *Das Naturrecht und die Idee des ewigen Friedens im 18. Jahrhundert*, Bochum, Universitätsverlag Drn. Brockmeyer, 1995, p. 65-121.

ZILJSTRA, C. P., *The Rebirth of Descartes : The Nineteenth-Century Reinstatement of Cartesian Metaphysics in France and Germany*. PhD thesis. University of Groningen, 2005.

ZIMMERLI, W. Ch., « Von der Verfertigung einer philosophie-historischen Größe : Leibniz in der Philosophiegeschichtsschreibung des 18. Jahrhunderts », dans A. Heinekamp, *Beiträge zur Wirkungs und Rezeptionsgeschichte von Gottfried Wilhelm Leibniz*, *Studia Leibnitiana Supplementa* 26, Stuttgart, F. Steiner Verlag, 1986 p. 148-167.

TABLE DES MATIÈRES

DEUXIÈME PARTIE
SCIENCES, MORALE ET THÉOLOGIE

TROISIÈME PARTIE
LA CONNAISSANCE

QUATRIÈME PARTIE
LA RÉCEPTION

Achevé d'imprimer par Corlet Numérique - 14110 Condé-sur-Noireau
N° d'Imprimeur : 143300 - Dépôt légal : novembre 2017 - *Imprimé en France*